second edition

MAN'S PAST AND PRESENT

A Global History—
An Abridgment of The World to 1500, *2nd ed.*
and The World Since 1500, *3rd ed.*

L. S. STAVRIANOS

PRENTICE-HALL, INC., ENGLEWOOD CLIFFS, NEW JERSEY

Library of Congress Cataloging in Publication Data

STAVRIANOS, L. S.
 Man's past and present.

 Includes bibliographical references and index.
 1. World history. I. Title.
D20.S832 1975 909 74-28215
ISBN 0-13-552091-6

PRINTED IN THE UNITED STATES OF AMERICA.

10 9 8 7 6 5 4 3

PRENTICE-HALL INTERNATIONAL, INC., *London*
PRENTICE-HALL OF AUSTRALIA, PTY. LTD., *Sydney*
PRENTICE-HALL OF CANADA, LTD., *Toronto*
PRENTICE-HALL OF INDIA PRIVATE LIMITED, *New Delhi*
PRENTICE-HALL OF JAPAN, INC., *Tokyo*

ACKNOWLEDGMENTS

Grateful acknowledgment is made to the following authors and publishers for permission for quotation of the epigraphs:

On page xiv: Étienne Gilson, *Les Metamorphoses de la Cité de Dieu* (Paris: Publications Universitaires de Louvain, 1942) and Lynn White, Jr., "The Life of the Silent Majority," in R. S. Hoyt, ed., *Life and Thought in the Early Middle Ages* (Minneapolis: University of Minnesota Press, 1967), pp. 85–86; Chapter 1: Geoffrey Barraclough, *History in a Changing World* (Oxford: Basil Blackwell & Mott, Ltd., 1955), p. 18; Chapter 2: Clyde Kluckhohn, *Mirror for Man* (New York: McGraw-Hill Book Company, 1949), p. 11; Chapter 3: R. J. Braidwood, "Near Eastern Prehistory," *Science*, Vol. 127 (June 20, 1958), 1419–30; Chapter 11: Robert Lopez, *The Birth of Europe*, © 1962 by Max Leclerc et Cie., Proprietors of Librairie Armand Colin and © 1966 translation by J. M. Dent & Sons, Ltd., and published in 1967 by M. Evans and Company Inc., New York, by arrangement with J. M. Dent & Sons, Ltd.; Chapter 12: Lynn White, Jr., "Tibet, India, and Malaya as Sources of Western Medieval Technology," *American Historical Review*, XLV (April, 1960), 515, 526; Chapter 15: William Carroll Bark, *Origins of the Medieval World* (Stanford: Stanford University Press, 1958), p. 66; Chapter 17: Lynn White, Jr., "Technology and Invention in the Middle Ages," *Speculum*, XV (1940), 156; Chapter 22: B. H. Sumner, *A Short History of Russia* (New York: Harcourt Brace Jovanovich, 1943), p. 1; Chapter 24: Herbert Butterfield, *Origins of Modern Science* (London: G. Bell & Sons, Ltd., 1957), p. 179; Chapter 25: John U. Nef, *War and Human Progress* (Cambridge, Mass.: Harvard University Press; copyright 1950 by the President and Fellows of Harvard College); Chapter 26: Peter Chaadayev, *Apology of a Madman*, in H. Kohn's *The Mind of Modern Russia* (New Brunswick, N.J.: Rutgers University Press, 1955), p. 50; Chapter 27: H. A. R. Gibb, "Social Change in the Near East," in P. W. Ireland, ed., *The Near East* (Chicago: The University of Chicago Press, 1942), p. 43; Chapter 28: Arnold J. Toynbee, *The World and the West* (London: Oxford University Press, 1953); Chapter 29: J. K. Fairbanks, "The Influence of Modern Western Science and Technology on Japan and China," from *Explorations in Entrepreneurial History,* VII, No. 4; Chapter 33: K. M. Panikkar, *Asia and Western Dominance,* published in England by George Allen & Unwin, Ltd., in the United States by The John Day Company, Inc.; Chapter 35: Winston Churchill, *The Second World War : The Gathering Storm* (London: Cassell & Co. Ltd. and Boston: Houghton Mifflin Co., 1948), pp. 221-22; Chapter 36; Arnold J. Toynbee, *Survey of International Affairs, 1931* (London: Oxford University Press, 1932, under the auspices of the Royal Institute of International Affairs); Chapter 41: René Grousset, *A History of Asia* (New York: Walker, 1963).

Dedicated to
Robert Wilson Kelso
and
Susie Starr Kelso
whose lakeside retreat facilitated
the writing of this and other works

CONTENTS

part four

MEDIEVAL CIVILIZATIONS OF EURASIA, 500–1500   124

. . . during this period history becomes, so to speak, an organic whole. What happens in Italy and in Libya is bound up with what happened in Asia and in Greece, all events culminating in a single result. . . . Consequently separate histories must be regarded as of very little use in arriving at a realistic conception of the total picture. For it is only by exposing side by side the threads that connect each event with the whole complex, and also by pointing out resemblances and differences, that it becomes possible to achieve this, and to be able to derive profit as well as enjoyment from the study of history.—Polybius

The throes of the contemporary world are those of a birth. And what is being born with such great pain is a universal human society. . . . What characterizes the events we witness, what distinguishes them from all preceding events back to the origins of history is . . . their global character.—Étienne Gilson

The novel task of our generation is to create a democratic culture to match our political and economic structures. History is central to such an adventure. We must write—and write from scratch—the history of all mankind including the hitherto silent majority, and not merely that of the tiny vocal fraction which dominated the rest.—Lynn White, Jr.

part one

MAN BEFORE CIVILIZATION

Part I is concerned with man's three million years before civilization. The other parts of the book are devoted to man's history since he became civilized, less than six thousand years ago. Thus, by far the longest phase of man's evolution will receive by far the briefest consideration. The reason for the disproportionate emphasis on the story of civilized man is the constantly accelerating tempo of human history. Geologic time is measured in billions of years, and man's prehistory in millennia; but since the advent of civilization, the chronological unit has shrunk progressively to centuries and to decades, until fateful events now daily crowd us, unceasingly and inexorably. Indeed the pace of change has reached such proportions that some question whether the human species is capable of adjusting with sufficient dispatch to avoid obsolescence, or even extinction.

The disparity in the pace of events, and the corresponding disparity in emphasis in this study, should not lead us, however, to minimize the significance of what happened during prehistory. During those millennia, two developments provided the bedrock foundation for all later history. One was the gradual transition from primate to man—from hominid to Homo sapiens. The other was the transformation of the human newcomer from a food gatherer who was dependent on the bounty of nature to a food producer who became increasingly independent of nature—the master of his destiny. These two epochal events—the making of man and the advent of agriculture—are the subjects of two chapters of Part I.

Although early man took those fateful first steps that were prerequisites for the future of his species, the fact remains that they were only first steps. In the process of becoming a thinking animal, man learned to use words and tools and fire; and in becoming a food producer, he learned to plant and to use the hoe and scythe. This technology placed him in an entirely different category from that of the animals about him, and yet it was a primitive technology compared to that which

1

was to follow. The contrast is apparent if a stone hatchet or a flint-tipped scythe is placed beside a modern computer or space ship. Though the difference is self-evident, it needs to be underscored here because it explains the steady extension of the range of human activity, to be noted in the introduction to each part of this book.

The more primitive the technology, the more constricted its range of operation; conversely, the more advanced the technology, the more extensive its range. In prehistoric times, the food gatherer perforce was restricted to the few square miles of his hunting grounds; the early cultivator, to his village and the surrounding fields and pastures. Thus the range of prehistoric human communities may be defined as being "local." The later history of man, depicted in the following pages, was in large part the history of the extension of that range from local dimensions to regional, interregional, global, and planetary.

chapter one

Introduction:
Nature of
World History

*. . . Universal history is more than the sum of its parts; it cannot be
divided and subdivided without being denaturalized, much as water,
separated into its chemical components, ceases to be water and
becomes hydrogen and oxygen.*—Geoffrey Barraclough

The distinctive feature of this book is that it is a *world* history. It deals
with the entire globe rather than with some one country or region. It is concerned not with Western man or non-Western man, but with all mankind. The
viewpoint is that of an observer perched on the moon, surveying our planet as
a whole, rather than that of one who is ensconced in London or Paris, or for
that matter, in Peking or Delhi.

I. WHY WORLD HISTORY?

This global approach to history represents a new departure in modern historiography. Since the days of the Enlightenment in the eighteenth century the emphasis has been on the nation rather than on mankind. But in recent years,
interest in world history has been growing largely as a reaction to the manifestly
global sweep of contemporary events. With astronauts and cosmonauts encircling
the entire planet in a few hours and even reaching the moon, and with newspaper
headlines concerned fully as much with Asia and Africa as with Europe and the
Americas, it is increasingly recognized that a wider angle of vision is needed.
World history is manifestly essential for the understanding of a world that has
become "one" in reality as well as in rhetoric.

This utilitarian function, however, is not the only reason for turning to world
history. Equally important is the fact that the story of man from its very beginnings has a basic unity that must be recognized and respected. Neither Western
nor non-Western history may be properly comprehended without a global
overview encompassing both. Only then is it possible to perceive the degree of
interaction amongst all peoples at all times, and the primary role of that interaction in determining the course of human history.

3

It is true that the interaction was fitful and inconsiderable until Columbus and da Gama set forth on their overseas explorations. Within a few decades they and their successors brought all parts of the world into direct contact, and the intimacy of that contact has grown steadily to the present day. By contrast, the various human communities prior to 1500 had existed in varying degrees of isolation. Yet this isolation was never absolute. During the long millennia before the European discoveries, the various branches of the human race in fact had interacted one with the other, though the precise degree varied enormously according to time and location. The details of this interaction comprise essentially the subject of this book for the period to 1500. And following that date, the earth, in relation to man's growing communication and transportation facilities, has shrunk at such an accelerating tempo that it is now a "spaceship earth," and "global village."

II. STRUCTURE OF WORLD HISTORY

If the fact of a common world history shared by all mankind is accepted, then there arises the question of its pedagogical viability. Frequently it is stated that since world history, by definition, encompasses all civilizations, it is far too broad a subject for classroom purposes. Western civilization, it is pointed out, is barely manageable by itself; how can all the other civilizations—including the Chinese, the Indian, and Middle Eastern—also be encompassed? The answer, of course, is that they cannot, and that world history, *thus defined,* is obviously impracticable. But such a definition is inaccurate and misleading. World history is *not* the sum of histories of the civilizations of the world, in the same manner that Western history is *not* the sum of histories of the countries of the West.

If the study of Western civilization involved successive surveys of British history, German history, French, Italian, Spanish, Balkan, and the rest, then this obviously would not be a feasible subject of study. Yet, in fact, it is feasible, and the reason is that the approach is not agglomerative. Rather it focuses on those historical forces or movements that affected the West as a whole, such as Christianity, Islam, the Crusades, the Renaissance, the Reformation, the French Revolution, the scientific and industrial revolutions, and so forth. So it is with world history, though the stage in this case is global rather than regional, and the emphasis consequently is on movements of worldwide influence.

In Paleolithic times, for example, there was the emergence in Africa of man himself and his gradual dispersal through Eurasia, Australia, and the Americas. During the Neolithic period occurred the fateful breakthrough to agriculture, followed by metalworking and assorted other crafts, and leading to urban life and civilization. This in turn led to the development of the great Eurasian civilizations—the Chinese, Indian, Middle Eastern, and European—which for millennia developed autonomously along parallel lines, though with varying degrees of interaction as a result of powerful interregional historical forces such as Hellenism, Christianity, Buddhism, and the recurring invasions from the Central Eurasian steppes. After 1500 this Eurasian balance gradually gave way to a global unity imposed by an emerging West and culminating in the nineteenth century in an unprecedented worldwide hegemony. Finally, the essence of twentieth-century world history is the growing reaction against this hegemony and the perilous groping toward a new world balance necessitated by the rapid diffusion of Western technology and ideology. Such, in capsule form, is the rationale and structure of world history.

III. GEOGRAPHY OF WORLD HISTORY

Just as the structure of world history is commonly assumed to be the sum of the histories of the world's civilizations, so the geography of world history is assumed to be the sum of the continents comprising the earth's surface. This latter assumption is as mechanical and misleading as the former. The traditional division of the globe into continents, useful though it may be for the student of geography, has little meaning for the student of world history. For the same reason that the structure of world history requires focusing on historical movements that have had major influence on man's development, so the geography of world history requires focusing on those regions that initiated those historical movements.

When this is done, one land unit stands out uniquely and unchallengeable: Eurasia, the veritable heartland of world history since Neolithic times. Eurasia encompasses two-fifths of the total land surface of the globe, and nine-tenths of the world's population. Within its confines developed the most advanced and most enduring civilizations. To an overwhelming degree, the history of man is the history of those Eurasian civilizations.

The distinguished anthropologist Franz Boas makes an observation that contains perhaps the chief reason for Eurasia's predominance:

The history of mankind proves that advances of culture depend upon the opportunities presented to a social group to learn from the experience of their neighbors. The discoveries of the group spread to others and, the more varied the contacts, the greater the opportunities to learn. The tribes of simplest culture are on the whole those that have been isolated for very long periods and hence could not profit from the cultural achievements of their neighbors.[1]

In other words, *if other geographic factors were equal,* the key to human progress has been accessibility. Those with the most opportunity to interact with other people have been the most likely to forge ahead. Indeed they were driven to do so, for there was selective pressure as well as opportunity. Accessibility involved the constant threat of assimilation or elimination if opportunity was not grasped. By contrast, those who were isolated received neither stimulus nor threat, were free from selective pressure, and thus could remain relatively unchanged through the millennia without jeopardizing their existence.

The Eurasian people obviously were the prime beneficiaries of this principle of accessibility. All were accessible to each other. They stimulated and threatened each other at an increasing tempo through the ages, as technological advances facilitated communication amongst the regions of Eurasia.

These regions need to be defined, for Eurasia is too large a land mass to be viewed as a single unit. Nor may Eurasia be defined as the combination of Europe and Asia, for this definition is both geographically and historically misleading. Geographically, Europe obviously is not equivalent or comparable to Asia. A glance at the map shows that Europe is a peninsula of the Eurasian land mass, corresponding, for example, to the Indian Peninsula. Historically, also, Europe is comparable not to Asia but to another Eurasian center of civilization, of which again India provides a good example. Thus Europe and India are intelligible equivalents in territorial extent, size and variety of population, and complexity of culture and historical traditions. From the viewpoint of world history, therefore, Eurasia should be viewed as comprising not the two continents of Europe and Asia, but five historically meaningful regions: the Middle East, India, China, Europe, and the Central Eurasian steppes.

The fertile river valleys and plains of the first four regions gave rise to the great historical civilizations that together have been responsible for the vital role of Eurasia as the heartland of world history. More specifically, the innovative center or "core" of the Middle East comprised the Nile and Tigris-Euphrates valleys and the Iranian Plateau; in India, the center was the Indus and Ganges valleys; in China, the Yellow and Yangtze valleys; and in Europe, the northern shore of the Mediterranean, which was economically and culturally dominant from Minoan times to the late Middle Ages. It should be added that Europe as defined here includes North Africa, because this area historically has usually had closer ties with Europe and the Middle East than with the lands south of the great Sahara barrier. It follows that the term "Africa" henceforth refers to sub-Saharan Africa.

The Central Eurasian steppes comprise the endless grasslands stretching from Manchuria in the east to Hungary in the west and provide an overland channel of communication amongst the centers of civilization strung out in Eurasia's periphery. These steppes supported nomadic herdsmen who were ever on the move with their flocks and who were always ready, when opportunity presented itself, to grasp at the riches of Peking, Delhi, Baghdad, and Rome. Fertile valleys and plains created the ancient core civilizations of Eurasia, but the steppes facilitated contact amongst these civilizations, either by peaceful communication along overland trade routes or by the ceaseless nomadic raids from the arid interior to the provocatively affluent periphery. Thus the history of Eurasia was to a great extent molded by this interaction between nomadic tribes and sedentary civilizations. The continual raids, which periodically built up into elemental and wide ranging movements of peoples, were regenerative as well as destructive. They swept away fossilized dynasties, institutions, and practices, introduced new peoples, techniques, and ideas, and determined in large degree the course of Eurasian history. The ancient, the classical, and the medieval periods of pre-1500 Eurasian history—the three broad historical periods that will be studied in this volume—were heralded by major turning points primarily attributable to these nomadic invasions.

The non-Eurasian world was made up of the three remaining land masses: Africa, the Americas, and Australia. Viewed in the light of the principle of accessibility, their disadvantage compared to Eurasia is apparent. They had no contact whatsoever with each other.

Africa alone had a physical connection with Eurasia, yet even here the interaction was tenuous and intermittent because of formidable geographic barriers between Africa and Eurasia, and within Africa itself. Nevertheless the progress of the Africans did rest in large part on outside stimuli such as the introduction of agriculture, of ironworking, and of new plants and animals. Consequently, in the Sudanic lands immediately to the south of the Sahara, Africans were able to organize a succession of medieval empires that were comparable in certain respects to those of contemporary Europe.

The American Indians, by contrast, were relatively handicapped by virtue of their complete isolation after crossing over from northeast Asia over 20,000 years ago. Their general level of development was not equal to that of the Africans, though they did develop impressive civilizations in Mexico, Central America, and Peru.

Finally, the Australian aborigines were the most retarded, having been cut off on their remote island continent for some 30,000 years. They all remained at the food-gathering stage, in contrast to the Africans, who had large Sudanic empires in addition to Hottentot and Pygmy food gatherers, and the American Indians, who had the advanced Aztec, Inca, and Maya civilizations along with food gatherers in California and Tierra del Fuego. Indeed Australia's isolation in the South Pacific had led not only to the retardation of human culture but also to the survival of archaic forms of flora and fauna, such as the eucalyptus plant, the monotremes, and the marsupials.

Such, then, was the understandable diversity of human societies encountered by the Europeans when they set out on their explorations from the fifteenth century onward. The spectrum ranged from the ancient and sophisticated civilizations of Eurasia, through the mixture of imperial structures and food-gathering bands in Africa and the Americas, to the unrelieved Paleolithic level prevailing throughout Australia.

This global pattern determines the organization of this book. For the period to 1500, the emphasis is on the Eurasian civilizations, which were incomparably more advanced and consequently made correspondingly greater contributions to human development during those millennia. Thus Parts II, III, and IV are devoted to the evolution of the Eurasian civilizations, while Part V summarizes the developments in the non-Eurasian world. The remaining parts are concerned with global developments since 1500: the emergence of the West, the establishment of Western global hegemony, and finally the current ambivalent phase of Western decline and triumph.

BIBLIOGRAPHY

A more complete and annotated bibliography is provided in the two volumes by L. S. Stavrianos: *The World to 1500* and *The World Since 1500* (Prentice-Hall, 1970)

SUGGESTED READING

G. BARRACLOUGH, *An Introduction to Contemporary History* (Penguin, 1965); K. N. CAMERON, *Humanity and Society* (Indiana Univ., 1973); V. GORDON CHILDE, *What Happened in History* (Penguin, 1942); W. H. McNEILL, *The Rise of the West: A History of the Human Community* (Univ. Chicago, 1963); R. TURNER, *The Great Cultural Traditions: The Foundations of Civilization,* 2 vols. (McGraw-Hill, 1941); UNESCO's multivolume *History of Mankind: Cultural and Scientific Development* (Harper, 1963 ff).

chapter two

Man
the Food Gatherer

Anthropology holds up a great mirror to man and lets him look at himself in his infinite variety.—Clyde Kluckhohn

One of the outstanding yet little-recognized achievements of modern man is his study and reconstruction of the past. The ancients had little comprehension of what had preceded them. Thucydides, the most objective of Greek historians, began his study of the Peloponnesian War by stating that nothing of great importance had happened before his time. His ignorance of history prevented him from recognizing the unique glory and contribution of Athens. By contrast, our age is more history minded than any other. We know more about the early history of the Egyptians, the Greeks, or the Chinese than they themselves knew. Furthermore, scientists in various fields—geology, archeology, anthropology, paleontology and biology—have extended our knowledge back before the beginning of civilization with its written records. This is of prime importance, for it was only about five thousand years ago that man learned to write, whereas his hominid beginnings have been traced back about three million years. We shall consider these long prehistoric millennia when man became man, yet at the same time contrived to sustain himself, as did the other animals about him, by collecting food wherever it was to be found, rather than by growing it as his agriculturist descendants were to learn to do.

I. ORIGINS OF MAN

Our earth is a minor planet spinning in a minor galaxy. Compared to the entire universe it is inconceivably small—literally like a speck of dust on the Pacific Ocean. It took form about 4.6 billion years ago, and the first life appeared on it some 1.5 billion years later as single-celled creatures. This life traditionally has been viewed as qualitatively different from nonlife, but scientists no longer accept this assumed dichotomy between organic and inorganic. Rather they view living matter as having evolved naturally from nonliving matter. They classify all matter in a hierarchy of states of organization. At a certain level in this hierarchy the transition occurs from inorganic to organic. More specifically, electrons, protons, and neutrons combine to form atoms, the atoms form molecules, and the molecules become more or less well-organized aggregates, one class of which constitutes living matter.

Organic matter in turn underwent a comparable hierarchical evolution: from the original microorganisms to primitive plants such as seaweeds, to animals without backbones such as jellyfish and worms, and to backboned animals. These vertebrates, with some of their invertebrate and plant cousins, began their successful adaptation to life on land about 300 million years ago. First came the amphibians, then the great army of prehistoric reptiles, the birds, and finally the mammals; and for the past sixty million years, mammals have been the dominant form of life on earth.

Scientists accept without question the proposition that man belongs to the animal kingdom—more specifically to the order of the Primates, which he shares with the lemurs, tarsiers, monkeys, and apes. The evidence accumulated from several fields of study all lead to this conclusion. The differentiation of the human stock occurred during the Pleistocene epoch with its six or seven glacial and five or six interglacial periods. These drastic environmental changes compelled all animals to adapt and readapt themselves continually to new conditions. Success in this crucial matter depended not upon brute strength nor upon the ability to resist cold, but rather upon the continuous growth of intelligence and the use of that intelligence to work out satisfactory adaptations. This, of course, is the secret of man's unchallenged primacy on earth. He has been, first and foremost, a generalist. He never adapted exclusively to one type of environment, as the gibbon did to the forest with his long lithe arms, or the polar bear to the arctic with his heavy white fur. Rather man adapted with his brain, which he then used to adapt to any environment.

Homo sapiens is the product of natural selection from a succession of manlike ancestors, or hominids, some of which were capable of using simple stone tools and weapons. The earliest of these hominids was Australopithecus, believed to have appeared first in the savannas of eastern and southern Africa some three million years ago, though recent findings in eastern Africa indicate that the date may go as far back as four or even five million years. The pelvis and leg of this hominid were strikingly similar to that of modern man, but his cranial capacity was only about one-third that of man, or hardly larger than that of living apes. Thus a manlike bipedal locomotive system was combined with an apelike brain. The low level of intelligence meant a correspondingly low level of speech and of toolmaking. The significance of this sequence is that the human brain did not appear first and then proceed to create human culture. Rather there was interaction back and forth. Speech and tool were both the causes and the effects of brain development.

Australopithecus gave way about half a million years ago to man's immediate ancestor, the hominid Homo erectus. His brain was about twice as large as that of his australopithecine predecessor, or two-thirds that of modern man. His generalized stone tool, the first hatchet, was more complex. It was the first overall designed tool, usually almond shaped, from six to eight inches long, several inches wide, and about one inch thick. The huge quantities of skeletal remains of large slaughtered animals—deer, rhinos, pigs, elephants, buffalo, hippos, horses, antelopes and gazelles—demonstrate the effective use made of this tool. Such large-scale hunting of big game also reflects efficient group organization and action, including speech communication. Another indication of social life is the first evidence of reverence for the dead. Fossils of hominid bodies have been found that had been covered with earth upon which red ochre or hematite had been scattered. Almost certainly this represented some kind of ritual burial. Along the same lines there is evidence of the dawn of the decorative sense in the beads and perforated teeth and shells that have been found in association with the fossils. Finally there are the all-important telltale signs of fire making—circular dark discs in the soil, five to six inches in diameter.

The mastery of fire had fundamental and far-reaching repercussions. It freed man's ancestors from the bondage of the limited energy supply of their own bodies. It helped them to survive the advancing glaciers of the ice ages. It increased tremendously the available food supply by making possible the cooking of a great range of roots and seeds that hitherto had been inedible. Fire further improved hominid diet as the cooking liberated protein and carbohydrate materials. Fire also made it possible for the hominids to break out of the warm savanna in which they had thus far been confined, to begin their dispersal throughout the globe, with repercussions being felt to the present day. (See Map I, "Global Distribution of Hominids and Homo Sapiens.")

II. MEANING OF MAN

The evolutionary process culminating in man was finally completed about 35,000 years ago with the appearance of Homo sapiens, or "thinking man." Viewed in broadest perspective, this represents the second major turning point in the course of events on this planet. The first occurred when life originated out of inorganic matter. After that momentous step, all living forms evolved by adapting to their environments through mutation and natural selection. That is, genes adapted to environment, as was evident during the climatic turmoil of the Pleistocene. But with the appearance of man, the evolutionary process was reversed. No longer did genes adapt to environment; instead, man adapted by changing the environment to suit his genes. Today, a third epochal turning point appears imminent, as man's growing knowledge of the structure and function of genes may soon enable him to modify his genes as well as his environment.

Man, and only man, has been able to create a made-to-order environment, or culture, as it is called. The reason is that only man can symbolize, or envision things and concepts divorced from here-and-now reality. Only he laughs, and only he knows that he will die. Only he has wondered about the universe and its origins, about his place in it and in the hereafter.

With these unique and revolutionizing abilities, man has been able to cope with his environment without mutations. His culture is the new non-biological way of having fur in the arctic, water storage in the desert, and fins in the water. More concretely, culture consists of tools, clothing, ornaments, institutions, language, art forms, and religious beliefs and practices. All these have served to adapt man to his physical environment and to his fellowman. Indeed, the story of man as related in the following chapters is simply the story of a succession of cultures that he has created, from his Paleolithic origins to the present day.

III. CULTURE OF THE FOOD GATHERERS

Just as Homo erectus had been able to fashion a more effective tool than his australopithecine predecessor, so now Homo sapiens with his superior intelligence developed the so-called "blade technique." He used the long, sharp flakes, or "blades," struck off the core of a stone to fashion a variety of new tools as well as "tools to make tools." Some of the new tools were composite, such as spears with hafted heads of bone, antler, or flint, and flint blades set in bone or wooden handles. Another departure was the construction of projectiles such as the bola, sling, spear thrower, and bow and arrow. The latter must have been relatively inefficient at first, but it was gradually improved until it became the most formidable weapon prior to modern firearms. Other inventions of the upper Paleolithic included bone and ivory bodkins, bone needles with eyes, belt fasteners, and even buttons—all of which indicate that the Magdalenian hunters wore sewn skin garments with fitting sleeves and trousers.

Although this technology of the late Paleolithic was advanced compared to that of the early Paleolithic half a million years earlier, it still was primitive in the sense that productivity was low. Food gatherers and hunters led a precarious hand-to-mouth existence. Normally they were able to support themselves and their dependents, but no surplus was left over for other purposes. This was profoundly significant, for it set inexorable limits to the evolution of the food gatherers' culture.

There was no possibility, for example, for an elaborate political structure for it simply could not be supported. Indeed, there was no formal political structure with full-time political leaders. Rather the hunters formed autonomous bands that usually numbered twenty to fifty persons, though larger groups were possible and did exist in areas that yielded plentiful food supplies, such as the American Northwest, with its inexhaustible salmon runs, and the Dordogne valley in southern France, with its great reindeer herds in Magdalenian times.

Social organization necessarily was as simple as the political, if indeed the two can be distinguished at this stage. The basic unit was the family, consisting of the parents and their immature and unmarried children. Extra wives usually were permitted but in practice polygamy was rare. Intra- and inter-family relationships rested on kinship ties. Each one had duties towards the others and in turn enjoyed rights and privileges. They helped each other in the quest for food and in providing shelter from the elements and defense from their enemies. Some fighting between tribal groups arose from personal feuds and from competition for hunting and fishing grounds. But Paleolithic society lacked both the manpower and the resources essential for sustained large-scale warfare, which was not possible until the coming of agriculture with its greatly increased productivity and correspondingly increased population.

This cooperation was evident in economic matters as well as social. No specialization was needed amongst hunters, except on a sex basis. Every man and woman possessed all the knowledge and skills proper to their sex and functioned accordingly. During the early Paleolithic, women collected fruits, nuts, and grains and grubbed up roots and insects, while men caught small game and fish. At that level there was little to choose between the sexes as food gatherers. But as tools improved, the males were able to organize large-scale hunting parties and to kill large animals, while the women remained close to camp to cook, care for the children, and collect available edibles.

Turning our discussion from social institutions and practices to general beliefs, we find that primitive man was basically ahistorical and nonevolutionary in his attitudes towards himself and his society. He assumed that the future would be identical to the present, as the present was to the past. Consequently there was no notion of change, and hence no inclination to criticize or to tamper with existing institutions and practices. Everything, including themselves, their culture, and their habitat, had appeared with creation and was destined to continue unaltered into the future. The creation myths of hunting peoples are strikingly similar, involving heroes who fashioned the landscape, stocked it with game, brought forth the people, and taught them the arts and their customs.

Primitive man was very knowledgeable concerning nature. He had to be, for his very existence depended on it. Yet he had little explanatory knowledge; he could give no naturalistic explanation if there were floods or droughts, or if the hunting or fishing was poor. This meant that he did not know how to cope with nature by naturalistic means, so perforce he resorted to the super-natural. He turned to magic and spent much time in efforts to persuade or fool nature to yield a greater abundance. By making each useful animal or plant the totem of a particular group, and by using images, symbols, and imitative dances, primitive man believed that the animal or food could be encouraged to flourish and multiply. As long as the rules of the totems were strictly observed, the reproduction of the group and of its food supply could be assured.

All group members seem to have participated at first in the ritual ceremonies, but towards the end of the Paleolithic part-time specialists in the form of medicine men or shamans seem to have appeared. These people were thought to have peculiar relations with the forces deemed to control those parts of the universe or environment that mattered—primarily food and fertility, but also health and personal luck. They were, to an increasing degree, relieved from the full-time work of food and tool production, and in return they exercised their magical arts for the common good. Shamans are still found today in nearly every surviving food-gathering culture, including those of the Bushmen, the Eskimos, and the Australian aborigines. Paleolithic technology, however, was not sufficiently productive to support anything approaching a priestly hierarchy. This in turn meant that no cohesive theology could be elaborated. Conceptions of gods and spirits were hazy, and much emphasis was placed on individual visions. Religion was not used as a method of social control. Benefits were coerced from the supernatural rather than being dependent on the morality of the individual.

By far the outstanding example of Paleolithic art consists of the extraordinary cave paintings, the best examples of which are located in southern France and northwestern Spain. The subjects of the drawings are usually the larger game: bison, bear, horses, woolly rhinoceros, mammoth, and wild boar. The best of the drawings are in full color, remarkably alive, and charged with energy. Despite their extraordinary artistic quality, the cave drawings apparently were designed for utilitarian reasons. They were executed in the darkest and most dangerous parts of the caves, although only the openings were inhabited. Also the artists commonly painted one picture over another, with no apparent desire to preserve their works. Hence it appears that these Paleolithic artists made their way to the depths of the earth and created as realistic a reproduction as possible of the animals they hunted in the belief that thereby they gained some sort of magic power over them.

In conclusion, Paleolithic culture was in many ways vastly appealing. It was thoroughly egalitarian, with warm bonds of kinship permeating and determining social relationships. It offered everyone specific and accepted obligations and rewards. There was no problem of alienation or of anxiety in the face of an uncertain or unpredictable future. To the present day, an Australian aborigine can take a piece of broken glass, fashion it skillfully into an arrow head or spear point, fit it to a spear thrower or to a bow that he has strung himself, set forth and kill his game, prepare his dinner with due attention to ceremony, and after dinner, round out the day with storytelling in which he shares the adventures of the day with the stay-at-homes. In this manner the Paleolithic hunter was a complete man to a degree that has not been approached since the agricultural revolution.

But the bonds that held Paleolithic society together were also constricting as well as comforting. The individual was wholly subservient to the band or tribe, which was viewed as a timeless procession of the dead, the living, and the unborn, attended by all the unseen powers of the spirit world. To this procession of life the individual was completely subject. It was this tradition, this stultifying and constraining tradition, that was the historically all-important other side of Paleolithic society. Today it is customary to distinguish between two modes of life: the "progressive" of the modern industrialized West, and the "traditional" of the underdeveloped agrarian non-West. The latter is indeed "traditional" compared to the former, but it is anything but traditional compared to the primitive tribal society that it superseded following the agricultural revolution.

We shall see that this agricultural revolution set off a chain reaction of urbanization, class differentiation, and social cleavage that undermined the appealing egalitarianism of primitive society. But in doing so it also broke the constricting bonds of tribal traditionalism and thereby launched man, for good or ill, on the fateful course that was to lead from hunting ground to megalopolis, from human muscle to atomic power. Before turning to the agricultural revolution, however, it is necessary to consider the dispersal of Paleolithic man throughout the globe and the ensuing repercussions felt to the present day.

IV. DISPERSAL AND RACE DIFFERENTIATION

It is commonly assumed that population explosion is a phenomenon peculiar to our times, but this is not so. Spectacular population spurts have occurred with each major technological breakthrough, and for the obvious reason that an advance in technology leads to increased productivity, which can support a larger number of people. At this time the differential between early and late Paleolithic technology did represent a major advance. This in turn led to a population jump from an estimated 125,000 hominids in the early Paleolithic to 5.32 million Homo sapiens on the eve of the agricultural revolution at the end of the Paleolithic ten thousand years ago. This increase of over forty-two times is thus comparable to the population explosions that, as we shall see, were to accompany each of the later technological revolutions. (See Map II, "World Population Growth.")

Another demographic pattern set at this time and repeated in the future was the disproportionate increase of any population that took the lead in technological innovation, and hence the spread of that population over larger areas. This pattern has prevailed since the first appearance of life on this planet. At all times, the best adapted species, or that which is most efficiently exploiting the physical environment, is the species that has prevailed and extended its domain. Thus the australopithecines, with their primitive pebble tools and lack of clothing, were unable to extend their range beyond the warm savanna lands. Homo erectus, by contrast, with his superior tools and his clothing and control of fire, was able to expand north from Africa to the temperate zones of Eurasia—hence the discovery of his widely scattered fossil remains such as Java man, Peking man, and Heidelberg man. Finally Homo sapiens, with his still more complex technology and correspondingly more efficient adaptation, was able to push further north into the Siberian tundra, as well as south into the African and Southeast Asian tropical rain forests.

Under these circumstances, Homo sapiens occupied the remaining continents by crossing one land bridge to Australia and another to Alaska. Once in the New World he fanned out in all directions. Thus man occupied all the continents except Antarctica, thereby becoming, together with his inseparable dog, the most widespread animal in the world.

Hand in hand with the dispersal of Homo sapiens went race differentiation. A variety of so-called races appeared, with distinguishing characteristics in skin color, hair texture, and facial structure. These races are believed to have emerged because of the relative isolation of the various human populations and their adaptation to differing local environments. The significant point concerning this differentiation within the human species is that it occurred so late—well *after* the emergence of Homo sapiens. All modern races, then, stem from a common stock *after* it had attained its full human development. This explains why the Europeans were able to interbreed with all races in all the lands they discovered. It also explains why, as virtually all anthropologists agree, there are no significant differences in the innate mental capacity among the living races of mankind. Representatives of late Paleolithic man or of the contemporary Australian aborigines would stand as much chance of graduating from a university as would representatives of any other races.

The precise circumstances under which the races appeared in various regions are not known, and probably never will be. Suffice it to note that by the end of the latest Ice Age about ten thousand years ago, the global distribution of races had assumed a roughly recognizable delineation. The Caucasoids occupied Europe, North and East Africa, and the Middle East, extending into India and Central Asia. The Negroids were in the Sahara (better watered then) and a bit southward, while the Pygmies and Bushmen, in contrast to later times, occupied the remainder of Africa. Other Pygmies, the Negritos, lived in the forests of India and Southeast Asia, while in the open country of these regions and in Australia were the Australoids. Finally in East Asia and the Americas were the Mongoloids.

Although this racial configuration bears a vague resemblance to the one we know, Map III, "Global Race Distribution," shows that basic changes had occurred by A.D. 1000 and still more by today. These changes, as we shall note later, came as a direct result of later technological revolutions. It was the failure to keep up with these revolutions that explains the virtual disappearance of the Bushmen and Pygmies and Australoids, as well as the swamping of the American Indians in most of the New World. Put in other words, it explains why 10,000 years ago blonds probably were no more numerous than Bushmen, whereas today there are 100,000 blonds for every living Bushman.

As noted in the preceding chapter, the differential in technological leadership, and hence in numerical strength, did not reflect a corresponding differential in genetic endowment. Rather it stemmed from the fact that the Mongoloids and Caucasoids were located in the Eurasian heartland, and the Negroids in a region of Africa easily accessible to Eurasian stimuli, whereas the Bushmen and Pygmies were unfortunate enough to be isolated in remote areas of Africa, and the Australoids on their distant island continent. The resulting differences in tempos of development have determined the very composition of the human family today, as well as the status and interrelations of the various members of the family.

SUGGESTED READING

K. W. Butzer, *Environment and Archeology* (Aldine, 1964); R. B. Lee and J. DeVore, eds., *Man the Hunter* (Aldine 1969); J. E. Pfeiffer, *The Emergence of Man* (Harper, 1969); M. Sahlins, *Stone Age Economics* (Aldine, 1972).

chapter three

Man
the Food Producer

It is probably very difficult for us now to conceptualize fully (or to exaggerate) the consequences of the first appearance of effective food production. The whole range of human existence, from the biological (including diet, demography, disease, and so on) through the cultural (social organization, politics, religion, esthetics, and so forth) bands of the spectrum took on completely new dimensions.—Robert J. Braidwood

During Paleolithic times man became man by learning to speak, to make tools, and to use fire. This gave him an enormous advantage over the other animals about him, and yet in one fundamental respect he remained akin to them. He was still a hunter among other hunters. He was still a food gatherer as were countless other species that were completely dependent on the bounty of nature. And being dependent on nature, he was dominated by nature. He had to be constantly on the move in order to follow animals and to locate berry patches or fishing grounds. He had to live in small groups or bands because not many could find enough food to support themselves in a given area. It is estimated that even in fertile areas with mild winters, only one or two food collectors could support themselves per square mile. And as much as twenty or even thirty square miles were needed for each human soul in regions of cold climate, tropical jungle, or desert.

Such subservience to nature left its imprint on all aspects of human society, as noted in the preceding chapter. But this subservience was greatly reduced when man made the epochal discovery that he could feed himself by growing his food as well as by gathering it. In doing so a new world with limitless horizons opened before him, as he left behind him the Paleolithic stage of his development and entered the Neolithic.

I. ORIGINS OF AGRICULTURE

Neolithic man differed from his Paleolithic predecessor in two respects: he made his stone tools by grinding and polishing rather than by chipping and fracturing, and he obtained his food wholly or primarily from agriculture and/or stock raising rather than from hunting animals or gathering plants. Of these two changes, the latter is by far the more significant. This is not to minimize the importance of the new ground tools, which were more durable than the earlier implements. Such highly important inventions as the plow and the wheel, which appeared towards the end of the Neolithic period, were facilitated by the availability of cutting tools made of ground stone. The fact still remains, however, that the trick of grinding a chipped or hewn ax to a smooth polished edge was a rather trivial matter compared to the transformation of man from a food collector to a food producer.

This transformation was not the result of sudden inspiration. Indeed the mechanics of plant growth were as widely known before the agricultural revolution as the fact that the earth was round was known before Columbus' voyage. It is well established that modern primitives who are wholly without agriculture nevertheless are thoroughly familiar with the nature and behavior of plants in their locales. They know that plants sprout from seeds, that they usually need water and sunshine to flourish, and that they grow better in one type of soil than in another. This type of knowledge is acquired naturally and unavoidably by modern primitives for the simple reason that their very existence depends upon such practical understanding of the surrounding flora and fauna. There is no reason for doubting, and plenty of evidence for believing, that prehistoric man acquired similar comprehension under comparable circumstances.

If the basic principles of plant life were known to man thousands of years before the agricultural revolution, then why did he delay so long in putting them into practice? One reason is that there was no incentive to do so. Contrary to what is commonly assumed, hunting peoples did not normally live on the brink of starvation. They did not increase in numbers to the limit that could be supported by the available food supply. Rather they resorted to practices such as infanticide, abortion, and lactation taboos in order to keep their numbers low enough to pull through the lean months of each year. Thus hunting societies continued to exist for millennia at a comfortable equilibrium and consequently lacked stimulus for radical change. Not only did the hunters under normal circumstances have plenty to eat, but they also had plenty of leisure. Once sufficient game had been killed or plant food collected, there was no particular incentive for working further. "There is abundant data," states one authority, "which suggests not only that hunter-gatherers have adequate supplies of food but also that they enjoy quantities of leisure time, much more in fact than do modern industrial or farm workers, or even professors of archeology."[1]

Another reason for man's delay in shifting to agriculture is the relative scarcity of domesticable plants and animals. Man has been able throughout history to domesticate only a few hundred plants and a few dozen animals that happen to possess certain essential characteristics. Plants must be potentially high-yielding and preferably should be adaptable to a variety of environments. If these requirements are not met, then plants will have little effect even though domesticated. Prehistoric Indians of present-day United States cultivated pigweed, marsh elder, lamb's quarter and sunflower, but none of these plants yielded enough to affect significantly the Indian way of life. Likewise animals, to be domesticable, must be capable of losing their instinctive flight-reaction before man, must breed under man's care, and must be willing to accept the diet provided by man. The peoples of the Old World were fortunate in having available a variety of such animals that provided them with meat, milk, wool, and beasts of burden. The American Indians, by contrast, were retarded by the lack of anything comparable; they had to do with a half-domesticated group of Andean cameloids: the llama, the alpaca, and the vicuña.

It follows from the above that no breakthrough to agriculture could be expected unless some change occurred which upset the comfortable equilibrium of the hunting societies, and even then, agriculture could occur only in areas where domesticable plants were available. This, in fact, is precisely what did happen. The end of the Pleistocene, as noted in the preceding chapter, was a period of drastic climatic fluctuations which upset the traditional balance between man and nature. And man, being Homo sapiens, adapted by using his knowledge of plant life to grow his own food.

This he had done innumerable times in various parts of the globe where he had experimented with a wide range of plants and animals. But now, in a few favored regions, he was able to increase the productivity of his domesticated plants and animals to the point where they provided such a high proportion of the diet that community life revolved primarily around the cultivation of the plants and the tending of the animals. This is what is meant by *agricultural revolution* as distinct from mere *domestication*. It was from the few centers of such agricultural revolution that food production as a new way of life gradually spread over large portions of the globe.

II. DIFFUSION OF AGRICULTURE

We know with certainty that the Middle East and Mesoamerica were independent centers of agricultural revolution, and recent research indicates that North China was also such a center. There is speculation, though no conclusive evidence, that other such centers may have evolved in Southeast Asia, West Africa, and the Andes. In the case of the Middle East and Mesoamerica, both regions had certain unique characteristics that seem to account for their pioneering role. Both enjoyed abundant variety of plants and/or animals.

In the Middle East were to be found the ancestors of modern wheat, oats, rye, and barley, as well as those of the modern goat, sheep, cattle, and pig. Likewise in Mesoamerica the two small republics of Costa Rica and Salvador, although comprising only one per cent of the area of the United States, yield as many plant species as do both the United States and Canada. This extraordinary diversity is the product of a corresponding diversity of habitats created by the wide range of altitude, temperature, and rainfall within a small area. Consequently, dozens of plants were successfully domesticated in Mesoamerica, the all-important ones being maize, amaranths, beans, and squashes.

Over a period of many centuries the various plants were adapted out of their particular local niches into a variety of environmental conditions, thereby culminating in a regional complex of multiple-species agriculture. This advanced type of agriculture had the great advantage of a high level of productivity and of "subsistence security." If one crop failed for climatic reasons, another with different requirements could survive, thus providing the dependable food supply essential for dense populations and for the civilizations that thereby were made possible.

It should be emphasized that the transition from the earliest domestication to agricultural revolution was very gradual and prolonged, and is known as the phase of "incipient agriculture." In the Middle East this phase spanned the period from roughly 9500 to 7500 B.C. In the New World it appears to have been even longer. One of the earliest centers of domestication in that area was the Mexican valley of Tehuacán, where incipient agriculture began approximately 7000 B.C. It is estimated that two thousand years later only 10 per cent of the diet of the local Indians was derived from their domesticated plants, primarily maize. By 3000 B.C., still only a third of the food came from this source. It was not until about 1500 B.C. that maize and other plants had been hybridized to the point where their yield was sufficiently high to provide most of the food, and thus to complete the transition from incipient agriculture to the agricultural revolution.

From these two original centers of full-fledged agriculture, and from others that might, and probably will, be identified in the future, the new mode of living spread to all parts of the globe. The diffusion process was sparked by two characteristics of this early agriculture. One was that it was an intermittent or shifting type of cultivation. The land was cleared and used for crop growing for a few years, whereupon it was abandoned to natural growth for eight or ten or more years in order to allow the fertility to be restored. This very extensive type of agriculture meant that the ratio of abandoned or recuperating land to that under cultivation at any one time was between five and ten to one. This, together with increasing population, necessitated constant extension of the limits of the tilled land into new regions. A closely related expansionist factor was overpopulation. Multiple-species agriculture yielded a greater and more reliable food supply, so that population increased correspondingly. When it reached the limit that could be supported by the prevailing level of agricultural productivity, the natural solution was emigration. Thus there was a continual "budding-off" or "hiving-off" from the agricultural settlements into the relatively sparsely populated lands of the food-gathering peoples. In this manner agriculture was diffused in all directions from the original centers, though in certain regions it never took hold, either because of excessive cold (arctic), excessive aridity (Sahara), or inaccessibility (Australia). (See Map V, "Expansion of Agriculturists," and Map V-a, "Dispersal of Agriculture.")

III. VARIETIES OF AGRICULTURE

This world wide diffusion of agriculture required adaptation to a variety of local conditions and hence led to the domestication of a corresponding variety of plants suitable to those conditions. In the Middle East wheat and barley had been from the beginning the most common crops. But as the farmers moved northward they found that these crops did not do as well as rye, which originally had been a weed sown unintentionally with the wheat and barley. Hence there was a shift to rye in Central Europe and, under similar circumstances, another shift further north to oats.

Likewise, the extension of agriculture to sub-Saharan Africa led to the cultivation of native millets and of one type of rice, while around the shores of the Mediterranean the olive became one of the most important sources of edible oil. Across the Iranian plateau and in northwest India an essentially Middle Eastern type of agriculture was practiced. But a dividing line running north and south through central India marks the transition to an entirely different climatic zone with correspondingly different plants. This is the monsoon world, with heavy seasonal rainfall, constant heat, and dense jungles. Seed-bearing plants of the Middle Eastern variety, which require plenty of sun, cannot thrive here, so in their place are to be found yam, taro, banana, and above all, rice. Finally, in the Americas the staple everywhere was maize, supplemented by beans and squash in North America and by manioc and potatoes of both the sweet and "Irish" varieties in South America.

The net result of the agriculture diffusion described above was, very generally speaking, three great cereal areas: the rice area in East and Southeast Asia; the maize area in the Americas; and the wheat area in Europe, the Middle East,

North Africa, and Central Asia to the Indus and Yellow River valleys. During the several millennia between the agricultural and industrial revolutions these three cereals were as fundamental for the history of man as coal and iron and copper were to become following the industrial revolution.

In the vast steppe and desert lands from the Sahara to Manchuria there is insufficient water for either rain-fed or irrigated agriculture, so that man was forced to depend on his domesticated animals rather than on plants. This pastoral nomadism was late in developing because it had to await the domestication of the horse and camel to provide suitable transport in open country. Once it got under way between 1500 and 1000 B.C., a variety of forms developed. Some pastoralists depended on a single animal—the camel in Arabia and cattle in Southwest Africa—while those of Central Asia had herds of horses, cattle, camels, sheep, and goats, which they adjusted to local climatic and grazing conditions. Regardless of the variety, nomadism required extensive grazing lands, so that the bands today rarely number more than 200 persons, and often less than 100. Population densities accordingly range mainly between 1 and 5 people per square mile.

These adaptive variations in the diffusion of agriculture and pastoralism were of profound significance for later history. Slash and burn agriculture and pastoral nomadism were not as productive per unit of land as the permanent irrigation type of agriculture that was developed later in the valleys of the Tigris-Euphrates, Nile, Indus, and Yellow rivers. Consequently it was these valleys, and certain other favored regions, that generated the material and human resources essential for the great civilizations that appeared later and were to dominate the globe to modern times. Also these opulent centers of civilization were to prove irresistible magnets to the comparatively poverty-stricken pastoral nomads of the Central Eurasian steppes, so that Eurasian history to modern times was in large part the history of the relations between the nomadic hordes of inner Eurasia and the surrounding river valley civilizations. Before turning to this history in the following chapters we will consider the manifold repercussions of the agricultural revolution on all aspects of human life.

IV. CULTURE OF THE FOOD PRODUCERS

The most obvious impact of the agricultural revolution was the new sedentary existence. Man now was able to settle down; in fact he had to in order to care for his newly domesticated plants and animals. Thus the Paleolithic nomadic band now gave way to the Neolithic village as the basic economic and cultural unit of mankind. Indeed it remained the basis for a pattern of life that was to prevail until the late eighteenth century and that persists to the present day in the vast underdeveloped regions of the world.

It is easy to romanticize Neolithic village life, but to do so would be grossly misleading. Everyone—men, women and children—had to work, and work hard, to produce food and a few handicraft articles. Productivity was low since man learned slowly and painfully about soils, seeds, fertilizers, and crop rotation. Despite the hard labor, famine was a common visitation, following upon too much or too little rain, or a plague of pests. Epidemics swept the villages repeatedly as sedentary life introduced the problem of the disposal of human excreta and other garbage. While dogs helped with sanitation and the cultural habits of personal modesty presumably demanded that stools be deposited at some distance from habitation, neither of these were sufficient to prevent the various diseases that follow the route from the bowel to the mouth. Also malnutrition was the rule because of inadequate food supply or unbalanced diet. Life expectancy under these circumstances was exceedingly low, but the high birth rate tended to increase village populations everywhere until famine, epidemic, or emigration restored the balance between food and mouths.

Yet Neolithic village life was not all misery and suffering. This was a time when man made technological progress at an infinitely more rapid rate than in the preceding millennia of the Paleolithic. The basic reason probably was not so much that he had more leisure time than the hunters, a common assumption that is now rejected, but rather that sedentism made a richer material existence physically possible. The living standards of the nomadic hunter were limited to what he could carry, whereas the Neolithic villager could indulge in substantial housing together with furnishings, utensils, implements, and assorted knick-knacks. Thus he learned to make pottery out of raw clay, at first imitating, naturally enough, the baskets, gourds, and other containers of preagrarian times. Gradually he grasped the potentialities of pottery materials and techniques and fashioned objects that no longer resembled the earlier containers. At the same time that man was developing the art of pottery making, he also acquired skills in the production of textiles. He used fibers of the newly domesticated flax, cotton, and hemp plants, and he spun and wove the fibers on spindles and looms that he gradually evolved. Neolithic man also learned to build dwellings that were relatively substantial and commodious, the materials usually being wood or adobe, depending upon local resources and climate.

Sedentism also made possible a tribal political structure in place of the individual bands of the hunting peoples. The inhabitants of the villages of a given region comprised the tribe, which was identified and distinguished from others by distinctive characteristics of speech and custom. Some tribes, usually those with primitive economies, were so amorphous and underdeveloped that they were almost at the hunting band level. Others boasted powerful chiefs and primitive nobilities as against the commoners, though the lines were blurred and never reached the class exclusiveness characteristic of the later civilizations.

The basic social unit of the Neolithic village customarily was the household consisting of two or more married couples and their children. This extended family was more common than the independent nuclear family because it was better suited for coping with the problems of wresting a livelihood. It could absorb the temporary or permanent loss of an individual producer and could function more efficiently during "choke" periods when many hands were needed for clearing forest, harvesting, or pasturing livestock.

The distinctive feature of the Neolithic village was social homogeneity. All families had the necessary skills and tools to produce what they needed, and, equally important, all had access to the basic natural resources essential for livelihood. This was assured because every family automatically was a component part of the village community, which had proprietary rights to farmlands, pastures, and other resources of nature. Hence there was no division between landed proprietors and landless cultivators in tribal society.

Precisely because of this egalitarianism, tribal societies, whether of Neolithic times or today, have a built-in brake on productivity. Output is geared to the limited traditional needs of the family, so there is no incentive to produce a surplus. This in turn means that labor is episodic, diversified, and correspondingly limited. The daily grind—the eight-hour day, five-day week—is conspicuously absent. The typical tribesman worked fewer hours per year than modern man and furthermore he worked at his pleasure. The basic reason was that he labored and produced in his capacity as a social person—as a husband or father or brother or village member. Work was not a necessary evil tolerated for the sake of making a living; rather it was a concomitant of kin and community relations.

The new life of the soil tillers also meant new gods—new religions. The spirits and the magic that had been used by the hunters were no longer appropriate. Now the agriculturists needed, and conceived, spirits who watched over their fields and flocks and hearths. Behind all these spirits stood a creator, usually vaguely conceived. But most important, almost everywhere was a goddess of the earth, or the goddess of fertility—the earth mother. She was the source of productivity of plants and animals, and of the fecundity of women. Life and well-being, the annual cycle of death and rebirth, ultimately depended upon her. Hence the proliferation of fertility goddess cults. This is manifested in the numerous clay figurines with exaggerated female characteristics—pendulous breasts and heavy thighs. Reflecting the spread of agriculture from the Middle East, these have been found throughout Europe and as far east as India.

V. DEMOGRAPHIC AND RACIAL REPERCUSSIONS

The agricultural revolution generated another population explosion comparable to that accompanying the advent of man. Improved tools developed by evolving man during the Paleolithic led to increased productivity and to a corresponding increase in population. Hence there was the jump from 125,000 man-apes one million years ago to 5.32 million Homo sapiens hunters 10,000 years ago, a 42-fold increase. (See Chapter 2, section IV.) Now, with the agricultural revolution, a given area yielded a larger and more dependable food supply, so that population figures rose even more dramatically than before. Between 10,000 and 2,000 years ago, the human population soared from 5.32 to 133 million, a 25-fold increase within 8,000 years as against the million year spread during the Paleolithic. (See Map II, "World Population Growth.")

This population increase was selective rather than generalized. As noted earlier, peoples that have led in technological innovation also have led in numerical growth. Consequently just as Homo sapiens earlier had outstripped and displaced his hominid predecessors, so now the agriculturists outstripped and displaced the hunters. The precise manner in which this "outstripping" and "displacing" functioned was probably somewhat as follows. Because of the extensive type of agriculture that was practiced, population pressure soon built up in the villages. The surplus population would "bud-off" to adjacent fresh lands, till the soil, and establish a new village. The relations with the native population varied according to local conditions. If there were marginal lands nearby that could not be used profitably by the agricultural immigrants, then the natives could find sanctuary there and thus preserve their identity. This happened in Africa, where the once widespread Pygmies and Bushmen were crowded into dense jungles and barren deserts respectively. Likewise, in North America the once widespread Shoshone-speaking Indian food gatherers were displaced by the Pueblo agriculturists. (See Map IV, "Recession of Hunters" and Map V, "Expansion of Agriculturists.")

Another type of relationship was of the symbiotic variety. An example of this prevails to the present day in the Congo forest, where Pygmy hunters provide Negro cultivators with meat, honey, and other forest products and receive in return cereals and iron weapons. Thus both peoples have been able to coexist and to preserve their identities.

The most common relationship between agricultural immigrants and local food gatherers has been intermarriage and gradual biological fusion. Then as population pressure built up again, the new hybrid population would "bud-off" in turn into fresh lands, where further interbreeding would take place with native peoples. In this way agricultural techniques and crops were transmitted long distances, and the people who emerged at the end of the line were of an entirely different racial type from the original initiators. Thus the immigrants who brought wheat, cattle, the wheel, and the plow into North China were thoroughly Mongoloid, even though these materials originated in the Middle East. Similar migrating and interbreeding occurred with the diffusion of agriculture westward from the Middle East to Europe, and from the savanna lands to southern Africa. Evidence of the latter is the presence today in southern Zambia of Negro-Bushman hybrids.

The net result of these migrations by which agriculture spread over the globe was that by A.D. 1000 the hunters, who 10,000 years ago comprised 100 per cent of the human race, had shrunk to little more than one per cent of the population. This occupational shift led in turn to a racial shift. Ten thousand years ago the race map of the globe showed a rough balance amongst six races—the Caucasoid, Mongoloid, Negroid, Bushman, Pygmy, and Australoid. (See Map III, "Global Race Distribution.") By A.D. 1000 this balance was drastically changed in favor of the agriculturist Mongoloids, Caucasoids and Negroids, and against the Bushmen-Pygmies who had remained food gatherers. The only reason the Australoids held their own was that their isolated island home had not yet been discovered by any agriculturists. This had to wait for the European explorers of the eighteenth century, and when the discovery did take place belatedly, the consequences were all the more catastrophic for the hapless aborigines.

The most striking racial repercussions of the agricultural revolution were in sub-Saharan Africa and East Asia. In the latter region the Mongoloids expanded in all directions at the expense of scattered Pygmy-Australoid peoples, thereby laying the basis for their present numerical superiority over all other races. Likewise, in Africa the Negroes enjoying the advantage of agriculture and iron working broke out of their original savanna homeland and worked their way through the rain forests to southern Africa. Thus, whereas there had been a fairly equitable racial balance in Africa as late as 4000 B.C. amongst Negroes, Bushmen, and Pygmies, by A.D. 1000 this balance had been completely upset in favor of the Negroes. Considering the globe as a whole, then, the racial effect of the agricultural revolution was to end the millennia-old racial equilibrium and to establish the Mongoloid-Caucasoid-Negroid predominance that persists to the present.

SUGGESTED READING

L. R. Binford and S. R. Binford, eds., *New Perspectives in Archeology* (Aldine, 1968); R. J. Braidwood and G. R. Willey, eds., *Courses Toward Urban Life* (Aldine, 1962); Ping-ti Ho, "The Loess and the Origin of Chinese Agriculture," *American Historical Review*, LXXV (October, 1969), 1–36; S. Struever, ed., *Prehistoric Agriculture* (Natural History Press, 1971); P. J. Ucko and G. W. Dimbleby, eds., *The Domestication and Exploitation of Plants and Animals* (Aldine, 1970).

part two

ANCIENT CIVILIZATIONS OF EURASIA, 3500-1000 B.C.

We have seen in Part I that after man became man, his first major achievement was the agricultural revolution. His next was the urban revolution, or the attainment of civilization. This involved an advance in technology that in turn, as noted in the introduction to Part I, led to a corresponding increase in the range of human activity. Whereas the food gatherer was restricted to the confines of his hunting grounds, and the Neolithic agriculturist to the environs of his village, civilized man of necessity operated far afield. He extended his control upstream to safeguard the water supply for his irrigation system and he sent forth soldiers and traders to obtain by whatever means necessary wood for the builders, the copper and tin for the metallurgists, and gold and silver for the craftsmen. Thus the range of the ancient civilizations was not limited to the immediate locality as had been the case with prehistoric communities. Rather it extended outward until it encompassed entire river valleys and even surrounding regions that yielded necessary raw materials.

chapter four

Origins
of Ancient Civilizations

The city came into being for the sake of life; it is for the sake of good life.—Aristotle

Every city is two cities, a city of the many poor and a city of the few rich; and these two cities are always at war.—Plato

The first light of civilization dawned on a desert plain scorched by the sun and nourished by two great rivers, the Tigris and the Euphrates. Although at one time it was believed that the Nile valley gave birth to civilization, it is now agreed that the earliest centers were in Sumer, the Old Testament's "land of Shinar." This area comprised the barren, wind-swept plains at the head of the Persian Gulf, in the southern part of what used to be known as Mesopotamia and is now the state of Iraq. It was about 3500 B.C. that certain communities of agriculturists that had developed techniques for cultivating this arid wasteland successfully completed the transition from Neolithic tribalism to civilization.

The date given is an approximation, and is pinpointed merely for the sake of convenience. In fact, no one year, or decade, or even century, can be specified in any meaningful sense. We have seen that the shift to food production did not suddenly occur when someone hit upon the idea of agriculture. Likewise the transition to civilization did not happen at the moment that someone conceived of urban centers and urban civilization. What happened, in short, was not an event but a process. The purpose of this chapter is to examine the nature and origins of this process.

I. NATURE OF CIVILIZATION

Precisely what is meant by the term civilization? Anthropologists point to certain characteristics found in civilizations that distinguish them from the preceding Neolithic cultures. These characteristics include urban centers, institutionalized political authority in the form of the state, tribute or taxation, writing, social stratification into classes or hierarchies, monumental architecture, and specialized arts and sciences. Not all civilizations have possessed all of these characteristics. The Andean civilization, for example, developed without writing, while the

Egyptian and Mayan lacked cities as commonly defined. But this cluster of characteristics does serve as a general guide for defining the attributes of the civilizations that emerged at various times in various parts of the world.

The end result was not a uniform type of civilization but rather a striking variety of "styles" of civilization. The earlier Neolithic cultures, as noted in the preceding chapter, represented adaptations to specific environments and hence differed markedly according to the balance between cultivation and stock breeding, and the varieties of plants cultivated and of animals bred. So now the various civilizations differed correspondingly, with the degree of distinctions depending on the degree of isolation in which they developed. Thus the Mayan, Aztec, and Inca civilizations, which emerged independently in the Americas, are clearly distinguishable from those which had taken form earlier in Eurasia. The Eurasian group in turn comprised a diversity of individual civilizations whose distinctiveness depended on their location in relation to the earliest center of civilization in the Middle East. Hence, China, being the most isolated behind desert expanses and mountain barriers, has from earliest times to the present been the most divergent of the Eurasian civilizations.

There remains the question as to why the step to civilization was taken in the first place, particularly in view of the manifold attractions of egalitarian Neolithic society. The answer is suggested by the experience in modern times of the Tanala of Madagascar. Their transition to civilization occurred recently enough to have been recorded by the anthropologist Ralph Linton. Before their shift, the Tanala cultivated dry rice by the slash and burn method. This gave them a good crop the first year, after which the yield progressively declined. Accordingly, the village moved frequently as the fields became exhausted. This mobility precluded individual ownership of land. The village as a whole held general proprietorship, the village elders parcelling out the land as equitably as possible amongst joint families. The several households in each of these joint families worked together, dividing the produce amongst themselves according to need. This was, then, a typical egalitarian tribal society, with no significant economic, political, or social differentiation.

All this changed when some of the families shifted to wet rice cultivation in imitation of neighbors to the east. Since the naturally wet lands were very limited in area, the labor force of an entire joint family was not needed, and the new type of farming therefore was carried on by individual families. These invested so much year-round labor in their rice terraces that they did not return them to the village for reallocation. And since little land was suitable for wet rice cultivation, the formerly classless Tanala society now became divided into a small class of landowners and a large majority who could not hope to own the more productive type of land.

This class division became an actual physical division when the dry-rice farmers were forced to move periodically to fresh lands, while the wet-rice farmers remained on their plots. Warfare also was affected by the new type of economy, as the permanently settled villagers now were willing to spend time and effort to build elaborate fortifications that discouraged the traditional raiding parties. The latter now concentrated on capturing stragglers for slavery, which was assuming new importance. Hitherto slaves had been of little use for slash and burn agriculture, but now they could be used for year-round work on the terraces. Also in place of the previous democracy there developed a society with an absolute king at the head, nobles who held land by royal assignment, commoners who formed the bulk of the population, and slaves who were war captives or their descendants. Finally, a new set of social values evolved, with property becoming the sole means of enhancing the ego. "It was a far cry," concludes the anthropologist Ralph Linton, "from the mobile, self-contained Tanala villages with their class-less society and strong joint families to the Tanala Kingdom with its central authority, settled subjects, rudimentary social classes based on economic differ-ences, and lineages of little more than ceremonial importance . . . the trans-formation can be traced step by step and at every step we find irrigated rice at the bottom of the change."[1]

This transformation of the Tanala is a replica in miniature of the process of change that undermined Neolithic society in the Middle East during the fourth millennium B.C. and culminated finally in the urban revolution and the emer-gence of civilization.

II. MESOPOTAMIAN ORIGINS

It was in the hills above the Tigris-Euphrates that man had learned to domesti-cate plants and animals and thereby to achieve the agricultural revolution. It was there also that man now began his next great adventure when he moved down to the river valley and gradually evolved a new and more productive irrigation agriculture and also new social institutions. The interaction of the new tech-nology and institutions set off a chain reaction that culminated eventually in civili-zation.

The move to the lowlands presented the Neolithic agriculturists with new problems—inadequate rainfall, searing heat, periodic floods, and lack of stone for building. But there were advantages that more than compensated—the date palms that provided plentiful food and abundant, though poor, wood, the reedy marshes with their wild fowl and game, the fish that furnished valuable protein and fat for the diet, and, above all, the fabulously fertile alluvial soil. The poten-tial of this new environment was challenging, and the pioneer agriculturists successfully responded to the challenge by a remarkable feat of adaptation. Thus during the fourth millennium B.C. occurred one of the great technological ad-vances of mankind.

Rainfall was barely sufficient for growing crops in the hilly uplands, but in the valleys below it was quite inadequate. Irrigation was necessary to bring the rich alluvial soils under cultivation, so the pioneer farmers dug short canals leading from the river channels to their fields. The crops were incredibly large compared to those that they had previously wrested from the stony hillsides. Documents dating to 2500 B.C. indicate that the average yield on a field of barley was eighty-six times the sowing! Food was now available as never before—more abundant, more varied, and, thanks to irrigation, more assured. The increased food meant increased population, which in turn made possible more irrigation canals, more new fields, and still more food.

While the technique of irrigation was being worked out, the new craft of metallurgy also was being mastered. This was particularly valuable for the valley settlements where flint was unavailable. At first native metals were treated as unusually tough and malleable stones, and worked cold by hammering and grinding. True metallurgy did not begin until it was learned how to reduce metals from their ores by smelting. Copper seems to have been the first metal so treated, and it was then discovered that upon heating it became liquid and assumed the shape of any container or mold. With cooling it hardened and could be given as good a cutting edge as stone. Furthermore by 3000 B.C. it was widely known in the Middle East and India that a more durable alloy could be produced by adding small quantities of other metals to the copper. Finally they hit on the ideal combination of copper and tin, the resulting bronze being decidedly superior to stone. It was particularly sought after for making weapons, since stone was too brittle to be dependable in battle. On the other hand, bronze was expensive because of the scarcity of both copper and tin, and hence was unavailable for general use, such as toolmaking.

Equally significant at this time was the invention of the plow. In the beginning this consisted simply of a sapling with one lopped and pointed branch left protruding two-thirds of the way down the trunk. A pair of oxen were yoked to the upper end of the trunk while the plowman steered by the lower end as the protruding branch was dragged through the earth. In the light soils of the semiarid Middle East this primitive contrivance was highly functional. By 3000 B.C. it was widely used in Mesopotamia and Egypt and was being introduced in India; by 1400 B.C. it had reached distant China. The significance of the ox drawn plow is that for the first time man was able to use motive power other than that of his own muscles. In this sense the plow was the precursor of the steam engine, the internal combustion engine, the electric generator, and the fission reactor.

By 3000 B.C., wind also was being harnessed to supplement human muscles—in this case to furnish power for water transport. Clumsy square sails appear to have been used first in the Persian Gulf and on the Nile River. They represented the first successful utilization of inorganic force to provide motive power. Crude though the early sail boats were, they offered a far more economic means for heavy transport than pack asses or oxcarts, so that much of the commerce of the ancient civilizations was waterborne.

Another basic invention of this creative millennium was the wheel. In the earliest Mesopotamian models, the wheel and axle were fastened together solidly and the wheels were disks. By 3000 B.C., the axle had been fixed to the cart with the wheel left separate, and shortly thereafter the spoked wheel appeared. Heavy and clumsy though these early carts were, they were much preferable to what had hitherto been available—human shoulders and the pack animal, usually the ass. The wheel also was used early for war chariots and for the potter's wheel, which made it possible to mass produce pottery, the first technical product for which this can be said.

These far reaching technological advances went hand in hand with correspondingly far reaching institutional changes. The increase in population enabled some of the villages to grow into towns dominated by a new elite of religious, and later, military and administrative leaders. Their appearance had been made possible by the increased productivity of agriculture, which resulted in food surpluses that could support the growing new class of priests, soldiers, and bureaucrats. This development was not a sudden or a simple one-way process. Technological and social change interacted, eventually precipitating the urban revolution and civilization. The Neolithic cultivators did not at some given time agree—nor were they forced—to provide a surplus for a ruling elite and thus to shift over from the status of tribesmen to that of peasants. Rather it was a gradual process in which *cause* and *effect* were functionally interrelated.

The genesis of the later class differentiation that distinguished civilization may be discerned in the modest village shrines that were centers of socio-religious life but not yet of a full-time priesthood. When the villages grew to towns, the shrines likewise grew to temples with retinues of priests and attendants—the first persons ever to be released from direct subsistence labor. That the priests should have been the pioneer elite group is understandable if they are viewed as the successors of the earlier tribal shamans. The latter had been most influential because of the importance of group agricultural ceremonialism, such as rain making, for Neolithic farmers. Now the new priesthood bore responsibility not only for the traditional supernatural phenomena but also for the growing managerial functions essential for an increasingly complex society.

The accumulative growth of technology and the increasing food surplus had made possible the emergence of the new priestly hierarchies, but the latter in turn contributed to both the technology and the economy. The earliest known examples of writing, which in itself was a priestly invention born of the need for keeping records, attest to the fact that the priesthoods supervised a multitude of economic as well as of religious activities. They kept the records necessary for calculating the time of the annual floods. They assumed the vital managerial functions indispensable for the proper functioning of the growing irrigation facilities, including the rationing of water and the construction and maintenance of dams and canals. They also provided at this time the main stimulus for the crafts, whose output was designed much more for temples than for secular markets.

At this point the growing heterogeneity of society, to which the religious elite had contributed so vitally, began to undermine the position of that elite. The larger and the more complex the towns grew, the more ineffective became purely religious sanctions. At the same time warfare was growing in scale and in frequency. This may have been due to the fact that population growth was outstripping agricultural resources, though the provocative wealth of the temples themselves may paradoxically have contributed to the disorders by inviting raids. The outcome was a shift of power from the priesthood to a new secular elite.

Previously, the occasional threat of outside attack had been met by the assembly of the community's adult males who selected a war leader for the duration. But as the intervals of peace became shorter, the tenure of these war leaders became longer, until they were ensconced as permanent military chiefs, and eventually as kings. Thus the palaces came to rival the temples, until a working partnership was evolved. The priests normally retained their great landholdings and continued their sacred services, while the palace officials constructed walls around their cities and raised large armies, which they employed against neighboring cities and, eventually, for empire building.

One effect of this rise of secular states and empires was a great increase in the output of nonagricultural commodities. The mass production of pottery, the prevalence of articles such as cylinder seals and metal utensils, and the hordes of assorted objects found in some of the more substantial houses, all suggest a new and significant middle class market. Also, a substantial quantity of luxury commodities was absorbed by the burgeoning palace retinues. In addition, the growing militarization required armaments on an unprecedented scale, including not only metal weapons and armor but also more elaborate equipment such as chariots. All this was a far cry from the relatively limited production of earlier times when crafts were geared mainly to meeting temple needs. It should be noted, however, that this change was almost exclusively in volume rather than in technique. What was new was the mass production and not a stylistic or technological innovation.

This mass production had important implications regarding foreign affairs. Most of the crafts were dependent on raw materials brought from the outside, since the lowlands were almost totally devoid of minerals and quality timber. Copper, for example, came from Oman, south of the Persian Gulf, silver and lead from the Taurus Mountains in Asia Minor, and timber from the Zagros Mountains of Iran and from Lebanon on the Mediterranean coast. In order to pay for such imports it was necessary for the various crafts to expand production to provide exports in exchange. The alternative was to conquer the sources of the needed raw materials. That this was not overlooked is evident in the career of Sargon, King of Akkad, in the middle of the third millennium B.C. His empire extended "from the Lower to the Upper Sea"—from the Persian Gulf to the Mediterranean—and he thereby controlled the sources of metals, stone, and timber.

The combined cost of the military and palace establishments bore so heavily on the resources of the early city states that it undermined the position of the traditional assemblies. The latter balked against the onerous levies necessary to meet the rising expenditures, with the result that the assemblies were increasingly bypassed and replaced by permanent, hereditary royal authority.

The centralization of political power was accompanied by growing class differentiation. This is strikingly evident in the corresponding differentiation in grave offerings. During the early period the disparity was minimal, but the more time passed the more pronounced it became. The great majority of the graves had only a few pottery vessels or even nothing at all, reflecting the poverty of the commoners. Those of the well-to-do exhibited "conspicuous consumption" in the form of copper vessels and beads of precious metal. The royal tombs, by contrast, were luxuriously furnished with beautifully wrought weapons and precious ornaments, and included large numbers of palace attendants—men-at-arms, harem ladies, musicians, charioteers, and general servants—who were sacrificed in order to accompany the royal occupant and attest to his power and wealth.

III. DIFFUSION OF CIVILIZATION

Such was the millennia-long evolution from autonomous farm villages to small theocratically-controlled states and eventually to dynastic empires with all of the attributes of civilization as defined above.

Once civilization took root in Mesopotamia and later in the several other regions of Eurasia and the New World, it spread out in all directions. Just as the agricultural revolution had replaced hunting societies with tribal ones, so now the tribal societies in turn were replaced by civilization. By the time tribalism had reached the peripheries of Eurasia, it was being superseded in its core areas. The displacement process continued inexorably as civilization spread out of the original river valleys and spanned adjacent areas of barbarism, until by the time of Christ it extended with virtually no interruption from the English Channel to the China Sea. (See Map VI, "Ancient Civilizations of Eurasia, 3500–1500 B.C.")

If 3500 B.C. is accepted as the approximate date for the emergence of civilization in Mesopotamia, then corresponding approximations may be given for the other centers of civilization: in Egypt, about 3000 B.C.; in the Indus Valley, about 2500 B.C.; in the Yellow River valley of China, about 1500 B.C.; and in Mesoamerica and Peru, about 500 B.C. It must be emphasized that these dates are rough estimates and that they are constantly being revised with new findings. Indeed, radiocarbon dating on which much prehistoric chronology has been based has been found recently to be off by several centuries. This is leading some scholars now to question the traditional assumption of cultural diffusion from the eastern Mediterranean to western Europe.

The New World civilizations, like New World agriculture, are believed to have developed independently of any Eurasian influences. Whether the beginnings of Chinese civilization were indigenous or stimulated indirectly from the Middle East cannot be answered at present. In the Nile and Indus valleys, civilization got under way as a result of stimulus diffusion from Mesopotamia, meaning that it was not specific techniques and institutions that were adopted, but rather the underlying ideas or principles. The *idea* of writing was taken from Sumer, but distinctive writing systems were evolved in Egypt and India; likewise with state organization, monumental architecture, and so forth. This, at least, is the traditional diffusionist view, but again it should be noted that it now is being questioned. Some scholars, for example, now believe that the Minoan-Mycenaean civilization of prehistoric Greece emerged independently of Mesopotamian or Egyptian influences.

Whatever the precise sequence, the end result was the evolution of several civilizations that shared a common general pattern but that nevertheless manifested distinctive characteristics of styles. These styles gradually took form and crystallized during these long millennia of autonomous development, so that to a considerable degree they persist to the present day.

SUGGESTED READING

R. M. ADAMS, *The Evolution of Urban Society* (Aldine, 1966); C. H. KRAELING and R. M. ADAMS, eds., *City Invincible: A Symposium on Urbanization and Cultural Development in the Ancient Near East* (Univ. Chicago, 1960); M. H. FRIED, *The Evolution of Political Society* (Random House, 1967); C. RENFREW, *Before Civilization: The Radiocarbon Revolution and Prehistoric Europe* (Knopf, 1973).

chapter five

Styles of Ancient
Civilizations

There are many sorts of food, and therefore there are many ways of life,
both of beasts and of men; they cannot live without food, and
differences in their food have made differences in their way of life.
—Aristotle

The development of man's first civilizations several millennia ago can be analyzed in terms of technological innovation, considerations of geography, and economic organization. Though these factors are vital to an understanding of the past, they leave us with little appreciation of the people themselves—how they looked at life, death, and one another. Each of the major ancient civilizations, whether in Mesopotamia, Egypt, Crete, the Indus River valley, or the Yellow River valley, had a distinctive view of life and style of living it. Expressed through art, philosophy, literature, and law, the life styles of the ancients take on substance and color.

Much remains conjecture, for even elementary questions cannot yet be answered. We still do not know, for example, who the Sumerians were, where they came from, and whether they were the first settlers in the Mesopotamian valley or whether they built upon foundations provided by earlier inhabitants. And concerning other ancient peoples, the degree of ignorance is even greater than it is for the Sumerians. Nevertheless certain distinctive life styles are discernible in the various regions, and these are the subject of this chapter.

I. MESOPOTAMIA

Geographic environment affected profoundly the styles of the ancient Eurasian civilizations as it had their preceding Neolithic cultures. In the case of Mesopotamia this is most apparent as regards location, which meant vulnerability to invasions that molded the development of that region from earliest times to the present. Indeed its history comprises in large part a millennia-long struggle between Indo-European invaders from the north and Semitic peoples from the south for control of the fertile river valley.

The first great builders of civilization in Mesopotamia, the Sumerians, appear curiously to have been neither Indo-European nor Semites. Similarities between their language and Chinese suggest some eastern place of origin. In any case it was they who in southern Mesopotamia established the first civilization by successfully harnessing the turbulent waters of the Tigris-Euphrates in an intricate network of irrigation canals. By 3000 B.C., Sumer consisted of twelve separate city states of which Uruk, for example, covered eleven hundred acres and housed perhaps as many as fifty thousand people. The cities fought continually for leadership, and the warfare became steadily more professional and costly. This weakened the Sumerians to the point where they fell subject to the Semites, whose famous leader, Sargon the Great, stands out in history as the first empire builder. Starting from his base at Akkad in the middle of the valley, he first conquered all Sumer and then marched far beyond, eventually winning an empire extending from the Persian Gulf to the Mediterranean.

This was a stupendous realm for the times but it proved short-lived. Sargon's grandson was defeated by new invaders from Iran, and the city state of Akkad was destroyed and disappeared from history. The individual Sumerian cities now reemerged and enjoyed a degree of independence until a strictly Sumerian empire was established by the ancient city of Ur. This lasted for a century from 2113 to 2006 B.C., when a new group of Semitic nomads, the Amorites, invaded the valley and, after protracted fighting, established the Babylonian Empire under their well-known ruler, Hammurabi (ca. 1704–1662 B.C.). As will be noted in the following chapters, this pattern of successive invasions was to persist to modern times, with the Amorites followed by Hittites, Assyrians, Persians, Macedonians, Romans, Arabs, and Turks.

Despite the parade of empires, ancient Mesopotamia was essentially a city civilization and commercial civilization. The cities were the basic units, and each was a sacred entity belonging to its main god. Temples and kings were large-scale capitalists, but much private capital also was invested in land, crafts, trading ventures, and money lending. The majority of citizens earned their livelihood as farmers, craftsmen, merchants, fishermen, and cattle breeders. Each city had a section reserved for the craftsmen—the masons, smiths, carpenters, potters, and jewelers. They sold their handicrafts in a free town market and were paid in kind or in money. The latter consisted of silver ingots or rings which had to be weighed after each transaction.

Outside the city walls were the fields on whose productivity the urban inhabitants ultimately were dependent. Most of the land was held in the form of large estates that belonged to the king or the priests or other wealthy persons. The workers on these estates were allotted individual plots along with seed, implements, and draft animals. In return they provided the labor and, through a variety of arrangements, yielded their surplus produce to the temple or palace or landowner. The basic crops were barley and wheat; the milk animals were goats and cows; sheep supplied the wool and that was the chief textile fabric of Mesopotamia. The most common vegetables were beans, peas, garlic, leeks, onions, radishes, lettuce, and cucumbers; the fruits included melons, dates, pomegranates, figs, and apples.

The management of the estates required the keeping of accounts such as the rents received from the tenant farmers, the size of the herds, the amount of fodder needed for the animals and of seed for the next planting, and the intricate details regarding irrigation facilities and schedules. These management and accounting records were inscribed with a reed stylus on clay tablets that were then baked in order to preserve them. This earliest form of writing, known as cuneiform, was obviously not invented for intellectual purposes; rather it was an instrument of administration.

At first the cuneiform consisted of pictographs, so that the scribe drew simplified pictures of oxen, sheep, grain, fish, or whatever was being recorded. Soon the pictographs were conventionalized rather than being left to the artistic fancy of each scribe. This assured uniform writing and reading of records, but a basic problem remained; pictographs could not be used to depict abstract concepts. Sumerian scribes met this difficulty by adding marks to the pictographs to denote new meanings, and, more important, by selecting signs that represented sounds rather than objects or abstractions. This was the essence of the phonetic alphabet that was evolved centuries later, but the Sumerians failed to apply the phonetic principle systematically and comprehensively. They reduced their signs from an original number of about two thousand to some six hundred by 2900 B.C. This was a substantial improvement, but cuneiform remained far more cumbersome than the alphabet developed later by the Phoenicians and the Greeks. Hence there was a need for scribes, who alone had mastered the difficult art of writing and who therefore enjoyed high status and privilege.

Although the origins of writing are to be found in the new circumstances arising from the production of economic surplus, its repercussions were extraordinarily far reaching and fateful. It stimulated intellectual development by making possible the recording and accumulation of factual data, and its transmission to successive generations. Equally significant, it promoted the definition and consolidation of individual cultures by giving permanent written form to religious traditions, which thereby became sacred books, to social customs, which became law codes, and to oral myths and stories, which became classics. Thus writing became the chief means for the cultural integration of the civilizations of mankind.

The Sumerians developed sciences and mathematics, as well as writing, in response to the concrete needs of their increasingly complex society. Their earliest mathematical documents were accounts of flocks, measures of grain, and surveys of fields. Their chief contribution was the development of the first systems for measuring time, distance, area, and quantity. Also, as early as 3000 B.C., they were carefully studying and recording the movements of heavenly bodies, and their motive again was utilitarian. They believed that the will of the gods determined celestial movements, and that knowledge of those movements would enable man to ascertain divine will and act accordingly. Thus Mesopotamian astrologers in the course of many centuries accumulated an enormous amount of data that later was used to develop scientific astronomy.

The religious beliefs of the Sumerians and their successors were profoundly affected by their physical environment, and particularly by the annual flooding of the Tigris-Euphrates. What impressed them was not the periodicity of inundation but the unpredictability of its timing and volume. The coincidence of heavy rains in the northern areas and deep snow in the Zagros and Taurus mountains frequently produced disastrous floods that devastated farmlands rather than filled irrigation canals. Fear of the annual floods, together with the ever-present danger of outside invasion, left the Sumerians with a deep feeling of helplessness in a world of uncontrollable forces. "Mere man—his days are numbered," reads a Sumerian poem, "whatever he may do, he is but wind." The Mesopotamian view of life was tinged with an apprehension and pessimism reflecting the insecurity of the physical environment. Man, it was felt, had been made only to serve the gods, whose will and acts were unpredictable.

The Mesopotamians sought to alleviate the insecurity prevailing between man and man by compiling detailed codes of law. The most outstanding of these was that of Hammurabi, which later served as the basis for the laws of other Semitic peoples, such as the Assyrians, Chaldeans, and Hebrews. The code begins with a prologue by Hammurabi stating that the gods of old had predestined Babylon to be supreme in the world, and predestined him "to cause justice to shine in the land, to destroy the wicked and the evil, that the strong might not oppress the weak." Then followed the laws themselves, some three hundred in all, seeking to regulate all social relationships, clearly and for all time. Thus the code illuminates the society as much as it does the legal system of ancient Babylon.

II. EGYPT

The next civilization to emerge—that of Egypt—owed a good deal to the original model that had taken form on the banks of the Tigris-Euphrates. It is believed that one point of contact was the area between the Nile and the Red Sea to which Sumerian traders were attracted by gold deposits. Another area of interaction was in Lebanon, where the Egyptians went to obtain timber. In the course of the trading that ensued, the Egyptians learned about the civilization of Sumer and were sufficiently stimulated so that certain forces already at work in their valley were speeded up, and the advent of civilization correspondingly hastened. But their creation was in no sense a copy of the Sumerian prototype; it was distinctive, reflecting the unique character of the Egyptian people and of their physical environment.

The Nile Valley, in contrast to the Mesopotamian, is exceptionally well protected against outside intervention by the Libyan Desert on the west, the Arabian Desert in the east, the Nubian Desert and precipitous cataracts on the south, and the harborless coast of the Delta on the north. The Egyptian people were left free in their sheltered valley to work out their own destiny. They did not have to cope with periodic inundations of either Semites or Indo-Europeans, and thus were able to preserve their ethnic identity from the time of the pharaohs to the present day. The fellaheen now working on the banks of the Nile resemble closely the figures carved and painted on the ancient temples and pyramids—the same short stature, slim physique, straight black hair, deep-set eyes, and slightly aquiline nose.

Egypt's sheltered existence allowed for political, as well as ethnic, stability. There was no kaleidoscopic succession of empires precipitated by periodic invasions. Instead the Nile River provided a natural cohesion that held the entire valley together as a stable and functioning unit. Its slow but steady current carried northbound traffic effortlessly, while the prevailing north-to-northwest winds made the return trip almost as simple. Thus the Egyptians were provided with a priceless means for reliable communication and transportation that facilitated the unification of the valley about 3100 B.C. under King Menes. Egypt now possessed the basic attributes of civilization, including a system of writing as well as professional administrators, soldiers, religious leaders, and artists.

The outstanding feature of the Dynastic Period was the remarkable political continuity. The so-called Old Kingdom, comprising six dynasties, endured for more than eight centuries from 3100 to 2270 B.C. No comparable period of political stability may be found in the annals of Mesopotamia. Towards the end of the Sixth Dynasty the authority of the kings no longer was absolute, and was increasingly challenged by independent provincial governors. An age of discord followed, known as the First Intermediate Period (2270–2060 B.C.). Upstart kings vied with one another for the support of the nobles, and invaders swept in from Libya and Asia. Finally the Eleventh Dynasty restored order and launched Egypt on the second period of stability, that of the Middle Kingdom (2060–1785 B.C.). The old pattern was repeated, though in obviously telescoped form. In less than three centuries Egypt was experiencing a Second Intermediate Period (1785–1580 B.C.), during which the country was invaded—and for the first time, conquered—by chariot-riding warriors, the Hyksos. As noted in the following chapter, these were but one group in an elemental movement of peoples that overran all centers of civilization in Eurasia in the course of the second millennium B.C.

The civilization of Egypt was generally stable and conservative, but by no means static. During the fifteen centuries between King Menes and the Hyksos, many changes in institutions and practices took place. Yet certain distinctive traits did persist through the centuries. One was the generally confident and optimistic world outlook of the Egyptians in contrast to that of the Sumerians. Just as the unpredictability and ferocity of the annual flooding of the Tigris-Euphrates contributed to the pessimism and insecurity of the Sumerians, so the predictability and gradualness of the Nile floods promoted opposite traits amongst the Egyptians. Whereas the Sumerians regarded their flood god as malevolent, the Egyptians viewed theirs as a deity "whose coming brings joy to every human being."

Egyptian religious beliefs and practices were extraordinarily complicated. They were made up of many elements—worship of the forces of nature, local sects devoted to the divinities of specific cities and nomes, the evolving beliefs of the priestly hierarchy, and diverse influences from abroad, especially from the East. The names of at least two thousand gods are known to us, yet none of these were regarded by their worshippers with complete submission or awe. The Egyptians believed instead that the deities were to be circumvented or manipulated for their personal or communal benefit. The aid of deities was invoked for unethical as well as ethical purposes, and the elaborate rituals performed in temples were as much incantations as acts of worship. During the later dynasties the idea that eternal afterlife was the reward for those who had been just and good in this life gradually developed. But Egyptian religion, with certain notable exceptions, had little ethical content. Also the mythology and theology lacked coherence, for the Egyptians were generally uninterested in the origins, characteristics, and relationships of their deities.

A predominant feature of Egyptian religious belief concerned death and the physical preparations for the afterlife, especially that of the king. Since his death was not final, his body was embalmed and placed in a gigantic tomb or pyramid, along with food and other necessities. The greatest of these pyramids was that of the Pharaoh Khufu, or Cheops, of the Fourth Dynasty. It covered 13 acres, rose to a height of 481 feet, and contained some 2,300,000 blocks, each weighing an average of $2\frac{1}{2}$ tons. And this was done with the simplest tools—ramps, rollers, and levers; no pulleys and no iron!

It has been said that the Egyptian peasants worked enthusiastically on these pyramids, believing that they were constructing the dwellings of a god on whom their collective well-being would depend. Whatever the justification for this statement—and it may be assumed that, enthusiastic or not, they had little choice in the matter—it does point up the presumed divinity of Egyptian kingship. From beginning to end the pharaoh was a god-king. No distinction was made between the sacred and the secular; indeed the notion was unthinkable. For this reason there was an absence in Egypt of anything corresponding to the Mesopotamian law codes. All law was the expression of the divine authority of the god-king.

This royal authority was enforced by a bureaucracy headed by the vizier—"the steward of the whole land," "the eyes and ears of the king." Other officials included the Royal Sealbearer, who controlled the Nile traffic, the Master of Largesse, who was responsible for all livestock, and the head of the Exchequer, who maintained branch offices with storehouses throughout the kingdom for the collection of taxes, and, probably, for the distribution of seeds and livestock in bad years. Also there were governors or *nomarchs* to rule each province, or *nome,* and below them came the mayors of the towns and villages. As in other empires, the nomarchs gradually accumulated large estates, became a hereditary official class, enhanced their power and status, and ultimately challenged central authority. This explains in large part the disruption of the Old Kingdom and the ensuing centuries of anarchy.

A final distinctive feature of Egyptian civilization was the overwhelming state domination of economic life. Individual property and enterprise were not unknown but neither were they as common as in Mesopotamia. The state not only controlled most production, both agricultural and handicraft, but also directed distribution. Huge government warehouses and granaries were filled with the taxes collected in kind—grains, animals, cloths, and metals. These served to defray state expenses and also provided reserves for years of scarcity. The king, it was said, is "he who presides over the food supplies of all." In addition to the taxes, each community had to provide men for the *corvée,* or forced labor. The pyramids are the best known examples of their work, but these laborers were also used for quarrying and mining and maintaining the irrigation canals.

Egyptian craftsmen were universally recognized for their skills, particularly in luxury products. Their jewelry can scarcely be excelled today; their enamel work and ivory and pearl inlay were superb; they discovered how to make glass in many colors; they were the first to bark-tan leather in the manner still followed in most of the world; and their linen cloth was as fine as has ever been woven. Egyptian technology was perhaps most precocious in devising artificial beauty aids. Medical papyri described procedures for removing wrinkles and darkening gray hair. Among the substances used for cosmetic purposes were kohl for lengthening the eyebrows and lining the outer corners of the eyes, malachite and lead ore for green and gray eye shadow respectively, red ocher for rouge, henna for dyeing the nails, the palms of the hand and the soles of the feet, and human hair for making wigs over which melted beeswax was poured. Ladies who wished to be in the height of fashion gilded their breasts and painted their nipples blue.

III. CRETE

The Minoan civilization of the island of Crete is named after its legendary king, Minos. Until the late nineteenth century the very existence of this civilization was unsuspected. The tales of heroes and gods recounted by Homer in the *Iliad* and *Odyssey* had been dismissed by scholars as folk myths. But they were believed by a German romanticist, Heinrich Schliemann, who vowed he would find and excavate Troy, where Greeks and Trojans had fought over Helen. He was sensationally successful, unearthing both Troy in Asia Minor and Mycenae in the Peloponnesus. The existence of a preclassical civilization in Greece had been proven, and at the end of the century the center of the Minoan civilization was unearthed by the English archaeologist Sir Arthur Evans at Knossos on Crete.

Neolithic communities had been long established on Crete when new settlers with new skills arrived from Asia Minor or Syria early in the third millennium B.C. These found a fertile land, well-known for its fish, its fruit, and especially its olive oil. Also its location in the middle of the eastern Mediterranean was ideal for trading purposes, the waters being safe and the climatic conditions favorable for small vessels propelled by oars or sails. Most Minoans doubtless tilled the soil, but their civilization definitely was amphibious—a thalassocracy, or sea civilization. The forests that covered their mountains provided the timber for constructing vessels in which they sailed from one end of the Mediterranean to the other. With their singlemasted ships they carried back and forth the foodstuffs, ivory, and glass of Egypt, the horses and wood of Syria, the silver, pottery, and marble of the Aegean Isles, the copper of Cyprus, and their own olive oil and pottery. Crete's location was ideal for cultural development as well as commercial. The Cretans were close enough to be stimulated by Mesopotamia and Egypt yet distant enough to be free to preserve their identity and express their individuality. This they did with such success that their civilization is indubitably the most graceful and zestful of the ancient world.

Minoan artists did not try to impress by mere size, nor did they concern themselves with remote and awful deities or divine kings. Instead they reproduced the life about them on their household utensils, on the walls of their houses, and in their works of art. They found models everywhere; in natural objects such as birds, flowers, sea shells, and marine life of all types; and in scenes from their own everyday life, such as peasants returning from their fields, athletes wrestling with bulls, and women dancing in honor of the Great Goddess. In architecture the Minoans were more interested in personal comfort than outward appearance. The royal palace at Knossos was a sprawling complex that apparently had grown over several centuries. It included not only a throne room, reception chambers, and living quarters, but also storehouses and workshops that occupied most of the complex, as befitted a trading people. Outstanding was an elaborate plumbing and sanitation system that was not surpassed until modern times.

The Minoans do not appear to have constructed great temples or monuments to their gods. Rather they set aside a few square feet in their homes to serve as private sanctuaries. The Knossos complex had a small room which seems to have been a chapel. The principal centers of worship were nature places—a mountain peak, a forest grove, or a limestone cave. The most important deity was female, the old Earth Mother, who was served by priestesses rather than priests. There are no indications of human or extensive animal sacrifices, the most common offerings being the fruits of the field.

Cretan communities seem to have been socially and economically more egalitarian than their counterparts on the mainland. In place of a few great temples and palaces surrounded by relative slums, the pattern on Crete was the open village, with its outdoor shrine as the center for community life. Families as a rule lived in individual houses built of timber and stucco. Domestic slaves probably were held, though not in large numbers. No buildings that may have been slave quarters have been found, so that the Cretan galleys presumably were rowed by freemen. None of the cities were fortified, indicating that Minoan sea power was deemed sufficient to protect the island. It suggests furthermore that the Cretan communities lived at peace with each other, in contrast to the traditional intercity warfare in Mesopotamia. All in all, it is understandable that ancient writers referred to Crete as "great, fat, and well-fed,"—the Isle of the Blessed.

IV. INDUS

About 2500 B.C., or approximately one thousand years after the appearance of man's first civilization at Sumer, another civilization emerged on the banks of the Indus River. It existed in solitary splendor until roughly 1500 B.C., when it petered out for reasons not yet entirely clear. Then it was completely forgotten, so that the Indians assumed their history began with the appearance of the Aryan invaders about 1500 B.C., just as the Greeks of the Classical Age assumed that their history began in 776 B.C., the year of the first Olympic games. In the 1920's archaeologists were attracted to a desolate spot on the lower Indus River containing several mounds and called by the local people Mohenjo-daro, or Place of the Dead. Excavations revealed that Mohenjo-daro was the site of a succession of flourishing cities, each built upon the ruins of the one before. Further excavations in other parts of the Indus Valley and surrounding territories uncovered an ancient civilization several times more widespread than either the Egyptian or Mesopotamian. It encompassed a triangular area roughly one thousand miles on each side, with the base of the triangle along the coast north and south of the mouth of the Indus, and extending northeastward to the foothills of the Himalayas.

Knowledge of this civilization is still at a rudimentary stage, so that further excavations may cause complete revision of current assumptions. The roots of the civilization have been traced back to an amalgam of indigenous Neolithic communities and immigrant farmers from the hills of Baluchistan who moved south into the Indus Valley early in the third millennium B.C. It is believed that the newcomers brought with them some knowledge of the cities and ways of Sumer, which facilitated the emergence of civilization on the Indus as it had earlier on the Nile. Like all the other ancient civilizations, that of the Indus was predominantly agricultural. Wheat and barley were the staples, but field peas, melons, sesame, and dates were also grown, as well as cotton, which was first used for cloth making in this valley. There was also considerable trade with the outside world, the items exported including peacocks, apes, pearls, cotton textiles, copper, ivory and ivory articles such as combs—the latter fashioned in the same pattern as the combs still used in India today, and still indispensable for combing lice out of the hair. Most of this foreign trade was with Mesopotamia and was carried on with sailing boats that followed the coast to the Persian Gulf. If driven out of sight of land, the sailors released crows that always flew toward the nearest point of coast. According to the Bible, this is precisely the method followed by Noah in the Ark when he wished to find out in which direction the land lay.

The Indus cities were unique for their time because they were carefully built according to a central plan rather than haphazardly like rabbit warrens. They were laid out on the grid pattern, with wide main streets encompassing large rectangular city blocks some four hundred yards in length and two hundred yards in width, far larger than the average city blocks of today. The buildings were constructed of bricks hardened in kilns, in contrast to the stone used in Egypt and the sun-dried bricks in Mesopotamia. The bricks everywhere were molded in two standard sizes (11 by 5.5 by 2.5 inches, and 9.2 by 4.5 by 2.2 inches), and weights and measures likewise were uniform throughout the Indus lands. Such orderliness and organization seem to have been all pervasive in this civilization. After it reached its maturity about 2500 B.C., it remained virtually static during the following millennium. This was carried even to the point of rebuilding the cities after each destructive flood in such a way that the new city was a duplicate of the old one. Such undeviating continuity of tradition has had no equal, even in Egypt, and has given rise to the theory that the authority regulating this disciplined society may have been spiritual. This hypothesis is supported also by the absence of military equipment and fortifications. But all this is mere speculation, and must remain so until more sites have been excavated and until the Indus script has been deciphered.

The causes and circumstances of the decline of the Indus civilization remain obscure. Hitherto it has been widely believed that Aryan invaders were primarily responsible, but it has recently been suggested that the civilization may have been literally drowned in mud. Subterranean volcanic activity, according to this theory, caused a huge upwelling of mud, silt, and sand that dammed the river and formed a huge lake that swamped Mohenjo-daro. After several decades the dam was worn down, the water drained through, and the river resumed its normal course, but in the meantime the city had been ruined. Judging from the multiple layers of silt found in Mohenjo-daro, this disaster occurred at least five times and perhaps more. The net result was irreparable damage to the heart of the Indus civilization, which left the outlying regions in the north too weak to resist the Aryan invaders, and in the south too weak to resist assimilation by native cultures.

V. SHANG

Not until about two thousand years after civilization first flowered in Mesopotamia did it appear in the valley of the Yellow River. There it was nourished by the fertile soil known as loess, which extends from the uplands of North China eastward to the sea. Another reason why the Yellow River valley was the center of the first Chinese civilization was that it is the most accessible region from the West. Nomads traversing the Central Eurasian steppes are deflected by mountain ranges towards North China rather than to the south. These nomads, as noted earlier were instruments of cultural cross fertilization as well as of raid and rapine. (See Chapter 1, section III.) This raises the question as to the degree to which the Shang civilization was indigenous or was stimulated by indirect contacts in the Middle East. The generally accepted theory is that the Shang were a relatively small group of Mongoloid invaders from the northwest steppes where they had indirectly acquired from the Middle East a knowledge of bronze and of war chariots. Exploiting the military advantage deriving from the technology, they conquered the Neolithic agricultural communities of North China.

Now a pattern of evolution ensued that was to appear repeatedly in the following millennia after each incursion into the country. The Shang enriched the local culture with the innovations they introduced, but were eventually assimilated, so that the Chinese traditions continued without interruption. The Shang civilization, then, comprised elements that doubtless were ultimately of Middle East derivation if traced back to their early Neolithic origins—elements such as barley, wheat, sheep, cattle, horses, bronze, and the wheel. Yet alongside these were indubitably native East Asian traits that, combined with the foreign adaptations, constituted the great and distinctive Chinese civilization that has persisted with an unequalled record of continuity from the Shang dynasty to modern times.

One of the uniquely Chinese culture traits was the raising of silkworms and the weaving of the fibers into delicate fabrics. Another was the eschewing of animal milk for human consumption, particularly noteworthy in view of the prominence of milk and milk products in the diet of Eurasian nomads. Ancestor worship has also been a prominent feature of Chinese religion from earliest times. Closely related was the importance attached to one's family name, which always preceded the personal name instead of following it as in the West. This reflected the traditional primary role in Chinese society of the family rather than of the individual, the state, or the church. The familiar Chinese style of architecture with the ornate roof supported by rows of wooden pillars also dates back to earliest times, as does the technique of bronze casting, which has never been surpassed anywhere in the world. The ritual bronze vessels were used in the preparation and offering of sacrificial meats, grain, and wine during the ancestor worship ceremonies. Most significant for the later history of China and all East Asia was the complex ideographic script found in Shang remains. This is the direct ancestor of modern Chinese writing, thus illustrating again the continuity of Chinese civilization. Whereas the hieroglyphics and cuneiform have for millennia meant nothing to the people of the Middle East, the Shang script is recognizable to modern Chinese.

As with the other Eurasian civilizations, the peasants here also were required to yield a portion of their crops to support the nobles, scribes, and officials gathered in the towns. Also they were obliged to serve under their lords in time of war as a light-armed infantry. Only the ruling warrior class could afford the two-horse chariots and the bronze helmets and plate mail that they wore into battle. This monopoly of bronze metallurgy buttressed the sharp class differentiation within Shang society. This was reflected in the contrast between the elaborate palaces and royal tombs on the one hand, and the crude pit dwellings of the common people on the other. It was illustrated also by the costly offerings that were placed in the tombs—bronze ritual vessels, fine silks, jades, marbles, musical instruments, and elaborate weapons. Even more impressive was the mass human slaughter, usually in multiples of ten, that accompanied royal burials. It is unknown whether the hapless victims, presumably slaves or prisoners of war, were sacrificed to propitiate vengeful gods or to become the slaves and concubines of the dead monarch.

SUGGESTED READING

B. and R. ALLCHIN, *The Birth of Indian Civilization: India and Pakistan Before 500 B.C.* (Penguin, 1968); R. GHIRSHMAN, *Iran* (Penguin, 1954); J. HAWKES, *The First Great Civilizations: Life in Mesopotamia, the Indus Valley, and Egypt* (Knopf, 1973); S. HOOD, *The Minoans* (Praeger, 1971); LI CHI, *The Beginnings of Chinese Civilization* (Univ. Washington, 1968).

chapter six

End of Ancient Civilizations

Since conquests are achieved only by dash and daring, a people accustomed to the nomadic life and the rough manners engendered by the desert can readily conquer a more civilized people, even though the latter be more numerous. . . .—Ibn Khaldun

In all civilizations there have been poets and thinkers who have looked to the past with longing. They have regarded prehistoric man as the "noble savage," untainted by the corrupting influence of civilization. Long ago, "in the beginning," during that wonderful first chapter of man's existence, there was paradise on earth. In the Hindu epics there are passages extolling an idyllic past in which castes were absent and man could enjoy life in freedom and security. Likewise Hesiod, an eighth century B.C. Greek poet, described a Golden Age of long ago, and then traced man's declining fortunes through the Silver and Iron ages to the deplorable present in which the author lived.

This concept of original bliss has some basis in historical fact, as its universality and persistence suggest. The various civilizations of the ancient world differed from each other in their respective "styles"—in their ways of looking at, and going through, life. But all of them were similar in one basic respect. They all changed man's relations with his fellow men in the same way. They all substituted a new class society for the classless society of precivilization times, with profound repercussions in every aspect of human society, including not only increased productivity, but also increased social fragility and consequent vulnerability to nomadic invasions. The purpose of this chapter is to analyze the historical significance of the ancient civilizations and the circumstances of the great invasions of the second millennium B.C. that laid the groundwork for the classical civilizations that followed.

I. HISTORICAL SIGNIFICANCE OF ANCIENT CIVILIZATIONS

So far as economic and social relationships were concerned, the tribesmen before the advent of civilization had enjoyed free and equal access to the natural resources necessary for livelihood. Economic equality and social homogeneity had

41

been the hallmark of their Neolithic villages. But when the tribesmen became peasants they no longer had free access to land and they no longer enjoyed the full product of their labor. Their specific obligations varied from region to region but the net result was everywhere the same. After making the payments required by the state, the priest, the landlord, and the moneylender, they were left almost invariably with only enough for sheer existence. In contrast to the egalitarianism of the Paleolithic hunting bands and the Neolithic villages, the ancient civilizations, as well as those of later periods, inevitably involved stratification into haves and have-nots.

What this meant in human terms was expressed as early as the third millennium B.C. by an Egyptian father taking his son to school and exhorting him to industry by contrasting the wretchedness of both peasants and workers with the blessings of learned scribes and officials.

Put writing in your heart that you may protect yourself from hard labor of any kind and be a magistrate of high repute. The scribe is released from manual tasks; it is he who commands. . . . Do you not hold the scribe's palette? That is what makes the difference between you and the man who handles an oar.

I have seen the metal-worker at his task at the mouth of his furnace, with fingers like a crocodile's. He stank worse than fish-spawn. . . . The stonemason finds his work in every kind of hard stone. When he has finished his labors his arms are worn out, and he sleeps all doubled up until sunrise. His knees and spine are broken. . . . The barber shaves from morning till night; he never sits down except to meals. He hurries from house to house looking for business. He wears out his arms to fill his stomach, like bees eating their own honey. . . . The farmer wears the same clothes for all times. His voice is as raucous as a crow's. His fingers are always busy, his arms are dried up by the wind. He takes his rest—when he does get any rest—in the mud. If he's in good health he shares good health with the beasts; if he is ill his bed is the bare earth in the middle of his beasts. . . .

Apply your heart to learning. In truth there is nothing that can compare with it. If you have profited by a single day at school it is a gain for eternity.[1]

The coming of civilization involved drastic change in political relationships. The Neolithic villagers had been subject to only rudimentary constraints, whether internal or external. But tribal chiefs and elders now were replaced by king or emperor, and by an omnipresent bureaucracy, including palace functionaries, provincial and district officials, judges, clerks, and accountants. Closely associated with this imperial administration was the ecclesiastical hierarchy that also was an integral feature of civilization. In place of the former shaman who had been a "leisure-time specialist," there now was the priest, a "full-time specialist."[2] This made possible the formulation of an official theology and the organization of a priestly hierarchy. Both the theology and the hierarchy served to buttress the secular order. They invested political institutions and leaders with divine sanction and attributes. The Mesopotamian *ishakku* was the vice-regent of his city's god, while the Egyptian pharaoh was the "living god." This coupling of divine and secular authority provided most powerful support for the *status quo*. It was a rare individual who dared risk swift retribution in this life and everlasting punishment in the hereafter.

As regards culture, the transformation wrought by civilization again was fundamental and enduring. The culture of a Neolithic village had been autonomous and homogeneous. All members had shared common knowledge, customs, and attitudes, and had not depended on outside sources for the maintenance of their way of life. But with civilization, a new and more complex society emerged. In addition to the traditional culture of the village agriculturist, there was now the new culture of the scribes, who knew the mysterious art of writing, of the priests, who knew the secrets of the heavens, of the artists, who knew how to paint and carve, and of the merchants, who exchanged goods with lands beyond deserts and seas. So there was no longer a single culture. Instead there developed what has been called *high culture* and *low culture*. The high culture was to be found in the schools, temples, and palaces of the cities; the low culture was in the villages. The high culture was passed on in writing by philosophers, theologians, and literary men; the low culture was transmitted by word of mouth among illiterate peasants.

The distinction between high and low culture has usually been overlooked because of our dependence upon written sources. Such sources naturally point up the existence of the various high cultures and their individual characteristics rather than the equally significant coexistence of high and low cultures within each civilization. In order to fully comprehend the experiences of mankind since the coming of civilization, it is essential to look within the individual civilizations as well as at them as a group. It is essential, in the words of the anthropologist Robert Redfield, to "slip in by the back entrance, through the villages. . . ."[3] If this is done, one finds everywhere the peasants in place of the Neolithic tribesmen. And all these peasant masses, in all parts of the civilized world, remained in many basic respects the same from the days of Sumer to the present time. Their skin color may have been brown or yellow or white. They may have grown rice or wheat or corn. Yet everywhere, as the historian Oscar Handlin has pointed out, "the peasant masses had maintained an imperturbable sameness."[4]

All the peasantries possessed in common a considerable body of factual information related to agriculture—information regarding the weather, the care of plants and animals, and the processes of combustion and fermentation. All the peasantries also regarded hard labor as a prime virtue and looked down upon townsmen as weaklings who were easily tired. Closely related was a common passion to own a plot of land, a few animals, and the simple tools of field and shop. This meant independence and security, and to attain this all peasantries stubbornly resisted outside intervention, whether by a landlord or by a present-day collective. This peasant "rugged individualism" was balanced, however, by the communal life and relationships of the village. The good neighbor was always ready to offer aid and sympathy when needed, as well as to participate in house raisings, warmings, harvest festivals, and other community affairs.

Relations between the high and low cultures normally were ambivalent and strained. On the one hand the peasants felt superior, regarding country life and agricultural work as morally "good," in contrast to urban life and professions. On the other hand, the elite regarded work as degrading and fit only for the masses who were capable of nothing better. Inevitably the Eurasian peasantries, in the course of millennia, internalized this attitude of their superiors and became servile and obsequious. And for those who refused to bend the knee, there was always ready at hand the physical violence of the soldier and the psychological violence of the priest. What scars this left on human beings is all too clear in the following report of present-day Indonesian peasants bowing and scraping before Dutch officials while Papuan tribesmen stand erect.

Netherlands officials who have seen service in Indonesia have had to do some considerable adjusting in New Guinea.

In Indonesia they came into a society that had its caste and class distinctions, its own ideas of authority and rights of rulers. They were masters and were treated as masters.

In New Guinea there are no masters and no slaves. Papuan life is a free sort of life. There are no village councils, no great lawgivers or authorities. A man's pretty much his own man, except for the influence on life of demons and spirits.

Between the Dutch and the Papuans there is no bowing and scraping. An Indonesian school-teacher who tried to convince Papuans that the proper way to show respect was to walk hunched over in front of superiors was told:

"We are men, and men walk straight."

A Dutch official walked into an office in Hollandia [New Guinea]. Seated at a table were an Indonesian official, still in the Netherland's service, and two Papuan village headmen. The Indonesian jumped to his feet and stood still. The Papuans looked up, smiled and remained seated.[5]

It is evident that the advent of civilization represented a setback for equality between man and man. On the other hand civilization also brought great gains and achievements. Viewed in the light of historical perspective, it constituted a major step forward in the evolution of man. In this respect it resembled the industrial revolution, which initially was responsible for painful social disruption and incalculable human suffering, but which in the long run advanced decisively man's productivity and well-being. So it was with the urban revolution and civilization. The average Neolithic tribesman probably led a more rounded and satisfying life than the average peasant or urban worker. But precisely because tribal culture was comfortable and tension-free, it was also relatively unproductive. (See Chapter 3, section IV.) The exactions of the tax collector, the priest, and the landowner were onerous, but they were also effective in stimulating output. Positive proof of the increased productivity was the enormous population increase in the river valleys. "The vast areas of the new cities as compared with any barbarian [Neolithic] village, the immense cemeteries attached to them, and the stupendous works executed by the citizens, place this conclusion beyond question."[6]

Living standards also rose along with population figures. Certainly the monarchs and the top officials, both secular and ecclesiastical, enjoyed a variety of food and drink, along with an opulence in clothing and accommodations that no tribal chieftain could ever have imagined. The new middle classes—merchants, scribes, lower officials, and clergy—also were able to lead lives that probably were as pleasant and refined as those enjoyed by their counterparts today. Even the masses may in some cases have been better off in the material sense, if not the psycho-social. A British archaeologist has pointed out that, "The sea-fish . . . brought to Lagash from the Persian Gulf and to Mohenjo-daro from the Arabian Sea were probably articles of popular consumption that a Stone Age peasant could never enjoy. The workmen's quarters at Harappa are more commodious than Neolithic huts."[7]

Civilization, with the new art of writing, also made possible the steady accumulation of knowledge and its transmission to successive generations. Innumerable examples of the astonishing technical triumphs of antiquity abound in present-day museums. Various sciences, including mathematics, astronomy, and medicine, also trace their beginnings back to these millennia. And the very affluence of the urban centers opened new horizons for architects, sculptors, painters, musicians, and poets.

It is true that these precious gains benefited the few much more than the many who, in the final analysis, bore the costs of the high culture. But the important point so far as the whole history of man is concerned is that the advances *were* made. And it was these advances, accumulating through the millennia, that finally enabled man in modern times to gain such mastery over nature and such productivity through science and technology, that the many are now benefiting along with the few. During the long intervening period the low culture of the villages remained largely unchanged. But the various high cultures underwent continual change—in their religions and philosophies and arts and sciences. These changes will be considered in parts III and IV, after the circumstances of the decline and fall of the ancient civilizations are examined in the following sections.

II. NOMADS ENTER HISTORY

The second millennium B.C. in Eurasia was a period of turbulence—a period of nomadic invasions, of the overthrow of old imperial structures, and of the disruption of old social systems. The ferment was profound and the dislocation was felt from one end of Eurasia to the other. For this reason, the second millennium was an age of transition in the course of which the ancient civilizations disappeared from the historical stage and their place taken by the classical civilizations.

Such wholesale fall and rise of empires, which has occurred more than once in the course of history, raises the question of causation. Was it internal rot or external force that was primarily responsible for political and social demolition throughout Eurasia? It is extremely difficult to answer such a broad question with certainty and precision. The degree to which, in the several regions involved, internal factors were operative as against external cannot be ascertained exactly, though it is safe to assert that both were major factors in determining the course of events.

Beginning with the internal weaknesses, there was first the scarcity and costliness of copper and bronze, which prevented the general use of these metals in making weapons and tools. This gave monarchs and their political and military allies a virtual monopoly of armaments and hence buttressed their privileged position at the top of the social pyramid. It also meant that only a small percentage of the total population was armed, a serious weakness when the old centers of civilization had to face the assault of nomads who were all armed.

The high cost of copper and bronze also deprived the peasantry of metal tools, and perforce they had to rely on stone axes and hoes, and on flint knives and sickles. This lowered productivity considerably, since stone tools were less efficient and durable than metal. Productivity also was curbed by the petering out of technological progress. "The thousand years or so immediately preceding 3000 B.C.," writes the British archaeologist V. Gordon Childe, "were perhaps more fertile in fruitful inventions and discoveries than any period in human history prior to the sixteenth century A.D."[8] This was the millennium, as noted earlier, when man learned to harness the power of wind and of animals, when he discovered the wheel, the art of writing, the technique of irrigation, and the chemical processes involved in metallurgy. (See Chapter 4, section II.) By contrast the third and second millennia B.C. witnessed nothing approaching this great creative outburst; the only comparable inventions during this later period were iron smelting (1400 B.C.) and a truly alphabetic script (1300 B.C.).

One partial explanation for the slowdown in technological growth, according to V. Gordon Childe, was the class differentiation noted in the preceding section. This differentiation undermined incentive for technological innovation. The ruling groups now had an abundant supply of docile labor available in the form of tenants or slaves, but the latter were unlikely to take the initiative in devising or adopting new techniques or devices when any increase in output would benefit others rather than themselves. This brake upon innovation because of social inequity persists to the present day, as indicated by the following comments made recently by a villager in India to an American missionary:

To a newcomer we may seem suspicious, obstinate, intolerant, backward—everything that goes with refusal to change. We did not choose these characteristics for ourselves. Experience forced them upon our fathers, and the warnings of our father, added to our experiences, have drilled them into us. Refusal to change is the armor with which we have learned to protect ourselves. If we and our fathers had accepted the new ideas and customs commended to us, we might have made greater progress. But greater progress would have drawn the eyes of a covetous world toward us. And then our lot would have been worse than before. . . . The plow that Bala's brother won at your exhibition last spring is better. It is light, like our plows, and good for ordinary plowing. But Bala's brother has not dared to use it. He is so prosperous that he is afraid of anything that makes a show of still greater prosperity. In that he may seem foolish to you. But we do not blame him for his caution.[9]

In addition to the weaknesses within, there was the constant threat of three nomadic groups without. In the southern deserts were the Semitic tribesmen, in the Eurasian steppes to the west the Indo-Europeans, and to the east the Mongol-Turkish peoples.

The Indo-Europeans, a cultural rather than a racial group, appear to have originated in the region of the Caspian Sea where they tended their herds of cattle and did a little farming on the side. Being primarily pastoralists, they were ever ready to pack their belongings into their great oxcarts and move on to more promising lands. Entire tribes participated in these migrations—women and children as well as the warriors. Thus they pushed westward to southern Russia and southeastern Europe, so that by 2000 B.C. they ranged in the broad belt from the Danubian Plain to the Oxus and Jaxartes valleys. From this far-flung base they increasingly threatened the centers of civilization that were geographically accessible to them—the Middle East, the Balkan Peninsula, and the Indus Valley.

The original dividing line between the Indo-European peoples in the western part of the steppes and the Mongol-Turkish in the eastern part consisted of the Altai and the Tien Shan Mountains. To the east of this line the steppes are higher and drier, and the climate generally more harsh. The pastures here are not as rich as in the west, and can support sheep, camels, and horses, but not cattle. This geographic imbalance produced a corresponding historic imbalance in the form of a persistent and powerful East-to-West gradient. The peoples of the eastern steppes were attracted to the west, both as refugees and as conquerors. A succession of tribes followed one upon the other—Scythians migrating from the Altai to the Ukraine; Turkish tribes replacing them in Central Asia and later following them westward; and finally the Mongols pushing from the rear until their great eruption in the thirteenth century during which they overran most of Eurasia. These eastern nomads, because of their geographic location, had access not only to Europe, the Middle East, and India, but also to China, where they broke through periodically when the opportunity presented itself.

Because of the East-to-West gradient, the racial composition of the peoples of the western steppes gradually changed from predominantly Caucasoid to predominantly Mongoloid, at least as far west as the Caspian Sea. The shift began late in the first millennium B.C. and continued until the end of the medieval period, when the tide was reversed by the Slavic Russians armed with the weapons of Western technology—muskets and cannon at first, and later machine guns and railroads.

Finally the Semites occupied roughly the area from the Mediterranean to the Tigris and from the Taurus to Aden. Successive waves have appeared through history, emerging apparently from the deserts of Arabia. They used the donkey for transportation until about 1100 B.C., when the domestication of the camel transformed their culture as the domestication of the horse did that of the steppe nomads. With the rise of civilization many Semitic tribes lived on the edges of the city, developing a symbiotic relationship with the urban dwellers, and always being ready to seize any chance for raid and plunder.

The old centers of civilization on the periphery of Eurasia were irresistible magnets for the surrounding tribesmen. The abundant crops, the barns swollen with grain, and the dazzling luxuries of the cities, all beckoned to the hungry nomads of steppes and deserts. Hence the periodic raids and invasions, particularly of the Mesopotamian cities, which were more vulnerable than those of Crete or the Nile or the Indus. But it was not until the second millennium B.C. that the balance of power throughout Eurasia shifted, and for the first time the nomads threatened the very existence of the great civilizations.

The new military capabilities of the nomads derived from two fateful developments—the domestication of the horse, and later, the smelting of iron. So far as is known, the earliest domestication of animals took place in the Middle East, where also occurred the earliest riding of animals. Both took place about 5000 B.C., but there was little riding at that early date for the simple reason that the only animals available were the ox, which was too slow, and the onager, or wild ass, which was too small. The practice of animal domestication, however, spread northward to southern Russia where both the onager and the wild horse were to be found. These two animals were domesticated there by 2500 B.C., and soon the horse became favored because it was larger, stronger, and faster. Furthermore the horse gradually increased in size with selective beeding by the southen Russian nomads.

The first military use that the nomads made of their horse was to harness it to a light-bodied chariot with two spoked wheels, which they developed as an improvement on the clumsy Mesopotamian cart with four solid wheels. The combination of the large horse and easily maneuverable chariot gave the nomads a formidable weapon—the war chariot. The first wave of nomadic invasions in the second millennium B.C. were invasions of charioteers. They rode hard into battle with one warrior in the chariot in charge of the horses and the others shooting arrows from their powerful compound bows. Few infantrymen could stand up for long to the volleys of arrows, let alone to the massed chariot charges that followed.

Towards the end of the second millennium the nomads further increased their military effectiveness by shifting from chariot to cavalry warfare. Their horses were now large and strong enough to bear directly the weight of the rider. Also the nomads developed the bridle and bit for guiding the horse, and the horned saddle and stirrup, which enabled them to ride with both hands free and to launch a shower of arrows at full gallop. This gave the Eurasian nomads unprecedented mobility, so that they were able to outride and outfight the armies defending the urban centers. This was the basis of nomadic military prowess through the Classical and Medieval ages, culminating in the extraordinary conquests of Genghis Khan in the thirteenth century. Not until the superiority of Western firearms was brought to bear were the centers of civilization relieved of the constant threat of nomadic invasion.

The counterpart of the horse for the desert nomad was the camel, of which there were two varieties—the one-humped Arabian, which is adapted to hot desert conditions, and the two-humped Bactrian relative, which is adapted to cold desert conditions. Both can live off land where even the ass would starve, and both can go for weeks on fat stored in their humps and on water stored in their multiple stomachs. Where and when the camel was first tamed is not clear, but by 1000 B.C., transportation and communication across the deserts of Central Asia and the Middle East were dependent on the "ship of the desert."

The discovery of the technique for smelting iron ore also enhanced nomadic military strength. It was not until the middle of the second millennium B.C. that the technique was developed in northeast Asia Minor, and not until the destruction of the Hittite Empire about 1200 B.C. that the local ironsmiths were scattered and their technique became generally known.

Iron ore, in contrast to copper and tin, is very widespread and correspondingly cheap. This meant that ordinary peasants now could afford iron tools. Agricultural productivity rose, and the limits of agriculture were extended into heavily wooded areas that hitherto had been impervious to the stone ax. (See Chapter 7, section I.) Equally significant was the effect of the cheap new metal on the Eurasian military balance. Hitherto the poverty-stricken nomads had not been able to afford the expensive bronze weapons in as large quantities as could the rulers of the urban centers. But now iron ore was available in almost every region, and every village smith could forge new weapons that were both superior to, and cheaper than, the old. Thus nomadic warriors now enjoyed not only superior mobility but also iron weapons that were as good and as plentiful as those of the soldiers guarding the civilized areas.

III. NOMADIC INVASIONS IN THE MIDDLE EAST

The combination of the horses and iron weapons precipitated two great waves of nomadic invasion that overwhelmed the centers of civilization. During the first, between roughly 1700 and 1500 B.C., the invaders usually arrived with horse-drawn chariots and bronze weapons; by the second wave between about 1200 and 1100 B.C. they commonly rode on horses and fought with iron weapons. These invasions should not be thought of as vast incursions of hordes that displaced native stock and completely changed ethnic patterns. Rather it was a case of relatively small numbers of invaders who used their superior military technology to establish themselves as warrior elites ruling over subject peoples that far outnumbered them.

The end result was the uprooting of civilization everywhere except in the Middle East. It was not that that region did not suffer invasions; indeed it endured the largest number because of its geographic accessibility. Empires rose and fell in the Middle East in rapid succession, yet civilization itself survived. One reason was that it had been established for a longer period in the Middle East and had sunk deeper roots. Also such large expanses of the Middle East had become civilized by 1700 B.C. that they could not all be overwhelmed and destroyed. Finally, the invaders in the Middle East usually were not raw barbarians fresh from the steppes or desert, but rather semicivilized barbarians who had settled earlier in surrounding lands and who consequently were already partially assimilated by the time of conquest.

About 2000 B.C. the Indo-European Hittites filtered into Asia Minor, probably through the Caucasus. They coalesced with the native peoples and in the course of the following centuries they organized an extensive empire that included much of Syria as well as Asia Minor. They even raided Babylon about 1590 B.C., though they never were able to establish themselves in Mesopotamia. The Kassites were another Indo-European group that came from the Zagros Mountains to the east of Mesopotamia. Taking advantage of the Hittite raid on Babylon they occupied that ancient capital and established a Third Babylonian Dynasty that lasted for several centuries (1600–1100 B.C.). Another invading tribe were the Hurrians, known in the Bible as Horites, who apparently came from the highlands of Armenia. To the north of Babylonia, in the region of Assyria, they created the Mitanni Empire, which reached its height about 1500 B.C. The Hurrians adopted much of Mesopotamian culture and transmitted it to surrounding peoples, including the Hittites in Asia Minor. Even well-protected Egypt did not escape unscathed during the centuries of turmoil. Between 1720 and 1570 B.C. that country was ruled by a very mixed, though predominantly Semitic, group of invaders known as the Hyksos. With their horse-drawn chariots and heavy type of sword and body armor they were able to dominate their country from their base in the delta, though they always remained the hated "Asiatic" foreigners.

By 1500 B.C. this first wave of invasions subsided in the Middle East and a reaction against the intruders set in amongst the indigenous peoples who comprised the vast majority. The Egyptians adopted the military techniques and weapons of the Hyksos to expel them in 1570 B.C. and to establish the Eighteenth Dynasty and the New Kingdom. After this experience with foreign domination the Egyptians sought security in imperial expansion. By the mid-fifteenth century B.C. they controlled Palestine, Syria, Phoenicia, and even reached the Euphrates. Local rulers were allowed to remain on their thrones but power rested with Egyptian garrisons and high commissioners. Likewise in Assyria native leaders successfully overthrew the Mitanni Empire and went on to conquer the Kassites. Thus they established the first Assyrian Empire, which dominated the Mesopotamian Valley. These developments left three major powers in the Middle East: the Hittite Empire in the north, the Egyptian in the south, and the Assyrian in the east.

This triangular balance was upset by the second wave of barbarian invasions, which got under way about 1200 B.C. The newcomers were not as devastating as those of the first wave, but they did leave a permanent imprint on the Middle East. They were aided by the fact that the Hittite and Egyptian empires had engaged in a long series of wars that left both exhausted and forced them to evacuate the Syrian-Palestine corridor. Three Semitic peoples moved into the vacuum. The Phoenicians established themselves on the Mediterranean coast where they founded important industrial and trading centers. The Arameans settled in Syria, Palestine, and northern Mesopotamia, and from their base in Damascus they became the masters of the caravan routes, as the Phoenicians were of the sea routes. Finally the Hebrews, who settled in Palestine and Syria, were destined to play a major role in history because of their religion. Meanwhile to the east other invaders such as the Indo-European Medes and the Semitic Chaldeans were infiltrating into Iran and southern Mesopotamia.

About 1100 B.C., a new center of power was taking form, the second Assyrian Empire. Iron weapons, a disciplined army, an efficient bureaucracy, and iron battering rams mounted on wheels enabled the Assyrians to steadily expand their rule. By the seventh century B.C. their empire, with its capital at Nineveh, included all Mesopotamia, portions of the Iranian plateau, Asia Minor, Syria, Palestine, and Egypt as far south as Thebes. But overextension of the empire and the implacable hostility of the subject peoples ultimately led to disaster. In 612 B.C. a coalition of enemies—Medes and Chaldeans, along with Scythian nomads from the north—destroyed Nineveh and ended forever the role of the Assyrians in history.

The fall of Nineveh was followed by a brief interlude during which the Medes and Chaldeans divided the legacy of the fallen empire. But a new colossus now emerged—the Persian Empire—that was by far the greatest imperial structure to date. The Persians, related to the Medes and formerly subject to them, first defeated their former overlords. Then under their King Cyrus (550–529 B.C.), and utilizing Assyrian military techniques, they overran in quick succession Asia Minor and the Chaldean Empire in Babylonia. Within a decade after Cyrus' death his successors had conquered both Egypt in the west and the Indian Punjab in the east. Thus the Persian Empire at its height ranged from the Nile River to the Indus and beyond. The entire Middle East now was under one rule and the barbarian tribes were effectively checked.

Despite the turbulence of these long centuries of invasion and the unceasing rise and fall of kingdoms and empires and their rulers, the significant fact is the remarkable degree of cultural continuity. As noted earlier, the demolition of political structures did not mean the extinction of civilization in the Middle East. Rather, the invading barbarians, beguiled by the luxuries of urban life and needing the cooperation of native scribes and bureaucrats and priests, soon adapted to the manners and traditions of their subjects.

IV. NOMADIC INVASIONS OF THE PERIPHERAL CIVILIZATIONS

Greece

In direct contrast to the Middle East, there was little cultural continuum in the peripheral regions of Greece, India and China. Their civilizations lacked the depth in time and space that bolstered those of Mesopotamia and Egypt, and consequently were wiped out in the course of the invasions of the second millennium B.C. In Greece, the first Indo-European invaders were the Achaeans who came sometime in the twentieth century B.C. They were charioteers with bronze weapons who traditionally have been thought to have infiltrated southward from the Danubian plains, though recent evidence suggests they may have crossed the Aegean from northwestern Asia Minor. Their general level of development was far behind that of the Minoan Cretans, but by 1600 B.C. the newcomers had absorbed much of the Minoan culture that had been transplanted to the mainland, and had established a number of small kingdoms from Thessaly down to the southern tip of the Peloponnesus.

The most advanced settlements were those in the Peloponnesus, being the closest to Crete. Mycenae was the outstanding center in the Peloponnesus, and has given its name to the emerging civilization. All settlements in Mycenaean Greece were strongly fortified, in contrast to the cities of Crete. Massive hilltop citadels were constructed, where the king and his retainers lived. The commoners built their dwellings outside the citadel but in time of danger sought refuge within its walls.

In contrast to the other Indo-European invaders, who had established themselves in the Middle East and the Indus Valley, the Mycenaeans took to the sea after the fashion of the Minoans and developed a formidable maritime power.

Depending on the opportunities at hand, they raided, they traded, and they founded overseas colonies in Rhodes, Cyprus, and the west coast of Asia Minor. The Mycenaeans exported pottery, olive oil, and hides in return for luxuries such as spices, ivory, and jewelry. In time, their goods were crowding out those of Crete in the markets of South Italy, Syria, and Egypt. Thus the Mycenaeans undermined the former economic hegemony of Crete in the Mediterranean, and by the fifteenth century B.C. they were raiding the great island itself. The un-·walled cities, including the capital of Knossos, were taken and destroyed. These disasters, together with a series of devastating earthquakes, led to the virtual extinction of the formerly great Minoan civilization by 1150 B.C.

Meanwhile the Mycenaeans were experiencing a similar fate at the hands of new invaders, the Dorians. Appearing about 1200 B.C. and armed with iron weapons, they captured the Mycenaean citadels and towns one by one. Administrative systems disintegrated, rural populations scattered, foreign trade withered, and Greece reverted to an agrarian and pastoral economy. A Dark Age descended and obscured Greece until the rise of the historical city states about 800 B.C.

The main Dorian settlements were in the Peloponnesus, from which the invaders pushed on overseas and founded colonies in Crete, in Rhodes, and on the adjacent coast of Asia Minor. Other Greeks, perhaps Mycenaean refugees, crossed from Athens to the Cyclades Islands and on to the central part of the west coast of Asia Minor. There they established settlements that became known as Ionia, which for a period was the most advanced region of the entire Greek world. Still further north other bands speaking the Aeolic dialect sailed from Thessaly and central Greece to the island of Lesbos and thence to northern Asia Minor. These new Greek colonies in Asia Minor were never able to expand into the interior because of the resistance of a numerous local population. They were confined to the coastal areas, yet they prospered and were destined to play a major role in the general history of the Greek people.

Much more is known of this Dark Age in Greece than of the corresponding post-invasion period in India. This is due in part to the fact that the Greeks had closer contacts with the ancient Middle Eastern civilizations than did the Indians. Traces of these contacts are available in archaeological remains and literary sources and provide clues to early Greek history and culture. More important is the precious heritage of the four great poems left by the Greeks themselves—Homer's *Iliad* and *Odyssey,* and Hesiod's *Works and Days* and *Birth of the Gods.* Homer wrote of war, adventure, and the life of nobles and kings, while Hesiod described the life and lore of the farmer, and the genealogies of the gods. Between them they have left a vivid picture of the primitive agricultural and pastoral society of these centuries. Households were largely self-sufficient, growing their own food and making their cloth with wool from their flocks of sheep. The monotony of the farm work was broken by the occasional visit of a bard who sang of the glories of war and of the exploits of illustrious ancestors.

Each community consisted of the noble families that governed and led in war, and the commoners, including freehold peasants, tenant farmers, and a few craftsmen, hired laborers, and slaves. At the top was the king, whose authority depended on his prowess in war and his leadership qualities in meetings of the council of nobles. Occasionally the king called a meeting of the assembly that included all adult males, but the purpose usually was to mobilize popular support for decisions already reached in conjunction with the nobles. These simple institutions, typical of the Indo-European tribes at this level of development, represented the embryo from which the Greek city state was to develop its organs of government.

India

In India, the Indus Valley civilization experienced the same fate as the Minoan of Crete. About 1500 B.C., it was overrun by tribesmen who had the military advantage of possessing iron weapons and horse-drawn chariots as against the copper weapons and ox-drawn carts of the natives. The invaders called themselves Aryans, and the land in which they settled Aryavarta, or land of the Aryans. They were of the Indo-European family of peoples, of which the western branches had invaded Mesopotamia and Greece, and the eastern, Iran, where some settled down while others continued eastward to the Indus. It was not a case of a concerted or planned campaign like those of the Muslims in later centuries. Rather the Aryans, in small groups, infiltrated a civilization that obviously had passed its peak and was unable to resist effectively.

As noted earlier, it is not clear whether the Indus civilization collapsed primarily because of the Aryan onslaught or because of seismic cataclysms. (See Chapter 5, section IV.) Whatever the reason, the fact remains that a primitive new society emerged in the latter half of the second millennium B.C. Information concerning this society is scanty because the Aryans left no concrete remains, for they used wood or mud for their dwellings and had no large cities. Thus material available for the reconstruction of Aryan life is the direct antithesis of that available for the Indus civilization. The latter left a wealth of material remains and no decipherable written records, whereas the Aryans left practically no remains and a wealth of literature in the form of Vedas. The word Veda means knowledge, and for the Hindus the Vedas are a primary source of religious belief as the Bible is for Christians and the Koran for Muslims. There were originally four Vedas, but the most important is the Rigveda, which is a primary source for study of the early Aryans as Homer's epics are for Mycenaean Greece.

The Aryans were tall, with blue eyes and fair skin, and very conscious of these physical features in contrast to those of the indigenous people whom they conquered. The latter are referred to in the Vedas as short, black, noseless, and as *dasas,* or slaves. The image of the Aryans that emerges from the Vedic literature is that of a virile people, fond of war, drinking, chariot racing, and gambling. When they first arrived in India the Aryans were primarily pastoralists. Their economic life centered around their cattle, and wealth was judged on the basis of the size of the herds. As the newcomers settled in the fertile river valleys, they gradually shifted more to agriculture. They lived in villages consisting of a number of related families. Several villages comprised a clan, and several clans a tribe, at the head of which was the king. As in Greece, the king's authority depended on his personal prowess and initiative, and was limited by the council of nobles, and in some tribes by the freemen.

The outstanding characteristic of this early Aryan society was its basic difference from the later Hinduism. Cows were not worshipped but eaten. Intoxicating spirits were not forsaken but joyously consumed. There were classes but no castes, and the priests were subordinate to the nobles rather than at the top of the social pyramid. In short, Aryan society resembled much more the other contemporary Indo-European societies than it did the classical Hinduism that was to develop in later centuries.

China

About 1500 B.C. charioteers with bronze weapons also invaded the distant valley of the Yellow River in North China. There they found a flourishing Neolithic culture from which evolved the Shang civilization. The current state of archaeological research does not allow definite conclusions as to the precise relationship between the invasions and the appearance of the civilization. It is generally agreed, however, that it was not a case of wholesale transplantation of foreign elements. Rather the indigenous Neolithic culture provided the solid base, to which the invaders contributed certain innovations and stimuli. Hence the Shang civilization was analyzed in the preceding chapter as one of the ancient civilizations. It follows that the intrusion of charioteers into North China did not produce a sharp cultural break as it did in Greece and India. Rather the distinctively Chinese Neolithic culture continued as a distinctively Chinese civilization, which persisted from the Shang period to the present.

This pattern of continuity is apparent in the transition from the Shang to the Chou dynasty in 1027 B.C. The Chou people had for long lived in the Wei Valley on the fringes of civilization, so that they shared the language and basic culture of the Shang at the same time that they borrowed military techniques from the sheep-herding "barbarians" to the north and west. Consequently when the Chou overran North China there was no interruption in the evolution of Chinese civilization. The writing system continued as before, as did ancestor worship and the division of society into aristocratic warriors and peasant masses. Political decentralization also persisted, and indeed became more pronounced under the Chou rulers who assigned the conquered territories to vassal lords. The latter journeyed periodically to the Chou court for elaborate ceremonies of investiture, but gradually this practice lapsed. The lords, ensconced in their walled towns, ruled over the surrounding countryside with little control from the capital.

In 771 B.C. the Chou capital was captured by "barbarians" allied with rebellious lords. The Chou dynasty resumed its rule from a center further to the east that was not so vulnerable to attacks from the borderlands. Thus the dynastic period before 771 B.C. is termed by the Chinese the Western Chou, and the period thereafter the Eastern Chou. During the latter time the Chou kings were rulers in name only. They were accorded certain religious functions and some ceremonial respect, but their domains were smaller than those of their nominal vassals, and their power correspondingly weaker. Indeed they managed to survive until 256 B.C. because they provided spiritual leadership. The dynasty was also a royal priesthood, and as such it was preserved as a symbol of national unity.

Although the Eastern Chou was a period of political instability, it was also a period of cultural flowering. It was a dynamic and creative age when the great works of literature and philosophy and social theory were written. This was the time when the classical Chinese civilization was taking form, corresponding to the classical Greek and Indian civilizations that were evolving at roughly the same time. The origin and nature of these classical civilizations is the subject of Part III.

SUGGESTED READING

O. LATTIMORE, *Inner Asian Frontiers of China* (Amer. Geographical Soc., 1940), and his *Studies in Frontier History: Collected Papers 1928–1958* (Mouton, 1962); W. M. McGOVERN, *The Early Empires of Central Asia* (Univ. North Carolina, 1939); E. D. PHILLIPS, *The Royal Hordes: Nomad Peoples of the Steppes* (Thames, 1965); G. VERNADSKY, *Ancient Russia* (Yale Univ., 1943).

part three

CLASSICAL CIVILIZATIONS OF EURASIA, 1000 B.C.-A.D. 500

The classical civilizations of Eurasia differed from the preceding ancient civilizations in several basic respects. One was their range, which, with the continuing advance of technology, expanded from river valleys to encompass entire regions such as China, the Indian peninsula, and the Mediterranean basin with its hinterland. No longer was it a case of valley civilizations surrounded by a sea of barbarism. Rather it was now the regional civilizations that expanded steadily outward until they were contiguous to each other, so that civilization stretched in an almost uninterrupted band across the breadth of Eurasia.

The classical civilizations were distinctive in content as well as in range. Like the ancient civilizations, each of these classical civilizations developed its special style. During these centuries, each evolved the social, religious, and philosophical systems that were to persist to modern times. Confucianism, Hinduism, Christianity, caste organization, and democratic government all emerged from the remarkable creativity of the Classical Age. This creativity, it should be noted, was not confined to one locality as had been the case at the time of the ancient civilizations. The Middle East then functioned as the center of initiative from which had diffused such fundamental innovations as agriculture, metallurgy, writing, and urban life. But now, during the centuries of the classical period, there existed an equilibrium amongst the Eurasian civilizations, and they interacted as equals. If anything, it was the Middle East that now lagged behind, while what had been the peripheral civilizations of Europe, India, and China now generated most of the innovations that distinguish the Classical Age.

chapter seven

Incipient Eurasian
Ecumene

Formerly the things which happened in the world had no connection among themselves. Each action interested only the locality where it happened. But since then all events are united in a common bundle.—Polybius

The most obvious and striking feature of the age of the classical civilizations was the existence for the first time of what might be termed an incipient Eurasian ecumene—a Eurasia that was on the way to becoming a functioning unit, an interacting whole. A comparison of the map of Eurasia about 1500 B.C. with that of about A.D 200 makes clear the substance of this Eurasian ecumene. (See Maps VI and X.) The empires of the early period were almost entirely restricted to their respective river valleys, and give the appearance of tiny islands in a vast sea of barbarism. By the first century A.D., however, the Roman, Parthian, Kushan, and Han empires spanned the breadth of Eurasia from the Scottish Highlands to the China Seas. This made possible a modest degree of interaction amongst empires. Of course there had always been certain interregional contacts even at the time of the ancient civilizations, as evidenced by the nomadic invasions in all directions. But now in the Classical Age these interregional contacts were substantially more close, varied, and sustained. And yet, even by the end of the Classical period the Roman and Chinese empires at opposite ends of Eurasia had not been able to establish direct official contact, and possessed no specific or reliable knowledge of each other. Thus Eurasian ecumenism remained at the incipient stage throughout these centuries. The origins, nature, and significance of this incipient ecumenism are the subject of this chapter.

I. ROOTS OF ECUMENISM

At the basis of the new Eurasian ecumenism was technological advance. This was to be expected, since from the very beginning of man's history the range of his activities had depended on the level of his technology. When he was at the food gathering stage, the range of the individual band was its hunting ground. As man learned agriculture and metallurgy and shipbuilding, we have seen that his range broadened to encompass, for example, the valley empires of Sargon and of the pharaohs. But now further technological advance made possible a much greater extension of agriculture and civilization, and hence the organization of regional empires that stretched contiguously across the breadth of Eurasia. And this technological advance was basically the discovery and increasingly widespread use of iron.

As noted earlier, iron smelting was developed first in Asia Minor in the middle of the second millennium B.C., and spread from there after the destruction of the Hittite Empire about 1200 B.C. (See Chapter 6, section III.) We have seen that the discovery facilitated the second wave of barbarian invasions at the end of the second millennium B.C., but some centuries elapsed before the new metal was available in sufficient quantities for everyday use. When hoes and axes and plows, as well as weapons, could be made of iron, then the economic, social, and political repercussions were immediate and far reaching.

This stage was reached slowly—about 800 B.C. in India, 750 B.C. in Central Europe, and 600 B.C. in China. In these and other regions the advent of cheap iron led first and foremost to the cutting down of heavy forests hitherto invulnerable to stone-edged axes and wooden plows. But farmers now were able to use their strong and sharp iron axes and their iron-shod plows to extend agriculture from the Middle East eastward across the Iranian plateau and westward across the Mediterranean lands and into Central and Northern Europe. Likewise in India the Aryan newcomers pushed eastward and cut down the forests of the Ganges Valley. At the same time agriculturists in China were extending their operations from the Yellow River Valley southward to the great Yangtze basin.

This expansion of the frontiers of agriculture made possible a corresponding expansion of the ecumene of civilization, which grew more in the half millennium from 1000 to 500 B.C. than in the preceding three millennia from 4000 to 1000 B.C. The basic reason for this was the tremendous increase in productivity that now took place. Not only was agriculture practiced in much larger areas, but the combination of soils and climate in Central Europe and in the monsoon Ganges and Yangtze basins was much more productive than in the comparatively arid Middle East and Indus and Yellow River valleys.

The jump in agricultural productivity meant that a surplus was now available for economic development and for state-building purposes. Trade increased in volume, especially along the rivers that constituted ready-made highways. Craftsmen appeared in increasing numbers to provide the services needed in the new agricultural communities and the products in demand for the new trade. At first goods and services were exchanged by barter, with obvious inconvenience for both buyer and seller. Then media of exchange were developed, such as measures of grain or, more common, bars of metal. But with every transaction the weight and purity of the metal had to be checked against fraudulent clipping and debasing.

About 700 B.C., the Lydians of western Asia Minor began stamping and guaranteeing pieces of metal as to both quality and weight. Various Greek city states soon improved on this by stamping flat circular coins on both sides. Thus gold and silver coins now facilitated large scale wholesale or interregional trade, and copper coins enabled farmers to sell rather than barter their produce, and artisans to work for wages rather than foodstuffs. The net effect was a great stimulus for all kinds of commerce, a corresponding stimulus for manufacturing and agriculture, and an overall increase in economic specialization with an attendant rise in efficiency and productivity. The manufacturer of cheap goods now had available for the first time a mass market, while the small landholder could turn from subsistence agriculture to specialized farming, whether the mulberry and silkworm in China or olive oil in Greece. The new iron tools also made possible the building of better and larger ships, which, in turn, led to longer voyages and to more trade and colonization. Overseas expansion was impeded at the outset by piracy, which was regarded as normal an activity as brigandage on land. *The Odyssey* describes the half-piratical, half-commercial expeditions of Menelaus and Odysseus in the Aegean Sea, and relates how all participants as a matter of course asked those whom they met whether or not they were pirates. But gradually maritime trade was developed on a regular large-scale basis, with great economic advantage. Transport by sea was many times cheaper than by land, and remained so until the development of an efficient horse harness in the Middle Ages and the building of good roads in the eighteenth century.

By the end of the Classical Age, trade routes circumscribed all of Eurasia in contrast to the local self-sufficiency that prevailed in most regions following the invasions of the second millennium B.C. In addition to the caravan routes across the interior of Eurasia, there were sea routes around the circumference—from the North Sea to the western Mediterranean, from the western Mediterranean to the Levant, from the Red Sea to India, and from India to Southeast Asia and, to a lesser degree, to China. This maritime commerce was accompanied by colonization, especially in the Mediterranean by the Phoenicians and Greeks, and later in Southeast Asia by the Indians.

Side by side with these economic developments were equally significant social and political changes. The military aristocracy that had risen to prominence with the invasions of the second millennium B.C. was being undermined by the new class of merchants, craftsmen, and mariners. The old tribal society was being transformed by monetization; personal services and allegiances were being superseded by the exigencies of the market place.

Equally disruptive was the political consolidation made possible by the economic growth. Tribal chiefs and their advisory councils and assemblies were being replaced by kingdoms and then by empires, whether in Italy or India or China. Nor was it a one way process of economic development stimulating political centralization. A reverse process also operated, for the great new regional empires spanning the Eurasian land mass enforced order and security that promoted long distance trade by land and sea. Regional empires also were able to build and maintain regional road networks that also facilitated commerce.

In the Persian Empire, for example, the so-called Royal Road ran 1,677 miles from Susa, located to the north of the Persian Gulf, westward to the Tigris, and thence across Syria and Asia Minor to Ephesus on the Aegean coast. The route was divided into 111 post-stations, each with relays of fresh horses for the royal couriers. Caravans took ninety days to travel this road from end to end, while the royal couriers traversed it in a week. As the empire was enlarged, branch lines were constructed southwest to Egypt and southeast to the Indus Valley. A few centuries later the Romans constructed their well-known system of roads that were so well engineered that some of them, along with their bridges, are still in use.

At the other end of Eurasia, the Chinese built an elaborate network of both roads and canals. They were able to transport goods from present-day Canton to the Yangtze Valley by an all-water route, thereby promoting their overseas trade. To the northwest they built roads that linked up with the long silk route, which, as will be noted in the following section, traversed the whole of Central

Asia to the Middle East. The main highways were lined with trees and provided with stations and guest houses. Road construction and maintenance was the responsibility of central and local officials who were subject to impeachment if they were derelict in their duties. Likewise in India the Royal Highway ran from the Ganges Delta to Taxila in the northwest, near the Khyber Pass, where it connected with the caravan routes west to the Middle East and north to Central Asia.

All these developments involved profound changes in social relationships, in political organizations, in ways of living and earning a livelihood. Such basic and all-inclusive disruption was unsettling and uncomfortable. It led to soul searching—to the posing of new questions and the seeking of new answers. Thinkers were moved to reconsider their respective traditions and to either abandon them or adapt them to the requirements of an age of transition. Speculation concerned such questions as the moral basis of ideal government, the functioning of the social order, and the origin and purpose of the universe and of life.

All over the civilized ecumene, such questions were being posed and discussed about the sixth century B.C. The answers constituted the great philosophical, religious, and social systems of the Classical Age. It was not happenstance, then, that the spokesmen for these systems were all contemporaries—Confucius in China, Buddha in India, Zoroaster in Persia, and the rationalist philosophers in Greece. In all these regions the disruption and the challenge was the same, but the answers varied greatly, and the several Eurasian civilizations set off in decidedly different directions. Indeed it was at this time that these civilizations developed their distinctive philosophical attitudes and social institutions that endured through the centuries and that have characterized them to modern times.

The specific nature of these attitudes and institutions will be analyzed in the following chapters devoted to each of the classical civilizations. The remainder of this chapter will be devoted to an examination of the interrelationships amongst these civilizations, or, in other words, the substance of the incipient Eurasian ecumene. Contemporary Eurasians could not have been aware of the parallel developments in their respective civilizations because they had little specific information about each other. But they were definitely aware that the historical stage was expanding—that life was becoming more complex and that a multitude of domestic and external forces impinged on them. Thus the Greek historian Polybius, when starting his history of events from 220 to 145 B.C., observed that, "during this period history becomes, so to speak, an organic whole. What happens in Italy and in Libya is bound up with what happened in Asia and in Greece, all events culminating in a single result."

Two aspects of this new "organic whole" were particularly evident, even to contemporaries. These were interregional commercial bonds and cultural bonds, the subjects of the following two sections.

II. COMMERCIAL BONDS

The principal interregional material bonds were commercial in character, though not exclusively so. This was a time when not only goods moved from one region to another, but people also moved about with their technological skills and their plants. There is a revealing letter, for example, written by the Persian ruler Darius to one of his governors, approving a proposal for transplanting plants and trees from one region to another. "I commend your plan," wrote the King, "for improving my country by the transplantation of fruit trees from the other side of the Euphrates, in the further part of Asia. . . .″[1] How wide-ranging was this interchange is indicated by the fact that cotton, sugar cane, and chickens, all first domesticated in India, spread to both China and western Eurasia during this period. Likewise the Chinese during these centuries obtained for the first time the grape vine, alfalfa, chive, cucumber, fig, sesame, pomegranate, and walnut. In return the Chinese gave to the rest of Eurasia the orange, peach, pear, peony, azalea, camellia, and chrysanthemum. There was a similar interchange of technology, as is evident in the case of that fundamental invention, the waterwheel. The first waterwheel in western Asia was that of Mithridates, king of Pontus, on the south shore of the Black Sea, about 65 B.C. The first waterwheel in China was built soon after, about 30 B.C. The difference between the two dates is much too small for direct diffusion in either direction, and strongly suggests diffusion in both directions from some unknown intermediate source. Such interaction between the various regions of Eurasia was intimately related to trade, and doubtless would have been much less substantial were it not for the efflorescence of local and long-distance trade during the centuries of the Classical Age.

This trade was conducted both by land across Central Eurasia and by sea around the periphery of the land mass. These two general routes were by no means exclusive or independent of each other. A large proportion of the goods were moved along some combination of the two routes, usually by sea between Egypt and India, and by one of several overland routes between India and China. Furthermore, the land and sea routes were competitive, so that excessively high charges or intolerable lack of security in one route normally deflected the trade to the other.

The maritime trade had gotten under way first at the time of the ancient civilizations. Egyptian traders ventured down the Red Sea to East Africa and along the Levant coast to Lebanon. Likewise, Sumerian merchants sailed down the Persian Gulf, along the Arabian peninsula, while their counterparts from the Indus Valley, in ways that remain obscure, appear to have worked their way westward until contact was established, perhaps at the Bahrain Islands in the Persian Gulf. But all of these early seafarers were mere landlubbers compared to the amphibious Minoans of Crete. These argonauts were the great maritime traders of ancient times, plying the Mediterranean from end to end as the unrivalled entrepreneurs of that inland sea.

With the invasions of the Achaeans and Dorians this far-flung commerce dried up and the eastern Mediterranean people sank back to an agrarian and autarchic type of existence. The first to resume the mercantile activities of the Cretans were the Phoenicians. A Semitic-speaking people who had settled along the narrow coastal plains of the eastern Mediterranean, they soon developed a flourishing trade as middlemen. (See Chapter 6, section III.) In the eleventh century B.C. they began trading with Cyprus where they also founded a colony. Thence they spread out over the Aegean and by the end of the ninth century B.C. they had entered the western Mediterranean and founded trading posts and colonies on the northwest coast of Africa, the south coast of Spain, and on Sicily, Malta, and the Balearic Islands. They even ventured beyond Gibraltar as far afield as Cornwall, England, whence came the eagerly sought after tin.

From about 1100 B.C. until the late eighth century B.C. the sailors and merchants of Phoenicia controlled most of the maritime trade of the Mediterranean. Then the Greeks appeared as competitors, spurred on by the same goad of population pressure. First they established trading posts, which later developed into agricultural settlements wherever the land resources made this possible. These settlements were quite independent of the mother city whence they sprang, even though the colonists reproduced the institutions and imitated the religious practices that they had left behind. Thus Greek colonization involved a multiplication of independent city-states rather than an imposition of imperialistic rule. The principal areas of Greek settlement were in Sicily, south Italy, southeastern France, northeastern Spain, and the Black Sea basin, which by the fifth century B.C. was ringed with flourishing Greek trading posts and settlements.

While the Greeks were prospering on the sea, the Persians were building their empire that eventually extended from the Nile Valley to the Indus. Although a mountain people and ignorant of things maritime, the Persians nevertheless were interested in opening sea routes to facilitate communications between their eastern and western provinces. For this purpose they made use of the experienced Phoenicians and Asia Minor Greeks, both of whom were their subjects. They appointed a Greek mariner, Scylax, to head an expedition that sailed about 510 B.C. from the Indus to Arsinoë at the head of the Red Sea. Trade flourished under these circumstances, and surpassed anything previously known in volume and in geographic range. Greek, Phoenician, Arab, and Indian mariners plied back and forth between India, the Persian Gulf, Egypt, and the numerous ports of the Mediterranean. Alexander and his successors continued the work of the Persians by dispatching more expeditions, which enhanced geographic knowledge, and by constructing a series of ports along the Red Sea, through which goods could be transported overland to the Nile and then shipped down the river to Alexandria.

All this proved to be but the prelude to the great expansion of trade between East and West that blossomed shortly before the Christian era, thanks to China's great westward expansion, which opened overland trade routes, and to the Roman conquest of the entire Mediterranean basin, which eliminated both pirates and tolls.

The Romans conducted a flourishing trade with all neighboring lands—with Scandinavia to the north, Germany across the Rhine, Dacia across the Danube, Africa south of the Sahara, and the eastern lands beyond the Red Sea. The eastern trade was greatly stimulated by the discovery that the monsoon winds could be used to speed the sailing back and forth across the Indian Ocean. "Roman" merchants, mostly Greeks and Syrians, did undertake such journeys, and a few even settled permanently in Indian cities, importing glass, copper, tin, gold coins, and linen and wool textiles from the West, and exporting in return spices, cotton textiles, and Chinese silk.

A few of the more adventurous "Roman" traders, the Marco Polos of their times, made their way still further east, sailing through the Malacca Straits and eventually reaching China. This direct contact between the Roman and Han empires seemed to portend a great new expansion of trade on all the seas surrounding Eurasia. In point of fact, the opposite happened because of a combination of internal convulsions and external barbarian attacks on both the Roman and Han empires. But if commerce between Egypt and India declined after the second century, the setback did not extend to the trade between India and Southeast Asia. At the time when Rome and China were left impotent during their time of troubles, India by contrast was reaching her apogee under the Gupta dynasty (A.D. 320–647). Indian civilization, as will be noted in Chapter 9, now came into full flower and exerted great influence on neighboring lands. To the north, across land frontiers, this influence, as described in the following section, was primarily religious and cultural: to the southeast, across the Bay of Bengal, it was also economic and political.

From very ancient times Indian merchants were attracted to Southeast Asia by its spices and mineral resources. Since the local peoples were relatively primitive, the Indians were able not only to control trade but also to propagate Hindu religion and customs and establish Indian kingdoms on the islands and mainland. Beginning in Malaya and Sumatra, the Indians by the fourth century A.D. were firmly ensconced in distant Borneo and Indochina. At the outset it was the island kingdoms that were most advanced, but toward the end of the third century A.D. they fell behind, perhaps because of the growth of piracy. The center of power shifted to the mainland where Indian immigrants were able to follow land routes across Malaya to Indochina. Kambuja, in present-day Cambodia, now emerged as a great Hindu kingdom.

The parallel between this Indian expansion in Southeast Asia and the Greek expansion several centuries earlier in the Mediterranean basin is apparent. In both cases merchants and colonists established footholds in far-flung coastal areas and transplanted their home institutions. The local populations, however, were neither Hellenized nor Hinduized en masse, so that the colonies eventually were assimilated, leaving behind only geographic names and architectural remains as mementoes of past enterprise. For Eurasian history, the significance of both Greater India and Magna Graecia is their contribution in extending the frontiers of civilization—in one case from the south Balkans to the Straits of Gibraltar and to south Russia, and in the other case from south India to Borneo and Indochina.

As far as overland trade was concerned, much depended on the degree to which order and security could be maintained. When large sections of the land routes were under the firm control of some authority, then trade could flourish; when anarchy prevailed, then trade withered. This pattern is clearly apparent in surveying commercial trends through these centuries. A general upward trend is evident in the volume of trade, the result of the technological advances and the expansion of the civilized ecumene. But within this overall trend there were dips and rises related to political conditions. For example, the centuries of the Scythian Empire in western Eurasia, the Chinese empires in eastern Eurasia, and the Mongol Empire embracing most of the continental land mass, were all centuries of secure trade routes and burgeoning commerce.

In the fifth century B.C. the Greek historian Herodotus wrote an elaborate account of the Scythians, the wagon-dwelling, mare-milking nomads who lived adjacent to the Greek cities on the north shore of the Black Sea and traded extensively with the colonists. Drawing on the resources of the extensive hinterland they controlled, they exchanged slaves, cattle, hides, furs, fish, timber, wax, and honey, for Greek textiles, wine, olive oil, and sundry luxury items. In the fourth and third centuries B.C. Scythian power was undermined by new nomadic incursions from the East. During the ensuing confusion long-distance trade evaporated, and over two centuries elapsed before it reappeared. The stimulant this time was provided by the Chinese at the other end of Eurasia who were extending their rule deep into what they called the "Western Region," that is, Central Asia. Their motivation was protection against their dangerous nomadic neighbors, the Hiung-nu, known in European history as the Huns.

Emperor Wu Ti (141–87 B.C.) sent a series of great expeditions against the Hiung-nu, eventually forcing the various tribes to submit or to flee into the desert. Indeed it was the Chinese victories that set off a chain reaction of westward migrations that eventually buffeted the Roman Empire and led to the fall of Rome. Later the Chinese attacked the remote kingdoms of Ferghana and Sogdiana, which had abused Chinese diplomatic missions, presumably feeling safe in their remote location behind the great Pamir Range. But Chinese armies, in a remarkable display of military might, crossed the Pamirs and forced submission to the Han emperor. Thus a great Chinese imperial wedge was driven across Central Asia, eventually establishing contact with the Kushan Empire in northwest India.

Trade now followed the victorious Chinese banners. Security was assured, and demand had been stimulated by the diplomatic missions, which, in accordance with the custom of the times, bore gifts peculiar to their respective countries. These official exchanges prepared the way for private traders by creating habits and desires. This was particularly true of Chinese silks, which everywhere were in great demand and which comprised at least 90 per cent of China's exports. In return, the Chinese received a wide range of commodities such as furs, woolens, jade, and livestock from Central Asia, amber from the Baltic, and from the Roman provinces, glass, corals, pearls, linen and wool textiles, and, above all, gold. These goods were transported back and forth by caravans along the famous Silk Road. The main line of this route began in northwest China at Ch'ang-an (Sian) went westward along the Kansu Corridor to the Tarim Basin, which it skirted along both its northern and southern edges, then crossed the Pamirs, continued through Samarkand and Merv in present-day Russian Turkestan, rounded the southern end of the Caspian Sea to Seleucia in modern Iraq, and thence continued to the Roman frontier in the Levant. (See Map X, "Incipient Eurasian Ecumene about A.D. 200.")

Despite the existence of this Silk Road, there was no direct commercial intercourse between the Roman Empire and Han China. Roman traders did not go directly overland to China, nor Chinese to Rome. Rather the commerce was conducted by various intermediaries, especially the Parthians of present-day Iran, who deliberately blocked direct contact between Romans and Chinese. The Romans retaliated by encouraging direct sea trade with India, thus eliminating the profiteering middlemen of Parthia. Instead of following the Silk Road westward, the caravans increasingly turned southward through Khotan to ports in northwest India. There the cargoes were picked up by "Roman" merchants, transported briskly across the Indian Ocean with the aid of the monsoons, and unloaded at Red Sea ports.

After the second century A.D., this flourishing trade declined gradually with the growing troubles of the Roman and Chinese empires. But it by no means dried up entirely. China continued to produce the silk; the oasis cities through which the Silk Road ran made every effort to maintain the trade on which they had grown rich; and in the West the consumer demand remained unsatiated. Even after Rome fell to the barbarians in the fifth century, Constantinople, or Byzantium, carried on as a great imperial capital with the customary demand for luxury products. But in the middle of the sixth century the Byzantines finally learned the secret of how the precious silk was made, and no longer were dependent on Chinese imports.

The final blow was the eruption of the Moslem Arabs who conquered the entire Middle East in the seventh century and then expanded into Central Asia where they defeated the Chinese in the battle of Talas in 751. Central Asia now became Moslem and for centuries was a barrier rather than a bridge between China and the West, and also between China and India. Hence the final closing of the overland routes and the shift of trade to the surrounding seas where the Arabs were becoming the leading mariners and merchants. Not until the thirteenth century, when the Mongols conquered all Eurasia from the Pacific Ocean to the Baltic and Black Seas, was it possible once more to reopen overland routes and thus clear the way for Marco Polo and his fellow merchants of medieval times.

Despite these various shifts in the direction of trade, one basic fact emerges from this survey. This is the qualitative increase in both the range and volume of commerce that occurred during the Classical Age in contrast to the preceding ancient period. No longer was the scope of commerce confined to individual regions, whether in the Mediterranean Sea or the Arabian Sea or some segment of the Eurasian steppes. Rather trade now became interregional with goods being carried from one end of Eurasia to the other both by sea and by land. This constituted the economic component of the new Eurasian ecumene; the following section will consider the cultural aspect of this ecumene.

III. CULTURAL BONDS

Commercial and cultural bonds were not unconnected or independent of each other. The transplantation of Indian civilization to Southeast Asia was in large part the work of Indian merchants. Likewise, the Greek merchants who followed Alexander's armies spread their Hellenistic culture throughout the Orient. And the course of the diffusion of Buddhism from India to China can be traced along the well-known Silk Road.

Cultural movements, however, had their own autonomous dynamism and were by no means entirely dependent upon merchants and trade routes. A fundamental factor affecting cultural developments in the classical world, exclusive of China, was the invention of a simple alphabetic script in the late second millennium B.C. Prior to that time only a handful of professional scribes had been able to read and write the complicated cuneiform script of Mesopotamia and the hieroglyphics of Egypt. The first alphabetic system was devised by Semitic traders in the Sinai Peninsula who adapted the Egyptian signs, with which they had become familiar, to indicate consonantal sounds. But they continued to use many additional symbols for words and syllables, and therefore failed to develop a strictly phonetic alphabet. The Phoenicians completed the transition in the thirteenth century B.C. by developing an alphabet of twenty-two signs denoting simple consonants. The Greeks improved the Phoenician alphabet by using some of its signs to indicate vowels. This Greek alphabet, with some modifications, was spread by the Romans westward and by the Byzantines eastward.

The significance of the alphabet is that it opened the world of intelligent communication to a far wider circle than that of the priests and officials of the old days. The scribes of Egypt and Mesopotamia naturally shunned the new style of writing, and continued to use their traditional scripts almost until the Christian era. China also, in her isolation, continued with her combination phono-pictographic system that has persisted with modifications to the present day. But elsewhere in Eurasia, alphabets were adopted with slight adjustments to fit the different languages. Everywhere the effect was to reduce somewhat, though by no means entirely, or even substantially, the gap between high and low cultures, between urban ruling circles and peasant masses, that had developed with the appearance of civilization. By challenging the monopoly of privileged intellectual cliques that generally supported the *status quo*, the simplified scripts generated a certain ferment in the body politic as well as in traditional piety and learning.

The overall cultural pattern noticeable amongst all Eurasian civilizations during these centuries of the Classical Age was the breakdown of local cultures, which were integrated into the new regional civilizations with their distinctive languages, religions, and social systems. It was much easier for these civilizations to exchange material goods than culture traits. Textiles, spices, and luxury products were universally usable and desirable, whereas ancestor worship, the caste system, and the city-state were irrelevant and unacceptable outside their places of origin. Thus the commercial interregional bonds during this period of incipient ecumenism were generally more extensive and influential than the cultural.

Yet the latter did exist and in some cases were of first-rate historical significance. The first outstanding instance was that of Hellenism which spread from the Greek world eastward to the Orient and westward to Europe. Toward the end of the classical period there were also the great universal religions, especially Christianity and Buddhism, with their claims to the allegiance of all men rather than of any one group.

Considering first Hellenism, derived from the Greek word "Hellas," meaning Greece, its diffusion throughout the Middle East was made possible by Alexander's famous conquest eastward to Central Asia and the Indus Valley. As will be noted in the following chapter, this empire lasted for only a few years during Alexander's lifetime. On his death in 323 B.C. it was divided among his generals, and later partitioned between Rome in the West and the Parthians in the East. It was during these fourth and third centuries B.C. that the military predominance of the Greek soldiers paved the way for the hundreds of thousands of Greek merchants, administrators, and professional men who flocked to the numerous cities built by Alexander and his successors.

Many of the Greek emigrants married local women, Alexander himself setting an example by taking a Persian noblewoman as wife and by arranging the mass marriage of three thousand of his soldiers with Persian women after their return from the Indian campaign. He also enlisted Persian soldiers in his regiments, and adopted the costume of the Persian king and the etiquette of his court. Even though the majority of its inhabitants usually were non-Hellenic, the typical city was basically Greek, with elected magistrates, a council, and an assembly of the citizens. A new form of the Greek language, the *Koine,* or common tongue, became the lingua franca throughout the Middle East. It could be learned relatively easily by those natives who became Hellenized as it was simpler than the Greek of the classical period. The most assimilated of the Middle Eastern peoples were those of Asia Minor who forgot their native languages and spoke the *Koine.* Elsewhere Greek manners, amusements, coinage, and arts were adopted by the upper classes in the cities.

The influence of Hellenism extended eastward to northern India and to Bactria and Sogdiana in Afghanistan. These Hellenic outposts deep in the heart of Asia exerted a certain recognizable and wide-ranging influence on surrounding peoples. First there were their coins, of brilliant craftsmanship, which constituted, in effect, the beginning of Indian coinage. Then there is the Buddhist text known as the *Questions of Milinda* (that is, Menander, Greek king of Bactria, who conquered part of northwest India) which introduces the Greek dialogue form into Indian literature. In the field of language, a number of Greek words were incorporated into Sanskrit, including those for horse-bit, pen and ink, book, and mine. In science, both Indian astrology and Hindu medicine contain Greek words among their technical terms. Most significant was the Greek impact on a school of religious art known as Gandharan, after the region of that name in northwest India, which had been under Greek rule. The main products were images of Buddha, with realistic anatomical details, in contrast to the traditional Buddha images, which projected a spiritual expression rather than an exact likeness. The transmission of Gandharan art style to China has been traced along the Silk Road, trod by Buddhist pilgrims, as well as by merchants.

Despite this impressive diffusion, Hellenism did not leave a permanent imprint on the Middle East, let alone the remainder of Asia. The basic reason was that its influence had been restricted to the cities where Greek settlers lived and where Greek dynasties had courts. Some of the native peoples were affected but they were almost exclusively of the small upper classes. The great majority in the countryside, and even in many of the cities, continued to speak their own languages and worship their own gods. Thus Hellenism did not sink deep roots and was incapable of surviving through the centuries. When the Islamic conquerors appeared during the Middle Ages they had little difficulty in overwhelming the little islands of Hellenistic culture, so that today, the Greek language and culture survive only in the Greek homeland on the southern tip of the Balkan Peninsula.

Hellenism in the western Mediterranean was slower to take root because the indigenous populations had not yet reached a sufficiently affluent and sophisticated level of civilization. But for that very reason the long-run impact of Hellenism in that region was more durable since there was less competition from the local culture.

As early as the sixth century B.C., the Romans were being influenced by the Greek colonies in southern Italy, but it was not until the third century onward, when the Romans conquered the heartland of Hellenism in the Balkans and the Levant, that they felt the full force of Greek culture. Roman soldiers and officials now came into direct contact with highly educated Greek rulers and administrators, while among the hostages and slaves brought to Rome were many Greeks who served in every capacity. Charmed by the beauties of Greek poetry, drama, and prose, educated Romans were content in the beginning with translations or imitations of the originals. But Roman patrons gradually demanded Roman themes and the expression of Roman values. A national literature came into being which, however, always bore the stamp of its Greek origins, both during the "Golden Age" of Vergil, Horace, and Ovid, and the "Silver Age" of Seneca, Tacitus, and Pliny the Elder and the Younger.

The most obvious manifestation of Greek influence was in the physical appearance of Rome and the other cities of the Empire. All three Greek orders were used—the Doric, Ionic, and Corinthian—as well as Greek sculpture, either originals or imitations. Thus towns and cities in Italy, as in the Middle East, began to take on a uniform physical appearance under the influence of Greek art and architecture. Indeed a basic contribution of the Romans to civilization was in appropriating and adapting Greek culture and then spreading it to diverse peoples who had never experienced direct contact with it—Gauls, Germans, Britons, and Iberians. Viewed from this perspective, the "fall" of Rome may be interpreted as the recession of Hellenism before the Germans and Celts, just as it receded in the Middle East before the Moslems.

Much more durable than the impact of Hellenism was that of the two great universal religions, Christianity and Mahayana Buddhism. They began their expansion in the late classical period from their respective places of origin in the Middle East and India, and during the course of the following centuries they won over all Europe in the one case, and most of Asia in the other. The reason for their success is to be found in certain novel characteristics that they shared in common. One was their emphasis on salvation and their promise of an afterlife of eternal bliss. Another was their egalitarianism, so that their brotherhood was open to all who sought admittance—women as well as men, rich and poor alike, slave or free. Finally, both religions stressed a high code of ethics, the observance of which was essential for salvation. This requirement, together with efficient ecclesiastical organization, enabled these two religions to exert effective influence on the daily lives of the faithful.

These features were particularly appealing in the later centuries of the Classical Age. These were times of social unrest and moral confusion, especially in the large urban centers. The multitudes in the cities felt uprooted and drifting. For such people, Christianity and Mahayana Buddhism offered solace, security, and guidance. It was not accidental that the earliest converts to Christianity were the lowly and dispossessed. Likewise, the greatest triumph of Mahayana Buddhism was in China during the time of troubles following the collapse of the Han dynasty, when there seemed to be no solution to man's worldly problems. Indeed, these satisfying and opportune characteristics of the two religions were evolved precisely in response to the needs of the times. They were not present either in the Judaism from which Christianity had emerged, or in the original Buddhism from which developed the later Mahayana variant.

Judaism was the parochial faith of the Jewish people who about the twelfth century B.C. adopted a national god, Jehovah. "I am Jehovah, thy God. . . . Thou Shalt have no other gods before me." This first of Jehovah's Ten Commandments did not say that Jehovah was the only god in the world. It said, rather, that he was the only god for the children of Israel. Also this Judaistic faith was at this time more social and ethical than mystical and otherworldly. But from the sixth century B.C. onward, the Jews changed their religious ideas under the influence of the religions of the Persians and other of their rulers. Also they were affected by the many Jews who lived outside Palestine where, exposed to the tenets of Hellenism, they sought to interpret Judaism in terms of Greek philosophy. Thus the Jews gradually adopted a belief in an afterlife—obedience to God's will would bring eternal happiness in heaven, and disobedience would bring eternal punishment in hell.

Nevertheless, Christianity was a Jewish cult during the lifetime of Jesus and immediately after his crucifixion. But it was universalized by Paul, a Hellenized Jew who lived in the city of Tarsus in Asia Minor. He preached that Christianity was not a sect of Judaism, but a new church, a church for Gentiles as well as for Jews. Hence the steady growth of the new religion despite the official persecution. Finally, in 313 it was tolerated by Emperor Constantine's Edict of Milan, and in 399 it was made the official state religion of the Roman Empire. Then, after the fall of the Empire, Christian missionaries carried the faith to the English and German peoples between 600 and 800, and to the Scandinavian and Slavic peoples between 800 and 1100. With the expansion of Europe, both missionaries and emigrants spread Christianity to all parts of the globe.

The evolution of Buddhism was somewhat similar in that it began, as will be noted in Chapter 9, section II, as a distinct Indian reaction against the injustice of the caste system and the exploitation by the Brahman priestly class. The founder, Siddhartha (ca. 563–483 B.C.), of the Gautama clan, was of noble rank, but he became so distressed by the suffering he saw about him that he gave up his family and material comforts for the life of a wandering ascetic. Finally, in a moment of revelation, he achieved enlightenment and thenceforth was known as Buddha, or the Enlightened One.

The four great truths of Buddhism are: (1) life is sorrow; (2) the cause of sorrow is desire; (3) escape is possible only by stopping desire; and (4) this can only be done by the "eight-fold path" consisting of right belief, right ambition, right speech, right conduct, right living, right effort, right thoughts, right pleasures. The objective of all this effort was Nirvana, literally meaning "emptiness," the "blowing out of the flame."

Buddha had not intended to establish a new religion but after his death his disciples preached his teachings and founded monastic communities that came to dominate the religion. The ideal of these communities was mental and physical discipline culminating in the mystic experience of Nirvana. Satisfying as this was for the monks, it failed to meet the needs of the everyday life of laymen. Hence the evolution of Mahayana, or the Greater Vehicle, as opposed to the Hinayana, or Lesser Vehicle. The Greater Vehicle was "greater" in the sense of its all-inclusiveness. It incorporated more of the concepts of pre-Buddhist Indian thought as well as the religious ideas of the people it converted. In doing so, it turned somewhat from its original contemplative bent and adopted precepts that were easier to comprehend and observe. Salvation now could be attained through faith, even an unthinking act of faith such as the mouthing of the name of Buddha. Also Nirvana changed, at least for the less sophisticated believers, to mean an afterlife in Paradise, and Paradise was more likely of attainment through good works that helped others.

This shift of emphasis from monasticism, asceticism, and contemplation, to charity, faith, and salvation, made Mahayana Buddhism more palatable to non-Indian peoples than the original religion had been, though both forms of the faith won foreign converts. Buddhism spread first to Ceylon and to northwest frontier regions of India in the third century B.C. Then in the first century B.C. it was carried into Central Asia and China, first by traders, then by Indian missionaries, and, most effectively, by Chinese converts who studied in India and then returned to win over their fellow countrymen. So successful were they that by the late fourth century A.D., nine-tenths of the population of northwest China was said to have been converted, and by the sixth century South China had followed suit. From China, Buddhism spread still further: to Korea in the fourth century A.D., to Japan in the sixth century, and later to Tibet and Mongolia. Meanwhile Buddhism in both its Hinayana and Mahayana forms had been penetrating into Southeast Asia. This did not occur at any particular period; rather it represented one aspect of the general Indianization of the region that took place over many centuries.

After these successes Buddhism declined in many countries. In China it reached its peak about 700 but thereafter suffered from internal decay and governmental hostility, and became merely one of "the three religions" (along with Taoism and Confucianism) in which the syncretic Chinese were interested. Likewise, in India, Buddhism eventually gave way to a revival of Hinduism, so that virtually no followers are to be found today in its own birthplace. (See Chapter 9, section II.) In Ceylon and in many parts of Southeast Asia, however, Buddhism of the Hinayana variety remains predominant to the present.

Despite this relative decline after its period of greatness, the fact remains that Buddhism in late classical and early medieval times was the predominant religion of Asia. It prevailed in the whole continent except for Siberia and the Middle East, thus giving that vast area a degree of cultural unity unequalled before or after. In doing so, it functioned as a great civilizing force in Asia as Christianity did at the same time in Europe. To many peoples Buddhism brought not only a religion and a set of ethics, but also a system of writing, a type of architecture, and all the other attributes of the great civilizations of India and China that the missionaries spread together with their religion. In the same way, at the other end of Eurasia, Christian missionaries were bringing to the barbaric Germanic and Slavic peoples the civilizations of Rome and of Constantinople, as well as the teachings of Christ. Such was the impact and historical significance of these powerful "cultural bonds" for the new Eurasian ecumene.

During the millennia of the ancient civilizations, the Middle East had been the center of initiative. It was the Middle East that during that period had made the fundamental contributions to mankind—contributions such as agriculture, metallurgy, urbanism, and imperial organization. But now in classical times this Middle Eastern predominance faded away, except in one area—that of religion. Not only Judaism but also Zoroastrianism have their roots in the Middle East. The latter religion, although observed today by only a handful of Parsis in India, had considerable influence in the Middle East when the Persian Empire was at its height. Furthermore, it stands out in the history of religions as a lofty faith that sought to replace the prevailing gross practices and superstitions of the Persian people with the principles of light, truth, and righteousness.

Yet the fact remains that apart from these religions and other related sects, the Middle East no longer was the vital source of innovation during the Classical Age. After the invasions of the late second millennium B.C., writes one authority, "the creative power of the Ancient Near East appears diminished . . . in the main we observe a codification and consolidation of acquired knowledge."[2] The new ideas and institutions which took shape in classical times, and which have persisted in many cases to the present, were the products of what formerly had been the peripheral regions of Eurasia. Accordingly, the following three chapters are devoted to the civilizations of these regions: the Greco-Roman, the Indian, and the Chinese.

SUGGESTED READING

J. N. Hillgarth, ed., *The Conversion of Western Europe 350–750* (Prentice-Hall, 1969); G. F. Hudson, *Europe and China: A Survey of Their Relations from the Earliest Times to 1800* (Arnold, 1931); J. Needham, *Science & Civilization in China* (Cambridge Univ., 1954–); H. G. Rawlinson, *Intercouse between India and the Western World* (Cambridge Univ., 1916); C. G. F. Simkin, *The Traditional Trade of Asia* (Oxford Univ., 1969); E. Zürcher, *Buddhism: Its Origin and Spread* (St. Martin's, 1962).

chapter eight

Greco-Roman
Civilization

*The pupils of Athens have become teachers of others, and she has
made the term Hellene no longer signify a race but a mental
outlook.*—Isocrates

Of the three chapters dealing with the three classical civilizations, this
one on the Greco-Roman civilization is the most lengthy. One reason is that two
distinct though related civilizations are involved, in contrast to the unitary civilizations of India and China. This bifurcation arises from a basic difference between the historical development at this time of the West on the one hand and
of India and China on the other. In all three instances, civilization spread out
from restricted centers of origin to encompass entire surrounding regions—from
the Greek peninsula to the western Mediterranean, from the Indus River valley
to South India, and from the Yellow River valley to South China. As noted in
Chapter 7, section I, iron tools made possible this expansion by facilitating the
extension of agriculture into forested regions, and of commerce and colonization
into new coastal areas. But at this point the common pattern ends. The newly
civilized regions in India and China remained generally subservient to the
original core areas, whereas in the West, Rome developed a military superiority
that enabled her to conquer not only the Greek homeland in the Balkans but
also the western portions of the ancient Middle East—Asia Minor, Palestine, Syria,
and Egypt. In doing so, Rome began a new phase of the history of the West, and
launched a new, though related, Western civilization. The history and nature of
these two sister civilizations, the Greek and the Roman, is the subject of this
chapter.

I. FORMATIVE AGE, 800–500 B.C.

With the Dorian invasions of the twelfth century B.C., Greece lapsed into a "Dark
Age." (See Chapter 6, section IV.) The Greece of this period was tribal, aristocratic, agricultural, and confined to the Aegean Basin. By the end of the sixth
century B.C. all this had changed. The tribe had given way to the city-state; other

social classes had risen to challenge the nobility; industry and commerce had come to play a considerable role; and Greek colonies were to be found scattered on all the Mediterranean shores. These changes constitute the comprehensive transformation of the Greek world that occurred during the formative age and that cleared the way for the subsequent Classical Age. (See Map VII, "Classical Age Empires in the Middle East and Europe.")

A basic factor behind these developments was the geography of the Greek lands, compartmentalized by crisscrossing mountain chains. Consequently there were no fertile river valleys or broad plains to support the elaborate imperial structures to be found elsewhere in Eurasia. Instead, dozens of little, relatively isolated, and fiercely independent city-states emerged. At the outset these city-states depended primarily on subsistence agriculture, herding, and fishing. But by the beginning of the eighth century B.C. this economic self-sufficiency was undermined by population pressure. Land-hungry peasants were forced to take to the sea as pirates or traders or colonists, or, as often happened, some combination of the three. By the fifth century the entire Mediterranean basin, including the Black Sea, was ringed with prosperous Greek colonies that constituted overseas replicas of the mother cities. (See Chapter 7, section II.) The colonies shipped raw materials and especially grain to overpopulated Greece and in return received wine, olive oil, and manufactured goods, such as cloth and pottery.

This economic revolution stimulated, and in return was stimulated by, social and political revolution. From the eighth century B.C. onward, the combination of foreign markets, money economy, and new luxuries left the small farmers vulnerable to mortgages, foreclosures, and even loss of personal freedom. Inevitably this led to bitter class conflict and to popular clamor for debt cancellation and land redistribution. Likewise in the cities new wealthy families emerged that aspired to political recognition commensurate with their economic strength. They could count on the support of the urban poor—artisans, stevedores, and sailors. All these discontented elements, then, struck out against the traditional political system that left power in the hands of the landowning aristocracy.

The movement for change was greatly strengthened in the seventh century when the aristocratic cavalryman was replaced as the decisive figure on the battlefield by the heavily armed and armored infantryman, the hoplite. Massed together in a solid block or phalanx, with a shield on the left hand and a long spear in the right, and trained to maneuver in unison, the hoplites could sweep bristling through the hitherto invincible horsemen. This innovation not only undermined the military basis of aristocratic political authority but also enhanced the status and influence of the independent farmer and artisan who could afford to equip himself for phalanx service.

The combination of economic and military change generated corresponding political change. Having started as monarchies in the Dark Age and having gradually changed to aristocratic oligarchies, the city-states in the seventh century came under the rule of dictators, or tyrants as they were called. These ambitious leaders, usually of noble birth, championed popular demands, won mass support, and seized personal power. The word "tyrant" referred to one who ruled without legal right, and carried with it no sense of moral reproach. Indeed, tyrants commonly favored the interests of the common people against the privileged classes, and often hastened the advent of democracy, though by no means invariably.

Sparta, in the southern Peloponnesus, was the classic example of the opposite trend. About 1000 B.C. the Dorian forefathers of the Spartans had overrun the rich valley of the Eurotas and reduced the native population to the status of *helots,* or serfs. Later in the eighth century the Spartans conquered the rich plains of neighboring Messenia. In order to keep down their large subject population the Spartans were forced to organize their state like a military camp. They became the best infantrymen in all Greece, but had no time or inclination for writing plays or carving statues or formulating philosophy.

Meanwhile the Athenians had been developing an altogether different type of society. Far from being a band of invaders camped amidst a hostile population, the Athenians prided themselves on being native inhabitants of Attica. Like the Greeks of other city-states, they began with a monarchy which gave way to an oligarchy of nine *archons* who were the chief executive officers and who were invariably aristocrats. But in contrast to Sparta, the subsequent evolution of Athens was towards democratization. The burgeoning trade created a strong middle class that joined forces with the dispossessed peasantry in demanding political liberalization. In 594 B.C. all parties agreed upon the appointment of Solon as chief magistrate with full powers for reform. In addition to ending enslavement for debts, he admitted propertyless citizens for the first time to the Assembly, made wealthy businessmen eligible to become *archons,* and diluted the power of the aristocratic Areopagus, or chief judicial body, by establishing new and more popular courts of justice. This social reform and political liberalization was continued by Pisistratus and Cleisthenes, so that by 500 B.C. Athens had emerged as a democracy while Sparta remained a militarized and regimented society.

II. CLASSICAL AGE, 500–336 B.C.

In his famous funeral speech commemorating the Athenian soldiers who had fallen in battle against the Spartans in 431, Pericles declared, "Our city is open to the world. . . . Athens is the school of Greece." This boast was fully justified. During the fifth century B.C. Athens overshadowed Sparta and all other Greek cities. This was the golden age of Periclean Athens which is synonymous with the golden age of Classical Greece.

One reason for the dazzling preeminence of Athens was the leading role of the city in the fateful defeat inflicted upon the great Persian Empire. The root of the war was the Persian conquest of the Greek city-states in Asia Minor during the mid-sixth century B.C. Heavy-handed Persian interference in their domestic affairs led the cities to revolt in 499. They appealed to the homeland cities for aid and received a positive response, partly because the Persian Empire at this time was expanding across southeastern Europe and menacing Greece from the north. Despite the naval assistance from across the Aegean, the Asia Minor cities were overwhelmed by 494. The Persian Emperor Darius now resolved to chastise the obstreperous Greeks and sent out an expedition that landed at Marathon, to the northwest of Athens, in 490. Although the Athenians fought almost alone, thanks to inter-city rivalries, their phalanxes inflicted a stunning defeat on the invaders.

Ten years later the Persians came again with much larger forces, and this time by land through Thrace and Thessaly. A mixed force under Spartan command fought gallantly to the last man at the pass of Thermopylae. The Persians pressed on to Athens, which they sacked, but the Athenian fleet destroyed the Persians in nearby Salamis. An allied Greek fleet followed the retreating Persians across the Aegean and won another naval victory. Soon the Asia Minor cities were freed from Persian rule, and the Greeks emerged as the victors over the greatest empire in the world.

The repercussions of the Greek triumph were momentous. First and foremost, it saved the Greeks from being engulfed in an oriental despotism, thereby allowing them to preserve their identity and to make their unique contribution to human civilization. Plato recognized this when he wrote: "If the common resolution of Athenians and Spartans had not warded off the impending enslavement, already we might almost say that the Greek communities would be jumbled together and Greeks confounded with Barbarians, as those under Persian tyranny now live broken up and tacked together in miserable confusion."[1]

The success of the Greeks, and especially of the Athenian fleet, also furthered the cause of democracy, for the rowers who drove the ships into battle were citizens who could not afford to equip themselves as hoplites. Thus the urban poor now assumed a military role even more important than that of the propertied hoplites. This naturally strengthened the movement for more democracy, which reached its apogee during the Age of Pericles (461–429 B.C.). Although an aristocrat by birth, Pericles was an earnest democrat who completed the transference of power to the Assembly, of which all adult male citizens were members. Pericles also introduced pay for service in most public offices so that the poor could afford to assume such offices. In addition he established an array of popular courts in which final decisions were rendered by juries on which all citizens could serve if chosen by lot. Pericles was quite justified, then, in proudly stating in his funeral oration in honor of the Athenian heroes who fell in battle with the Spartans in 431: "Our form of government does not enter into rivalry with the institutions of others. We do not copy our neighbor, but are an example to them. It is true that we are called a democracy, for the administration is in the hands of the many and not of the few."

Finally the prominent role of Athens in the Persian Wars led the city to a course that eventually culminated in imperialism. Whereas Sparta was immobilized by her static economy and the constant threat of a helot revolt, Athens took the lead in organizing a confederacy of Asiatic Greeks and islanders. Known as the Delian Confederation because its headquarters were originally on the small island of Delos, its purpose was collective security against possible further Persian attacks. It was theoretically an alliance of equals, but from the start Athens provided the executive leadership and the generals and also collected tribute from cities unable or unwilling to furnish ships. Step by step Athens tightened her hold, until by 450 B.C. the Confederation had become an empire, and the power of Athens extended, in the words of Euripides, from Ionia "to the outward Ocean of the West."

Athenian imperialism was relatively enlightened and beneficent, but the outbreak of the Peloponnesian War in 431 B.C. was probably inevitable, given the expansionist dynamism of Athens and the resulting apprehension of Sparta. Since one was a maritime power and the other a land power, the fighting dragged on indecisively for ten years. The Spartan armies raided Attica each year but could not penetrate the long walls that joined Athens to the sea and protected her supplies. The Athenians for their part, badly hurt by the great plague of 429 B.C. which carried off almost half the population, including Pericles, could only make random raids on the coast of the Peloponnesus. Then in 415 the fatal decision was made to send the fleet to capture Sicily and cut off Sparta's grain supply. "Fleet and army," wrote Thucydides, "perished from the face of the earth, nothing was saved." Athens' allies now revolted; the Spartans finally destroyed the long wall; and Athens was starved into capitulation in 404 B.C. Athens was left shorn of its fleets, its empire, and even its vaunted democracy, for the Spartan victors imposed a short-lived oligarchic regime.

This ruinous war left the Greek world exhausted and solved none of its problems. Spartan high-handedness caused Thebes and Athens to unite together in a new league for mutual protection. Internecine rivalries prevailed again and the city-states once more were engulfed in a confused anarchy of shifting alliances and petty wars. The stage was set for the subjugation and forcible unification of Greece by foreign power. In 338 B.C. Philip of Macedon smashed the combined armies of Thebes and Athens at Chaeronea. He deprived the Greek cities of most of their autonomy, but before he could proceed further he was assassinated in 336 B.C. His successor was his world famous son, Alexander the Great.

The Classical Age was over; the Hellenistic Age was beginning. Before turning to the latter we shall pause to consider the civilization of the Classical Age, generally accepted as one of the great triumphs of the human mind and spirit.

III. CIVILIZATION OF THE CLASSICAL AGE

The "Golden Age of Pericles," "the Greek Miracle," "the Glory That Was Greece"—these are some of the hyperboles commonly used in referring to the civilization of fifth-century Greece.

We shall see that this civilization had its shortcomings, yet this extravagant praise is understandable and largely deserved. Why is this so? What was the basis of the Greek "genius"? It may be safely assumed that it was not literally a matter of genius—that the Indo-Europeans who migrated to the south Balkans did not happen to be genetically superior to those who migrated to the Middle East or India or Western Europe. Rather the answer must be sought by comparing the historical development of the Greeks with that of the other Indo-Europeans who settled in other regions of Eurasia.

Such comparison suggests two explanations for the extraordinary achievements of the Greeks. In the first place they were located close enough to the earliest centers of civilization in Egypt and Mesopotamia to profit from their pioneering accomplishments, and yet not so close that they could not retain their individuality. The second factor was the emergence and persistence of the polis, which provided the essential institutional framework for the cultural blossoming. The polis, it should be noted, was not a uniquely Greek institution. In India, for example, the Aryan immigrants in the earlier stage of their development also had what amounted to city-states in certain regions. But these were eventually absorbed by the territorial monarchies that came to dominate the Indian peninsula. The Greeks alone were able to preserve their city-states for several centuries.

One reason was the mountainous terrain, which did not afford a geopolitical base for an enveloping regional empire. (See section I of this chapter.) Another was the direct access to the sea enjoyed by most of the Greek city-states, which gave them economic sustenance and strength as well as intellectual stimulation. It is true that the Greeks paid a heavy price for their polis fragmentation in the form of continual wars that eventually led to unification imposed from the outside by Macedon and then by Rome. But in return they enjoyed their centuries of freedom within their respective states, and this appears to have been at least a prerequisite for the great creative outburst of the fifth century.

The classical Greek civilization was not pristinely original. Like all civilizations, it borrowed heavily from what had gone before, in this case the Middle Eastern civilizations. But what the Greeks borrowed, whether art forms from Egypt or mathematics and astronomy from Mesopotamia, they stamped with the distinctive quality of their minds. And this was, in the final analysis, an open-mindedness, an intellectual curiosity, an eagerness to learn, a common-sense approach. When the Greeks traveled abroad, which they did more than others as traders, soldiers, colonists, and tourists, they did so with a critical eye and skeptical mind. They questioned everything and tested all issues at the bar of reason. In Plato's *Apology,* Socrates maintains that the individual must refuse, at all costs, to be coerced by human authority or any tribunal, to do anything, or think anything, which his own mind condemns as wrong—". . . the life which is unexamined is not worth living. . . ."

This free thought was uniquely Greek, at least in such pervasiveness and intensity. Unique also was the secular view of life, the conviction that the chief business of existence was the complete expression of human personality here and now. This combination of rationalism and secularism enabled the Greeks to think freely and creatively about human problems and social issues and to express their thoughts and emotions in their great literary, philosophical, and artistic creations, which are relevant and compelling to the present day.

These unique qualities of the Greeks are reflected clearly in their religious thought and practices. They viewed their gods as being similar in nature to themselves, differing only in superior power, longevity, and beauty. By believing in such divinities the Greeks felt securely at home in a world governed by familiar and comprehensible powers. The quality of this religion becomes evident when contrasted with that of the Mesopotamians. According to Mesopotamian explanations of the origins of things, the human race had been specifically created to build temples for the gods and to feed them with offerings. How different was the conception of the sixth-century Greek philosopher Xenophanes:

Mortals think that the gods are begotten, and wear clothes like their own, and have a voice and a form. If oxen or horses or lions had hands and could draw with them and make works of art as men do, horses would draw the shapes of gods like horses, oxen like oxen; each kind would represent their bodies just like their own forms. The Ethiopians say their gods are black and flat-nosed; the Thracians, that theirs are blue-eyed and red-haired.[2]

Religion in Classical Greece was an integral element in polis life and accordingly penetrated every aspect of that life. It offered an interpretation of the natural world, a consecration of daily work and of social institutions, and also was one of the chief sources of inspiration for poets and artists. Every Greek temple was a focus of local and national culture. Many specialized, more or less accidentally, in the development of particular arts. Round the worship of the legendary Aesculapius on the island of Cos grew up a brotherhood of miracle-workers who became the first scientific physicians. Outstanding was the renowned Hippocrates, whose medical treatises were resolutely clinical in tone. He diagnosed each case on the basis of objective observation, eschewing magical causes or cures for disease. Regarding the "sacred" disease, epilepsy, he wrote, "It seems to me that the disease called sacred is no more divine than any other. It has a natural cause, just as other diseases have. Men think it divine because they do not understand it. . . . In Nature all things are alike in this, that they can all be traced to preceding causes."[3]

Likewise round the worship of Dionysus, the wine god, grew up a company of actors who passed from dramatizing the ritual cult of the god to creating profound tragedy and uproarious comedy. This literature is inconceivable apart from its setting in fifth-century Athens. The plays were produced before the assembled citizens at regularly held religious festivals organized and financed by the state. This close relation between the author and his audience was responsible for the balance and normality of Athenian drama. Aeschylus, in his *Persians,* presented a dramatized version of the victory at Salamis before the very citizens who had won that victory. Sophocles in his tragedies referred frequently to the gods, yet he was not interested primarily in religious problems. Rather he was chiefly concerned with human beings, noble and admirable, confronted with forces beyond their control, committing awful deeds, and suffering terrible retribution. The heroism and suffering of Oedipus in the face of overwhelming adversity are the essence of tragedy and express something of the meaning of human life and of the problems common to all men.

If Sophocles was not deeply interested in conventional religion, Euripides was positively skeptical. He wrote unsparingly of the weakness of the gods and satirized those who deemed them superior to men. Euripides was generally critical and a dedicated fighter for unpopular causes. He championed the rights of the slave and the foreigner, urged the emancipation of women, and attacked the glorification of war. The same is even more true of Aristophanes, whose comedies were filled with social satire. Himself a conservative who yearned for the good old days, he ridiculed democratic leaders and policies. In the *Lysistrata* he presented a group of women who, appalled by the endless bloodshed, refused to sleep with their husbands until they forsook war.

Greek art also was the distinctive product of a polis civilization. Art and architecture found their highest expression in the temples, the civic and religious core of polis culture. These temples were the revered dwelling places of the protecting gods and goddesses, such as Athena for whom the Parthenon was built as a shrine in Athens. Sculpture, the handmaiden of architecture, served to decorate the houses of the gods. Master sculptors, such as Phidias and Praxiteles, worked on temple walls and pediments and also carved statues for the interiors. Nor should Greek coins be overlooked in this connection, for they afford some of the finest examples of the sculpture of the times. In conclusion, all of Greek art embodied the basic Greek ideals of balance, harmony, and moderation. This is evident in a comparison of the Parthenon with an Egyptian pyramid or a Mesopotamian ziggurat, or of a Greek statue with the relatively crude and stilted sculptures of most Middle Eastern peoples to that time.

The same contrast is manifest in philosophical speculation. The sixth-century rationalist philosophers of Ionia on the Asia Minor coast were the first to challenge the traditional supernatural explanations of the nature of the world. They posed the basic question "What is the stuff of which the world is made?" Thales speculated that everything originally was water, because this substance is found in liquid, solid, and vapor form. Heraclitus thought fire was the prime element because it was so active and could transform everything. Anaximenes believed it was air, arguing that it became fire when rarefied, and wind, cloud, water, earth, and stone when condensed. In the light of modern science these efforts may appear naive, but what is important is that the question was asked and the answer was sought by the free use of reason and without recourse to divine intervention.

In response to the growing complexity of Greek society, philosophers about the mid-fifth century B.C. turned their attention from the physical universe to human beings and their problems. This was particularly true of the Sophists, of whom Protagoras was the outstanding spokesman. "Man is the measure of all things," he maintained, by which he meant that there are no absolute truths since everything is relative to the needs of man himself. This emphasis on man led the Sophists to condemn slavery and war, and to espouse most popular causes. On the other hand many Greeks, especially those of conservative persuasion, feared that the relativism of the Sophists endangered social order and morality. Typical was Socrates, who was profoundly disturbed by the political corruption of his day and by the absence of any certain guide to correct living. Out of his never ending conversations with his friends evolved the science of dialectics, which tests provisional definitions through questions and answers until universally recognized truths are reached. In this way, Socrates maintained, concepts of absolute truth or absolute good or absolute beauty could be discovered. And these would provide enduring guides for personal conduct, in contrast to sophist relativism, which had been used to rationalize private license and public corruption.

Socrates' disciple Plato (427–374 B.C.) was an aristocrat who shared with his friends their pride in Athens and their distrust of the Athenian people. Distrust deepened into hatred when Athenian democracy condemned Socrates to death. Plato's goal, therefore, was a society that preserved aristocratic privileges and yet was acceptable to the poorer classes. Accordingly he divided the citizens of his ideal Republic into four grades: guardians, philosophers, soldiers, and the masses that did the work. This class differentiation was to be permanent, and was to be justified by a myth or "noble lie" about God creating men of four kinds: gold, silver, brass, and iron.

The other great thinker of this period was Aristotle (384–322 B.C.), who began as Plato's disciple but who, following his master's death, founded the Lyceum. Aristotle was a collector and rationalizer rather than a mystic, a logician and scientist rather than a philosopher. He took all knowledge for his province, so that he ranged more widely than anyone before or since. His outstanding contributions were in logic, physics, biology and the humanities; indeed he established these subjects as formal disciplines. As a great encyclopedist, he sought orderliness in every aspect of nature and of human life. Thus he balanced the classes of the social world with corresponding orders in the natural world, beginning with minerals at the bottom, then vegetables, animals, and finally man at the top. This gradation justified the division of human beings into born masters and born slaves:

. . . from the hour of their birth some are marked out for subjection, others for rule; . . . the art of war is a natural art of acquisition, for it includes hunting, an art which we ought to practice against wild beasts and against men who, though intended by nature to be governed, will not submit; for war of such a kind is naturally just.[4]

No account of Classical Greece would be complete without reference to Herodotus and Thucydides, who related the stirring events of their times and in doing so created a new literary genre—history. Herodotus ascribed the epochal defeat of the Persians to the democratic constitution of the Athenians, so that his *History* is the first great tribute to democracy. Thucydides' history was very different, being of the Peloponnesian War in which Athens, after twenty-seven years of bitter struggle, was finally beaten to her knees. Whereas Herodotus eulogized victory and glory, Thucydides analyzed defeat and suffering. His sympathies were unquestionably with Athens, whose armies he had led as a general. But he sternly suppressed his emotions and set for himself the task of ascertaining objectively the causes of the disaster. Although he did not use the phrase, he nevertheless said in effect that he was seeking to create a science of society.

Of the events of the war I have not ventured to speak from any chance information, nor according to any notion of my own; I have described nothing but what I either saw myself or learned from others of whom I made the most careful and particular enquiry. The task was a laborious one, because eye-witnesses of the same occurrences gave different accounts of them, as they remembered or were interested in the actions of one side or the other. And very likely the strictly historical character of my narrative may be disappointing to the ear. But if he who desires to have before his eyes a true picture of the events which have happened, and of the like events which may be expected to happen hereafter in the order of human things, shall pronounce what I have written to be useful, then I shall be satisfied. My history is an everlasting possession, not a prize composition which is heard and forgotten.[5]

Having presented the remarkable achievements of the Greeks in so many fields, it is customary to point out certain failings. Women were accorded inferior status; slaves were exploited; and these slaves, together with the *metics,* or resident aliens, though comprising a majority of the population, were denied Athenian citizenship. All this is true but largely irrelevant. Classical Greece should be judged by contemporary standards rather than by present-day practices, by what it did rather than by what it failed to do. If this be the criterion, then the contributions and their historical significance stand out clearly and overwhelmingly. The spirit of free inquiry, the theory and practice of democracy, the major forms of art and literature and philosophical thought, and the emphasis on individual freedom and individual responsibility—all these comprise the splendid legacy of Greece to mankind.

IV. HELLENISTIC AGE, 336–31 B.C.

The Hellenistic Age derives its name from the new civilization that emerged with the diffusion of Classical Greek culture throughout the Middle East following Alexander's conquests. (See Chapter 7, section III.) On succeeding his father, Philip, in 336 B.C., Alexander first crushed a revolt in Thebes with a severity that persuaded the other Greek cities to acquiesce in his rule. Then in 334 B.C., he led his Macedonian soldiers eastward in an extraordinary series of victorious campaigns that extended as far as the Punjab in India. Only the refusal of his men to advance any further persuaded Alexander to return to Babylon where he died of malarial fever in 323 at the age of thirty-three.

Rival generals now fought for control of the great empire until by the beginning of the third century three succession states emerged: Macedonia in the Balkan Peninsula, Egypt under the Ptolemies, and the Asian provinces under the Seleucids.

Although Alexander's empire proved ephemeral, these succession states did survive more or less intact until they were conquered by Rome in the first century B.C. During those centuries, the Middle East became Hellenized. Thousands of Greek merchants, administrators, teachers, professional men, and mercenary soldiers emigrated from their city-states to Egypt and the Asian provinces, attracted by the unprecedented opportunities afforded by those rich lands. Thus were laid the foundations for the new Hellenistic civilization, a hybrid creation that differed from the classical parent stock in virtually every respect.

The political framework was altered basically because the polis was undermined and rendered sterile. The city-states in Greece tried to survive by experimenting with federal unions—the Achaean League and the Aetolian Federation—but they proved ineffective and eventually succumbed to the Roman legions. As for the cities in the succession states, they were quite different from the classical polis, being rent internally by dissension between the Greek immigrants and the native peoples. Furthermore, real decisions were made in imperial courts rather than in meetings of popular assemblies. Thus the citizens understandably concentrated on accumulating wealth and enjoying life, leaving the poor and the slaves to shift for themselves as they could. The civic spirit and social cohesion of the old polis gave way to self-centeredness and class strife.

Economic conditions and institutions also changed fundamentally. The Greek homeland suffered economic as well as political eclipse. It had depended on the export of wine, oil, and manufactured goods in return for foodstuffs and raw materials from the overseas colonies. But by the fourth century these colonies had taken root and developed their own industries and vineyards and olive orchards. The home cities now were dwarfed by their former colonies just as Europe after the nineteenth century was dwarfed by the United States and the Soviet Union, and essentially for the same reason.

Although the Greek lands suffered economic decay, many Greeks waxed rich by emigrating to the Middle East, which was now open to them. They had much to contribute with their enterprising spirit and their advanced commercial and banking methods. The net result was an increase in regional economic integration with a corresponding increase in regional commerce and productivity. The proceeds, however, were grossly maldistributed. Speculators took advantage of rising profits to reap great fortunes, while slaves increased in number and free workmen declined in status. It was a period, in short, of greater productivity but also greater economic inequality and social strife.

The average person during this Hellenistic Age was buffeted not only economically but also psychologically. He felt lost in the large new cities with their teeming multitudes uprooted from their traditional milieu. In the old polis, life had been relatively simple. Law, morality, religion, and duties were all clearly defined and generally accepted. Now all this was gone and the citizen found himself in a formless world, particularly since the Hellenistic cities frequently were torn by racial and cultural as well as class divisions. The rulers tried to cultivate a mystique of personal loyalty, adopting titles such as Savior and Benefactor. But such expedients offered no lasting solution. Each person remained confronted with the question of how to conduct himself in face of the impersonal and overwhelming forces of his time.

The response of intellectuals tended to be withdrawal from worldly affairs and turning from reason to mysticism. This was reflected in the vogue for romantic adventure and utopian literature. It was reflected also in the philosophies of the day, such as Cynicism, Skepticism, Epicureanism, and Stoicism. Though very different in many respects, they were generally concerned with the pursuit of personal happiness rather than of social welfare. Their underlying motive was to reconcile politically impotent man to the uncertainties of life in an economically insecure and war-ridden world. If philosophy was the religion of the cultivated upper classes, very different was the religion of the lower classes. They turned to cults of oriental origin—Mithraism, Gnosticism, the Egyptian mother-goddess Isis, and the astral religion of the Chaldeans. All these had in common the promise of salvation in afterlife. All satisfied the emotional needs of the harried masses with comforting assurances of a paradise to come. Thus the secularism and rationalism of Classical Greece now gave way to mysticism and otherworldliness.

In view of these trends in philosophy and religion, it is surprising to note that more progress was achieved in science in the Hellenistic Age than in any other period prior to the seventeenth century. This was due in part to the economic opportunities afforded by Alexander's conquests. The greatly expanded markets provided incentive to improve technology in order to increase output. Also the continual wars amongst the succession states, and between them and outside powers, created a demand for more complex war engines. Equally stimulating was the direct contact between Greek science and that of the Middle East—not only of Mesopotamia and Egypt, but also, to a certain extent, of India. Finally, the Macedonian rulers of the Hellenistic states, brought up in the aura of the prestige of Greek learning, generously supported scientific research. This was particularly true in Egypt, where the Alexandria Museum and Library constituted in effect the first state-supported research institute in history. All these factors explain the galaxy of outstanding scientists during these centuries—Euclid in geometry, Hipparchus and Aistarchus in astronomy, Eratosthenes in geography, and Galen in medicine.

In conclusion, the historical significance of the Hellenistic Age is that it brought the East and West together, breaking the separate molds that had formed through history. Men now for the first time thought of the entire civilized world as a unit—an ecumene. At first the Greeks and Macedonians went to the East as conquerors and rulers, and imposed a pattern of Hellenization. But in the process they themselves were changed, so that the resulting Hellenistic civilization was an amalgam rather than a transplantation. And in the long run the religions of the East made their way West and contributed substantially to the transformation of the Roman Empire and medieval Europe.

V. EARLY REPUBLIC, TO 264 B.C.

In 217 B.C. a peace conference was held in Greece to try to end the incessant wars amongst the city-states. A delegate of the Aetolian League, pointing to the titanic struggle between Rome and Carthage in the western Mediterranean, warned that whoever won would be a menace to Greece. "For it is evident even to those of us who give but scanty attention to affairs of state, that whether the Carthaginians beat the Romans or the Romans the Carthaginians in this war, it is not in the least likely that the victors will be content with the sovereignty of Italy and Sicily, but they are sure to come here."[6] The warning proved prophetic. Peace was patched up, but within five years there was war again. During the following century, Rome, having destroyed Carthage, turned eastward and imposed her rule upon both Macedon and the Greek cities, and ultimately upon the entire Hellenistic East.

What were the origins of this Italian city that was to affect so profoundly the course of world history? Actually many similarities are noticeable between the early histories of the Greeks and the Romans. Both were of the same ethnic stock, for just as the Indo-European Achaeans and Dorians filtered down the Balkan peninsula to Greece, so the Indo-European Latins filtered down the Italian peninsula to the south bank of the Tiber River. Among the Latin communities formed at the time was Rome, located at the lowest point at which the Tiber could be conveniently forded and the highest to which small ships could ascend. This strategic position, similar to that of London on the Thames, made Rome from the outset more mercantile and more open to foreign influences than other Latin settlements.

The chief foreign influences came from two civilized peoples who had come from overseas to settle in Italy—the Etruscans and the Greeks. (See Chapter 7, section II). About 500 B.C. Rome expelled its last Etruscan king and began its career as an independent city-state. Within a few years it had conquered the surrounding peoples and controlled the entire Latin plain from the Apennine Mountains to the sea coast. Roman institutions during this formative period were similar to those of the early Greek cities. The king originally held the *imperium,* or sovereign power, restrained only by an advisory council of aristocrats and a popular assembly that could only approve or disapprove legislation. Then, as in Greece, the monarchy was abolished and the patricians became the dominant element in society. The *imperium* formerly held by the king was now delegated to two consuls who were elected for one year periods and who were always patricians. The Senate, which was the principal legislative body, also was an aristocratic body and remained so even after some commoners, or plebians, were admitted.

The divergence between the development of Rome and of the Greek city-states occurred when Rome accomplished what had proven beyond the capacity of the Greek cities—the conquest and unification of the entire peninsula. Why was it that Rome could master the Italian peninsula whereas no Greek city was able to unify the Greek lands, let alone the whole of the Balkan peninsula? One reason was the marked difference in terrain. The Balkans are a jumble of mountains, whereas in Italy there are only the Apennines which are not difficult to cross and which run only north and south without transverse ranges. Consequently the Italian peninsula is not so compartmentalized, and is correspondingly easier to unite and keep united. Another reason for the success of the Romans was their enlightened treatment of the other Italian peoples. Athens had levied tribute and never extended its citizenship. Rome granted full citizenship to about a fourth of the population of the peninsula, and Latin citizenship to the remainder, which carried substantial but not complete privileges. This policy saved Rome, for her Italian allies remained loyal during the critical years when Hannibal was rampaging irresistibly up and down the length of the peninsula. Finally the Romans prevailed because of the superiority of their legions, each consisting of 3,600 men who were trained to disperse and fight if necessary in small units of 120.

By 295 B.C. the Romans had won central Italy and pushed south against Tartentum, the prosperous Greek city in the "instep" of the peninsula. The Tarentines called in the help of the Greek king Pyrrhus of Epirus, ranked by Hannibal as second only to Alexander in generalship. Pyrrhus won two "Pyrrhic victories," but he could not afford his heavy losses, whereas the Romans, though losing even more, could draw from a pool of 750,000 Italian fighting men. So Pyrrhus withdrew in 272 B.C. with the insightful observation "What a battleground I am leaving for Rome and Carthage!" Only eight years later, in 264 B.C., Rome and Carthage were at war in Sicily.

VI. LATE REPUBLIC, 265–27 B.C.

The transformation of Rome from an Italian republic to a great empire was sudden and spectacular and was reminiscent of the conquests of Alexander. Indeed there were certain common basic factors that help to explain the explosive expansion of both Macedon and Rome. Each had evolved superior military instruments and techniques, and each enjoyed the vital advantage of social vigor and cohesion in contrast to the social decrepitude and fragmentation of the Persian Empire and the Hellenistic succession states.

Rome's great rival, Carthage, had started as a Phoenician colony and then had waxed rich and powerful because of her near monopoly of the transit trade in the western Mediterranean. At first there was no direct conflict between Rome and Carthage for the simple reason that the one was a land power and the other a sea power. But they did clash when the Romans conquered southern Italy, for they feared Carthage's growing influence on the island of Sicily that was so close to their newly-won possessions.

The First Punic War (264–241 B.C.) forced the Romans for the first time to turn to the sea. They built a fleet and by turning naval battles into boarding operations they doggedly wore down the Carthaginians and conquered Sicily. The struggle to the death between the two great powers was now inevitable. Rome spent the next twenty years subduing the Celtic tribes in the Po Valley, thereby increasing her reserve of peasant soldiers. Carthage, to compensate for the loss of Sicily, consolidated her hold on Spain. It was from this base that the great Carthaginian strategist, Hannibal, carried out his daring invasion of Italy in 218 across the Alps, thus beginning the Second Punic War (218–201). He defeated the Romans in battle after battle, particularly in his great masterpiece of Cannae (216). But the loyalty of Rome's allies robbed him of victory. When a Roman army landed near Carthage, Hannibal was recalled, undefeated, from Italy, to be defeated on his home ground. Once again Rome had exhausted her opponent, and in 201 Carthage was forced to accept a peace leaving her only her small home territory, her walls, and ten ships—enough to chase off the pirates. Despite this catastrophic defeat, the Carthaginians made a remarkable economic recovery. But this served only to alarm Rome to the point of ruthlessly provoking the Third Punic War (149–146). Carthage itself was captured, the city completely destroyed, and the populace enslaved.

With these Punic Wars, Rome was caught in a chain reaction of conquest leading to further conquest. One reason was her overwhelming strength; with Carthage out of the way she was now the number one power in the Mediterranean. Also conquest was manifestly profitable, as booty, slaves, and tribute poured in from each new province. Finally, there were the inevitable commitments and challenges associated with far-flung imperial frontiers. For example, Philip V of Macedon had aided Hannibal during the Second Punic War, so Rome, after having disposed of Carthage, turned on Macedon. The ensuing war proved to be the first of a series in which the Romans skillfully played off against each other the several Middle Eastern powers—Macedon, Seleucid Syria, Ptolemaic Egypt, and the rival Aetolian and Achaian leagues of Greek city-states.

Thus the Romans overran and annexed in quick succession Macedon, Greece, the Asia Minor states of Pergamum, Bithynia and Cilicia, then Seleucid Syria, and finally Egypt in 31 B.C. In this manner the Romans took over the Hellenistic succession states of the East, though in Asia they acquired only the provinces along the Mediterranean coast. All the interior had fallen to Parthia, which henceforth was to be Rome's chief rival in the East. Meanwhile Julius Caesar had gained fame by conquering (58–49 B.C.) all of Gaul between the English Channel and the Mediterranean. Finally the permanent occupation of Britain was begun in the first century of our era and was consolidated with the construction of a line of fortifications between the firths of Clyde and Forth. This marked the limits of Roman rule in northern Europe.

Rome did not treat her newly acquired provinces as generously as she had her earlier Italian allies. The Senate appointed governors who were given a free hand so long as they sent back home an adequate flow of tribute, taxes, grain, and slaves. The result was unconscionable exploitation and extortion. The maladministration of Governor Gaius Verres in Sicily (73–71 B.C.), described in the following indictment by Cicero, was neither exceptional nor atypical:

Sicilian soldiers and sailors, our allies and our friends, were starved to death; fine fleets, splendidly equipped, were to the great disgrace of our nation destroyed and lost to us.

Famous and ancient works of art, some of them the gifts of wealthy kings . . . —this same governor stripped and despoiled every one of them. Nor was it only the civic statues and works of art he treated thus; he also pillaged the holiest and most venerated sanctuaries; in fact, he has not left the people of Sicily a single god whose workmanship he thought at all above the average of antiquity or artistic merit.[7]

The Roman homeland was affected almost as adversely by these policies as the subject territories. Many of the small farmers in Italy had been ruined by the ravages of Hannibal's campaigns and by the long years of overseas service during the following wars. Then came the influx of cheap grain and of droves of slaves from the conquered provinces. The peasants were forced to sell out to the new class of ultrarich who were eager to accumulate large estates because agriculture still was considered the only respectable calling for gentlemen. Thus the second century B.C. saw the growth in Italy of large plantations (*latifundia*) worked by slaves and owned by absentee landlords. The dispossessed peasantry drifted to the towns where they lived in squalid tenements and competed once again with slaves for such work as was available. The authorities took care to provide them with "bread and circuses" (*panis et circenses*) in order to keep them quiet. Despite the insecurity and rootlessness, city life at least was exciting and alluring. Poets were loud in their praise of rustic virtues, but the peasants themselves thought otherwise and continued to flock to Rome—the "common cesspool" as it was termed by the contemporary historian Sallust.

The political fruits of empire were as bitter as the economic. The Senate, which had directed the victorious overseas campaigns, gained greatly in prestige and power. Also the new urban mobs offered no basis for popular government since they were always ready to sell their votes or to support any demagogue who promised relief from their troubles. Equally disruptive was the changing character of the armed forces. Imperial obligations required a large standing army, so that it no longer sufficed to call up property owners for short-term militia service. Rather the ranks were opened to volunteers, and so dispossessed peasants enlisted for long periods. Rome's legions accordingly changed from a citizen army to a professional one. The soldiers' first loyalty now was not to the state but to their commanders to whom they looked for a share of the booty and of any land that might be available for distribution. The generals increasingly came to regard the legions entrusted to them as their client armies and used them to advance their personal fortunes.

The cultural repercussions of imperial expansion also were disruptive. The traditional Roman virtues had been those of poor, hard-working peasants. But when wealth began to pour into the capital, the ancient homilies concerning thrift, abstinence, and industry were soon forgotten. The last days of the Republic were marked by a wild scramble for money, the sort of ostentatious waste to be expected from *parvenues,* and a callous indifference to all human values.

In light of the above, it is understandable that the period from the end of the Punic Wars in 146 B.C. to the end of the Republic in 27 B.C. was one of crisis—of class war, slave revolts, and increasing military intervention in politics. A gallant reform effort was made at the outset by Tiberius Gracchus and his brother Gaius. They sought to use their elective positions as Tribunes to push through a moderate program of land distribution. But the oligarchs would have none of it and resorted to violence to gain their ends. Tiberius was murdered in 133 B.C. along with three hundred of his followers. Twelve years later Gaius was driven to suicide, and the senatorial class resumed its sway.

The fate of the Gracchi brothers made it clear that no leader could prevail without superior forces at his disposal. So now it was generals such as Marius and Sulla who took the stage and fought virtual civil wars until Julius Caesar, the conqueror of Gaul, became the undisputed master of the empire. His murder in 44 B.C. was followed by political jockeying and armed strife between his adopted son and heir Octavian and the political adventurer Mark Antony. With his naval victory over Antony and Cleopatra at Actium (31 B.C.), Octavian was supreme. He was only thirty-three years old at the time, the age at which the great Alexander had died. But Octavian had forty-four years of life ahead of him, during which he laid the foundations for two golden centuries of imperial peace and stability.

VII. EARLY EMPIRE, 27 B.C.–A.D. 284

In 27 B.C. the Senate conferred upon Octavian the titles of Augustus and Imperator, symbolizing the transformation of Rome from republic to empire. Octavian professed to prefer the republican title of "First Citizen" (*Princeps*), but in practice he played the role of emperor to the full. He created a centralized system of courts under his own supervision and assumed direct control over provincial governors, punishing them severely for graft and extortion. He standardized taxes and made their collection a state function rather than a private business operated by rapacious tax farmers. He kept close check on the army, seeing to it that the soldiers were well provided for and that they swore allegiance directly to him. He also created a permanent navy that suppressed piracy and safeguarded the transportation of both commodities and troops to all parts of the empire.

By these measures Augustus, as he came to be known, created an efficient administrative system that ensured the *Pax Romana* that was to prevail for two centuries. It is true that the four emperors following Augustus—Tiberius (14–37), Caligula (37–41), Claudius (41–54), and Nero (54–68)—were unworthy of their high office. But the empire weathered their misrule and then blossomed under a succession of "five good Emperors"—Nerva (96–98), Trajan (98–117), Hadrian (117–138), Antoninus Pius (138–161), and Marcus Aurelius (161–180). It was during these reigns that the Roman Empire reached its apogee, both in geographic extent and in the quality of its civilization.

In the extreme north, the imperial frontier was defined by the fortifications built from the Forth to the Clyde. In the northeast, the Rhine and the Danube provided a natural frontier. Both Asia Minor and Egypt were Roman possessions, but between the two the frontier ran close to the Mediterranean coast, leaving the interior to the Parthians and, after A.D. 224, to the Sassanians. Likewise in North Africa the Romans controlled the coastal territories between Egypt and the Atlantic, with the Sahara as their southern limit.

This huge area, with its strong natural frontiers, constituted a prosperous and virtually self-sufficient economic unit. Various factors contributed to the flourishing nature of the imperial economy during these centuries, including the honest and efficient administration, the monetary stability, the large-scale public works, and the extensive trade, both within and without the empire. Thanks to the thriving domestic and foreign trade, staples and luxuries poured into the capital from as near as Gaul and as far as China—enough staples to feed and clothe over a million people, and enough luxuries to satisfy the extravagances of the rulers of the Western world.

In the cultural field, a basic achievement of the Romans was the extension into Central and Western Europe of urban civilization with all that that entailed.

In this respect their role in the West was similar to that of the Greeks in the Middle East. In the third century B.C., after Alexander, the Greeks founded dozens of cities from which Hellenistic culture spread as far as the Indus and the Jaxartes. So now the Romans founded cities such as London and Colchester in Britain, Autun and Vaison in Gaul, and Trier and Cologne in Germany. These cities, with their public bathhouses and theaters and markets comprised the basic cells of the imperial culture as well as of the imperial body politic.

The great city of the empire, of course, was Rome. It sprawled over five thousand acres and its population during the second century A.D. is estimated at a little over one million. This was gigantic for a period when there was little of the technology that makes modern cities viable. Thus a modern visitor to ancient Rome would have been impressed by the complete absence of street lighting and of sanitary facilities in the crowded tenements of the poor. He would have been impressed also by the teeming streets reverberating with the noise of hawkers bawling their wares, money changers ringing their coins, tinkers pounding their hammers, snake charmers playing their flutes, and beggars rehearsing their misfortunes to passersby. Life under such conditions was made tolerable by mass state facilities and entertainments—chariot races, gladiatorial contests, and sumptuous baths with exercise quarters, lounging halls, gardens, and libraries.

Finally Rome was also the center of imperial culture. This culture, as noted earlier, was essentially Greek-derived, particularly in such fields as literature, art, and philosophy. (See Chapter 7, section III.) But in engineering and law, the Romans, with their bent for practicality, had important contributions of their own to make. Typically, the Romans achieved little in abstract science but excelled in the construction of aqueducts, sewer systems, bridges, and roads, the latter being so well engineered that they continued to be used through the Middle Ages, and in some cases even to the present day. Likewise, Roman achitecture, in contrast to the Greek, was concerned primarily with secular structures such as baths, amphitheaters, stadia, and triumphal arches. And new building materials—concrete, brick, and mortar—made possible vaulting on the grand scale for their large buildings.

Perhaps the most important single intellectual contribution of the Romans was their body of law based on reason rather than custom. Their original laws, as set down in the Twelve Tablets about 450 B.C., were simple and conservative, typical of a peasant people. With the growth of commerce and of empire, life became more complicated and these laws no longer sufficed. Hence the formulation of a new body of law—the *jus gentium,* or law of the peoples—which they accepted as applicable to themselves as well as to others. The Romans also evolved the legal concept of *jus naturale,* or natural law. This stemmed not from judicial practice but from the Stoic idea of a rational god ruling the universe. Or, in Cicero's words, it was law above mere custom or opinion, "implanted by Nature, discoverable by right reason, valid for all nations and all times." While jurists did not regard this as an automatic limitation upon Roman civil law, they did view it as an ideal to which human legislation should conform. This basic principle represents one of Rome's great contributions and remains operative to the present day. In fact, Roman law, as systematized later in Justinian's Code in the mid-sixth century, constitutes the basis for the present legal systems of the Latin countries of Europe, of the Latin American states, of the Province of Quebec, and of the state of Louisiana.

VIII. LATE EMPIRE, A.D. 284–467

The great days of Rome came to an end with the death of Marcus Aurelius in 180. His son Commodus avoided his duties as head of the empire and spent most of his time at chariot races and gladiatorial contests. After his assassination in 193 he was followed by rulers who were for the most part equally incompetent. The Praetorian Guard, a highly trained and well-paid body created by Augustus to protect the security of the capital, now got out of control, and an emperor remained in power only while he had the support of this body. During the period from 235 to 284 there were almost two dozen emperors, and only one of them died a natural death. This disintegration in the center inevitably weakened the frontier defenses. Outlying provinces were overrun by the German tribes in the West and by the revived Persian Empire of the Sassanians in the East.

This imperial decay of the third century was checked with the advent of the strong and capable emperors Diocletian (284–305) and Constantine (312–317). Among the policies they adopted to hold the empire together was a rigid regimentation, including controls of prices and interest rates and export prohibitions on "strategic products," such as iron, bronze, weapons, army equipment, and horses. These controls were extended to the point of a virtual caste system. Constantine required every soldier's son to be a soldier unless unfit for service. Similarly agricultural laborers were tied to the land on a permanent and hereditary basis. The tendency was to extend this to all crafts and professions that were deemed indispensable or that had recruitment difficulties.

Another policy during this time of troubles was decentralization, which proved necessary with the deterioration of the imperial economy. Diocletian divided his realm in two, keeping the eastern half for his own administration and appointing a co-emperor for the western. This division was hardened when Constantine built a new capital on the site of the old Greek colony of Byzantium on the Bosphorus. Constantinople, as the new city soon came to be called, became one of the great cities of the world and served as the proud capital of the East Roman, or Byzantine, Empire for centuries after Rome and the Western empire had passed away.

It was Constantine also who made the fateful decision to seek imperial stability and cohesion through cooperation with Christianity rather than its suppression. This represented the culmination of a centuries old trend in religious attitudes and practices. The vicissitudes of daily life during this later imperial phase were leading increasing numbers to turn for solace to salvation religions, as had happened earlier in the Hellenistic East. (See section IV of this chapter.) Spiritual needs no longer were satisfied by the cult of emperor and the official polytheism. Brotherhoods that celebrated the mysteries of Oriental gods now provided satisfying explanations of the world, rules of conduct, and release from evil and from death.

The most successful of the new religions was Christianity. It offered the doctrine of One God, the Father Omnipotent, in place of the polytheism of the Greco-Roman gods and the diffuse monotheism of the oriental cults. It brought the solace of a Redeemer, Jesus, who was not an ambiguous figure in a mythological labyrinth, but who miraculously lived an earthly life, even though he was the Son of God. Christianity also guaranteed salvation to the believer, but instead of a starry eternity, it restored him to life through a personal resurrection foreshadowed by the Resurrection of Christ himself. Perhaps most important of all, Christianity provided fellowship when times were disjointed and common people felt uprooted and forsaken. All Christians assisted one another, and by their devotion and self-denial they set an inspiring and contagious example. Thus at a time when the laws and philosophy of the old order were becoming irrelevant and unviable, Christianity offered relevance and hope for the meek and the humble.

By the time of the great fire of 64 the Christians had become so numerous that Nero deemed it politic to blame them for the disaster and to begin the first of numerous persecutions, but this merely hallowed the memory of the martyrs and spurred the proselytizing efforts. After a final major persecution early in the fourth century, Emperor Constantine issued the Edict of Milan (313) excusing Christians from pagan rituals and granting their religion the same toleration accorded to all others. Finally Emperor Theodosius (379–395) made Christianity in effect the state church. The old Roman aristocracy and the apostate Emperor Julian (361–363) fought a stubborn rearguard action to preserve pagan practices, but by the end of the fourth century Christianity reigned supreme.

Just as the emperors adopted Christianity with the aim of furthering social cohesion, so for the same reason they adopted the pomp and circumstance of oriental court etiquette. In contrast to Augustus who had dubbed himself "First Citizen," Diocletian took the name of Jovian, the earthly representative of Jupiter, while Constantine, after his conversion to Christianity, assumed sacred status. The power of the emperor henceforth was considered to be derived from the gods rather than delegated by citizens. Accordingly, court ritual now made the emperor remote and unapproachable, bedecked in a jeweled diadem and a robe of purple silk interwoven with gold. All subjects were required to prostrate themselves, while a privileged few were allowed to kiss the border of the emperor's robe. High imperial officials were correspondingly beatified—the treasurer became "count of the sacred largesses," and the imperial council was known as the "sacred consistory."

With these measures the emperors of the third and fourth centuries strove valiantly to halt the imperial decline. If resolve and effort alone were needed, they would have been spectacularly successful. In fact they did stabilize the situation somewhat, but only temporarily. The net effect of their herculean endeavors was to postpone rather than to avert the end. Beginning in 406 the West Roman emperors were powerless to prevent permanent large-scale incursions of Franks, Burgundians, Visigoths, and Vandals in Gaul, Spain, and Africa. Nor could they prevent the ultimate indignity of the sack of Rome by barbarians in 410 and again in 455. Finally in 476 Romulus Augustulus, the last of the West Roman emperors, was forced to abdicate by Odoacer, the German, or Hunnic, leader of a band of mercenary soldiers.

Though generally taken to mark the end of the West Roman Empire, this incident, which attracted little attention at the time, was merely the culmination of a process of disintegration that had extended over two centuries. To understand the reason for this "fall of Rome," if the traditional cataclysmic phrase may be used, it is necessary to determine the dynamics of this prolonged but inexorable descent to oblivion. The instrument responsible for the "fall" was, of course, the German barbarians. Thus a French historian has concluded, "Roman civilization did not die a natural death. It was murdered."[8] These is some justification for this verdict, particularly if it is kept in mind that the innumerable small tribes known to the Romans in the earlier centuries amalgamated later to form the larger political units of the Franks, the Alamanni, and the Goths. Yet even then it was not a case of irresistible hordes sweeping everything aside by sheer weight of numbers. Historians estimate that only about 100,000 Ostrogoths invaded Italy, and an equal number of Visigoths subjugated Spain and southern France. The Vandal force that crossed the Straits of Gibraltar to North Africa totalled about 80,000 men, or 1 per cent of the native population of that province.

So the question still remains—why the "fall"? An American historian has recently stated that "though war was the apparent cause of death . . . the organic disease of the Empire was economic."[9] In fact, this "organic disease" is discernible not only in the Roman Empire but in the Hellenistic states, in Classical Greece, and even in the earlier ancient civilizations. All were afflicted by the same basic problem of low productivity. This stemmed from the failure to advance technology significantly after the Neolithic age, which had produced such core inventions as metallurgy, the plow, the wheel, the sail, and the solar calendar.

The underlying cause for this technological retardation appears to have been the institution of slavery, which was an integral and universally accepted part of all these civilizations. Even in Classical Greece, where slavery never was as rampant as in Rome, Aristotle, as noted above, asserted that some men were born to rule and some to be ruled, and if the latter refused to accept their preordained fate, then it was "naturally just" that they should be hunted down as though they were "wild beasts."

The repercussions of this slavery institution were manifold and pernicious. It deprived the slave of any incentive to improve on the traditional operations of his craft. It also deprived the master of any incentive to technological innovation so long as plenty of slave labor was available. Thus when an obelisk was to be erected during the reign of Vespasian in the present-day Piazza San Pietro in Rome, an inventor of the time suggested an engineering technique that would have greatly facilitated the operation. But the emperor preferred manual slave labor so as not to leave the slaves unemployed. Likewise the water-mill, though known in the eastern provinces of the empire as early as the first century B.C., was not adopted in Rome until the fourth century when the supply of slaves had shrunk.

Equally harmful was the natural tendency of a slave-owning society to associate manual labor with slaves and hence to regard such labor as beneath the dignity of freemen. Thus the Greek essayist Plutarch stated that the great Archimedes

. . . did not think the inventing of military engines an object worthy of his serious studies, but only reckoned them among the amusements of geometry. . . .

The first to turn their thoughts to mechanics, a branch of knowledge which came afterwards to be so much admired, were Eudoxus and Archytas, who confirmed certain problems, not then soluble on theoretical grounds, by sensible experiments and the use of instruments. But Plato inveighed against them, with great indignation, as corrupting and debasing the excellence of geometry, by making her descend from incorporeal and intellectual, to corporeal and sensible things, and obliging her to make use of matter, which requires much manual labor, and is the object of servile trades. Mechanics were in consequence separated from geometry, and were for a long time despised by philosophers.[10]

In these various ways, then, the institution of slavery tended to inhibit technological innovation during the millennia following the egalitarian Neolithic age. Slavery also had the economic effect of depressing the internal market by restricting domestic purchasing power, since slaves obviously were not able to purchase the fruits of their labor.

For some time these basic structural weaknesses were masked by imperial expansion, with the resulting flood of booty, tribute, foodstuffs, and slaves. But there were limits to the expansion of empires at that level of technological development—limits set by logistical and communications requirements. Thus Rome, like China, was able to advance just so far and no further. When that point was reached, and the imperial frontiers became fixed, or even began shrinking, then the hitherto hidden structural defects became visible.

The army, which hitherto had been a profitable source of slaves and material wealth, now became a heavy but inescapable burden. Likewise the bureaucracy, having become swollen during the period of expansion, now proved insupportable in a period of contraction. The excessive expenditures led to inflation that eventually reached runaway proportions. In Egypt, for example, a measure of wheat that cost 6 drachmai in the first century A.D. rose to 200 in 276, 9,000 in 314, 78,000 in 334, and to more than 2 million soon after 334. With such inflation, coinage became worthless and there was some reversion to barter. This trend was hastened by the growing diffusion of industry to the countryside and to the provinces. The diffusion occurred for a variety of reasons, including the deterioration of imperial communication facilities and the drop in the supply of slaves which necessitated tapping new labor pools. The shift of industry from the cities to villages and large country estates meant the agrarianization of the empire. The large estates became increasingly self-sufficient, boasting craftsmen of every kind as well as agricultural laborers. And the more self-sufficient they became, the more the imperial economy disintegrated into autarchic units.

This economic decentralization inevitably was accompanied by political decentralization. With the decline of trade and the shrinkage of state revenues, the imperial edifice no longer could be supported and slowly it began to crumble. This was a factor behind the desperate efforts of Diocletian and Constantine to buttress the structure by imperial fiat. But the disease was "organic" rather than superficial, so all the regimentation, with its propping and bracing, was of no avail in the long run. Regimentation, however, was not the cause of imperial decay, but an ineffective remedy that was tried to halt the decay. "Crisis preceded regimentation," as an economic historian has pointed out.[11]

It follows that a major reason why the West Roman Empire "fell" and the East did not, was precisely that the economy of the West was less advanced and less strong. Italian agriculture was never as productive as that in the alluvial valleys of the Middle East. The grain harvest in Italy "was on an average no more than four times the sowing."[12] The rich soils of Central and Northern Europe had to await medieval technological advances for effective exploitation. Likewise industry in the West was of relatively recent origin and generally lagged behind that in the East. This was true of Italy, and much more so of Gaul, the only other western province where industry had taken root. Thus although the whole Roman Empire was wracked by "organic disease," the western part, being the least robust, was the first to succumb, while the eastern survived to live for another millennium.

Despite its demise, the West Roman Empire did leave a rich legacy. Most apparent are the material remains—the amphitheaters, arenas, temples, aqueducts, roads, and bridges. Equally obvious is the linguistic bequest in the form of the Romance (or Romanized) languages of Europe. Roman law, as noted above, is very much alive in the legal systems of numerous countries in Europe and the Americas. The organization and ritual of the Catholic church owe much to

Roman imperial structure and religious traditions. Finally the *Pax Romana,* which had brought two centuries of relative peace and prosperity, left a tradition of imperial unity in place of the city-state particularism of the Greeks. It was this tradition during the following centuries that fired the imagination and ambition of barbarian princes throughout Europe to become *imperator* or *basileus* or tsar.

SUGGESTED READING

R. H. BARROW, *The Romans* (Penguin, 1951); J. B. BURY, *A History of Greece to the Death of Alexander the Great,* 3rd ed. (Macmillan, 1951); J. FERGUSON, *The Heritage of Hellenism* (Harcourt, 1973); D. KAGAN, ed., *Decline and Fall of the Roman Empire* (Heath, 1962); C. ROEBUCK, *The World of Ancient Times* (Scribners, 1966); M. ROSTOVT-ZEFF, *Social and Economic History of the Hellenistic World,* 3 vols., (Clarendon, 1941); W. W. TARN and G. T. GRIFFITH, *Hellenistic Civilization* (Arnold, 1952); T. B. L. WEBSTER, *Athenian Culture and Society* (Univ. California, 1973).

chapter nine

Indian Civilization

Government is the science of punishment.—Kautilya

I consider that my duty is the good of the whole world.—Ashoka

Turning from Greece and Rome to India, we enter an altogether different world. The differences are not simply those that might naturally emerge from contrasting physical environments—differences in occupations, diet, habitation, dress, and the like. The differences were much more far reaching and fundamental. There was nothing in the West remotely resembling basic Indian concepts and institutions such as caste, *ahimsa,* or nonviolence, reincarnation, and *karma,* or the law of moral consequences. These were not merely esoteric abstractions of Indian thought. Rather they constituted the bedrock of Indian civilization, molding the thought and daily lives of all Indians. And the pattern that resulted was so distinctive and so enduring that Indian civilization to the present day has distinguishing characteristics that mark it off from all other Eurasian civilizations.

Such distinctiveness also characterizes the civilization of China, as will be noted in the following chapter, but this is to be expected, given the unparalleled geographic and historical isolation of that country. In India, by contrast, the beginnings appeared to be basically similar to those of the other regions to the west where Aryan invaders had settled—the Iranian plateau and the Balkan and Italian peninsulas. As noted earlier (Chapter 6, section IV), the Aryan tribes that descended upon India about 1500 B.C. possessed the same physical features, the same pastoral economy, the same social institutions, the same gods, and the same epics as did, for example, the Achaeans and the Dorians. Furthermore the Indo-Aryans were not isolated in their subcontinent to anywhere near the degree that the Chinese were on the eastern extremity of Eurasia. The mountain ranges of northwest India are not impassable, so that armies and merchants and pilgrims crossed back and forth through the centuries. In fact, during much of the time there was more interaction between northern India and the Middle East and

Central Asia, than between northern India and the southern part of the peninsula.

The question naturally arises, then, why the Indo-Aryans should have developed a civilization so basically different from those of their kinsmen to the west. The scanty evidence available does not allow for a specific or definitive answer, but the most simple and plausible explanation is that the Indo-Aryans were Indianized. In contrast to the Achaeans or Dorians or Latins, who settled in relatively uncivilized areas, the Indo-Aryans encountered in the Indus Valley a highly developed civilization with large urban centers and a dense population. (See Map VIII, "Classical Age Empires in India.") This native population, although subjugated and despised, was too numerous and too advanced to be exterminated or pushed aside or assimilated, leaving few traces of the original culture. Instead, as the Aryan pastoralists settled down and took up agriculture, they perforce lived in close proximity with the prior inhabitants of their new land. After some centuries of such coexistence and intermarriage, the inevitable result was a cultural synthesis. The circumstances and nature and consequences of this synthesis are the subject of this chapter.

I. ARYAN IMPACT

Following their penetration into the Indus Valley, the Aryans gradually spread eastward into the heavily forested basin of the Ganges. Their expansion was slow at first, with only stone, bronze, and copper axes being available. But iron was introduced about 800 B.C. and their pace gained speed. The main occupation now shifted from pastoralism to agriculture. Furthermore, the monsoon climate of the Ganges Valley made possible rice cultivation, which was much more productive than the wheat and barley grown in the Punjab. Thus the center of population density shifted from the northwest to the east, which consequently became the seat of the first powerful kingdoms.

The shift to agriculture stimulated various crafts necessary for the new villages, including carpentry, metallurgy, weaving, and tanning. Agriculture also promoted trade, with the river serving as the natural highway for transporting surplus foodstuffs. Barter was the common practice at first, with the cow as the unit of value in large-scale transactions. When coins appeared, the earliest weight standards, significantly enough, were exactly those of the pre-Aryan Indus civilization. Towns grew out of villages that were strategically located for trade or that had specialized in particular crafts.

This economic growth in turn facilitated political consolidation. Originally the Indo-Aryans, like their relatives in the West, were organized under tribal chiefs assisted by councils of elders and general assemblies. With economic development the tribes gave way to kingdoms in the Ganges plain and to republics in the Punjab and in the foothills of the Himalayas. Of these early states the kingdom of Magadha in the lower Ganges soon rose to preeminence because of its location on two main trade routes and its control over rich iron ore deposits. With these advantages Magadha was to serve as the base for the formation of both the Maurya and Gupta empires.

The Nanda dynasty in the fourth century B.C. was the first to exploit systematically the resources of Magadha for state building purposes. They built canals, organized irrigation projects, and established an efficient administrative system for the collection of taxes. The Nandas have been described as the earliest empire builders of India. In fact, they laid the foundations of empire but were not destined to actually fashion the first imperial structure. This was to be the historic role of Chandragupta Maurya, the young adventurer who usurped the Nanda throne in 321 B.C. and went on to build the famous empire named after him.

These economic and political developments were paralleled by fateful changes in social structure. Originally the Indo-Aryans, like other Aryans, were divided into three classes, the warrior nobles, the priests, and the common people. They had none of the restrictions associated with caste, such as hereditary professions, rules limiting marriages to within castes, and taboos as to dining companions. But by 500 B.C. the caste system was functioning with all its essential features. Although many theories have been advanced as to its origins, it is generally agreed that color was a basic factor. Being so conscious of the difference in complexion between themselves and the dark natives, the Aryan newcomers dubbed them *Dasas*, or slaves. With their strong sense of racial superiority, the Aryans strove to prevent admixture with their despised subjects. Accordingly they evolved a system of four hereditary castes. The first three comprised their own occupational classes, the priests (*Brahmans*), the warrior nobles (*Kshatriyas*), and the farmers (*Vaishyas*). The fourth caste (*Shudras*) was reserved for the Dasas, who were excluded from the religious ceremonies and social rights enjoyed by their conquerors.

This arrangement ceased to correspond to racial reality with the passage of time. Aryan tribes frequently made alliances with Dasa tribes to wage war against other Aryan tribes. Also Aryan settlers mingled with the natives who then adopted Aryan speech and customs. In such cases the Dasas' priests became Brahmans, and their chiefs, Kshatriyas. In response to these realities, traders and some landowners were classified as Vaishyas, while cultivators and general laborers became Shudras. Within these four broad divisions have grown up a bewildering variety of castes which have four basic features in common. One is characteristic employment, so that bankers and merchants often belong to the Vaishya caste. Another feature of caste is the hereditary principle, expressed in complex marriage regulations and restrictions. Caste also involves further restrictions as to food, water, touch, and ceremonial purity. Finally each caste has its *dharma,* or moral code, which stipulates such duties as maintenance of the family unit and performance of prescribed ceremonies at marriage, birth, and death.

Outside this system are the pariahs, or untouchables, comprising today about a seventh of the Indian population. They are condemned to trades or crafts regarded as unclean because their function involves some ritual defilement or the taking of human or animal life. These occupations include hunters, fishermen, butchers, executioners, gravediggers, undertakers, tanners, leather workers, and scavengers. Involvement in these occupations has led in turn to social segregation. Untouchables live in isolated villages or in quarters outside town limits, and are required to use their own temples and wells and to avoid polluting members of the castes by any kind of physical contact. The untouchables are further subjected to psychological disabilities as crippling and degrading as the physical. The doctrine of karma holds that one's status in present life has been determined by the deeds of previous lives. The untouchables therefore are held responsible for their present plight because of past sins, and their only hope for improved status in future lives is dutiful performance of present duties.

It is this combination of social and religious sanctions that has enabled caste to function to the present day. It should be added that with its manifold provisions for mutual aid, caste does provide security so long as one abides by its injunctions. Thus it continues to serve as the steel framework of Hindu society.

And although it has been attacked by reformers and undermined by the exigencies of modern industrial society, caste nevertheless remains essentially in operation in rural India where three-fourths of the total population continues to live.

II. REFORMATION AND COUNTER-REFORMATION

Caste, with its basic tenets of dharma, karma, and reincarnation, is part and parcel of the Hindu religious system. Originally the Aryans had typical tribal gods personifying natural forces, such as Indra, god of thunder and war, Agni, god of fire, and Soma, god of their sacred intoxicant of the same name. Gods of this nature were appropriate for pastoralists, but as the Aryans settled down to agriculture they perforce turned to new deities. Hence the advent of the "great gods" of Hinduism—Brahma, the Creator, Vishnu, the gracious Preserver, and Shiva, the Mighty and the Destroyer. It is not accidental that these new gods, particularly Shiva, bear striking resemblances to finds in the Indus Valley sites. At this time, the Aryans naturally appropriated native religious ideas and practices that had evolved through the millennia in the ancient agriculture-based civilization.

With the new gods came also a growing concentration of power in the hands of the priestly class, or Brahmans. This innovation also was derived probably from pre-Aryan religious tradition. Whatever the historic prototypes, the Brahmans effectively exploited their mastery of the Vedas, or hymns, that were recited aloud during rituals and sacrifices. These were transmitted orally through the generations, and were considered so sacred that they were memorized word for word, sound for sound. As the custodians and transmitters of this precious heritage, the Brahmans were able to assert and enforce their claims as the leaders of Hindu society, superior to the Kshatriya, or secular heads.

With time the Brahmans challenged even the status of the deities by emphasizing the significance of the rituals over which they presided. They set forth these claims in the Brahmanas, or prose manuals designed to interpret the Vedas and guide the ritual. These often consisted of a combination of puerile speculation and shrewd formulas that buttressed priestly pretensions. At a more mundane level the Brahmans enjoyed numerous prerogatives and exemptions because of the sacred nature of their functions. Donors of gifts were assured definite reward in this, as well as in subsequent, lives. "Gift of land" was rated most highly for it "liberated from all sin." Thus the Brahmans acquired vast estates, including entire villages. Also they were exempt from all taxes since they were deemed to have discharged such debts through "acts of piety." And being sacrosanct, the Brahmans could not be sentenced to death or to any type of corporal punishment. Finally the doctrines of karma, reincarnation, and dharma provided virtually irresistible means for Brahman control of the mind. There was little chance for individual assertiveness when one's station in life was the inescapable result of one's own past actions, and when hope in future life rested exclusively on faithful observance of stipulated caste duties, regardless of how onerous or degrading they might be.

The Brahman pretensions and exactions were one factor in the religious reformation in India in the sixth and fifth centuries B.C. Another was the economic growth noted above, which created a wealthy merchant, or Vaishya, caste that resented the special privileges enjoyed by the two upper castes. Finally there was the tension between the Brahmans and the non-Aryans who had been admitted to the Hindu fold but who resented the priestly domination. This combination of factors lay behind the ferment in Indian religious and intellectual circles during these centuries. The demand arose for moshka, or freedom—for something more meaningful and satisfying than prescribed rituals and rigid doctrines.

One manifestation of the unrest was a trend towards asceticism. Some of the most active minds, alienated by the society about them, concentrated on pure introspection. They developed techniques for disciplining or "yoking" (yoga) the senses to an inward focus, culminating in that state of trance or ecstasy which mystics describe as "enlightenment" and sceptics call "self-hypnotism." Out of this inward searching and speculating developed many reform movements, of which only two have survived to the present—Jainism and Buddhism. The founders of both, it might be noted, began as ascetics and then challenged in more practical and systematic fashion the Brahman establishment.

Jaina ideas were in circulation as early as the seventh century B.C., but it was the teacher Mahavira (ca. 540–467 B.C.) who gave them shape and institutional organization. A basic tenet of his teaching was that not only animals and insects, but "sticks and stones and trees" had each a separate soul. Accordingly he stressed the importance of respecting life in any form. The Jaina priest going about his duties will sweep the path before him to avoid stepping on any insects, and the pious Jaina wears a cloth over his nose to prevent insects being drawn up his nostrils. About a million Jainas live today in West India (Gujarat), but their influence on Hindu society has been far greater than this number suggests. They, together with the Buddhists, were responsible for the central doctrine of ahimsa, or nonviolence, which eventually was accepted within the general body of Hinduism. Mahatma Gandhi, although not a member of this sect, was strongly influenced by its teachings.

Jainism never spread outside India, but Buddhism became a powerful force in Central Eurasia and in East and Southeast Asia. In doing so it played a major role in the creation of a Eurasian ecumene during the Classical Age. (See Chapter 7, section III.) So far as India was concerned, the significance of Buddha's teachings is that they posed a more fundamental challenge to Hinduism than did Jainism. He had no place for caste or for Brahmans, and, like the later Protestants, he held that the scriptures should be understood by the laity. Apart from its spectacular successes in the outside world, Buddhism within India was a serious rival to Hinduism for several centuries. But it never became the dominant faith, and after A.D. 600 it went into decline. By the end of the twelfth century, when the Moslem Turks arrived, it survived only in a few localities and in a debased form.

One reason for this paradoxical disappearance of a great religious movement from the land of its birth was that it failed to provide for the usual crises of life. It offered no ceremonies for birth, marriage, death, and other critical turns in the lives of the laity. By contrast the Brahmans were ready with their rites, which fact assured their survival despite the attacks of the reformers. More important, the Brahmans themselves embraced reform. In their philosophical texts, the Upanishads, they set forth their own paths to moshka—to freedom and release.

The supreme spirit permeating the universe, they taught, was Brahman, a being capable of all knowledge and feeling. He was the universal soul and the all-pervading breath; all else was illusion. The individual soul—Atman—was a spark of the supreme being. By transmigration it passed from state to state until it attained release by reabsorption into Brahman. This identification of the individual soul and the Soul of the universe was the ultimate goal that holy men sought to reach by discipline, meditation, and withdrawal from the world of the senses. Thus seekers after truth now could abandon the world within the fold of Hinduism.

Although Buddhism as a practicing faith disappeared in India, it has survived to the present by virtue of its basic tenets being incorporated in Hinduism. The Hindu counter-reformation triumphed precisely because it accepted Buddhist ideas in partnership. The original Hinduism with its nature worship and sacrifice and power propitiation was transformed by the philosophy of the Upanishads, by the compassion of ahimsa, and by the spiritual and moral discipline of dharma.

III. MAURYA EMPIRE

Turning from religious movements to political developments, the outstanding event was the emergence of India's first imperial structure, the Maurya Empire. As noted earlier in this chapter, the migration of the Aryans to the Ganges Valley had shifted the center of gravity to that region, and particularly to the kingdom of Magadha. Meanwhile the northwest provinces had been going their own way, dissociated from the rest of India by virtue of their close ties with Persian civilization. In fact, Emperor Darius crossed the Hindu Kush mountains about 518 B.C. and made the western Punjab the twentieth satrapy of his empire. Two centuries later, in 327 B.C., Alexander conquered the region, although his intrusion was more a raid than a full-fledged invasion. He stayed only two years, and less than a decade after his departure Greek authority in the Punjab had completely disappeared. Not a mention of Alexander is to be found in contemporary Indian sources. And yet his campaign did have significant influence on the future development of India.

Least important are the accounts left by Alexander's companions of their impressions of India. Unfortunately none of these has survived, though information taken from them has been passed down as fragments in the writings of later historians and geographers. More practical was the contribution of Alexander's army and fleet in opening or reinforcing land and sea trade routes. This swelled the east-west trade from northwest India through Afghanistan and Iran to Asia Minor and Levant ports.

Most important for Indian history was Alexander's role in creating a political vacuum in northwest India by overthrowing several local kingdoms and republics. Chandragupta Maurya promptly filled the void and founded the empire named after him. In 322 B.C., three years after Alexander's departure, Chandragupta, then an ambitious young general, unseated the Nanda dynasty of Magadha and founded his own. In the following years he extended his rule steadily northwestward until his empire extended from the Ganges to the Indus, including the deltas of both rivers. At the same time he organized a powerful army and an efficient administration to sustain his realm. Thus when Seleucus became king of the Middle East as one of the successors to Alexander and attempted to recover Alexander's Indian provinces, Chandragupta easily repelled the Greek forces.

A year later, in 304, Seleucus was forced to accept a peace by which he abandoned the Indian provinces to the Maurya emperor and bestowed upon him the hand of a Greek princess in marriage. In return he obtained 500 elephants, which he used to good effect against his rivals in the Hellenistic world. This settlement marked the advent of the Maurya Empire as one of the great powers of the age. In the capital of Pataliputra, in Magadha, resided for several years the Greek ambassador, Megasthenes, whose observations are a valuable source, even though available now in only secondary form. Chandragupta's son, Bindusara (ca. 298–273 B.C.), appears to have conquered the Deccan, while his grandson, the famous Ashoka (273–232 B.C.), subjugated Kalinga, or eastern India. Thus the Maurya Empire under the latter ruler encompassed the entire Indian peninsula except for the southern tip.

The structure and functioning of this empire is indicated in the book *Arthashastra* [The theory of political economy], by Chandragupta's mentor, Kautilya. A thoroughgoing realist, Kautilya was devoted to "the goddess of wealth, whom thousands of kings have rejected." His efforts appear to have met with substantial success. Well kept highways thronged with merchants and soldiers, royal couriers and mendicant fakirs, and enough vehicles to necessitate a regular highway code. The conquest of Kalinga on the east coast stimulated trade, and an Admiralty department maintained waterways and harbors. Numerous temple inscriptions attest to the wealth and generosity of trade and craft guilds that provided endowments. The capital, Pataliputra, known as the "city of flowers," was famous for its parks, its public buildings, its river frontage of over nine miles, and its educational institutions to which students flocked from all parts of the empire and from abroad. All this was supported by "the king's sixth" of the harvest, which in practice was more commonly raised to a fourth, leaving the peasants with barely enough for existence.

Ashoka's reign represented a basic and unique departure from this traditionally harsh type of imperial rule. Having conquered the kingdom of Kalinga in a particularly bloody campaign, Ashoka underwent a spiritual experience and thereafter devoted himself to promoting and materializing the teachings of the Buddha. After the fashion of the Persian rulers, he inscribed his edicts on rocks, in caves, and on specially built pillars. These edicts were more in the nature of state sermons than formal laws. They enjoined typically Buddhist virtues—simplicity, compassion, mutual tolerance, and respect for all forms of life. His numerous public works included hospital and medical care at state expense, orchards and resting places on highways, distribution of alms to all sects, and Buddhist missions to several foreign countries. Ashoka did not make Buddhism the state faith, nor did he persecute the other sects. To the contrary, he made generous contributions to Brahmans and Jainas and helped the worthy of whatever denomination. It was not a change of religion, then, but of general attitude. He laid most stress on toleration and non-violence, not only because they were morally desirable but also because they would promote harmony in his huge and diverse empire.

This proved successful during his reign, for Ashoka ruled with popular acclaim for forty-one years. But within half a century after his death his dynasty was overthrown and his empire destroyed. This has been the pattern of Indian history to modern times. In contrast to China, where imperial unity was interspersed with short intervals of fragmentation, in India it was precisely the opposite—brief unity and prolonged fragmentation. This is not to say that India did not possess unity. She did, but it was cultural rather than political. And this culture emphasized loyalty to the social order rather than to the state, as evidenced in the higher status accorded to caste than to any political institution. Thus the culture that enhanced unity in one sphere undermined it in another.

IV. INVADERS, TRADERS, AND MISSIONARIES

With the end of the Maurya Empire early in the second century B.C. there followed five hundred years of confusion and obscurity. But one constant factor is discernible throughout this period. This is the increasing interaction between India and the outside world, with manifold repercussions in all areas—political, economic, and cultural.

First there was the impact of the Greeks, known in India as the Yavanas, who remained a force in the northwest for two centuries after Alexander. As noted in Chapter 7, section III, they stimulated Gandharan art, set a model for Indian coinage, and, above all, promoted trade between India and the Middle East. Next came a series of invaders who displaced the Greeks and in some cases pushed further to the south. The Parthians, called Pahlavas by the Indians, originated in the Caspian Sea area, and first wrested control of Iran and Mesopotamia from the Seleucids. Then, from about 140 B.C., bands of these people infiltrated into northwest India, forcing the Greeks northward and finally occupying the lower Indus Valley. After the Parthians came the Scythians, or Shakas as they were known in India. Forced out of Central Asia, they overwhelmed the Greeks in Bactria about 130 B.C., crossed the Hindu Kush Mountains, spread into the Punjab, and finally settled in Gujarat. There they mixed with the native population to form the Maratha people who were to figure prominently in later Indian history.

Finally came the Kushans, who crossed the Hindu Kush Mountains into the Punjab in the first century B.C. In the next century they extended their rule southward, probably as far as the Narbada River between Hindustan and the Deccan. Under their best known ruler, Kanishka, who ruled from about A.D. 130 to 160, their empire included the Punjab, Kashmir, the Indus and Upper Ganges valleys, Afghanistan, and parts of present-day Chinese Turkestan. It was an empire that straddled the busiest commercial routes of the time and encompassed regions permeated by Indian, Hellenistic, Persian, and, to a lesser degree, Chinese influences. Kushan coins have been found in Scandinavia, Ethiopia, and various Roman provinces, as well as in Asian Lands. These coins bear the names and effigies of gods from the Hellenic, Persian, and Indian pantheons. Kanishka depicted both the Buddha and Persian divinities on his coins and protected Jainism and Brahmanism impartially. Likewise he adopted at one and the same time the Indian imperial title *maharaja* ("great king"), the Parthian title, which in Sanskrit was *rajatiraja* ("king of kings"), and the Chinese title, which in Sanskrit was *devaputra* ("son of Heaven").

During the third century the Kushan Empire declined and faded out. The immediate reason appears to have been the advent of the vigorous Sassanian dynasty in Persia (A.D. 226), which expanded eastward into Afghanistan. This disrupted the ties between the original Central Asian base of the Kushans and their provinces in India. By the end of the third century the Kushan empire had disintegrated, leaving a power vacuum between the Ganges basin and the borders of Persia. This cleared the way for the next great Indian empire, the Gupta, just as a similar vacuum earlier had preceded the empire of the Mauryas.

In retrospect, the unprecedented interaction between India and the outside world during this half millennium between 200 B.C. and A.D. 300 stands out clearly. The empires of the Greeks, the Pahlavas, the Sakas, and the Kushans all were based at least as much in Central Asia or the Middle East as in India. All fostered the profitable trade along the routes running from northern India westward to the Middle East and northward to Central Asia and China. This was also the period of flourishing overseas commerce that brought Roman traders to southern and western India, and Indian traders to Southeast Asia. (See Chapter 7, section II.)

In the realm of culture, Indian Buddhist missionaries during these centuries were carrying their message to all the surrounding countries. The begging priest could move among hostile or disordered peoples with impunity since he was too poor to be worth robbing and also was surrounded with the aura of supernatural dedication. There was little incentive for robbing or injuring such a man, since the only return was the possibility of retribution from above. Hence the diffusion of Buddhism and Brahmanism from India to the surrounding countries, with all the cultural accretions involved in such transfer of religions. (See Chapter 7, section III.) Nor was the culture flow exclusively one-sided. The succession of invaders from the north brought with them a variety of Greek, Persian, and Central Asian influences. And by sea there came to India in the first century A.D. a new religion—Christianity. According to legend, St. Thomas arrived about A.D. 52 on the Malabar coast of southwest India where he established a number of churches and where considerable Christian communities exist to the present day.

V. GUPTA CLASSICAL AGE

In the fourth century A.D. the great Gupta Age began—a time when the invaders of the preceding centuries were assimilated and when various cultural trends reached fruition. This was the classical period of Indian civilization, comparable to the Early Empire or Augustan Age in the West. The Gupta Empire, like the Maurya, had as its base the Magadha state in the Ganges Valley. This state had managed to preserve its independence following the Maurya collapse, and then, with the end of the Kushans, it began to expand once more into the resulting vacuum.

The Gupta era began with the accession of Chandragupta I about 320, and reached its height under his grandson, Chandragupta II, who reigned from 375 to 415. He expanded his empire until it stretched from the Indus to the Bay of Bengal, and from the northern mountains to the Narbada River. These frontiers constitute the traditional limits of Hindustan, a point deserving emphasis. Politically, the Gupta Empire was a north Indian empire and did not encompass the entire peninsula. Indeed south India at this time was in many ways a world apart, with the Vindhya range still an effective barrier dividing the peninsula in two. The peoples of the south spoke Dravidian languages—Tamil, Telugu, and Kanarese—in contrast to the Indo-Aryan speech of the north. On the other hand, the south had accepted the Hindu and Buddhist religions and social customs and used Sanskrit as its language of scripture and learning. Thus a single civilization bound together the diverse peoples despite their disparate ethnic and linguistic backgrounds and the existence in the south of several independent kingdoms.

The Gupta Empire appears to have enjoyed marked prosperity. This was enhanced by the currency reform of Chandragupta II who introduced standard gold and silver coins. The volume of trade reached new heights, both within the peninsula and with outside countries. One of the chief industries was textiles—silk, muslin, calico, linen, wool, and cotton—which were produced in large quantities for both domestic and foreign markets. Other important crafts included metallurgy, pottery, carving, and the cutting and polishing of precious stones. Judging from the reports of Chinese Buddhist pilgrims, Gupta rule was milder than that of the Maurya. Fa-hien, who spent the years 401 to 410 in India, travelling from monastery to monastery, was impressed by the state services and by the general prosperity. Although the dynasty was Hindu, he observed no discrimination against Buddhists. The countryside was peaceful and prosperous, and not overrun by police and spies as under the Maurya.

In linguistics and literature, this was the period of the triumph of Sanskrit. Hitherto the learned and rather archaic language of the Brahmans, Sanskrit now staged a comeback, spreading to administration and secular literature. Poetry and prose flourished with the stimulus of lavish royal patronage. Outstanding were the works of Kalidasa, "the Indian Shakespeare," who rendered ancient legends and popular tales into both dramas and lyrics. Perhaps the greatest cultural achievement of the Gupta era was the redaction into final form of the two great national epics, the Mahabharata and the Ramayana. Dating back to many centuries before Christ, the early versions of these works have been entirely lost. Today they are known only in the form in which they were left by Gupta writers. In this form they have remained the classics of Hindu literature and the repositories of Hindu tradition. Their heroes and heroines are a part of the life of the people; their mine of stories has been used by generations of writers and their philosophical poem, the *Bhagavad Gita,* is the supreme scripture of the Hindus.

In the field of science the Gupta period was outstanding. Contact with Greeks resulted in mutually beneficial exchange of ideas. Aryabhata, born in A.D. 476 at Pataliputra, is one of the greatest figures in the history of astronomy. He taught that the earth is a sphere, that it rotates on its own axis, that lunar eclipses are caused by the shadow of the earth falling on the moon, and that the length of the solar year is 365.3586805 days—a calculation with a remarkably slight margin of error. Another great scientist, Varamihira, was learned in Greek sciences and was so gifted that he made significant contributions to virtually all natural sciences.

The greatest achievement doubtless was the formulation of the theory of zero and the consequent evolution of the decimal system. The base could have been any number; the Hindus probably chose ten because they counted on their fingers. With this system, individual numbers were needed only for 0, 1, 2, . . . 9. By contrast, for the ancient Greeks each 8 in 888 was different. And for the Romans, 888 was DCCCLXXXVIII. The difficulty of division and multiplication with these systems is apparent. The simple Hindu numerals were carried westward by Arab merchants and scholars, and so became known as "Arabic numerals." Despite their obvious advantage they were long scorned as pagan and as too vulnerable to forgery; one stroke could turn 0 into 6 or 9. It was not until the late fifteenth century that Hindu-Arabic numerals prevailed in the West and the door was opened to modern mathematics and science. In retrospect, this Indian contribution stands out as comparable to the invention of the wheel, the lever, or the alphabet.

SUGGESTED READING

A. L. BASHAM, *The Wonder That Was India* (Sidgwick, 1956); W. T. DEBARY, *et al.,* *Sources of Indian Tradition* (Columbia Univ., 1958); M. EDWARDES, *Everyday Life in Early India* (Batsford, 1969); P. SPEAR, *India: A Modern History* (Univ. Michigan, 1961); R. THAPAR, *A History of India,* Vol. I (Penguin, 1966).

chapter ten

Chinese Civilization

When the right men are available, government flourishes. When the right men are not available, government declines.—Confucius

Chinese civilization is characterized by cohesion and continuity as compared with the disparateness and discontinuity of Indian civilization. There has been no sharp break in China's evolution comparable to that occasioned in India by the appearance of the Aryans or the Moslems or the British. There were, of course, numerous nomadic incursions into China, and even a few dynastic take-overs. But it was not the Chinese who were forced to adopt the language or the customs or the pastoralism of the invader. Rather it was the invader himself who invariably was quickly and completely Sinicized.

One reason for this was the greater isolation of China, so that she was invaded only by the nomads of the northwest. She did not have to cope with the succession of peoples with relatively sophisticated cultures who invaded India and who consequently were able to retain in varying degrees their ethnic and cultural identity. The Chinese were all Mongoloids to begin with, as were their nomadic invaders and the relatively primitive tribes that they assimilated in the course of their expansion eastward to the Pacific and southward to Vietnam. Thus the Chinese enjoyed racial and cultural homogeneity throughout their history. During the Classical period this homogeneity was further cemented, as we shall see, by the standardization of the writing system, which enabled speakers of widely differing dialects to communicate with each other. In India, by contrast, there are today fourteen "national languages," one of which is English, which serves, in Nehru's words, as "the link" amongst the other thirteen.

As important as cultural homogeneity in China has been the remarkable political unity that has persisted through the ages. This can be explained to a considerable degree by the unique secularism of Chinese civilization—the only great civilization that has at no time produced a priestly class. To be sure, the emperor was also a priest who made the sacrifices to heaven in behalf of all his subjects, but this religious function was always secondary to the business of governing. Consequently, the great division between religious and laity, between Church and State, which existed in the other Eurasian civilizations, had no place in China. Nor was there any counterpart to India's epics, steeped in metaphysics and concerned with personal salvation. Rather the Chinese had their classics which emphasized the life of man in society, and particularly the relations between the members of a family and between a king and his subjects. This strong secular bent provided a firm underlying foundation for political organization and stability. This was further cemented during these centuries by a unique Chinese institution—a civil service recruited on the basis of public competitive examinations. It was two thousand years before anything comparable appeared in the West, or anywhere else for that matter.

These, then, are some of the background factors that help explain the Chinese civilization and history that will be analyzed in this chapter.

I. AGE OF TRANSITION

The period of the Eastern Chou (771–256 B.C.) was on the surface inauspicious, with its powerless dynasty and its feudal lords constantly at war with one another. (See Chapter 6, section IV.) Yet this was also a period of basic socio-economic change that determined the course of China's evolution decisively and permanently. The root cause for this change here, as in India, was the introduction of iron. It came late in China, not appearing significantly until about 600 B.C. But by the fifth and fourth centuries B.C. it was leaving its mark on Chinese society and government.

The pattern of its impact was familiar. New and more efficient iron tools made possible the extension of agriculture from the original Yellow River place of origin southward towards the heavily-wooded Yangtze basin (corresponding to the diffusion in India from the Indus to the Ganges). Iron tools also facilitated extensive drainage projects in the valleys, canal building for long-distance hauling of bulky commodities, and well digging for irrigation purposes in the dry northwest lands.

All this meant a very substantial increase in productivity, which in turn stimulated trade and industry and culminated in the monetization of much of the economy. Money had been used earlier, usually in the form of cowrie shells. Now copper coins appeared and were increasingly used in all branches of the economy. Most involved in this monetization was a new class of free and wealthy merchants and craftsmen. They were no longer dependent on feudal lords as they had been in the past. Rather they now constituted a new monetary aristocracy that soon challenged the primacy of the feudal lords. With this monetization, land now became a form of property that was bought and sold. Wealthy merchants acquired large holdings, and nobles sought to increase their revenues by appointing agents to collect more rent directly from the peasants instead of the customary amount traditionally obtained from the village headman.

This economic change was accompanied by political change—by a fundamental shift from feudal decentralization to state centralization. The economic growth and monetization provided the rulers of the various feudal states with the financial resources needed for centralization. This was particularly so because the newly reclaimed lands could be administered outside feudal relationships and hence rents were contributed directly to the princes' exchequers. Also the princes increasingly established profitable monopolies in the production and distribution of iron and salt. The result was that the princes were able to transform fiefs they had formerly parcelled out to nobles into administrative units staffed by officials of their own central government. This was a gradual development, but where it did occur, it greatly increased the resources and power of the ruler, and correspondingly enfeebled the Chou dynasty in the capital. Indeed a basic reason for the success of the rulers of Ch'in in conquering all China was precisely that they pioneered in these measures and profited accordingly. We will discuss this in section III of this chapter.

II. PHILOSOPHERS AND CLASSICS

The disruption and reorganization that we have described profoundly affected Chinese thinkers. It forced them to reassess their traditions and to either abandon them or adapt them to the requirements of a period of transition. Thus the Eastern Chou period was a time of great intellectual ferment and creativity, reminiscent of the achievements under comparable circumstances of the rationalist philosophers in Greece and of the Buddha and other religious reformers in India. So intense was this intellectual activity that the Chinese refer to this as the period of the "Hundred Schools." Here we shall consider a few of these schools that persisted through the centuries and influenced significantly the evolution of Chinese civilization.

Although the founders of these various schools often were bold innovators, almost all of them looked for inspiration in a supposedly golden age in the distant past. This tendency is to be found in most civilizations; golden ages are depicted in the *Iliad,* the *Aeneid,* and the Vedas, as well as in Chinese writings. But consciousness and veneration of the past was exceptionally strong amongst the Chinese. Hence they carefully preserved and studied the writings of earlier ages, which they considered indispensable for the conduct of both private and public affairs.

The most important of these ancient works were the *Five Classics* associated with Confucianism. According to the order in which they are usually discussed, the first of these is the *Classic of Changes,* or *Book of Divination,* replete with popular omen lore and auguries. The second work is the *Classic of Documents,* or *Book of History.* This consists of historical documents and speeches from the early Chou centuries, though some of the materials are now known to be later forgeries. The third is the *Classic of Songs,* or *Book of Poetry,* an anthology of some three hundred poems dating mostly from the early Chou period. The fourth work is the *Record of Rituals,* or *Book of Rites,* a collection of materials ranging from the broadest philosophical pronouncements to the most detailed rules for the conduct of everyday life. The final work is the *Spring and Autumn Annals,* a brief chronicle of events between 722 and 481 B.C. that affected the state of Lu or occurred in that state. This was Confucius' native state, and according to tradition he compiled the *Annals* from earlier local records.

Turning from these Classics to the philosopher-teachers that studied and made use of them, the most outstanding by all odds is Confucius. His influence has been so overwhelming and enduring that the Chinese way of life during the past two thousand years can be fairly characterized with one word—Confucianism. Born in 551 B.C. to an impoverished family of the lower aristocracy, Confucius (the Latinized form of K'ung-fu-tzu, or Master Kung) had to make his own way in the world. And the world he faced was unpromising, with feudal anarchy rampant, and no higher power, spiritual or temporal, to attract national loyalty. Confucius was moved by this to wander from court to court seeking a ruler who would adopt his ideas for successful government. His influence in the world of practical politics was negligible, so he turned to the teaching of young men who, he hoped, might be more effective in implementing his precepts.

Confucius at last had found himself. He proved to be a teacher of rare enthusiasm and skill. What he taught, and the nature of his personality, are set forth in the *Collected Sayings,* or *Analects,* which reflect an engaging personality—sensible, kindhearted, distressed by the folly of his age, convinced that he could restore tranquility, and withal, possessing a saving sense of humor.

Confucius' teachings were fundamentally conservative. But while insisting on the right of the rulers to rule, he was equally insistent that they should do so on the basis of sound ethical principles. Like Plato, he wanted the kings to be sages, and this could be if they possessed the five virtues of a gentleman—integrity, righteousness, loyalty, altruism, and love, or human-heartedness. Confucius also was a rationalist in an age of gross superstition and fear of the supernatural. While recognizing spirits and Heaven, he largely ignored them in his teachings. "If you do not know about the living, how can you know about the dead?"

Confucius' teachings were far from being generally accepted, let alone implemented, during his lifetime. Yet in the end they prevailed and became the official creed of the nation. One reason was his basic conservatism, his acceptance of the *status quo,* which naturally appealed to those at the top. Another was his emphasis on ethical principles, which he insisted were the prerequisites for the proper exercise of authority. Finally Confucius provided a philosophy for officialdom, for the bureaucrats who became indispensable with the establishment of imperial government two and a half centuries after his death. Thus in the second century B.C. Confucianism was declared the official dogma of the empire, and the Classics became the principal study of scholars and statesmen. Until the fall of the Manchu dynasty more than two thousand years later, in 1911, the teachings of Confucius reigned supreme in the land.

After Confucianism, the most influential Chinese philosophy was Taoism. This is understandable, for the two doctrines supplement each other neatly, satisfying between them both the intellectual and emotional needs of the Chinese people. While Confucianism emphasized decorum, conformity, and social responsibility, Taoism stressed individual whim and fancy, and conformity to the great pattern of nature. This pattern was defined as Tao, or the Road or Way, so that the disciples are known as Taoists. The key to conforming with Tao was abandonment of ambition, eschewing of honors and responsibilities, and a meditative return to nature. The ideal subject had big bones, strong muscles, and an empty head, while the ideal ruler "keeps the people without knowledge and without desire . . . and fills their stomachs. . . . By non-action nothing is ungoverned."

Altogether different from both Confucianism and Taoism were the doctrines of the Legalists. They were practicing statesmen rather than philosophers and were interested in reorganizing society in order to strengthen the princes they served and to enable them to wage war and unite the country by force. They viewed the nobility as an anachronism to be replaced by state military forces, whereas the mass of the people were to be coerced into productive work. They regarded merchants and scholars as nonessential and diversionary, and therefore not to be tolerated. All aspects of life were to be regulated in detail by laws designed to promote the economic and military power of the state. The efficacy of these doctrines was demonstrated when they were adopted by the Ch'in rulers, who proceeded to subjugate the other princes and to establish the first empire. They then extended their regimentation with customary ruthlessness to the entire country, but the result, as we shall see, was a reaction that led to the overthrow of the empire a few years after the death of its founder. Legalism was discredited and Confucianism, as noted, was enthroned permanently as the official creed.

III. CH'IN EMPIRE

China's millennia-long history has been marked by three great revolutions that basically changed her political and social structure. The first in 221 B.C. ended the feudal system and created a centralized empire; the second in 1911 ended the empire and established a republic; while the third in 1949 put in power the current Communist regime.

The first of these revolutions was engineered by the leaders of the northwest state of Ch'in in the Wei Valley. This location in itself contributed to the victory, for the valley is largely inaccessible and easy to defend. The Ch'in rulers were able to attack the other states to the east without fear of any enemy action in their rear. The frontier location also served to keep the Ch'in military forces in fighting trim because of the constant wars against the barbarian nomads. In fact the Ch'in were amongst the first Chinese to use steel in place of bronze weapons, and cavalrymen in place of charioteers. Important also in the Ch'in triumph was the conquest in 318 B.C. of the great food-producing plain of Szechwan. This added greatly to the area and strength of Ch'in, placing it in somewhat the same relationship to the other Chinese states as Macedonia had been to the Greek cities. Finally the Ch'in rulers were able and ambitious realists who pioneered in applying Legalist doctrines and concentrating all power in their hands. (See Map IX, "Classical Age Empires in China.")

With these advantages, the Ch'in leaders extended their possessions steadily, overcoming the surrounding states one by one. Contemporaries referred fearfully to the "wild beast of Ch'in," and likened its relentless expansion to that of a "silkworm devouring a mulberry leaf." By 221 B.C. the Ch'in ruler was master of all China, and he adopted the title of *Shih Huang-ti,* or "First Emperor." His successor would be "Second Emperor," and so on down the generations for "ten thousand years," meaning forever.

The new emperor proceeded to apply to all China the Legalist doctrines that had succeeded so brilliantly in his home state. He abolished all feudal states and kingdoms, reorganizing his vast realm into administrative areas, or commanderies, each with a set of officials appointed by, and responsible to, the central government. Also he disarmed all soldiers except his own, required the old aristocratic families to reside in his capital where they could be kept under surveillance, and planted Ch'in garrisons throughout the country. The new emperor also imposed economic centralization by standardizing weights, measures, and coinage.

In the light of future history, one of the most important innovations was the adoption of a standardized script that was intelligible from one end of China to the other. This proved to be a most effective and enduring bond of unity because of the nature of Chinese script. This is based not on a limited number of signs expressing the phonetic elements of a word; it consists rather of a large number of symbols or characters, each one of which denotes an object or an abstract concept. The system is precisely that used in the West for figures. All Westerners know what the symbol "5" means, even though they call it five, fünf, cinque, or cinq. So it is with Chinese characters, or ideographs, which have meaning but no sound. They are ideas, like numerals, which every reader can sound according to his own dialect. Thus the new Ch'in standardized script, which has continued with modifications to the present, could be read and understood by all educated Chinese, even though they spoke dialects that often were mutually unintelligible. And for the same reason, the script was equally comprehensible to foreign peoples, so that educated Japanese, Koreans, or Vietnamese can read Chinese without being able to speak a word of it. The significance of this for future Chinese national unity and for Chinese cultural influence throughout East Asia can well be surmised.

Whatever their justification in the light of later history, these innovations at the time impinged on many vested interests and aroused passionate opposition. This was especially true of the scholars, for whom Legalist doctrines and policies were anathema. The First Emperor accordingly decided to deprive them of their intellectual props by ordering the "Burning of the Books." All the Classics were consigned to the flames, except those dealing with subjects of utilitarian value, such as medicine, agriculture, and divination. The plan really failed, for scholars hid their books at great risk or else memorized entire texts before surrendering them. Later, after the fall of the dynasty, the greater part of the traditional literature was recovered from the hidden books and from the memories of old men. The persecution, however, effectively dampened the intellectual ferment that had characterized the Chou period; the Golden Age of Chinese thought was over.

This intellectual loss should be balanced against the indubitable economic gain through more efficient utilization of human and natural resources. The standardization of weights, measures, and coinage facilitated economic growth. Also a network of trunk roads was built, radiating from the capital to the most distant frontiers. To maximize the value of these roads, the emperor standardized the length of the axles of the two-wheeled Chinese carts—an essential measure because the wheels cut deep ruts in the friable sandy soil, so that every cart had to follow the existing ruts or be fitted with new axles. The emperor also utilized the new national unity and strength to extend the frontiers southward to present-day Vietnam. To the northwest the nomads were beaten back, and to keep them back the famous Great Wall was built, running 1400 miles from Inner Mongolia to the ocean. So great was the loss of life on this stupendous project that even today, more than two thousand years later, people still speak of the fact that a million men perished at this task, and that every stone cost a human life. Just as the scholars cursed the emperor for the "Burning of the Books," so the common people cursed him for the building of the Great Wall.

It was this general detestation, together with the lack of a competent successor, that explains the popular revolt and the end of the dynasty in 207 B.C., only four years after the death of the First Emperor. But although Ch'in rule was so shortlived, it left a deep and permanent imprint on China. The country had been transformed from a congeries of feudal states into a centralized empire, which it remained until the twentieth century. It is only appropriate that the occidental name for China is derived from the Ch'in.

IV. HAN EMPIRE

The First Emperor had abolished feudalism in one stroke, but the succeeding Han emperor, more pragmatic and cautious, first restored feudalism a bit and then whittled it away to insignificance. The imperial structure erected by the First Emperor was gradually restored, though without the original terror and oppression. Thus the Han Empire flourished for four centuries, about the same length of time as the Roman Empire. The Han Empire also resembled the Roman Empire in its vast territorial expanse. During the first sixty years the Han rulers concentrated on national recuperation and dynastic consolidation. But under the "Martial Emperor," Wu Ti (141–87 B.C.), the imperial frontiers were gradually extended in all directions. Tribal territories in the south were incorporated, though several centuries of Chinese immigration and assimilation of the local peoples were necessary before this part of the empire became predominantly Chinese-speaking. The greatest expansion occurred to the west, where Chinese expeditions drove across Central Asia, establishing contact with the Kushan Empire in northwest India and vastly increasing the volume of trade along the Silk Road. (See Chapter 7, section II.)

The Han Empire was comparable to the Roman Empire in population as well as territorial extent. A census taken in the year A.D. 1, and believed to be reasonably accurate, showed the empire to have 12.2 million households with a total of 59.6 million people. By contrast the population of the Roman Empire at the time of Augustus (27 B.C.–A.D. 14) is estimated at 30 to 50 million people in Europe, somewhat fewer in Asia, and not quite 20 million in Africa.

At the head of the Han realm stood the emperor, entrusted with full temporal authority but also responsible for the physical well-being and prosperity of his subjects. Below the emperor were two senior officials corresponding to a modern prime minister and a head of civil service. These men were in constant touch with the emperor and were responsible for the actual operation of government. Beneath them were nine ministries entrusted with the following functions: religious ceremonials, security of the palace, care of the imperial stables, punishment of criminals, receipt of homage and tribute from foreign leaders, maintenance of records of the imperial family, collection of state revenues, and management of the imperial exchequer.

In addition to the central government there was a provincial bureaucracy that administered, in descending order, commanderies, prefectures, districts, and wards. Officials at the grass roots level were assigned such basic tasks as collection of tax in grain, textiles, or cash; arresting of criminals; maintenance of roads, canals, and granaries; and upkeep of the imperial post, with its horses and chain of stations.

In the first century B.C. this bureaucracy is said to have comprised some 130,000 officials, or only one for every 400 or 500 inhabitants. This small number in relation to the total population was typical throughout Chinese history, and is to be explained by the restricted role of the imperial government. Chinese governments did not assume responsibility for the social services taken for granted in the modern world, as is evident from the ministerial duties listed above. Rather the main role of government was collection of revenue and defense of the country against external attack, and of the dynasty against internal subversion.

The bureaucracy was a privileged, but not hereditary, elite. During the Han period, a unique system was originated for the selection of civil service personnel by means of competitive public examinations. In principle the examinations were open to all, but candidature involved such a prolonged study that only the sons of the well-to-do could qualify. On the other hand, poor boys not infrequently were given the opportunity to study by village, clan, or guild endowments. Because the examinations were based on the Confucian Classics, the empire in effect was run by Confucianists and according to Confucian principles. Each official was assigned to a post outside his home province to ensure that he would not use his position to build up local family power. The result was an administrative system that was far more efficient and responsive than any other prior to modern times. Indeed this civil service based on merit was a major factor in the continuity of the Chinese imperial system from the time of the First Emperor to the twentieth century. There was another side, however, to this examination system. Being based on total acceptance of a single body of doctrine, it engendered a rigid orthodoxy and an intellectual arrogance that was to prove China's undoing centuries later with the intrusion of the West.

Although China was to suffer grievously in modern times because she lagged in science and industry, during the Han period it was a very different story. China then drew technologically abreast of the rest of Eurasia, and in many fields took a lead that she was to maintain until recent centuries. Some of the more important Chinese inventions of these centuries were the water-powered mill, the shoulder collar for horses, which greatly increased their efficiency, and the techniques for iron casting, paper making, and pottery glazing. Rag paper, dating from about A.D. 100, soon replaced cumbersome wooden and bamboo slips for writing. But paper is not as durable as wood, and since it was developed by the Chinese long before printing, it can be held responsible, paradoxically, for the loss of certain books. Pottery glazes, however, which were eventually developed into porcelain or china, were an undiluted blessing. They not only reached the level of artistic creation, but they also represented a major advance in hygiene, since smooth porcelain was more sanitary than the rough pottery or wooden utensils hitherto available.

The outstanding Han contribution in literature was in the field of historical writing. This was to be expected from a people who looked to the past for guidance in dealing with the present. Their Five Classics contained a good deal of assorted historical materials. But now in the first century B.C. appeared a history much more comprehensive and sophisticated than any to that date. This was the *Shih chi,* or *Historical Records,* written by a father-son team, though authorship is commonly attributed to the son, Ssu-ma Ch'ien, who wrote the major part. As court astrologer, he had access to the imperial library and archives. Also he had the advantage of extensive travelling throughout the empire, during which he made use of the resources of local libraries. The history he wrote was not so much an original work as a compilation of all available historical materials. As he explained modestly, "My narrative consists of no more than a systematization of the material that has been handed down to us. There is therefore no creation; only faithful representation."

This method had obvious disadvantages, especially the lack of dramatic quality and stylistic unity found in early historians such as Herodotus. On the other hand it did assemble and preserve for posterity a tremendous quantity of historical materials from contemporary books and archives. The *Historical Records* was in effect a universal history, equivalent to a work of approximately 1,500,000 words. Its 130 chapters included chronological records and tables of the various dynasties, biographies of Han notables, and essays on varied topics such as rituals, music, astrology, astronomy, economic matters, and foreign peoples and lands. Future Chinese historians paid Ssu-ma Ch'ien the tribute of copying his method, so that Chinese historiography has transmitted through the millennia a mass of data unequalled by that of any other country over so long a period.

All Chinese historians also shared a belief in the "Mandate of Heaven" concept. They held that a king ruled as the deputy of Heaven only so long as he possessed the virtues of justice, benevolence, and sincerity. When he no longer demonstrated these virtues and misruled his kingdom, he was automatically deprived of the Mandate of Heaven, and rebellion against him was then not a crime but a just punishment from Heaven through the medium of the rebels.

Thus Chinese historians, although often aware of the social and economic factors behind dynastic decline, subordinated them to what they considered to be a more basic underlying consideration—the moral qualifications of the ruler. Chinese historiography, then, tended to be more a compilation of sources than the personal analyses of individual historians, and the organizational framework was based on the rise and fall of dynasties interpreted in accordance with the workings of the Mandate of Heaven.

V. IMPERIAL DECLINE

The traditional interpretation of Chinese history as a succession of repetitive dynastic cycles obscured fundamental changes that occurred in certain periods behind the cyclical facade. It is true, of course, that dynasties did rise and fall. The founder of a line naturally was a man of ability, drive, and action. But his descendants, after a few generations of upbringing in a court atmosphere, were likely to be effete and debauched. Sometimes a strong ruler or a capable and devoted minister managed to halt the deterioration. But the overall trend was downhill, until successful revolt removed the dynasty and restarted the familiar cycle.

More fundamental than this dynastic cycle, however, was what might be termed the economic-administrative cycle. This began with the security and prosperity common at the outset of every major dynasty. The restoration of peace led to population increase, greater production, correspondingly greater revenues, and full government coffers. But a combination of personal ambitions, family influences, and institutional pressures inevitably led the emperors sooner or later to overextend themselves. They squandered their human and financial resources on roads, canals, fortifications, palaces, court extravagances, and frontier wars. Thus each dynasty began to experience financial difficulties about a century after its founding.

To meet the deficits the government raised taxes, which bore most heavily on the small peasant proprietors that were the backbone of Chinese society. At the beginning of each dynasty they constituted the majority of the peasantry. But as taxes increased, more and more of them lost their plots to the large landowners and became tenants. The landowners, having political influence commensurate with their wealth, paid negligible taxes, so that the more their holdings increased, the more the government revenues declined, and the more the taxes rose on the diminishing number of small peasants. Thus a vicious circle was set in motion—rising taxes, falling revenues, neglected roads and dikes, declining productivity, and eventually, famines, banditry, and full scale peasant uprisings. Meanwhile frontier defenses were likely to have been neglected, inviting raids across the frontiers by the nomads. Often it was the combination of internal revolt and external invasion that brought down the tottering dynasty and cleared the way for a new beginning.

This was essentially the pattern of the Earlier Han dynasty. The "Martial Emperor," Wu Ti (141–87 B.C.), had won great victories and extended China's frontiers deep into Central Asia. But in doing so he overstrained the imperial resources. He resorted to a variety of measures to cope with the crisis, including currency debasement, sale of ranks, and reinstitution of government monopolies on salt, iron, and liquor. Although he managed to remain solvent for the duration of his reign, his successors sank deeper into trouble as the number of tax-paying small peasants declined. Large-scale revolts broke out, and even at the court various omens were interpreted as portents from Heaven that the end of the dynasty was drawing near.

In fact the dynasty was briefly ousted (A.D. 9–25) by Wang Mang, a powerful minister who had already dominated the court for some three decades. He boldly tackled the basic economic problem by decreeing nationalization of the great private estates and their distribution amongst the tax-paying peasants. This and other reforms alienated the wealthy families, who opposed the usurper bitterly. At the same time a disastrous change in the lower course of the Yellow River made millions homeless and drove the uprooted peasants into banditry and rebellion. The nomads took advantage of the disorders to invade the country and sack the capital, where Wang Mang died at their hands in A.D. 23. He was succeeded on the throne by a distant cousin of the former Han emperor.

The history of the Later Han (A.D. 25–222) was basically the same as that of its predecessor. During the lengthy wars of the interregnum many of the old aristocrats and landowners had been wiped out. Tax returns, therefore, were adequate at the beginning of the revived dynasty. But again the tax-paying peasantry began to be squeezed out, and the downward spiral once more was under way. Great rebellions which broke out in 184 in East China and in Szechwan were not crushed until 215. The dynasty never recovered from this ordeal.

The situation resembled that of the last days of Rome. The decimation of the small peasants had decimated also the original peasant draft army. This was replaced by professional troops, whose first loyalty was to their generals, who thus were able to ignore the central government. Great landowners also defied the government by evading taxes and enlarging their holdings by various legal and extra-legal means. Helpless peasants, fleeing the barbarian invaders or government tax collectors, became the virtual serfs of these landowners in return for economic and physical security. The great families converted their manors into fortresses, virtually taking over the functions of government in their respective localities. Their estates were largely self-sufficient, so that trade declined and cities shrank correspondingly. Thus the Han dynasty passed from the historical stage in A.D. 222 in a swirl of peasant revolts, warlord coups, and nomadic raids. China entered a prolonged period of disunity and disorder similar to that in the West following the collapse of the Roman Empire.

SUGGESTED READING

H. G. Creel, *Confucius, the Man and the Myth* (Day, 1949); G. B. Cressey, *Land of the 500 Million: A Geography of China* (McGraw-Hill, 1955); W. T. deBary, *et al.*, *Sources of Chinese Tradition* (Columbia Univ., 1960); M. Loewe, *Everyday Life in Early Imperial China* (Putnam, 1968); J. Needham, *Science and Civilization in China* (Cambridge Univ., 1954); E. O. Reischauer and J. K. Fairbank, *East Asia: The Great Tradition* (Houghton, 1958).

chapter eleven

End of
Classical Civilizations

*All in all, the invasions gave the Coup de Grace to a culture which had
come to a standstill after reaching its apogee and seemed doomed to
wither away. We are reminded of the cruel bombings in our own day
which destroyed ramshackle old buildings and so made possible the
reconstruction of towns on more modern lines.*—Robert Lopez

The great civilizations of Greece, Rome, India, and China dominated
the Eurasian ecumene in classical times. Yet in the end, the nomads and pastoralists of the frontier regions overran these civilizations and fundamentally altered
the course of global history. Beneath the seeming invulnerability of the empires
lay roots of decline that invariably brought on decay and eventual disintegration.
Technological stagnation and arrested productivity combined to expose the
classical civilizations to the onslaught of the barbarians from the third to the
sixth centuries.

The effect of the nomadic invasions varied from region to region. Northern
China and northern India were overrun but retained their distinctive civilizations. Southern China and southern India escaped invasion because of their remoteness. Byzantium and Persia proved powerful enough to repel the invaders.
The West, however, suffered repeated and protracted incursions by Germans,
Huns, Moslems, Magyars, and Vikings, so that the old order was uprooted to a
degree unequalled anywhere else in Eurasia. Ironically, however, this destruction
was a primary reason for the primacy of the West in modern times, for a new
civilization was able to emerge out of the ashes of the old, a civilization better
adapted to the demands of a changing world. The purpose of this chapter is to
describe the significance and decline of the classical civilizations and to determine
how and why the West started on the road to global dominance.

I. HISTORICAL SIGNIFICANCE OF
CLASSICAL CIVILIZATIONS

The classical civilizations, like the preceding ancient civilizations, were by definition founded on class differentiation. They rested in the final analysis on the
labor of peasant masses that furnished the surplus that supported the ruling elites.

Despite differences in detail, the overall social structure of the various Eurasian civilizations was similar. At the head of each was the ruling king or emperor. Next came the nobility and top officials—Roman senators, Iranian warrior-nobles, Indian princes, and Chinese marquises and Grand Administrators. Another privileged group in all civilizations was the priestly hierarchy—Indian Brahmans, Iranian magi, Christian priests, and the secularist Confucian literati. Traders and merchant enterprisers were also present everywhere, carrying on manufacturing, mining, wholesale and retail trade, organized transportation, and moneylending. Finally at the bottom of the pyramid, and comprising the great majority of the total population, were the workers in agriculture and the crafts. Some were free; others were serfs or slaves, with the proportion varying according to region and period.

Greece at first was an exception to this general pattern, consisting of small city-states with elected magistrates, and governments based on citizen assemblies and councils. But this Greek exception proved short-lived. It is true that Xerxes failed to conquer Greece, and that Alexander instead conquered Persia, but this did not represent a victory for the Greek city-states. Alexander and his successors adopted the manners, methods, and institutions of the Persian autocracy. Likewise in Rome the republic gave way to autocratic emperors who created a vast imperial bureaucracy on models derived from Egypt and Persia via the Hellenistic kingdom. By the time of Constantine, the Roman Empire bore a far greater resemblance to the Persian Empire than it did to Periclean Athens or Cicero's Rome.

Inextricably bound up with this social stratification was economic stratification. Everywhere there was gross inequity in the distribution of wealth. Everywhere the privileged lived in provocative luxury as contrasted with the poverty and misery of the rural and urban workers. Two very different standards of living inevitably meant two very different cultures within each civilization. Neolithic cultural homogeneity had given way with the advent of the ancient civilizations to the low culture of the villages and the high culture of the schools, temples, and palaces of the cities. (See Chapter 6, section I.) This bifurcation continued in the classical civilizations, with the core of all the Eurasian high cultures now being the "sacred books"—the Iranian Zend-Avesta, the Indian Vedas, the Buddhist Canon, the Chinese Classics, and the Christian Old and New Testaments. Since these texts were the basis of knowledge, they dominated education. This was often carried to the point of wholesale memorization and arid scholasticism. The Chinese examination, the Indian debate, and the Hebrew and Christian colloquies between masters and pupils, all tested students' mastery of an approved body of learning.

The sacred books also were used to inculcate loyalty and obedience. Repudiation of official teachings or challenge to the social order were branded as crimes punishable in this world and in the next. The "hells" which were so prominent in all high cultures were eternal concentration camps for those who dared resist their secular or religious leaders. Normally this threat of punishment in the afterlife effectively buttressed the *status quo,* though peasant wit everywhere suggests that not all were unquestioning believers. "There are three blood suckers in this world," runs a north Indian proverb, "the flea, the bug, and the Brahman."

Low culture in the classical civilizations remained essentially the same as in the ancient civilizations. There was the same body of lore related to the everyday occupations in the fields, workshops, and homes. And to appease or control the feared supernatural forces, there were everywhere similar rites, rituals, and superstitions that had little relationship to the official religions professed by the high cultures. In India, for example, the peasantry was unaware of the lofty philosophical formulations of the Upanishads. But it was all too aware of cruel goblins, of vampires that ate raw flesh, and of spirits stalking the earth at night, vomiting fire, and devouring the putrefied flesh of corpses.

In addition to this common class basis, the classical civilizations also shared a common durability and permanence. Despite the interaction amongst these civilizations, reflecting the new Eurasian ecumenism, the fact remains that they all retained their individuality during these centuries. There was no case of one dominating or imposing a permanent imprint on the other. The impact of Hellenism on the Middle East proved ephemeral, while Buddhism failed to displace Confucianism in China, and was Sinicized in the process.

The reason for this regional independence is that the agrarian-based civilizations of pre-modern times lacked the technical and economic resources for extending their control beyond their respective regions. Interregional hegemony was not feasible until the scientific and industrial revolutions of modern times, which were to provide the West with the power and the dynamism to overwhelm not only Eurasia but the entire globe. Since all the Eurasian civilizations had the same agricultural base, none of them had power and organization sufficiently superior to overcome the regional pride and self-consciousness that had developed everywhere. For this reason the individual classical civilizations endured to modern times. Only with the disruptive expansionism of the West did the philosophies and religions and social institutions of the Classical Age begin to give way in the various regions of Eurasia. And even so, they are still very much alive today, as demonstrated by the continued vitality of Roman law and of the Roman Catholic church in the West, and of Hinduism and of caste in India.

II. ROOTS OF DECLINE

The classical civilizations were all able to preserve their identity because they all remained agricultural civilizations. Or, in other words, they all remained technologically stagnant through the millennia. John Maynard Keynes perceived and emphasized this immobility.

The absence of important technological inventions between the prehistoric age and comparatively modern times is truly remarkable. Almost everything which really matters and which the world possessed at the commencement of the modern age was already known to man at the dawn of history. . . . At some epoch before the dawn of history . . . there must have been an era of progress and invention comparable to that in which we live today. But through the greater part of recorded history there was nothing of the kind.[1]

Keynes's observation is fully justified. The Neolithic age preceding civilization had been, in fact, remarkably precocious in its technology. It was then that man invented the wheeled cart, the sailboat, and the plow, discovered the chemical processes involved in metallurgy, worked out an accurate solar calendar, and learned how to harness the power of animals and of the wind. After the urban revolution, this headlong advance was arrested. During the following millennia only three discoveries were made that compared in significance with those of the earlier period. These were iron, the alphabet, and coinage. All three, significantly enough, were discovered not in the old centers of civilization along the Nile and the Tigris-Euphrates, but rather in peripheral and less constraining environs—the Caucasus frontier region and the Aegean commercial cities.

Apart from these three great inventions, the advances made at this time were based on the earlier discoveries, merely refining the skill with which they were used or increasing enormously the scale on which they were applied. Since labor productivity was not raised by new inventions, wealth could be increased only by bringing new areas under cultivation, or by conquest and exploitation. But virgin lands were not limitless; indeed extensive fertile regions throughout the Mediterranean basin now were being eliminated as sources of food because of large-scale erosion that was becoming a serious problem. Likewise empires could not expand indefinitely, for there were strict limits beyond which they could not extend because of the level of their military technology. Thus a point of diminishing returns was inescapable when the pressure of burgeoning military and bureaucratic establishments became too much for the productive capacities. A vicious circle then set in, as noted above, particularly in the case of the fall of the Han and Roman empires concerning which more information is available. Rising taxes and increasing impoverishment fomented uprisings in the cities and countryside, which invited nomadic incursions and ultimately led to successful internal revolt or external invasion, or a combination of the two. Hence the cyclical nature of imperial history in pre-modern times. A historian, analyzing the decline of the Roman Empire, emphasized, in conclusion, technological backwardness:

The Roman Empire, we must not forget, was technically more backward than the Middle Ages. In agriculture a two-field system of alternate crops and fallow was usually followed, and the potentially richest soils were little exploited. The horse collar had not been invented, so that oxen had to be employed for plowing and for carting. Water mills existed, but seem to have been relatively rare, and corn was generally ground by animals or by human labor in hand querns. Yet with this primitive technique, agriculture had to carry an ambitious superstructure far heavier than that of any medieval state. No medieval kingdom attempted, as did the Roman Empire, to support, as well as a landed aristocracy and the church, a professional standing army, and a salaried bureaucracy.[2]

In retrospect it is clear that the cycle could have been broken only by technological advances that would have provided the economic underpinnings necessary for the imperial edifices. But technology was moribund, and the basic reason was that the ruling establishments everywhere knew how to expropriate existing wealth but did not know how to create new capacity for producing more wealth. They were capable of siphoning off astonishingly large surpluses from their peasant subjects, as evident in the stupendous amounts of capital and labor invested in pyramids, ziggurats, cathedrals, and palaces. But technological innovation required something more than efficient organization and coercion, and all the agricultural civilizations failed to achieve this *something more*—which was why they remained agricultural.

The widespread presence of slavery was one reason for the technological standstill. It was usually simpler and cheaper to put slaves to work than to design and construct new machines. Thus the inventors of the time usually produced gadgets intended not to save labor but to amuse or to facilitate religious ritual. Hero of Alexandria in the first century A.D. used his knowledge of steam power to construct a device that opened temple doors. Likewise, in the same century, Emperor Vespasian in Rome forbade the use of a machine that would erect columns inexpensively, commenting, "Let me provide food for the common folk." Laudable though this sentiment might be, the fact remains that it made the cities of the classical empires parasites of the country rather than centers of productive industry.

Slavery also inhibited technology by fostering a negative attitude toward work.

Since labor was the lot of the slaves, it came to be regarded as demeaning for any free citizen. Even in civilizations where slavery was not so prevalent, this attitude toward labor existed; witness the cult of the long fingernail in China. Sharp social stratification naturally promoted an upper-class contempt for work and workers, and slavery merely served to accentuate this attitude. The Roman philosopher Seneca, in a letter to Lucilius in A.D. 65, expressed scorn for manual labor, which, he said, should be proffered with "bowed body and lowered eyes":

Some things we know to have appeared only within our own memory; the use, for example, of glass windows which let in the full brilliance of day through a transparent pane, or the substructures of our baths and the pipes let into their walls to distribute heat and preserve an equal warmth above and below. . . . Or the shorthand which catches even the quickest speech, the hand keeping pace with the tongue. All these are the inventions of the meanest slaves. Philosophy sits more loftily enthroned: she doesn't train the hand, but is instructress of the spirit. . . . No, she's not, I say, an artisan producing tools for the mere everyday necessities.[3]

Precisely this isolation of the philosopher from the artisan arrested the technological growth of the Eurasian civilizations. It was the interaction between the two—the ordered speculation of the philosopher and the practical experience and traditional lore of the artisan—that enabled the West to achieve its great scientific and industrial revolutions in modern times, and thereby make its unique contribution to man's development. But such interaction proved impossible in the classical civilizations because of the sharp social cleavages and the resulting social attitudes. The lofty intellectual lacked interest and the depressed artisan lacked incentive.

This technological stagnation explains the cyclical nature of Eurasian imperial history during the pre-modern millennia. Empires rose and fell in a basically similar pattern. None was able to break through to a new level of development. Hence the repetitive cycles in contrast to the dynamism of modern industrialized societies. W. W. Rostow has described as follows this common feature of the agricultural civilizations prior to Britain's epochal and pioneering "take-off" with her industrial revolution.

. . . limitations of technology decreed a ceiling beyond which they could not penetrate. They did not lack inventiveness and innovations, some of high productivity. But they did lack a systematic understanding of their physical environment capable of making invention a more or less regular current flow, rather than a stock of *ad hoc* achievements inherited from the past. . . .

It followed from this productivity ceiling that food production absorbed 75 per cent or more of the working force and that a high proportion of income above minimum consumption levels was spent in non-productive or low-productive outlays: religious and other monuments, wars, high living for those who controlled land rents; and for poorer folk there was beggar-thy-neighbor struggle for land or the dissipation of the occasional surplus in an expensive wedding or funeral. Social values were geared to the limited horizons which men could perceive to be open to them; and social structures tended to hierarchy. . . .[4]

III. BARBARIAN INVASIONS

The period from the third to the sixth centuries was one of Eurasia-wide invasions comparable to the bronze and iron invasions of the second millennium B.C.

And just as the earlier invasions effectuated the transition from the ancient to the classical civilizations, so these later invasions ended the classical civilizations and heralded the medieval. (See Map XI, "Barbarian Invasions in Eurasia, 4th and 5th Centuries A.D.")

The general direction of nomadic movement was from east to west because of the geographic steppe gradient—the lure that the better watered and more fertile lands of the western steppes held for the nomads of the east. (See Chapter 6, section II.) The main invasion routes followed the corridor of grassland that stretched across Central Eurasia, beginning in the environs of Peking and ending in the Hungarian plains of Central Europe. A basic factor behind the invasions was the constantly increasing interaction between the nomads and the surrounding centers of civilization. In many of these centers, nomads were used as slave or mercenary soldiers, a practice that frequently proved the entering wedge for either a military coup in the imperial capital or for an invasion by the fellow-tribesmen of the barbarian mercenaries. Another factor was the gradual settling down of nomadic peoples, often in regions adjacent to imperial frontiers. This shift from nomadism to agriculture normally led to population growth and greater economic and military strength, which invariably was used if imperial weakness held out the promise of success. Invasions also were often the end result of a lengthy shock transmission process. A defeat before the Great Wall of China or the formation of an aggressive tribal confederacy in Mongolia frequently deflected the train of nomadic buffer shocks westward, culminating eventually in nomadic incursions across the Oxus or Danube or Rhine rivers.

Because of the Eurasia-wide scope of the invasions, a great variety of peoples were involved. Han China, Gupta India, and Sassanian Iran usually were assaulted by Turco-Mongols, often referred to as Huns. But the Roman Empire, being at the western terminal of the invasion route, was the object of attack, at one time or another, of all the peoples along that route, as well as of surrounding barbarians. The procession included assorted Germanic tribes, Iranians, Balto-Slavs, and Vikings, as well as the Turco-Mongols.

The outcome of the invasions varied as much as their personnel. In China, the Han Empire finally succumbed to Turco-Mongol invaders in A.D. 222. Three separate kingdoms emerged, Wei, north of the Yangtze, Wu, in the south, and Shu, in the west. After decades of warfare, Wei defeated its rivals and established in 265 a new dynasty, the Chin. This dynasty ruled all China until 316, when a new wave of invaders overran the entire northern half of the country. The Chin court fled south to Nanking, whence it ruled the Yangtze Valley and those regions of the south settled by the Chinese. China remained divided in two in this manner until finally reunited by the Sui dynasty in 589.

These centuries are called by Chinese historians the "Age of Confusion." The southern half of the country was ruled by a succession of Chinese kings, while the northern part was governed by assorted Turco-Mongol conquerors. The Chinese considered the southern kings to be the legitimate heirs to the Han dynasty and denied the title Emperor to the northern rulers. In reality both halves of the country during these centuries were usually fragmented. But it was northern China that suffered the most disruption, being exposed to the long succession of barbarian invasions. "Under their impact," observes one authority, "a pastoral economy might conceivably have replaced the agricultural economy of North China, and Altaic language might have taken the place of the Chinese."[5]

The West Roman Empire under similar circumstances did undergo, as we shall see, such a basic transformation. But North China was saved, primarily because the native Chinese population so greatly outnumbered the nomadic invaders. The north at that time was still by far the most populous part of the country, and therefore was able to absorb the nomadic influx without undergoing radical change. In fact large numbers of Chinese migrated from north to south during these troubled centuries to escape the barbarian ravages, so that not only did the north remain Chinese, but the south was substantially Sinicized. Consequently the partial barbarization of the north was counterbalanced by the southward expansion of Chinese culture, providing an enormous hinterland depth of China from north to south. Thus with reunification of the entire country by the Sui dynasty in 589, China resumed her normal course, as distinctively Chinese as during the Han period.

Turning to India, the invasions there occurred much later, for the Gupta Empire was at its height when China already was beset with her "Age of Confusion." During the fifth century, however, the eastern branch of the Huns, or the "White Huns" as they are called, crossed the Oxus River and drove south to India, while the western branch advanced over the Russian steppes to Europe. Under the impact of the Hun onslaught the Gupta Empire disintegrated during the first half of the sixth century. Very little is known of events during the remainder of the century, so that it may be presumed that there was much strife and probably further invasions.

The veil of obscurity lifted briefly during the first half of the seventh century when a feudatory ruler, Harsha, succeeded by a combination of diplomacy and force of arms in uniting most of northern India. His empire was loosely organized, however, consisting of powerful independent monarchs who recognized his suzerainty more as a personal homage than as subordination to imperial authority. Thus with Harsha's death in 647, after a brilliant reign of forty-one years, his ramshackle structure fell to pieces. Once more the veil of obscurity descended upon India, and remained down until the thirteenth century when the Moslem Turks appeared and gradually imposed their rule over most of the country.

The intervening several centuries were marked by recurring invasions and disunity. No empires emerged with bureaucratic organization like that of the Maurya or Gupta. Instead there were transitory clan supremacies or kingdoms based upon individual personalities. Also there were migrations into India on a large enough scale to form new cultural and social groups. An outstanding example is that of the Rajputs, a sturdy and brave people who gave their name to the area known as Rajputana in northwest India. They were a military aristocracy who were soon absorbed into the Hindu caste of Kshatriyas, or warriors. They became intensely proud of their Hinduism and for some time dominated north and central India. In fact they remained prominent to the nineteenth century, and to a degree even to the present.

Their experience is significant because it helps explain why India, despite the long centuries of turmoil and invasions, was not fundamentally changed. The newcomers were assimilated into the prevailing caste system, so that it was much more a case of their adapting to India's civilization than the other way around. Thus India, like China, emerged from her time of troubles with the civilization that she had evolved during classical times modified but not transformed.

IV. GERMANS AND HUNS IN THE WEST

In Europe, however, the pattern of events was precisely the opposite; there it was transformation rather than modification. The most numerous invaders in that region of Eurasia were the Germans who occupied the Central and East

European lands from the Baltic to the Danube, and from the Rhine to the Russian plains. They were organized in tribes, amongst the more important being the Franks, Vandals, Lombards, and the Ostrogoths and Visigoths. All shared the same general religious beliefs and institutions, and all spoke closely related dialects, so that they could understand each other. The social organization of these tribes consisted of three main elements. At the top were the nobles who were usually hereditary and who were the large landholders. Most Germans were freemen who customarily owned their own plots of land. Those who did not were obliged to work for the nobles as sharecroppers. At the bottom was a class of men neither free nor slaves. They were bound to the land but could not be sold apart from it. This form of bondage, similar to that of the Roman *colonus*, was the source of the institution of serfdom that prevailed in Western Europe in medieval times.

The main source of authority in these tribes was the assembly of freemen. It selected the king, if there was one, and also the military leader for each campaign. Tacitus noted that the Germans usually chose their kings on the basis of inheritance, but their war chiefs by their valor and ability on the battlefield. Young men were given the right to carry a sword after solemn rites that were the origin of the later medieval ceremony by which a squire was raised to knighthood. Each outstanding warrior leader had a retinue of young followers, or *comitatus*, who fought beside him in battle and owed him loyalty and obedience. In return the chief provided arms and subsistence as well as a share of the war booty. This institution contributed to the later system of feudalism, which was based on the loyalty of knights to their feudal lords.

Tacitus described the Germans as great eaters, heavy drinkers, and confirmed gamblers. On the other hand he praised their high moral standards, which he held up as a model for his fellow Romans. He also stressed their hospitality as universal and unstinted. During the winter season groups would go from house to house, staying at each until the owner's supplies were exhausted. This is reminiscent of the later medieval arrangement by which a king or noble was entitled, as a part of his feudal dues, to so many days of entertainment for himself and his entourage. The general cultural level of these Germans is suggested by the fact that they knew how to weave and to make metal implements and wheeled vehicles, but did not know how to write.

Such were the people who began to press upon the imperial frontiers as early as the first century B.C. At that time the Roman legions were strong enough to hold the line with little difficulty. But with the decline of the empire the army also weakened and the Romans were hard pressed to maintain control. They resorted to diplomacy to play off one tribe against another, and they also accepted, since they had no choice, the settlement of whole bands of German warriors on the Roman side of the border in return for their aid against the tribes on the other side. This policy worked so long as the Romans were able to keep their allies in check. But by the fourth century they could no longer do so and the floodgates burst.

The onslaught was triggered by dread new invaders that the Europeans had never seen before—the Huns. Their appearance and their deliberate policy of frightfulness terrorized both the Romans and the Germans. The contemporary Roman historian, Ammianus Marcellinus, described them as "almost glued to their horses," and "so monstrously ugly and misshapen that you might suppose they were two-legged animals. . . ." Apparently displaced from their original pasture lands in Central Asia by a newly-formed confederacy, the Huns headed westward and crossed the Volga in 372. There on the Russian steppes they quickly defeated the eastern-most German tribe, the Ostrogoths, and then terrorized the neighboring Visigoths into seeking refuge across the Danube River on Roman territory. Two years later, in 378, the Visigoths, exasperated by what they considered to be harsh treatment by Roman officials, defeated and killed the East Roman Emperor in the Battle of Adrianople. This destroyed the legend of Roman invincibility, so that during the following decades Italy and Gaul as well as the Balkan Peninsula felt the scourge of German and Hunnic invasions.

The Visigoths under Alaric marched to Italy, sacked Rome in 410 (an event that shocked the imperial world at the time but that soon was to be repeated), and eventually settled in southern Gaul and northern Spain where they founded the first German kingdom on Roman territory. Behind the Visigoths came the Huns who established their base on the Hungarian plains whence they raided both the eastern and western provinces of the empire. Under their feared leader, Attila, they appeared in 452 before the undefended gates of Rome, where according to an implausible tradition, Pope Leo I persuaded the Hun chieftain to spare the capital. In any case Attila turned northward without sacking the capital, and with his death a year later his empire collapsed and the Huns disappeared from European history.

The Hunnic devastations, however, had shattered Roman control over the western provinces and German tribes now migrated across the frontiers virtually at will—the Vandals to North Africa, the Franks to Gaul, and the Angles, Saxons, and Jutes to England. Thus it was that the West Roman Empire passed under the control of new German succession kingdoms, a passing symbolized by the deposition of the last emperor, Romulus Augustulus, by the German Odoacer, in 476. (See Chapter 8, section VIII.)

To this point the course of events in Europe was familiar. The West Roman Empire had succumbed to the barbarians as had the Han and Gupta empires. Furthermore it appeared in the sixth century that the aftermath of imperial disintegration in the West would be the same as that in China. Just as the Sui dynasty had finally united China in 589, so Europe at about the same time seemed to be on the road to reunification by the Frankish kings and the East Roman emperors.

Under the leadership of the Merovingian kings, the Franks had become the most powerful people in the West. The most outstanding of the Merovingians was Clovis (481–511), who united the Frankish tribes, defeated the Romans, Byzantines, and Visigoths, and welded together a kingdom stretching from the Pyrenees across Gaul and well into Germany. A principal reason for his success was his conversion to Catholicism, which won him the support not only of the Pope but also of the indigenous Gallo-Roman population. It appeared that the Merovingians might be able to recreate the West Roman Empire, enlarged by the addition of the Frankish lands on the eastern bank of the Rhine.

This imperial ambition was shared by the rulers at Constantinople. While the West Roman Empire had been falling apart, the East Roman Empire remained intact, thanks to its naval power, its superior financial resources, and the natural strength of its capital located on the straits between Europe and Asia. Thus Constantinople survived the barbarian invasions which overwhelmed Rome, and, in fact, endured another half millennium before falling to the Turks in 1453. During those centuries the empire developed a distinctive civilization, a mixture of Greek, Roman, Christian, and Eastern elements. To emphasize this distinctiveness, the empire is commonly referred to as the Byzantine Empire, so named after the original Greek colony on the site of Constantinople.

After the western provinces had become German kingdoms, the suzerainty of the Byzantine emperors perforce was restricted to the eastern half of the original empire—that is, to the Balkan Peninsula, Asia Minor, Syria, and Egypt. This contraction was unacceptable to Justinian the Great (527–565) who was an Illyrian by birth and a westerner at heart. He spoke and thought in Latin, and was determined to recover the western lands and to restore the original Roman Empire. One of his generals, Belisarius, with a small number of heavily armed troops, conquered the Vandal kingdoms in North Africa in one year. Southeast Spain also was recovered from the Visigoths, but eighteen years of bitter fighting was needed to subdue the Ostrogoths in Italy. Thus within two decades almost all the Mediterranean had become once more a Roman lake, and Justinian expressed the hope "that God will grant us the remainder of the empire that the Romans lost through indolence."

V. CONTINUED INVASIONS IN THE WEST

But this was not to be. The West did not follow the path of China. Instead a new wave of invasions smashed the fragile new imperial structures of the Franks and the Byzantines, and left the West once more in turmoil and disunity. Again it was a confederacy in Mongolia that pushed hordes of refugees westward along the invasion route to Europe. Like their Hunnic predecessors, these Avars, as they came to be known in the West, used the Hungarian plains as a base from which they launched raids in all directions.

These raids set off migrations that had far reaching repercussions. They forced the Germanic Lombards into Italy (568) where they drove out the Byzantines from most of the peninsula, thus blasting Justinian's hopes for an imperial restoration. The Avars also pushed Slavic tribes southward into the Balkan Peninsula where they dispersed the Latinized Illyrians and Dacians into isolated mountain areas. The Slavic newcomers sank roots in the northern Balkans as agriculturists, while the dispossessed Illyrians and Dacians remained in obscurity until modern times when they reappeared as the Albanians in the western Balkans and as the Rumanians north of the Danube. Thus during the seventh century the Balkan Peninsula attained its modern ethnic pattern, with Greeks in the south, the Albanians in the west, the Rumanians in the northeast, and the Slavs occupying a broad band from the Adriatic to the Black Sea.

In the eighth century hopes were aroused again for western imperial unity by the spectacular successes of the Carolingian dynasty, which had replaced the Merovingians. The successors of Clovis had proven a sorry lot—the *Rois fainéants,* or "do-nothing kings." The kingdom was held together, however, by strong willed ministers who held the office of "mayor of the palace." The most outstanding of these was Charles Martel, the Hammer, who was the power behind the throne from 714 to 741. His greatest achievement was the defeat at the Battle of Tours (732) of the Moslems who had overrun North Africa and Spain, and had advanced into Southern France. (See Chapter 13, section III.)

Martel's son, Pepin the Short, was not content to remain the minister of "do-nothing" kings and in 751 deposed the last Merovingian and established what came to be known as the Carolingian dynasty. The name is derived from Charlemagne, the son of Pepin, and the most famous of the line. During his long reign from 768 to 814 Charlemagne campaigned ceaselessly to extend his frontiers. He conquered the Saxons in northwest Germany, dispersed the Avars in Hungary, annexed the Lombard kingdom in Italy, and forced the Moslems back over the Pyrenees. By the end of the eighth century he was the undisputed master of the

West, his empire extending from the North Sea to the Pyrenees and from the Atlantic Ocean to the Slavic lands in Eastern Europe. In recognition of his supremacy, Pope Leo III crowned him as emperor on Christmas Day in the year 800. And the assembled multitude, relates Charlemagne's secretary and biographer, shouted, "To Charles Augustus, crowned of God the great and pacific Emperor of the Romans, life and victory!"

The scene reflects the tenacity of the dream of imperial unity. But it was destined to remain a dream, for soon after Charlemagne's death Europe was inundated by new waves of attacks from the south, the east, and the north. In the south, Moslem pirates and adventurers conquered the islands of Crete and Sicily, and also raided all the Mediterranean coasts with devastating effect on maritime trade. In the east, still another nomadic host from Central Asia, the Magyars, reached the Hungarian plains in 895 and followed the example of the preceding Huns and Avars in raiding the surrounding lands.

Most wide ranging were the incursions of the Norsemen, or Vikings. They were the equivalent on sea of the nomads on land. In place of horses they built fast ships with shallow draught that gave them unrivalled speed and mobility. The Vikings from Norway sailed westward to Iceland, Greenland, and North America. With their comrades from Denmark they raided the British Isles and the west coast of Europe, and even forced their way through the Straits of Gilbraltar and ravaged both shores of the Mediterranean. Since Sweden faces eastward, the Vikings from that country crossed the Baltic to the Russian rivers and followed them to their outlets in the Caspian and Black seas.

Thus the whole of Europe was enveloped by these daring raiders. At first, in the late eighth and ninth centuries, they were interested only in plunder, and they destroyed countless monasteries and towns. In the tenth and eleventh centuries the Vikings began to settle down in the overseas territories, thus occupying and ruling large parts of northern France and the British Isles. But wherever they settled they were eventually absorbed into the existing Christian state. The king of France, for example, in the hope of forestalling further depredations by the Vikings, recognized their leader in 911 and gave him the title of duke of what came to be known as Normandy, a name derived from the Norsemen who settled there. One of the descendants of this Duke Rollo of Normandy was William the Conqueror who successfully invaded England in 1066.

Meanwhile the Carolingian Empire had crumpled under the impact of the triple assault of Moslems, Magyars, and Vikings. Western Europe once more was reduced to a shambles. The lowest point was reached in the tenth century. At no time since the end of the Roman Empire did the present seem so wretched and the future so bleak. (See Map XII, "Continued Barbarian Invasions in the West, 9th and 10th Centuries.")

VI. HISTORIC UNIQUENESS OF THE WEST

From this survey of the invasions marking the transition from the classical to the medieval eras, it is apparent that the various regions of Eurasia were affected quite differently. South China and South India were unscathed, being geographically too remote to be reached by the invaders. The Byzantine Empire, with its resourceful diplomacy, financial resources, and naval strength, successfully repelled through the centuries a long succession of assailants—Germans, Huns, Avars, Slavs, Persians, and Arabs. Persia was equally successful under its Sassanian dynasty, which replaced the Parthians in A.D. 226. The Sassanians united the country by appealing to Persian pride, by reviving Zoroastrianism as a state religion, and by organizing a force of heavily armored cavalrymen. Thus Persia was able to repel waves of nomads along the Oxus River while fighting Byzantium to an exhausting draw that left both empires easy prey for the oncoming Moslem Arabs.

China and India, as noted earlier, did not fare so well in their northern regions. Both were overrun by barbarians yet both were able to preserve the distinctive civilizations that they had developed during the Classical Age. Thus a Chinese of the first century B.C. Han period would have felt quite at home had he been resurrected, for example, in the early eighth century A.D. He would have found the contemporary T'ang dynasty essentially the same as the Han, and he would have noted the same people, the same language, the same Confucianism and ancestor worship and imperial administration and so forth.

This points up the uniqueness of the historical experience of the West. If a Roman of the first century B.C. had been resurrected in the Europe of 1000 or 1500 or 1800, he would have been astonished by the German peoples in many parts of the old empire and by the strange new ways of life. He would have found the Latin language replaced by several new Germanic and Romance languages; the Roman togas replaced by blouses and trousers; the ancient Roman gods cast aside for the new Christianity; the Roman imperial structure superseded by a conglomeration of new nation states; and the old ways of earning a living rivalled by new agricultural techniques, by commerce with hitherto unknown parts of the globe, and by new crafts with strange machines that saved labor and that ran without the traditional human or animal power.

The explanation, of course, is that only in the West was a classical civilization permanently submerged and superseded by something fundamentally new. Everywhere else in Eurasia the various regional civilizations either escaped the invaders (South China and South India), or repelled them (Byzantium and Persia), or endured and survived them (North China and North India). Only in the West was the classical civilization shattered beyond recall despite repeated attempts at restoration over several centuries.

Since it was precisely this uniqueness that made possible the global primacy of the West in modern times, its origins require attention. As noted in section II of this chapter, technological stagnation was a basic structural weakness of the classical civilizations. But since this was true of all of them, why did only the West European civilization founder?

A comparison of West European institutions and experiences with those of the rest of Eurasia points to certain conclusions. In the first place Western Europe was not as productive in classical times as, for example, China. The monsoon winds provide most of East Asia with ample rainfall during the summer growing months, in contrast to Europe where most of the rain comes in the sterile winter months. This, together with the greater solar heat in the lower latitudes, allows more intensive and prolonged cultivation in East Asia, including two crops per year in many localities. Furthermore, rice, the principal crop of East Asia, produces a much larger yield per acre than wheat, rye, and the other cereals grown in the West. According to one estimate, rice on a given plot of land yields caloric value that is five times as great as that of wheat on the same land.[6] The net result was a far greater productivity in China than in the West, which led to the correspondingly denser population found in China from the advent of agriculture to the present day. This superiority in productivity and in population in turn made China more capable of supporting the empire's bureaucratic and military establishments, and of resisting, or, if necessary, absorbing, barbarian invaders.

Another was the absence in the West of anything comparable to the Chinese writing system, which provided lasting cultural homogeneity, and to the Chinese examination system, which provided administrative efficiency and stability. Finally, the Roman Empire had to cope with more formidable enemies on its frontiers. Being located on the western receiving end of the steppe invasion route, Europe bore the brunt of attacks by virtually all the nomadic peoples. Furthermore, the Roman Empire's Germanic neighbors were more numerous than the nomads on China's northwestern frontier, while the neighboring Persians and Arabs were more advanced and posed a more serious and lasting military threat than did China's nomadic neighbors. Hence the prolongation of the invasions in the West far beyond their duration in the rest of Eurasia.

It will be recalled that at one point North China faced the prospect of pastoralism replacing agriculture and of Altaic languages replacing Chinese. The restoration of unity and order by the Sui dynasty eliminated this prospect, but in the West the invasions continued in prolonged succession. The Avars undid the work of Justinian and Clovis, and the Moslems, Magyars, and Vikings demolished the empire of Charlemagne. Furthermore Western Europe lacked the great hinterland depth of China from north to south. There was no counterpart in Western Europe to the simultaneous Chinese retreat from old lands in the north and development of rich new lands in the south. The Mediterranean and the North African littoral could not provide the Western Europeans with the refuge and the new resources that the southern provinces did for the Chinese. Likewise the Western Europeans lacked the advantages of the Byzantines with their hinterland in Anatolia and the Near East, combined with their sea power in the Mediterranean, Adriatic, and Black Seas. Hence the unique denouement in the West—the irrevocable dissolution of the imperial structure and of its classical civilization.

This outcome is of such significance that it can fairly be described as a major turning point in world history. It was such a fateful turning point because the wholesale demolition cleared the ground for long overdue innovation. A historian recently presented the following conclusion concerning the demise of the Roman Empire: "All in all, the invasions gave the *coup de grace* to a culture which had come to a standstill after reaching its apogee and seemed doomed to wither away. We are reminded of the cruel bombings in our own day which destroyed ramshackle old buildings and so made possible the reconstruction of towns on more modern lines."[7] But this "culture" was no different from the others of Eurasia, which also were at a "standstill." Those others, however, managed to survive the invasions and to gain a new lease on life. But it was the old life that was prolonged, while the West, with the death of the Roman Empire, was able to start a new life—to make a new beginning.

The import of this new beginning becomes evident if it is recalled that during the classical period the Middle East had been the center of initiative from which had diffused the fundamental innovations of those millennia. But during the classical period it was Europe, India, and China that generated most of the innovations, while the Middle East lagged behind. And the reason was precisely that the ancient civilization of the Middle East had survived the invasions of the second millennium B.C., while the ancient civilizations of the peripheral regions had gone under, leaving the way clear for a fresh start—for the emergence of the new classical civilizations.

So it was during the transition from the classical to the medieval civilizations. But this time the existing classical civilizations survived everywhere except in the West. For this reason the West alone was free to strike out in new directions and to evolve during the medieval age a new technology, new institutions, and new ideas—in short, a new civilization. And in modern times this new civilization proved its superiority over the "standstill" civilizations of the rest of Eurasia— indeed of the entire world—as inevitably and irresistibly as at an earlier time the agricultural civilizations had triumphed over tribal cultures.

SUGGESTED READING

W. C. BARK, *Origins of the Medieval World* (Stanford Univ., 1958); G. JONES, *A History of the Vikings* (Oxford Univ., 1968); F. LOT, *The End of the Ancient World and the Beginning of the Middle Ages* (Knopf, 1931); O. J. MAENCHEN-HELFEN, *The World of the Huns* (Univ. California, 1973); S. MAZZARINO, *The End of the Ancient World* (Faber, 1966); E. A. THOMPSON, *A History of Attila and the Huns* (Clarendon, 1948), and his *The Goths in Spain* (Oxford Univ., 1969).

part four

MEDIEVAL CIVILIZATIONS OF EURASIA, 500-1500

Like the Classical Age, the Medieval Age was heralded by invasions— by the Dorians, Aryans, and Chou in the first instance, and by the Germans, Huns, and Turks in the second. There the parallel ends, however, for the medieval centuries, unlike the classical, were punctuated by continued invasions that affected virtually all regions of Eurasia. Beginning in the seventh century, there were the invasions of the warriors of Islam who overran not only the entire Middle East where they originated, but eventually North Africa, Spain, the Balkans, India, Southeast Asia, and much of Central Asia. Even more extensive were the conquests of the Turks and the Mongols during the half millennium between 1000 and 1500, encompassing as they did the great bulk of the Eurasian land mass from the Baltic Sea to the Pacific Ocean.

These great conquests, despite their fury and range, nevertheless did not uproot civilization in most of Eurasia as the earlier incursions of the Dorians, Aryans, and Chou had done. By medieval times most civilizations had sunk roots too deep to be extirpated so easily. Thus the traditional civilizations everywhere survived. In China, for example, the native Ming dynasty supplanted the Mongol Yuan, and the country reverted with a vengeance to age-old ways. In the sprawling Moslem world the indigenous Greco-Roman, Iranian, Semitic, and Egyptian traditions were not obliterated but rather fused into the syncretic civilization of Islam. Likewise the East Roman Empire continued without interruption for a full millennium as the Byzantine Empire, so that its inhabitants referred to themselves in modern times as "Romaioi," or Romans.

The one exception to this general pattern, as noted in the preceding chapter, was in the West. There, and there alone, the prevailing classical civilization was torn up root and branch. Only in the West, therefore, was the ground sufficiently cleared for the emergence of a new civilization that was free to develop along fresh lines in contrast to the traditional civilizations of the rest of Eurasia.

It was this unique feature of the West that enabled it to develop the economic vigor, the technological proficiency, and the social dynamism to expand overseas and to gain control of the sea routes of the world. With this fateful development the Medieval Age came to an end. But it ended, it should be noted, not with land invasions by Eurasian nomads, as did the ancient and classical periods, but rather with the maritime enterprise of the West. The overseas activities of Western explorers, merchants, missionaries, and settlers marked the transition from medieval to moden times, and from the Eurasian to the global phase of world history.

chapter twelve

Eurasian Ecumene

What has emerged is a sense of the remarkable complexity of the interplay between the Occident and East Asia from Roman and Han times onward. This involved a two-way traffic, in many items, along many routes, and of varying density in different periods . . . . despite difficult communication, mankind in the Old World at least has long lived in a more unified realm of discourse than we have been prepared to admit.—Lynn White, Jr.

Just as an incipient Eurasian ecumene differentiated the Classical Age from the Ancient Age, so now a full-fledged Eurasian ecumene differentiated the Medieval Age from the Classical Age. The incipient stage had been attained as a result of improved technology, particularly the large-scale production of iron, with its manifold repercussions in all aspects of life. (See Chapter 7.) Likewise the full ecumene was now facilitated by further technological advance, especially in shipbuilding and navigation. But more significant during these centuries was a political consideration—the existence for the first time of tremendous empires that encompassed not merely river valleys as in the Ancient Age, or entire regions as in the Classical Age, but that reached across several regions to embrace a large proportion of the entire Eurasian land mass.

It has been seen that the great Alexander knew nothing of the Ganges Valley or of China, and that virtually no direct relations existed between the Roman and the Han empires at the opposite ends of Eurasia. The reason is that Alexander's empire was pretty much confined to the Middle East, with only a precarious foothold in India, while the Roman and Han empires were for all practical purposes restricted to the western and eastern tips of Eurasia. In striking contrast, the medieval period witnessed first the Islamic Empire, which by the mid-eighth century stretched from the Pyrenees to the Indian Ocean, and from Morocco to the borders of China. In later centuries Islam expanded much further into Central Asia, Southeast Asia, and Africa's interior. Even more impressive was the thirteenth century Mongol Empire that included Korea, China, all of Central Asia, Russia, and most of the Middle East—the greatest Eurasian empire to that time and ever since. (See Map XIV, "Mongol Empire at the Death of Kublai Khan, 1294.")

Empires of such unprecedented dimensions eliminated the age-old regional isolation by making possible direct contact and interaction amongst the various parts of the land mass. This chapter will consider the nature of the resulting new bonds—commercial, technological, religious, and intellectual.

I. EURASIAN SEA TRADE

In classical times, the existence of the large Roman and Han empires at the opposite ends of the Eurasian trade routes stimulated commerce all along the line, and conversely, the disintegration of these empires undermined and reduced this commerce. It revived, however, and reached new heights during medieval times with the appearance of the Islamic, and later the Mongol, Empire.

The Moslem conquests unified the entire Middle East, through which ran all the trans-Eurasian trade routes—both the land routes that terminated at various Black Sea and Syrian ports, and the sea routes that ran through the Red Sea and the Persian Gulf. Particularly flourishing was the trade across the Arabian Sea with the Malabar coast of southwest India. Sizeable settlements of Moslem merchants, mostly Arabs and Persians, grew up in the ports of India and Ceylon. From west to east were shipped horses, silver, wrought iron objects, and linen, cotton, and woolen fabrics, which were exchanged for silks, precious stones, teak, and assorted spices.

Moslem merchants went on from India and Ceylon to Kalah Bar (Kedah) on the Malay coast, whence some sailed on to Sumatra and Java, while others went through the Malacca Straits and then north to Kanfu (Canton) in South China. The customary schedule was to leave the Persian Gulf in September or October, sail with the northeast monsoon to India and Malaya, and arrive in the China Sea in time for the southern monsoon to Canton. There the Moslem merchants spent the summer, and then returned with the northeast monsoon to the Malacca Straits and across the Bay of Bengal, arriving back in the Persian Gulf in the early summer—making a round trip of a year and a half.

After the first Moslem reached Canton in 671, considerable numbers settled there and prospered as middlemen between China and the overseas world. With the advent of the Sung dynasty (960–1127), the Chinese made considerable progress in shipbuilding and navigation, so that by the end of the twelfth century they were replacing the Moslems in the waters of East and Southeast Asia. By the time the Mongols conquered China and founded the Yuan dynasty (1279–1368), Chinese ships were the largest and best equipped, while Chinese merchants were settling in various ports in Southeast Asia and India. Marco Polo, who in 1291 accompanied a Mongol princess around southeast Asia to Iran, witnessed and described the vigor of Chinese maritime enterprise, as did also the Arab traveller Ibn Battuta, who fifty years later chose to make his way from India to China on a Chinese junk.

During the Ming dynasty (1368–1644), Chinese maritime activity reached its height, culminating in a remarkable but short-lived naval domination of the Pacific and Indian Oceans in the early fifteenth century. This was manifested by the series of seven expeditions sent out between 1405 and 1433 under the superintendency of the chief court eunuch, a certain Cheng Ho. These expeditions were unprecedented in their magnitude and in their achievements. The first comprised 62 ships and 28,000 men, and sailed as far as Java, Ceylon, and Calicut. On the return a flotilla of Sumatran pirates tried to block the way but they were completely annihilated. The later expeditions pressed on further, reaching as far as the east coast of Africa and the entrances to the Persian Gulf and the Red

Sea. More than thirty ports in the Indian Ocean were visited by the Chinese, and everywhere they persuaded or compelled the local rulers to recognize the suzerainty of the Ming emperor. And all this at a time when the Portuguese were just beginning to feel their way down the coast of Africa, not reaching Cape Verde until 1445! (See Map XVII, "Early 15th-Century Chinese and Portuguese Voyages.")

These extraordinary Chinese expeditions were suddenly halted by imperial fiat in 1433. The reasons for their beginning as well as for their ending remain a mystery. It is surmised that the expeditions may have been launched to compensate for the loss of foreign trade over the land routes with the disintegration of the Mongol Empire, or to enhance the prestige of the imperial court, or to find the emperor's predecessor who had disappeared underground as a Buddhist monk. Likewise it is speculated that the expeditions may have been halted because of their excessive cost or because of the traditional rivalry between court eunuchs and Confucian bureaucrats. In any case the withdrawal of the Chinese left a power vacuum in the waters of East and South Asia. Japanese pirates harried the coasts of China, while in the Indian Ocean the Moslem Arabs regained their former primacy. But adept though they were as merchants, the Arabs lacked the unity and the resources to develop the formidable naval power that the Chinese had briefly marshalled. Thus when the Portuguese sailed round Africa into the Indian Ocean in 1498, they encountered no effective resistance, and proceeded to establish their hegemony of the West.

II. EURASIAN LAND TRADE

Meanwhile a great revolution in land trade had occurred with the rise of the Mongol Empire. For the first and only time in history one political authority extended across the breadth of Eurasia—from the Baltic Sea to the Pacific, and from Siberia to the Persian Gulf. A mid-fourteenth century Italian handbook summarized the commercial significance of this *Pax Mongolica* in describing a trade route running across Central Asia from its beginning point at Tana at the mouth of the Don River.

> The road you travel from Tana to Cathay is perfectly safe, whether by day or by night, according to what the merchants say who have used it. . . . You may reckon that from Tana to Sarai [on the Volga] the road is less safe than on any other part of the journey; and yet even when this part of the road is at its worst, if you are some sixty men in the company you will go as safely as if you were in your own house.[1]

When Kublai Khan in 1264 moved his capital from Karakorum in Mongolia to Peking, this automatically opened China to the European merchants trading along the trans-Eurasian routes. The first Europeans to arrive at Kublai's new court were not diplomatic emissaries but two Venetian merchants Nicolo and Maffeo Polo. Of greater economic importance than this access to China was the access for the first time to the source of spices in India and the East Indies. Hitherto spices had reached Europe via two routes: through the Red Sea and Egypt, or to the Persian Gulf and then by caravan routes to ports on the Black Sea or the eastern Mediterranean. The first route was controlled by the Arabs who shipped the spices to Egypt, and by the Venetians who loaded cargoes at Alexandria for distribution in Europe. The second route was dominated by the Mongol ruler (Ilkhanate) of Persia and Mesopotamia, and by the Genoese who awaited the spices at the port terminals.

The Genoese, however, were not content only to sail the Black Sea. They ascended the Don River from the Azov Sea in small, light vessels, which they transported, probably on ox-wagons, across the narrow neck of land to the Volga and thence to the Caspian Sea and to Persia. Thus the Genoese were able to reach the Persian Gulf and to go directly to India and the East Indies where they discovered how cheap the spices were in their places of origin and what fabulous profits had been made during the past centuries by the succession of middlemen between the producers in Southeast Asia and the consumers in Europe.

This revival of overland trade during the *Pax Mongolica* proved short-lived. One reason was the expulsion of the Mongols from China in 1368 and the general disintegration of the Mongol Empire. This led to a recrudescence of fragmentation in Central Asia and hence to the disruption of trans-Eurasian trade. More important was the conversion of Ilkhan Ghazan (1295–1304) to Islam, which automatically barred to European merchants the transit route to the spice islands. Almost all spices henceforth were shipped along the Red Sea-Nile route, with golden profits for the Arab and Venetian middlemen. But other Europeans were unwilling to continue paying exorbitant prices, particularly since they now knew from where the spices came and at what cost. Hence the search for a new route around the Moslem barrier—a search that was to culminate in da Gama's epochal voyage around Africa.

III. TECHNOLOGICAL DIFFUSION

The great Moslem and Mongol empires affected not only the flow of trade within Eurasia but also the diffusion of technology. An outstanding example is the lateen sail, a tall, triangular, fore-and-aft sail that has always been used on Arab craft. In the Mediterranean, by contrast, the Egyptians, Phoenicians, Greeks, and Romans had used a square sail which is easier to handle in bad weather. But the Arab sail is much more maneuverable, being able to keep closer to the wind and to tack on rivers and narrow waters. For this reason it soon superseded the square sail in the Levant, and by the eleventh century it had become the normal rig throughout the Mediterranean. Today this triangular sail is known as the "Latin," or "lateen," sail, though it was the Arabs who, with the Moslem invasions, introduced it into the Mediterranean. And from there it spread to the Atlantic where, during the fifteenth century, Portuguese and Spanish ship designers combined the square sail on the foremast with the lateen on the main and mizzen. The resulting hybrid three-masters were capable of sailing in all reasonable weathers, and thus made possible the long ocean voyages of Columbus and da Gama.

The Moslem Empire, straddling North Africa, the Middle East, and South Asia, had contact with all regions of Eurasia and thus served as a conduit or intermediary in the interchange of knowledge and techniques as well as of articles of trade. In the medieval period, the direction of the technological diffusion was usually from east to west. In earlier times, it is true, it had been the other way around. During the ancient and classical periods such basic inventions as the wheel, windlass, and pulley diffused in all directions from Mesopotamia, the swape and crank from Egypt, the windmill from Persia, and iron smelting from Asia Minor. But during the first fourteen centuries of the Christian era, China was the great center of technological innovation, and transmitted to the rest of Eurasia a multitude of inventions. The English philosopher Francis Bacon wrote in 1620:

It is well to observe the force and virtue and consequences of discoveries. These are to be seen nowhere more conspicuously than in those three which were unknown to the ancients, and of which the origin, though recent, is obscure and inglorious; namely, printing, gunpowder, and the magnet. For these three have changed the whole face and state of things throughout the world, the first in literature, the second in warfare, the third in navigation; whence have followed innumerable changes; insomuch that no empire, no sect, no star, seems to have exerted greater power and influence in human affairs than these mechanical discoveries.[2]

All three of these inventions, whose historical significance Bacon correctly appraised, were of Chinese origin. The oldest existing example of block printing—printing in which a single block of wood is engraved for each page printed—is a Chinese Buddhist sacred text from the year 868. The first invention of separate movable type also is Chinese, the work of a simple artisan who between 1041 and 1049 made movable type of baked clay. In later centuries the Chinese substituted wood and various metals for the clay. The diffusion of these inventions has been traced from China to the Middle East and thence to Europe, where the first example of block printing dates back to 1423, followed in 1456 by the first book printed with movable type—Gutenberg's *Bible*.

Gunpowder was used in China for fireworks as early as the T'ang dynasty (618–906). By 1120 the Chinese had evolved a weapon known as the "firelance" comprising a stout bamboo tube filled with gunpowder. This was almost certainly the precursor of the metal-barrel gun, which appeared about 1280, though it is not known whether it was first contrived by Chinese or Arabs or Europeans.

The earliest definite reference to magnetism is found in a Chinese book of about 240 B.C., but for centuries thereafter the compass was used only by geomancers for magical purposes. By 1125, however, it was applied for navigation purposes, and apparently the Arab merchants who came to China learned of this instrument and introduced it into Europe.

Other Chinese inventions that spread throughout Eurasia with profound repercussions were paper, the stern-post rudder, the foot-stirrup, which made possible the heavily-armored feudal knights of medieval Europe, and the breast-strap harness, which rests on a horse's shoulders and allows it to pull with full force without choking as had been the case with the old throat harness. Finally the Chinese domesticated numerous fruits and plants which were spread throughout Eurasia, usually by the Arabs. These include the chrysanthemum, the camellia, the azalea, the tea rose, the Chinese aster, the lemon, and the orange, the latter still being called the "Chinese apple" in Holland and Germany.

In conclusion it should be noted that the transmission of these and other inventions occurred in clusters that obviously relate to facilitating political events. Thus the Crusades may be considered responsible for the twelfth-century cluster of the compass, stern-post rudder, paper-making, and the idea of the windmill, while the *Pax Mongolica* likewise stimulated the fourteenth-century cluster of gunpowder, silk machinery, printing, and the blast furnace for cast iron.

IV. EURASIAN RELIGIONS

The medieval period was characterized not only by an unprecedented trans-Eurasian exchange of goods and technologies, but also by an unprecedented diffusion of religious creeds. In the case of Christianity and Buddhism, this began towards the end of the classical period and continued during the medieval. (See Chapter 7, section III.) But by all odds the outstanding religious innovation during the medieval centuries was the appearance of Islam. Apart from its teachings, which will be noted in the following chapter, the new religion profoundly affected extensive regions of Eurasia and Africa as a result of its spectacular eruption from the Arabian Peninsula following the death of Mohammed in A.D. 632.

The expansion of Islam, the details of which will be noted later, occurred in two stages. During the first, from 632 to 750, it spread over the Middle East and then west to the Pyrenees and east to Central Asia. The net effect was the virtual transformation of the Mediterranean into a Moslem lake. But the second stage of expansion between 1000 and 1500 made the Indian Ocean also a Moslem preserve, for during these centuries Islam expanded much further—into India, Southeast Asia and Africa.

The vast extension of the domains of Islam naturally alarmed the beleaguered rulers of Christendom who were now effectively isolated on the western tip of Eurasia. This explains their ambivalent reaction to the appearance of the Mongols in the thirteenth century. They were appalled and terrified by the devastation and slaughter that marked the seemingly irresistible advance of the Mongol horsemen. Yet, as seen through Western eyes, the picture was not all black. The Mongols had subjugated the Christian Russians, who were adherents of the schismatic Greek church. Furthermore the most crushing blows had been dealt by the Mongols against Islamic Persia and Mesopotamia. When the Moslems in desperation appealed to the Christian rulers for aid, the normal reaction was that expressed by the Bishop of Winchester: "Let us leave these dogs to devour one another." Some Westerners went further and cherished the hope that the new barbarians might be converted to the true faith as the Magyars and Vikings had been before them. Being ignorant of civilization and with no sophisticated religious beliefs or organized priesthood to sustain them, the Mongols seemed ripe for conversion and for assimilation.

The Western Christians, however, were not alone in their designs on the Mongols. Representatives of three other religions were then competing for the soul of Asia. Most aggressive was Islam, which then was spreading from Persia across the Oxus River into Central Asia, where it won over some Turkish tribes. Buddhism also had become familiar to the Mongols in the course of its diffusion from its Indian home to China along the Silk Road of Turkestan. Finally there were the Nestorian Christians, whose origins go back to the Council of Ephesus (431) when they were condemned as heretics. They then withdrew from the Roman Empire into Persia, and later, under pressure from advancing Islam, moved along the overland routes through Central Asia to China. Thus they were able to convert various Turkish tribes, and then as the Mongol Empire expanded, these Christianized Turks entered its service as administrators, translators, interpreters, and envoys.

While these Nestorian Christians naturally entertained high hopes of converting the Mongols, the Western Christians dispatched two missions to the court of the Grand Khan in Karakorum in northern Mongolia. The first (1245–47) was led by the Italian Franciscan John de Plano Carpini, and the second (1253–55) by the Flemish Franciscan William de Rubruquis. They found the Khans interested in all foreign religions, but the traditional magicians, or shamans, were very influential at the court, and the friars were unable to win over any members of the royal family. Also an alliance against Islam proved impossible, for the Mongols demanded submission rather than partnership—"all of you, without exception," declared Mangu Khan, "must come to tender us service and pay us homage . . . the Commandments of the Eternal are what we impart to you."[3]

The missions were successful, however, in providing the West with the first reliable information concerning the appearance, customs, and military tactics of the new barbarians.

In the West, hope still was held for the great but mysterious realm of Cathay, which was known to be free of Islam. Neither Carpini nor Rubruquis had reached China, but they were told that it was only twenty days' journey from Karakorum and that it was a country of unparalleled wealth. When Kublai Khan in 1264 moved his capital to Cambaluc (from Khan Baliq or the Khan's headquarters—the modern Peking) China for the first time became accessible to Europeans. The first to arrive were two Venetian merchants, Nicolo and Maffeo Polo. Later, in 1289, Pope Nicholas IV sent John of Montecorvino, a veteran of fourteen years' missionary work amongst the Moslems of the Levant, to the Mongol court. Friar John took the sea route from the Persian Gulf to India, the Malacca Straits, and Kanfu (Canton), whence he went overland to Cambaluc (Peking). He was allowed to remain in the capital and to preach, so that within six years after his arrival in 1292 he had built a church with a campanile and with a choir of 150 boys whose Gregorian chants pleased the imperial ear. When the Papacy learned of this success it sent reinforcements, enabling Friar John to start another mission in Kanfu. By the time of the friar's death in 1328 several thousand converts had been won over in China.

This progress had been made possible by the positive attitude of the Mongol rulers who deliberately encouraged all alien religions, whether Moslem, Buddhist, or Christian, as counterweights to the dominant Confucian establishment in China. Accordingly the Christian missionaries received liberal allowances from the imperial treasury that enabled them to build a friary with "apartments fit for any prelate." This unexpected affluence proved short-lived, however, for it depended entirely on the support of the Khan. But as Marco Polo reported, "All the Cathaians detested the Great Khan's rule because . . . he put all authority into the hands of Tartars, Saracens, or Christians, who were attached to his household and devoted to his service, and were foreigners in Cathay." Thus when the Mongols were expelled from China in 1368, the various foreign elements they had patronized were expelled along with them, including the Catholic missions. Western Christianity was not to gain a foothold in China again until da Gama's voyage established a direct sea route between the two extremities of Eurasia and paved the way for the arrival of the Jesuits in the sixteenth century.

V. EXPANDING HORIZONS

Although the Europeans failed to win over the Mongols as allies or as coreligionists, they did, thanks to the *Pax Mongolica,* broaden immeasurably their horizons and gain a new Eurasian perspective. This was very different from the early medieval period when the collapse of the Han and Roman empires severed the trans-Eurasian ties of classical times. Parochialism set in, and in the West this was accentuated by the tenets of triumphant Christianity. The Bible became the main source of geographical knowledge, so that Jerusalem was regarded as the center of the earth, while the Nile, Euphrates, and Ganges were believed to have a common source in the Garden of Eden.

The expansion of Islam in the seventh and eighth centuries further narrowed European horizons by erecting a constricting barrier across North Africa and the Middle East. It was not until the twelfth century when the Crusaders began to return from the Levant with their tales that first-hand information of the outside world again became available. Yet even then the Mediterranean remained the axis of the world, and knowledge of the lands to the east and south was meager in the extreme.

The great breakthrough came with the *Pax Mongolica,* which made possible the transition from a Mediterranean to a Eurasian perspective, just as Columbus and da Gama later were to effect a corresponding transition from a Eurasian to a global perspective. The travels of merchants, missionaries, and prisoners of war revealed the existence of a great empire in the Far East that not only equalled but surpassed Europe in population, wealth, and level of civilization. Nor was this a one-way process, for the East now became aware of the West as well as vice versa. Marco Polo, who opened the eyes of the West to Cathay, had his counterparts in China and the Middle East.

We know of Chinese trading colonies in Moscow, Tabriz, and Novgorod during this period, while Chinese engineers were employed on irrigation projects in Mesopotamia. Also there are records of Chinese bureaucrats who accompanied Genghis Khan on his campaigns and inspection tours from one end of Eurasia to the other. In addition there was the Nestorian monk Rabban Bar Sauma, who was born in Peking and who travelled in 1278 to the Ilkhan's court in Baghdad. From there he was sent by the Mongols to Europe to seek Christian help against Islam. Starting out in 1287, he travelled to Constantinople, Naples, Rome, Paris, and London, meeting en route both Philip IV of France and Edward I of England. The most wide-ranging of these medieval travellers was the Moslem Ibn Battuta (1304–1378). Starting from his native Morocco, he made the pilgrimage to Mecca and journeyed on through Samarkand to India where he served as judge and also as ambassador to China. Returning later to Morocco, he resumed his travels, crossing north to Spain and then south to the interior of Africa, where he reached Timbuktu. When he finally returned to Morocco and settled down, he had travelled no less than 75,000 miles.

By all odds the most important traveller for the Western world was the famous Marco Polo. Accompanying his father and his uncle on their second journey to China, he arrived at Kublai Khan's court in 1275. He favorably impressed the Khan and served him for seventeen years in various capacities that required him to travel throughout the country. As an official he carefully observed the inhabitants and resources of the lands through which he journeyed, noting such things as "a kind of black stone, which is dug out of the mountains like any other kind of stone and burns like wood." In 1292 he escorted a Mongol princess on a voyage around southeast Asia and across the Indian Ocean to Persia where she was to be the bride of the Ilkhan. Marco Polo then continued westward to his native Venice, arriving there in 1295 after an absence of twenty-five years. Shortly afterward he was captured in a battle with the Genoese, and while in prison he dictated his account of his travels.

The book opens with this passage, which gives some idea of what a thrilling eye-opener it was for the people of the time.

Emperors and Kings, dukes and marquesses, counts, knights, and burgesses, and all ye, whoever ye be, who wish to know of the various races of men, and of the diversities of the different regions of the world, take this book and have it read to you. You shall find in it all the mighty wonders, all the great singularities of the vast regions of the East—of the Greater Armenia, of Persia, of Tartary, and of India, and of many a country besides —set down by us clearly and in due order, as they were recounted by Messer Marco Polo. . . . And all who read this book or hear it read, must believe it, as all the things contained in it are true. For I tell you that ever since the Lord our God did with his own hands mould our first father Adam, there never was up to the present day any man,

Christian or Pagan, Tartar or Indian or of any other race whatsoever, who knew and explored so great a part of the various regions of the world and of its great marvels, as this Messer Marco knew and explored. . . .[4]

Marco's stories seemed so fantastic and exaggerated that he was dubbed Il millione, "the man who talks in millions." Actually he provided Europeans with the most comprehensive and authoritative account of China available to the mid-sixteenth century. The title of his book is significant—*The Description of the World.* In fact this work had suddenly doubled the size of the known world for westerners. Marco Polo opened up new vistas for his contemporaries fully as much as Columbus was to do two centuries later. Indeed it was his tantalizing picture of Cathay and the Spice Islands that beckoned the great explorers onward as they sought a direct sea passage after the Moslems had blocked the overland routes.

SUGGESTED READING

G. F. Hourani, *Arab Seafaring in the Indian Ocean in Ancient and Early Medieval Times* (Princeton Univ., 1951); G. F. Hudson, *Europe and China: A Survey of Their Relations from the Earliest Times to 1800* (Beacon 1961); D. F. Lach, *Asia in the Making of Europe* (Univ. Chicago, 1965); R. E. Latham, trans., *The Travels of Marco Polo* (Penguin, 1958); J. Needham, *Science and Civilization in China* (Cambridge Univ., 1954); C. G. F. Simkin, *The Traditional Trade of Asia* (Oxford Univ., 1969); A. Toussaint, *History of the Indian Ocean* (Univ. Chicago, 1966).

chapter thirteen

Rise of Islam

The burden of the desert of the sea. As whirlwinds in the south pass through; so it cometh from the desert, from a terrible land.—
Isaiah 21:1

*We have revealed to thee an Arabic Koran, that thou mayest warn Mecca, the Mother of Cities, and those who are about her; that thou mayest give warning of the Day of Judgement, of which is no doubt —when part shall be in Paradise and part in the flame.—*Koran,
Sura XLII

The centuries between 600 and 1000 witnessed the emergence of Islam, a major turning point in Eurasian and world history. The spectacular conquests of the Moslem warriors united once more the entire Middle East as Alexander the Great had done almost a millennium earlier. The subsequent disruption of Alexander's empire, followed eventually by the imposition of Roman rule in Asia Minor and Syria, led to the division of the Middle East into two parts with the Euphrates River as the dividing line. The eastern part was the center of Persian civilization and consisted of Iran and Iraq, while the western part, the abode of Byzantine civilization, encompassed the Balkans, Asia Minor, Syria, Egypt, and North Africa. The Islamic conquests of the seventh and eighth centuries ended this division by uniting under the star and crescent all the territories from the Pyrenees to the Sind and from Morocco to Central Asia.

More remarkable than these military exploits were the cultural achievements of Islam. Although the conquered territories were the centers of the most ancient civilizations of mankind, nevertheless they were by the eleventh century linguistically Arabized and culturally Islamized. Arabic became the language of everyday use from Persia to the Atlantic, while a new Islamic civilization emerged that was an original synthesis of the preceding Judaic, Perso-Mesopotamian, and Greco-Roman civilizations. This linguistic and cultural transformation persists to the present day, so that an Iraqi and a Moroccan now have as strong linguistic and cultural ties as an Englishman and an Australian.

I. ARABIA BEFORE ISLAM

The Middle East on the eve of the Moslem invasions was dominated by two great empires: the Byzantine, which from Constantinople controlled the lands of the eastern Mediterranean, and the Sassanian, with its capital at Ctesiphon, ruling the Tigris-Euphrates valleys and the Iranian plateau. The hostility between these two states was chronic, one being Christian with a Greco-Roman culture, and the other Zoroastrian with Perso-Mesopotamian traditions. Between 603 and 629 they fought a series of exhausting wars that left both vulnerable to the gathering storm in the Arabian deserts.

Arabia at this time was regarded by its civilized neighbors as an obscure land of nomadic barbarians. Apart from the south where agriculture and monarchical government were feasible, the rest of the peninsula was pastoral and tribal. The *sheikhs,* or elective tribal leaders, were merely the first among equals, being bound by traditional custom that governed all. Their principal functions were to lead in time of war and to serve as custodians of holy places. Most of the tribes were pagan, worshipping trees, fountains, and stones that were regarded as the dwelling-places of vaguely defined powers. There was also a belief in more personal gods, which were subordinate to a higher deity called Allah. Both Judaism and Christianity had penetrated Arabia from the north, winning over entire tribes in the border region as well as isolated groups in the remainder of the peninsula. Compared to these faiths, the polytheistic idolatry, tribal warfare, and political disunity of Arabia must have seemed shamefully primitive to thoughtful Arabs. Indeed we hear of several "prophets" appearing about the beginning of the seventh century, reflecting a striving towards an indigenous monotheism. Like every successful preacher, Mohammed gave voice and form to the need and longing of his time.

II. MOHAMMED

Mohammed was born in 569 in Mecca, a prosperous city located at the crossing of trade routes running north to Syria, south to the Yemen, and also east to the Persian Gulf and west to the Red Sea port of Jedda and the sea lane to Africa. He was the posthumous son of a Mecca merchant, and because his mother died when he was six, he was brought up first by his grandmother and subsequently by his uncle. Little is known of his youth, though tradition has it that at the age of twelve he was taken by his uncle on a caravan to Syria. In the course of that journey he may have picked up some Jewish and Christian lore. At the age of twenty-five he married a wealthy widow who bore him several daughters and two sons who died in infancy.

About his fortieth year Mohammed went through a period of intense spiritual tension, in the course of which he became convinced that God had chosen him to be a prophet, a successor to Abraham and Moses and Jesus. Asked to describe the process of revelation, he answered that the entire text of the Koran existed in Heaven and that one fragment at a time was communicated to him, usually by the archangel Gabriel who made him repeat every word. Others who were near Mohammed on some of the occasions neither saw nor heard the archangel. His convulsions may have been epileptic seizures, particularly since he reported hearing sounds like the ringing of bells—a frequent occurrence in epileptic fits. In any case Mohammed now believed that he had received a divine call to attest the unity and transcendence of Allah, to warn his people of the Day of Judgment, and to tell them of the rewards for the faithful in Paradise and the punishment of the wicked in Hell.

His teachings were written down soon after his death and became the sacred scripture of the new religion known as Islam, meaning "submission to God's will." Mohammed did not establish an organized priesthood nor did he prescribe specific sacraments essential for salvation. But he did call on his followers to perform certain rituals known as the Five Pillars of Islam. These are: (1) Once in his life the believer must say with full understanding and absolute acceptance, *la ilaha illa llah: muhammed rasulu'llah*—"There is no God but Allah; Mohammed is the Messenger of Allah." (2) Five times daily he must pray—at dawn, at noon, in mid afternoon, at dusk, and after it has become dark. Facing in the direction of Mecca, the worshipper prays on a carpet, with his shoes removed and his head covered. (3) The Moslem must give alms generously, as an offering to Allah and an act of piety. (4) The Moslem must fast from daybreak to sunset during the whole month of Ramadan. (5) Once in his life the Moslem, if he can, must make the pilgrimage, or Hadj, to Mecca.

These rituals provided the believers with an extraordinarily powerful social cement. They prayed and fasted together, they assumed responsibility for their less fortunate brothers, and they journeyed to Mecca together—rich and poor, yellow, white, brown, and black. Furthermore the Koran provided guidance for all phases of the life of the faithful—for manners and hygiene, marriage and divorce, commerce and politics, crime and punishment, peace and war. Thus Islam was not only a religion but also a social code and a political system. It offered to its followers not only religious commandments but also specific precepts for private and for public life. There was no cleavage between the secular life and the religious, between the temporal and the spiritual, as was the case in the Christian world. What is Caesar's, in Islam, is God's, and what is God's is also Caesar's. The *Shari'a,* or Holy Law, was until recently the law of the land throughout the Moslem world, and it is still so to a great extent in individual countries.

To these teachings Mohammed slowly won converts, the first being members of his immediate family and personal friends, who later enjoyed great prestige as "Companions of the Prophet." As the little band of converts grew, the wealthy Meccan merchants became alarmed for fear that Mohammed's teachings would undermine the older religious beliefs and discourage pilgrims from coming to worship at the shrine of the Black Stone in their city. Because of the growing opposition, Mohammed accepted an invitation to go to the nearby city of Medina, which was rent by dissension between its Arab and Jewish inhabitants. Gradually Mohammed persuaded the Medina Arabs to accept his religion and he organized a theocratic state based on his teachings.

From his base in Medina, Mohammed organized attacks on the Mecca caravans. Such raiding was an accepted and popular economic activity amongst Arab nomads, who now flocked to the banner of the Prophet in the hope of winning booty, and incidentally salvation. By 630 the Moslems were strong enough to capture Mecca, whereupon Mohammed made the Black Stone, housed in the Ka'ba, the chief shrine of his religion. Thus he effected a compromise by which he preserved the basic tenets of his faith and yet rooted it in traditional Arab custom. By the time of his death in 632, most—though by no means all—of the Arab tribes had recognized his overlordship and paid him tribute.

Mohammed, who had found his native land a flotsam of idolatrous practices, now left it with a religion and a revealed book, and with a community and a state sufficiently well organized and armed to dominate the entire peninsula. Within a century his followers were to march on from victory to victory, building an imposing empire across the breadth of Eurasia and propagating his creed, which today boasts half a billion adherents throughout the world. If influences on the course of events be the criterion, then Mohammed surely stands out as one of the giants of history.

III. AGE OF CONQUESTS

Precisely because the Moslem community was the product of Mohammed's genius, it now seemed likely with his death to break up into its component elements. To forestall this, foreign raids were undertaken and were enthusiastically supported by Bedouins eager for booty. The leader of the raids was the caliph, or deputy, who was chosen in the place of the Prophet in his secular capacity. There was no question, of course, of a successor to Mohammed as Prophet, but a secular chief of the community was essential. Thus when Abu Bakr, Mohammed's father-in-law, was selected as caliph, it signified that he was the defender of the faith rather than religious leader.

Under Caliph Omar, who succeeded Abu Bakr in 634, the early raids blossomed into full-fledged campaigns of conquest. They did so because the outwardly formidable Byzantine and Persian empires were soon discovered to be hollow shells. They not only had been weakened by the series of wars between them, but in addition their subjects were seriously disaffected because of heavy taxation and religious persecution. Furthermore the Moslem forces now were being transformed from raiding parties to large-scale armies as entire tribes from all Arabia migrated northward, attracted by reports of dazzling riches. Thus the great conquests that followed represented the expansion not of Islam but of the Arab tribes, who on many occasions in earlier centuries had pushed northward into the Fertile Crescent. The unprecedented magnitude of the expansion at this time derived partly from the exceptional weakness of the two empires and partly from the unity and élan engendered by the new Islamic faith.

Once the invasions were under way the Arabs made good use of their experience in desert warfare. Being mounted on camels, in contrast to the horses of the Byzantines and Persians, they were able to attack at will, and, if necessary, to retreat back to the safety of the desert. Just as the Vikings later were to be able to ravage the coasts of Europe because of their command of the sea, so now the Arabs used their "ships of the desert" to attack the wealthy empires. It was not accidental that in the provinces they conquered the Arabs established their main bases in towns on the edge of the desert. They used existing cities like Damascus when they were suitably located, and when necessary created new ones like Kufa and Basra in Iraq, and Fustat in Egypt. These garrison towns met the same need for the emerging Arab Empire that Gibraltar, Malta, and Singapore later did for the British sea empire.

In 636 the Arabs won a decisive victory over the Byzantines in the ravines of the Yarmuk River, a tributary of the Jordan. Attacking in the midst of a blinding sandstorm they almost annihilated a mixed force of Greek, Armenian, and Syrian Christians. Emperor Heraclius fled to Constantinople, abandoning all of Syria to the victors. Caliph Omar now turned against the rich adjacent province of Iraq. Its Semitic, partly Christian, population was alienated from its Persian and Zoroastrian masters. This contributed to the great victory won by the Arabs in the summer of 637 at Qadisiya. The Persian emperor hastily evacuated his nearby capital Ctesiphon and fled eastward.

The astonishing triumphs at Yarmuk and Qadisiya left the Moslems with unheard of riches, which further swelled the flood of Bedouin tribesmen from the southern deserts. Their pressure on the frontiers was irresistible, and the Arab armies rolled onward, westward into Egypt and eastward into Persia. Within two years (639–641) they had overrun the whole of Egypt, but in Persia for the first time they encountered stiff resistance. Although the imperial leadership was incompetent and unpopular, nevertheless the nation was ready to fight for its freedom and its Zoroastrian religion. Not until 651 was the country subdued, and long before then, in 644, Omar had been assassinated by a Persian captive.

Omar's successors in the caliphate bore the banners of Islam still further afield, driven on by the momentum of victory, of religious enthusiasm, and of nomadic cupidity. In North Africa the Arab forces, supplemented by native Berber converts, fought their way clear across to Morocco and then crossed the Straits of Gibraltar into Spain. In 711 they defeated Roderick, the last Visigothic king of Spain, and advanced to the Pyrenees and on into France. There, however, they were defeated by Charles Martel at Tours in 732. This battle is often designated as a major turning point in the history of Western Europe, though it is doubtful that the Moslems, even if successful, could have advanced much further in a region so distant from their home base. The same is true of the expansion of the Moslems to the east. In 715 they conquered the province of Sind in northwest India but were unable to push further until several centuries later when their Turkish coreligionists invaded India from the north. Likewise in 751 the Moslems defeated the Chinese at Talas in Central Asia, but again were unable to advance further towards China. Thus Talas, Sind, and the Pyrenees marked the limits for Moslem expansionism given the level of their military technology.

This points up the exceptional significance of the Arab failure to take Constantinople after a full year's siege in 717–18. Since this city was so close to the center of their empire, they presumably would have been able to overrun much of Eastern Europe had they prevailed at Constantinople. This, of course, is precisely what the Moslem Turks did in the fifteenth century, but if it had occurred nearly a millennium earlier, much of Eastern Europe would have been Arabized and Islamized, and would constitute today an integral part of the Moslem Middle East.

Despite these setbacks, the fact remains that what had started out as a simple desert religion had grown in little more than one century into a great Eurasian empire. By 750 Islam ruled over the vast territories stretching from the Pyrenees to Sind, and from Morocco to the frontiers of China. (See Map XIII, "Expansion of Islam to 1500.")

IV. ARAB KINGDOM TO ISLAMIC EMPIRE

With the phase of expansion completed, the Arabs now settled down to enjoy the fruits of victory. They were virtually an army of occupation in their subject lands, residing mostly in the strategically located camp cities whence they controlled the surrounding countryside. Since Caliph Omar had decided at the outset that his followers should not be allotted fiefs in the conquered provinces, they now were supported by government pensions. The funds for these pensions were derived from lands confiscated by the Islamic state and from taxes which were levied at a higher rate upon non-Moslems than upon Moslems. Apart from this discriminatory taxation, the non-Moslems were left virtually undisturbed. No effort was made to convert them; indeed conversion was not at all welcomed for it involved under the circumstances a decline in revenue. Thus Islam was in effect a perquisite of the Arab warrior-aristocracy that ruled over the much more numerous subject peoples.

This arrangement was soon disturbed by the appearance in increasing numbers of the *Mawali,* or non-Arab Moslems. These converts flocked to the cities where they served the needs of the Arab aristocracy as servants, artisans, shop-keepers, and merchants. Being Moslems they claimed equality with the Arabs but this was not conceded. As the empire expanded and wealth poured into the cities from the subject provinces, the *Mawali* increased in numbers and wealth. But they remained excluded from the ruling circles, so they became a disaffected urban element, determined to gain status commensurate with their economic power. Thus the Arab Umayyad dynasty of caliphs, which had moved the capital from Medina to Damascus in 661, came to be regarded with much justification as a parasitic clique that had outlived its usefulness once the conquests were completed. The opposition to the Arab aristocracy, therefore, was both a national and a social movement of protest.

A disputed accession to the throne precipitated a decade of civil strife culminating in the accession of the Abbasid caliphate in 750. This represented much more than a mere change of dynasty. The *Mawali,* and particularly the Persians, now replaced the old redundant aristocracy. The Arabs no longer were a privileged salaried soldiery, being replaced by a royal standing army that was at first largely Persian. The former garrison cities became great commercial centers under *Mawali* control. Some of the Arabs became absorbed into the mass of towns-people and peasants, while others reverted to nomadism.

The imperial structure also changed radically, especially with the shift of the capital from Damascus eastward to Baghdad in 762. In effect this meant that the Abbasid caliphate was turning its back on the Mediterranean and looking to Persia for traditions and support. The caliph no longer was an Arab sheikh but a divinely ordained autocrat—the "Shadow of God upon Earth." His authority rested not on tribal support but on a salaried bureaucracy and standing army. Thus the caliphate became an oriental monarchy similar to the many that had preceded it in Ctesiphon and Persepolis and Babylon. Under the order and security imposed by this monarchy, a syncretic civilization that was an amalgam of Judaic, Greco-Roman, and Perso-Mesopotamian traditions, evolved during the ensuing centuries. Islam ceased to be merely the code of a ruling warrior-aristocracy and became instead a new and distinctive civilization.

V. ISLAMIC CIVILIZATION

Within a century after Caliph Mansur had selected Baghdad as the Abbasid capital, it numbered about a million people. In the center was a citadel some two miles in diameter in which were the caliph's residence and the quarters of his officials and guards. Beyond the citadel walls a great commercial metropolis sprang up, supported by the plentiful produce of the fertile Mesopotamian valley. The main crops were wheat, barley, rice, dates, and olives. The Abbasids increased the output when they extended the area of cultivated land by draining swamps and by enlarging the irrigation works. They also were less extortionist than the previous rulers in their tax and labor levies on the peasants, though this improvement was soon nullified by the speculations of wealthy merchants and landowners and by the introduction of slave labor on the large estates.

The provinces contributed rich supplies of metals—silver from the Hindu Kush, gold from Nubia and the Sudan, copper from Isfahan, and iron from Persia, Central Asia, and Sicily. Industry also flourished, textiles being the most important in the number of workers employed and the value of the output. Linen, cotton, and silk goods were produced in many parts of the empire, both for local consumption and for export. Carpets also were made almost everywhere, those of Tabaristan and Armenia being considered the best. The art of papermaking, learned from Chinese prisoners taken at Talas in 751, spread rapidly across the Islamic world, reaching Spain by 900. Other industries included pottery, metalwork, soap, and perfumes. Such a rich economy, extended across the breadth of the far-flung Abbasid Empire, stimulated interregional trade on an unprecedented scale. Moslem merchants, as noted in the preceding chapter, traded overland through Central Asia, and overseas with India, Ceylon, Southeast Asia, China, and Africa.

With this solid economic base, the Abbasid caliphs were able to indulge themselves in their dazzlingly luxurious palaces. The *Thousand and One Nights* portrays Harun al-Rashid (786–809), the best known of these caliphs, as a gay and cultured ruler, surrounded by a galaxy of poets, musicians, singers, dancers, scholars, and wits. Among the popular indoor games were chess, dice, and backgammon, while outdoor sports included hunting, falconry, hawking, polo, archery, fencing, javelin throwing, and horse racing. Harun was contemporary with Charlemagne, but their respective capitals, Baghdad and Aix-la-Chapelle, were quite incomparable—as incomparable as Baghdad and Paris today, but in the reverse sense.

The Abbasid caliphate was noted not only for its affluence and splendor but also for its relative toleration in religious matters in an age when this quality was markedly absent in the West. The explanation is to be found partly in the religious law of Islam. The sacred law recognized the Christians and Jews as being, like the Moslems, People of the Book. Both had a scripture—a written word of revelation. Their faith was accepted as true, though incomplete, since Mohammed had superseded Moses and Jesus Christ. Islam therefore tolerated the Christians and Jews. It permitted them to practice their faith, though subject to discriminatory taxation and to certain restrictions concerning clothes, churches, and the like. Despite this, their position was clearly superior to that of comparable dissenters in the West. They could practice their faith, enjoy normal property rights, and belong to craft guilds. They were often appointed to high state office, and were spared the martyrdom or exile endured, for example, by Jews and Moslems in Spain following the Christian conquest.

The Abbasid caliphate also was noteworthy for its achievements in the field of science. It is true that the tendency here was to preserve and to pass on rather than to create something new. One of their greatest scientists, al-Biruni (973–1048), stated, "We ought to confine ourselves to what the Ancients have dealt with and to perfect what can be perfected."[1] Nevertheless the sheer size of the empire, its contacts with literally all regions of Eurasia, and its almost overpoweringly rich legacy from the several great centers of civilization that it encompassed all contributed to the very real achievements of Islamic science. Baghdad, for example, boasted a "House of Wisdom" consisting of a school of translators, a library, an observatory, and an academy. The scholars associated with it translated and studied the works of Greek scientists and philosophers, as well as scientific treatises from Persia and India.

In astronomy the Moslems generally accepted the basic tenets of their Greek predecessors and made no significant advances in theory. But they did continue without interruption the astronomical observations of the ancients, so that the later Renaissance astronomers had available some nine hundred years of records which provided the basis for their crucial discoveries. Mathematics was of great interest to Moslems because it was needed both in astronomy and in commerce.

Thanks to Babylonian and Indian influence they made important advances, especially in popularizing the Hindu system of numbers based on the decimal notation. (See Chapter 9, section V.) Misleadingly called Arabic numerals, this system did for arithmetic what the discovery of the alphabet had done earlier for writing. It democratized mathematics, making it available for everyday use by nonspecialists.

In geography, as in astronomy, the Moslems made little theoretical progress, but the extent of their empire and of their commerce enabled them to accumulate reliable and systematic data concerning the Eurasian land mass. The Moslems also prepared charts and maps in which they naturally located Mecca in the center, as the contemporary Christian cartographers did for Jerusalem. Islamic medicine was based on that of the Greeks, but the greater geographical spread of Islam made possible a knowledge of new diseases and drugs. Moslems established the first apothecary shops and dispensaries, founded the first medieval school of pharmacy, required state examination and certification for the practice of medicine, and operated well-equipped hospitals, of which some thirty are known. The great Islamic doctors, such as Muhammad al-Razi (844–926) and Abu Ali al-Husein ibn Sina (980–1037), famous in Europe as "Rhazes" and "Avicenna," were brilliant men of wide knowledge ranging from astronomy through botany to chemistry, and wrote texts that were used in European medical schools until the seventeenth century.

Even more significant for the general advance of science were the Moslem contributions in chemistry. To the traditions and practices of the Babylonians, Egyptians, and Greeks, they added the extensive chemical knowledge of the Indians and Chinese. They expended much talent and energy in the quest for the two ancient will-o'-the-wisps: the philosopher's stone for transforming base metals into precious ones, and the elixir for prolonging life indefinitely. Yet their treatises show that they were the first to evolve sophisticated laboratory techniques for handling drugs, salts, and precious metals. Thus they were able to develop localized chemical industries for the production of soda, alum, iron sulphate, nitrates, and other salts for industrial purposes, especially in textiles.

The highest achievement of the Arabs in their own estimation was their poetry. In pre-Islamic times it had a public and social function, with the poet often serving as a eulogist or a satirist. The main themes were war, valor, love, praise of a patron, abuse of an enemy, and glorification of one's tribe or camel or horse. Under the Abbasids, Arabic poetry was enriched by the contributions of many non-Arabs, especially Persians. But there was no borrowing from Greco-Roman literature, which explains why Arabic literature remained strange and unknown to the West. Moslem scientists became familiar to Westerners, but not Moslem poets. Yet to the present day the Arabs find much pleasure and inspiration in their poetry with its intoxicating verbal effect and the hypnotic power of its monotonous rhyming.

In addition to their own original achievements, the Moslems made an invaluable contribution in translating and transmitting ancient works. The Umayyad caliphs had distrusted all non-Arabs and were uninterested in their civilizations. The Abbasids, by contrast, had been strongly supported by Christians, Jews, and Zoroastrian Persians, and were much more tolerant and broad-minded. The "House of Wisdom" in Baghdad included a large staff of translators, one of the outstanding ones being a Christian, Hunain ibn-Ishaq (809–873). He visited Greek-speaking lands to collect manuscripts, and with his assistants he translated a large number of them, including works of Hippocrates, Galen, Euclid, Ptolemy,

Plato, and Aristotle. Another great translation center was in the city of Toledo in Moslem Spain, where the translators during the twelfth and thirteenth centuries included Jews, Spaniards, and foreign scholars from all over Europe. This activity was of utmost significance, for Western Europeans had lost direct acquaintance with Greek learning and for long were unaware even of its existence. Thus Moslem scholarship preserved the Greek works until Western Europe was ready once more to resume their study.

In conclusion it should be emphasized that two basic bonds held together the diverse peoples of the sprawling caliphate: the Arabic language and the Islamic religion. Much more remarkable than the Arab conquests was the diffusion of the Arabic language. By the eleventh century Arabic had superseded the old Greek, Latin, Coptic, and Aramaic languages and prevailed from Morocco to Persia, as it does to the present day. This common language explains the feeling of common identity prevailing in this region, even though it includes Negroid Sudanese as well as the prevailing Semites, and Christian Lebanese and Coptic Egyptians as well as the prevailing Moslems. Even beyond this vast area that was permanently Arabized, Arabic exerted a profound influence on other Moslem languages. Arabic words are as common in these other languages as Greek and Latin words in English, and some of these languages (Urdu, Malay, Swahili, and Turkish until World War I) are written in Arabic script.

The Islamic religion also is a powerful bond—much more powerful than Christianity in this respect because it is not only a religion but also a social and political system and a general way of life. (See section II of this chapter.) Religion thus provides the basis for Islamic civilization as language does for the Arabic world. We have seen that the Islamic civilization evolved during the centuries following the conquests as a fusion of Christian, Jewish, Zoroastrian, and Arab religious elements, and Greco-Roman and Perso-Mesopotamian administrative, cultural, and scientific elements. The end product was not a mere mosaic or agglomeration of previous cultures, but rather a fusion that represented a new and original civilization. It was diverse in its origins and strands, yet uniquely molded by the distinctive imprint of Arabic Islam.

VI. DECLINE OF THE CALIPHATE

The Abbasid caliphate reached its height during the reign of Harun al-Rashid, and thereafter declined under circumstances reminiscent of the collapse of the Roman Empire. There was first the matter of sheer size—a very real problem in an age when communications were dependent on horse and sail. The outlying provinces were three thousand miles distant from the capital, so that it is not surprising that they should be the first to break away: Spain in 756, Morocco in 788, and Tunisia in 800.

Also, as in the case of Rome, there was the problem of imperial expenditures that were excessive and insupportable in relation to the prevailing economy and technology. The rampant luxury of the Baghdad court and the overweight of the inflated bureaucracy were not counterbalanced by technological progress. The resulting financial crisis forced the caliphs to appoint provincial governors as tax farmers in the areas they administered. With the revenues they collected, these governors maintained the local soldiery and officials, and remitted an agreed sum to the central treasury. This arrangement left the governors-farmers the real rulers of the provinces, together with the army commanders with whom they soon reached working agreements. By the mid-ninth century the caliphs were losing both military and administrative control, and were being appointed and deposed at will by Turkish mercenaries. The thirteenth-century Moslem historian al-Bundari describes clearly this transition from centralized empire to feudal autonomy:

It had been the custom to collect money from the country and pay it to the troops and no one had previously had a fief. Nazim al-Mulk [eleventh-century official] saw that the money was not coming in from the country on account of its disturbed state and that the yield was uncertain because of its disorder. Therefore he divided it among the troops in fiefs, assigning to them both the yield and the revenue. Their interest in its development increased greatly and it returned rapidly to a flourishing state.[2]

Imperial weakness, as usual, invited barbarian attacks. Just as the Roman Empire had been invaded across the Rhine and the Danube, so the caliphate now was assaulted from the north, south, and east. From the north came the Crusaders who overran Spain, Sicily, and Syria, aided by Moslem discord in all three areas. In Sicily the end of the local dynasty in 1040 was followed by civil war, which facilitated the invasion of the island by the Normans from southern Italy. By 1091 the whole of Sicily had been conquered and the mixed Christian-Moslem population came under the rule of Norman kings.

Likewise in Spain the Umayyad dynasty was deposed in 1031 and the country was split up into numerous petty states ruled by "parties" or factions reflecting diverse ethnic groups. These included the Arabs, the Berbers, the indigenous pre-Moslem Iberian stock, and the "Slavs," or European slaves. The latter, mostly from Central and Eastern Europe, had been employed as mercenary soldiers by the Umayyads as the Turks were by the Abbasids, and like them had come to dominate their masters. This fragmentation of Moslem Spain enabled the Christian states of the north to expand southward. By 1085 they captured the important city of Toledo, and by the end of the thirteenth century only Granada on the southern tip of the peninsula was left to the Moslems.

The loss of Sicily and Spain to Christendom proved permanent, but such was not the case with Syria. Here also the fratricidal warring of several Moslem states enabled the Crusaders from 1096 onward to advance rapidly down the coast of Syria into Palestine. They established four states, Edessa (1098), Antioch (1098), Jerusalem (1099), and Tripoli (1109), all organized along western feudal lines. But these states lacked roots, never assimilating their Moslem Arab subjects. Their existence depended on the sporadic arrival of recruits from Europe. Also they were all confined to the coastal areas and hence vulnerable to resistance movements organized in the interior. These states could exist only so long as the surrounding Moslem world remained divided. The disunity was ended by Salah ad-Din, better known in the West as Saladin. By uniting Moslem Syria and Egypt he surrounded the Crusader principalities and began the counterattack in 1187. By the time of his death in 1193 he had recaptured Jerusalem and expelled the westerners from all but a narrow coastal strip. During the following century this also was overrun and the Moslem reconquest was completed.

In addition to these Crusader onslaughts from the north, the caliphate was attacked by Berbers from southern Morocco and the Senegal-Niger area, and by the two Arab Bedouin tribes of Hilal and Sulaim from Upper Egypt. These tribes swept across Libya and Tunisia, wreaking havoc and devastation. It was this invasion rather than the earlier seventh-century Arab irruption that gutted civilization in North Africa. The famous fourteenth-century Arab historian Ibn Khaldun, himself a native of North Africa, noted the ruination of his homeland as follows:

In Tunisia and the West, since the Hilal and Sulaim tribes passed that way at the beginning of the fifth century [the middle of the eleventh century A.D.] and devastated these countries, for three hundred and fifty years all the plains were ruined; whereas formerly from the Sudan to the Mediterranean all was cultivated, as is proved by the traces remaining there of monuments, buildings, farms and villages.[3]

Finally the third group of invaders were the Turks and Mongols from the East. Their incursions, persisting through several centuries and encompassing virtually the entire Eurasian land mass, constitute a major chapter of world history. The Turco-Mongol invasions are comparable to the Arab-Islamic conquests in scope and impact. Indeed the two are intimately related, for many of the Turco-Mongols were converted to Islam, and they then extended the frontiers of their faith into distant new regions. The course and significance of these Turco-Mongol invasions is the subject of the following chapter.

SUGGESTED READING

T. Arnold and A. Guillaume, eds., *The Legacy of Islam* (Clarendon, 1931); F. Gabrieli, *Muhammad and the Conquests of Islam* (World Univ. Library, 1968); H. A. R. Gibb, *Mohammedanism: An Historical Survey* (Home Univ. Library, 1953); P. K. Hitti, *History of the Arabs from the Earliest Times to the Present*, 5th ed. (St. Martin's, 1951); R. A. Nicholson, *A Literary History of the Arabs* (Cambridge Univ., 1969).

chapter fourteen

Turco-Mongol Invasions

*Nay, it is unlikely that mankind will see the like of this calamity,
until the world comes to an end and perishes, except the final
outbreak of Gog and Magog. For even Antichrist will spare such as
follow him, though he destroy those who oppose him; but these
[Tartars] spared none, slaying women and men and children, ripping
open pregnant women and killing unborn babes.—Ibn Al-Athir
(Moslem historian, 1160–1233)*

By all odds the most visible and spectacular development during the half millennium from 1000 to 1500 was the great swarming of Turco-Mongol peoples from the vast racial hive of Central Asia. These nomads overran literally the whole of Eurasia except for its distant extremities: Japan, Southeast Asia, southern India and Western Europe.

Three stages are discernible in the course of the nomadic expansion during these centuries. The first, between 1000 and 1200, marked the emergence of the Turks, first as mercenaries and then as masters of the Abbasid caliphate. They infused vigor and aggressiveness into the now moribund world of Islam, and extended its frontiers into Asia Minor at the expense of Byzantium and into northern India at the expense of Hindustan. The second stage, during the thirteenth century, witnessed the Mongol irruption which engulfed not only Central Asia, East Asia, and Russia, but also the Moslem Middle East, thereby halting abruptly the expansionism of the Moslem Turks. The final stage, between 1300 and 1500, involved the disintegration of the Mongol Empire, which cleared the way for the resurgence of the Turks and the resumption of the Turkish-Islamic advance into Christian Europe and Hindustan.

This chapter will consider each of these stages in turn, and their implications for general world history.

I. TURKISH PREDOMINANCE IN THE ISLAMIC WORLD

The Turks are a linguistic rather than an ethnic group, their common bond being that they all speak one form or another of a Turkish family of languages. Although an ethnically mixed people, they are generally Caucasoid in appearance rather than Mongoloid. By the mid-sixth century they dominated the extensive steppe lands from Mongolia to the Oxus, or Amu Darya. From the eighth century onward they came increasingly under Islamic influence as a result of the Arab conquest of Persia and defeat of the Chinese at Talas (751).

The response of the Turkish tribesmen to the brilliant Abbasid caliphate across the Oxus River was very similar to that of the Germans to the Roman Empire across the Rhine. First there was the cultural impact as the primitive Turkish pagans succumbed to the teachings of Islam and to the material allurements of a sophisticated civilization. At the same time the tribesmen were entering the military service of the caliphate, as the Germans earlier had entered that of Rome. As mounted bowmen of great mobility, they soon demonstrated their superior military qualities and increasingly replaced the Arabs and Persians in the caliph's armed forces.

As the caliphs became weaker, the Turkish mercenaries, like their German counterparts, became masters rather than servants. They made and unmade rulers in Baghdad, holding successive caliphs in tutelage. About 970 a branch of the Turkish people known as the Seljuks were crossing over unhindered into Moslem territory and soon had gathered power into their hands. This was formally recognized in 1055 when the caliph proclaimed the Seljuk leader, Tughril Beg, the "sultan," or "he who has authority." Although the caliphs remained the nominal heads of the empire, the *de facto* rulers henceforth were the Turkish sultans. Under their aggressive leadership, the frontiers of Islam now were further extended into two regions.

One was Asia Minor, which had remained for centuries a bastion of Christian Byzantine power against repeated onslaughts by Arabic Islam. But in 1071 the Seljuks won a crushing victory at Manzikert in eastern Asia Minor, taking prisoner the Byzantine Emperor Romanus IV. This proved to be a decisive turning point in Middle Eastern history, for the battle was followed by civil war between rival Byzantine factions. In fact, this factionalism had been largely responsible for the defeat at Manzikert, and its continuation now enabled Turkish tribesmen to pour unopposed into Asia Minor. The quarreling Byzantine bureaucrats and generals, bidding against each other for the services of the Turkish tribal chieftains, handed over many towns and forts to the invaders. Furthermore the peasantry, alienated by the corruption and exploitation of Byzantine officials, accepted their new masters with passivity, if not relief. Thus between the eleventh and the thirteenth centuries the larger part of Asia Minor was transformed from a Greek and Christian to a Turkish and Moslem region, and it remains so to the present day. Furthermore Byzantium was gutted by this loss of Asia Minor, a province that hitherto had provided the bulk of the imperial revenue and army manpower. Constantinople now was like a huge head atop a shrivelled body. The roots of the fall of Constantinople in 1453 go back to 1071.

For the Seljuks, the victory at Manzikert was a giant step forward in their reconstitution of the moribund caliphate. Under Malik Shah (1073–1092) the Seljuk sultans reached their height, ruling Syria, Mesopotamia, and Iran, as well as Asia Minor. A brilliant cultural renaissance occurred under their aegis, with Persian language, literature, and art in the ascendancy. But Seljuk predominance proved short-lived. The empire disintegrated after Malik because of rivalry amongst his heirs and because of the granting of fiefs that became hereditary. (See Chapter 13, section VI.) This imperial disintegration made it possible for the Crusaders to conquer the Holy Land in the twelfth century. Another result was the emergence in western Asia Minor of the Ottoman Turks, who were destined to carry the banners of Islam to the walls of Vienna and to dominate the entire Middle East until the twentieth century.

While the Seljuks had been pushing westward in search of fame and booty, other Turks had been similarly engaged in the east, fighting their way towards the vast treasure house of India. Outstanding was a certain Mahmud (997–1030), who, from his base at Ghazni in Afghanistan, raided the Indian lands almost annually and finally annexed the Punjab, which has ever since remained Moslem. Mahmud's zeal in destroying Hindu temples and smashing their idols, a zeal that was based on the Islamic tenet that any visible representation of the deity was sinful, earned him the epithet "the image breaker." The successors of Mahmud were replaced in the twelfth century by another Turkish dynasty based in Ghor, also in Afghanistan. Under a certain Mohammed, the Ghori Turks advanced southward to Gujarat and eastward into the Ganges Valley. They captured Delhi in 1192 and made it the capital of the Turkish sultanate in India. During this campaign, Buddhist monasteries were destroyed and Buddhist monks were slaughtered on such a scale that Buddhism never recovered in its place of origin.

The relative ease with which the Turks ensconced themselves in a land in which they were hopelessly outnumbered is to be explained partly by the archaic Indian military tactics, which were the same as those that had proven inadequate against Alexander fifteen hundred years earlier. The infantry were usually an undisciplined rabble, while their vaunted elephants were useless against the Moslem cavalry. Equally damaging, and a more fundamental weakness, was the Hindu caste system, which left the fighting to only the Kshatriya, or warrior caste. The rest of the population was untrained and largely indifferent, particularly because class differentiation separating oppressive landlords from their peasants was added to caste fragmentation. Thus the masses either remained indifferent or else welcomed the invader and embraced his faith. This response was to be repeated frequently in the future and explains why in modern times the British Raj was able to rule from Delhi as Turkish Sultans had before.

II. GENGHIS KHAN

While the Turks were becoming the masters of the Moslem world, an obscure chieftain in far-off Mongolia was beginning his career of conquest that was to culminate in the greatest empire of history. Genghis Khan (spelled also Chinggis, Chingis, Jenghiz, etc.), whose personal name was Temujin, was born about 1167, the son of a minor clan leader. When Temujin was twelve years old his father was poisoned and as a result the future Khan spent a childhood of misery. He was able to overcome these humble beginnings by mastering the complicated art of tribal politics, which called for a creative mixture of loyalty, cunning, and ruthless treachery, as well as physical prowess. After turning against his overlord and eliminating various rivals he finally was able to weld the various Mongol-speaking tribes into a single unit. At a *kuriltai,* or assembly of Mongol chieftains, held in 1206 he was proclaimed supreme head of his people with the title Genghis Khan, signifying "ruler of the universe."

He was now in a position to satisfy his natural nomadic impulse for conquest and booty. In this respect Genghis Khan was no different from the long line of steppe conquerors who had gone before him. Why then was he alone destined to become the master of the greater part of Eurasia? This question is particularly intriguing because, as a Mongol, Genghis Khan did not have the manpower resources of other nomad conquerors, who were almost invariably Turks. All the Mongol tribes together numbered about one million men, women, and children, which afforded Genghis Khan a maximum of 125,000 warriors. With such limited resources, how was he able to come so close to becoming literally the "ruler of the universe"?

Genghis Khan began with the built-in advantage enjoyed by all nomad warriors—the fact that their daily life was a continuous rehearsal of campaign operations. Clad in leather and furs, leading extra horses as remounts, and capable of riding several days and nights in succession with a minimum of rest and food, these warriors introduced *blitzkrieg* into the world of the thirteenth century. Normally they lived off the countryside, but if necessary they drank the blood of their horses and the milk of their mares. Their skills in the hunt, acquired from boyhood, enabled them to coordinate the operations of flying horse columns over long distances. Their favorite tactic was feigned flight, during which the enemy might pursue the fleeing Mongols for days, only to be lured to ambush and destruction. Other tactical maneuvers included the tying of branches to the tails of horses to stir up dust in order to give the impression of large forces on the march, and also the mounting of dummies on spare horses for the same purpose.

The basic Mongol weapon was the compound large bow, more powerful than the English longbow, and capable of killing at 600 feet with its armor-piercing arrows. This was a fearful weapon in the hands of Mongol horsemen who were able to shoot their supply of thirty arrows at full gallop. Other equipment included a steel helmet, light body armor made of hide, a saber, and sometimes a lance with a hook and a mace. The Mongol horses grazed only on the open range, with no shelter during the long bitter winter and no hay or grain for supplementary feed. This made them somewhat stunted in size but very tough and adaptable. To these traditional nomad techniques Genghis Khan added new skills and equipment learned mostly from the Chinese. These included powerful catapults, battering-rams, and sappers who tunnelled under walls and blew them up with gunpowder. Thus Genghis Khan supplemented his incomparable mounted bowmen with the siege weapons necessary for capturing fortified cities.

The Mongols were also masters of espionage and psychological warfare. Before undertaking a campaign they collected all possible intelligence regarding the enemy's roads, rivers, fortifications, and political and economic conditions. They also used agents to spread demoralizing stories about the size of the Mongol forces and the futility of resistance. In the course of the campaigning they used ruthless terror tactics to undermine enemy morale. Prisoners of war were forced to lead the assault against their own people, and entire populations were put to the sword when any resistance was offered.

Finally Genghis Khan's grand strategy was unique in that he was careful to overcome his nomadic neighbors before assaulting the great empires. He was familiar with the traditional Chinese strategy of divide and rule, or as they put it, "Use barbarians to control barbarians." Thus many nomad chieftains in the past had been destroyed by simultaneous attacks by imperial armies and rival tribesmen. Genghis Khan's strategy, therefore, was first to unite "all the people of the felt-walled tents."

III. EARLY CONQUESTS

Even with his military genius and superb fighting machine, Genghis Khan would not have been able to become a world conqueror had he not appeared at the right historical moment. A strong and united China, such as had existed under the Han and the T'ang, could have stopped him with ease, as could also the Moslem

Arabs at the height of their power. But the Eurasian balance of power was quite different in the early thirteenth century. China was divided then into three fragments, with the Chin dynasty ruling the north, the Sung the south, and the Tibetan Tanguts ensconced in the northwest with their kingdom of Hsi Hsia. To the west was the state of Kara-Khitai based on oasis cities such as Bokhara and Samarkand. Beyond that, on the Oxus River, was the Moslem kingdom of Khorezm, and still further west the Abbasid caliphate at Baghdad, both far past their prime.

Genghis Khan first subjugated the Hsi Hsia state between 1205 and 1209, and forced it to a tributary status. In 1211 he attacked North China, first overrunning the region north of the Great Wall and then in 1213 piercing the Wall and penetrating to the Yellow River plain. By 1215 he had captured and pillaged Peking and also gained the services of Chinese who knew how to besiege cities and others who knew how to administer and exploit agricultural societies. In accordance with his overall strategy, Genghis Khan now turned to the surrounding nomadic territories. Manchuria fell in 1216, Korea in 1218, and Kara-Khitai in the following year.

These conquests brought him to the frontiers of Khorezm, which he overran in 1219–1221. Rich and ancient cities such as Bokhara, Samarkand, and Balkh were pillaged and their inhabitants massacred, with the exception of skilled artisans who were sent to Mongolia. The stricken ruler of Khorezm perished on a small island in the Caspian Sea where he had sought refuge, while his son fled eastward to India. Relentless Mongol detachments defeated him again on the banks of the upper Indus, but he escaped to Delhi where the Turkish sultan, aghast at the carnage, granted him asylum.

Not content with these spectacular triumphs in the Middle East and India, the Mongols swung north to the Caucasus where they defeated the Georgians. Advancing on to the Ukraine they crushed a numerically far superior army of 80,000 Russians in 1223. Meanwhile Genghis Khan had returnd to Mongolia to direct another victorious campaign against the Hsi Hsia kingdom, which had revolted against his rule. This proved to be his final exploit, for he died soon after in 1227.

IV. MONGOL EMPIRE

After a two-year interregnum, Genghis Khan's son, Ogodai, was selected as successor. During his reign from 1229 to 1241 the campaigning was resumed in the two extremities of Eurasia—China and Europe—some five thousand miles apart. In China the remnants of the Chin state in the north were liquidated by 1234 and then the Sung in the south were immediately attacked. They resisted stoutly, but the war which lasted forty-five years ended in their complete destruction. At the same time Genghis Khan's grandson, Batu, was sent with a force of 150,000 men to the European West. Crossing the middle Volga in the fall of 1237 he fell upon the principalities of central Russia. Town after town was captured, including the then comparatively unimportant Moscow. By March 1238 he was approaching Novgorod near the Baltic Sea, but he feared that the spring thaw would mire his horsemen in mud so he withdrew suddenly to the south.

Two years later, in the summer of 1240, the Mongols attacked southern Russia again, this time from their bases in the Caucasus. By December they had captured the ancient Russian capital of Kiev. Such was Mongol frightfulness that a contemporary monk recorded that the few survivors "envied the dead." The following year the Mongols pressed on into Poland and Hungary, defeated a German army of 30,000 at Liegnitz in Silesia, crossed the frozen Danube, captured Zagreb, and reached the Adriatic coast. Thus Mongol armies now were operating across the breadth of Eurasia from the Adriatic to the Sea of Japan. In the spring of 1242 came news of the death of Ogodai Khan in Mongolia, so Batu withdrew through the Balkans to the lower Volga Valley where he laid the foundations of the khanate known as the Golden Horde, a name derived from the golden tent of its khan.

Such was the impact of these strange horsemen from the east that in far-off St. Albans, near London, the monk Matthew Paris recorded in his Chronicle:

Swarming like locusts over the face of the earth, they have brought terrible devastation to the eastern parts of Europe laying it waste with fire and carnage. After having passed through the lands of the Saracens, they have razed cities, cut down forests, overthrown fortresses, pulled up vines, destroyed gardens, killed townspeople and peasants. For they are inhuman and beastly, rather monsters than men, thirsting for and drinking blood, tearing and devouring flesh of dogs and men, dressed in ox-hides, armed with plates of iron, short and stout, thickset, strong, invincible, indefatigable, their backs unprotected, their breast covered with armour; drinking with delight the pure blood of their flocks, with big, strong horses, which eat branches and even trees, and which they have to mount by the help of three steps on account of the shortness of their thighs. They wander about with their flocks and their wives, who are taught to fight like men. And so they came with the swiftness of lightning to the confines of Christendom, ravaging and slaughtering, striking everyone with terror and incomparable horror.[1]

Whether or not this dreadful scourge would return was the great question facing Europeans. It was answered by the course of Mongol politics. After Ogodai's death, five years elapsed before the election of his son, Guyuk, as his successor. Major expeditions were impossible during this period of uncertainty, as they were also during the short two-year reign of the alcoholic Guyuk. Another interregnum of three years now ensued, ending with the accession of a capable Genghis Khan grandson, Mangu (1251–1259), who sent his brothers Kublai and Hulagu to complete the conquest of South China and to take over the Abbasid caliphate of Baghdad. In their China campaigns the Mongols demonstrated once more their consummate skill in great strategic envelopment movements. In addition to pushing down the Yangtze and taking the Sung capital of Hangchow, Kublai outflanked the Sung from the west and south. In wide-ranging campaigns he overran Szechwan, Yunnan, Annam, and Tonking, thus surrounding the Sung kingdom on all sides. In 1277 he captured Canton, the great port in the south, and three years later the conquest was completed with the destruction of the Sung fleet off Hainan island. In the meantime Mangu had died in 1259 during the Szechwan operations, and Kublai had been selected his successor. Kublai, as the Great Khan, moved the Mongol capital from Karakorum in the homeland to Peking in North China. True to the original idea of world conquest formulated by Genghis Khan, Kublai after his victory over the Sung launched new campaigns on land against Indochina and Burma, and overseas against Java and Japan. Little wonder that Marco Polo wrote that Kublai Khan, whom he served for seventeen years, was "the most puissant of men, in subjects, land and treasure, that there is on earth or ever was, from the time of our first father Adam to this day."

Hulagu in the meantime had crossed the Oxus and rampaged through Persia, Mesopotamia, and Syria. When the Abbasid capital, Baghdad, fell in 1258, its 800,000 inhabitants are reported to have been massacred with the exception of a few artisans whose skills were prized. The hapless caliph was rolled up in a carpet and trampled to death by horses in order to avoid the shedding by the sword of royal blood, forbidden by Genghis Khan's injunctions. After the taking of Aleppo and Damascus in similar fashion, it appeared that nothing could prevent the Mongols from advancing on to Egypt and North Africa, thus completing the conquest of the entire Moslem world.

But now occurred an unexpected and fateful reversal at Ain Jalut (Goliath's Spring), Palestine, where in 1260 the Egyptian Mamlukes defeated the Mongols. One reason for the setback was that the death of Mangu Khan in 1259 had disrupted the unity of the Mongol ruling families. Hulagu supported the candidacy of his older brother Kublai for the vacant throne, but was opposed by his cousin Berke, head of the Golden Horde in Russia. In fact Berke, a convert to Islam, was so outraged by Hulagu's destruction of the caliphate that the two men were drifting towards open war. As a precautionary measure Hulagu had recrossed the Euphrates to Persia, leaving in Palestine a depleted force of mostly non-Mongol units. The defeat of this force saved Islam and marked the beginning of the end of the Mongol Empire.

V. MONGOL DECLINE

Despite the setback in Palestine, the Mongol Empire at that time was an extraordinarily impressive edifice, encompassing Russia, the Middle East, and South China, in addition to the original conquests of Genghis Khan. Mongol armies were active from the Baltic coast to Burma, while naval units were attacking Japan and Java. And yet this gigantic empire already was beginning to fall apart, and only a few decades later was to be virtually nonexistent.

The reason, of course, was not simply the defeat by the Mamlukes. Few Mongol units had been involved in that battle, and swift retribution could be expected, as had always happened before to the few opponents who had won individual engagements. But the pattern was not repeated this time, and the reason was the process of imperial disintegration already under way.

The disintegration was in part a function of sheer overextension. After reaching the extremities of Eurasia, even the Mongols, with their extraordinary mobility, found that they were bogging down. In addition to the defeat at Goliath's Spring, Mongol raids into India between 1285 and 1303 were repelled by the Turkish sultans of Delhi, and likewise in Burma and Vietnam the Mongols discovered that jungle fighting was altogether different from cavalry raids across the steppes. Mongol naval expeditions overseas proved equally ineffective. The fleet sent in 1291 against the Liuch'iu Islands failed even to find them. An expeditionary force sent to Java two years later was withdrawn after suffering heavy losses. The greatest overseas effort was made against Japan, where large expeditions were sent in 1274 and 1281. The Japanese fought with great bravery and finally were saved by a southwest typhoon which destroyed the enemy ships and which they gratefully dubbed the "divine wind," or *Kamikaze*. Thus the sea, like the jungle, set limits to Mongol expansionism.

It was not merely a case, however, of being unable to conquer the extremities of Eurasia and the offshore islands. It was much more serious, for the Mongols found they could not retain what they already had won. The basic difficulty was that they were too few in number and too primitive in relation to their subject peoples. The Mongols, as Pushkin put it, were "Arabs without Aristotle and algebra." This left them vulnerable to assimilation as soon as they dismounted from their horses and settled down to enjoy their conquests. In this respect they differed fundamentally from the Arabs who had both a language and a religion that their subjects were willing to adopt and that served as strong bonds for imperial unity. The Mongols, being less advanced than the Arabs, enjoyed no such advantage. Rather the opposite was the case with them, for they adopted the languages, religions, and cultures of their more advanced subjects and thereby lost their identity. This was the root reason why their empire dissolved so soon after its creation.

Indicative of the assimilation process was Kublai Khan's decision to move the Mongol capital from Karakorum to Peking. Inevitably he became a Chinese-style emperor, ruling from a palace of Chinese design, conducting elaborate Confucian ceremonies, and building new Confucian temples. As the Grand Khan, he was nominally the suzerain of all the Mongol khanates. Actually his authority did not extend beyond China. His brother, Arikboga, had contested his election as Grand Khan, and only after a four-year struggle had Kublai Khan prevailed. Then he was challenged by his cousin, Kaidu, who controlled Turkestan, and the ensuing forty-year civil war ended in stalemate. Thus the Mongol Empire was shattered by dynastic rivalries as well as by cultural assimilation.

While Kublai Khan was becoming a Chinese emperor, Hulagu was becoming a Persian ruler. With Tabriz as his capital he established the so-called Ilkhanate. (The term Ilkhan means "subject Khan," and was applied to the Mongol rulers of Persia as subordinates to the Grand Khan.) His successor's adoption of Islam in 1295 as the official religion both reflected and accelerated the Mongol's assimilation into their Iranian-Islamic milieu. Likewise the Golden Horde across the Caucasus went its own way, influenced by the native Christian Orthodox culture and by the official Islamic creed. Before long the only remaining pure Mongols were those in ancestral Mongolia where they came under the influence of Buddhism and sank into impotent obscurity.

VI. MOSLEM TURKISH RESURGENCE

Since the Mongols were so few in numbers, they had incorporated an ever increasing proportion of Turks into their armies. Then with the break-up of the empire these Moslem Turks quickly came to the fore, as they had earlier in the caliphate before the Mongol onslaught. A succession of military adventurers now rose and fell in the struggle for control of the Central Eurasion steppes. The most remarkable of these was Timur, known to Europe as Tamerlane. He seized Samarkand in 1369, and from there struck out in all directions. First he destroyed the Ilkhanate in Persia and Mesopotamia, then defeated the Golden Horde in Russia and the Ottoman Turks in Asia Minor, and he even invaded India and sacked Delhi. He was resolved to make his capital, Samarkand, the finest city in the world, and after each campaign he sent back caravans loaded with booty, together with craftsmen, artists, astrologers, and men of letters. At its height, his empire extended from the Mediterranean to China, and Timur was preparing to invade the latter country when he died in 1405. His empire then disintegrated even more rapidly than that of the Mongols.

After Timur, the outstanding development was the extension of Moslem Turkish power in India and in Byzantium. During the thirteenth century the Turkish sultans of Delhi, under the pressure of the Mongol threat, had confined themselves to consolidating their position in north India. In the fourteenth century, with the threat removed, they expanded two-thirds down the length of the peninsula to the Kistna River. Then in the aftermath of Timur's raid, north and central India were left a congeries of small Turkish-ruled states with none strong enough to revive the Delhi sultanate. Meanwhile the expansion of Islamic power over a large part of India had provoked a Hindu reaction in the form of the large Hindu state of Vijanagar, comprising the whole of India south of the Kistna River. Such was the fragmented state of the Indian peninsula when unity was imposed from without during the sixteenth century by another Moslem Turkish dynasty, the Mughal.

Meanwhile in the Middle East the frontiers of Islam were being extended at the expense of Byzantium by the Ottoman Turks. These newcomers from Central Asia had entered the Seljuk Empire in its decline and settled in the north-west corner of Asia Minor, less than fifty miles from the strategic straits separating Asia from Europe. In 1299 the leader of these Turks, Uthman, declared his independence from his Seljuk overlord, and from these humble beginnings grew the great Ottoman Empire, named after the obscure Uthman.

The first step was the conquest of the remaining Byzantine portion of Asia Minor. This was accomplished by 1340, thanks to the disaffection of the Christian peasantry and the plentiful supply of *ghazis,* or warriors of the faith, who flocked in from all parts of the Middle East to battle against the Christian infidels. Next the Turks crossed the straits, winning their first foothold in Europe by building a fort at Gallipoli in 1354. They hardly could have selected a more favorable moment for their advance into Europe. The Balkan Peninsula was divided by the strife of rival Christian churches and by the rivalries of the Byzantine, Serbian, and Bulgarian states, all past their prime. Also the Christian peasants of the Balkans were as disaffected as their counterparts in Asia Minor. And Western Christendom was too divided to go to the aid of the Balkans even if there was the will to do so, which was not the case because of the ancient antipathy between Catholic and Orthodox Christians. Thus the way was clear for the Ottoman Turks, and they took full advantage of the opportunity.

They surrounded Constantinople by taking Adrianople in 1362 and Sofia in 1384. Then they were diverted for some decades when their sultan was defeated and captured by Timur in 1402. But Timur was a flash in the pan, and his death, in 1405, left the Ottomans free to rebuild and to resume their advance. Finally in 1453 they took beleaguered Constantinople by assault, ending a thousand years of imperial history. Before the end of the century they were the masters of the entire Balkan Peninsula to the Danube River, with the exception of a few Venetian-held coastal fortresses. (For details, see Chapter 15, section IV.)

VII. SIGNIFICANCE OF TURCO-MONGOL INVASIONS

One result of the Turco-Mongol invasions between 1000 and 1500 was the emergence of a new Eurasian balance of power in which Islam was the central and decisive force. When the West began its overseas expansion in the late fifteenth century, Islam already was expanding overland in all directions. The Ottomans were crossing the Danube into Central Europe; Central Asia was completely won over with the exception of the eastern fringes; and the Mughals were about to begin their conquest of virtually the entire Indian peninsula. Furthermore, Islam was advancing far out onto the peripheries of the Eurasian ecumene. In Africa it was spreading steadily into the interior of the continent from two centers. From the North African coast it was carried across the Sahara to West Africa where a succession of large Negro Moslem kingdoms flourished. Likewise from the Arab colonies on the East African coast, Islam spread inward over lands that included the Christian kingdom of Nubia, which was conquered and converted.

Islam also was carried by Arab and Indian merchants to Southeast Asia. Here, as in Africa and other regions where the local peoples had not reached a high level of civilization, conversion was easy because of the simplicity and adaptability of the new faith. All one had to do to become a Moslem was to repeat the words, "I bear witness that there is no God but Allah and that Mohammed is the Messenger of Allah." Local practices and traditions usually were accepted and sanctified by the addition of Islamic ritual. Thus the faith was spread not by the sword, but by the unobtrusive work of traders who won over the populace by learning their language, adopting their customs, marrying their women, and converting their new relatives and business associates.

Marco Polo found many Moslems in Ferlec (present day Atjeh) when he visited there in 1292. "You must know that the people of Ferlec used all to be idolaters, but owing to contact with Saracen merchants, who continually resort here in their ships, they have all been converted to the law of Mahomet."[2] By the end of the fifteenth century, Islam had spread as far east as Mindanao in the Philippines. The Moslem state of Malacca played a key role in the diffusion of Islam because of its preeminence as a trade center, controlling all commerce through the straits. Not only did it draw traders from India and all Southeast Asia, but it also attracted religious teachers by offering opportunities to instruct wealthy patrons. Malacca's greatest achievement was the conversion of Java, signalled by the success of the Javanese Moslem princes in overthrowing the old Hindu kingdom of Majapahit. Considering Southeast Asia as a whole, the main Moslem centers, as might be expected, were those areas with the most active trade contacts: the Malay Peninsula and the Indonesian archipelago.

This diffusion of Islam throughout Eurasia during these five centuries almost tripled the territory of the Moslem faith, with important repercussions on the course of world history. The initial stage of Islamic expansion in the seventh and eighth centuries had made the Mediterranean a Moslem lake; this later stage of expansion made the entire Indian Ocean a Moslem lake. This meant that virtually all the goods reaching Europe from Asia now were carried along Moslem-controlled land or sea routes, especially after the Ilkhanate embraced Islam in 1295. Thus the several decades after 1240 during which the Mongol Empire permitted safe travel and trade across Eurasia proved to be but an interlude between earlier and later eras in which Arab-Turkish control of Central Asia and the Middle East constituted a barrier between China and the West. The continued expansion of the Moslem faith also served to make Islam by 1500 a world force rather than simply a Middle Eastern power. This has affected profoundly the course of world affairs to the present day. It explains why today the Indian peninsula is divided into two parts, why Moslem political parties are so influential in Southeast Asia, why Islam is a powerful and rapidly growing force in Africa, and why it is now the faith of one-seventh of the people of the world.

The Turco-Mongol invasions are significant also because of the cross-fertilization that they stimulated within Eurasia. In the technological field we have seen that *Pax Mongolica* was responsible for the transmission of a cluster of Chinese inventions, including gunpowder, silk, machinery, printing, and the blast furnace for cast iron. (See Chapter 12, section III.) Another example of cross-fertilization is the case of Ilkhanid Persia, which, by its location, was exposed to influences from both East and West. We know of Chinese artillerymen who reached Persia in the service of the Mongol armies; also of one Fu Meng-chi who propounded the principles of Chinese astronomy, of Chinese physicians at the Ilkhan's court, and the Chinese artists who left an indelible impression on Persian miniature painting. From the opposite direction, European influence was mostly in the field of trade and diplomacy. A colony of Italian merchants flourished in the capital of Tabriz, and from their numbers the Ilkhans recruited the ambassadors and interpreters for their various missions to Europe. And then there was, of course, Marco Polo, who escorted from China to Persia a Mongol princess to be the Ilkhan's bride, and then proceeded on to Venice.

Finally, the opportunities offered by this cross-fertilization were fully exploited only by the new civilization developing in Europe—a profoundly significant fact that was to mold the course of world history to the present day. All the other Eurasian civilizations proved too set in their ways. At first it appeared that the Islamic world would have no difficulties in adapting and changing. Despite the primitive background of Arabia from which it had emerged, Islam had proven itself remarkably adept and receptive in borrowing from the great established civilizations and creating something new and impressive. But this involved an inescapable built-in tension between the dogma of the Islamic faith and the rationalist philosophy and science of the Greeks. In the early years the Caliph al-Mamun (813–833) had generously supported the translation of the ancient classics and had espoused the rationalist doctrine that the Koran was created and not eternal. But his successors were quite different and gave their support to conservative theologians who rejected all scientific and philosophical speculation as leading to heresy and atheism.

This represented the triumph of scholasticism, in the sense that seeking God was deemed more important than understanding nature. Such scholasticism had prevailed also in the early medieval West following the barbarian invasions. The Papacy had then dominated the intellectual life of the age, and theology was the accepted queen of the sciences. The same development occurred now in the Islamic world following its series of barbarian invasions—Crusaders, Berbers, Bedouins, Seljuks, and Mongols. Here, as in the West, men turned to religion for succor and consolation in the face of material disaster. But whereas in the West scholasticism eventually was challenged and superseded, in the Moslem world it remained dominant through the nineteenth century.

In his *Incoherence of Philosophy,* the outstanding theologian of Islam, al-Ghazzali (1058–1111), strongly attacked the whole secular school. He argued that the ultimate source of truth is divine revelation and that the intellect should be used to destroy trust in itself. He was challenged by the famous Moslem Aristotelian philosopher ibn Rushd of Cordova, Spain, known in the West as Averroes (1126–1198). In his *Incoherence of the Incoherence,* he asserted that knowledge should be subject to the test of reason and that philosophy was not inimical to the Faith. But he was by no means a freethinker, maintaining that the masses, whose intelligence neither desired nor was capable of philosophical reasoning, should be educated "theologically." The educated classes, which he believed could be educated "philosophically," nevertheless rejected his position, accusing him of hypocrisy and suspecting him of atheism.

The extent of orthodox reaction is reflected in the work of the great historian and father of sociology, Ibn Khaldun (1332–1406). He was the first to view history not as the conventional annalistic and episodical writing of his time, but as the science of the origin and development of civilizations. And yet this erudite and creative thinker rejected philosophy and science as useless and dangerous: "It should be known that the opinion the philosophers hold is wrong in all its aspects. . . . The problems of physics are of no importance to us in our religious affairs or our livelihoods. Therefore we must leave them alone. . . . Whoever studies it [logic] should do so only after he is saturated with the religious law and has studied the interpretation of the Koran and jurisprudence. No one who has no knowledge of the Moslem religious sciences should apply himself to it. Without that knowledge, he can hardly be safe from its pernicious aspects."[3]

Thus intellectual growth and innovation in the Moslem world ceased, and at a time when Europe's universities were in full ferment, the Islamic *madrasas* were content with rote memorization of authoritative texts. Whereas the Moslem world had been far ahead of the West between 800 and 1200, by the sixteenth century the gap had disappeared, and thereafter it was the West that boomed ahead while Islam stood still and even retrogressed. The disparity between the two worlds has been well described as follows: "Islamic medicine and science reflected the light of the Hellenic sun, when its day had fled; and shone like a moon, illuminating the darkest night of the European Middle Ages; some bright stars lent their own light; but moon and stars alike faded at the dawn of a new day—the Renaissance."[4]

A similar disparity developed between the West and the other Eurasian civilizations, for the simple reason that only the West negotiated the fateful transition to modernism. Both India and Byzantium were conquered by Islam and enveloped in its stagnancy. China, reacting against the Mongols who were expelled in 1368, manifested a strong ethnocentrism—an almost instinctive hostility and scorn for all things alien and hence barbarian. Russia also succeeded in 1480 in throwing off the Mongol yoke, but permanent scars remained. The country had been closed to fresh winds from the West for two and a half centuries, and both Mongol ideas and usages had paved the way for the absolutism of the Muscovite state and of the Orthodox church.

The West alone was the exception to this general pattern. Only there occurred the great mutation—the emergence of modern civilization with a new technological base that quickly proved its superiority and diffused not only throughout Eurasia but the entire globe. This uniqueness of the West stems, as noted earlier (Chapter 11, section VI), from the shattering impact of the barbarian invasions, which plowed under the classical civilizations and allowed new concepts and institutions to take root and flourish. The following chapters will consider first the traditional Byzantine and Confucian civilizations that flanked the Islamic world on each side, and then will analyze the contrasting revolutionary civilization of the West.

SUGGESTED READING

C. CAHEN, *Pre-Ottoman Turkey* (Sidgwick, 1968); *The Cambridge History of Iran,* Vol. 5, *The Seljuk and Mongol Periods,* ed. J. A. BOYLE (Cambridge Univ. 1931): H. INALCIK, *The Ottoman Empire: The Classical Age 1300–1600* (Weidenfeld & Nicolson, 1972); E. D. PHILLIPS, *The Mongols* (Thames, 1969); T. T. RICE, *The Seljuks* (Thames, 1961); *The Mongols on the Eve of Europe's Expansion,* ed., J. J. SAUNDERS (Prentice-Hall, 1966) and his *The History of the Mongol Conquests* (Harper, 1972).

chapter fifteen

Traditional
Byzantine Civilization

*A thousand years of Byzantium produced extinction; a thousand years
of medieval effort [in the West] produced the Renaissance, the modern
state, and ultimately the free world.*—William Carroll Bark

Edward Gibbon's verdict on the thousand years of Byzantium's existence as "a uniform tale of weakness and misery" has long since given way to respect and appreciation for its manifold contributions to human civilization. Yet the precise manner and context in which Byzantium's history should be presented remain somewhat of a puzzle. Should this millennium be depicted as the epilogue to Roman history, or as the background for Slavic civilization, or as the prelude to the Ottoman Empire?

Each of these approaches is valid if Byzantine history is viewed from the perspective of one region or another. But if the angle of vision is global, as is the case in this volume, then Orthodox Byzantium falls into place naturally and obviously as one of the several traditional Eurasian civilizations that survived the barbarian invasions and continued without interruption from the Classical Age to modern times. (See Chapter 11, section VI.)

This unbroken sweep of history, however, eventually meant obsolescence and extinction, especially in the political sense. Because it was the most vulnerable, the Byzantine civilization was the first to suffer this fate. China, for example, faced nomadic invasions only from the northwest and was so far out of the way on the eastern tip of Eurasia that the aggressive West was not able to break in until the mid-nineteenth century. Byzantium, by contrast, faced not only a succession of barbarian invasions from across the Danube, which were comparable to those menacing China, but also endured the onslaught of the expanding West in the form of Venetian merchants and Norman knights, as well as the assault of a resurgent East embodied first in the Sassanian Persian irruption and then in the Moslem Arab and Turkish invasions. Thus, whereas the traditional Chinese civilization endured to 1912, the Byzantine collapsed first in 1204, then was partially revived in 1261, and survived in a palsied state until the death blow in 1453. (See Map XVIII, "Decline of the Byzantine Empire.")

I. EMERGENCE OF BYZANTIUM

No Western capital approaches the proud record of the Byzantine capital, Constantinople, in continuity and scope of imperial rule. It was already an old city when rebuilt by Constantine in A.D. 330 to be the New Rome. In the following centuries it stood impregnable before the barbarian assaults to which the first Rome eventually succumbed. For one thousand years Constantinople played its new role as the capital of Byzantium, until it fell to the Ottoman Turks in 1453. Then it became the capital of a new empire, and as the Ottoman warriors pressed their conquests, the dominion of Constantinople spread to new frontiers, reaching from Morocco to Persia, and from Vienna to the Indian Ocean. Constantinople presided over this vast region up to modern times, when the Ottoman Empire gave way to the Turkish Republic, and Kemal Ataturk moved his capital from the shores of the Bosphorus to the safety of the Anatolian plateau.

This remarkable history of Constantinople is due in large part to its commanding position on the Straits between Europe and Asia. This bestowed strategic as well as commercial strength to the capital. It is protected by two marine gates that can be closed to hostile ships from either the Aegean or Black seas. The Byzantine emperors supplemented these natural defenses with two great walls on the land side, the first 4 miles long, and the second, some 30 miles further west, 40 miles long and 20 feet wide. These double ramparts, together with the natural bulwark of the Balkan Mountains, protected the land approaches to Constantinople. Thus the city was able to hold out during the ten centuries of Byzantium, although it was a beleaguered fortress for much of this period.

The references to the Roman and Byzantine phases of Constantinople's history raise the question of when the first ended and the second began. It was not with the deposition of Romulus Augustulus in A.D. 476, for the tradition of imperial unity persisted for centuries more. The Eastern emperors continued to regard themselves as the heirs of the Caesars, even though Italy, Gaul, Britain, Spain, and North Africa had all been lost to the barbarians. The conservative, backward-looking Justinian (527–565) devoted himself to making this imperial myth a reality, but his efforts proved ephemeral and pyrrhic. (See Chapter 11, section IV.) His campaigns in the western Mediterranean left the imperial treasury depleted and the Balkan and Asiatic provinces neglected and vulnerable. Within a decade after his death a new barbarian tribe, the Lombards, had overrun most of Italy. Likewise on the Danube frontier, the Avars, with their Slav and Bulgar subjects, were penetrating into the Balkans, displacing the Latinized Illyrians and weakening imperial control. In the East the Persians, who had been bribed into peace during Justinian's reign, now set out under their ambitious King of Kings, Chosroes II, to eliminate altogether the East Roman Empire. By 615 they had overrun Syria, Palestine, and Egypt, and were encamped on the shores of the Bosphorus opposite Constantinople.

With the accession of the great Emperor Heraclius (610–614), Byzantium was able to mobilize the resources and the will necessary to avert impending disaster. Even though a joint Avar-Persian force was besieging Constantinople, Heraclius took the offensive and in 627 decisively defeated the Persians in the same locality in Mesopotamia where Alexander the Great also had defeated them one thousand years earlier. The following year the Persians were forced to sign a peace returning all their conquests.

Having disposed of the danger in the East, Heraclius now discovered that the Slavs in the meantime had occupied and sunk roots in large parts of the northern Balkans. Making a virtue of necessity, he assigned to them definite areas, in return for which they acknowledged his suzerainty and agreed to pay annual tribute. Thus the Slavic new-comers changed gradually from invaders into settlers. With the passing of a few centuries these widely scattered Balkan Slavs had developed along different lines and crystallized into four major groups: the Slovenes at the head of the Adriatic, the Croatians between the Drave River and the Adriatic, the Serbs in the central Balkans between the Adriatic and the Danube, and the Slavs, who shortly were to adopt the name of their Bulgarian conquerors, in the remaining territory to the Black Sea. The second two groups organized great though short-lived medieval kingdoms, which borrowed their culture from Byzantium. In contrast, the Slovenes and Croatians, because of their position in the western part of the peninsula, became subjects of the Holy Roman Empire and were influenced by Rome rather than Constantinople in their cultural development.

The struggle against the Avars and the Persians proved but a prelude to the greater and more fateful contest with the Moslem Arabs. As noted earlier in Chapter 13, section III, the warriors of Islam speedily overran most of the Middle East during the 630's and 640's. A millennium of Greco-Roman rule in Syria, Palestine, and Egypt was now ended within two decades, despite the desperate efforts of the aging Heraclius. Later in the century the very existence of the Byzantine Empire was threatened by the combination of Moslem sea raids and Bulgar land attacks. In a remarkable feat of adaptation the Arabs developed a naval power with which they conquered Cyprus and Rhodes, and then besieged Constantinople on several occasions, beginning in 669. At the same time Byzantium was threatened from the north by the Bulgars, an Asiatic people originally used by the Byzantines against the Avars. But now the Bulgars were occupying for themselves the territory between the Danube and the Balkan Mountains, and from this base threatened Constantinople.

Once more Byzantium was saved by inspired imperial leadership, this time in the person of Leo III the Isaurian (717–741). A military commander of Syrian origin, he seized power when Constantinople was under siege by the Arabs. He not only lifted the siege but drove the Arabs back out of Asia Minor. By the end of his reign the imperial frontiers were secure, but they were drastically shrunken frontiers compared to those of Justinian. Italy had been lost to the Lombards, the northern Balkans to the Slavs and the Bulgars, and Syria, Palestine, Egypt, and North Africa to the Arabs.

This reduced empire, however, was a more homogeneous empire, for the eastern provinces had been predominantly Monophysite and non-Greek. Under the circumstances Byzantium was strengthened rather than weakened by the withdrawal to the Taurus Mountains separating Greek Asia Minor from what was now becoming the heartland of the Islamic world. This demarcation was reinforced by internal convulsions within the Moslem world culminating in the accession of the Abbasid Caliphate (750), which moved the Islamic capital from Damascus to Baghdad. The orientation of Islam now was to the east rather than towards the Mediterranean, so that the Byzantine and Moslem empires were able to coexist peacefully until the appearance of the militant Turks in the eleventh century.

A demarcation similar to that between Byzantium and Islam was developing between Byzantium and the West. With the Lombard invasion the Roman

Popes had looked to Constantinople for protection, but to no avail because of Byzantine preoccupation with the Arabs. The Popes accordingly turned to the Franks, and the resulting partnership culminated in the famous Papal coronation of Charlemagne in 800. Constantinople reluctantly conceded to Charlemagne in 812 the title of *Basileus,* thereby recognizing the political entity of the West. During the following centuries Byzantium and the West drifted apart not only in politics but also in language, in ecclesiastical matters, and in general culture.

The emerging Byzantine Empire of the eighth century was much smaller than Justinian's short-lived creation, but it was also much more homogeneous. The diverse racial, cultural, and religious elements of the eastern and western provinces had been shed, and the remaining core was basically, though by no means exclusively, Greek. In this manner, then, the transition was completed from the East Roman Empire of the sixth century to the Byzantine Empire of the eighth—an empire with a culture clearly distinct from both that of Islam to the east and from that of the new Europe to the west.

II. BYZANTIUM'S GOLDEN AGE

The Byzantine Empire reached its apogee during the period between the early ninth and early eleventh centuries. Imperial administration was soundly based on the *themes,* or provinces, each headed by a *strategos,* or general, who was in charge of both civil and military affairs. This militarization of administration had been effected by Heraclius as a means of expediting action at a time of imminent foreign danger. Imperial lands in the *themes* were divided amongst the peasants in return for military service. Under strong emperors this *theme* arrangement assured effective administration, a reliable military reserve, and a well-filled treasury, since the peasants assumed much of the tax burden.

Byzantium's economy also was solidly founded on free peasant communities that functioned alongside the estates of the great landowners. In the urban centers that had survived since Greco-Roman classical times, craftsmen worked at a high level of competence. Arab writers described the quality of Byzantine handicrafts, especially the luxury products, as being equaled only by those of China. Equally important was the great volume of goods that passed through Constantinople from all regions of Eurasia—slaves and salt from the Black Sea lands, spices, perfumes, and precious stones from India, papyrus and foodstuffs from Egypt, silk and porcelain from China, and silver, wrought iron objects, and linen, cotton, and woolen fabrics from the West.

This political, economic, and military strength enabled the Byzantine emperors to launch reconquest campaigns that were more realistic if not as ambitious as those of Justinian. Crete and Cyprus were recovered, thereby curbing Arab naval raids in the Aegean waters. The imperial frontiers were extended also into northern Syria, Armenia, and Georgia. In the northern Balkans where the Bulgars were a constant threat to the empire, Basil II won such a crushing victory in 1014 that he was known thereafter as *Bulgaroktonus,* or "the Bulgar-Slayer."

In cultural matters this was a period of stability and homogeneity. The Byzantines still called themselves *Romaioi,* or Romans, but Greek, in either its literary or popular forms, was the universal language of the empire. Religious homogeneity also had been promoted with the loss of the dissident eastern provinces to Islam and with the resolution of the violent and protracted dispute between iconoclasts and iconodules—that is between breakers and worshippers of images. The compromise settlement barred religious sculpture but did allow paintings, which remain to the present day an important feature of Orthodox religious life.

The Byzantine church also demonstrated its vitality with the conversion of the Moslems on reconquered Crete, and of the Slavs in the northern Balkans. In 865 the Bulgarian Khan Boris accepted Christianity from Constantinople in return for imperial recognition of his conquests. In the following years Byzantine missionaries provided the Bulgarians with an alphabet, translated the Scriptures into their language, and prepared a Slavonic liturgy. About the same time the Serbian tribes also were converted to Orthodoxy, as were the Russians of the Kievan state. (See section VI of this chapter.) Further to the west, however, the Latin church prevailed among the Croatians and Slovenes, who followed in the wake of the neighboring Catholic Italians, Hungarians, and Germans. Imperial stability was enhanced also by the intimate, mutually supporting relationship between emperor and patriarch. The principle of a subservient state church was traditional and accepted, the emperor calling himself not only *autokrator* but also *isapostolos,* or the equal of the apostles.

In conclusion, Byzantium during these centuries was reminiscent of China under the Ming dynasty—stable, powerful, wealthy, self-satisfied, and rather inward looking now that a reasonable coexistence had evolved with both the Western and Moslem worlds.

III. BYZANTIUM'S DECLINE

When Basil, "the Bulgar-Slayer," died in 1025 the Byzantine Empire appeared unchallengeably secure in its splendid eminence. The northern frontier rested solidly on the Danube, Arabic Islam was divided and was no longer a threat, and whatever was emerging in the West was patently primitive and insignificant in comparison to the Second Rome on the Bosphorus. Yet within half a century after Basil's death the empire was in serious trouble, and less than two centuries later, in 1204, its capital had fallen to the despised barbarians of the West.

One reason for the dramatic reversal was the undermining of the imperial military system with the growing insubordination of the *strategoi,* or generals, in charge of the *themes,* or provinces. Basil II had been strong enough to keep the military in check, but his weak successors were unable to do so, especially when the *strategoi* joined forces with the great provincial landowners. Repeatedly the *strategoi* rebelled against civilian authority in Constantinople, using the peasant levies originally intended for frontier defense. In retaliation the bureaucrats disbanded the peasant levies, commuting the military service of the peasants to cash payments. The funds thus collected were used to hire mercenaries, including foreign Normans, Germans, Patzinaks, and Armenians. But in comparison with the former peasant forces, these mercenaries proved notoriously unreliable, often turning against the empire they ostensibly were defending when their pay was not forthcoming.

A closely related cause for imperial decline was the political problem of the feudalization of society. The *strategoi* and the local landowners accumulated vast estates, so that entire provinces fell under the domination of a few families. The emperors issued frequent orders against this trend, but to no avail, and for the simple reason that their implementation depended on the very class against which they were directed. After Basil II even these efforts largely ceased, and instead the emperors began to grant state properties in usufruct to those who had rendered valuable service. These grants, or *pronoia,* became associated with military service, and thus came to resemble the fiefs of the West, except for the absence of homage and subinfeudation. Indeed when the Latins conquered Byzantium in 1204 and divided it into fiefs, the Greek aristocracy recognized the fiefs as the Latin version of their own *pronoia.*

The empire was plagued also by serious economic ailments. The large private monastic estates reduced imperial revenues, especially when Basil's successors relieved the large landowners of most taxes. At the same time imperial expenditures were rising because of court extravagances and the cost of the mercenary army. Equally serious were the mounting raids of Patzinaks and Seljuk Turks, which left certain regions devastated and unproductive. The Byzantine gold *solidus,* which had remained stable for seven centuries, now suffered successive debasements.

In Byzantium, as in many other empires, internal weakness attracted external aggression. In the West were the Norman adventurers who originally had served as Byzantine mercenaries but who now turned against the weakened empire and overran its possessions in southern Italy that had survived since the time of Justinian's conquests. Likewise in the east were the Seljuk Turks who had infiltrated from their Central Asian homeland into the Islamic Empire where they were employed as mercenaries by the Baghdad caliphs. Gradually the mercenaries became masters, and in 1055 they captured Baghdad and founded the Seljuk Empire. These Turks reanimated the moribund Islamic world, reuniting the lands between India and the Mediterranean and pressing upon the Taurus Mountain frontier that for centuries had separated the Byzantine and Islamic worlds. (See Chapter 14, section I.)

This was the background of the two disasters that befell Byzantium in 1071, marking the beginning of centuries of decline. One occurred at Bari in southern Italy where the Normans conquered the sole surviving Byzantine foothold. The other, and much more decisive setback, was at Manzikert, where, as noted earlier, Turkish victory led to the gradual changing of Asia Minor from the bedrock of Greek Byzantine power to the heartland of the Turkish nation.

The Byzantine Empire was saved from what appeared to be imminent dissolution by the astuteness and tenacity of Emperor Alexius Comnenus (1081–1118). He granted valuable commercial concessions to the Venetians in return for their support against the Normans who were threatening to attack Constantinople. He also appealed to Western Christendom for assistance against the Moslem Seljuks. Instead of a limited number of mercenaries that he had hoped for, he was confronted by hordes of undisciplined Crusaders, led in part by the Normans that Alexius had excellent reason to distrust. This contact between two societies resulted in mutual suspicion and open hostility. Greeks and Latins disliked each other's languages, religions, politics, and ways of life.

Alexius adroitly encouraged the Crusaders to cross over to Asia Minor where, together with the Byzantines, they recovered some regions from the Seljuks. But relations between Greeks and Latins became increasingly strained during the Second and Third Crusades. Also the Byzantines suffered a disastrous setback when they rashly set out to attack the Seljuk capital of Konia in central Asia Minor. On the way they were crushed by the Turks at Myriocephalon (1176), a defeat that ended whatever possibility that might have remained for a Byzantine comeback in Asia Minor. Meanwhile the Venetians were undermining the economic foundations of Byzantium with the commercial privileges they had extracted from the hard-pressed emperors. They had complete freedom from tolls or duties throughout the empire, a concession that gave them a decisive advantage over Byzantine merchants who were subject to heavy taxes. Thus not only did the Italians get a stranglehold on the empire's trade, but the treasury at Constantinople was deprived of a prime source of revenue. The contrast between Venetian affluence and Byzantine poverty provoked riots in 1183 in which many Latins were killed and their properties looted.

Such was the background of the Fourth Crusade, appropriately nicknamed the "businessmen's crusade." The economic designs of Venetian merchants, the quest for loot and lands by Western adventurers, the blandishments of a Byzantine pretender, and the long pent-up grievances harbored by Latins against what they considered to be the cunning, effeminate, grasping, and heretical Greeks, all combined to deflect the Fourth Crusade from its original goal of liberating Jerusalem to an assault upon Constantinople. A mixed force of French, Venetians, Flemings, and Germans stormed the capital in the spring of 1204 and subjected it to three days of merciless looting and slaughter. "Even the Saracens," observed a Byzantine chronicler, "would have been more merciful." Paradoxically, the end result of the Fourth Crusade was to pave the way for Islamic domination of the entire Middle East. Although the Byzantine Empire was restored in 1261, it never recovered from the traumatic shock of the Latin conquest, and remained in helpless impotence until the Ottoman capture of Constantinople in 1453.

IV. END OF BYZANTIUM

The victorious Latins set up their feudal states on the ruins of Byzantium. They established a Latin empire at Constantinople, a Latin kingdom at Thessaloniki, and several Latin states in Greece. The commercially minded Venetians occupied a whole quarter of Constantinople and annexed numerous islands and ports strategically located on their route to the Levant. These new states, however, were doomed from the outset. The native Greek Orthodox populations remained bitterly hostile to the end. Furthermore the Latin conquerors had won only a few isolated toeholds on the fringes of the Balkan Peninsula, and were surrounded on all sides by enemies. They faced not only the Serbian and Bulgarian kingdoms in the Balkan interior, but also three Greek succession states located at Arta in Epirus, at Trebizond on the southern shore of the Black Sea, and at Nicaea in western Asia Minor. The first of these Greek states was too poor to provide effective leadership, and the second was too isolated. So it was Nicaea, with its strategic location and adequate resources as well as able leadership, that organized Greek resistance to Latin rule.

By skillful diplomacy and force of arms the Nicaean rulers steadily reduced the Latin empire until only the city of Constantinople itself remained. Finally in 1261 the Latin emperor and the Venetian settlers fled from Constantinople without offering resistance. The Nicaean emperor, Michael Palaeologus, made his solemn entry into the capital and, amidst popular acclamation, took up his residence in the imperial palace.

The final phase of Byzantine history comprised the period between 1261, when Michael Palaeologus recovered Constantinople, and 1453, when his successor, Constantine Palaeologus, was killed at a gate of the capital fighting the Turks. During these two centuries the restored empire consisted merely of the cities of Constantinople and Thessaloniki, with small fluctuating areas around each, and two separate appanages: Mistra, in the Peloponnesus, and Trebizond, in northern Asia Minor.

The outlook for this pitiful remnant of empire was scarcely more promising than that of its Latin predecessors. In Asia it faced the formidable Turks, and in Europe it was surrounded by small Latin states that remained in Greece, and by the Serbians and Bulgarians to the north. To these external dangers were added internal difficulties. Economically the empire was bankrupt. The Italian stranglehold on commerce continued unbroken, so that in the mid-fourteenth century the Genoese quarter in Constantinople was collecting seven times as much as the imperial government in customs revenues. Increased taxes commonly were avoided by the politically influential rich. The poor rose in revolt against the aristocracy of birth and wealth, so that cities were torn by social strife.

Between 1342 and 1349 Thessaloniki was ruled by revolutionary leaders known as the Zealots. They reduced taxes on the poor, annulled their debts, confiscated and distributed monastery lands, and introduced participatory democracy with mass rallies and popularly elected officials. Their political program appears to have been influenced by the example of the republican city-states in Italy. But a dying Byzantine Empire could not sustain the political and social innovations then emerging naturally in the vigorous and expanding West. With Serbian and Turkish aid the emperor suppressed the Zealots and ended their republic.

In addition to this socio-economic fragility, the empire was weakened by religious dissension. Hoping to obtain Western aid against the approaching Turks, the emperors on three separate occasions had agreed to the submission of the Orthodox Church to the Papacy (Unions of Lyons, 1274; Rome, 1369; and Florence, 1439). These agreements proved meaningless, for the West gave insignificant aid, while Byzantium was further torn by the bitter popular opposition to any concessions to the hated Latins. "Better Islam than the Pope" was the defiant popular response to the barbarities of the Fourth Crusade and to the exploitation by Italian merchants.

The cry of preference for the Turks had been heard frequently in the past, but in the mid-fifteenth century the situation was unique because the Turks then were in a position to accept the invitation. As noted in Chapter 14, section VI, the Ottoman Turks had taken over from the Seljuks, conquered the remaining Byzantine enclaves in Asia Minor, crossed the Straits to Europe, defeated the Bulgars and Serbs, and finally by 1453 were ready to close in on the beleaguered Byzantine capital.

Constantinople's population by this time had shrunk to between fifty and seventy thousand. The total force available for the defense of the city, including a small number from the West, amounted to no more than nine thousand. This was totally inadequate to man the extensive series of walls and to repair the breaches pounded by the enemy cannon. The Ottoman army, led by the capable Sultan Mohammed II, numbered at least eighty thousand. Yet the defenders, under the courageous leadership of Emperor Constantine, repulsed the attackers from April 2 when the siege began to May 29 when the final assault prevailed. The city was then given over to the soldiery for the promised three-day sack. The contemporary Byzantine historian Ducas describes as follows this ending of a thousand years of Byzantium.

Three days after the fall of the city he [Mohammed] released the ships so that each might sail off to its own province and city, each carrying such a load that it seemed each would sink. And what sort of a cargo? Luxurious cloths and textiles, objects and vessels of gold, silver, bronze and brass, books beyond all counting and number, prisoners including priests and lay persons, nuns and monks. All the ships were full of cargos, and the tents of the army camps were full of captives and of the above enumerated items and goods.

And there was to be seen among the barbarian host one wearing the sakkon of an arch-bishop, another wearing the gold epitrahelion of a priest, leading their dogs clothed in-stead of with the usual collars with gold brocaded amnous (ecclesiastical vestments). Others were to be seen seated at banquets, with the holy discs before them containing fruit and other foods, which they were eating, and with the holy chalices from which they drank their wine. And having loaded all the books, reaching unto a number beyond numbering, upon carts, they scattered them throughout the east and west. For one nomisma ten books could be bought (and what kind of books), Aristotelian, Platonic, theological, and every other kind. There were gospels which had every type of embel-lishment, beyond number, they smashed the gold and silver from them and some they sold, others they threw away. And all the icons were thrown into the flame, from which flame they broiled their meat.[1]

V. BYZANTIUM'S LEGACY

In the light of retrospect Byzantium obviously made significant contributions in various fields. One was in its role as a protective shield behind which the West was left free to develop its own civilization. The full meaning of this became clear when, after the fall of Constantinople in 1453, the Turks within barely a century reached the heart of Europe and besieged Vienna. Equally important was Byzantium's stimulus to trade and general economic development. For centuries Byzantium was the economic dynamo for the entire Mediterranean basin, while its currency served as the standard international medium of exchange. Its mer-chants and its commodities did much to lift Western Europe out of its feudalized self-sufficiency and to start the Italian city-states on the road to commercial domination of the Mediterranean.

In the realm of culture, Byzantium salvaged the intellectual and artistic treasures of antiquity and transmitted them to posterity along with her own legacy. From Byzantium came Roman law codified by Justinian, a religious art that only recently has been properly understood and appreciated, and the literary and scholarly masterpieces of classical and Hellenistic times as compiled, anno-tated, and preserved by conscientious scholars. Finally, as will be noted in the following section, Byzantium was for the eastern Slavs what Rome had been for the Germans—the great educator, the great initiator, the source both of religion and of civilization.

These achievements belie Gibbon's well known verdict concerning the histor-ical significance of Byzantium. Yet at the same time it is apparent that Byzantium lacked the freshness and luster of classical Athens, even though the latter was territorially and chronologically insignificant by comparison. The reason is that the role of Byzantium was conservative in the proper sense of the word. This is not to say that Byzantium was static. From beginning to end it was adjusting itself to changing times and circumstances. But the fact remains that its destiny was to conserve rather than to create. It was born an aged state and lived in the shadow of past power and glory which it sought to maintain or recover. It pro-duced a remarkable succession of outstanding leaders—administrators, generals, scholars, and theologians—but because of the context in which they worked very few of them were genuinely creative.

The fact that the East Roman Empire survived that of the West by a full millennium constituted a great advantage at the outset. Between the fifth and the eleventh centuries the West was primitive and insignificant in comparison to the Second Rome on the Bosphorus. But these were centuries when the West, pre-cisely because it had to start afresh, was laying the foundations for a new civilization, while Byzantium was living on its splendid but overpowering patrimony. This is why from the eleventh century onward the West was able to forge ahead with its booming economy, rising national monarchies, new intellectual horizons, and a dynamic expansionism that manifested itself first in local crusades and then in an overseas thrust that was to lead within a few centuries to global hegemony. And, in pitiful contrast, during these later centuries Byzantium proved incapable of breaking the bonds to the past and thus became an obsolete anachronism that fought a gallant but foredoomed holding action until the ignominious but inevitable end in 1453.

VI. BYZANTIUM AND THE SLAVS

Although Byzantium had passed off the historical stage, Byzantine institutions and culture lived on amongst the Slavs to the north, as indeed they did in large part amongst the Balkan Christians who had passed under Turkish rule. Originating in the swampy borderland between present-day Russia and Poland, the Slavs fanned out in a great arc, the surrounding plains beckoning them in all directions.

Those who migrated westward comprise the Czechs, Slovaks, and Poles of today, and are known as the Western Slavs. Because of their location they fell under Western influence, so that their religion is Catholic and their alphabets Latin. Those who migrated across the Danube to the Balkan Peninsula are known today as the Slovenes, Croats, Serbs, and Bulgars. As noted in section I of this chapter, the first two of these South Slavic peoples adopted Western cultural forms, in contrast to the Serbs and Bulgars who were influenced by Constantinople rather than Rome in their cultural development. Finally to the east migrated the ancestors of the present-day Slavic peoples of the Soviet Union. These Eastern Slavs are known today as the Great Russians of the northern part of the country, the Little Russians, or Ukrainians, of the southern regions, and the White, or Byelo, Russians of the western borderlands where the earliest Slavs apparently originated.

The Eastern Slavs settled on the broad plains stretching from the Arctic shores in the north, to the Black Sea in the south, and to the Urals in the east. In the northern plains the colonists remained within the shelter of the forests, where they encountered little opposition from scattered and loosely organized Finnish and Lithuanian tribes with whom they intermarried or easily pushed aside. In the southern plains, by contrast, where the forests gradually gave way to the open steppes, the settlers were always vulnerable to the attacks of the peoples who ranged the great nomad route from Central Asia across the Ukraine to the Danube Valley.

These Eastern Slavs, or Russians, engaged in trapping, fishing, and primitive slash-and-burn agriculture. Consequently, scattered homesteads and small hamlets were the general rule, rather than compact villages or towns. The few towns that did appear grew up as trade centers along main river routes. This was the case with Kiev on the Dnieper River carrying the north-south traffic, and with Novgorod on Lake Ilmen commanding the east-west commerce. Kiev emerged as the center of a loose confederation of Russian principalities strung out along the river routes.

The early Russians borrowed certain basic culture traits, especially Christianity from Byzantium. Hitherto the pagan Russians had worshipped forces of nature personified in certain deities such as Dazhbog, god of heat and light, Perun, god of thunder and lightning, and Striborg, god of wind. Neither temples nor priests existed, and religious ritual was limited to sacrifices offered to crude images of the deities erected in open spaces. Prince Vladimir of Kiev deemed this native Slavic pantheon inadequate and, according to the Chronicle compiled by monks at Kiev in the late eleventh and twelfth centuries, he pondered the arguments of representatives of various faiths who told him of their beliefs, and he even sent envoys to the countries where these faiths were practiced to report back to him. About the year 988, Vladimir, on the basis of their reports, decided in favor of Orthodox Christianity, his envoys having been overwhelmed by the services they had beheld in the Hagia Sophia of Constantinople: ". . . we knew not whether we were in heaven or on earth. For on earth there is no such splendor or such beauty, and we are at a loss how to describe it."[2]

Vladimir's adoption of Orthodox Christianity involved much more than a mere change of religion; the repercussions affected profoundly and pervasively the institutions and future history of the Russian people. An ecclesiastical hierarchy based on the Byzantine model was now organized. The head was the Metropolitan of Kiev, appointed by, and subject to, the jurisdiction of the Patriarch of Constantinople. For two centuries the Metropolitans were all Greeks, though bishops appointed by the Metropolitans were mostly Russians after the first few generations. Christianity also brought with it a new religious and legal literature, including translations of the Bible, Byzantine collections of the writings of the church fathers, lives of saints, and law books. Byzantine art also was now introduced in the form of stone churches, mosaics, frescoes, paintings, and particularly icons, in which the Russians excelled and developed their distinctive Russo-Byzantine style. The Orthodox Church also brought with it Byzantine ecclesiastical law and established ecclesiastical courts. As in Western Europe, these courts had very wide jurisdiction, including all cases involving morals, beliefs, inheritance, and matrimonial matters.

In the realm of politics the new church served to strengthen the authority of the prince. Just as in Western Europe the Papacy had transformed the Frankish kings from tribal chieftains to the Lord's anointed, so now Russian Orthodoxy transformed the heads of the principalities from mere leaders of bands of personal followers to "servants of the lord" and hence rulers by divine right. Furthermore the Russian church, in accordance with Byzantine tradition, accepted secular authority and control. There was no counterpart in Moscow, as there had been none in Constantinople, of Gregory VII or Innocent III in Rome, demanding and exacting obedience from emperors and kings alike. After the disappearance of Byzantium and of its emperor, this submissiveness of Eastern Orthodoxy manifested itself in the subservience of the Russian church to the Russian emperor, which persisted with fateful consequences until the Tsarist empire followed the Byzantine to extinction.

It is apparent from the above that Byzantine influence in Russia constituted a great stimulus, yet at the same time it also proved to be an anesthetic. What the Russians borrowed was already fully evolved and relatively static, whether it was doctrine, ritual, music, or architecture. In this sense Byzantium had a rather stultifying effect on an awakening people, discouraging rather than encouraging creativity and originality. Futhermore, in adopting the Byzantine form of Christianity, the Russians inherited and sustained the Catholic-Orthodox feud, thereby erecting a barrier between themselves and the West. This was a distinct setback, for the Russians heretofore had developed numerous ties—commercial, dynastic and diplomatic—with the rest of Europe. Prince Yaroslav in the eleventh century, for example, had marriage connections with the leading dynasties of Europe, his sister being married to Casimir I of Poland, his son to a princess of Byzantium, and his two daughters to Henry I of France and to Harald III of Norway.

These associations between Russia and the West were dissolved not only by religious issues, but even more by the Mongol invasion and occupation. Kiev always had been extremely vulnerable to invasion, being located at the point where the forest zone gives way to the steppe. The threat of attack by the nomads hung over the city like the sword of Damocles. The sword descended in 1237 when the Mongols swept over the Russian lands as they did over most of Eurasia. Kiev and other Russian cities were razed, Novgorod being the only one of any size that escaped conquest because of its location in the far north. In the words of a chronicler, "No eye remained open to weep for the dead."

VII. THIRD ROME

Whereas the Mongols voluntarily withdrew from Central Europe, in Russia by contrast they chose to remain, establishing the kingdom, or khanate, of the Golden Horde. Its capital was Sarai, located strategically on the Volga, where the river bends furthest to the west. The ensuing two centuries of Mongol rule inevitably left a deep imprint on the Russian people. They were forced to abandon their small settlements on the steppe and to withdraw into the secure fastnesses of the forests. There they were left to their own devices so long as they recognized the suzerainty of the Mongol khan and paid him annual tribute. Indeed the khans issued certain charters, or *yarlyks,* granting the Russian church freedom from taxation and recognizing the Metropolitans' juridiction over Orthodox Christians. In return the Russian clergy offered prayers for the khans and their kin who, though they were Moslems rather than Christians, naturally welcomed such affirmations that lessened the likelihood of revolt.

Gradually the Russians recovered their strength and developed a new national center—the principality of Moscow, located deep in the forest zone away from the dangerous steppe. (See Map XIX, "The Growth of Muscovy.") Moscow had advantages other than its relative inaccessibility to the nomads. It was located at the crossroads of important land and river trade routes. And the principality enjoyed the advantage of a line of rulers who were peaceful, frugal, and calculating. These rulers added to their possessions patiently and ruthlessly, until Moscow became the new national nucleus.

Ivan III (1462–1505) was particularly successful in his "gathering of the Russian lands," so that he may be regarded as the first of the national rulers of Russia. He conquered several neighboring principalities such as Yaroslav, Tver, and Rostov, which at one time had been more powerful than Moscow but which had since fallen behind. Most outstanding was his victory over mighty Novgorod, which had built up a vast trading empire of its own. By the end of his reign Ivan III had extended his frontiers from within a few miles of the Baltic to the Arctic Ocean in the north and the northern Urals in the east.

Ivan also successfully challenged the rule of the Mongols by exploiting divisions that had developed amongst them, and playing off contending factions against one another. More important was the fact that the Russians, in contrast to the Mongols, were able to import cannon and small arms from the West, and also possessed arsenals for the manufacture of these weapons. With these advantages, Ivan was able to renounce formally the suzerainty of the Golden Horde, and the khan proved incapable of enforcing his authority.

Noteworthy also is Ivan's marriage in 1472 to Sophia, niece of the last Byzantine emperor, who had perished on the walls of Constantinople in 1453. The Russian church and court earlier had strongly opposed the agreement of the Greeks at Florence (1439) for union with Rome. Indeed the Russians interpreted the eventual fall of Constantinople to the Turks as divine retribution for unprincipled surrender to the Latins. With Constantinople fallen, the Russians now regarded Moscow as the home of the true faith, which they were divinely ordained to defend and to preserve in its original purity. This conviction was explicitly articulated at the end of the fifteenth century by the monk Philotheus who wrote to Ivan:

> The church of ancient Rome fell because of Apollinarian heresy; as to the second Rome—the church of Constantinople—it has been hewn by the axes of Ishmaelites, but this third new Rome—the Holy Apostolic church—under thy mighty rule, shines throughout the entire world more brightly than the sun. All the Orthodox Christian realms have converged in thine own. Thou art the sole Autocrat of the universe, the only Tsar of the Christians. . . . Observe and hearken, O pious Tsar, two Romes have fallen, but the third stands, and no fourth can ever be.[3]

Ivan understandably welcomed this credo which so exalted his status and mission. With the encouragement of Sophia he adopted Byzantine court etiquette and chose the Byzantine double-headed eagle as his emblem. He became tsar and autocrat, in imitation of the past emperors of Constantinople, and his title was correspondingly grand and resplendent: "Ivan, by the mercy of God, Emperor of All Rus and Grand Prince of Vladimir and Moscow and Novgorod and Pskov and Tver and Perm and Ugra and Bolghar and the rest."

Thus Byzantium lived on in the Russian lands as the Third Rome. This Third Rome survived because it possessed vast resources and an impregnable base encompassing the great Eurasian plains and, before long, the limitless trans-Ural territories of Siberia. This was altogether different from the shrunken Byzantium that had dragged out a precarious existence for centuries prior to 1453. Cardinal Bessarion's call for modernization had evoked no response from this foredoomed anachronism (See Chapter 17, section III), but in Russia certain tsars were to appear who assumed themselves the role of Bessarion. And as the autocratic rulers of a vast empire, they possessed both the authority and the resources to translate, however imperfectly, their desires into reality, and thereby to assure, as the monk Philotheus had prophesied, that this Third Rome would not suffer the fate of the Second.

SUGGESTED READING

J. BLUM, *Lord and Peasant in Russia from the Ninth to the Nineteenth Century* (Princeton Univ., 1961); *Cambridge Medieval History,* Vol. IV (Cambridge Univ. 1966); M. T. FLORINSKY, *Russia: A History and an Interpretation,* 2 vols. (Macmillan, 1947); G. OSTROGORSKY, *History of the Byzantine State* (Rutgers Univ., 1957); G. VERNADSKY, *The Mongols and Russia* (Yale Univ., 1953); S. VRYONIS, *Byzantium and Europe* (Harcourt, 1967).

chapter sixteen

Traditional
Confucian Civilization

*I am happy because I am a human and not an animal; a male, and
not a female; a Chinese, and not a barbarian; and because I live in
Loyang, the most wonderful city in all the world.*—Shao Yung
(Neo-Confucianist, 1011–1077)

The fact that the Han dynasty eventually was succeeded by the Sui
and T'ang dynasties ensured that civilization in China was to continue along
traditional lines, in contrast to the unique mutation that was taking form in the
West following Rome's collapse. (See Chapter 11, section III.) The ensuing millennium proved to be for the Chinese people a great Golden Age. During the Han
period China had succeeded in catching up to the other Eurasian civilizations,
but now, during the medieval period, China was able to forge ahead and to
remain the richest, most populous, and, in many ways, the most culturally advanced country in the world.

The millennium between the sixth century, when the Sui dynasty restored
imperial unity, and the sixteenth, when the Westerners began their intrusion by
sea, was for China an era of unparalleled political, social, and cultural stability.
But this stability paradoxically proved to be a curse as well as a blessing. It was
a blessing because Chinese society during this millennium provided more material and psychological security for more people than any other society in the
world. But the stability was also a curse because it was so successful and comfortable that China remained relatively unchanged, though by no means completely
static. At the same time, however, as we shall note in the following chapter, the
West was being transformed by its technological precociousness, its economic
vitality, and its social and political pluralism, all of which engendered a dynamism that was to culminate in global hegemony. The end result, then, was the
disruption of the beautifully balanced but conservative Chinese society by the
irresistible expansionism of the West. This denouement, however, should not
be allowed to obscure the fact that for a full millennium the civilization of China
led the world by its sheer viability and by its contributions to the human heritage.

I. SUI RESTORES UNITY

The Sui dynasty (589–618) played the same role in Chinese history as the Ch'in dynasty some eight centuries earlier. Both dynasties reunited China after long periods of disorder, and both then proceeded to make fundamental contributions to the development of the country. But in doing so they drove their people so hard and antagonized so many vested interests that both scarcely survived their founders.

The great contribution of the Ch'in rulers was the imperial unity they forced upon China through road and canal building, construction of the Great Wall, standardization of weights, measures, and script, and extension and strengthening of the frontiers. The efforts of the Sui emperors were very similar and equally exhausting. They reconstructed the Great Wall, parts of which had fallen into disrepair. They built the main sections of the gigantic Grand Canal system linking the Yangtze Valley, which had become the economic center of the country, with the North, which remained the political center.

Just as exhausting as these domestic projects were the series of campaigns that extended the imperial frontiers to include Formosa, Annam and Champa in Indochina, and Kansu in the northwest. But the attempts to conquer the most northern of the three kingdoms into which Korea was then divided proved disastrous. Four successive invasions were repulsed by the resolute Korean defenders. The disaffected soldiers mutinied, while the overtaxed peasants rose in rebellion in various parts of the country. The emperor fled to South China where he was assassinated in 618. The victor in the ensuing struggle among several pretenders established the T'ang dynasty, regarded by many Chinese and Western historians as the most illustrious of them all.

II. T'ANG EMPIRE

The most manifest characteristic of the T'ang dynasty was its imperial expansionism. In a series of great campaigns, it extended the frontiers even beyond those of the Han emperors. In Central Asia it established Chinese suzerainty over the Tarim Basin and beyond the Pamirs to the states of the Oxus Valley and even to the head waters of the Indus in modern Afghanistan. Other vast territories that now were constrained to accept Chinese suzerainty were Tibet in the south, Mongolia in the northwest, and Korea and Manchuria in the northeast. The only other comparable empire in the world at the time was that of the Moslem Arabs in the Middle East.

These foreign conquests were made possible by the reestablishment of strong central government at home. As noted earlier (Chapter 10, section V), the Han dynasty had been undermined by powerful local families that had accumulated huge, self-sufficient, and tax-free estates on which they built fortress-like manor houses from which they successfully defied central authority. This disintegration was furthered by the appearance of Buddhist monasteries, which, with their extensive and growing landholdings, offered another challenge to the imperial government.

An antidote to this political fragmentation gradually evolved during the centuries of the interregnum and was perfected by the Sui and T'ang bureaucrats. It consisted of the "equal field" system by which all able-bodied peasants were assigned plots of about nineteen acres by the central government. This did not deprive the powerful families of their holdings, for the land was obtained from other sources, such as reclamation projects and fields that had been abandoned during the wars. Also the free peasants alone received the land grants, and by no means all of them in actual practice. Nevertheless the "equal field" system did help somewhat to loosen the grip of the great families and to strengthen the T'ang regime. It halted for some time the growth of the large semifeudal estates. It increased government revenues, since the small peasants paid taxes whereas the politically powerful great landholders did not. Furthermore the peasants were given military training and organized into a regular militia, thereby strengthening the military position of the imperial government.

The T'ang dynasty consolidated its authority also by developing a competent bureaucracy to administer the empire. The Sui earlier had reinstated the Han system of civil service based on competitive public examinations. The T'ang continued and expanded this system in accordance with the basic Confucian tenet that matters of state are better met by recruiting men of talent than by the legal and institutional change that is typical of the West. When fully evolved, the system consisted of a series of examinations held amidst an elaborate series of rituals. The first, in the district and prefectural cities, occurred every two or three years, and the approximately 2 percent of the candidates who passed these took the prefectural exams a few weeks later. Survivors (about half the candidates) became eligible for appointment to minor posts and for further examinations held every three years in the provincial capitals. Success here entitled one to take the imperial examinations at the capital. Only 6 percent passed this hurdle and became eligible for appointment to high office; and only a third of these normally passed the climactic palace examination in the presence of the Emperor himself and were admitted to membership in the most exalted fraternity of Chinese scholarship, the Hanlin Academy, from which were selected the historiographers and other high literary officers.

At first the examinations were fairly comprehensive, emphasizing the Confucian classics but including also subjects like law, mathematics, and political affairs. Gradually, however, they came to concentrate on literary style and Confucian orthodoxy. The net result was a system that theoretically opened offices to all men of talent, but that in practice favored the classes with sufficient wealth to afford the years of study and preparation. Also, it was a system that stifled originality and bred conformity. So long as China remained relatively isolated in East Asia, it provided stability and continuity. But with the intrusion of the dynamic West it served instead to prevent effective adjustment and response, until it was finally abolished altogether in 1905.

The three top government bodies in the capital were the Imperial Secretariat, which operated directly under the emperor and formulated policy, the Imperial Chancellery, which reviewed the decisions of the first body and returned them for reconsideration when deemed necessary, and the Secretariat of State Affairs, which implemented the decisions of the other two organs. Under the Secretariat of State Affairs were six Ministries, or Boards: Personnel, Revenue, War, Justice, Public Works, and Rites; the last of these was entrusted with the conduct of the civil service examinations.

The capital in which these and other government bodies met was Ch'ang-an, a magnificent city of probably over one million people. Its broad thoroughfares, criss-crossing in checkerboard fashion, often were crowded with Persians, Indians, Jews, Armenians, and assorted Central Asians. They came as merchants, missionaries, and mercenary soldiers, for China under the T'ang was more open to foreigners than at any other time with the exception of the short-lived Mongol Yüan interlude.

This openness was most apparent in matters of religion. The extension of imperial frontiers and the reopening of land and sea trade routes led to a great influx of foreign religious ideas and missionaries. This was particularly true of Buddhism, which first entered China from India (see Chapter 7, section III) during the Han dynasty and which began to seriously challenge the official Confucianism during the chaotic interregnum following the Han. In that time of trouble Confucianism was increasingly questioned because its emphasis on filial piety and family loyalty appeared to weaken an already weak state. Consequently Buddhism gained rapidly during the interregnum and reached the height of its influence during the early T'ang, which is sometimes called the "Buddhist period" of Chinese history. Although Buddhism attained great wealth and influence in China, it became in the process thoroughly Sinicized, and also contributed fundamentally to Neo-Confucianism.

Eventually the imperial government turned against Buddhism and resorted to outright persecution. The Buddhist emphasis on the salvation of the individual rather than on his obligation to the family was too contrary to basic Chinese traditions. So was the complete withdrawal from society of monks and nuns, which was considered unnatural and antisocial. And, above all, the government coveted the vast treasures and estates that the monasteries had accumulated through the centuries. Hence the series of persecutions that crippled Buddhism in China, though it did not disappear altogether as it did in India. The persecution was restricted to the institutions and their clergy, and did not include the rank-and-file believers, as was the case in comparable situations in the West. The end result of this Buddhist interlude was minimal so far as the overall evolution of Chinese civilization was concerned. Buddhism did make significant contributions to Chinese philosophy, metaphysics, art, and literature, but it did not remold Chinese society as a whole, as Christianity had remolded the European.

During the last century and a half of their reign, the T'ang rulers were faced with the usual problems of a dynasty in decline. Imperial expenses outstripped revenues. Population growth likewise outstripped land supply, so that peasant families no longer could be provided with individual plots. The "equal field" system broke down, and the wealthy families once more enlarged their estates at the expense of the peasants. Since the revenue system was based on per capita taxes, the burden of paying for the mounting imperial expenses fell on the peasants at a time when their holdings were shrinking.

The government responded by shifting increasingly from per capita to land taxes. This produced more revenue, but it did not halt the decline in the number of free peasants. This decline meant a corresponding decline in the supply of manpower for militia and corvée duty. Imperial defense was entrusted increasingly to mercenaries and border "barbarian" tribes who were not as dependable as the former militia. Thus in 751 Chinese armies were defeated both in Yunnan in the south and at Talas in Central Asia. The latter battle was particularly decisive for it enabled the Moslem Arab victors to begin the Islamization of a vast area that had been one of the earliest strongholds of Buddhism.

The T'ang emperors managed to hang on for another century and a half, but it was a period of steady deterioration. Incompetence and provocative luxury in the capital combined with successive droughts and widespread famine to provoke rebellions in many provinces. The end came in 907, when one of the rebel leaders deposed the last T'ang ruler and sacked Ch'ang-an. The empire now broke into fragments, and the ensuing half century is known as the interregnum of the "Five Dynasties." An able general finally was able to restore unity and to found a new dynasty, the Sung, which, like its predecessor, endured for about three centuries (960–1279).

It should be noted that this brief half century interlude between dynasties now became the pattern for future Chinese history. Never again was the country to experience several centuries of anarchy, as it had following the Han collapse. The reason is that from the T'ang onward, Chinese civilization was too massive and deep-rooted to remain disrupted for prolonged periods. Perhaps this civilization might have become more innovative and creative if imperial unity had been supplanted by the pluralism and diversity of the West. This is an "if" of history that must remain speculative. The only certainty is that the Chinese themselves regarded disunity and the attendant turmoil as abnormal and deplorable. "Just as there cannot be two suns in one sky," went an old saying, "so there cannot be two Chinese states or two rulers of China."

III. SUNG GOLDEN AGE

The Sung emperors were markedly passive in their external relations compared to their Han and T'ang predecessors. They did not begin with great campaigns reestablishing imperial frontiers in the heart of Eurasia. Instead the second Sung emperor modestly attempted to regain from nomad control merely the territory between Peking and the Great Wall. But he was disastrously defeated, and his successor gave up claim to this region, and even paid the nomads an annual "gift," which in fact was thinly veiled tribute. Thus the Sung never recovered the northeast territories in Manchuria, nor the northwest territories that provided access to the overland routes to the west.

This was a grave weakness for the Sung dynasty, leaving it vulnerable to nomadic incursions. The policy of paying "gifts" proved viable for a century and a half, but disaster came when a Sung emperor made a rash attempt to recover the northeastern lands. He was encouraged to do so when the ruling nomads in that region were defeated by newcomers from North Manchuria. Taking advantage of what appeared to be an opportunity, the emperor sent his armies into Manchuria. Instead of easy victory they sustained a crushing defeat that was followed by massive invasion of North China. The Sung defenses crumpled and the dynasty was left only with the Yangtze Valley in central China, and the lands to the south. Consequently the second half of the dynasty, from 1127 to 1279, is known as the Southern Sung; the first half, between 960 and 1127, is called the Northern Sung.

This dynasty was much berated by later Chinese historians for failing initially to regain the outlying provinces, and then suffering the loss of the entire northern half of the country. This criticism cannot be denied, yet it is also true that in many respects Chinese civilization reached its apogee during the centuries of the T'ang and the Sung. This was particularly so in the field of culture. During these centuries appeared the vast encyclopedias of Buddhist texts and Confucian classics; the comprehensive dynastic histories written by teams of scholars; the masterpieces of scores of great poets and artists; the art of calligraphy, depicted on scrolls prized as highly as paintings; the beautiful porcelain as thin as glass and almost as transparent; the priceless invention of printing that was utilized for the mass duplication and distribution of Buddhist scriptures; and the extraordinary advances in science and technology which are only now being adequately comprehended. (See Chapter 12, section III.)

In addition to its cultural attainments, the Sung period is noteworthy for a veritable commercial revolution that was quite significant for all Eurasia. The roots are to be found in a marked increase in the productivity of China's economy. Steady technological improvements raised the output of the traditional industries. Agriculture likewise was stimulated by the introduction of a quickly maturing strain of rice that allowed two crops to be grown each season where only one had been possible before. Also new water control projects undertaken by the Sung greatly expanded the acreage of irrigated paddy fields. Thus it is estimated that the rice crop doubled between the eleventh and twelfth centuries.

This increasing productivity made possible a corresponding increase in population, which in turn further stimulated production in interacting fashion. The volume of trade also rose with the quickening tempo of economic activity. For the first time large cities appeared in China that were primarily commercial rather than administrative centers. Even more marked than this spurt in domestic trade was that in foreign trade. Considerable overseas commerce had been carried on since Han times, but during the T'ang, and more especially during the Sung, the volume of foreign trade far surpassed all previous records. The basis for this burgeoning trade was the unprecedented productivity of China's economy, the initiative of Moslem merchants and mariners who were active in Asian seas, and the improvements in maritime technology, including the use of the compass, of an adjustable centerboard keel, and of cotton sails in place of bamboo slats.

The end result was that for the first time the seaports rather than the old overland routes became China's principal contact with the outside world. Indicative of China's economic leadership at this time is the fact that her exports were mostly manufactured goods such as silks, porcelains, books, and paintings, while the imports were mostly raw materials such as spices, minerals, and horses. Finally it should be noted that during the Sung the Chinese themselves for the first time engaged on a large scale in overseas trade, no longer depending largely on foreign intermediaries. In conclusion, China during the Sung was well on the way to becoming a great maritime power. But the all important fact, for world history as well as for Chinese, is that this potentiality was never realized. And, equally significant, this veritable commercial revolution of the Sung era had none of the explosive repercussions on Chinese society that a corresponding commercial revolution had on Western society. (See section V of this chapter.)

IV. YÜAN MONGOL RULE

The rule of the Southern Sung, though confined to only half the country, proved exceptionally peaceful and prosperous. Meanwhile North China was under the Chin, a people of Manchurian origin. About 1215 they appealed to the Southern Sung for help against the formidable Mongols who had driven them out of Peking. The Sung, not aware of the deadly power of the Mongols, supported them by sending infantry skilled in siege warfare. When the Chin were overwhelmed by 1234, the Sung emperor rashly attempted to secure North China for his own empire. The Mongols retaliated by promptly invading South China. The war dragged on for decades because the Mongols were preoccupied elsewhere, but the end came in 1279 when the last Sung pretender perished in a naval battle. A new

Mongol dynasty that took the name Yüan now began its rule that was to endure to 1368.

This was the first and only time that China was ruled by full nomads who had not already been partly Sinicized by earlier contact with the empire. The immediate reaction of the rude conquerors was to level the cities and to incorporate their new subjects into the traditional Mongol tribal society. But they realized that this was impossible and instead they established an administrative apparatus essentially similar to that of their Chinese predecessors. At the same time they were able to preserve their identity because their nomadic background separated them from their subjects as regards language, customs, and laws. They also took care to employ in their service many foreigners to counterbalance the suspect Chinese majority. Marco Polo is the best known of these foreign-born bureaucrats, though most of them were Central Asian Moslems.

Kublai Khan, who moved the Mongol capital from Karakorum to Peking and became essentially a Chinese emperor, dutifully performed the traditional Confucian imperial rites. Also he sought to appease the Confucian literati by exempting them from taxation, but they remained largely alienated. They resented the large number of foreigners in what had become virtually an international civil service, and they resented also the Mongol toleration and patronage of various foreign religions, including Islam and Nestorian Christianity. (See Chapter 14, sections IV and V.)

Because of its nature and relatively short duration, Mongol rule in China did not leave a deep imprint on the country. Perhaps the most lasting contribution was the selection of Peking as the capital. Situated in the North China plain on the routes leading westward to Central Asia and eastward to Manchuria, Peking has remained an important military, economic, and administrative center to the present day. Mongol rule also stimulated a sharp rise in overland trade since China now was part of a huge empire encompassing most of Eurasia. (See Chapter 12, section II.) Commerce was also facilitated by the widespread use of paper money, which was introduced by the Sung but developed further by the Mongols.

The able Kublai Khan died in 1294 at the age of eighty and was succeeded by his equally able grandson, Timur. But he died young, and the following Khans were incompetent and debauched by palace life. Fratricidal conflicts broke out within the dynasty, and even worse, frequent flooding of the Yellow River produced widespread famine in North China. Rebellions broke out in most of the provinces, and finally the turmoil was ended by an able commoner who, like the founder of the Han, rose through sheer native ability in a time of crisis and opportunity to become the Son of Heaven. Thus the Chinese Ming dynasty was established in 1368 and remained in power to 1644.

V. MING ETHNOCENTRISM AND WITHDRAWAL

Two dynasties, the Ming (1368–1644) and the Ch'ing (1644–1912), ruled China during the more than half millennium between the overthrow of the Mongols and the advent of the republic. These centuries comprise one of the great eras of orderly government and social stability in human history. A main reason for this unprecedented durability was the unchallenged primacy of a new Confucian metaphysics known as Neo-Confucianism. This renaissance of Confucian thought took place mostly during the time of troubles following the collapse of the T'ang dynasty, when the needs of the age patently called for something more than the mere memorization of Confucian classics. Accordingly a number of scholars undertook a searching reappraisal of the problems of man and of the universe.

A leader in this undertaking was Chu Hsi (1129–1200), who in his youth had studied both Buddhism and Taoism. Satisfied with neither, he turned to the Confucian classics, and with his remarkable talent for synthesis he evolved an interpretation that incorporated elements of Buddhism and Taoism and that was more satisfyingly relevant for his age. His approach was essentially that of the empirical rationalist. He taught that the universe is governed by natural law, which should be comprehended and respected. He also believed in the goodness of man and in his perfectability. He compared man to a mirror covered with dust which, if cleaned, will be as bright as ever. Evil, therefore, was the result of neglect and of defective education, and hence was correctable.

Chu Hsi's influence in the Confucian world was comparable to that of Thomas Aquinas in Western Christendom. Just as Aquinas soon was to weave Aristotle and St. Paul into the official scholastic philosophy, so Chu Hsi now integrated contemporary Chinese thought into the Neo-Confucian synthesis. And by his very comprehensiveness and persuasiveness Chu Hsi, like Aquinas, discouraged further philosophical development. This was particularly true during the Ming period when, as a reaction against the preceding foreign Mongol domination, there was a pronounced ethnocentrism and a looking backward to past traditions. In such an atmosphere, Chu Hsi came to be regarded as the absolute and final authority. "Ever since the time of the philosopher Chu," declared a Ming scholar, "the Truth has been made manifest to the world. No more writing is needed: what is left to us is practice."[1]

Since the Confucian classics, with Chu Hsi's commentaries, became the basis of the civil service examinations, this Neo-Confucianism constituted the official orthodoxy of the empire until the late nineteenth century. Its effect was to reinforce the growing social rigidity with an intellectual supplement and rationale. It contributed fundamentally to the unequalled continuity of Chinese civilization, but the cost was a stultifying conformism adverse to all originality or new ideas from the outside.

Chinese society owed its stability not only to Neo-Confucianism but also to the entrenched power of the so-called gentry ruling class, a power based on its combined possession of land and office in an agrarian-based bureaucratic empire. As landlords and as money lenders the gentry dominated the economic life of the villages and towns. Shortage of land and of capital enabled them to impose extortionate rents and interest rates. Frequent natural disasters forced bankrupt mortgagees to become virtual contractual serfs of the local gentry families. It was common for these families by late Ming times to have several thousand indentured peasant households of this sort.

The gentry also were degree holders; indeed this is what the Chinese term for "gentry" literally denotes. But landowning was virtually a prerequisite for financing the years of study necessary to become a degree holder, and hence gain eligibility for a post in the bureaucracy. Thus the association between the local gentry and the imperial bureaucracy was intimate and mutually supporting. Frequently the government official who appeared at his provincial post found the native dialect quite incomprehensible, in which case he was completely dependent on the local gentry for orientation and guidance.

Ming and Ch'ing China were ruled by the bureaucracy and the gentry together, if a meaningful distinction can be made between the two. Both the imperial establishment and the local gentry were interested in preserving the mutually beneficial *status quo,* and they cooperated to that end. Whereas earlier dynasties occasionally had attempted to force through land redistribution and other such reforms, the Ming and the Ch'ing carefully avoided any challenges to the gentry hegemony.

By contrast, the merchant class was treated altogether differently. This was a basic and most meaningful difference between the Western and Chinese societies. In the West the bourgeoisie, because of the pluralism of the society in which it appeared, enjoyed from the outset considerable autonomy, and was able to increase it with the passage of time. In China there did exist a corresponding merchant class which during the Sung enjoyed a veritable commercial revolution. Furthermore China originated most of the basic technological inventions of medieval times. Yet the commercial revolution and the technological advances together failed to bring about in China the revolutionary repercussions that completely transformed society in the West. The basic reason for this, as noted in Chapter 11, section VI, was the continuity of Chinese history—the fact that the Han dynasty was continued in essentials by the Sui, and the Sui in turn by the T'ang and the Sung, and so on in unbroken succession until the end of imperial history in 1912. Thus the traditional bureaucracy-gentry ruling establishment, buttressed by the intellectual props of Neo-Confucianism, was able to absorb the effects of the new technology and of economic growth. But in the West, Rome came to an end with no imperial successor. Instead, a new pluralistic civilization emerged in which gunpowder, the compass, the printing press, and the ocean-going ship were not muffled but rather exploited to their full potential with explosive consequences, first for Europe, and then for the entire world, including China.

No such explosive repercussions were possible in China because the imperial establishment there was too enveloping and restricting. For example, Chinese merchants and industrialists customarily organized themselves into local guilds headed by chiefs, but these guild chiefs were certified by the government which held them responsible for the conduct of individual members. Boat traders also were organized under harbor chiefs similarly responsible to the government. More important were the government monopolies in the production and distribution of numerous commodities that the court and the administration consumed, including arms, textiles, pottery, leather goods, apparel, and wine. The government also controlled completely the production and distribution of basic commodities such as salt and iron that were necessities for the entire population. Such restraints deprived Chinese merchants of the opportunity for unrestricted entrepreneurship, and the economy of the possibility for unfettered growth. The restraints also promoted official corruption, for members of the imperial court used their privileged positions to manipulate the state monopolies for personal gain.

Another example of the restrictive, inward-looking policies of China's ruling establishment was its active opposition to overseas enterprise. Chinese emigrants had trickled down to Southeast Asia before the arrival of the Europeans. In 1603, thirty-two years after the founding of Manila as a Spanish settlement, the Chinese population there was about 20,000, compared with perhaps 1,000 Spaniards. And these Chinese virtually controlled the economic life of the settlement, and were extending their control to the other islands of the Archipelago. When in that year, 1603, the Manila Chinese suffered one of the massacres which they and their compatriots in Southeast Asia have periodically endured to the present day, an official of the nearby mainland province of Fukien condoned the massacre and denounced all overseas Chinese as deserters of the tombs of their ancestors and men who were unworthy of the emperor's concern. Likewise an imperial edict of 1712 forbade Chinese to trade and reside in Southeast Asia. Five years later another edict allowed those already abroad to come home without fear of punishment, and in 1729 still another edict set a date after which those overseas would not be allowed to return. How explicit and striking the contrast with the Western states, which soon were to be actively promoting overseas settlements and trading companies, and were to be ever ready to take up arms against any threats to these enterprises.

The most dramatic and fateful manifestation of this negative official Chinese attitude to overseas activities is to be found in the bizarre history of the early fifteenth-century Ming voyages with their technological preeminence and their astonishing range, which proved conclusively China's world leadership in maritime undertakings. Then came the imperial order forbidding further overseas expeditions and the unhesitating enforcement of that order. (See Chapter 12, section I.) Although the precise motives behind this edict are unknown, the significant fact is that its issuance was possible because Chinese merchants lacked the political power and social status of their Western counterparts. It was this fundamental difference in institutional structure and outward-thrusting dynamism that deflected Chinese energies inward at this fateful turning point in world history, and left the oceans of the globe open to Western enterprise. The inconceivable yet inevitable sequel was the eclipse within a few centuries of the great "Celestial Kingdom" by the barbarians of the West.

VI. CHINESE CIVILIZATION IN JAPAN

Since the Chinese civilization and Chinese empires persisted in unbroken continuity to modern times, they have dominated East Asia in a way that no Western country has dominated the West. Consequently there did not develop in East Asia the political and cultural diversity that has prevailed in the West since the fall of Rome. The only exception has been in the steppes and deserts of the far north and west, where agriculture is climatically impossible and where the nomads accordingly developed a distinctive, non-Chinese, pastoral way of life. By contrast, in the neighboring Vietnamese, Korean, and Japanese lands, there was no climatic obstacle to the development of agriculture and hence to the diffusion of Chinese civilization. Of these three lands, Japan was able to remain the most independent of the Chinese colossus, both politically and culturally, and hence played a correspondingly more significant role in both East Asian and world history. The remainder of this chapter therefore, will concentrate on the evolution of Japan to the eve of the Western intrusion.

Japanese history has been shaped to a considerable degree by the influence of geographic location. In this respect there is a close parallel with the British Isles at the other end of the Eurasian landmass. The Japanese islands, however, are more isolated than the British Isles; 115 miles separate them from the mainland, compared with the 21-mile width of the English Channel. Thus before their defeat by the United States, the Japanese had been seriously threatened by foreign invasion only in the thirteenth century. The Japanese, therefore, have been close enough to the mainland to benefit from the great Chinese civilization, but distant enough to be able to select and reject as they wished. In fact, the Japanese have been unusually sensitive and alert to what they have imported from abroad. Although popularly regarded as a nation of borrowers, they have independently evolved, because of their isolation, a larger proportion of their own culture than have any other people of comparable numbers and level of development.

The Japanese are basically a Mongoloid people who migrated from Northeast

Asia, but the hairy Caucasoid Ainu who originally inhabited the northern islands contributed to their racial composition; Malayan and Polynesian migrants from the south probably did also. Early Japan was organized into a large number of clans, each ruled by a hereditary priest-chieftain. Toward the end of the first century after Christ, the Yamato clan established a loose political and religious hegemony over the others. Its chief was the emperor, and its clan god was made the national deity.

This clan organization was undermined by the importation of Chinese civilization, which began on a large scale in the sixth century. Buddhism, introduced from Korea, was the medium for cultural change, fulfilling the same function here as Christianity did in Europe among the Germans and Slavs. Students, teachers, craftsmen, and monks crossed over from the mainland, bringing with them a new way of life as well as a new religion. More significant was the role of those Japanese who journeyed to the "Celestial Kingdom" and returned as ardent converts. The impetus for change culminated in the Taika Reform, which began in 645 and sought to transform Japan into a centralized state on the model of T'ang dynasty China. In accordance with the Chinese model, the country was divided into provinces and districts ruled by governors and magistrates who derived their power from the emperor and his council of state. Also, all land was nationalized in the name of the emperor and allotted to peasant households. The new owner-cultivators were responsible for paying to the central government a land tax in the form of rice and a labor tax that sometimes involved military service.

These and other changes were designed to strengthen imperial authority, and they did so in comparison with the preceding clan structure. But in practice, the Japanese emperor was far from being the undisputed head of a highly centralized state. The powerful hereditary aristocracy forced certain modifications in this Chinese-type administration that ultimately brought about its downfall. Although officials supposedly were appointed, as in China, on the basis of merit through examination, actually the old aristocracy succeeded in obtaining positions of status and power. Likewise, they retained many of their large landholdings, which were usually tax exempt and became manors outside the governmental administrative system. During this period the Fujiwara family perfected the dyarchy, or dual system of government. They did the actual work of ruling, furnishing the consorts for the emperor, and filling the high civil and military posts. Meanwhile, the emperor passed his life in luxurious seclusion, not bothered by affairs of state or degraded by contacts with common men. His prime responsibility was to guarantee unbroken succession for ages eternal. This dyarchical system of government, which had no parallel in China, remained the pattern in Japan until the country was opened up by the Europeans in the nineteenth century.

In cultural matters there was the same adaptation of Chinese models. The Japanese borrowed Chinese ideographs but developed their own system of writing. They borrowed Confucianism but modified its ethics and adjusted its political doctrines to suit their social structure. They accepted Buddhism but adapted it to satisfy their own spiritual needs, while retaining their native Shintoism. They built new imperial capitals, first at Nara and then at Kyoto, that were modeled after the T'ang capital, Ch'ang-an. But there was no mistaking the Japanese quality of the temples, pavilions, shrines, and gardens. The imperial court became the center of highly developed intellectual and artistic activity. Court life is delightfully described in Lady Murasaki's famous eleventh-century novel, *The Tale of Genji*. But this novel also reflects a society grown effeminate and devoted almost exclusively to the pursuit of aesthetic and sensual pleasures. This degeneration, which worsened in the next century, contributed to the coming of the new age of feudalism, when political power shifted from the imperial court to virile rural warriors.

VII. JAPANESE FEUDALISM

The Chinese system of imperial organization introduced by the Taika Reform of 645 worked effectively for a long period. By the twelfth century, however, it had been undermined and replaced by a Japanese variety of feudalism. One reason was the tendency of provincial governors, who were too fond of the refinements of Kyoto, to delegate their powers and responsibilities to local subordinates. Another was that powerful local families and Buddhist communities were always hungry for land and often able to seize it by force. They were willing to bring new land under cultivation so long as the incentive of tax exemption was maintained. These trends reduced the amount of tax-paying land, which meant an increased tax load for the peasant owner-cultivators, who in turn either fled to the northern frontier areas where the Ainu were being pushed back by force of arms, or else commended themselves and their lands to lords of manors. This relieved them of taxes and provided them with protection, but at the cost of becoming serfs. The net result of this process was that by the end of the twelfth century, tax-paying land amounted to 10 percent or less of the total cultivated area, and local power had been taken over by the new rural aristocracy.

At the same time, this aristocracy had become the dominant military force because of the disintegration of the imperial armed forces. The Taika Reform had made all males between the ages of twenty and sixty subject to military service. But the conscripts were required to furnish their own weapons and food and were given no relief from the regular tax burden. This arrangement proved unworkable and was abandoned in 739. Government military posts became sinecures generally filled by effeminate court aristocrats. As a result, the campaigns against the Ainu were conducted by the rural aristocrats. They became mounted warriors and gradually increased their military effectiveness until they completely overshadowed the imperial forces. A feudal relationship now developed between these rural lords and their retainers, or *samurai* (literally, "one who serves"). This relationship was based on an idealized ethic that was known as *bushido,* or "way of the warrior." The *samurai* enjoyed special legal and ceremonial rights, and in return were expected to give unquestioning service to their lords.

By the twelfth century, Japan was controlled by competing groups of feudal lords. For some time the Fujiwara were able to maintain a balance of power by throwing what strength they had on one side or another. In the end, one of these lords, Minamoto Yoritomo, emerged victorious. In 1192 the emperor commissioned him *Seii-Tai-Shogun* (Barbarian-Subduing-Generalissimo), with the right to nominate his own successor. As Shogun, Yoritomo was commander-in-chief of all the military forces and was responsible for the internal and external defense of the realm. From his headquarters at Kamakura, Yoritomo controlled the country in the name of the emperor, who continued to remain in seclusion in Kyoto. It was during this Kamakura Shogunate that the Mongols made their two attempts to invade Japan, in 1274 and 1281. On both occasions the Mongols were able to land, were fiercely resisted by the Japanese, and then were scattered by great storms that destroyed the expeditionary forces. The Japanese, believing their deliverance due to the intervention of the gods, called these storms "divine winds," or *kamikaze*.

In 1333 the Kamakura Shogunate was brought to an end, largely as a result of intrigues at the imperial court as well as growing disaffection among the warrior class. The Ashikaga family now obtained the title of Shogun, but their authority never extended far beyond the environs of Kyoto. In the rest of Japan, local lords struggled to gain control of as much land as possible. The outcome was the rise of great territorial magnates known as *daimyo* ("great name"). At the beginning of the sixteenth century there were several hundred of these daimyo, each seeking to attain hegemony over all Japan.

VIII. JAPAN'S WITHDRAWAL AND ISOLATION

The period of daimyo control witnessed rapid economic growth with important repercussions for Japanese society. Important technological advances were made in agriculture as well as in handicrafts, so that production per acre apparently doubled or even tripled in some parts of the country. The increased productivity stimulated more trade and a shift from a barter to a money economy. Towns gradually developed in the fifteenth and sixteenth centuries at strategic crossroads or coastal harbors or major temples. In these towns appeared the Japanese guilds, or *za*, which, like their Western counterparts, sought to gain monopoly rights in the production or transportation of certain goods, or in the exercise of certain trades or professions. They obtained these monopoly rights by paying fees to certain local authorities, thereby gaining greater freedom and higher status for their members.

Foreign and domestic trade quickened with the rising productivity of the Japanese economy. As early as the twelfth century enterprising Japanese had ventured overseas to Korea and then to China, prepared both for trade and for piracy. Gradually they extended the range of their operations, so that by the late fourteenth century these pirate-traders were active throughout Southeast Asia. Japanese settlers and soldiers of fortune also were widely scattered, especially in Indochina, Siam, and the Philippines.

These socio-economic developments began to undermine feudalism in Japan, as they had done earlier under similar circumstances in the West. If this trend had continued without interruption, Japan presumably would have followed the West European example and developed into a modern unified nation-state with an overseas empire. But Japan did not do so; instead she withdrew into seclusion.

A prime reason for this appears to have been the intrusion of the Western powers into the waters of Southeast and East Asia. This blocked the natural course of Japanese expansionism. If the Westerners had not appeared, the Japanese probably would have secured footholds in Formosa and in various parts of Southeast Asia. But now the Japanese were alarmed by the obvious superiority of Western military technology on the seas, as well as by the surprising effectiveness of Western missionaries on the home islands. Their response was to withdraw into the almost complete seclusion adopted in the early seventeenth century by the Tokugawa Shogunate.

All missionaries were forced to leave and their converts required to renounce their faith. Eventually all foreigners had to depart, with the exception of a few Chinese and Dutch who were allowed to trade under restricted conditions on the Deshima islet in Nagasaki harbor. In addition, Japanese subjects were forbidden to go abroad on penalty of death. Thus began over two centuries of seclusion for Japan.

The end result, then, was not a modern expansionist nation-state. Rather, Japanese feudalism was preserved and shielded from outside influences by the Tokugawa walls of seclusion. The cost for Japan, as for China, was institutional rigidity and obsolescence. Yet there was a fundamental difference between the two countries. Japan was not saddled with a monolithic, overpowering imperial structure as was the case in China. Rather the Tokugawas had merely papered over the cracks, so that when the West intruded in the nineteenth century, Japan, unlike China, was able to respond positively and creatively.

SUGGESTED READING

On China, see bibliography for Chapter 10 and also the following studies: W. BINGHAM, *The Founding of the T'ang Dynasty* (Waverly Press, 1941); M. ELVIN, *The Pattern of the Chinese Past* (Stanford Univ., 1973); C. O. HUCKER, *The Traditional Chinese State in Ming Times, 1368–1644* (Univ. Arizona, 1961). On Japan, there are the following: D. KEENE, *Japanese Literature: An Introduction for Western Readers* (Grove, 1955), and his *Anthology of Japanese Literature from the Earliest Era to the Mid-Nineteenth Century*, 2 vols. (Grove, 1955); E. O. REISCHAUER, *Japan Past and Present*, rev. ed. (Knopf, 1953); G. B. SANSOM, *Japan: A Short Cultural History*, rev. ed. (Appleton, 1944), and the same author's three-volume *A History of Japan* (Stanford Univ., 1958–64); R. TSUNODA et al., *Sources of the Japanese Tradition* (Columbia Univ., 1958).

chapter seventeen

Revolutionary
Western Civilization

*The chief glory of the later Middle Ages was not its cathedrals or its epics or its scholasticism: it was the building for the first time in history of a complex civilization which rested not on the backs of sweating slaves or coolies but primarily on non-human power.—*Lynn White, Jr.

The British philosopher-scientist Francis Bacon observed in 1620 that printing, gunpowder, and the compass, three inventions that were "unknown to the ancients," had in his day "changed the whole face and state of things throughout the whole world." The significance of this statement is that all three of the inventions that he perceptively selected had originated in China, and yet they had little effect on that country in comparison with their explosive repercussions in the West. Chinese civilization was too deeply rooted and Chinese imperial organization too pervasive to allow such inventions to disrupt traditional institutions and practices. Thus printing was used to disseminate old ideas rather than new; gunpowder reinforced the position of the emperor rather than of emerging national monarchs; and the compass, despite the remarkable expeditions of Cheng Ho, was not used for worldwide exploring and trading and empire building as was done by the Westerners.

The root of this fateful difference is to be found in the unique characteristics of the new Western civilization—pluralistic, adaptable, and free of the shackles of tradition that bound all the other Eurasian civilizations. The result was a historic mutation that transformed not only the West but also, as Bacon foresaw, the entire globe as it endured the dynamic expansionism of the revolutionary new society.

I. PLURALISM IN THE WEST

"In order to escape the evils which they saw coming, the people divided themselves into three parts. One was to pray God; for trading and ploughing the second; and later, to guard these two parts from wrongs and injuries, knights were created."[1] This analysis by the secretary of Philip VI of France depicts simply but essentially the division of medieval Western society into priests, workers, and warriors. Although these three classes were to be found in all Eurasian civilizations, yet their status and interrelationships were unique in the West because of the disintegration of the Roman Empire and the failure to reconstitute an imperial structure. Precisely how these classes functioned under these circumstances will be considered now within the context of the three institutions they personified: feudalism, manorialism, and the church.

Feudalism was a system of government in which those who possessed landed estates also possessed political power, so that state authority was replaced by contractual agreements between lords and vassals. Feudalism appeared when the German kings who had usurped Roman imperial authority lacked the funds to maintain a bureaucracy, a judiciary, and armed forces. The alternative was to grant estates as reward for service, but the recipients, or vassals, tended to administer them as private realms. Charlemagne was strong enough to exact and enforce oaths of loyalty from his vassals, but under his weak successors political power shifted to the vassals, whose estates or fiefs became virtually inalienable. These powerful lords in turn subdivided their holdings into lesser fiefs which they allocated to followers that were dependent on them rather than on the king. The feudal contract between these lords and vassals specified certain mutual obligations. The most important were that the lord should provide protection as well as the fief, while the vassal rendered military service for as long a time each year as local custom required—usually about forty days.

This process of feudalization proceeded apace within each of the feudal kingdoms that took form following the disintegration of Charlemagne's empire. Since the legal justification for fiefs of the great lords derived nominally from royal authority, the lords were careful to select a king even though they had no intention of respecting his sovereignty. But as Western Europe settled down after 1000 with the cessation of foreign invasions, the rulers gradually were able to assert their feudal rights and to begin the building of strong monarchies. The ensuing struggle between kings and nobles was the essence of Western political history during the following centuries.

Just as feudalism emerged with the collapse of large-scale political organization, so manorialism emerged with the collapse of large-scale economic organization. Consequently the manor was a self-sufficient village that was worked by serfs who were not free to leave, and who with their labor supported a hierarchy of lay and clerical lords. The size of the manor varied considerably, its inhabitants numbering in the scores or hundreds. Unlike a slave, the serf had recognized rights as well as responsibilities. He was entitled to protection, he was assured a plot for the support of himself and his family, and he enjoyed numerous religious holidays and harvest festivals that provided respite from toil. In return he was required to till those strips in the cultivated fields reserved for the lord, to perform other domestic and farm chores for the lord, and to give him a portion of any income from any source.

The manor of necessity provided almost all its own needs because of the virtual disappearance of long distance trade, of centralized handicraft production, of imperial currencies, and the like. Despite, or perhaps because of, this self-sufficiency, manorial technology was not at all primitive compared to that of Roman times. With imperial economic disintegration there was a loss of luxury crafts, irrigation works, aqueducts, and road systems. But the self-sufficient villages, because of their self-sufficiency, had no need for imperial organization. They functioned, and with steadily improving efficiency, on a local, village-to-village basis. The manors kept and improved the mills and smithies and used more iron than ever before, since it could be produced locally. Thus agricultural technology in the medieval West, as will be noted in section III of this chapter, advanced substantially beyond Greco-Roman standards, with far-reaching repercussions on all aspects of life.

Turning to the church, we find a similarly paradoxical development; that is, the Pope emerged more powerful precisely because of the fall of Rome. He did not have to contend against imperial domination as did the bishops of Constantinople, Alexandria, and Antioch against the dictates of the Byzantine emperor. It is true that Justinian's conquest of Italy enabled him and his successors to dominate the Papacy, so that no less than eleven of the thirteen Popes between 678 and 752 were Greeks or Syrians by birth. But with the Lombard invasion of Italy and the Islamic conquest of Egypt, Syria, and North Africa, the Byzantine emperors' ability to intervene in the West was severely curtailed. (See Chapter 15, section I.) The Papacy now turned from beleaguered Constantinople to the Franks, with whom it concluded an alliance that culminated in the crowning of Charlemagne by Pope Leo III in 800. Meanwhile the Papacy was further consolidating its supremacy in the West through its missions to convert the pagan northlands. With their success, new churches were founded which accepted the pope's "Catholic," or "universal," discipline, including the English church in 597, the Lombard and Frisian in the seventh century, and the German in the eighth.

Such, then, were the components of the new pluralistic society emerging in the West: an independent church instead of dictation by the emperor; a congeries of feudal kings and lords in place of imperial authority; autonomous manors individually taming the wilderness instead of the slave plantations of Roman times; and, before long, a rising merchant class operating with unique effectiveness from its urban bases against nobles, prelates, and, ultimately, monarchs. How this society, and this alone in all Eurasia, evolved and adapted during the half millennium after 1000 and eventually developed the strength and dynamism for overseas expansion is the subject of the following sections.

II. GEOGRAPHIC BACKGROUND

Geographic considerations comprise a significant factor in Europe's thrust forward ahead of other regions during the medieval period. One of these considerations was an advantageous location. Being on the western tip of the Eurasian landmass, Europe escaped invasions after year 1000. The significance of this remoteness of Western Europe is evident in the light of the disastrous Mongol conquest of Russia in the thirteenth century, of the Ottoman Turkish conquest of the Balkan Peninsula in the fifteenth and sixteenth centuries, and of the repeated Berber assaults in North Africa.

Equally significant was Europe's exceptionally favorable endowment of natural resources. The prevailing westerly winds from the Atlantic sweep unhindered across all Europe and deep into Russia. Hence Europe north of the Mediterranean basin enjoys a relatively moderate climate and constant rainfall, which together with the fertile soils provide an ideal combination for productive agriculture. Rivers usually run ice free and full, providing convenient means of transportation and communication. This advantage is further enhanced by the deeply indented coastline, which gives inland regions relatively easy access to coastal outlets. Some plateaus and mountain ranges interrupt the sweep of the great plains, but they are not so high or massive that they interfere seriously with transportation. Rather these mountains are an asset, being rich in minerals that historically have been quite important. These natural resources had, of course, always been available, but it was not until medieval Europe had effected its technological advances that they could be effectively exploited. The resulting increase in productivity had profound repercussions, including the shift of the economic and political center of Europe northward from its traditional site in the Mediterranean basin.

III. TECHNOLOGICAL PRECOCITY

More technological progress was made in medieval Western Europe than had been made during the entire history of classical Greece and Rome. One reason for this was the absence of slavery, a practice that tended to inhibit technological innovation. Another was the prevalence of frontier conditions that placed a premium on labor-saving devices. The manorial system of the medieval West also contributed to technological progress. The social strata under this system ranged not from a "divine" emperor to a subhuman slave, but from a serf with very definite rights, as well as duties, to a manorial lord who was sufficiently in touch with his serfs to have some real knowledge of the processes of production. Accordingly manual labor acquired a status and respect that were unknown in the old slave-based civilizations. Finally technology in the West was stimulated by the humanitarian ethic of Christianity, which itself began as a revolt against the inhumanity of the old imperial society. The monks in the monasteries insisted that manual labor was an integral part of the spiritual life. They were the first to combine brainpower and sweat, and in doing so, they aided technological advance. It was not accidental that it was a friar, Roger Bacon, who in the thirteenth century foresaw many of the technological achievements of the future.

Machines may be made by which the largest ships, with only one man steering them, will move faster than if they were filled with rowers; wagons may be built which will move with unbelievable speed and without the aid of beasts; flying machines can be constructed in which a man may beat the air with mechanical wings like a bird . . . ; machines will make it possible for men to go to the bottom of the rivers. . . .[2]

Bacon's insight reflects the unique nature of Western society as well as his own genius. Such a statement would have been inconceivable in classical Greece and Rome, just as it had no counterpart anywhere else in contemporary Eurasia. And it helps to explain why so many inventions that were of Chinese origin or that had been known to the Greco-Romans, were fully developed and exploited only by the Western Europeans.

The specific technological achievements of the West included basic inventions in the primary occupation of agriculture. One was the "three-field" rotation system of farming, which was gradually adopted from the eighth century onward and which raised productivity substantially, since only a third of the land lay fallow at any one time instead of the half left by the former "two-field" system. Another was the development of a heavy wheeled plow with a sharp iron point that made possible the cultivation of rich bottom lands with heavy soils and dense vegetation. Agriculture was aided also by more effective use of horsepower with the invention of a new type of collar that enabled the horse to pull without choking, thereby increasing tractive performance four to five times. Also significant was the invention of horseshoes, which facilitated the use of the horse for hauling as well as for plowing.

Finally, note should be made of the all-important watermill and windmill, both of which were known in Greco-Roman times but little used because of the abundance of slave labor and the scarcity of streams dependable the year around. With both these obstacles absent in the northern lands, the mill and the miller soon were to be found in almost every manor. And whereas the water wheel had been employed in the Mediterranean basin as a specialized device for grinding grain, in the course of the Middle Ages it was developed into a generalized prime mover. Thus water power came to be used for forge hammers and forge bellows, for saw-mills and lathes, and for fulling mills making cloth, pulping mills making paper, and stamping mills crushing ore. Indeed 5,000 mills were listed in England's Domesday Book of 1086. This represented one for every fifty households, certainly enough to substantially affect living standards.

This unique progress of the West is reflected in the changing relations with the traditional neighboring civilization of Byzantium. When the Western Crusaders began their siege of Constantinople in 1203, they were awestricken by the wealth and magnificence of that ancient capital, remarking that they "could not believe that there could be in all the world so rich a city." Two and a half centuries later, by contrast, a Greek scholar, Cardinal Bessarion, wrote a letter expressing a very different attitude. Having lived many years in Rome, the cardinal was impressed by the advanced state of handicrafts in Italy. So in 1444 he wrote to Constantine Palaeologos, then ruler of the autonomous Byzantine province of Peloponnesus (Morea), suggesting that "four or eight young men" be sent to Italy surreptitiously to learn Italian craft skills, and to learn Italian "so as to be conversant with what is said." Bessarion was particularly impressed by the water-driven saw mills which eliminated hand labor. He referred to "wood cut by automatic saws, mill wheels moved as quickly and as neatly as can be." Likewise he had in mind water-driven bellows when he wrote that "in the smelting and separation of metals they have leather bellows which are distended and relaxed untouched by any hand, and separate the metal from the useless and earthy matter that may be present." Bessarion also reported that in Italy "one may easily acquire knowledge of the making of iron, which is so useful and necessary to Man." The significance of this testimony is apparent. The technological advances made by medieval Western Europe had been of such magnitude that for the first time an Easterner was recommending that pupils should be sent to the West to learn the "practical arts."[3]

IV. DEVELOPING ECONOMY

Technological advance was matched by corresponding economic advance. There was steady economic growth from 900 to 1300. Then came the fourteenth-century slump, brought on by a combination of factors: a series of crop failures and famines, especially during 1315 and 1316; the Black Death, which carried off between one-third and two-thirds of the urban populations when it first struck in 1349, and which recurred periodically thereafter for generations; and the Hundred Years' War between England and France, and other conflicts in Germany and Italy. Shortly after 1400, however, a revival set in, and the trend from then on was generally upward.

This overall economic progress naturally was related to the technological advances which stimulated productivity in agriculture and handicrafts. The complete relief from foreign invasion during these centuries also contributed to the economic growth. Also there was a population increase of about 50 percent between the tenth and fourteenth centuries. This rate of increase seems insignificant in the present age of global population explosion, but it was unmatched at the time in any equivalent world area. The demographic spurt stimulated improvements in agriculture to support the growth of population, and the increased food supply in turn made possible further population increase.

Europe's economic development was evident in all fields. New mining methods led to rising output of salt, silver, lead, zinc, copper, tin, and iron ore in Central and Northern Europe. Likewise the rich timber and naval stores of Britain, Scandinavia, and the Baltic now were exploited more extensively than ever before. The same was true of the northern fisheries, particularly the cod of Iceland and Norway, and the herring of the Baltic. Most important, of course, was the rising productivity in agriculture in which most of the population was engaged. Peasants first brought under cultivation the waste lands around their own villages, of which there was plenty because in the twelfth century only about half the land of France, a third of the land of Germany, and a fifth of the land of England was under cultivation. Peasants not only cultivated unused lands in their midst, but with population growth they emigrated to the vast underpopulated frontier regions. Just as the United States had its westward movement to the Pacific Ocean, so Europe had its eastward movement to the Russian border. German colonists were moving beyond the Elbe at the expense of the Slavic and Baltic peoples of Eastern Europe, and other colonists were following the *reconquista* into Spain, and the Anglo-Saxon push into Wales, Scotland, and Ireland.

The combination of population increase and rising output in agriculture, mining, fishing, and forestry stimulated a corresponding growth of commerce and of cities. In the tenth century, merchants were to be found in Europe, but they trafficked mostly in luxuries. By the fourteenth century, however, commerce had advanced from the periphery to the center of everyday life. Goods exchanged included raw wool from England, woolen cloth from Flanders made from English wool, iron and timber from Germany, furs from Slavic areas, leather and steel from Spain, and luxury goods from the east. Although this commerce never engaged more than a small minority of the total population, nevertheless its great expansion in late medieval times had important repercussions for the whole of society. Towns slowly appeared, beginning as centers of local trade and local administration. The lead was taken in Italy where the inhabitants of such centers as Venice, Amalfi, and Naples were cut off from their hinterland by the Lombard invaders and so took to the sea for a living. Later other cities appeared along inland trade routes and along the Baltic coast. Important also for the distribution of goods were the great fairs that developed along the trade routes, outstanding being those in the county of Champagne, located strategically equidistant from Flanders, Italy, and Germany.

Western European cities were insignificant in medieval times compared to those of China, India, or the Middle East, as regards population or volume of trade. But they were quite unique because of their growing autonomy and political power. Precisely because they were starting afresh, and within the framework of a politically fragmented Europe rather than a monolithic empire, the burghers from the beginning exhibited a self-confidence and independence that had no parallel anywhere else in Eurasia.

As they acquired power and financial resources, they normally extracted from the king a royal charter licensing them to unite in a single commune, with the right to act as a corporation, to make agreements under its corporate seal, and to have its town hall, court of law, and dependent territory outside the walls. The charter also permitted merchants and craftsmen to organize into guilds, or sworn voluntary associations designed for protection and mutual aid, including the regulation of manufacturing standards, prices, and working hours. Thus towns gradually came to be recognized as a new element in society, their inhabitants being outside feudal law. This was reflected in the custom that if a serf escaped to a town and lived there for a year and a day without being apprehended, he became a free man. As a saying put it at that time, "Town air makes a man free."

In certain regions, groups of cities banded together to form leagues which became powerful political, as well as economic, entities. When the Hohenstaufen emperors attempted to force the wealthy cities of northern Italy—Milan, Brescia, Parma, Verona, and others—to pay taxes and accept imperial administration, they organized themselves into the Lombard League which with Papal aid successfully waged war against the emperors. Likewise various Baltic towns—Bremen, Lübeck, Stettin, Danzig, and others comprising a total of ninety in 1350—organized themselves into the Hanseatic League which fought against pirates, pressed for trading privileges in foreign countries, and virtually monopolized the trade of Northern Europe.

This evolution gave the European merchant a status, as well as power, that was unique in Eurasia. In China, government was carried on by scholars; in Japan, by soldiers; in the Malay lands and in the Rajput states of India, by the local nobility; but nowhere by merchants. Nowhere, that is, except in Europe, where they were steadily gaining in political as well as economic power. There they were becoming lord mayors in London, senators in the German Imperial Free Cities, and grand pensioners in Holland. Such social status and political connections meant more consideration and more consistent state support for mercantile interests and, later on, for overseas ventures.

V. RENAISSANCE FERMENT

The medieval West experienced cultural and intellectual developments as innovative and significant as the technological and economic. The centuries from the fall of Rome to about the year 1000 constitute a "Dark Age" in the sense that there was a complete absence of cultural creativity. The weight of poverty, insecurity, and isolation was too great to permit the production of literary, artistic, or scholarly masterpieces. It is true that the monks in the monasteries did manage to preserve certain parts of classical culture, but they naturally concentrated on those parts that conformed to their own religious convictions, while ignoring what was more secular. The result was a "Christianized" or "clericized" culture that was supplementary to, and dependent upon, the church.

In the eleventh century, cathedral schools were established by the bishops for the education of the priests of their dioceses. A century later the first universities evolved out of the cathedral schools. A distinctive feature of these universities was that they were self-governing corporations with a legal identity of their own. Also they did not consist of only a liberal arts faculty, as did the cathedral schools, but in addition usually had faculties of canon law, civil law, medicine, and theology. The first universities appeared in the twelfth century at Bologna, Paris, and Oxford. In the following century others were founded at Padua. Naples, and Salamanca; and in the fourteenth century they spread to Central Europe—to Prague, Cracow, and Vienna. All these universities were primarily institutions for training the clergy. This emphasis was natural and proper at a time when the clergy had a monopoly of literate occupations and administrative positions.

This educational and intellectual environment changed with the Renaissance ferment of the period from roughly 1350 to 1600. The Renaissance got under way first in Italy, and hence reflected the conditions and values of contemporary Italian society. This was a bustling urban society based on flourishing industries and on the profitable commerce between Western Europe and the wealthy Byzantine and Islamic Empires. Prosperous cities such as Venice, Genoa, Florence, Milan, and Pisa were dominated by the great merchants who controlled politics as well as trade and crafts. These families were the patrons of Renaissance artists and writers, and their needs, interests, and tastes colored the Renaissance cultural revival, even though the patrons included ducal families such as the Sforzas of Milan, as well as Popes such as Nicholas V, Pius II, Julius II, and Leo X. This accounts for the secularism and humanism of the Renaissance—its concern with this world rather than the hereafter, its focus on pagan classics rather than Christian theology.

This secularism and individualism of the Renaissance was reflected in its scholarship and education. The so-called father of Renaissance literature, Francesco Petrarca or Petrarch (1304–1374), stressed the value of the classics as a means for self-improvement and a guide to social action. Likewise the new board schools of the Renaissance trained not priests, but the sons of merchants. The curriculum emphasized classical studies and physical exercise and was designed to educate the students to live well and happily and to function as responsible citizens.

The Renaissance spirit is most strikingly expressed in its art. Since the church no longer was the sole patron, artists were encouraged to turn to subjects other than the traditional Biblical themes. Such themes continued to appear quite commonly, but in the works of such masters as Leonardo da Vinci, Michelangelo, Raphael and Titian, the emphasis increasingly shifted to portraits designed to reveal the hidden mysteries of the soul and to paintings intended to delight the eye with striking colors and forms.

The Renaissance was not an exclusively Italian phenomenon. Its innovations spread to Northern Europe in the sixteenth century, the instruments of diffusion being Italian diplomats and generals who were employed by northern monarchs, and the printing press, which speeded up the circulation of books and ideas. Printing was particularly influential in Northern Europe because literacy was more widespread there than in the southern and eastern regions of Europe. The flood of printed matter certainly fomented popular agitation concerning political and religious issues, thereby contributing substantially to the Reformation and the ensuing religious and dynastic wars.

In conclusion, what is the significance of the Renaissance in the perspective of world history? It is apparent that the new emphasis on man and on what he could accomplish was more conducive to overseas expansion than the preceding medieval outlook. On the other hand, this point can easily be exaggerated and needs serious modification. The fact is that Renaissance Europe was not science oriented. The leading figures tended to be more aesthetic and philosophical than objective and skeptical. The Iberian pioneers of overseas expansion definitely were not Renaissance men. "However Renaissance may be defined," states a distinguished historian of European expansion, ". . . Prince Henry and his captains were, in the main, men of the Middle Ages. Even Columbus . . . embarked on his famous enterprise with an intellectual equipment which was mainly medieval and traditional."[4]

The Renaissance ferment, then, explains not so much the origins of European expansion before 1500, as its impetus and irresistible power after 1600. The latter, however, is vastly significant in its own right. The fact remains that there was an intellectual ferment in Western Europe and that it had no counterpart in the rest of Eurasia. This is a fundamental difference of enormous import.

In the Ottoman Empire, for example, the Moslem medressehs or colleges emphasized theology, jurisprudence, and rhetoric at the expense of astronomy, mathematics, and medicine. The graduates of these schools were uninformed about what was being done in the West and quite uninterested in finding out. No Moslem Turk could believe that a Christian infidel could teach him anything of value. Now and then, a rare, far-sighted individual warned of the dangers of this intellectual iron curtain that separated the Ottoman Empire from neighboring Christendom. One of these voices was Katib Chelebi, the famous Turkish bibliographer, encyclopedist, and historian who lived in the first half of the seventeenth century. Coming from a poor family, he was unable to obtain a formal higher education. This proved to be a blessing in disguise. He was spared the superficial, hair-splitting specialization on Moslem sacred studies that characterized Ottoman education at this time. The fact that he was self-taught explains in large part his open-mindedness towards Western learning. One of Chelebi's works was a short naval handbook that he compiled following a disastrous defeat of the Ottoman fleet in 1656. In the preface of this work, Chelebi emphasized the need for mastering the science of geography and map-making.

For men who are in charge of affairs of state, the science of geography is a matter of which knowledge is necessary. They may not be familiar with what the entire globe is like, but they ought at least to know the map of the Ottoman State and of those states adjoining it. Then, when they have to send forces on campaign, they can proceed on the basis of knowledge, and so the invasion of the enemy's land and also the protection and defense of the frontiers becomes an easier task. Taking counsel with individuals who are ignorant of that science is no satisfactory substitute, not even when such men are local veterans. Most such veterans are entirely unable to sketch the map of their own home regions.

Sufficient and convincing proof of the necessity for learning this science is that fact that the heathen, by their application to and their esteem for those branches of learning have discovered the New World and have over-run the markets of India.[5]

Chelibi grasped the connection between Europe's intellectual advance and her overseas expansion. In his last work before his death in 1657, Chelebi warned his countrymen that if they did not abandon their dogmatism, they would soon "be looking at the universe with the eyes of oxen." His prediction proved prophetic. The Turks remained steeped in their religious obscurantism, and like other non-Western peoples, they paid a high price. The Christian infidels with their new learning eventually became the masters not only of the New World but of the ancient empires of Islam and of Confucianism.

VI. RISE OF NATIONAL MONARCHIES

Political developments were as significant as the economic and cultural developments in the evolution of the medieval West. The emerging national monarchies provided the means for mobilizing and focusing Europe's resources and energies on overseas enterprise. The roots of the monarchies go back to the tenth century when Western Europe had become a mosaic of petty feudal states that had acquired, bit by bit, the land and authority of the defunct Carolingian Empire. Several traditions and interests operated during the following centuries at cross purposes. There were feudal kings engaged in continual conflict with their feudal vassals, who often held larger fiefs and wielded more power. There were feudal principalities, both lay and clerical, that raised the prickly investiture issue. There were also city-states that sometimes combined in powerful organizations such as the Lombard and Hanseatic Leagues. And in opposition to the particularist interests of the preceding three groups, there was the striving for a united Latin Christendom headed by the pope in Rome, or by a "Roman" emperor as the successor to Charlemagne and his predecessors. This complex of conflicting interests produced an infinite variety of constantly changing alliances and alignments at all levels of political life.

In very broad terms, the political evolution of Western Europe after Charlemagne may be divided into three stages. Between the ninth and eleventh centuries, popes and emperors generally cooperated. The popes helped the emperors against the German secular lords, and in return were supported against the Byzantine opponents to papal authority. In 1073 a period of papal supremacy began with the accession of Pope Gregory VII. The investiture dispute between the papacy and the emperors—the struggle to control the investiture of German bishops—was won by Gregory, thereby undermining imperial administration and power. By the thirteenth century Pope Innocent III was involved in the affairs of virtually every European state, making and breaking kings and emperors. For over two centuries, the papacy generally was recognized as the head of Latin Christendom, particularly because of a succession of pious French and English kings.

The period of papal supremacy ended suddenly and dramatically when Pope Boniface VIII issued the bull *Unam sanctam* (1302) in which he set forth uncompromisingly the doctrine of papal authority: ". . . we declare, state, define and pronounce that it is altogether necessary to salvation for every human creature to be subject to the Roman pontiff." But what had been acceptable in previous centuries was no longer so. The monarchs and their councillors now were placing the welfare of their kingdoms ahead of the wishes of popes. Boniface was subjected to threats and mistreatment by an agent of the French king and died soon after his humiliation. In 1305 a French archbishop was elected pope as Clement V, and instead of going to Rome he took up residence at Avignon in southeastern France. During the next seventy years the Avignonese popes, as the pawns of the French monarchy, lost their predecessors' commanding position in Latin Christendom.

The new power of European kings was derived in large part from their informal alliance with the rising merchant class. The burghers provided financial support to the monarchs, and also managerial talent in the form of chamberlains, overseers, keepers of the king's accounts, managers of the royal mint, and so forth. These originally had comprised the king's household in charge of the monarch's private affairs. Now strong centralized governments evolved as the king's household was employed to administer the realm as a whole. More specifically, it laid the foundation for a bureaucracy, a judiciary, and a system of taxation in collaboration with some representative assembly.

The monarchs in return provided the burghers with protection against the incessant wars and arbitrary exactions of the feudal lords and bishops. They also served merchant interests by ending the crazy-quilt pattern of autonomous local authorities, each with its own customs, laws, weights, and currencies. As late as the end of the fourteenth century there were thirty-five toll stations on the Elbe, over sixty on the Rhine, and so many on the Seine that the cost of shipping grain 200 miles down the river was half its selling price. With the removal of such encumbrances and the enforcement of royal law and order, national monarchies emerged by the fifteenth century encompassing roughly the territories of modern England, France, Portugal, and, after the marriage of Ferdinand and Isabella, also Spain.

VII. REFORMATION

These emerging national monarchies were decisively strengthened by the Reformation of the sixteenth century. From the viewpoint of European history the Reformation stands out as the great religious upheaval that shattered irrevocably the unity of western Christendom. But from the perspective of world history the Reformation is significant for its role in transferring power from church to state, and thereby providing the Western monarchies with the political and economic dynamism that powered Europe's overseas drive.

Considering first the Reformation as a religious movement, it got under way with Martin Luther's protest against the selling by the Papacy of a particularly blatant indulgence that promised absolution "from all thy sins, transgressions, and excesses, how enormous soever they may be . . . so that when you die the gates of punishment shall be shut, and the gates of the paradise of delight shall be opened. . . ." It was in protest against this "unbridled preaching of pardons" that Luther, then a priest at the University of Wittenberg, posted his ninety-five theses on the church door. Such a gesture was not unprecedented in the history of the church. Many reformers and rebels had taken similar stands in the past, only to be silenced by the Papacy through persuasion or force. Thus Pope Leo X dismissed Luther's protest as a "squabble amongst monks." But the course of events was to demonstrate that Luther was destined for a role infinitely more fateful than that of a squabbling monk.

One reason was the weakening of the church during the fourteenth century "Babylonian Captivity" when two Popes, one in Rome and one in Avignon, each claimed to be the legitimate successor of Saint Peter and excommunicated the other. At least as important was the growth of national feelings in northern Europe, so that both monarchs and subjects increasingly viewed the Popes as foreigners with no right to meddle in national affairs or to raise revenue within national frontiers.

This sentiment explains the enthusiastic popular response to Luther's stand. The ensuing public debate led Luther to spell out the revolutionary implications of his basic doctrine of justification by faith—that is—that the priestly offices and ministrations of the Church were unnecessary intermediaries between the individual and God. In October 1520 Luther burned a papal bull of excommunication, and the following year, when summoned to appear before an Imperial Diet, he refused to recant "unless I am convinced by the testimony of the Scriptures or by clear reason."

Emperor Charles V was unable to move decisively against the spreading Lutheran heresy because he was involved in wars with the French and the Turks. By the time he became free of these distractions in 1546, the Lutheran princes were too strong and well organized to be crushed in the manner of past heresies. They banded together in the Schmalkaldic League and successfully resisted the Emperor until he accepted the Peace of Augsburg (1555), which granted each

German prince the right to select either the Catholic or Lutheran faith and to impose it on his subjects.

The Augsburg settlement recognized only Lutheranism as an alternative to Catholicism, but Luther's fundamental doctrine of individual interpretation of the Scriptures led inevitably to diverging interpretations and to a rising flood of heresies. In Switzerland, for example, John Calvin preached predestination—each individual's fate was decreed by God before birth. The radical Anabaptists, carrying to its logical conclusion Luther's doctrine that every man should follow the dictates of his conscience, demanded full religious liberty, separation of church and state, and an end to military service and to class and status differentiation.

The prevailing factor determining the religion of a state almost invariably was the decision of its prince. If he favored a break with Rome, the Reformation triumphed; if he opposed a break, the Reformation was doomed. Very substantial benefits awaited the prince who opted in favor of Protestantism. His political power increased for he became the head of his national church rather than having to accept the ecclesiastical suzerainty of the international Papacy. His economic position also improved as he could confiscate Church lands and movable wealth, and also check the flow of revenue to Rome. Despite these advantages of turning against the Pope, as many princes remained loyal as chose to break away. One reason was the threat of attack by the imperial forces of Charles V, who was supported by the Pope. Also many princes found they could extract as many political and economic concessions from the Papacy by remaining Catholic as they were likely to obtain as Protestant princes. It was a hodge-podge religious map of Europe that evolved after Luther's death. Thanks to the Catholic Reformation and its militant instrument, the Jesuit order, Catholicism continued to be the official faith in southern Europe and in most of Central Europe. The remaining states of Europe embraced either Lutheranism, Calvinism, or Anglicanism.

Thus the legacy of the Reformation was the splintering of the universal medieval Church into numerous territorial churches—some national, some princely, some provincial, and some confined to a single city. This brings us to the significance of the Reformation for world history as distinct from European. The common feature of all these new territorial churches was their control by secular rulers. Regardless of whether the church remained Catholic in doctrine or adhered to one of the Protestant faiths, it was the secular authority that controlled ecclesiastical appointments and church finances. This meant the transfer of power from church to state, and a corresponding strengthening of the national monarchs. The large new political entities proved to be efficient instruments for mobilizing the human and material resources needed for overseas enterprise. It was not accidental that although most of the early explorers were Italian navigators, their sponsors were the new national monarchies rather than their miniscule home city-states. The Spanish and Portugese courts provided the backing for Columbus and da Gama, and the English and French courts quickly and eagerly followed up with backing for Cabot, Verrazano, and many others in the following centuries.

VIII. WESTERN EUROPE'S EXPANSIONISM

Between the fourth and tenth centuries Europe was invaded by Germans, Huns, Magyars, Vikings and Moslems. But from the tenth to the fourteenth centuries this situation was dramatically reversed as Europe took the offensive on all fronts. (See Map XVI, "Expansionism of the Medieval West.") Assorted crusaders pushed back the Moslems in Spain, southern Italy, Sicily, and the Holy Land, and even overran the Christian Byzantine empire. Meanwhile in northeast Europe, German frontier lords were winning lands east of the Elbe. As this German expansion was continued east of the Oder against the pagan Prussians, it was conducted as a crusade by the Teutonic Knights. By the end of the fifteenth century large areas formerly occupied by Slavic and Baltic peoples had become thoroughly German from top to bottom: lords, bishops, townsmen, and peasants.

These crusades were considered at one time to have been responsible for stimulating practically every constructive development in the later Middle Ages, including the growth of trade and towns, and the advances in culture. This interpretation no longer is accepted, and instead it is generally agreed that the crusades basically were the consequence rather than the cause of this progress. Without the preceding technological advances, commercial revival, intellectual ferment and political consolidation, the crusades would have been quite inconceivable. This dynamism continued and picked up speed after the fourteenth century slump, and the result was the extension of the expansionist crusading drive to overseas territories.

The uniqueness of this West European dynamism is apparent in the variety of Eurasian responses to the expansion of the Moslem world in the fifteenth century. As noted in Chapter 14, section VI, Islam at that time was fanning out from the Middle East in all directions. The Turks, after capturing Constantinople, overran the Balkan Peninsula and then crossed the Danube and pushed through Hungary to the walls of Vienna. Likewise in the east the Turks under the colorful Babur were striking southward from Afghanistan, beginning their founding of the great Mogul Empire that was to rule India until the British takeover in the nineteenth century. In Africa also, Islam was spreading steadily into the interior from its bases on the northern and eastern coasts of the continent. Finally Moslem merchants dominated the Eurasian sea routes running from the Red Sea and the Persian Gulf across the Indian Ocean and around Southeast Asia to the China seas.

With these advances by its soldiers, merchants, and preachers, the world of Islam had become the heartland of Eurasia. It occupied the strategic center of the great landmass, and the more it expanded, the more it isolated the Chinese at the eastern end of Eurasia and the Europeans at the western. The completely different responses of the Chinese and the Europeans to this encirclement profoundly influenced the course of world history from that time to the present.

The Chinese, as noted earlier, withdrew voluntarily, even though their Cheng Ho expeditions had demonstrated conclusively that they possessed both the technology and the resources to dominate the oceans. (See Chapter 12, section I, and Chapter 16, section V.) But during this Ming period, after the interlude of Mongol domination, the Chinese were turning their backs to the outside world. And their merchant class, lacking the political power and social status of its Western counterpart, was unable to challenge imperial edicts banning overseas enterprise. Thus the Chinese turned their formidable talents and energies inward, thereby deliberately relinquishing a lead role in Eurasia, and ultimately, world affairs.

The response of the Europeans was precisely the opposite. Their geographic horizons and commercial ambitions had been immeasurably broadened by *Pax Mongolica,* so that the sudden disintegration of the Mongol empire had left them with acute frustration and yearning. Likewise the loss of the crusaders' outposts in the Levant, the Islamization of the Il-Khanate in Persia, and the Turkish conquest of the Balkans, all served to deprive the Europeans of access to the Black Sea, to the Persian Gulf and to the Indian Ocean. Thus the Europeans were effectively fenced in on the western tip of Eurasia. It is true that the all-important spice trade still flourished, as Italian merchants continued to meet Arab traders in the ports of the Levant and to pick up cargoes for transshipment to the West. This arrangement was satisfactory for the Italians and the Arabs who reaped the golden profits of the middleman. But other Europeans were not so happy, and they sought earnestly for some means to reach the Orient to share the prize.

Their search was bound to succeed, given their technical skills, their economic strength, and their political pluralism. There was no emperor in Europe to issue restraining orders; instead there were rival national monarchies competing strenuously in overseas enterprises. Also there was in Europe a genuine need and strong demand for foreign products, and the merchants were sufficiently powerful to ensure satisfaction of the need. Thus if Columbus had not discovered America and if da Gama had not rounded the Cape, then others assuredly would have done so within the next few decades. In short, Western society had reached the take-off point. It was ready to burst out, and when it did, it found the ocean ways clear, and it spread irresistibly over the entire globe.

SUGGESTED READING

M. BLOCH, *Feudal Society*, 2 vols. (Univ. Chicago, 1961); G. R. ELTON, *Reformation Europe* (Harper, 1966); W. K. FERGUSON, *The Renaissance* (Torchbook, 1940); J. R. LEVENSON, ed., *European Expansion and the Counter-Example of Asia, 1300–1600* (Prentice-Hall, 1967); R. S. LOPEZ, *The Birth of Europe* (Lippincott, 1966); R. L. REYNOLDS, *Europe Emerges: Transition Toward an Industrial World-Wide Society 600–1750* (Univ. Wisconsin, 1961); B. H. SLICHER VAN BATH, *The Agrarian History of Western Europe, 500–1850* (Arnold, 1963); L. WHITE, JR., *Medieval Technology and Social Change* (Clarendon, 1962).

part five

NON-EURASIAN
WORLD TO 1500

In dealing thus far with the millennia to 1500, attention has been focused exclusively upon the Eurasian part of the globe. The reason, as explained in Chapter 1, section III, is the overwhelming primacy of Eurasia in world affairs during those millennia, together with the fact that human history prior to 1500 was essentially regional rather than global in scope. Once Homo sapiens dispersed to all the continents, the primitive level of his technology limited strictly the range of his operations. During the following millennia he lived and functioned in regional isolation. The peoples of Australia and of the Americas were completely isolated on their respective continents, while those of Africa were largely, though not exclusively, isolated also.

During those millennia when human history was primarily regional history, the inhabitants of the great Eurasian landmass comprised the great majority of the world's total population, and, living in proximity to each other, they interacted in varying degrees through the ages. This interaction stimulated a relatively rapid pace of development in Eurasia, and, conversely, the isolation and lack of outside stimuli retarded development in the non-Eurasian regions. This explains why, during the pre-1500 era, the overwhelming majority of the historically significant advances in human civilization were Eurasian in origin, and why, perforce, the world of today is essentially a Eurasian world. Hence the concentration thus far in this study on Eurasian peoples and civilizations.

In the fifteenth century this regional phase of world history came to an end with Europe's overseas expansion, bringing peoples of all regions into direct contact with each other. This outward thrust traditionally is viewed from the West's angle of vision. The emphasis is on Columbus and da Gama and Magellan and on their discoveries and the subsequent repercussions. This approach, however, is inadequate for global history. A global perspective requires consideration not only of the expanding West but also of the regions into which the West expanded. The peoples of these regions, after all, comprised an appreciable proportion of the human race, so that their evolution must be considered, albeit not as painstakingly as that of the historically more prominent Eurasians. Also the lands and peoples and institutions of the non-Eurasian world were as significant in determining the outcome of Western expansionism as were the Westerners themselves. For these reasons, then, the following two chapters are devoted to Africa and to the Americas and Australia.

chapter eighteen

Africa

Geographers, in Afric's maps,
with savage creatures filled the gaps;
And o'er unhabitable downs
Placed elephants for want of towns.—Dean Swift

       If degree of accessibility to outside stimuli is a decisive factor in determining the tempo of a region's development, then a casual glance at a map suggests that Africa is tolerably well located. To the north the continent is separated from Europe by the Mediterranean, a narrow and easily crossed body of water that historically has functioned more as a highway than as a barrier. To the east the Sinai Peninsula provides a bridge to Asia, while the Red Sea is even narrower and easier to cross than the Mediterranean. Finally the great expanses of the Indian Ocean are neutralized by the monsoon winds, which facilitate communication back and forth between East Africa and South Asia.

       Yet historically Africa has been much more isolated from Eurasia than these impressions would indicate, and this isolation has remained a prime and constant factor in the continent's development. This chapter will consider first the geography behind the isolation, and then the peoples involved and the nature of their historical evolution.

I. GEOGRAPHY

Africa, as defined in this study, refers to the part of the continent south of the Sahara Desert. The reason for this definition, is that the Sahara is the great barrier, the great divider, while the Mediterranean by comparison is a connecting boulevard. This explains why historically the people of North Africa have had more interaction with the other peoples around the Mediterranean basin than with those to the south of the desert barrier. Thus sub-Saharan Africa, the subject of this chapter, is in effect an island, the northern shore of which is the Sahara Desert rather than the Mediterranean.

      The Sahara is by no means the only obstacle to contact with the outside world. On the east of the great desert, along the upper reaches of the Nile, are the enormous swamps of the Sudd, which historically have constituted a formidable barrier. Also contributing to Africa's inaccessibility is a coastline unbroken by bays, gulfs, or inland seas. Consequently this coastline is shorter than Europe's, though Africa has thrice the area. This lack of anything corresponding to the Mediterranean, the Baltic, or the Black Sea means that Africa's interior is relatively closed to the outside world.

Effective barriers are to be found also in the form of thousand-mile-long sand-bars along the east and west coasts, and in the tremendous swells on both coasts, which make landing in a small boat quite hazardous. And if the bars and breakers are successfully negotiated, there remains still another obstacle—the rapids and waterfalls created by the rivers tumbling down a succession of escarpments from the interior plateau to the low coastlands. Historically the coastal waterfalls meant that there was no counterpart in Africa to the smooth-flowing St. Lawrence and Amazon, which provide easy access to the interior of the Americas, or to the Rhine and Danube, which do likewise for Europe. Also, the approaches to Africa are beset by the hot, humid climate of the low-lying coastal areas and by the tropical diseases accompanying such a climate. The interior uplands generally have a healthy bracing climate but the coastal regions have presented a serious health hazard to those seeking to penetrate inland.

As significant as this external inaccessibility, has been the internal—that is, the difficulty of crossing from one part of Africa to another. Viewing the continent as a whole, it begins with small fertile strips at the extreme northern and southern tips. These soon yield to the great desert expanses of the Kalahari in the south and the Sahara in the north. Next are the rolling grasslands or savannas, known in the north as the Sudan, the Arab term meaning "the country of the black people." Then come the tropical rain forests, which in their densest parts are more difficult to penetrate than the deserts.

These extremes of nature, together with the absence of nearby coastal outlets and of unencumbered river systems, have combined to inhibit interaction amongst the various regions of the continent. Inevitably this has retarded the overall development of its peoples and explains the simultaneous existence of large and complex empires in the savannas, and of hunting bands in remote desert and forest areas.

This geographic setting helps to explain also the paradoxical difference in the timing of European penetration of Africa compared to that of the Americas. As late as 1865, when the Civil War was ending in the United States, only the coastal fringe of Africa was known, together with a few insignificant portions of the interior. This imperviousness of Africa to Europe's dynamism was due in part to the geographic conditions that combined to make the continent unusually resistant to outside intrusion. But geography was not the only factor involved. At least as important was the African's general level of social, political, and economic organization, which was high enough to effectively block the Europeans for centuries. But before considering the culture of the Africans, we shall first examine their ethnic composition.

II. PEOPLES

In contrast to what is sometimes assumed, the African peoples are far from ethnically homogeneous. Various strains are to be found south of the Sahara, and have existed throughout history. Their origins and diffusion remain in large part a mystery, however, and authorities are far from agreement. The ethnic classification that, for the present at least, meets with the fewest objections recognizes four major peoples: (1) Bushmen, who speak the Khoïsan language, (2) Pygmies, whose original language is unknown because they adopted those of their later conquerors, (3) Negroes, who speak the Niger-Congo language, and (4) Caucasoids, known also as Capsians, Cushites and Hamites, who speak the Afroasiatic language. These four peoples may have originated in the region of Lake Victoria, whence the Bushmen migrated south to southern Africa, the Pygmies west to the Congo, and the coastal rain forests of West Africa, the Negroes west to West Africa and northwest to the then fertile Sahara region, and the Caucasoids northwest to Egypt and North Africa, as well as northeast to Arabia and West Asia.

These categories and migrations, it should be reemphasized, are by no means universally accepted. Indeed, one authority has summarized current knowledge, or lack of knowledge, as follows:

. . . we can say little more than this: if one stands at Suez and looks south and southwest, people tend to get darker the further one goes. One must, even in this generalization, except the Bushmanoids. . . . The fact of the matter is that, empirically, Egyptians are more or less Mediterranean Caucasoids; that as one goes south and southwest, there is a gradual change; along the Guinea Coast or in the Congo forests, the Negro stereotype is dominant. There is not, however, an undisputed "line" that can be drawn on a map, or distinctions that can be made between tribes (in other than statistical terms) with the claim that one is unequivocally Caucasoid and the other Negroid. In even the most dominantly Negroid tribes, there are to be found individuals with light skin and green eyes. . . .[1]

III. AGRICULTURE AND IRON

The cultures of Africa were the outcome of a much greater degree of interaction with the outside world than had been possible in the Americas or Australia. Agriculture, for example, which originated in Mesopotamia and then took root in Egypt in the fifth millennium B.C., may have spread from there to the Sudan stretching from the Ethiopian highlands to the Atlantic coast. Some authorities, it should be noted, believe that agriculture was invented independently in this zone, along the upper reaches of the Niger River. Whether or not this is so, the fact remains that the great majority of the plants that eventually were cultivated in sub-Saharan Africa were importations. The most important of these were: from Mesopotamia and Egypt via the Nile—barley, wheat, peas, and lentils; from Southeast Asia—bananas, sugar cane, the Asian yam, and new forms of rice; from the New World via the Portuguese and later slave traders—tobacco, corn, lima and string beans, pumpkins and tomatoes. Prior to the advent of iron tools, these plants were grown largely in the grasslands of the Sudan. Little agriculture was practiced in the rain forests because the edible fruits and vegetables available there provided an adequate food supply without the hard labor needed to fell trees and till soil with stone implements.

As basic for Africa as the introduction of agriculture was that of iron metallurgy. The latter was definitely an importation, with three separate sources being likely. One was Carthage, whence the art probably was spread by traders who, by 500 B.C. and perhaps earlier, had developed two regular caravan routes across the Sahara. The desert was not as wide and formidable at that time, so the traders were able to cross with carts and chariots pulled by donkeys and horses, as we know from rock engravings found along the routes. Later, when the desert passage became more difficult, the Romans solved the problem by introducing camels from Central Asia.

A second source of iron metallurgy was the kingdom of Kush located on the upper Nile, with its capital at Meroe, a little north of Khartoum. The Kushites were predominantly Negroids and known to the ancient Egyptians as Nubians. Originally they had suffered raids by the armies of the pharaohs, but gradually they built a strong enough state structure so that by 751 B.C. they conquered Egypt and ruled the country for one century. Then Assyrian armies from the east forced the Kushites to withdraw, but it was from these Assyrians that the art of ironmaking was learned. The Kushites were able to put their knowledge to good use, for their country, unlike Egypt, had abundant resources of iron ore and fuel. Meroe soon became a great iron-producing center. The huge mounds of slag still to be seen around the ruins of the capital suggest that it had served as the Pittsburgh of Central Africa. After more than a thousand years' existence, the Kushan kingdom declined during the fourth century A.D., but not before ironmaking had spread far to the south and west.

A prime cause for the Kushan decline was invasion from Ethiopia, the third source of the introduction of iron metallurgy into sub-Saharan Africa. The ancestors of the Amharic people of modern Ethiopia built an empire about A.D. 50 with Axum as the capital. These Axumites were traders who exchanged their goods in the Indian Ocean lands, the Middle East, and East Africa. Although details are not yet known, they introduced both metallurgical and advanced agricultural techniques in East Africa.

The Carthaginians, the Kushites, and the Axumites together were responsible for the widespread diffusion of the art of ironmaking in sub-Saharan Africa. By about 500 B.C. the local populations had begun to make their own tools and weapons. The technique had spread westward as far as central Nigeria by 200 B.C., and southward to the Zambezi by the first century A.D. In this manner Africa entered the iron age, with repercussions as far-reaching as those noted earlier in the case of Eurasia.

Iron-tipped hoes and iron-shod axes made possible the extension of agriculture into the forests of Africa, as earlier they had into the forests of Central Europe and of the Ganges and Yangtze valleys. The resulting increase in agricultural output left a surplus available for trading purposes. As in Eurasia, this in turn led to social differentiation—to the division of peoples into rulers and ruled in place of the former simple kinship relationships. Hence the appearance about the ninth century A.D. of definite state structures with military and administrative services and with the revenue sources necessary for their support.

Another repercussion in Africa was the radical change in the ethnic composition of the continent. It was the accessible Negroes and Caucasoids of the Sudan, rather than the inaccessible Pygmies and Bushmen of the rain forests and the southern regions, who adopted and profited from agriculture and iron metallurgy. Consequently, it was they also who increased disproportionately in number and who were able, with their iron tools and weapons, to push southward at the expense of the Bushmen and Pygmies. This explains why they were the predominant ethnic groups by the time the Europeans arrived, whereas a millennium earlier they had shared the continent fairly evenly with the Bushmen and Pygmies.

IV. ISLAM

The repercussions of agriculture and metallurgy were all accentuated by another profoundly significant historical force emanating from Eurasia, that is, Islam. Its rapid sweep across North Africa in the seventh century encountered little resistance from the Byzantine rulers but a good deal from the native Berber populations. The latter, however, were eventually won over to Islam, and they then joined the Arabs in conquering Spain and in extending the Moslem faith and culture across the Sahara to the Sudan. Berber traders converted their African counterparts that they encountered along the trans-Sahara trade routes. Tolerant Negro rulers allowed Moslems full liberty both to practice and to propagate their religion. Thus Islam first made its appearance in the markets of the western Sudan about the ninth century. By the thirteenth century it had become the state religion of the great Mali empire of the time, and spread steadily with official support.

On a much smaller local scale Islam also gained a foothold in East Africa, where Moslem Arab communities had been established from an early date. Inter-marriage of the Arab settlers with Bantu women created a new people, the *Sawahila,* or "coastalists," whose language became the lingua franca of East Africa. Their settlements were confined to coastal enclaves or to islands which offered more security against mainland tribes. No attempt was made to conquer the interior, so that Islam never obtained a massive base in East Africa comparable to that in North Africa and the Sudan.

The impact of Islam upon Africa was varied and profound. It was evident most obviously in the externals of life—names, dress, household equipment, architectural styles, festivals, and the like. It was evident also in the agricultural and technological progress that came with enlarged contact with the outside world. In East Africa the Arabs introduced rice and sugar cane from India. Islam also stimulated commerce by linking the African economy to the far-flung net-work of Eurasian trade routes controlled by Moslem merchants. From their bases in North Africa the Moslems used the camel much more than had the Romans, and increased correspondingly the number of trans-Saharan trade routes and the volume of trade. They exchanged cloth, jewelry, cowrie beads, and, above all, salt, in return for ivory, slaves, ostrich feathers, and, most important, gold from the upper Niger, Senegal, and Volta rivers. Much of this gold ultimately found its way to Europe, and in such large quantities that it became important for redressing medieval Europe's adverse balance of trade with the East. Such was the mutually stimulating interaction between the Sudanese economy and foreign trade that by 1400 the whole of West Africa was crisscrossed with trading trails and dotted with market centers.

Meanwhile a similar trading pattern had been developing in East Africa. Moslem middlemen on the coast sent agents into the interior who bought ivory, slaves, gold from Rhodesia, and copper from Katanga. These commodities then were exported through Indian Ocean trade channels, controlled at the time by Moslem merchants. In later centuries iron ore also was obtained from the interior, shipped to southern India, and made into the so-called Damascus blades. In return for these African products were received Chinese and Indian cloth, and various luxury goods, especially Chinese porcelain, remains of which still can be found along the coast. This trade was the basis for the string of thriving ports and city-states along the East African coast. By the thirteenth century two of them, Kilwa and Zanzibar, had established mints of their own, striking copper coins in considerable quantity.

Returning to the role of Islam in Africa, it served also to stimulate greatly the intellectual life of the Sudan. Literacy was spread with the establishment of Koranic schools. Scholars could pursue higher learning at various Sudanese universities, of which the University of Sankore at Timbuktu was the most out-standing. This institution was modeled after other Moslem universities at Fez,

Tunis, and Cairo. It was the custom for scholars to move about freely among these universities and others in the Moslem world, to study at the feet of particular masters. The Moslem traveler Leo Africanus, who visited Timbuktu in 1513, found that the flourishing state of learning was due to the support it received from the ruler, Askia the Great. "Here [in Timbuktu] are great store of doctors, judges, priests, and other learned men, that are bountifully maintained at the king's cost and charges. And hither are brought divers manuscripts or written books out of Barbarie [North Africa], which are sold for more money than any other merchandize."[2]

The adoption of Islam also enhanced the political cohesion of the Sudanic kingdoms. Their rulers traditionally could claim the allegiance only of their own kinship units or clans, and of such other related kinship units that recognized descent from a great founding ancestor. But when the kingdoms were enlarged into great empires, this kinship relationship obviously became inadequate as the basis for imperial organization. The more widely an empire was extended, the more alien its emperor appeared to a large proportion of the subjects. Local chiefs could not be depended upon to serve as faithful vassals; they tended instead to lead their own people in resistance to imperial rule. Islam helped to meet this institutional problem by strengthening the imperial administration. Moslem schools and colleges turned out a class of educated men who could organize an effective imperial bureaucracy. These men were not dominated by their kinship alliances; their own interests were tied to imperial authority, and they normally could be counted upon to serve that authority loyally.

V. SUDAN EMPIRES

It was this combination of agricultural and metallurgical progress, corresponding growth in economic productivity, flourishing interregional trade, and the stimulus from Islam, that explains the process of state building that went on in Africa from the eighth century onward. Not surprisingly, the most complex political structures appeared in the Sudan, where long distance trade was most highly developed and where Islamic influence was the strongest. Hence the emergence in that region of three great empires: Ghana (700–1200), Mali (1200–1500), and Songhai (1350–1600). (See Map XX, "African Empires and Trade Routes.")

These empires had certain fundamental characteristics in common. They were all based primarily upon trade, so that each extended its authority northward to control the import of salt, and southward to control the purchase of gold. Each derived most of its revenues from levies on the buying and selling of these and other commodities. The revenues from these duties made possible progressively greater sophistication in imperial administration. Thus the Songhai Empire was more complex than its two predecessors. It was divided into defined provinces, each with a governor on long-term appointment. It also boasted the beginnings of a professional army and even of a number of ministries—for finance, justice, home affairs, agriculture, and forests, as well as for "White People," that is, the Arabs and Berbers on the Saharan frontiers of the empire.

The Mali and Songhai empires owed much to Islam for furthering trade, providing a trained bureaucracy, and stimulating intellectual life. Islam also transformed the Sudan from an isolated African region to an integral part of the Moslem world. Thus the fourteenth century Arab traveller Ibn Battuta included Mali in his journeys which ranged as far east as China. Arriving at the

Mali capital in June 1353 he was favorably impressed by the imperial administration and by the habits of the people.

> The negroes possess some admirable qualities. They are seldom unjust, and have a greater abhorrence of injustice than any other people. Their sultan shows no mercy to anyone who is guilty of the least act of it. There is complete security in their country. Neither traveller nor inhabitant in it has anything to fear from robbers or men of violence. They do not confiscate the property of any white man who dies in their country, even if it be uncounted wealth. On the contrary, they give it into the charge of some trustworthy person among the whites, until the rightful heir takes possession of it. They are careful to observe the hours of prayer, and assiduous in attending them in congregations, and in bringing up their children to them. On Fridays, if a man does not go early to the mosque, he cannot find a corner to pray in, on account of the crowd.[3]

Although Islam played a key role in the formation and functioning of the Sudanic empires, it should be noted that it was primarily an urban faith. It was the merchants and townspeople who became Moslems, while the country folk by and large remained loyal to their traditional pagan gods and beliefs. Thus the reliance of many of the emperors and of their imperial establishments on Islam was a source of weakness as well as of strength. Islam, we have seen, had much to contribute, but its base was narrower than it seemed to contemporary observers who naturally visited urban centers and travelled along trade routes. Thus in times of crisis the town-centered empires proved unexpectedly fragile and quickly fell apart.

Another weakness of the Sudanic empires was their vulnerability to attack from the North by Berbers looking for the sources of African gold or seeking to impose their particular version of the true faith. The fanatical Almarovids were responsible for the overthrow of Ghana in 1076, and likewise an invasion from Morocco destroyed Songhai in 1591. The latter catastrophe marked the end of the Sudanic imperial era. In the words of a seventeenth-century Timbuktu historian: "From that moment everything changed. Danger took the place of security; poverty of wealth. Peace gave way to distress, disasters, and violence. . . ."[4]

VI. KINGDOMS AND TRIBES

The three empires noted above are the best known African medieval political creations. In the rest of the continent, however, there existed a great variety of other political structures. In Southeast Africa, for example, there were certain similarities to the situation in the Sudan. Just as the Sudan was famous in the Mediterranean basin for its gold exports, so Southeast Africa was famous for the same reason in the Indian Ocean basin. And just as the Sudanic empires and North African states were nourished by the one trade pattern, so by the fifteenth century the Monomotapa empire in the interior and the Kilwa city-state on the coast were supported by the other.

Monomotapa, a word adapted by the Portuguese from the royal title *Mwenemutapa*, encompassed modern Rhodesia and Mozambique, thereby controlling the sources of the gold and the routes to the coast, after the fashion of the Sudanic empires. It was the monarchs of Monomotapa who raised the Great Temple of Zimbabwe, a massive enclosure with walls 32 feet high, constructed to provide an appropriate setting for the conduct of royal ceremonial rites. Kilwa's merchant rulers, who called themselves sultans, were middlemen who controlled the flow of goods from Monomotapa to the Moslem trading ships that ranged the Indian Ocean and even beyond to the China seas. "Kilwa is one of the most beautiful and well-constructed towns in the world. The whole of it is elegantly built," wrote Ibn Battuta—the same Battuta who later was impressed also by Mali.[5]

Just as the Sudanic kingdoms were ravaged by Berber invaders from the north, so Monomotapa and Kilwa were destroyed by Portuguese intruders from overseas. Within a decade after Vasco da Gama's rounding of the Cape of Good Hope in 1497, the Portuguese had sacked many of the coastal cities of southeast Africa and were carrying on in the Indian Ocean as though it were a Portuguese lake. Later the Portuguese made their way up the Zambezi river and similarly undermined the Monomotapa empire. They settled in various strategic locations along the river and extended their influence in all directions until the inevitable showdown in 1628. With their firearms the Portuguese easily defeated two Monomotapa armies, so that several petty kingdoms now arose on the ruins of the former empire.

The diversity of the African scene is manifest if one turns from southeast to northeast Africa, where Christian kingdoms existed in obscure isolation amongst the Ethiopians and the Nubians. Until the fourth century A.D. the Axumites of Ethiopia had been pagans, whose gods were those of south Arabia. In A.D. 333 Christianity was introduced by a Syrian, Frumentius, who converted the king. Since that time Christianity has remained the official religion and has permeated all phases of Ethiopian life. The Moslem conquests of the seventh century cut off Ethiopia from the Mediterranean, and the loss of the Red Sea ports to the Moslems between the eighth and tenth centuries left the country completely cut off from the outside world. But Ethiopia possessed a sufficiently large interior of mountains and plateaus to survive in substantial isolation to modern times. Under these conditions a distinctive society took form and endured—a Christian feudal society with a court comprised of priests, officials, and army commanders, and with a king who, like his early medieval European counterparts, was forced by economic necessity and political pressures to move his court continually from region to region.

The Kush kingdom in Nubia, as noted in section III of this chapter, had been destroyed by Axum in 325. The succession states that followed were converted to Byzantine or Coptic Christianity in the sixth century by a mission from Alexandria. The hold of the new faith is reflected in the large number of churches, some with superb murals still glowing in their original colors, having been preserved by covering sand. Like Ethiopia, these Christian Nubian kingdoms were isolated by the seventh-century Islamic conquest of Egypt. Despite border warfare with the Moslems, Nubian Christianity survived for another six centuries, unknown to the outside world. But in the thirteenth century Egypt came under the rule of the militant Saracens who, being at war with the Western Crusaders in the Holy Land, were unwilling to tolerate other Christians nearer to home. Thus they overran most of Nubia in the late thirteen century, though isolated areas held out for another two centuries.

In this sampling of diverse African societies—and it is a mere sampling rather than a comprehensive survey—the most primitive should not be overlooked, for their continued existence reflected the extreme physical compartmentalization of the continent. The Pygmies and Bushmen, constricted and isolated in inaccessible deserts and rain forests, remained at the food gathering stage of development. The world passed them by as they continued with man's original mode of livelihood as hunters and food collectors. But this does not mean that their cultures are of no significance or interest. Those few who have closely observed the Pygmies report highly developed talents in dancing, choral song, acting, mimicry, and storytelling. Likewise the Bushmen are famous for their rock-paintings and engravings, executed with natural and easy rhythmical lines, and depicting animals, hunting and battle scenes, and dancing ceremonial activities.

VII. CONCLUSION

Allowing for the difference between the Moslem and the Christian intellectual climates, a citizen of fourteenth-century Timbuktu would have found himself reasonably at home in fourteenth-century Oxford. In the sixteenth century he would still have found many points in common between the two university cities. By the nineteenth century the gulf had grown very deep.[6]

This point made by the British Africanist, Thomas Hodgkin, describes a process that is certainly not unique to Africa. It is clear from the preceding chapters that this is a worldwide process, and for the simple reason that the West pioneered in modernization and consequently pulled ahead of all other societies. Yet the fact remains that the gap between the West and Africa opened much wider than those between the West and other Eurasian regions. Constantinople, Delhi, and Peking did decline in relation to London, Paris, and Berlin, but they did not decline to virtual extinction as did Timbuktu. The problem as to why the West took the lead in modernization and forged ahead of other regions has been considered in Chapter 17. But we face here another problem—namely, why did Africa fall behind not only the West but also Eurasia in general?

This question has scarcely been posed, let alone answered. The preceding chapters analyzing the evolution of various Eurasian civilizations suggest certain factors that may be relevant and that are here presented tentatively for consideration. Their relative significance, if indeed they are significant, cannot be assessed without much more research and reflection.

One distinctive feature of Africa's development that quickly comes to mind is that the general stimulus generated by agriculture, metallurgy and long-distance trade soon reached a plateau and failed to develop further. There was no counterpart in Africa to the chain-reaction upsurge that occurred in northern Europe and in the Ganges and Yangtze valleys, when they were opened up and exploited with iron tools. Perhaps one reason was the absence in Africa of regions of corresponding fertility and potential productivity. The combination of poor soils, climatic extremes and the tsetse fly made it impossible for the African agriculturists and craftsmen to be as productive as their Eurasian counterparts. Even the favored Sudan was excessively dependent on the export of gold and slaves, which could not provide a broad enough base for continued economic growth.

Africa's development appears to have been stunted also by the external and internal isolation, described in the first section. For example, Africa did not have anything comparable to Europe's rivers and coastal outlets, nor did it enjoy the advantages of being near the advanced Byzantine and Islamic civilizations as Europe did. Instead there were deserts and rain forests within, and oceanic expanses without. This prevented effective exploitation of even the limited output that the natural resources allowed. It is true that Africa, unlike the Americas, was close enough to Eurasia to benefit from the diffusion of basic technology such as agriculture and metallurgy. But Africa was too remote to receive, for example, the long series of inventions that were exchanged in the course of millennia amongst the Eurasian regions, to their mutual advantage.

Finally Africa suffered from vulnerability to outside attack, for retarded development means weakness, and weakness everywhere invites aggression. The disastrous effects of Berber invasions of the Sudan, and of the Portuguese onslaught on southeast Africa have been described above. They are particularly relevant in view of the fact that Western Europe, by contrast, suffered no invasions whatsoever during the critical five centuries prior to 1500 when she rose to global prominence. This vulnerability factor was to manifest itself in particularly virulent form with the later infliction of the slave trade, which not only depopulated vast areas but also caused economic and political chaos.

These various factors may explain why Africa's development stopped far short of the levels reached by the Eurasian societies. This retardation is reflected in the continued collective ownership of land and in the failure of urban centers to dominate the economies of any African regions. On the other hand this, in turn, made possible the preservation of the appealing egalitarianism and leisurely pace of life that prevail where kinship ties and communal land ownership remain in force. (See Chapter 3, section IV.) The British Africanist Basil Davidson has concluded that ". . . comparison between Africa and Europe is likely to be in Africa's favor. . . . So far as the comparison has any value, daily life in medieval Europe was likely to be far more hazardous or disagreeable for the common man and his wife."[7]

This positive judgment doubtless is justified, but from the perspective of world history the noteworthy point is that the appealing features of African society had survived precisely because it lacked the dynamism and continued growth of Eurasian societies. So long as the Africans remained relatively isolated from the outside world, they could preserve and enjoy a way of life that had long since been lost in the Eurasian civilizations. But when Western expansionism reached the African shores, a heavy price had to be paid. For the greater the underdevelopment, the greater the vulnerability and the resulting disruption. This was true when Bantu agriculturists expanded throughout Africa at the expense of "underdeveloped" hunting peoples, and it was to be equally true in modern times when the representatives of the industrialized West burst out over the globe at the expense of "underdeveloped" agriculturists, and especially of those who had remained at a Neolithic level of organization.

Finally, it should be noted that although the Africans had not kept up with the Eurasians, they surpassed the more isolated American Indians and Australian aborigines. This explains to a large degree why the Europeans were so much slower in penetrating into the interior of Africa than into the Americas or Australia. Geographic factors also were involved here, as noted in section I, but more basic was the higher level of development reached by the Africans, particularly those with whom the Europeans had dealings. These naturally were the most advanced, because that meant they were also the most productive, and hence offered the most opportunity for profitable trade.

The commerce that developed with the coming of the Europeans was novel for the advanced Africans only in its scale. Mercantile activity was not, in itself, something strange, since they for a long time had maintained trade ties with areas as far removed as Morocco and Egypt. It follows that the Africans reacted to the Portuguese very differently from the manner in which the American Indians were reacting to the Spaniards at the same time. It is true that the forest dwellers, who had not had direct contact with the Arabs, were astonished by the white skin of the Europeans, by the loud noise of their firearms, and by the fact that these newcomers came from the sea, which was much revered by the coastal peoples. Yet the fact remains that the arrival of the Portuguese did not produce the demoralization and disintegration in Africa that the Spaniards did in the Americas. Accordingly, the Africans traded with the Europeans on terms that they themselves dictated. For centuries the coastal chieftains refused to allow the Europeans to penetrate inland because they wished to maintain their profitable position as middlemen between the European buyers and the producers in the interior. A British official wrote in 1793 that Africa remained an unknown continent "rather from the jealousy of the inhabitants of the sea coasts, in permitting white men to travel through their country, than from the danger or difficulty attending the penetration." This jealousy he attributed to the middlemen's fear "that the advantages of their trade with Europe should be lessened and transferred from them to their neighbours; or that the inland kingdoms by obtaining European arms" would become dangerous rivals.[8]

Adam Smith, writing in 1776, was aware of this difference between the American Indians and the African Negroes in their capability for resisting European penetration.

Though the Europeans possess many considerable settlements both upon the coast of Africa and in the East Indies, they have not yet established in either of those countries such numerous and thriving colonies as those in the islands and continent of America. Africa, however, as well as several of the countries comprehended under the general name of the East Indies, are inhabited by barbarous nations. But those nations were by no means so weak and defenceless as the miserable and helpless Americans; and . . . they were besides much more populous. . . . In Africa and the East Indies, therefore, it was more difficult to displace the natives, and to extend the European plantations over the greater part of the lands of the original inhabitants.[9]

SUGGESTED READING

B. DAVIDSON, *The African Past: Chronicles from Antiquity to Modern Times* (Little, 1964), and his *The African Genius: An Introduction to African Social and Cultural History* (Atlantic, Little, Brown, 1970); J. D. FAGE, *An Atlas of African History* (Arnold, 1965); R. GREY and D. BIRMINGHAM, eds., *Pre-Colonial African Trade* (Oxford Univ., 1970); R. HALLETT, *Africa to 1875* (Univ. Michigan, 1970); R. A. LYSTAD, *The African World: A Survey of Social Research* (Praeger, 1965); G. P. MURDOCK, *Africa: Its Peoples and Their Culture History* (McGraw-Hill, 1959); R. OLIVER and J. D. FAGE, *A Short History of Africa* (Penguin, 1962).

chapter nineteen

Americas and Australia

To the nations, however, both of the East and West Indies, all the commercial benefits which can have resulted from these events [the expansion of Europe] have been sunk and lost in the dreadful misfortunes which they have occasioned.—Adam Smith

The Vikings had stumbled upon North America in the eleventh century, and for about one hundred years they tried to maintain settlements there, but without success. In the fifteenth century Columbus likewise stumbled upon the New World, but this time the sequel was altogether different. Instead of failure and withdrawal, discovery now was followed by massive and overwhelming penetration of both North and South America. The contrast reflected the extent of the increase in European power and dynamism during the intervening half millennium.

Equally striking was the contrast between the rapid European penetration and exploitation of the Americas, and the centuries that elapsed before the same could be done in Africa. One reason was geography; the New World was physically more accessible and inviting. The other reason, as noted by Adam Smith, was "the miserable and helpless" plight of the Indians. Although they were far from all being at the same level of development, yet the overall nature of the Indian cultures was such that effective resistance was impossible. And if this was true of the American Indians, it was much more so of the Australian aborigines who were still at the food-gathering stage. In this chapter we shall consider the physical setting and the cultural background of the fateful developments that followed the landings of Columbus in the West Indies and of Captain James Cook in New South Wales.

I. LAND AND PEOPLE

The Americas, in contrast to Africa, were exceptionally open to newcomers from Europe. No sandbars obstructed the approaches to the coasts. Harbors were much more frequently available along the indented coastline of the Americas than along the unbroken coastline of Africa. Also the Americas had a well-developed pattern of interior waterways that were relatively free of impediments and offered easy access to the interior. There was no counterpart in Africa to the majestic and smooth-flowing Amazon, Plata, Mississippi, or St. Lawrence. The climate of the Americas, too, is generally more attractive than that of Africa. The Amazon basin, it is true, is hot and humid, and the polar extremities of both continents are bitterly cold, but the British and the French settlers flourished in the lands they colonized north of the Rio Grande, and the Spaniards likewise felt at home in Mexico and Peru, which became their two principal centers.

Until recently it was believed that the Indians first began crossing over from Siberia to the Americas about 10,000 years ago. New archaeological findings, together with the use of carbon-14 dating, have forced drastic revision of this estimate. It is now generally agreed that man certainly was in the New World 20,000 years ago, and probably 20,000 years or more before that. The last major migration of Indians took place about 3,000 years ago. The actual crossing to the New World presented little difficulty to these early newcomers. The last of the Ice Ages had locked up vast quantities of sea water, lowering the ocean level by 460 feet and thus exposing a 1,300-mile-wide land bridge connecting Siberia and Alaska. A "bridge" of such proportions was, in effect, a vast new subcontinent, that allowed ample scope for the vast diffusion of plants and animals that now took place. Even after rising temperatures lifted the sea level and submerged the connecting lands, the resulting narrow straits easily could have been crossed in crude boats without even losing sight of shore.

Most of those who crossed to Alaska moved on into the heart of North America through a gap in the ice sheet in the central Yukon plateau. They were impelled to press forward by the same forces that led them to migrate to America—the search for new hunting grounds and the continual pressure of tribes from the rear. In this manner both the continents were soon peopled by scattered tribes of hunters. Definite evidence has been found that indicates that the migrants from Asia reached the southern tip of South America by 11,000 years ago.

As regards racial traits, all Indians may be classified as Mongoloids. They have the characteristic straight black hair, sparse on the face and body; high cheekbones; and the Mongolian spot that appears at the base of the spine in young children. Considerable variation exists, however, among the different tribes: the earliest varieties of American Indian are much less Mongoloid than the later ones, because they left Asia before the Mongoloids, as we know them today, had fully evolved. That the immigrants at once spread out and settled in small, inbred groups in a variety of climates also explains the presence of individual physical types.

II. CULTURES

The migrants to the New World brought little cultural baggage with them since they came from northeast Siberia, one of the least advanced regions of Eurasia. They were, of course, all hunters, organized in small bands, possessing only crude stone tools, no pottery, and no domesticated animals, except perhaps the dog. Since they were entering an uninhabited continent they were completely free to evolve their own institutions without the influences from native populations that the Aryans had been subject to when they migrated to the Indus Valley, or the Achaeans and Dorians when they reached Greece.

During the ensuing millennia the American Indians did develop an extraordinarily rich variety of cultures, adapted to one another as well as to the wide range of physical environments they encountered. Some remained at the hunting band stage while others developed kingdoms and empires. Their religions encompassed all known categories, including monotheism. They spoke some 2,000 distinct languages, some as different from one another as Chinese and English. This represents as much variation in speech as in the entire Old World, where about 3,000 languages are known to have existed in A.D. 1500. Nor were these languages primitive, either in vocabulary or in any other respect. Whereas Shakespeare used about 24,000 words, and the King James Bible about 7,000, the Nahuatl of Mexico used 27,000 words, while the Yahgans of Tierra del Fuego, considered to be one of the world's most retarded peoples, possess a vocabulary of at least 30,000 words.[1]

Taking all types of institutions and practices into account, anthropologists have defined some twenty-two culture areas in the New World—the Great Plains area, the Eastern Woodlands, the Northwest Coast area, and so forth. A simpler classification, on the basis of how food was obtained, involves three categories: hunting, gathering, and fishing cultures; intermediate farming cultures; and advanced farming cultures. This scheme is not only simpler but it is also meaningful from the viewpoint of world history, for it helps to explain the varied responses of the Indians to the European intrusion.

The advanced farming cultures were located in Mesoamerica (central and southern Mexico, Guatemala, and Honduras) and the Andean highland area (Ecuador, Peru, Bolivia, and northern Chile). The intermediate farming cultures were generally in the adjacent regions, while the food-gathering cultures were in the more remote regions—the southern part of South America, and the western and northern part of North America.

This geographic distribution of culture points up the fact that, in contrast to Africa, the most advanced regions in the Americas were not located closest to Eurasia. One reason is that northeast Siberia was not a greater center of civilization, as was the Middle East and the Mediterranean basin that contributed so much to the Africans. Also, climatic conditions in Alaska and the Canadian Arctic obviously were not conducive to rapid cultural development as was the case in the Sudan savannah zone. Thus the tempo of advance in the Americas depended not on proximity to Eurasia but rather on suitability for the development of agriculture. It is significant, then, that agriculture was first developed in the Americas in regions that were strikingly similar to the Middle East where agriculture originated in Eurasia—that is, highland regions not requiring extensive clearing of forests to prepare the fields for crops, with enough rainfall to allow the crops to mature, and with a supply of potentially high-yielding native plants available for domestication.

Chapter 3, section I describes the origins of agriculture in Mesoamerica about 7000 B.C. and the long stage of "incipient agriculture" to 1500 B.C. before food growing finally became the determining factor in society. The Indians domesticated over one hundred plants, or as many as were domesticated in all Eurasia, a truly extraordinary achievement. Agriculture in turn made possible the development of large empires and sophisticated civilizations comparable in certain respects to those of West Africa. Unfortunately, these indigenous American civilizations were suddenly overwhelmed by the Spaniards and thus left little behind them other than their precious domesticated plants.

III. CIVILIZATIONS

The three major Amerindian civilizations were the Mayan, in present-day Yucatan, Guatemala, and British Honduras; the Aztec, in present-day Mexico; and the Inca, stretching for 3,000 miles from mid-Ecuador to mid-Chile. (See Map XXI, "Amerindian Empires.") The Mayans were outstanding for their remarkable development of the arts and sciences. They alone evolved an ideographic form of writing in which characters or signs were used as conventional symbols for ideas. They also studied the movements of the heavenly bodies in order to measure time, predict the future, and set propitious dates for sacrifices and major undertakings. So extensive was the astronomical knowledge compiled by highly trained priests that it is believed to have been at least equal to that of Europe at that time.

Maya cities, if they may be so called, were ceremonial centers rather than fortresses or dwelling places or administrative capitals. This was so because the Mayans practiced slash and burn agriculture, which exhausted the soil within two or three years, requiring constant moving of the village settlements. To balance this transitory mode of life, the Maya cultivators expressed their social unity by erecting large stone buildings in centers that were devoted primarily to religious ceremonies. These buildings were large temple pyramids and also community houses in which the priests and novices probably lived. This architecture, produced entirely with stone tools, was decorated with sculpture that was unsurpassed in the Americas and that ranks as one of the great world arts.

The Maya civilization flourished between the fourth and tenth centuries, but then declined for reasons that remain obscure. It may have been soil exhaustion, or epidemic disease, or, more plausibly, peasant revolutions against the burden of supporting the religious centers with their priestly hierarchies. In any case the great stone structures were abandoned to decay and were swallowed by the surrounding forest, to be unearthed only in recent decades with archaeological excavations.

The Aztecs were brusque and warlike compared to the artistic and intellectual Mayas—a contrast reminiscent of that between the Romans and the Greeks in the Old World. The Aztecs actually were latecomers to Mexico, where a series of highly developed societies had through the centuries succeeded one another. These had been vulnerable to attacks by barbarians from the arid north who naturally gravitated down in response to the lure of fertile lands. The last of these invaders were the Aztecs, who had settled on some islands on Lake Texcoco, then filling much of the floor of the valley of Anáhuac. As their numbers grew and the islands became overcrowded, the Aztecs increased their arable land by making *chinampas,* floating islands of matted weeds, covered with mud dredged from the lake floor, and anchored to the bottom by growing weeds. To the present day, this mode of cultivation is carried on in certain regions. Before each planting the farmers scoop up fresh mud and spread it over the *chinampa,* whose level steadily rises with the succession of crops. The farmers then excavate the top layers of mud, which they use to build a new *chinampa,* thus beginning a new cycle.

The *chinampas* enabled the Aztecs to boom in numbers and wealth. Early in the fifteenth century they made alliances with towns on the lake shore, and from that foothold they quickly extended their influence in all directions. Raiding expeditions went out regularly, forcing other peoples to pay tribute in kind and in services. By the time the Spaniards appeared on the scene, Aztec domination extended to the Pacific on the west, to the Gulf of Mexico on the east, almost to Yucatan on the south, and to the Rio Grande on the north. The capital, Tenochtitlán, was by then a magnificent city of 200,000 to 300,000 people, linked to the shore by causeways. The conqueror Cortes compared the capital to Venice and judged it to be "the most beautiful city in the world."

Aztec power was based on constant war preparedness. All men were expected to bear arms, and state arsenals were always stocked and ready for immediate use. With their efficient military machine the Aztecs were able to extract a staggering amount of tribute from their subjects. According to their own extant records, they collected in one year fourteen million pounds of maize, eight million pounds each of beans and amaranth, and two million cotton cloaks in addition to assorted other items such as war costumes, shields, and precious stones.[2]

The Spaniards were not only dazzled by the wealth and magnificence of the Aztec state, but also horrified by the wholesale ritual massacre of a continual procession of human victims. These were slaughtered at the top of the ceremonial pyramids that abounded everywhere and that the Spaniards soon realized functioned as altars for human sacrifice. Indeed the Aztecs waged war to take captives for sacrifice as well as to exact tribute for their capital. The first objective they considered even more important than the second, for their priests taught that the world was in constant danger of cataclysm, especially the extinguishing of the sun. Hence the need for offering human victims to propitiate the heavenly deities. But this practice trapped the Aztecs in a truly vicious circle: sacrificial victims were needed to forestall universal disaster; these could be obtained only through war; successful war could be waged only by sacrificing victims, but these in turn could be secured only through war.

Finally, the Incas of Peru were one of the numerous tribes of Quechua stock and language that raised llamas and grew potatoes. In the twelfth century they established themselves in the Cuzco valley which they soon dominated. At this early stage they evolved a dynasty from their war chiefs, while their tribesmen constituted an aristocracy amongst the other tribal peoples. The combination of a hereditary dynasty and aristocracy, which was unique in the New World, constituted an effective empire-building instrument. From their imperial city of Cuzco in the Peruvian highlands, the Incas sent forth armies and ambassadors, west to the coastal lands, and north and south along the great mountain valleys. By the time of the Spanish intrusion they had extended their frontiers some 2,500 miles from Ecuador to central Chile, a much larger empire than that of the Aztecs.

This empire was held together physically by a road system which still can be traced for hundreds of miles and which included cable bridges of plaited aloe fibre and floating bridges on pontoons of buoyant reeds. Equally important was an extensive irrigation system, parts of which are still in use, and which made the Inca empire a flourishing agricultural unit. Communications were maintained by a comprehensive system of post-stations and relays of runners who conveyed messages swiftly to all parts of the empire.

Imperial unity was furthered also by elaborate court ritual and by a state religion based on worship of the sun, of which the king, or Inca, was held to be a descendant, and in whose ceremonial worship he played an essential role. Other techniques of imperial rule included state ownership of land, mineral wealth, and herds, careful census compilations for tax and military purposes, deposition of local hereditary chieftains, forced population resettlement for the assimilation of conquered peoples, and mass marriages under state auspices. Not surprisingly, the Inca empire is considered to be one of the most successful totalitarian states the world has ever seen.

IV. CONCLUSION

Impressive as were these attainments of the American Indians, the fact remains that a handful of Spanish adventurers was able to easily overthrow and completely uproot all three of the great New World civilizations. And this despite the fact that the Aztec empire had a population of over ten million, and the Inca empire, over six million. The explanation for the one-sided Spanish triumph is to be found ultimately in the isolation of the Americas. This isolation, it should be noted, was, as in the case of Africa, internal as well as external. That is to say, not only were the American Indian civilizations cut off from stimulating interaction with civilizations on other continents, but also they were largely isolated from each other.

"With respect to interrelations between Peru and Mesoamerica," reports an archaeologist, "it is sufficient to state that not a single object or record of influence or contact between these areas has been accepted as authentic from the long time span between the Formative period [about 1000 B.C.] and the coming of the Spaniards. . . ."[3] In other words, there is no reliable evidence of interaction between the Mesoamerican and Peruvian civilizations over a span of 2,500 years. And during those millennia, as we have seen, the various regions of Eurasia, and to a lesser extent sub-Saharan Africa, were in continual fructifying contact. The end result was that the American Indians—even those of the Andes and Mesoamerica—lagged far behind the Eurasians and especially behind the technologically precocious Europeans. By A.D. 1500 the New World had reached the stage of civilization that Egypt and Mesopotamia had attained about 2500 B.C.

Precisely what did this mean when the confrontation occurred with the arrival of the Spaniards? It meant, in the first place, that the Indians found themselves economically and technologically far behind the civilization represented by the invaders. The highly developed art, science, and religion of the Indians should not be allowed to obscure the fact that they lagged seriously in more material fields. The disparity was most extreme in Mesoamerica, but it also prevailed in the Andean area. In agriculture, the Indians were brilliantly successful in domesticating plants but much less effective in actual production. Their cultivation techniques never advanced beyond the bare minimum necessary for feeding populations that rarely reached the density of those of the Old World. Their tools were made only of stone, wood, or bone. They were incapable of smelting ores, and though they did work with metal, it was almost exclusively for ornamental purposes. The only ships they constructed were canoes and seagoing rafts. For land transportation they made no use of the wheel, which they knew but used only as a toy. Only the human back was available for transportation, with the exception of the llama and the alpaca, which were used in the Andes but which could not carry heavy loads.

The immediate significance of this technological lag should not be exaggerated. The Indians obviously were at a grave disadvantage with their spears and arrows against the Spaniards' horses and guns. But after the initial shock, the Indians became accustomed to firearms and cavalry. Furthermore, the Spaniards soon discovered that the Indian weapons were sharp and durable, and they came to prefer the Indian armor of quilted cotton to their own.

This suggests that factors in addition to technological disparity lay behind the Spanish victories. One was the lack of unity amongst the Indian peoples. In both Mexico and Peru the Spaniards were able to use disaffected subject tribes that had been alienated by the oppressive rule of Cuzco and Tenochtitlán. The Indians were also weakened by over-regimentation. They had been so indoctrinated and accustomed to carrying out orders without question that when their leaders were overthrown they were incapable of organizing resistance on their own.

This passivity was compounded by religious inhibitions. Both Cortes in Mexico and Pizarro in Peru were at first believed by the natives to be gods returning in fulfillment of ancient prophecies. This explains the suicidal vacillations of Atahualpa in Cuzco and of Montezuma in Tenochtitlán. To Atahualpa the Spaniards were the creator-god Viracocha and his followers, and, for this reason the ruler waited meekly for Pizarro, who with his 180 men quickly seized control of the great empire. Likewise, to Montezuma, Cortes was the god Quetzalcoatl who was returning to claim his rightful throne, so that again the ruler waited listlessly for the Spaniards to ensconce themselves in his capital.

Equally disastrous for the Aztecs was their concept of war as a short-term ritual endeavor. Their main interest in war was to capture prisoners, whose hearts they offered to their gods. Accordingly their campaigns frequently were ceremonial contests during which prisoners were taken with minimal dislocation and destruction. This type of military tradition obviously was a serious handicap. The Spaniards killed to win; the Aztecs tried to take prisoners.

If the great civilizations of the New World lacked the power and the cohesion to resist the Europeans, this was even more true of the less developed food gathering and intermediate farming culture areas. Precisely because they were less developed, they also had smaller populations, so that when the Europeans appeared they simply lacked the numbers to hold their ground. Their weakness in this respect was accentuated by the diseases that the first explorers brought with them. The Indians, lacking immunity, were decimated by the epidemics, so that the early colonists often found abandoned fields and deserted village sites that they could take over.

Later, when the full flood of immigration from Europe got under way, the Indians were hopelessly overwhelmed. First came the traders who penetrated throughout the Americas with little competition or resistance, for the Americas, unlike Africa, had no rival native merchant class. Then appeared the settlers who, attracted by the combination of salubrious climate and fertile land, came in ever-increasing numbers and inundated the hapless Indians. When the latter occasionally took up arms in desperation, they were foredoomed to failure because they lacked both unity and the basic human and material resources. Thus, the unequal contest ended relatively quickly with the victorious white man in possession of the choice lands and the Indians relegated to reservations or to the less desirable regions that did not interest the new masters.

It is apparent that the balance of forces was quite different in America from what it was in Africa. Geography, relatively small population, and a comparatively low level of economic, political, and social organization all worked against the Indian to make it possible for the Europeans to take over the Americas at a time when they were still confined to a few toeholds on the coasts of Africa. Adam Smith was indeed justified in referring to the Indians as "miserable and helpless Americans" in contrast to the Africans.

V. AUSTRALIA

Australia is the most isolated large landmass in the world, being more extreme in this respect than the southern tips of South America and of Africa. This isolation made it possible for archaic forms of life to survive to modern times, including plants such as the eucalyptus family, and mammals such as the monotremes and the marsupials. In Australia archaic human types also survived that were still in the Paleolithic stage when the first British settlers arrived in the late eighteenth century. As in the case of the American Indians, the date of the first appearance of the aborigines in Australia has not been determined. Archaeological excavations have led to the pushing of the date progressively back, the latest findings indicating an arrival date of at least 31,000 years ago. Three different ethnic groups ferried over to Australia at that time when only narrow straits separated the continent from the Indonesian archipelago. These three strains are discernible in the present-day aboriginal population. The majority are slender, long-limbed people with brown skins, little body hair, and wavy to curly head hair and beards. They have survived in substantial numbers because they live in desert areas that are of little use to the white man. In the cool and fertile southeastern corner of the continent are a few survivors of a very different native stock—thick set, with light brown skin, heavy body hair, and luxuriant beards. Along the northeastern coast, in the only part of Australia covered with dense tropical rain forest, lives the third ethnic group. Part of the Negroid family, they are small, of slight build, and with woolly hair and black skins.

The culture of these peoples was by no means uniform. The most advanced were those in the southeast, where rainfall was adequate for permanent settlements. But throughout the continent, the aborigines, thanks to their complete isolation, had remained Paleolithic food gatherers. Their retardation was particularly evident in their technology and in their political organization. They wore no clothing except for decorative purposes. Their housing consisted, in dry country, of simple, open windbreaks, and, in wet country, of low, domed huts thrown together of any available material. Their principal weapons were spears, spear throwers, and boomerangs, all made of wood. They were ignorant of pottery, their utensils consisting merely of a few twined bags and baskets and occasional bowls made of bark or wood. As food gatherers and hunters they were highly skilled and ingenious. They had a wide range of vegetable, as well as animal, foods, and an intimate knowledge of the varieties, habits, and properties of these foods. They did all in their power to keep up the rate of reproduction of the plants and animals on which they depended. But not being food producers, their method of ensuring an adequate food supply was one of ritual rather than of cultivation. A typical ceremony was the mixing of blood with earth in places where the increase of game or plants was desired.

The poverty of Australian technology was matched by an almost equal poverty of political organization. Like most food-gathering peoples, the aborigines lived in bands, groups of families who normally camped together and roamed over a well-defined territory. They had no real tribes, but only territorial divisions characterized by differences in language and culture. Consequently, they did not have chiefs, courts, or other formal agencies of government. Yet these same aborigines had an extraordinarily complex social organization and ceremonial life. The hunter who brought in game or the woman who returned from a day of root digging was required to divide his take with all his kin according to strict regulations. Among the northern Queensland natives, when a man sneezed, all those within hearing slapped themselves on their bodies, the place varying according to their precise relationship to the sneezer.

So involved were these nonmaterial aspects of Australian society that they have been a delight to students of primitive institutions. But precociousness in these matters was of little help to the aborigines when the Europeans appeared in the late eighteenth century. If the American Indians with their flowering civilizations and widespread agricultural communities were unable to stand up to the white man, the Paleolithic Australians obviously had no chance. They were few in numbers, totaling about 300,000 when the Europeans arrived. This meant one or two persons per square mile in favorable coastal or river valley environments, and only one person every 30 to 40 square miles in the arid interior. In addition to this numerical weakness, the aborigines lacked both the arms and the organization necessary for effective resistance. And unlike the American Indians and the African Negroes, they showed little inclination to secure and use the white man's "fire stick." Thus the unfortunate aborigines were brutally decimated by the British immigrants, many of whom were lawless convicts shipped out from overcrowded jails. The combination of disease, alcoholism, outright slaughter, and wholesale land confiscation reduced the native population to 45,000 today, together with some 80,000 mixed breeds.

SUGGESTED READING

A. A. ABBIE, *The Original Australians* (Muller, 1969); R. M. and C. H. BERNDT, *The World of the First Australians* (Univ. Chicago, 1964); P. FARB, *Man's Rise to Civilization as Shown by the Indians of North America*. . . . (Dutton, 1968); A. M. JOSEPHY, JR., *The Indian Heritage of America* (Knopf, 1968).

MAPS

221

The range of human activity throughout history has been determined by the level of technological development. The more primitive the technology, the more constricted the range; and, conversely, the more advanced the technology, the more extensive the range. Consequently, in Map I, Global Distribution of Hominids and Homo Sapiens, the Australopithecines with their primitive pebble tools and lack of clothing are restricted to the warm African savannas; Homo erectus with his superior tools and clothing and control of fire has expanded into the temperate zones of Eurasia; while Homo sapiens with his still more complex technology has pushed further into northern Eurasia, the Americas, and Australia.

Technological advance has involved not only range extension but also population growth. The more advanced the technology, the more efficient the exploitation of the physical environment and hence the larger the population that can subsist in a given region. Map II, World Population Growth, depicts the population "explosions" resulting from each technological revolution from Paleolithic times to the present.

The population explosions were naturally limited to those races that participated in the technological revolutions. Consequently, as shown in Map III, Global Race Distribution, certain races have increased to their present dominant status, while others have dwindled to insignificance.

With the agricultural revolution, the disparity in population growth not only resulted in the rise of certain races and the fall of others, but also caused an increase of agriculturists and a decrease of hunters. The agriculturists, possessing the more advanced technology, far outstripped the hunters, as depicted in Map IV, Recession of Hunters, and in Map V, Expansion of Agriculturists.

The agricultural revolution made possible the rise of civilizations, which were at first limited to the fertile river valleys where agriculture was most productive. Thus the early civilizations, as shown in Map VI, Ancient Civilizations of Eura-

sia, 3500–1500 B.C., were small islands in the surrounding seas of barbarism. These ancient civilizations were overwhelmed during the second millennium B.C. by Indo-European and Semitic nomadic invasions, which thereby cleared the ground for the succeeding classical civilizations.

The classical civilizations and empires encompassed entire regions rather than isolated river valleys. The development of these regional empires in Europe, India, and China is presented in Maps VII, VIII, and IX. These regional empires together comprised a Eurasian ecumene—a continuous belt of civilizations and imperial structures across the breadth of Eurasia. The political, religious, and economic components of this new entity are depicted in Map X, Eurasian Ecumene About A.D. 200.

The classical civilizations, like the ancient ones, were in many cases overthrown by a new wave of Eurasia-wide invasions, as pictured in Map XI, Barbarian Invasions in Eurasia, 4th–5th Centuries A.D. In most of Eurasia, imperial structures eventually were reconstituted and stabilized, but in the West the short-lived Carolingian Empire was overthrown by a new wave of invasions by Moslems, Magyars, and Vikings (Map XII, Continued Barbarian Invasions in the West, 9th–10th Centuries). Two other great waves of invasions profoundly affected medieval Eurasia—that of Islam beginning in the 7th century, and that of the Mongols in the 13th century (Map XIII, Expansion of Islam to 1500, and Map XIV, Mongol Empire at the Death of Kublai Khan, 1294).

Destructive though these invasions were initially, they did forge bonds and create a Eurasian ecumene more closely knit than that of the classical period (Map X). This new medieval ecumene, with its network of trade routes and wide-ranging travellers, is depicted in Map XV, Eurasian Ecumene about 1300.

In the late Middle Ages, Western Europe passed from an attitude of self-defense, as depicted in Map XII, and took the offensive. This expansionism was the product of a combination of factors, including technological advances, economic growth, population upsurge, and religious militancy. The result was a series of crusades, motivated at least as much by secular considerations as by religious ones, and launched in all directions, as depicted in Map XVI, Expansionism of the Medieval West.

Because of Western Europe's lead in global exploration, it is often overlooked that in the early 15th century the Chinese undertook a series of expeditions that were far more ambitious and wide ranging than anything in the West at that time, as illustrated in Map XVII, Early 15th-Century Chinese and Portuguese Voyages.

As striking as the difference between the Chinese and Portuguese voyages was the contrasting fate in Eastern Europe of the Byzantines and the Russians. The Byzantine Empire, which had encompassed the Mediterranean basin under Justinian I, shrank during the following centuries, albeit with periodic comebacks, until by the fifteenth century it comprised only two minuscule footholds, one in the Peloponnesus and the other around the city of Constantinople. This contraction is depicted in Map XVIII, Decline of the Byzantine Empire. To the north, by contrast, the gathering of the Russian lands was being achieved under the leadership of Muscovy. Map XIX, The Growth of Muscovy, depicts this unifying process to the end of Ivan III's reign in 1505.

Meanwhile developments comparable to those in Eurasia had been unfolding in the non-Eurasian world, though at a slower pace. The advent of agriculture and iron metallurgy in sub-Saharan Africa stimulated economic growth, commerce, and empire building (Map XX, African Empires and Trade Routes). In the Americas, agriculture was developed independently and most successfully, as reflected in the large number of plants that were domesticated. But the Americas suffered from isolation, so that iron metallurgy never reached the New World as it did sub-Saharan Africa from Eurasia. Nevertheless, the flourishing agriculture did provide a base for state structures comparable to those of sub-Saharan Africa, as shown in Map XXI, *Amerindian Empires.*

As a result of the historical evolution depicted in the above maps, the various regions of the world had reached varied levels of development by 1500, when the Europeans began their overseas expansion which for the first time brought all the regions into direct contact with each other. This disparity in development, as shown in Map XXII, *Culture Areas of the World about 1500,* is of basic historical significance, for it determined the course and speed of European expansion during the following centuries. The more retarded the overseas territories, the more swift and overwhelming the European intrusions, and, conversely, the more advanced the overseas territories, the more effective and prolonged their resistance to the Europeans.

Until the fifteenth-century Iberian discoveries, man had lived in regional isolation. Australia and the Americas had been completely isolated, Africa largely so, and even the various regions of Eurasia had interacted only intermittently. With European overseas expansion this regional compartmentalization gave way to global unity, as illustrated in Map XXIII, *Western Man's Knowledge of the Globe, A.D. 1 to 1800.* Since the West took the lead in overseas expansion, it dominated world trade routes and established colonies in the underdeveloped portions of the globe (Map XXIV, *World of the Emerging West, 1763*).

The Industrial Revolution, in which the West also pioneered, further increased Western Europe's power and influence in world affairs. One result was the extension of European political domination throughout the world, as described in Map XXV, *Russian Expansion in Europe and Asia,* and Map XXVI, *World of Western Dominance, 1914.*

This Western global hegemony of the nineteenth century stimulated a reaction in the twentieth century that culminated in national and social revolution in the colonial territories. Thus the world of today is altogether different from that of the pre-World War I era, as illustrated in Map XXVII, *World of New Global Relationships, 1974.*

GLOBAL DISTRIBUTION OF HOMINIDS AND HOMO SAPIENS

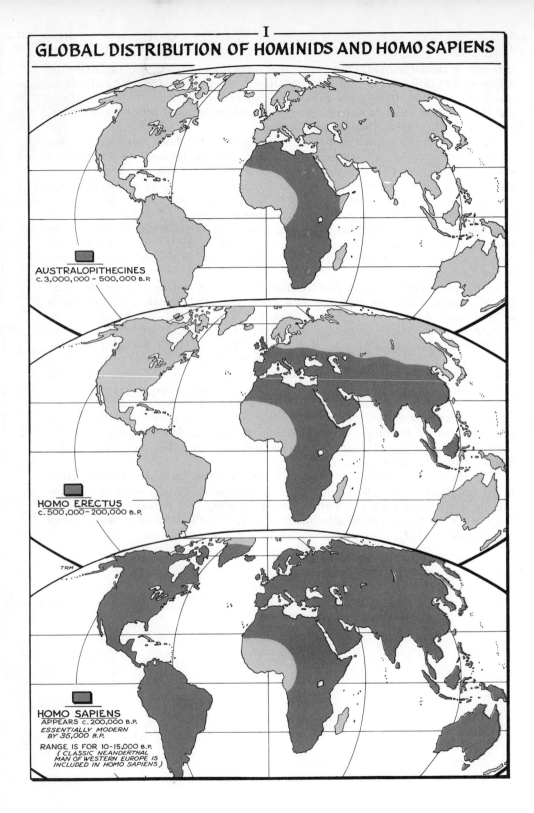

AUSTRALOPITHECINES
c. 3,000,000 – 500,000 B.P.

HOMO ERECTUS
c. 500,000 – 200,000 B.P.

HOMO SAPIENS
APPEARS c. 200,000 B.P.
ESSENTIALLY MODERN BY 35,000 B.P.

RANGE IS FOR 10–15,000 B.P.
(*CLASSIC NEANDERTHAL MAN OF WESTERN EUROPE IS INCLUDED IN HOMO SAPIENS*)

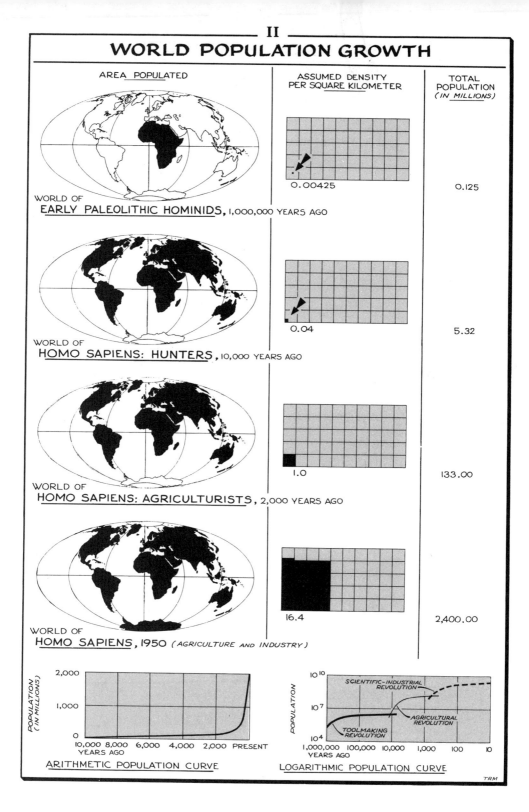

WORLD POPULATION GROWTH

AREA POPULATED	ASSUMED DENSITY PER SQUARE KILOMETER	TOTAL POPULATION (IN MILLIONS)

WORLD OF
EARLY PALEOLITHIC HOMINIDS, 1,000,000 YEARS AGO

0.00425   0.125

WORLD OF
HOMO SAPIENS: HUNTERS, 10,000 YEARS AGO

0.04   5.32

WORLD OF
HOMO SAPIENS: AGRICULTURISTS, 2,000 YEARS AGO

1.0   133.00

WORLD OF
HOMO SAPIENS, 1950 (AGRICULTURE AND INDUSTRY)

16.4   2,400.00

POPULATION (IN MILLIONS)

2,000

1,000

0

10,000 8,000 6,000 4,000 2,000 PRESENT
YEARS AGO

ARITHMETIC POPULATION CURVE

POPULATION

10^{10}

10^{7}

10^{4}

SCIENTIFIC-INDUSTRIAL REVOLUTION

AGRICULTURAL REVOLUTION

TOOLMAKING REVOLUTION

1,000,000 100,000 10,000 1,000 100 10
YEARS AGO

LOGARITHMIC POPULATION CURVE

TRM

227

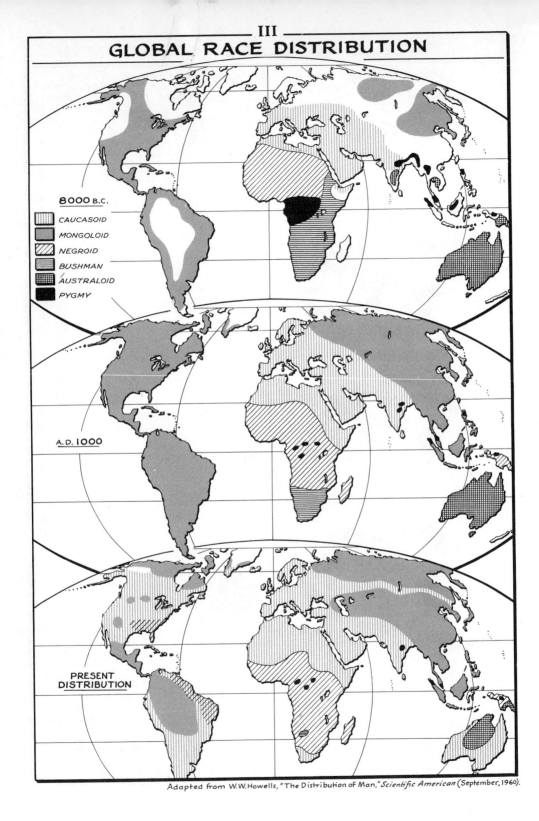

III
GLOBAL RACE DISTRIBUTION

8000 B.C.

CAUCASOID
MONGOLOID
NEGROID
BUSHMAN
AUSTRALOID
PYGMY

A.D. 1000

PRESENT
DISTRIBUTION

Adapted from W.W. Howells, "The Distribution of Man," *Scientific American* (September, 1960).

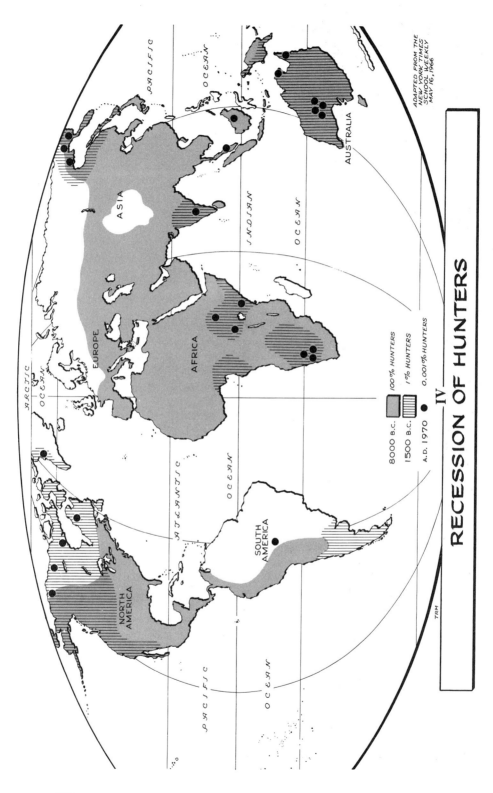

RECESSION OF HUNTERS

ADAPTED FROM THE NEW YORK TIMES SCHOOL WEEKLY MAY 16, 1966

ASIA

EUROPE

AFRICA

AUSTRALIA

NORTH AMERICA

SOUTH AMERICA

PACIFIC OCEAN

ARCTIC OCEAN

ATLANTIC OCEAN

INDIAN OCEAN

PACIFIC OCEAN

8000 B.C.   100% HUNTERS

1500 B.C.   1% HUNTERS

A.D. 1970   0.001% HUNTERS

IV

TRH

EXPANSION OF AGRICULTURISTS

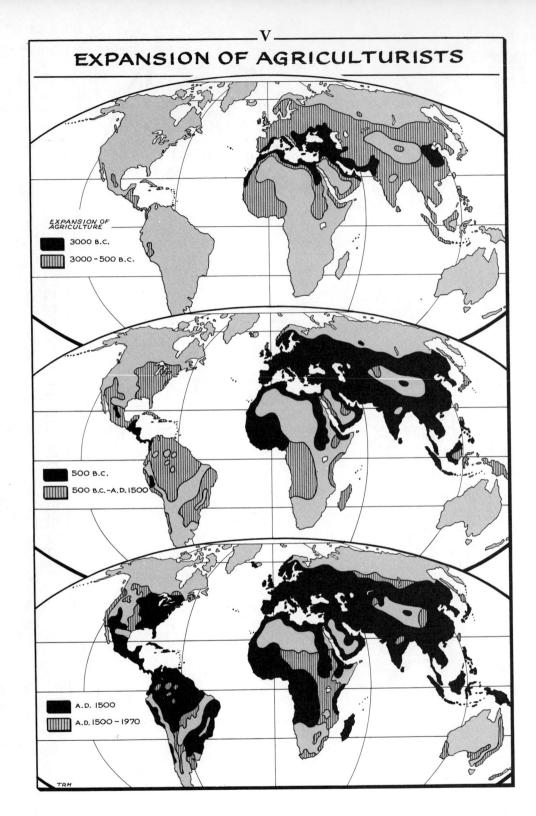

EXPANSION OF
AGRICULTURE

■ 3000 B.C.
▥ 3000 – 500 B.C.

■ 500 B.C.
▥ 500 B.C.–A.D. 1500

■ A.D. 1500
▥ A.D. 1500 – 1970

TRM

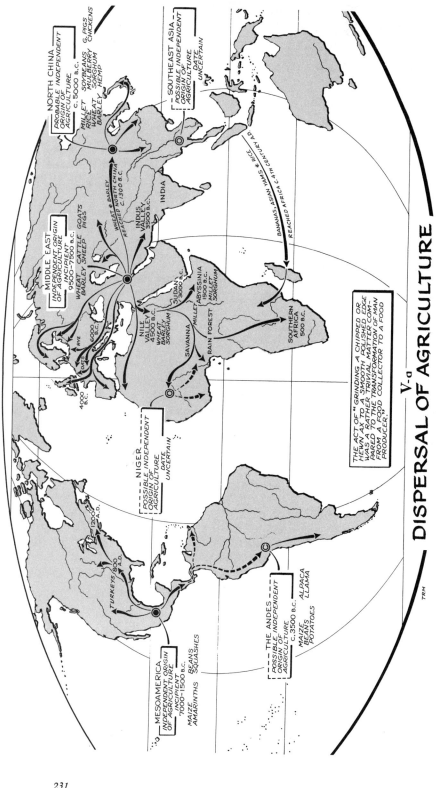

DISPERSAL OF AGRICULTURE

V-a

TRM

ARROWS SHOW MOVEMENT OF SOME IMPORTANT
CEREAL DOMESTICATES.
MILLET WAS PROBABLY DOMESTICATED
IN SUBSAHARAN AFRICA AFTER THE
DISPERSAL OF AGRICULTURE FROM
THE NORTH.

DATES INDICATE ACHIEVEMENT
OF A "SETTLED FARMING"
WAY OF LIFE BY SOME PEOPLE
IN THE REGION.

NORTH CHINA
PROBABLE INDEPENDENT
ORIGIN OF
AGRICULTURE
c. 5000 B.C.
MILLET
RICE
WHEAT
BARLEY

G. PIGS
CHICKENS
SOYBEANS
MULBERRY
SORGHUM
HEMP

SOUTHEAST ASIA
POSSIBLE INDEPENDENT
ORIGIN OF
AGRICULTURE
DATE
UNCERTAIN

MIDDLE EAST
INDEPENDENT ORIGIN
OF AGRICULTURE
INCIPIENT
9500-7500 B.C.
WHEAT CATTLE GOATS
BARLEY SHEEP PIGS

WHEAT & BARLEY
REACHED NORTH CHINA
c. 1300 B.C.

INDUS
VALLEY
3500 B.C.

INDIA

6000
B.C.

RYE

OATS

4000 B.C.

NIGER
POSSIBLE INDEPENDENT
ORIGIN OF
AGRICULTURE
DATE
UNCERTAIN

NILE
VALLEY
4500 B.C.
WHEAT
BARLEY
SORGHUM

SUDAN
3000 B.C.

SAVANNA

MILLET-ABYSSINIA
1500 B.C.

RAIN FOREST

MILLET
SORGHUM

SOUTHERN
AFRICA
500 B.C.

BANANAS, ASIAN YAMS & RICE c.A.D.
REACHED AFRICA c. 4TH CENTURY A.D.

THE ACT OF "GRINDING A CHIPPED OR
HEWN AX INTO A SMOOTH POLISHED EDGE
WAS A RATHER TRIVIAL MATTER COM-
PARED TO THE TRANSFORMATION OF MAN
FROM A FOOD COLLECTOR TO A FOOD
PRODUCER."

TURKEYS 800
A.D.

1200
A.D.

MESOAMERICA
INDEPENDENT ORIGIN
OF AGRICULTURE
INCIPIENT
7000-1500 B.C.
MAIZE   BEANS
AMARINTHS SQUASHES

THE ANDES
POSSIBLE INDEPENDENT
ORIGIN OF
AGRICULTURE
c. 3500 B.C.
MAIZE   ALPACA
BEANS   LLAMA
POTATOES

231

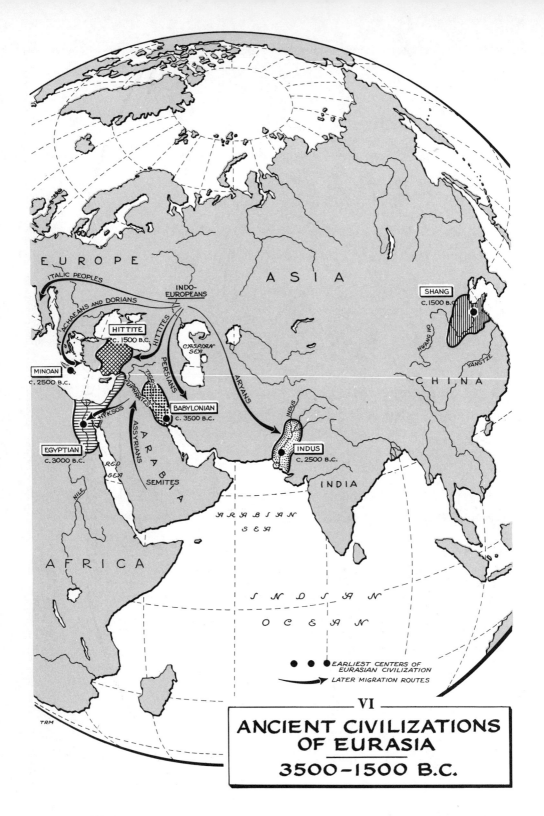

EUROPE

ASIA

ITALIC PEOPLES

ACHAEANS AND DORIANS

INDO-
EUROPEANS

SHANG
c. 1500 B.C.

HITTITE
c. 1500 B.C.

HITTITES

CASPIAN
SEA

MINOAN
c. 2500 B.C.

PERSIANS

HYKSOS

BABYLONIAN
c. 3500 B.C.

EUPHRATES

TIGRIS

ARYANS

CHINA

HWANG HO

YANGTZE

INDUS

EGYPTIAN
c. 3000 B.C.

ASSYRIANS

A R A B I A

NILE

RED
SEA

SEMITES

INDUS
c. 2500 B.C.

INDIA

A R A B I A N
S E A

AFRICA

I N D I A N

O C E A N

● ● ● EARLIEST CENTERS OF
EURASIAN CIVILIZATION

LATER MIGRATION ROUTES

VI

ANCIENT CIVILIZATIONS
OF EURASIA

3500–1500 B.C.

TRM

232

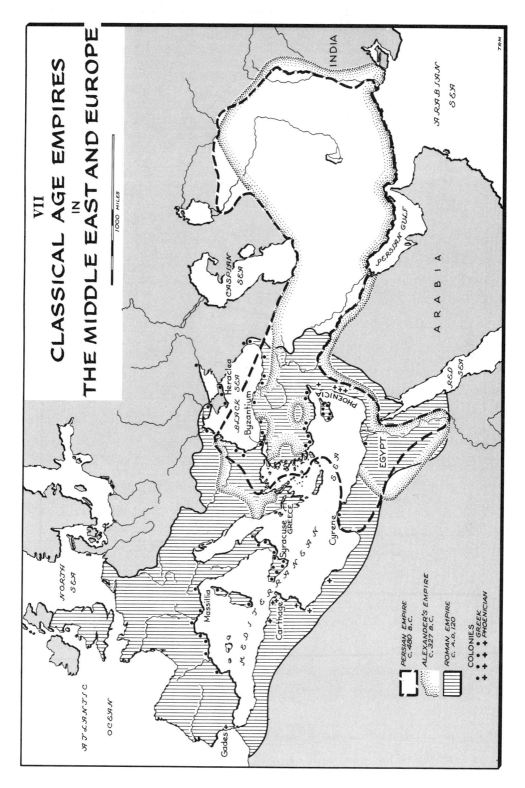

VII

CLASSICAL AGE EMPIRES
IN
THE MIDDLE EAST AND EUROPE

1000 MILES

INDIA

ARABIAN SEA

CASPIAN SEA

PERSIAN GULF

ARABIA

RED SEA

Heraclea

BLACK SEA

Byzantium

PHOENICIA

EGYPT

Cyrene

GREECE

Syracuse

AEGEAN SEA

Massilia

MEDITERRANEAN

Carthage

Gades

NORTH SEA

ATLANTIC OCEAN

PERSIAN EMPIRE
C. 480 B.C.

ALEXANDER'S EMPIRE
C. 327 B.C.

ROMAN EMPIRE
C. A.D. 120

COLONIES
GREEK
PHOENICIAN

TRM

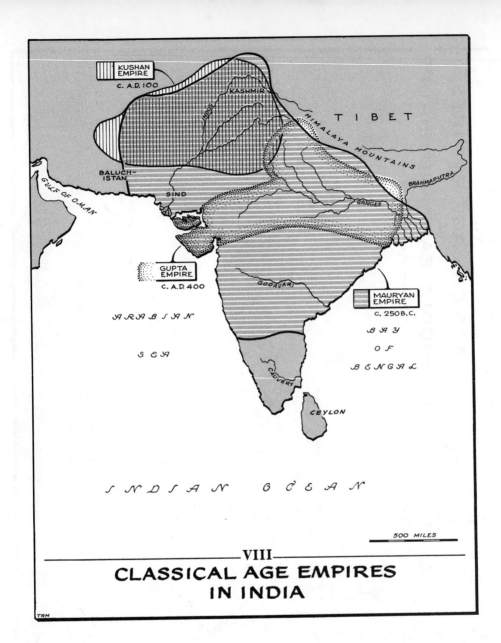

KUSHAN EMPIRE
C. A.D. 100

GUPTA EMPIRE
C. A.D. 400

MAURYAN EMPIRE
C. 250 B.C.

TIBET

HIMALAYA MOUNTAINS

KASHMIR

INDUS

BRAHMAPUTRA

BALUCH-ISTAN

SIND

GANGES

GULF OF OMAN

GODAVARI

ARABIAN

SEA

BAY

OF

BENGAL

CAUVERY

CEYLON

INDIAN OCEAN

500 MILES

VIII

CLASSICAL AGE EMPIRES IN INDIA

TRM

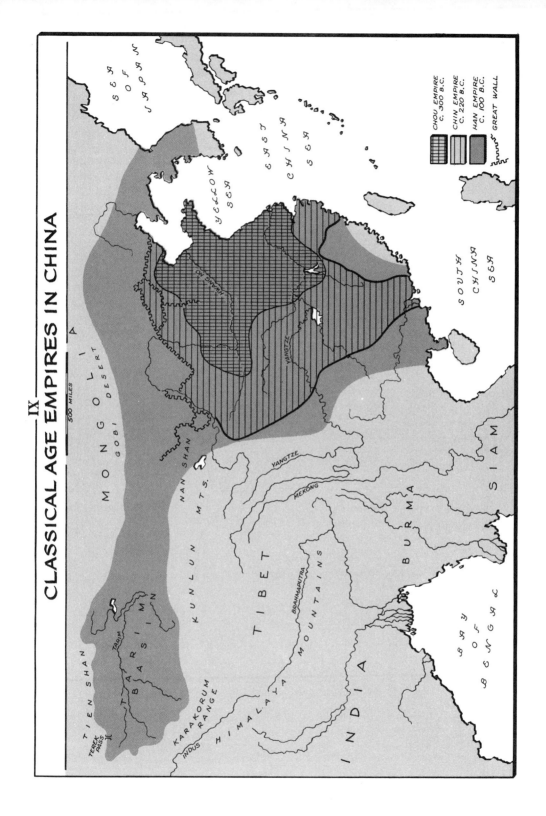

CLASSICAL AGE EMPIRES IN CHINA

IX

500 MILES

CHOU EMPIRE
C. 300 B.C.

CHIN EMPIRE
C. 220 B.C.

HAN EMPIRE
C. 100 B.C.

GREAT WALL

SEA OF JAPAN

EAST CHINA SEA

YELLOW SEA

SOUTH CHINA SEA

MONGOLIA

GOBI DESERT

HWANG HO

YANGTZE

NAN SHAN MTS.

KUNLUN

YANGTZE

MEKONG

TIBET

BRAHMAPUTRA

HIMALAYA MOUNTAINS

BURMA

SIAM

INDIA

BAY OF BENGAL

TIEN SHAN

TARIM

TAREK PASS

KARAKORUM RANGE

INDUS

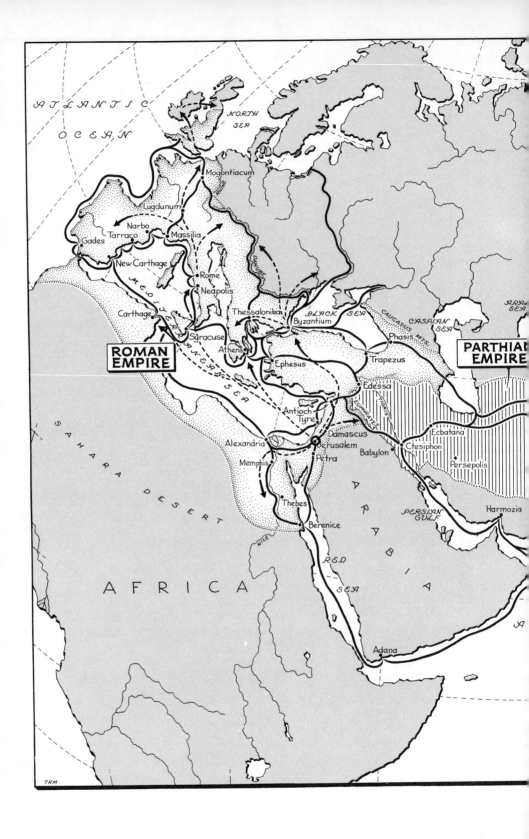

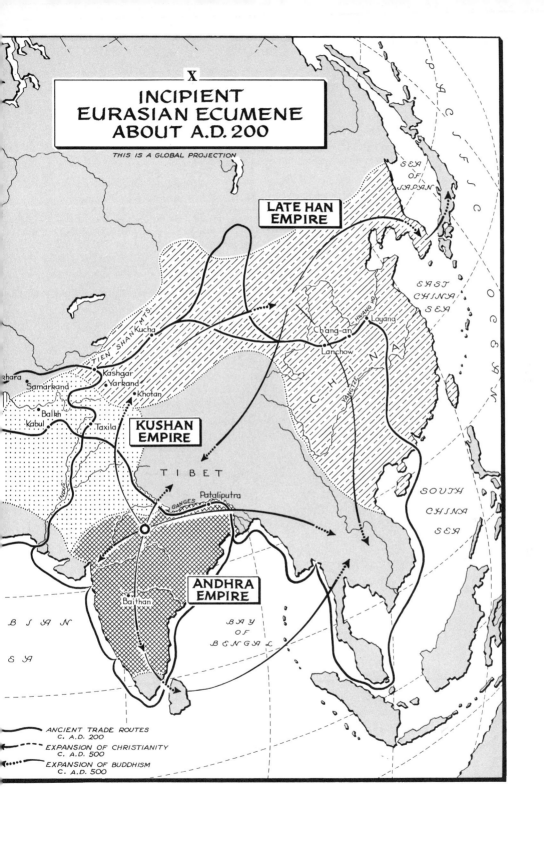

INCIPIENT EURASIAN ECUMENE ABOUT A.D. 200

X

THIS IS A GLOBAL PROJECTION

LATE HAN EMPIRE

KUSHAN EMPIRE

ANDHRA EMPIRE

SEA OF JAPAN

PACIFIC OCEAN

EAST CHINA SEA

SOUTH CHINA SEA

BAY OF BENGAL

ARABIAN SEA

TIEN SHAN MTS.

TIBET

C H I N A

HWANG HO

YANGTZE

GANGES

INDUS

Kucha
Kashgar
Yarkand
Khotan
Samarkand
Balkh
Kabul
Taxila
hara
Ch'ang-an
Loyang
Lanchow
Pataliputra
Baithan

ANCIENT TRADE ROUTES
C. A.D. 200
EXPANSION OF CHRISTIANITY
C. A.D. 500
EXPANSION OF BUDDHISM
C. A.D. 500

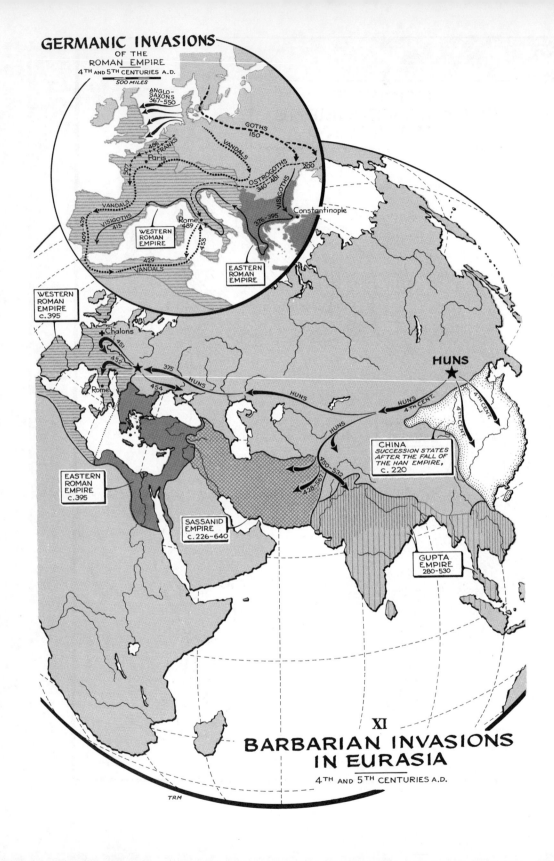

GERMANIC INVASIONS
OF THE
ROMAN EMPIRE
4TH AND 5TH CENTURIES A.D.
500 MILES

ANGLO-SAXONS 367-550

GOTHS 150

VANDALS

FRANKS 486

Paris 507

OSTROGOTHS 340-481

200

VISIGOTHS

Constantinople

VANDALS

VISIGOTHS 415

376-395

Rome 489

WESTERN ROMAN EMPIRE

455

429 VANDALS

EASTERN ROMAN EMPIRE

WESTERN ROMAN EMPIRE c.395

+ Chalons

451

452

375

Rome

454

HUNS

HUNS

HUNS

HUNS

HUNS 4TH CENT.

4TH CENT.

4TH CENT.

CHINA
SUCCESSION STATES AFTER THE FALL OF THE HAN EMPIRE, c. 220

EASTERN ROMAN EMPIRE c.395

450-551

428-561

SASSANID EMPIRE c. 226-640

GUPTA EMPIRE 280-530

XI
BARBARIAN INVASIONS IN EURASIA
4TH AND 5TH CENTURIES A.D.

TRM

XII
CONTINUED BARBARIAN INVASIONS IN THE WEST
9TH AND 10TH CENTURIES

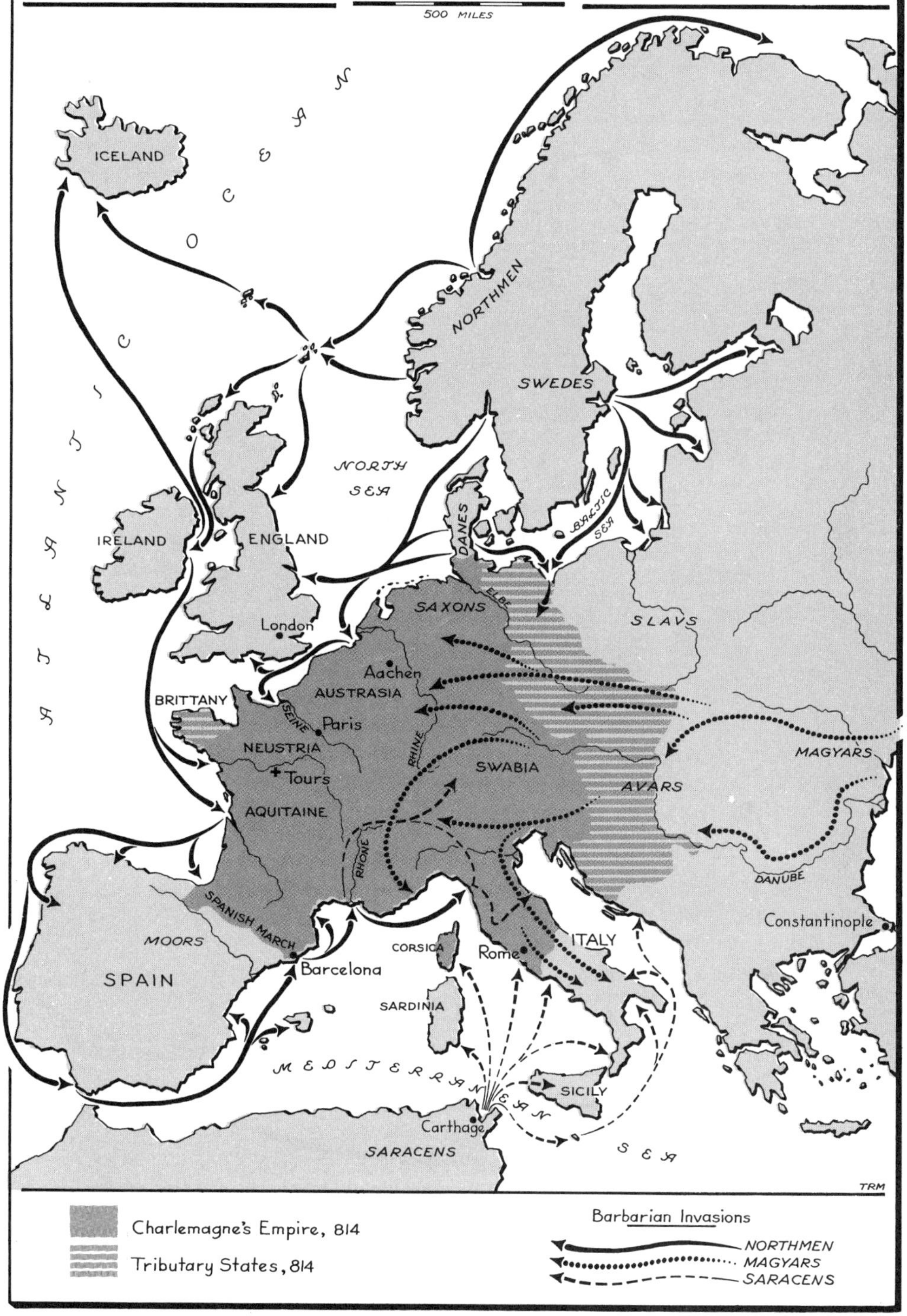

500 MILES
ATLANTIC OCEAN
ICELAND
NORTHMEN
SWEDES
NORTH SEA
BALTIC SEA
DANES
IRELAND
ENGLAND
London
SAXONS
ELBE
SLAVS
Aachen
AUSTRASIA
BRITTANY
SEINE
Paris
NEUSTRIA
RHINE
Tours
SWABIA
MAGYARS
AVARS
AQUITAINE
RHONE
DANUBE
SPANISH MARCH
MOORS
SPAIN
Barcelona
CORSICA
Rome
ITALY
Constantinople
SARDINIA
MEDITERRANEAN SEA
SICILY
Carthage
SARACENS
TRM
Charlemagne's Empire, 814
Tributary States, 814
Barbarian Invasions
NORTHMEN
MAGYARS
SARACENS

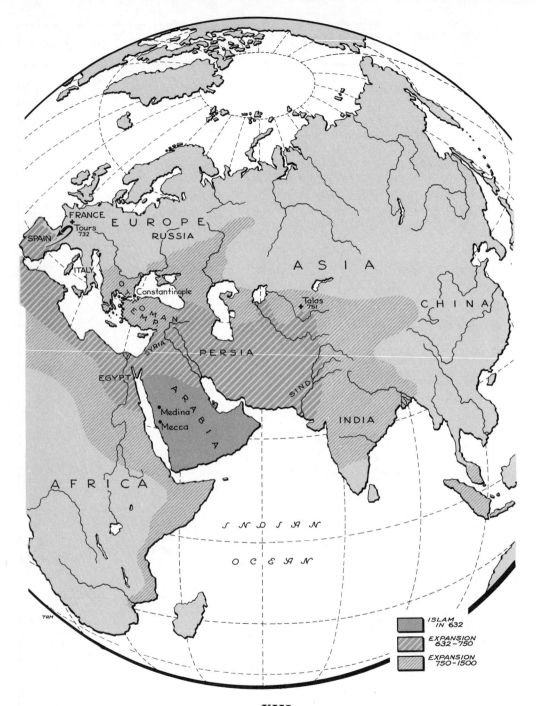

	ISLAM IN 632
	EXPANSION 632–750
	EXPANSION 750–1500

XIII
EXPANSION OF ISLAM TO 1500

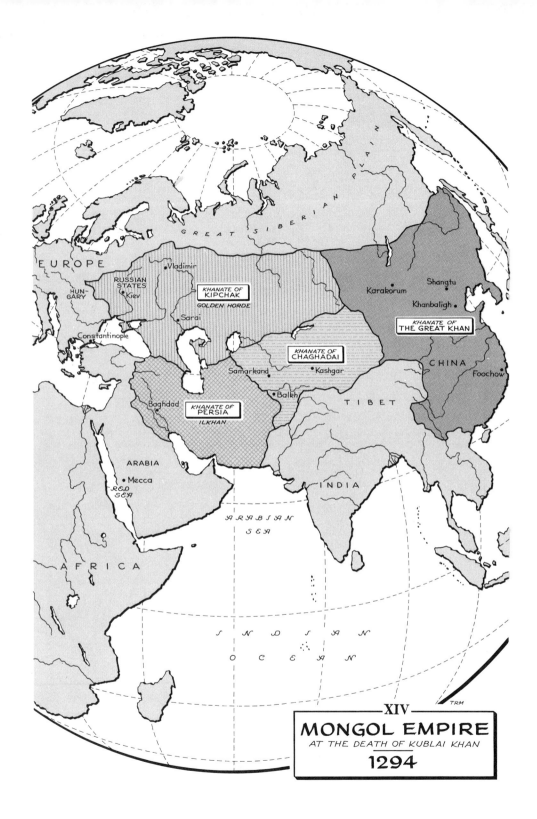

EUROPE

RUSSIAN
STATES

HUN-
GARY
• Kiev

• Vladimir

GREAT SIBERIAN PLAIN

KHANATE OF
KIPCHAK
GOLDEN HORDE

• Sarai

Constantinople

KHANATE OF
CHAGHADAI

• Samarkand
• Kashgar

KHANATE OF
PERSIA
ILKHAN

• Baghdad

• Balkh

TIBET

ARABIA

• Mecca
RED
SEA

INDIA

ARABIAN
SEA

Karakorum

Shangtu

Khanbaligh •

KHANATE OF
THE GREAT KHAN

CHINA

Foochow

AFRICA

I N D I A N

O C E A N

TRM

XIV

MONGOL EMPIRE

AT THE DEATH OF KUBLAI KHAN

1294

241

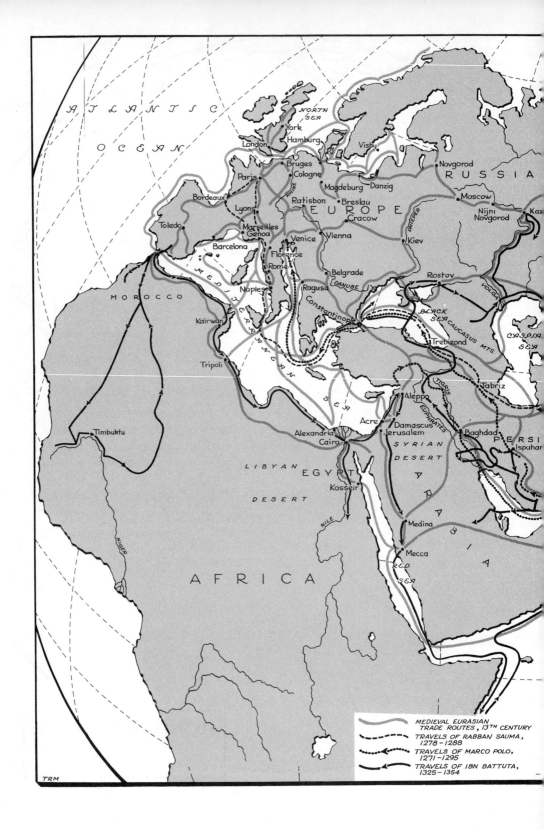

ATLANTIC OCEAN

NORTH SEA

York
London
Hamburg
Visby
Novgorod
RUSSIA
Bruges
Cologne
Magdeburg
Danzig
Paris
RHINE
Moscow
Ratisbon
Breslau
Nijni
Novgorod
Bordeaux
EUROPE
Cracow
Kaz
Lyons
DNIEPER
Toledo
Marseilles
Genoa
Venice
Vienna
Kiev
Barcelona
Florence
Rome
Belgrade
Rostov
VOLGA
Naples
Ragusa
DANUBE
Constantinople
BLACK SEA
CAUCASUS MTS.
MEDITERRANEAN
Kairwan
Trebizond
CASPIA
SEA
Tripoli
TIGRIS
Tabriz
SEA
Aleppo
Acre
EUPHRATES
PERSI
Damascus
Baghdad
Alexandria
Jerusalem
Ispahan
MOROCCO
Cairo
SYRIAN
DESERT
LIBYAN
EGYPT
DESERT
Kosseir
DESERT
ARABIA
NILE
Medina
Mecca
RED SEA
Timbuktu
NIGER
AFRICA

MEDIEVAL EURASIAN
TRADE ROUTES, 13TH CENTURY

TRAVELS OF RABBAN SAUMA,
1278 – 1288

TRAVELS OF MARCO POLO,
1271 – 1295

TRAVELS OF IBN BATTUTA,
1325 – 1354

TRM

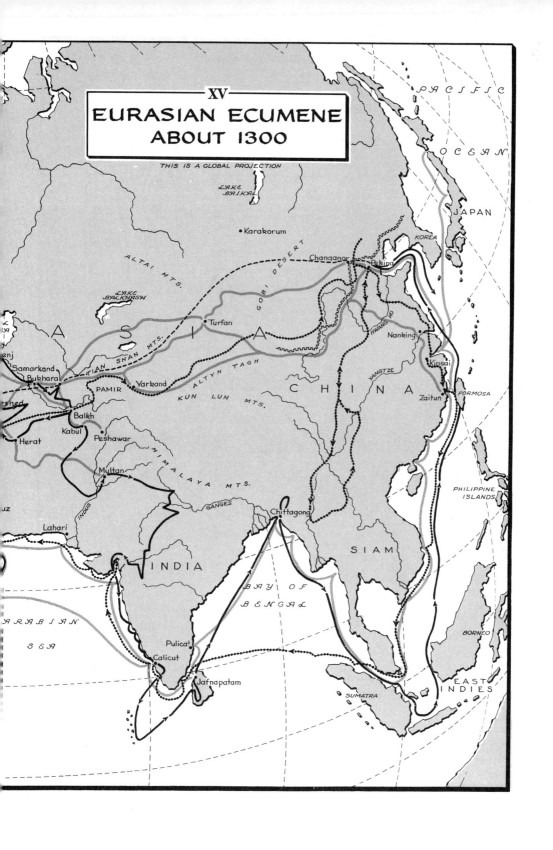

XV
EURASIAN ECUMENE
ABOUT 1300

THIS IS A GLOBAL PROJECTION

PACIFIC

OCEAN

JAPAN

KOREA

LAKE
BAIKAL

Karakorum

ALTAI MTS.

GOBI DESERT

Changanor

Peking

LAKE
BACKHASH

ASIA

Turfan

TIAN SHAN MTS.

HWANG HO

Nanking

Samarkand
Bukhara

PAMIR

Yarkand

ALTYN TAGH

KUN LUN MTS.

CHINA

Kinsai

FORMOSA

YANGTZE

Zaitun

Balkh

Kabul

Peshawar

Herat

HIMALAYA MTS.

PHILIPPINE
ISLANDS

Multan

GANGES

INDUS

Lahari

INDIA

Chittagong

SIAM

BAY OF

BENGAL

ARABIAN

SEA

Pulicat

BORNEO

Calicut

Jafnapatam

SUMATRA

EAST
INDIES

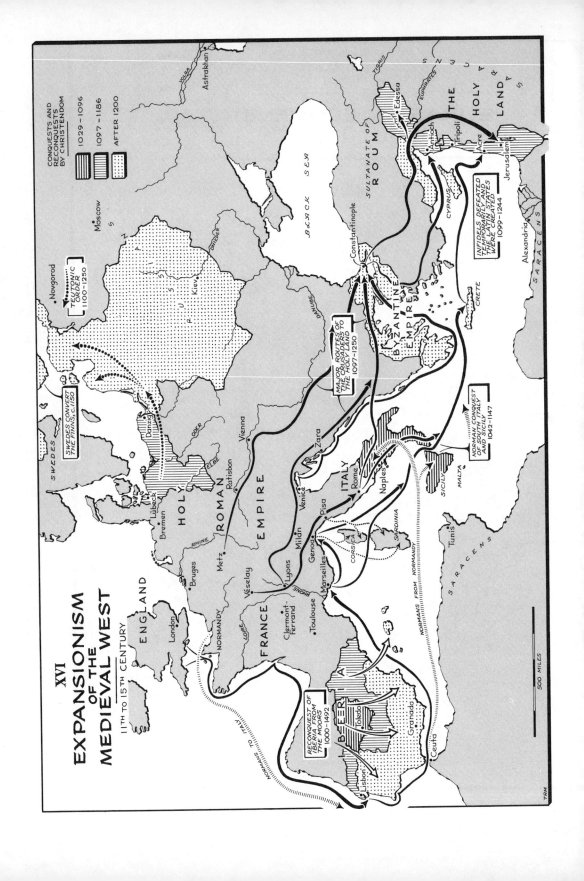

XVI

EXPANSIONISM
OF THE
MEDIEVAL WEST

11TH TO 15TH CENTURY

CONQUESTS AND
RECONQUESTS
BY CHRISTENDOM

1029 – 1096
1097 – 1186
AFTER 1200

SWEDES CONVERT
THE FINNS, c.1150

TEUTONIC
ORDER
1100-1250

MAJOR ROUTES OF
THE CRUSADERS TO
THE HOLY LAND
1097-1250

NORMAN CONQUEST
OF SOUTH ITALY
AND SICILY
1042-1147

INFIDELS DEFEATED
TEMPORARILY AND
CRUSADER STATES
WERE CREATED
1099-1244

RECONQUEST OF
IBERIA FROM
THE MOORS
1000-1492

500 MILES

SWEDES

Novgorod
Moscow

VOLGA
Astrakhan

DNIEPER

Kiev

P O L A N D

DON

ELBE
ODER

Danzig
Lübeck
Bremen
Bruges
RHINE

H O L Y
R O M A N
E M P I R E

Ratisbon
Metz
Vienna
DANUBE

BLACK SEA

SULTANATE OF
ROUM

Constantinople

TIGRIS
EUPHRATES
Edessa
Antioch
Tripoli
Acre
Jerusalem
THE
HOLY
LAND

CYPRUS
CRETE
Alexandria
SARACENS

BYZANTINE EMPIRE

Zara
Venice
Milan
Genoa
Pisa
RHONE
Lyons
Vézelay
Toulouse
Clermont-
Ferrand
Marseilles
F R A N C E
LOIRE
NORMANDY
London
E N G L A N D

ROME
Naples
I T A L Y

CORSICA
SARDINIA
MALTA
SICILY
Tunis
SARACENS

NORMANS FROM NORMANDY
NORMANS TO ITALY

Lisbon
Toledo
Granada
Ceuta
I B E R I A

TRM

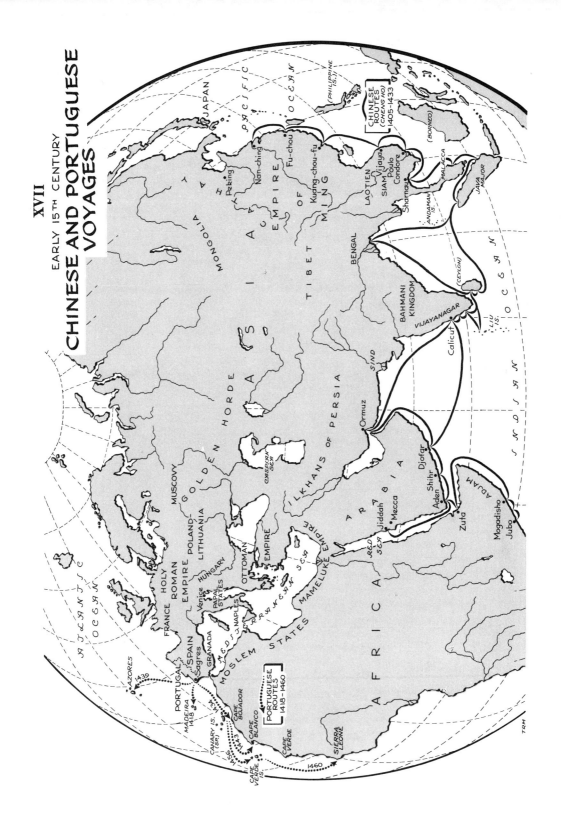

XVII

EARLY 15TH CENTURY

CHINESE AND PORTUGUESE VOYAGES

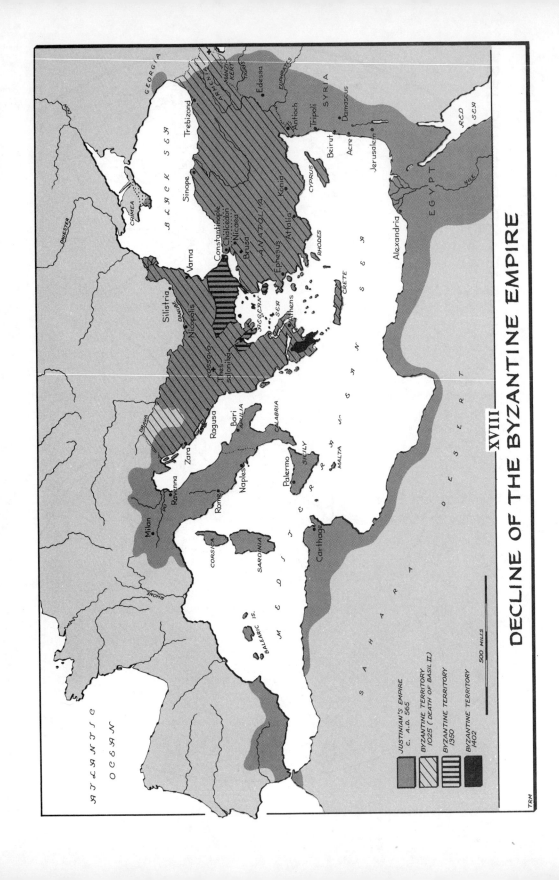

DECLINE OF THE BYZANTINE EMPIRE

XVIII

JUSTINIAN'S EMPIRE
C. A.D. 565

BYZANTINE TERRITORY
1025 (DEATH OF BASIL II)

BYZANTINE TERRITORY
1350

BYZANTINE TERRITORY
1402

500 MILES

ATLANTIC OCEAN

GEORGIA

BLACK SEA

CRIMEA

DNIESTER

DNIEPER

Trebizond

Sinope

Varna

Silistria

Nicopolis

DANUBE

MANZIKERT

ARMENIA

Edessa

TIGRIS

EUPHRATES

SYRIA

Antioch

Tripoli

Damascus

Beirut

Acre

Jerusalem

RED SEA

EGYPT

NILE

Alexandria

CYPRUS

Konia

ANATOLIA

Ephesus

Attalia

RHODES

CRETE

Constantinople

Chalcedon

Nicaea

Brusa

AEGEAN SEA

Athens

DRINA

Thessalonika

KOSOVO

Zara

Ragusa

Bari

APULIA

CALABRIA

SICILY

MALTA

Palermo

Naples

Rome

Ravenna

PO

Milan

CORSICA

SARDINIA

BALEARIC IS.

RHONE

MEDITERRANEAN SEA

Carthage

SAHARA DESERT

TRM

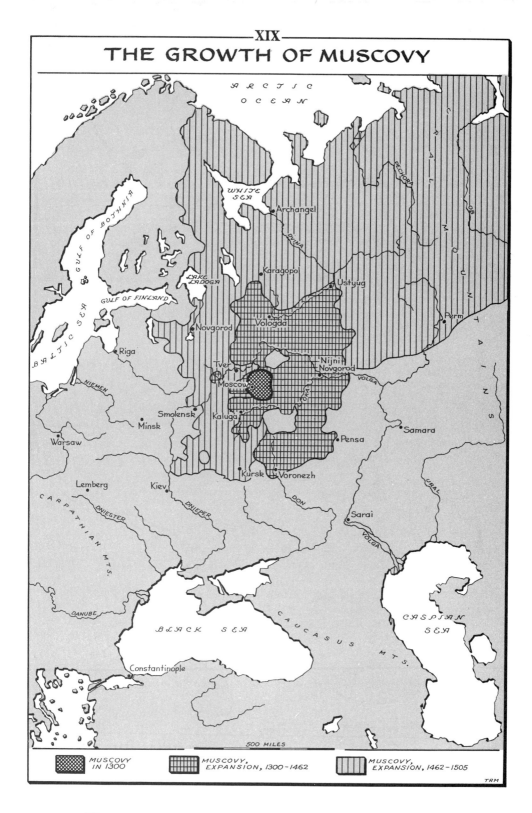

THE GROWTH OF MUSCOVY

XIX

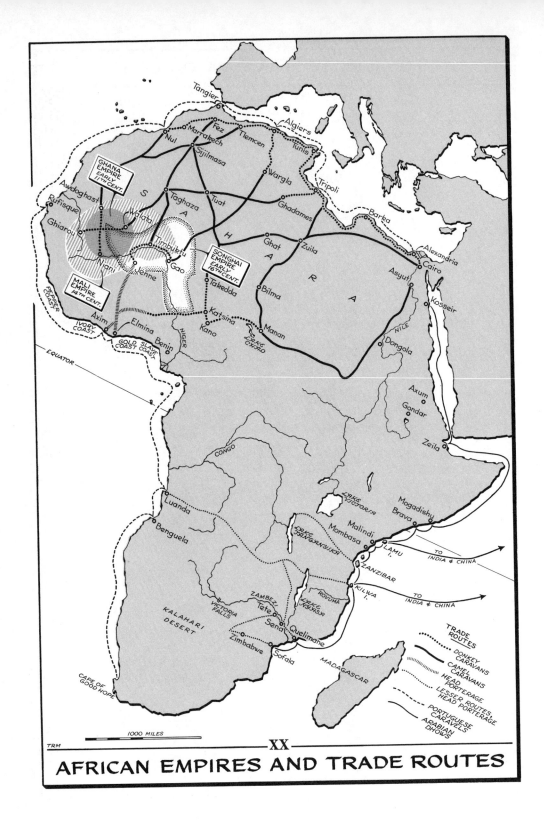

AFRICAN EMPIRES AND TRADE ROUTES

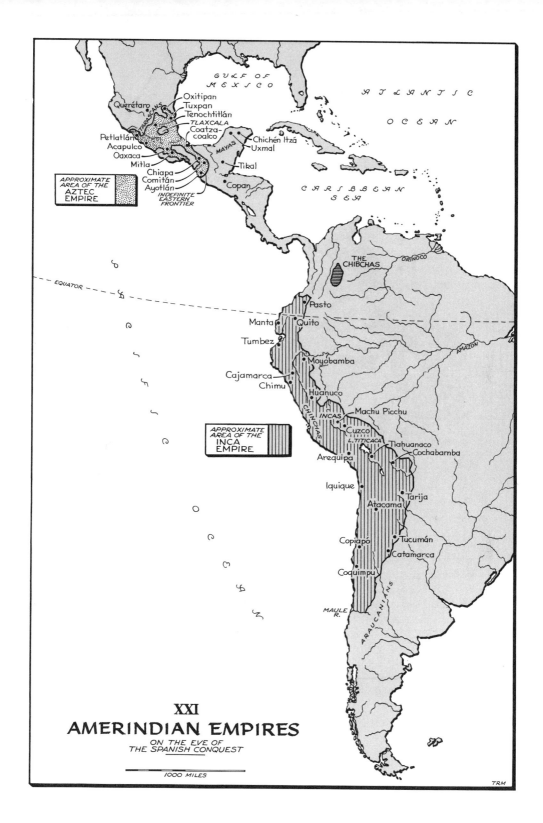

GULF OF MEXICO

ATLANTIC OCEAN

Querétaro
Oxitipan
Tuxpan
Tenochtitlán
TLAXCALA
Coatza-
coalco
Petlatlán
Acapulco
Oaxaca
Mitla
Chiapa
Comitán
Ayotlán
Chichén Itzá
Uxmal
Tikal
Copan
MAYAS

TARASCANS

APPROXIMATE
AREA OF THE
AZTEC
EMPIRE

INDEFINITE
EASTERN
FRONTIER

CARIBBEAN SEA

EQUATOR

THE CHIBCHAS

ORINOCO

Pasto

Manta
Quito

Tumbez

Moyobamba

AMAZON

Cajamarca
Chimu

Huanuco

Machu Picchu

INCAS
Cuzco
L. TITICACA
Tiahuanaco
Cochabamba

CHINCHAS

Arequipa

APPROXIMATE
AREA OF THE
INCA
EMPIRE

Iquique

Atacama
Tarija

Copiapó
Tucumán
Catamarca

Coquimpu

MAULE R.

ARAUCANIANS

PACIFIC OCEAN

XXI

AMERINDIAN EMPIRES

*ON THE EVE OF
THE SPANISH CONQUEST*

1000 MILES

TRM

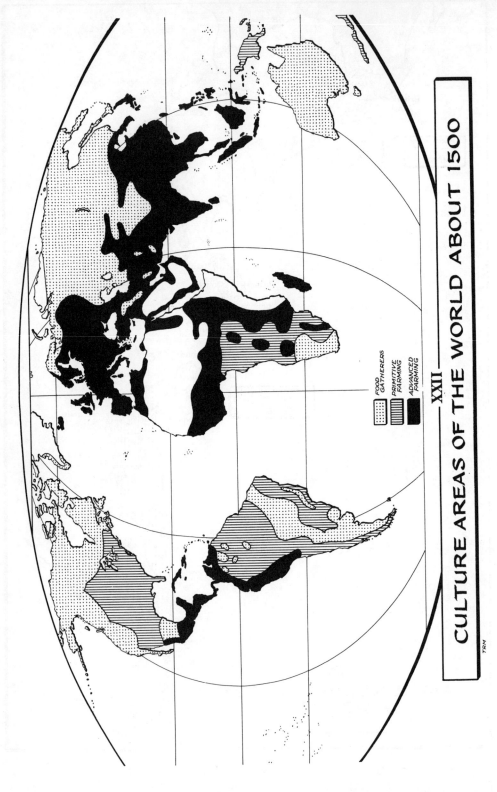

FOOD
GATHERERS

PRIMITIVE
FARMING

ADVANCED
FARMING

XXII

CULTURE AREAS OF THE WORLD ABOUT 1500

TRM

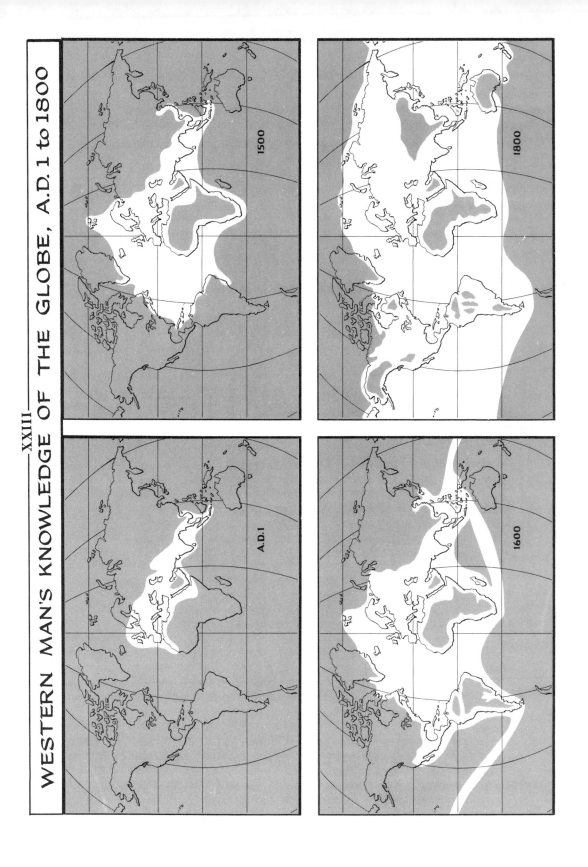

WESTERN MAN'S KNOWLEDGE OF THE GLOBE, A.D. 1 to 1800

A.D. 1

1500

1600

1800

WORLD OF THE EMERGING WEST, 1763

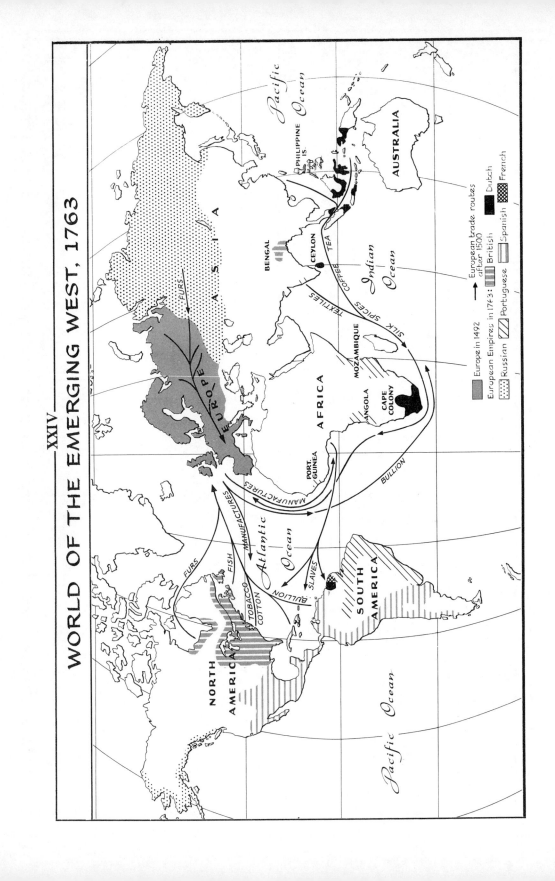

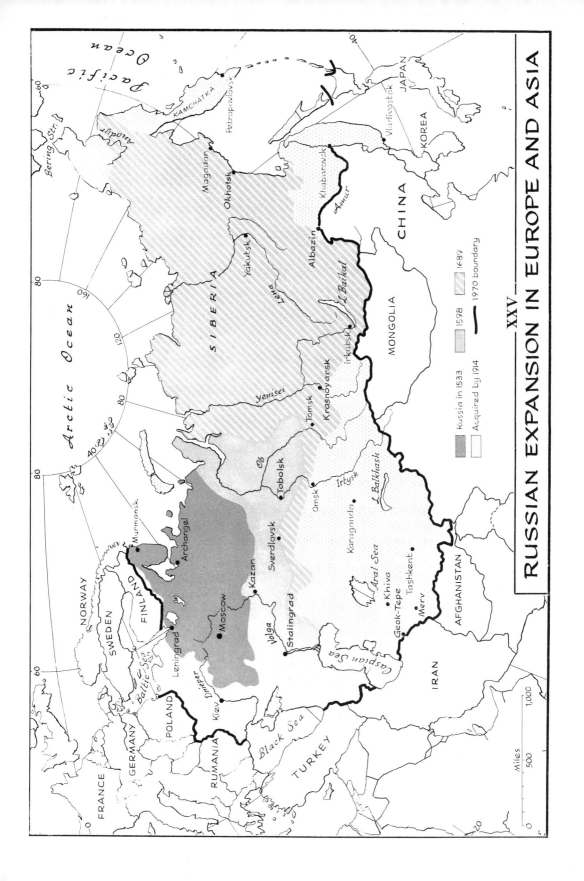

RUSSIAN EXPANSION IN EUROPE AND ASIA

Russia in 1533
Acquired by 1914

1598
1689
1970 boundary

XXV

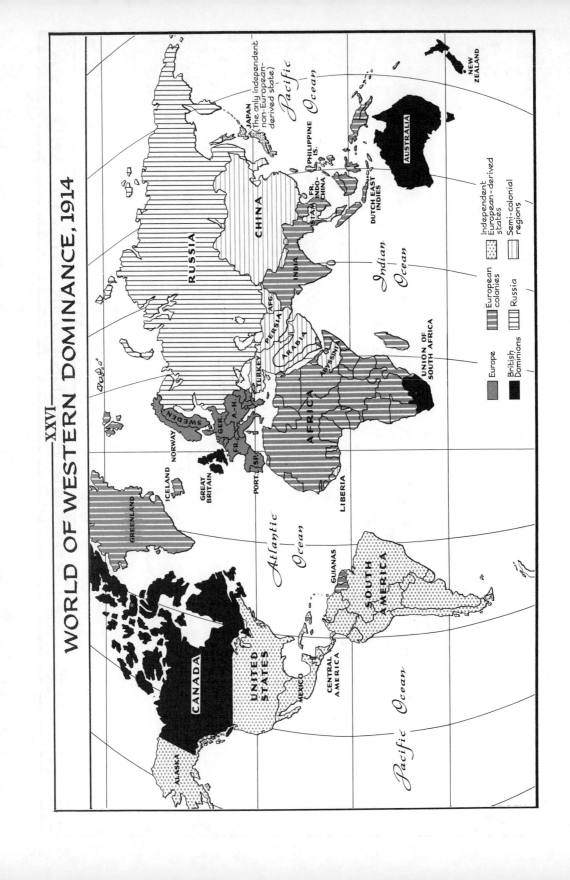

WORLD OF WESTERN DOMINANCE, 1914

XXVI

Legend:
- Europe
- British Dominions
- European colonies
- Russia
- Independent European-derived states
- Semi-colonial regions

Labels on map:

GREENLAND

CANADA

UNITED STATES

ALASKA

MEXICO

CENTRAL AMERICA

GUIANAS

SOUTH AMERICA

Atlantic Ocean

Pacific Ocean

Pacific Ocean

ICELAND

NORWAY

SWEDEN

GREAT BRITAIN

PORT.

SP.

FR.

GER.

A.-H.

TURKEY

PERSIA

AFG.

ARABIA

ABYSSINIA

LIBERIA

AFRICA

UNION OF SOUTH AFRICA

RUSSIA

CHINA

INDIA

SIAM

FR. INDO-CHINA

PHILIPPINE IS.

DUTCH EAST INDIES

Indian Ocean

JAPAN (The only independent non-European-derived state)

Pacific Ocean

AUSTRALIA

NEW ZEALAND

WORLD OF NEW GLOBAL RELATIONSHIPS, 1974

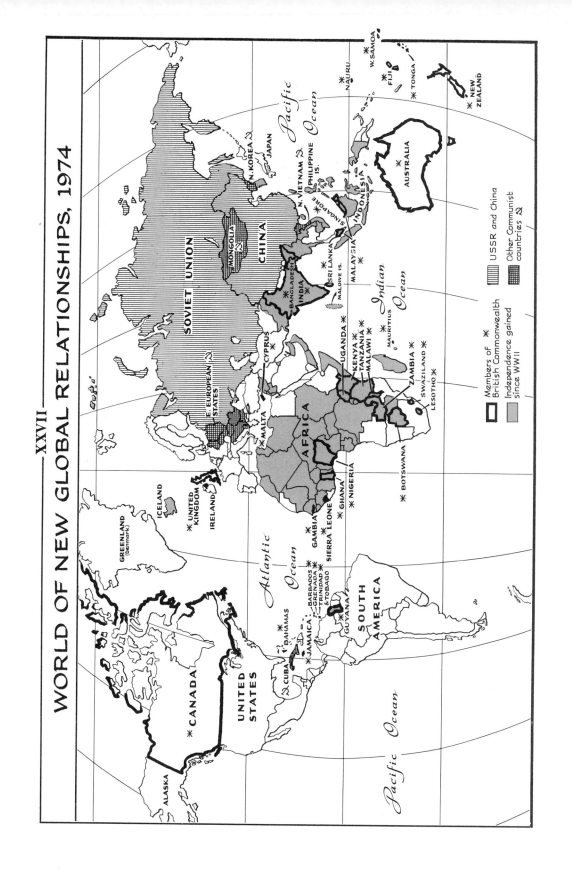

part six

WORLD OF THE EMERGING WEST, 1500-1763

During much of the medieval period the Western Europeans felt iso-
lated and threatened on the western tip of Eurasia. In the twelfth century the
English chronicler William of Malmesbury complained that the Moslem enemy
held Asia and Africa, leaving only a part of Europe for the Christians. "This
little portion of the world which is ours is pressed upon by warlike Turks and
Saracens: for three hundred years they have held Spain and the Balearic Islands,
and they live in hope of devouring the rest."[1]

In early modern times this global balance of power was completely upset. As
early as 1625 an Ottoman observer was complaining that the Islamic lands were
being encircled and exploited by the Europeans.

Now the Europeans have learnt to know the whole world; they send their ships every-
where and seize important ports. Formerly, the goods of India, Sind, and China used to
come to Suez, and were distributed by Muslims to all the world. But now these goods are
carried on Portuguese, Dutch, and English ships to Frangistan, and are spread all over
the world from there. What they do not need themselves they bring to Istanbul and
other Islamic lands, and sell it for five times the price, thus earning much money. For
this reason gold and silver are becoming scarce in the lands of Islam. The Ottoman Em-
pire must seize the shores of Yemen and the trading passing that way; otherwise before
very long, the Europeans will rule over the lands of Islam.[2]

This perceptive analyst was describing the advent of an entirely new age—the
age of the "emerging West." The earlier Classical and Medieval ages had been
heralded by land invasions by nomads who utilized their superior mobility to
break into the centers of civilization when imperial weakness presented the op-
portunity. The modern age, by contrast, was heralded by sea invasions by the
Westerners, who functioned with equal mobility on the world's oceans and thus

1 Cited by W. Clark, "New Europe and the New Nations," Daedalus (Winter, 1964), p. 136.
2 Cited by B. Lewis, The Emergence of Modern Turkey (New York: Oxford Univ., 1961), p. 28.

were free to operate on a global scale. Part VI deals with the overseas activities of the Iberians and of the northwest Europeans, and also with the contemporaneous overland expansion of the Russians across Siberia to the Pacific.

The resulting global relationships developed during this period between 1500 and 1763 constituted an incipient global ecumene. Just as the "Incipient Eurasian Ecumene" of the classical period had paved the way for the full-fledged "Eurasian Ecumene" of medieval times, so now the "Incipient Global Ecumene" of the early modern centuries was the precursor of the Western-dominated "Global Ecumene" that flourished between 1763 and 1914.

chapter twenty

West European Expansion: Iberian Phase, 1500-1600

The discovery of America, and that of a passage to the East Indies by the Cape of Good Hope, are the greatest and most important events recorded in the history of mankind.—Adam Smith

The two countries of the Iberian Peninsula, Spain and Portugal, took the lead in the expansion of Europe in the sixteenth century. This seems paradoxical in view of the fact that after the sixteenth century these countries declined rapidly, and throughout modern times have remained quite insignificant. What, then, is the explanation for the short-lived but brilliant expansion of Spain and Portugal? This chapter is concerned first with this problem of the origins of Iberian expansionism, then with the process of empire building in the East and in the New World, and finally with the causes and symptoms of Iberian decline.

I. ROOTS OF IBERIAN EXPANSIONISM

Religion was an important factor in European overseas expansion, but nowhere was it so important as in the Iberian Peninsula. Both the Spaniards and the Portuguese were impelled by memories of their long anti-Moslem crusade. To other peoples of Europe, Islam was a distant menace, but for the Iberians it represented a traditional and ever-present enemy. Most of the peninsula at one time had been under Moslem rule, and now, in the fifteenth century, Granada in the south still remained a Moslem stronghold. Furthermore, the Moslems were in control of the nearby North African coast, and growing Turkish seapower was making itself felt throughout the Mediterranean.

Prince Henry the Navigator first won fame in 1415 for his gallant role in the capture of the town and fortress of Ceuta across the Straits of Gibraltar. Likewise Queen Isabella, moved by intense religious conviction, began her crusade against Granada in 1482, and pressed on, village by village, until final victory in 1492. Immediately thereafter, the Spaniards crossed the Straits and captured the city of Melilla. It is not surprising that this deep-rooted drive should have been continued across the oceans where there were more Moslems to be exterminated, and new heathen to be delivered from idolatry. God as well as gold was in the minds of the explorers and colonizers.

Geography, in addition to religion, lured the Iberians overseas. Spain and Portugal were strategically situated for overseas enterprise, and, furthermore, there were four groups of islands—the Canaries, the Madeiras, the Azores, and the Cape Verdes—stretching westward across the Atlantic and southward down the coast of Africa. These were highly attractive, partly because they were fertile and productive, but also because they provided strategic bases and ports of call. After appeals to the Pope and savage local fighting, the Spaniards acquired the Canaries and conceded the other three groups to the Portuguese. Throughout the fifteenth century, Iberian sailors had been discovering islands located far out into the ocean. It was natural that they should assume the existence of more islands awaiting discovery and exploitation. The agreement that Columbus reached with Isabella in 1492 provided that he should head an expedition "to discover and acquire islands and mainland in the Ocean Sea."

It was Portugal, however, rather than Spain, that took the lead in overseas enterprise during the fifteenth century. One reason for Portugal's head start was its small size and its location on the Atlantic coast, surrounded on three sides by Spanish territory. This effectively safeguarded the Portuguese from temptation to squander their resources in European wars. Thanks to the leadership of Prince Henry, they turned instead to oceanic projects. The other reason was Portugal's superior knowledge of navigation, gained primarily from the Italians. Lisbon was on the route of Genoese and Venetian sea traffic with Flanders through the Straits of Gibraltar, and the Portuguese took advantage of this, by employing Italian captains and pilots in the royal navy. Prince Henry followed up by assembling a galaxy of talented seamen, including Italians, Catalans, and even a Dane. Furthermore, Henry's work was continued by the crown following his death, so that the Portuguese became the most knowledgeable of all Europeans in seamanship and geography.

Portugal's interest in exploration quickened following the capture of Ceuta in 1415. Moslem prisoners divulged information concerning the ancient and profitable trade across the Sahara with the Negro kingdoms of the Sudan. (See Chapter 18, section I.) For centuries the latter had provided ivory, slaves, and gold in return for various manufactured goods and salt. Since Western Europe in general and Portugal in particular were then suffering from a serious shortage of bullion, Prince Henry was intrigued by the possibility of tapping this gold trade. Thus when he sent his captains down the coast of Africa, his original objective was the gold trade across the Sahara rather than the spice trade of the East Indies.

A major step forward in early Portuguese exploration was taken when Prince Henry's captains passed the desert coast in 1445 and found below it a verdant new land "covered with palms and other green and beautiful trees, and it was even so with the plains thereof."[1] By the time of Henry's death, the coast had been explored down to Sierra Leone, and a number of coastal stations had been established which enabled the Portuguese to attract at least a part of the caravan trade that they were after. Meanwhile, Portuguese aspirations had come to encompass India as well as Africa. Because Europe at this time was blocked from access to the East by the Moslem power that controlled all of North Africa and the Middle East, the Mediterranean was for the Europeans a prison rather than a highway. Therefore, with the exception of the Venetians, who profited as middlemen, they eagerly sought a new route to the spice islands. Thus as the Portuguese ventured further down the coast of Africa, their horizons expanded. It is significant that when Albuquerque urged his followers before Malacca to "quench the fire of the sect of Mahamede," he also emphasized the prospects for material gain. "I hold it certain that if we take this trade of Malacca away from them (the Moors) Cairo and Mecca will be entirely ruined and Venice receive no spiceries unless her merchants go and buy them in Portugal."[2]

II. COLUMBUS DISCOVERS AMERICA

In view of Portugal's pioneering work in the theory and practice of oceanic navigation, it is paradoxical that the first great discovery—that of the New World—was effected under Spanish auspices. It is even more paradoxical that the reason for this outcome is that the Portuguese were more advanced in their geographical knowledge than the Spaniards and figured correctly that Columbus was wrong in his calculations. It was common knowledge among informed people by the fifteenth century that the world was round. The question was not the shape of the world but its size, and the relationship of the continents to the oceans. By combining Marco Polo's estimate of the east-west extent of Asia, which was an overestimate, the same traveler's report of the distance of Japan from the Asian mainland—1,500 miles—an extreme overestimate, and Ptolemy's estimate of the circumference of the globe, which was an underestimate, Columbus concluded that less than 3,000 miles of ocean separated Europe from Japan. Accordingly, he believed that the shortest and easiest route to Asia was by a short voyage across the Atlantic, and this was the project that he proposed before various courts. The Portuguese, thanks to Prince Henry, had more practical experience and were better informed of the most advanced knowledge of the day. They were convinced that the globe was larger than Columbus held, that the oceans were wider, and that the shortest route to the Orient was around Africa rather than across the Atlantic. For this reason the Portuguese king turned Columbus down when he applied for financial assistance in 1484. Two years later Columbus was at the Spanish court where, after a preliminary rejection, he finally won the support of Queen Isabella.

On August 2, 1492, Columbus set sail from Palos with three small ships manned by reliable crews with capable and seasoned officers. By mid-October he landed at one of the Bahama Islands, which he named San Salvador. Columbus was convinced that this island was very near to where Japan ought to be, and the next step was to find Japan itself. The Spanish monarchs loyally supported him, outfitting three additional expeditions during which he discovered numerous islands and explored the mainland coast from Honduras to Costa Rica. The results were disappointing, for only small quantities of gold were found. But several thousand adventurers who had flocked to the New World persisted in their probings until finally they stumbled upon riches beyond their wildest dreams in the Aztec and Inca empires. It is ironic that the Spaniards eventually triumphed because they clung to their delusion that they had reached the coast of Asia. Had they realized that they had stumbled instead on a great continental barrier between Europe and Asia, they might very well have turned away from what appeared to be an unprofitable wilderness, particularly because Portugal's Vasco de Gama had in the meantime opened up the profitable Cape route to India.

III. PORTUGAL IN ASIA

The Portuguese had been making considerable profit from their trade along the African Guinea Coast. Coarse pepper, gold, ivory, cotton, sugar, and slaves now entered European commerce through Portugal. Prince Henry's successors continued his work of opening up the West African coast. A breakthrough occurred in 1487 when Bartholomeu Dias, while probing along the coast, was caught by a gale that blew his ships south for thirteen days out of sight of land. When the wind moderated, Dias steered for the West African coast but discovered that he had already passed the Cape without knowing it. He landed at Mossel Bay on the Indian Ocean, and wished to explore further, but his weary and frightened men forced him to return. On the homeward passage he first sighted the great cape, and named it the Cape of Storms. It was the Portuguese king who, upon Dias' return, renamed it the Cape of Good Hope.

The king did not follow up on this rounding of the Cape because of political and financial complications. The result, as noted, was that Columbus was the first to reach the New World, which he persisted in claiming to be the Orient. The more knowledgeable Portuguese were dubious from the beginning, but they now hastened to open and secure the Cape route to India. On July 8, 1497, Vasco da Gama left Portugal with four ships, and sailed around the Cape to Milindi on the East African coast where he picked up an Arab pilot who guided him across the Indian Ocean to Calicut on the west coast of India.

Da Gama did not receive a warm welcome in Calicut. The resident Arab merchants were naturally alarmed by this threat to their traditional monopoly and did their best to throw obstacles in the way of the European intruders. Furthermore, the Portuguese trade goods—mostly trinkets and woolen cloth—were unsuitable for the Indian market because Portugal (and all Europe) produced little at this time that was of interest to the Eastern peoples. European manufactures were generally inferior in quality and higher in price than the goods produced in the East. One of Vasco da Gama's companions relates that "We did not . . . effect these sales at the prices hoped for . . . for a very fine shirt which in Portugal fetches 300 reis, was worth here . . . only 30 reis, for 30 reis in this country is a big sum."[3]

With much effort da Gama collected a cargo of pepper and cinnamon and cleared for home, arriving in September, 1499. The cargo proved to be worth sixty times the cost of the entire expedition. Dazzling horizons opened up before the delighted Portuguese, and King Manuel assumed the titles "Lord of the Conquest, Navigation, and Commerce of Ethiopia, Arabia, Persia, and India." These titles were taken quite seriously. The Portuguese were determined to monopolize the trade along the new route and to exclude, not only other Europeans, but also the Arabs and other Eastern peoples who had traded in the Indian Ocean for centuries. To enforce their claims, the Portuguese resorted to ruthless terrorism, particularly when they encountered the hated Moslems. Da Gama, on a later voyage, found some unarmed vessels returning from Mecca. He captured the vessels and, in the words of a fellow Portuguese, "after making the ships empty of goods, prohibited anyone from taking out of it any Moor and then ordered them to set fire to it."[4]

Such was the nature of the epochal meeting of two Eurasian cultures brought face to face for the first time after millennia of regional isolation. The Portuguese were the aggressive intruders. Numbering only about two million, they gained mastery over the vast Indian Ocean basin with its teeming millions and great natural resources. One reason was that the Portuguese had the great good fortune of being able to utilize the vast bullion supply that soon was to start pouring in from the treasures of the Aztec and Inca empires and from the Mexican and Peruvian silver mines. Without this providential windfall the Portuguese would have been most seriously restricted, because they had neither natural resources nor manufactured goods that were of interest to the Eastern peoples. The fact that Portuguese-made shirts cost ten times as much as Indian, as da Gama discovered, suggests that the Portuguese would have had difficulty finding something to exchange for the spices they wanted. That something was provided by the New World silver mines. The East was always eager to accept bullion. Hence the observation that "The voyage of Columbus was an imperative supplement to that of da Gama."[5]

Another reason for the triumph of the Portuguese was the disunity of the Indian Ocean lands. India was divided between the Mogul invaders in the north and petty Hindu rulers in the south, while Southeast Asia was exceptionally vulnerable because of the withdrawal of Ming China and the disintegration of the Hindu-Javanese Majapahit Empire. Thus the way was clear for the Portuguese who, following da Gama's voyage, sent out naval and merchant fleets to exploit the golden opportunity. Furthermore the Portuguese enjoyed naval predominance, thanks to their superior artillery and to their ability to execute squadron maneuvers and to use their ships as floating batteries rather than as transports for boarding parties.

The great weakness of the Portuguese was their limited manpower. Accordingly their aim was not to conquer a land empire but to monopolize the spice trade and, where possible, to smite the Moslems and propagate the faith. To attain these objectives the great Alfonso de Albuquerque, governor general from 1509 to 1515, seized control of the narrow sea passages leading to and from the Indian Ocean. He captured the islands of Socotra and Hormuz, which were the keys to the Red Sea and the Persian Gulf respectively. In India he failed in an attempt to seize Calicut and took instead the city of Goa located in the middle of the Malabar Coast. He made Goa his main naval base and general headquarters, and it remained a Portuguese possession until 1961. Further to the east he captured Malacca, commanding the strait through which all commerce with the Far East had to pass. Two years later, in 1513, the first Portuguese ship to reach a Chinese port put into Canton. This was the first recorded European visit to China since Marco Polo's day. The Portuguese at first had trouble with the Chinese government because the ruler of Malacca had recognized Chinese suzerainty and had fled to Peking with complaints against the violent and barbarous Europeans. But in due course the Portuguese secured the right to establish a warehouse and a settlement at Macao, a little downstream from Canton, and from where they carried on their Far Eastern operations.

The Portuguese Empire in Asia was negligible in its actual extent, comprising only a few islands and coastal posts. But these possessions were so strategically located that they gave the Portuguese command of trade routes spanning half the globe. Each year Portuguese fleets sailed down the African coast, which was dotted with stations for provisioning and refitting the ships. After rounding the Cape, they put in at Mozambique in East Africa, another Portuguese possession. Then they sailed with the monsoon across to Cochin and Ceylon, where they loaded the spices that had been brought in from the surrounding territories. Further east was Malacca, which gave them access to the trade of East Asia, for which they served as middlemen and carriers. Thus, the Portuguese profited from purely Asian trade—between China and Japan and the Philippines, for example—as well as from the trade between Europe and the East.

With this network of trading stations and strong points, Albuquerque had broken the traditional monopoly of the Arab merchants in the Indian Ocean, and in doing so he was competing with the Venetian merchants for the "spiceries" that they had customarily obtained in the ports of Levant. The extent of his success may be gauged from the fact that in the four years 1502–1505, the Venetians were able to obtain an average of only 1 million English pounds of spices a year at Alexandria, whereas in the last years of the fifteenth century they had averaged 3.5 million pounds. Conversely, Portuguese spice imports rose from 224,000 pounds in 1501 to an average of 2.3 million pounds in the years 1503–1506.

These statistics explain why the Egyptians, with full Venetian support, sent a naval expedition in 1508 to aid the Indian rajas to drive the Portuguese interlopers out of the Indian Ocean. The effort failed, but the Turks, who conquered Egypt in 1517, continued the campaign against the Portuguese and sent several fleets during the following decades. They were all unsuccessful, and the spices continued to flow around the Cape to Europe. Yet it should not be assumed that the old routes through the Middle East fell into complete disuse. In fact, after the initial dislocation, they regained much of the lost trade.

As it turned out, all the advantages were by no means on the side of the oceanic route. It is true that Portuguese ships could take relatively large cargoes compared to the limited carrying loads of the caravans plying from the Red Sea and Persian Gulf to Mediterranean ports. Furthermore, the Cape route involved only one long haul, in contrast to the numerous and expensive loadings, unloadings, and reloadings from the Spice Islands to India to the Red Sea and Persian Gulf and thence to the Levant ports and Italian ports before reaching the West European consumer.

On the other hand, shipwrecks on the long voyage around the Cape were frequent and costly. And, since the Portuguese had no goods to offer for profitable outward freight, they shipped out New World bullion for the spices, and thus had to sell the spices at prices sufficiently high to meet the costs of both the outward and homeward passages. As a result, Portuguese-imported spices often were little cheaper in Western Europe than those brought by land from the Middle East. Furthermore, it was widely believed that spices tended to lose their aroma during the long sea voyage. Perhaps this was a story put out by the Venetians, but it may very well have had some foundation in fact. Portuguese cargoes were carried in bags, in leaky ships, and through latitudes with extreme weather fluctuations.

The Portuguese, besides, were unable to establish a total monopoly on the ocean route, because corrupt Portuguese officials usually were willing, for a consideration, to allow Arab shipping to enter the Red Sea and the Persian Gulf. The net result was that the Arabs and the Venetians, far from being put out of business following da Gama's voyage, competed successfully with the Portuguese throughout the sixteenth century. It was not until the following century, with the appearance in the Indian Ocean of the more efficient and economically powerful Dutch and English, that the old Italian and Arab middlemen were supplanted and that the traditional Middle Eastern trade routes were overshadowed by the oceanic.

IV. DIVISION OF THE WORLD

The discoveries of Columbus and of da Gama raised the question of sovereignty over the newly found areas. This problem had never agitated medieval Europe because all the territory with which its rulers had any practical concern was already possessed by states sufficiently alike in sentiment and organization to be capable of entering into mutual relations. When Europe began to expand, there was adopted by tacit mutual agreement the convenient doctrine that Christian states had the right to possess themselves of the lands of the heathen and infidel without regard for the native peoples concerned. Another doctrine that was accepted, at least by Portugal and Spain, was the right of the Pope to allot temporal sovereignty to any lands not possessed by a Christian ruler. As early as 1454, Pope Nicholas V issued a bull granting to the Portuguese title to the territories they were discovering along the African coast toward India.

When Columbus returned from his first voyage with the conviction that he had reached the Indies, the Spanish court feared Portuguese counterclaims and therefore pressed Pope Alexander VI for recognition of Spanish sovereignty. On May 4, 1493, Pope Alexander defined a line of demarcation running 100 leagues west of the Azores and Cape Verde Islands, and granted to Spain all lands to the west of it, and to Portugal all lands to its east. On June 7, 1494, Spain and Portugal negotiated an agreement, the Treaty of Tordesillas, moving the line 270 leagues further west. The effect of this change was to give Portugal a claim to Brazil in the New World. At the time, the Spaniards thought they had the better of the bargain, believing that the route to the Indies was westward. Actually the demarcation line left to Portugal the only route to India feasible at the time.

The riches that Portugal reaped from the spice trade following da Gama's voyage goaded the other European countries to a frantic search for another route to the Indies. The successive failures of Columbus to find Cathay did not kill the hope of reaching Asia by sailing west. It might still be possible to thread a way between the various masses of inhospitable land so far discovered. The hope was encouraged by the chance discovery of a Spanish adventurer, Vasco Nuñez de Balboa, who, while exploring for gold in the Isthmus of Darien, came within sight of the Pacific. The new knowledge that a narrow strip of land separated the two oceans encouraged the explorers seeking the elusive passage to the East.

Under these circumstances a new class of professional explorer appeared in the early sixteenth century. Mostly Italians and Portuguese (they being the best informed and the most experienced explorers at that time), they were men whose national allegiance sat lightly upon them and who undertook explorations for any monarch willing to finance them. The Italians included Amerigo Vespucci, who sailed for Portugal and Spain, John Verrazano who sailed for France, and the two Cabots, father and son, who sailed for England. The Portuguese included Juan de Solís, Juan Fernandez, and Ferdinand Magellan, all of whom sailed for Spain.

Only Magellan found the passage to Asia. Spain sent him out because, with regular spice cargoes arriving in Lisbon, it realized that it was being beaten in the race for the Spice Islands. Claiming that the line of demarcation defined by the Tordesillas Treaty ran right round the globe, Spain dispatched Magellan west for Asia, hoping that he would find at least some of the Spice Islands on the Spanish side of the line. His expedition is one of the great epics of seafaring. He set out from Seville on September 10, 1519, with a fleet of five ships, each about 100 tons. On September 3, 1522, one surviving ship limped into Seville harbor, the others having been lost during the rounding of Cape Horn and the interminable crossing of the Pacific, and in clashes with natives in the Philippines and with Spaniards in the Spice Islands. Yet the single cargo of spices was valuable enough to defray the expense of the entire expedition.

The Spaniards sent out another expedition which reached the Spice Islands in 1524. But it proved to be a disastrous failure because the Portuguese were too firmly established to be challenged profitably. Furthermore, the Spanish king was desperately in need of money at this time to finance his war with France. So in

1529 he signed the Treaty of Saragossa with Portugal, by which, in return for 350,000 ducats, he gave up all claims to the Spice Islands and accepted a demarcation line fifteen degrees east of them. This treaty marked the end of a chapter in the history of discovery. The Portuguese held on to the Spice Islands until they lost them to the Dutch in 1605, while the Spaniards continued to show interest in the Philippines and eventually conquered them in 1571, even though the islands were east of the line stipulated by the Saragossa Treaty. Long before this, however, Spain had shifted her attention to the New World, where great treasures had been found equal in value to the spices of the East.

V. AGE OF CONQUISTADORS

The year 1519, in which Magellan left Seville on his famous voyage around the world, was also the year in which Hernando Cortes left Cuba on his equally famous expedition against the Aztec Empire. In doing so, Cortes heralded what might be termed the age of the conquistadors. The preceding decades, from 1500 to 1520, had been the age of the explorers, when numerous navigators under various flags probed the entire length of the Americas in search of a passageway. In the thirty years that followed, a few thousand Spanish adventurers won the first great European overseas empire.

One of these soldiers of fortune was Hernando Cortes, who arrived in Hispaniola in 1504, and five years later participated in the conquest of Cuba. Distinguishing himself during this campaign he was selected to head an expedition to Yucatan to investigate reports of civilized city dwellers living in the interior. In March, 1519, Cortes landed on the mainland coast near present-day Veracruz. He had only six hundred men, a few small cannon, thirteen muskets, and sixteen horses. Yet with this insignificant force he was to win fabulous riches and become master of an exotic, highly advanced empire. The reasons for this spectacular success have already been noted—the courage, ruthlessness, and superior weapons of the Spaniards, the impractical fighting tactics of the Indians, and their bitter dissensions that Cortes exploited cleverly and decisively.

Cortes began by scuttling his ships to show his men that they had no hope of returning to Cuba in case of setbacks. Then, after some fighting, he reached agreements with various tribes that were hostile to their Aztec overlords. Without the food, the porters, and the fighting men provided by these tribes, Cortes could not have won the victories he did. By playing upon the superstitions of Montezuma, the Aztec war-chief, Cortes was able to march peacefully into the capital, Tenochtitlan. He was graciously received by Montezuma, whom he treacherously took prisoner and kept as a hostage. This was a brazen bluff that could not be maintained for long. The Indians were vastly superior in numbers, and their priests were stirring them up to rebellion. The Spanish policy of destroying native temples provoked an uprising during which Montezuma was killed. Cortes fought his way out of the capital by night, losing a third of his men and most of his baggage in the process. But his Indian allies remained loyal, and he received reinforcements from Cuba. A few months later he returned and laid siege to the capital with a force of 800 Spanish soldiers and at least 25,000 Indians. The fighting was bitter and dragged on for four months. Finally, in August, 1521, the surviving defenders surrendered their city, which was almost entirely reduced to rubble. Today, Mexico City stands in its place, with hardly a trace left of the original Aztec capital.

Even more audacious was the conquest of the Inca Empire by a Spanish expedition led by Francisco Pizarro and comprising 180 men, 27 horses, and 2 cannon. After preliminary explorations from which he learned the general location of the Inca Empire, he set forth in 1531, with his four brothers, on his great adventure. After a long delay in crossing the Andes, Pizarro reached the deserted city of Cajamarca on November 15, 1532. The following day the Inca ruler, Atahualpa, who was curious about these strange "men with beards," paid a formal visit to Pizarro. In imitation of Cortes, Pizarro captured the unarmed and unsuspecting emperor and massacred many of his followers. The emperor paid an enormous ransom for his freedom—a room 22 feet by 17 feet piled 7 feet deep with gold and silver articles—but he was nevertheless executed by the Spaniards. The Inca Empire now was left leaderless, and the Indian population, accustomed to paternalistic regimentation, offered little resistance. A few weeks later Pizarro entered and looted the capital, Cuzco. The next year, 1535, he left for the coast, where he founded Lima, still the capital of Peru.

The triumphs of Cortes and Pizarro inspired other conquistadors to march through vast areas of both the American continents in search of more booty. They found nothing comparable to the Aztec and Inca treasures, but in the process they did determine the major configuration of all South America and of a large part of North America. By the middle of the sixteenth century they had followed the Amazon from Peru to its mouth. By the end of the century they were familiar with the entire coastline of South America, from the Gulf of California south to Tierra del Fuego and north to the West Indies. Likewise in North America, Francisco de Coronado, in his search for the fabled Seven Cities of Cibola, traversed thousands of miles and discovered the Grand Canyon and the Colorado River. Hernando de Soto, who had been prominent in the conquest of Peru, explored widely in the southeast of what was to become the United States. He landed in Florida in 1539, made his way north to the Carolinas and west to the Mississippi, and followed that river from its junction with the Arkansas River to its mouth. These men, and many others like them, opened up the New World for the Spaniards in the same manner that La Salle and Lewis and Clark opened it for the French- and English-speaking peoples.

VI. EUROPE'S FIRST COLONIAL EMPIRE

By 1550 the conquistadors had completed their work. The way was now clear for the Spaniards to proceed with the development of their overseas possessions. Since the native populations were not so dense or so highly organized as those of Africa and Asia, it was possible for the Iberians to settle in considerable numbers in the New World and to impose their cultures. Thus they built up Europe's first true colonial empire—something quite different from the purely commercial empires in Africa and Asia.

The swashbuckling conquistadors were effective as empire builders but quite ineffective as empire administrators. They could not settle down; they fell to fighting among themselves, decimating their ranks during prolonged feuding and internecine warfare. Had these conquistadors been left to themselves, they probably would have gradually developed scattered and virtually independent feudal communities based on the exploitation of native labor. But the Spanish crown, which had curbed feudal tendencies within Spain, would not tolerate the emergence of a new feudal aristocracy overseas. Accordingly, the conquistadors were replaced by bureaucrats who imposed royal authority and royal justice.

At the apex of the imperial administrative structure was the Council of the

Indies, located in Spain and closely supervised by the crown. It made all important appointments and exercised general jurisdiction over colonial affairs. Supreme authority in the New World was entrusted to two viceroys who sat in Mexico City and Lima, respectively. The official in Mexico City headed the viceroyalty of New Spain, which comprised all the Spanish territories in North America together with the West Indies, Venezuela, and the Philippines. The Lima official presided over the viceroyalty of Peru, comprising the remaining Spanish possessions in South America. These two vast viceroyalties were subdivided into smaller units ruled by *audiencias,* or councils, modeled on bodies that had been established in Spain to administer territories newly liberated from the Moslems. These audiencias were staffed by professional lawyers who usually had no excessive family pride or military ambition and therefore made ideal royal servants. In the sixteenth century there were ten such audiencias in the New World.

A basic problem of Spanish administration in the Americas was the treatment of the Indians. The crown granted to deserving conquistadors, known as "protectors," or encomenderos, the right to draw specified tribute from assigned Indian villages and also to levy forced labor. In return, the encomenderos were required to give military service and to pay the salaries of the parish clergy. The provision for forced labor obviously opened the door to abuse, so it was modified in the mid-sixteenth century. The natives still could be made to work, but the compulsion was provided by public rather than private authority, and official wage rates had to be paid to the laborers so recruited. It is unnecessary to add that these safeguards were not always enforced, the colonies being too far from Madrid and too isolated from each other.

The all-important fact for the economy of the Spanish colonial empire is the great flood of gold and silver. First there were the countless treasure objects that were seized as booty, and then the Spaniards discovered rich silver veins in Mexico and Bolivia, which they worked with native labor. They were required to register their claims with royal officials and to bring all precious metals to the royal offices to be stamped and taxed at the rate of one-fifth their value, the royal quinto. Between 1503 and 1660 Spain received from America a total of 18,600 registered tons of silver and 200 registered tons of gold. Unregistered bullion smuggled into Spain has been variously estimated at from 10 to 50 per cent of the total, the smaller percentage probably being nearer the truth.

Apart from mining, the principal occupations in Latin America were agriculture and stock raising in the haciendas, and plantation monoculture in the tropical coastlands. The haciendas employed Indian labor and produced foodstuffs for their own use and for sale to nearby cities and mining settlements. The plantations were quite different, employing mostly imported African slaves and producing only one crop for the European market. The first plantations were evolved for the growing of sugar on the Atlantic islands—the Azores, Madeiras, Cape Verdes, and Canaries. Later this institution was further developed, first in the sugar plantations of Brazil and the West Indies, and later in the tobacco, cotton, and coffee plantations of North and South America.

VII. IBERIAN DECLINE: CAUSES AND SYMPTOMS

The Iberian countries led Europe in empire building, but by the end of the sixteenth century they were falling behind badly. One reason was their involvement in a succession of dynastic and religious wars that exhausted their material and human resources. Charles V, grandson of Ferdinand and Isabella, inherited from his forebears the united Spanish Kingdom, together with the Spanish possessions in the New World and in Italy, the hereditary Hapsburg lands in Central Europe, and the Burgundian possessions, including the wealthy Netherlands. This sprawling empire, the largest since that of Charlemagne seven centuries earlier, aroused fears and precipitated a long series of Hapsburg-Valois wars fought primarily by the French and the Spaniards. At the same time Charles had to contend with the Turks who almost captured Vienna in 1529, and with the Protestant heretics that were splitting Western Christendom into two camps. (See Chapter 17, section VII.)

In 1556 Charles abdicated his throne, worn out by forces too vast to control. His son, Philip II, faced the same dynastic struggle with France and religious struggle with Protestantism. Particularly exhausting was the long war with the Dutch Protestants that eventually involved also the English and led to the destruction of the Invincible Armada in 1588. Contemporaries called the Netherlands "the graveyard of Spain." Obviously the rulers of Spain overextended themselves in attempting to play the leading role on sea as well as on land. Spain paid dearly for a century of lavish squandering of manpower and resources. On the other hand it is doubtful that this was the primary cause for Spain's collapse to the status of a third-rate power. Holland, after all, was very much involved in these wars, and the country repeatedly was ravaged by Spanish armies. Yet Holland emerged as the dominant naval power and trading nation of Europe.

Although the Iberian states indisputably were weakened by foreign entanglements, a more substantive cause for their chronic decline was the fact that for long they had been economic dependencies of northwest Europe. They had been so before they began their overseas expansion and they remained so afterwards. As a result they were unable to exploit the economic opportunities offered by their newly won empires, and instead these empires, like their mother countries, fell under the domination of the northwest European states as their colonies or semicolonies.

The economic subservience of the Iberian countries was a part of the general shift of the economic center of Europe in the late Middle Ages from the Mediterranean basin to the north. The reason for this shift was the accelerating productivity of northern Europe (see Chapter 17, section III), which enabled the new mass trade of the Baltic-North Sea area (grain, lumber, fish, and coarse cloth) to surpass the traditional luxury trade of the Mediterranean (spices, silks, perfumes, and jewelry). As the European economy grew and living standards rose, the mass trade catering to the general populace increased much more rapidly than the luxury trade for the wealthy few.

The northern commerce was controlled by the Hanseatic League, which played the same role in the Baltic and North Sea as Venice and Genoa did in the Mediterranean. In the sixteenth century the Hansa was dislodged by the Dutch who built such a large and efficient merchant marine that they soon extended their domination to the Atlantic seaboard. Hitherto the Atlantic trade had been controlled by the Venetians and Genoese sailing northward with luxury commodities, but now it was controlled by the Dutch sailing southward with bulk cargoes. In this new trade pattern, the economic subservience of the Iberian states was evident in their exports which were almost exclusively raw materials— wine, wool, and iron ore from Spain, and African gold and Setubal salt from Portugal. In return they received back their own wool, which had been manufactured abroad into cloth, as well as metallurgical products, salt, and fish.

These economically backward Iberian states were able to take the lead in overseas expansion only because of a fortunate combination of favorable geographic location, maritime technology, and religious drive. But economic strength and dynamism were not behind this expansion, which explains why the Iberian states were unable to exploit their new empires effectively. They lacked the shipping necessary for imperial trade, as well as the industries to supply the manufactured goods needed in the Spanish American colonies. It is true that Spanish industry for a few decades was stimulated by the burgeoning overseas market for manufactures, but the industrial growth stopped about 1560, and chronic decline then set in.

One reason, paradoxically enough, was the great inflow of treasure, which produced a sharp inflation. Prices rose approximately twice as high in Spain as in northern Europe, and Spanish wages lagged only slightly behind the soaring prices, while wages in the rest of Europe were kept far down. This penalized Spanish industry, making its products too expensive to compete in the international market.

At least as important as this price and wage inflation was the ruinous influence of the Spanish aristocrat, or hidalgo, on the national economy and national values. Although the aristocrats, together with the higher ecclesiastics, comprised less than 2 per cent of the population, they owned from 95 to 97 per cent of the land. If follows that the peasants, about 95 per cent of all Spaniards, were almost all landless. The remaining 3 per cent—clerics, merchants, and professional men, many of whom were Jews—were not a middle class in any economic or social sense. They were completely overshadowed by the nobility, who had social status and prestige. Because the nobility looked down upon careers in commerce or industry as demeaning for any gentleman, this prejudice became the national norm. Nor was this mere empty vanity, for the hidalgo had all the advantages—honors, exemption from taxation, and territorial wealth that was more secure than commercial or industrial riches. Consequently, the ambition of successful merchants was to acquire estates, buy titles, which were sold by the impoverished crown, and thus abandon their class and become hidalgos. The blighting influence of this hidalgo spirit was felt in all branches of the economy—in the favoritism shown towards sheep farming as against agriculture, in the expulsion of the industrious Jews and Moslems, and in the negative attitude of the Cortes towards commercial and industrial interests. Hence the ultimate failure of the economic spurt that occurred in Spain in the first half of the sixteenth century.

This failure ended any possibility of overcoming the traditional Iberian economic backwardness and subservience to northwest Europe. It also doomed the Iberian colonial possessions to a corresponding backwardness and subservience. First the Dutch and then the British controlled most of the carrying trade with the Spanish and Portuguese colonies. The northwest Europeans also were soon supplying up to 90 percent of the manufactured goods imported by Brazil and Spanish America, as well as a high proportion of similar goods consumed in the Iberian Peninsula itself. The merchant guild of Seville enjoyed a monopoly of all trade with the colonies, in which foreigners were forbidden by law to participate. But it was the foreigners who possessed the shipping and the manufactured goods needed in the colonies. Inevitably the Spanish merchants exported in their own name goods that belonged to foreign firms and were of foreign manufacture. Also, through an elaborate series of fictions, foreign merchants and financiers became members by proxy of the Seville guild. Thus the legal members conducted a vast commission business for foreigners that soon surpassed their own legitimate trade. The end result is apparent in the following complaint of a contemporary Spaniard: "All that the Spaniards bring from the Indies after long, prolix, and hazardous navigations, and all that they harvest with blood and labour, foreigners carry off to their homelands with ease and comfort."[6]

It is ironic that the net effect of Spanish overseas enterprise was to further fuel the booming capitalist economy of northwest Europe, while in the Iberian Peninsula it provided just enough wealth to forestall pressures for the basic institutional reforms that were long overdue. This is the root cause for the sudden and irreversible decline that followed so soon after the few decades of imperial glory.

The exploitation of the American colonies, Mexico and Peru, made the restructuring of the Spanish semifeudal, land-based, aristocratic economy and society unnecessary. . . . After 1600 when the modernizing states of Europe were questioning concepts of practices of privilege, of the "absolute state," of the church militant, of private usufruct of public power, of bullion rather than production as wealth, these institutions and attitudes took new root in Spain and Spanish America.[7]

SUGGESTED READING

E. W. Bovill, *Caravans of the Old Sahara* (Oxford Univ., 1933); C. R. Boxer, *The Portuguese Seaborne Empire 1415–1825* (Hutchinson, 1969); K. M. Panikkar, *Asia and Western Dominance* (Day, 1954); J. H. Parry, *The Age of Reconnaissance: Discovery, Exploration and Settlement 1450–1650* (World, 1963), and his *The Spanish Seaborne Empire* (Knopf, 1966); S. J. and B. H. Stein, *The Colonial Heritage of Latin America* (Oxford Univ., 1970).

chapter twenty-one

West European
Expansion:
Dutch, French, British Phase,
1600-1763

I should like to see Adam's will, wherein he divided the earth between Spain and Portugal.—King Francis I

The period between 1600 and 1763 witnessed the overtaking and surpassing of Spain and Portugal by the powers of northwestern Europe—Holland, France, and Britain. This development was of prime significance for the entire world. It made northwestern Europe the most influential and dynamic region of the globe. The countries of northwestern Europe were to dominate the world—politically, militarily, economically, and, to a certain degree, culturally—until 1914. Their practices and institutions became the models for peoples everywhere.

The world hegemony of northwestern Europe did not actually materialize until after 1763. But it was during the years between 1600 and 1763 that the basis for this hegemony was laid. These were the years when the British gained their first foothold in India, when the Dutch drove the Portuguese out of the East Indies, when all the northwestern powers set up stations on the coasts of Africa, and when the British and the French became the masters of North America above the Rio Grande, and also controlled much of the commerce of the Iberian possessions south of it.

This chapter will analyze the roots of northwest European primacy, and the struggles of Holland, France, and Britain for leadership, culminating in 1763 with the emergence of Britain as the dominant colonial power of the world.

I. ROOTS OF NORTHWEST EUROPEAN PRIMACY

Northwest Europe did not rise from utter obscurity to the leading position in Continental commerce and in overseas enterprise. As noted in the preceding chapter, the foundation was laid during the late Middle Ages when the economic center of Europe shifted from the Mediterranean basin northward, and the principal trade routes likewise shifted from the Mediterranean to the Atlantic. In addition to economic superiority, northwest Europe possessed a social structure and a cultural climate that were particularly responsive to economic interests.

Far from regarding business enterprise with disdain, the patriciate of Holland and the nobility of England, and even of France, were already ready to participate in any business venture that promised profit. Also there was much more class mobility in the north, with merchants and financiers entering the ranks of the nobility just as gentlemen participated in commerce. Daniel Defoe observed in 1726 that "trade in England makes gentlemen, and has peopled this nation with gentlemen; for the tradesmen's children, or at least their grandchildren, come to be as good gentlemen, statesmen, Parliament men, privy counsellors, judges, bishops, and noblemen, as those of the highest birth and the most ancient families."[1] The social attitude reflected in this statement was the precise opposite of the myopic hidalgo spirit that contributed so much to Iberian decadence.

Finally northwest Europe was aided by a price-wage-rent differential. Prices rose 256 per cent in England during the sixteenth and seventeenth centuries, while wages rose only 45 per cent. Rents also lagged badly behind prices in northwest Europe, an English squire complaining in 1549 that landlords were becoming impoverished because "the most part of the landes of this Realme stand yet at the old Rent." This meant that of the three main elements of society—the laborers, landlords, and entrepreneurs—the entrepreneurs were the ones who reaped golden profits during these centuries of inflation. These profits were plowed back into mining ventures, industrial establishments, and commercial enterprises, with the result that the economy of northwestern Europe boomed ahead at an unprecedented rate. The famous British economist John Maynard Keynes has described the period from 1550 to 1650 as follows: "Never in the annals of the modern world has there existed so prolonged and so rich an opportunity for the business man, the speculator, and the profiteer. In these golden years modern capitalism was born."[2] That it was born in northwestern Europe explains why the northwestern countries forged ahead of Spain and Portugal and attained a predominant position in world affairs, a position they were to retain until the outbreak of World War I.

II. EARLY NORTHWEST EUROPEAN EXPANSION

The countries of northwestern Europe were naturally envious of the lucrative empires of Spain and Portugal. But for long they refrained from poaching on these imperial preserves, not out of respect for Papal Bulls, but rather for fear of Iberian power. Accordingly, the English and the French turned to the North Atlantic, which was beyond the limits of Iberian activity. Henry VII of England sent out John Cabot in that direction in 1496, the year of Columbus' second return, and Cabot discovered a resource that proved in the long run to be even more valuable than the silver mines of the Spaniards: he found fish. The sea off Newfoundland was teeming with fish—probably the most important article of trade in fifteenth and sixteenth century Europe, the mainstay of the people in the winter and their diet on fast days throughout the year.

The Portuguese were the first to exploit the Newfoundland Banks, but the French and the English soon followed. As the number of ships increased, the nature of the trade changed from the immediate sale of "green" fish to the marketing, at longer intervals, of much larger quantities of "dry" fish. The fishermen set up temporary shelters ashore during the summer months in order to dry and repair nets and to smoke and salt the catch. The scale of operations reached such proportions that it affected Europe significantly in at least two respects. The regular supply of immense quantities of cod represented a great windfall for a continent where many people at that time lived near starvation level for part of every year. And the Newfoundland fisheries bred successive generations of mariners who were trained and fitted for ocean navigation. The ships that later probed the Arctic for a northeast or a northwest passage; the expeditions that began the settlement of North America; the English and the Dutch fleets that fought the armadas of Spain and Portugal—all these were largely manned by seamen trained in the hard school of the Banks fisheries.

The maritime states of northwestern Europe were by no means satisfied with cod. They still hankered after spices, but they were not yet prepared to challenge Portugal's mastery of the Cape route. So they began their long and fruitless series of expeditions in search of a northeast or northwest passage to the Orient. They reasoned that since the Tropics had proved passable, contrary to all expectations, the Arctic should be also. In 1553 an expedition of three ships left England with the express intention of sailing to China by way of the northeast. The ships were separated during a gale, and two of them, under Willoughby, reached the Barents Sea. There they were frozen in for the winter, and the crews all perished. The remaining ship under Richard Chancellor reached a settlement at the mouth of the Dvina River in the White Sea. After long haggling with the local people, Chancellor and some of his officers set off on an astonishing journey in horse-drawn sleighs, in winter, from the White Sea to Moscow. It proved to be a historic trip. Chancellor learned of the power and wealth of the Russian Tsar, Ivan IV, or the Terrible. The latter in turn was delighted to establish for the first time direct communications with a western European country. The Muscovy Company was organized in 1555 to exploit the new trade opportunity.

Other attempts to discover a northeast passage invariably ended before a wall of ice. Interest therefore shifted to the possibility of a northwest route. The search began here with the three voyages of the Englishman Martin Frobisher, between 1576 and 1578. He was followed by a long line of explorers, including John Davis (who explored between 1585 and 1587), Henry Hudson (1607–1611), and Robert Bylot and William Baffin (1615–1616). They were all Englishmen, for, alone among the early exploration projects, the search for a northwest passage was a largely English enterprise. None of them was successful in sailing through to the Pacific, but they did discover the Hudson Strait and Hudson Bay, which together provided a back entrance to the richest fur-producing region of the New World. This knowledge later enabled the English to compete in a region that otherwise would have been monopolized by the French.

The failure of the northern Europeans to find new routes to the East drove them to encroach on the preserves of the Iberian powers. Because Portugal's eastern possessions were still too strongly guarded, the northerners struck first at the more vulnerable Spanish colonies in the Americas. The French, operating from La Rochelle, had begun engaging in piracy and privateering on the Spanish Main with the accession of Charles V in 1516. The English interlopers who were showing up in Spanish America at this time tried to carry on trade on a peaceful, commercial basis. They wanted not to plunder but to take advantage of the opportunities offered by the inability of the weak Spanish industry to meet the needs of the colonies. Of the two commodities most in demand in the Spanish colonies—cloth and Negro slaves—the English produced the first and could purchase the second in West Africa.

Sir John Hawkins won fame and fortune as the founder of the English slave trade because he was shrewd enough to sense the possibilities of this situation and bold enough to act without regard for legal niceties. In 1562 he made his first voyage, picking up slaves in Sierra Leone and exchanging them in Hispaniola

(Haiti) for hides and sugar. The profits were so spectacular that Queen Elizabeth and several of her Privy Councilors secretly invested in his second voyage. He followed the same procedure as before and returned with a cargo of silver that made him the richest man in England. A third voyage ended in disaster, but the opportunities for profit were too great for the English and the other northerners to refrain and forget. During the following decades numerous Protestant sea captains visited the Spanish Indies as pirates and privateers.

Furthermore, other events in Europe at this time were bringing closer a showdown between the Catholic and Protestant powers—the Dutch revolt against Spanish rule, the Pope's excommunication of Queen Elizabeth, the murder of thousands of French Protestants on St. Bartholomew's Eve, and the launching of the Spanish Armada in 1588. Formal war with Spain (which at this time had absorbed Portugal) removed any inhibitions that may have restrained the Protestant powers. They broke boldly and openly into the Iberian imperial preserves—into the Portuguese East as well as into Spanish America. And the more they penetrated, the more they were encouraged to go on by the unexpected weakness that they encountered. The Dutch were the ones who were first able to exploit this opportunity afforded by Iberian decline. The seventeenth century was to be for Holland *Het Gouden Eeuw*—"the Golden Century."

III. HOLLAND'S GOLDEN CENTURY

The remarkable rise of Holland to power and prosperity in the seventeenth century was in part a result of its favorable geographic location. Stretching across the estuaries of great rivers—the Scheldt, Maas, and Rhine—Holland was provided with excellent harbors looking westward to England and the Atlantic. Backed by the great hinterland of Germany, Holland also was strategically located along the ancient trade routes of Europe running north-south from Bergen to Gibraltar, and east-west from the Gulf of Finland to Britain. With such an advantageous location the Dutch early engaged in the carrying trade. Their merchant marine owed its start to the local coastal fisheries and later to the North Sea herring fishery. The Dutch preserved their catch by salting and smoking, and exported it to all parts of Europe in return for grain, timber, and salt. With the building of the Iberian overseas empires, the Dutch picked up cargoes of the new colonial products in Seville and Lisbon for distribution through Europe, bringing in return grain, fish, naval stores, and textiles.

Early in the sixteenth century the Dutch wrested control of the Atlantic trade from the Italians and became the leading carriers of Europe. Their primacy was based on their *fluyt*, or flyboat, an inexpensive general carrier with enormous capacity. Hitherto the typical merchantman had been built with heavy timbering and galleried transom so that it could mount cannon and serve, when necessary, as a man-of-war. The Dutch were the first to take the risk of building a merchant packet deliberately designed to carry only goods and no guns. The *fluyt's* broad beam, flattened bottom, and restricted cabin accommodations gave it maximum hold space and unusual economy of building material. This slow and ugly but cheap and capacious boat was the mainstay of the Dutch merchant marine that came to dominate the seas of the world. As early as 1600 the Dutch had 10,000 ships in operation, by far the world's largest merchant marine.

A combination of circumstances at the end of the sixteenth century drove the Dutch to challenge Portugal's hegemony in the East openly. One was Sir Francis

Drake's famous voyage around the world (1577–1580), which revealed that the Portuguese, so far from being the masters of the East, were defending immensely long trade routes and widely scattered strongholds against a host of enemies. The Portuguese East Indies no longer seemed so invulnerable. Furthermore, the union of the Spanish and Portuguese crowns in 1580 led the Protestant nations to regard Portugal with the fear and hatred they had formerly reserved for Spain. Portugal now was seen as an enemy in Europe and overseas, and her empire became fair game for the Protestant powers. Then, too, the Netherlands revolt interfered with the distribution of colonial goods in northern Europe because the Dutch no longer were able to pick up cargoes in Iberian ports. Under these pressures, the Dutch decided that because they could no longer obtain their spices in Lisbon, they would fetch them directly from the Indies.

The first task was to collect reliable data concerning the long Cape route in the face of stringent Portuguese censorship. A break-through occurred in 1595 with the publication of the *Itinerario,* a geographical description of the world by Jan Huyghen van Linschoten. He had lived in India for seven years as a servant of the Portuguese archbishop of Goa, so that he was able to provide detailed sailing instructions for the Cape route. His work was used the year it was published to guide the first Dutch fleet to the East Indies. Despite heavy losses in manpower and equipment, substantial net profit remained, and the next expedition cleared a 400 per cent profit.

The Dutch now swarmed into the Eastern waters, no less than five fleets, comprising twenty-two ships, sailing in the year 1598. From the beginning they outmatched the Portuguese. They were better sailors, they could transport spices more cheaply in their *fluyten,* and their trade goods were cheaper and better constructed because their home industry was superior to that of the Iberian states. In 1602 they amalgamated their various private trading companies into one great national concern, the Dutch East India Company. Under the terms of the charter that the company received from the States-General, it enjoyed a monopoly of trade, so far as the Dutch were concerned, between the Cape and Magellan's Strait. It was empowered to make war or peace, seize foreign ships, establish colonies, construct forts, and coin money.

The company utilized these powers to the full in its dealings with the native potentates and in its successful drive against the faltering Portuguese. The English had organized their own East India Company two years earlier, in 1600, but they proved to be no match for the Dutch, who, nevertheless, at first tolerated the English competition. They were still fighting for independence from Spain and could not afford to add to their enemies. But when the Dutch concluded a truce with Spain in 1609, they turned against the English. The outcome of the struggle for monopoly was never in doubt. The Dutch had five times as many ships, and they had built a string of forts that gave them control of the key points in the Indonesian Archipelago. Furthermore, the Dutch had the services of a governor-general of genius, Jan Pieterszoon Coen, who did for his country what Albuquerque had done for Portugal. During his term of office (1618–1629) he drove the Portuguese from the East Indies and made it possible for his successors to expel them from Malacca (1641) and from Ceylon (1658). Coen also harassed the English out of the archipelago, compelling them to retreat to their posts in India. Equally important was Coen's cultivation and development of inter-Asiatic trade, much greater in volume than the traffic that rounded the Cape to Europe. The Portuguese had participated in this trade, but Coen went much further, establishing a base on Formosa (Taiwan) and from there controlling the commerce routes to China, Japan, and the Indies.

At first the Dutch East India Company consciously sought to avoid acquisition of territorial possessions, attributing the decline of Portuguese power in the East to the dissipation of energy and capital in territorial conquest. But in its efforts to establish a trade monopoly, the company was led step by step to the territorial expansion it wished to avoid. Monopoly could be enforced only by a network of fortified posts. The posts required treaties with local rulers, treaties led to alliances, and alliances to protectorates. By the end of the seventeenth century the Dutch were actually administering only a small area, but numerous states comprising a much greater area had become protectorates. Then during the eighteenth and nineteenth centuries the Dutch annexed these protectorates outright and built up a great territorial empire.

The export of spices to Europe diminished in value after about 1700, but the inter-Asiatic trade that Coen had developed made up for the shrinkage. Moreover, the Dutch developed a new economic resource at about that time by introducing coffee bushes into the East Indies. In 1711 they harvested 100 pounds of coffee, and by 1723 they were marketing 12 million pounds. Thus, as Europe acquired a taste for coffee, the Dutch became the principal suppliers of this exotic beverage. Through these various means the Dutch East India Company averaged annual dividends of 18 per cent throughout the seventeenth and eighteenth centuries.

Dutch overseas activities were not confined to the East Indies, however. In the Arctic waters around Spitzbergen the Dutch virtually monopolized the whaling industry. In Russia they badly outdistanced the English Muscovy Company. In the New World, the Dutch founded New Amsterdam on Manhattan Island in 1612. This colony never became large, numbering only 1,900 in 1663. But it served as a base and clearing house for a great volume of Dutch shipping that ran a lucrative though illicit carrying trade between Europe and the Spanish, English, and French colonies in America. In fact, the English captured New Amsterdam in 1664 largely in order to plug what had become an intolerable leak in their mercantile system.

Further south in the Americas, the Dutch operated through their Dutch West India Company, established in 1621. Its purpose was to exploit the loosely held riches of the Spanish and Portuguese colonies in the New World. After a decade of intermittent fighting, the Dutch won control of the Brazilian coast all the way from Bahia to the Amazon. But the company was unwilling and unable to shoulder the expense of maintaining adequate garrisons, and the coastal strip was all lost by 1654. The Dutch West India Company also founded colonies at Caracas, Curaçao, and in Guiana in the Caribbean, where they left a lasting imprint by introducing sugar cane cultivation.

The Dutch colony that proved to be the most durable of all was the small settlement established in 1652 on the Cape of Good Hope in South Africa. This was not a trading station but a true colony founded to provide fuel, water, and fresh provisions for the ships en route to the East. One of the company officers wished to settle the Cape with Chinese, knowing them to be the cheapest colonists that could be had. It is interesting to speculate how different the future course of events might have been if his proposal had been adopted. But the Dutch officials in the East Indies refused to supply Chinese coolies, and instead a number of Boers, or peasants, were induced to migrate from Holland, along with some French Huguenots. The colony soon proved its value. The fresh meat and vegetables it provided to Dutch and other ships helped keep down scurvy and saved the lives of thousands of seamen. Today the descendants of these Boers comprise two-fifths of the three million Europeans residing in South Africa. They constitute the only overseas nucleus of Dutch language and culture that persists to the present. This is in striking contrast to the great English-speaking nations that today occupy a large portion of the earth's surface. The contrast explains in part the inability of the Dutch to retain the primacy that they enjoyed during their golden seventeenth century.

During the eighteenth century Holland fell behind Britain and France in economic development and in overseas activity. One reason for this decline was the persistent efforts of the French and British governments to build up their merchant marines by discriminatory decrees against the Dutch. Examples of this legislation were the several Navigation Acts passed from 1651 onward providing that no goods should be imported into or exported from any English colony except in English ships—that is, ships built, owned, and at least three-quarters manned in England or an English colony.

The Dutch were weakened also by a series of exhausting wars—with Britain from 1652 to 1674 over mercantile disputes, and with France from 1667 to 1713 over the territorial ambitions of Louis XIV. The Dutch were peculiarly vulnerable to their enemies during these wars. Their merchantmen were slow and virtually unarmed. Their regular navy was usually neglected because of the concentration on the merchant marine. Thus, the English and French privateers reaped a golden harvest preying on the Dutch ships as they came together from all corners of the world and ran the gauntlet through the English Channel to their home ports. Within two years after the beginning of war in 1652, the English had seized about 1,700 merchant ships as prizes from the Dutch.

The Navigation Acts and the wars with Britain and France do not entirely explain Holland's decline. In fact, the volume of Dutch trade reached its peak in the period 1698 to 1715, and during those years the Dutch merchant marine was still twice the size of England's and probably nine times that of France. But at the same time Holland's share of the total trade was falling. What was taking place, therefore, was a relative rather than an absolute decline. The Dutch were not slipping, but the French and English were catching up. And the basic reason for this was that the Dutch lacked the resources to maintain their original rate of expansion. The French had a large population, a flourishing agriculture, and a rich homeland with outlets on both the Atlantic and the Mediterranean. The English also had much greater natural resources than the Dutch and enjoyed the great boon of an insular location, which spared them the cost of periodic invasions. Furthermore, the English had behind them the rapidly growing wealth and strength of their overseas colonies, whereas the Dutch had only the one small and isolated settlement on the tip of South Africa. Thus we find that the value of British exports rose from £8 million in 1720 to £19 million in 1763, and that French exports increased from 120 million livres in 1716 to 500 million in 1789. The Dutch, who had already reached their peak, were simply incapable of matching such growth. In the final analysis, Holland gave way to Britain and France in the eighteenth century for the same reason that Britain and France were to give way to the United States and the Soviet Union in the twentieth.

IV. ANGLO-FRENCH RIVALRY

The eighteenth century was marked by a struggle between Britain and France for colonial supremacy. The two countries were in face-to-face rivalry throughout the globe—in North America, in Africa, and in India.

In North America, the British and French possessions had many characteristics in common. They were settled at about the same time. They were located on the Atlantic seaboard and in the West Indian islands. The native populations were relatively sparse and primitive, so that the British and the French, unlike the Spanish, could not hope to live off native labor, although they did depend on Negro slave labor in the sugar islands. Since the British and French found no precious metals, they had to support themselves by agriculture, fishing, lumbering, commerce, and fur trading.

The English colonies fell roughly into three groups: Virginia and its immediate neighbors, which produced mostly tobacco; New England with its little groups of nonconformist settlements, which engaged in fishing, lumbering, commerce, and the fur trade; and the British West Indies, by far the most highly prized because of their extremely profitable sugar plantations. One characteristic of these English colonies, taken as a whole, was their populousness, which was much greater than that of the French. Their other chief characteristic was their political intractability. Every colony had a governor, an executive council, and a judiciary, all appointed from England. Nearly every colony also had an elective legislative assembly, and as a rule it was at loggerheads with the appointed officials and the imperial authorities. A central issue was the regulation that all colonial products be sent to England in English ships. This seemed to the royal officers a reasonable requirement, because they in turn gave the colonies a monopoly of the home market for their products. But the colonial merchants and planters protested bitterly when they were not allowed to use the cheaper Dutch shipping and to export their products to more profitable non-English markets.

The French settlements in North America were outstanding because of their strategic location. The first French posts were established in Acadia, or Nova Scotia, in 1605, in Quebec in 1608, and in Montreal in 1642. Using the St. Lawrence River valley as their main base of colonization, the French took advantage of the incomparable inland water system to push westward to Lake Superior and southward to the Ohio River. In 1682 a French nobleman, La Salle, paddled down the Mississippi and laid claim to the whole basin, a claim that was soon backed with a string of forts along the waterways. Thus the English colonies along the Atlantic seaboard were effectively encircled by a great arc running from the Gulf of St. Lawrence to the Gulf of Mexico. The French also had the considerable advantage of discipline and cohesion. There were no obstreperous elective bodies in the French colonies. Paris appointed the governors, who were responsible for the defense of each colony, and the intendants, who handled economic affairs. These officials gave the orders, and their subordinates carried them out without question.

The French and English were neighbors also in the West Indies. The chief French possessions in this region were Martinique and Guadeloupe; the English were Jamaica, Barbados, and the Bahamas. These colonies were valuable as stations for trade with the Spanish and Portuguese colonies to the south, but their greatest asset was their tropical produce—sugar, tobacco, and indigo—which supplemented the economies of France and Britain.

In Africa, the French by the beginning of the eighteenth century had established themselves in Madagascar, at Gorée, and at the mouth of the Senegal River, while the English were in Gambia and on the Gold Coast. These footholds on the African coast served as stations for trade in gold, ivory, wax, and—most important, especially after the development of the West Indian sugar colonies increased the demand for a labor force there—slaves. Africa, however, was little affected by the Anglo-French rivalries of the eighteenth century. The real struggle for that continent was not to come until the nineteenth and twentieth centuries.

India, by contrast, was the scene of sharp Anglo-French conflicts, paralleling those in North America. The British had fallen back on the Indian subcontinent when they were driven out of the East Indies by the Dutch in the early seventeenth century. By the end of the century they had four major footholds in India: Calcutta and Madras on the eastern coast, and, on the western, Surat and Bombay. The French had organized an East India Company of their own in 1604, and by the end of the century the French were ensconced in two major posts—Chandarnagar near Calcutta, and Pondichéry near Madras.

During the seventeenth century all Europeans who resided and traded in India did so on the sufferance of the powerful Mogul emperors. The latter could easily have driven the Europeans into the sea if they did not behave themselves and submit humble petitions for the privilege of carrying on their commercial operations. During the eighteenth century the situation was completely reversed. From barely tolerated alien merchants confined in a few coastal outposts, the Europeans changed to aggressive intruders who gradually won control of entire provinces of India.

The reason for this transformation is the disintegration of the Mogul Empire. After the great and enlightened Emperor Akbar died, in 1605, his successors failed to follow his wise policies of religious toleration and light taxation. This was especially true of Aurangzeb, the last great Mogul emperor, who came to the throne in 1658. A Moslem fanatic whose religious persecution, especially in his later years, alienated his Hindu subjects, Aurangzeb was forced to wage continual warfare, which in turn led to heavier taxes and to further popular disaffection. With his death in 1707 the Mogul Empire began to fall apart. There was no settled rule of succession, so that for two years his sons disputed the throne. Then between 1712 and 1719 five puppet emperors ruled at Delhi. Under these circumstances the provincial governors began to assert their independence and to establish hereditary local dynasties. The Marathas, who represented Hindu nationalism in a vague and incipient sense, expanded from their capital of Satara, about a hundred miles south of Bombay on the west, to within two hundred miles of Calcutta on the east. This disintegration of central authority gave the British and the French East India Companies the opportunity to transform themselves from mere commercial organizations to territorial overlords and tribute collectors. They built forts, maintained soldiers, coined money, and entered into treaties with surrounding Indian potentates, with no central authority in India capable of denying them the exercise of such sovereign rights.

V. ENGLAND'S TRIUMPH

Such, then, was the line-up of the rival British and French empires in India, Africa, and the Americas. The duel between the two empires during the seventeenth and eighteenth centuries ended in an overwhelming British triumph. One reason was that France was less interested in overseas possessions than in European hegemony. Since the sixteenth century, the French Bourbons had concentrated primarily on gaining ground in Italy and on combating the Hapsburgs in Austria and Spain. When in 1758 the valiant General Montcalm sent an emissary to Paris to explain the desperate military situation in Canada and the need for immediate assistance, he was informed that one does not attempt to save the stables when the house is on fire. It was not until the nineteenth century, after the Bourbon dynasty had been overthrown, that France turned again to overseas enterprise and expansion.

Another reason for Britain's triumph was that many more Englishmen than Frenchmen emigrated to the colonies. By 1688 there were 300,000 English settlers concentrated in the narrow piedmont region of the Atlantic coast compared to a mere 20,000 Frenchmen scattered over the vast areas of Canada and the Mississippi valley. This disparity arose in part from the refusal of Paris to allow the French Protestants, or Huguenots, to emigrate to the colonies, whereas Massachusetts was populated in large part by Nonconformists who left England because they could not abide Anglicanism. Another significant factor was the richness of the French soil compared to that of England. The peasant masses of France were deeply attached to their holdings and were able to earn enough so that they did not have to resort to emigration. In England, on the other hand, large-scale enclosures had been taking place for some time in order to produce more wool for the growing textile industry and more foodstuffs for the burgeoning towns. Both these commodities could be produced more efficiently on consolidated, scientifically operated holdings than on the small, separate field strips inherited from the Middle Ages. Enclosures meant more productivity, but they also meant mass dislocation and distress. It was the dispossessed who provided the basis for the large-scale emigration from England to the colonies.

This combination of factors explains the tremendous discrepancy in the volume of emigration from France and from England. The significance of the discrepancy can scarcely be overestimated. At the time of the American Revolution the population of the English colonies amounted to no less than two million, or a third of the total population of the English-speaking world. This mass transplantation explains in large part the victory of Britain over France in 1763, and of the American Republic over Britain two decades later.

The remarkable development of Britain's industry also contributed to her success in overseas competition. Her industrial growth during the century between 1550 and 1650 was to be surpassed only by that during the Industrial Revolution after 1760. In fact, it was during the earlier period that there was laid the foundation for the later development of heavy industry. This initial spurt of English industry occurred partly because of the Thirty Years' War on the Continent (1618–1648), which created a demand for war materials. In responding to the demand, the British expanded their mining, metallurgical, and chemical industries tremendously, aided by many new techniques introduced by the refugees and immigrants from France, Germany, and Flanders. Of the new industries, coal mining grew most spectacularly. Coal was now used widely as a fuel and in industries—such as sugar refining—that required intense heat. The output of coal increased from some 200,000 tons in 1550 to 3 million tons in 1700. This expansion involved improvement of mining equipment and of draining machines, which stimulated the later development of the steam engine. Water power also was harnessed more extensively than before, and water-driven hammers were used in forges. Other industries that expanded markedly at this time were those producing cannon, gunpowder, saltpeter, glass, paper, alum, and salt.

French industry was about equal to the English in volume of output. But it should be kept in mind that the population of France was more than three times that of England. And the French tended to manufacture luxuries, in contrast to the cloth and hardware produced in England. Furthermore, technological advance in France was hampered by the guild system, which was very highly organized and powerful in that country. In general, it may be said that commercial and industrial interests did not receive so much encouragement in France as in England because they lacked the political power of their counterparts across the Channel.

England's flourishing economy helped her overseas enterprises in various ways. It made more capital available for colonial development, and this was an important consideration because both the English and the French colonies required heavy initial expenditures. Unlike the Spanish colonies, they yielded no bullion and they afforded no native labor force that could be exploited. The English and the French promoters of colonization were forced therefore to transplant whole communities with a complete labor force of Europeans. They had to provide these people with transportation, tools, seed, and equipment. All this involved a heavy capital outlay, and as a rule it was more likely to be forthcoming from London than from Paris. There was more money per capita in England, and, rather than being invested in a large standing army and an elaborate court, as was the case in France, it was in an available liquid form. England's industries also provided cheaper and more durable goods, which gave English colonists and traders an advantage over their French rivals. In North America, for example, the English fur traders were able to offer the Indians cheaper and better blankets and kettles and firearms in return for their pelts. Finally, English industry was better equipped for naval construction. This fact, together with the greater awareness in English ruling circles of the importance of sea power, explains in large part the superiority of the British navy during the long series of Anglo-French wars.

The colonial and commercial rivalry between Britain and France did not lead to blows until the late seventeenth century. Before that time the English had been much more at odds with the Dutch, their points of conflict ranging the globe—fisheries in the North Atlantic, commercial posts in the East, settlements in America, and slave trading in Africa and the West Indies. These issues precipitated a series of three Anglo-Dutch Wars between 1652 and 1674. Then the situation changed as the British realized that the French were replacing the Dutch as their most formidable rivals. Holland had limited resources and had passed its prime; France was a much richer and more populous country, and was stepping up its overseas activities drastically. The Glorious Revolution in Great Britain (1688) also contributed to the estrangement of Britain and France; it ousted the Stuart dynasty, which had looked to Louis XIV for friendly aid in the creation of absolutism and the reinstatement of Catholicism in England. In the place of the Stuarts came William III, Prince of Orange, Stadholder of the Dutch Netherlands, a firm Protestant, and an archenemy of Louis XIV. Thus the accession of William III served to bring together England and Holland against France. In 1689 began a series of four Anglo-French wars that dragged on for almost a century until England's great victory in 1763.

All these wars had two phases, one European and the other overseas. The European revolved about dynastic ambitions, especially those of Louis XIV of France and Frederick the Great of Prussia. The overseas operations were fought over diverse issues—the balance of power in India, conflicting territorial claims in America, terms of trade in the Spanish colonies, and control of the world trade routes. The dichotomy between the European and overseas aspects of these wars was sufficiently marked so that each one was known by one name in Europe and another in America. Hence the wars have come down in history as the War of the League of Augsburg or King William's War (1689–1697), the War of the

Spanish Succession or Queen Anne's War (1701–1713), the War of the Austrian Succession or King George's War (1743–1748), and the Seven Years' War or the French and Indian War (1756–1763).

The first three wars were not decisive in their overseas aspects. In Europe they did settle important matters: Louis XIV was effectively checkmated, and Frederick the Great successfully seized the province of Silesia and catapulted Prussia into the first rank of European powers. But in America, where most of the overseas engagements were fought, there were only isolated and inconclusive campaigns. The French enjoyed the support of most of the Indian tribes, partly because their missionaries were far more active than the English, and also because the few French settlers did not represent so great a threat to the Indians as the inexorably advancing tide of English settlement that was beginning to spill over the Appalachians. With their Indian allies, the French repeatedly harried and burned the English frontier villages. The English, on the other hand, used their superior manpower and naval strength to attack the French possessions in present-day Nova Scotia and Cape Breton Island that were vulnerable by sea.

The net result of these first three wars was that the British acquired Nova Scotia, Newfoundland, and the Hudson Bay territories. But these conquests left unsettled the basic question of whether the French would retain Canada and the Mississippi Valley, and thereby restrict the English to the Atlantic seaboard. This question was answered conclusively by the fourth war, which also settled the future of India.

The Seven Years' War was fought between 1756 and 1763 in Europe, but in America it began two years earlier because of the growing rivalry for the possession of the Ohio Valley. British colonials had already begun to stream westward through the mountains into the valley when in 1749 the British government chartered the Ohio Company, organized by Virginia and London capitalists for the colonization of the valley. This company built a fort in 1754 at the strategic junction of the Monongahela and Allegheny rivers. The French promptly captured it, enlarged it, and christened it Fort Duquesne in honor of the governor of Canada. In the following year the British General Braddock arrived in America with a regular army to retake Fort Duquesne. But he refused to heed the advice of his colonial officers on how to wage frontier warfare, and his forces were badly defeated and he himself killed. The British reverses continued through 1756. The French commander was the Marquis de Montcalm, a European-trained general who, however, readily adapted himself to frontier conditions and brilliantly led his French and Indian forces. The turning point of the war came in 1757, largely by reason of the entrance of William Pitt (the Elder) into the British cabinet. He concentrated his resources on the navy and the colonies, while subsidizing his ally, Frederick of Prussia, to fight on in Europe. His strategy was, as he put it, to win an empire on the plains of Germany.

His strategy succeeded brilliantly. His reinforced navies swept the French off the seas, while the American colonists, stirred by his leadership, joined the British regulars to form a force of about 50,000 men. This was a huge host by the standards of American warfare, and it overwhelmed one French fort after another. The climax came with the siege of Quebec, the heart of French Canada and a great natural stronghold defended by the redoubtable Montcalm. The sheer cliffs rising from the banks of the St. Lawrence River seemed invulnerable to assault. Sickness weakened the besieging forces and defeat appeared unavoidable. The British commander, thirty-three-year-old General James Wolfe, decided in despair to risk a hazardous operation. Thirty-six hundred of his men were ferried in the dead of night to a point above the city where they disembarked and scrambled through the bushes and over rocks up a precipitous path to a high plateau, the famous Plains of Abraham overlooking the town of Quebec. That morning, September 13, 1759, the decisive battle was fought. Both Wolfe and Montcalm were killed, but the British veterans prevailed. Quebec surrendered a few days later. The next year Montreal also fell to the advancing British. This was the end of the French colonial empire in America, for Britain's command of the sea precluded any relief from Paris.

In India the success of the English was no less complete. The situation was quite different from what it was in America, in that neither the British nor the French government had territorial ambitions in India. This was true also of the directors of the English and French East India Companies, who insisted that their agents in India attend strictly to business. They were interested only in profits, and they resented every penny or sou spent on non-commercial objectives. But it took a year or more to communicate with the agents in India, and the latter frequently took advantage of this fact to act independently and involve their companies in Indian affairs. They did so because the disintegration of the Mogul Empire that was taking place at this time offered dazzling opportunities for personal financial aggrandizement and for empire building.

The first European to intervene on a large scale in Indian affairs was the French governor Joseph Dupleix. Even he does not seem to have been interested, at the outset at least, in territorial expansion for its own sake. Rather he wished to acquire territory so that, from taxes and other political revenues, he could obtain more capital for commercial operations. Dupleix had limited French forces under his command, but he extended his influence by drilling native Indians along European military lines. These trained troops, or sepoys, enabled him to back claimants to various Indian thrones and to build up a clientele of native rulers under obligation to himself. This procedure was very effective, because a few European troops or sepoys could overcome much larger numbers of purely Indian forces in pitched battle. But Dupleix was recalled to France in 1754 because the company was apprehensive that his aggressive tactics would lead to war with Britain.

War did come to India in 1756 with the outbreak of full-scale hostilities between Britain and France. At the outset the French, thanks to Dupleix' activities, were in the stronger position. They held more territory, they had more than double the fighting force, and they wielded wider political influence among the native princes. But in the end the British won a crushing victory. Again naval superiority was the deciding factor. Britain was able to transport troops, money, and supplies from Europe while preventing France from doing likewise. The British, too, had the inspired leadership of Robert Clive, a company official who had come out years before as a clerk. Clive possessed both outstanding military talents and an ability to comprehend Indian politics. In 1756, on hearing of the war in Europe, he marched on Bengal. With the support of Indian merchants who had waxed wealthy by virtue of the trade with Europe, Clive defeated the pro-French Moslem ruler at the Battle of Plassey in 1757, put his own puppet on the throne, and extorted huge reparations both for himself and for his company. During the rest of the war the British navy enabled Clive to shift his forces at will from one part of India to another, and at the same time severed the communications of the French posts with each other and with France. The end came with the surrender in 1761 of the main French base at Pondichéry.

The overseas phase of the Seven Years' War was decided by the fall of Quebec in America and of Pondichéry in India. But the war dragged on in Europe until 1763, when the belligerents concluded the Peace of Paris. Of her American possessions, France retained only Guiana in South America, the insignificant islands of St. Pierre and Miquelon on the Newfoundland coast, and a few islands in the West Indies, including Guadeloupe and Martinique. Britain therefore received from France the whole of the St. Lawrence valley and all the territory east of the Mississippi. These were almost empty territories, and were not considered as valuable as the sugar islands, Guadeloupe and Martinique, which were returned to France. In fact, they were returned on the insistence of the British planters in the West Indies, who feared the competition of the French sugar islands if they were included within the British imperial commercial structure.

Spain had entered the war late on the side of France and was, therefore, compelled to cede Florida to Britain. As compensation, France gave her western Louisiana, that is, the territory west of the Mississippi River. In India the French retained possession of their commercial installations—offices, warehouses, and docks —at Pondichéry and other towns. But they were forbidden to erect fortifications or pursue political ambitions among the Indian princes. In other words, the French returned to India as traders and not as empire builders.

When the Treaty of Paris was signed, the British political leader Horace Walpole remarked, "Burn your Greek and Roman books, histories of little people." This farseeing observation points up the long-range, worldwide implications of the peace settlement. So far as Europe was concerned, the treaty allowed Prussia to keep Silesia and to become Austria's rival for the leadership of the Germanies. But of much more significance for world history were the overseas repercussions of the Paris Treaty. France had lost North America and India. This meant that America north of the Rio Grande was to develop in the future as a part of the English-speaking world. Bismarck later observed that the fact that the United States and Britain spoke the same language was the most important single element in modern diplomacy. France's expulsion from India was also a historical event of global significance, for it meant that the British were to take the place of the Moguls there. Once installed in Delhi, the British were well on their way to world empire and world primacy. It was the incomparable base offered by the vast and populous sub-continent that enabled the British in the nineteenth century to expand into the rest of South Asia and then beyond to East Asia.

SUGGESTED READING

C. R. Boxer, *The Dutch Seaborne Empire 1600–1800* (Knopf, 1965); E. P. Hamilton, *The French and Indian Wars: The Story of Battles and Forts in the Wilderness* (Doubleday, 1962); J. H. Parry, *Trade and Dominion: The Overseas European Empires in the Eighteenth Century* (Praeger, 1971); H. I. Priestly, *France Overseas Through the Old Regime: A Study of European Expansion* (Appleton, 1939); W. B. Willcox, *Star of Empire: A Study of Britain as a World Power, 1485–1945* (Knopf, 1950); C. Wilson, *Profit and Power: A Study of England and the Dutch Wars* (Longmans, 1957); T. Woodrooffe, *Vantage at Sea: England's Emergence as an Oceanic Power* (St. Martin's, 1958).

chapter twenty-two

Russian Expansion

in Asia

*Throughout Russian history one dominating theme has been the
frontier; the theme of the struggle for the mastering of the natural
resources of an untamed country, expanded into a continent by the
ever-shifting movement of the Russian people and their conquest of
and intermingling with other peoples.*—B. H. Sumner, *A Short History
of Russia*

At the same time that the Western Europeans were expanding overseas
to all corners of the globe, the Russians were expanding overland across the entire length of Eurasia. The mastering of the continental expanses of Siberia is an
epic story comparable to the westward expansion of the United States to the
Pacific. In fact, the ever advancing frontier has left as indelible a stamp on the
Russian character and Russian institutions as it has on the American.

It should not be assumed that the Russians are alone among the European peoples in having been affected by a frontier. During the medieval period, large parts
of Central and Eastern Europe were lightly populated. (See Chapter 17, section
IV.) For centuries, various European peoples, and particularly the Germans,
pressed a line of settlement eastward along the Baltic coast and down the Danube
valley. But this internal colonization ceased to be a dominating theme with the
end of the Middle Ages. Overseas colonization took its place, and the peoples of
Western Europe concentrated their energies on opening and exploring new frontiers in new worlds. The Russian people, by contrast, continued to expand overland into the vast Eurasian plain stretching out from their doorstep. This was a
stupendous undertaking which proceeded apace for several centuries until the
last of the Moslem khanates in Central Asia had been subdued in 1895. It is not
surprising, then, that the frontier has been a major factor throughout the course
of Russian history, as it has been throughout American. In this chapter we shall
examine the nature and the course of Russian expansion into Siberia and the
Ukraine.

I. GEOGRAPHY OF RUSSIAN EXPANSION

In order to understand the remarkable Russian expansion across the plains of
Eurasia it is necessary to understand the geography of those plains. A glance at
the map shows first and foremost their staggering proportions. They comprise a

sixth of the land surface of the globe, a larger area than the United States, Canada, and Central America combined. Another prominent characteristic of the Russian landmass is its remarkable topographical uniformity. It is in very large part a flat plains area. The Ural Mountains do run across the plains in a north-south direction, but they are a single, narrow, worn-down chain of mountains with an average altitude of only two thousand feet. Furthermore, they do not extend further south than the 51st parallel, leaving a wide gap of flat desert country stretching down to the Caspian Sea. Under these circumstances the whole plain must be looked upon as a single geographic entity—the subcontinent of Eurasia.

The Eurasian plains that comprise most of present-day Russia are surrounded by a natural boundary stretching from the Black Sea to the Pacific Ocean. This boundary consists of an uninterrupted chain of mountains, deserts, and inland seas—from the Caucasus Mountains in the west to the Caspian Sea, the Ust Urt Desert, the Aral Sea, the Kizil-Kum Desert, the Hindu Kush, Pamir, and Tian Shan ranges, the Gobi Desert, and the Great Khingan Mountains east to the Pacific Ocean. The ring of mountains surrounding the Eurasian plains keeps out the moisture-laden winds from the Pacific and the warm monsoons from the Indian Ocean, and explains both the desert climate of Central Asia and the cold, dry climate of Siberia. The whole expanse of Siberia, from the Baltic to the Pacific, has essentially the same continental type of climate, with short, hot summers and long, cold winters. The uniformity of climate, like that of topography, facilitated Russia's eastward expansion, for the frontiersman felt equally at home throughout the five-thousand-mile expanse of plains. The Central Asian deserts, on the other hand, he found to be strange and forbidding. He also found that they were held by militarily powerful Moslem khanates in contrast to the weak tribes in Siberia. The result was that the Russians did not master the Central Asian deserts until 250 years after they had reached the Pacific further north.

Russian expansion was affected by river systems as well as by topography and climate. Because of the flat terrain, Russian rivers are generally long, wide, and unencumbered by rapids. Consequently they have proven invaluable as routes and as vehicles for commerce, colonization, and conquest. West of the Urals the outstanding rivers are the Western Dvina flowing into the Baltic, the Dniester, the Dnieper, and the Don flowing south to the Black Sea, and the Volga flowing first east and then south to the Caspian. East of the Urals the Siberian plains are watered by four vast river systems, the Ob in the west, the Yenisei in the center, the Lena in the northeast, and the Amur in the southeast. Since the whole of Siberia tilts downward from the massive Tibetan ranges, the first three of these rivers flow northward into the Arctic, while the fourth makes its way eastward to the Pacific. The Arctic outlet of the Ob, the Yenisei, and the Lena has negated in large part their economic usefulness. But the fact remains that these rivers, together with their numerous tributaries, provided a natural network of highways extending all the way to the Pacific. Once the Russians crossed the Urals they were able to make their way, with few portages, from one waterway to another. Thus they advanced in zigzag fashion, ever eastward, in pursuit of the furred animals.

A final geographic factor in the pace and course of Russian expansion is the combination of soil and vegetation prevailing in various parts of the country. Four major soil-vegetation zones run in east-west layers across Russia. In the far north, along the Arctic coast, is the barren tundra, frozen the year round except for a six-to-eight week growing period in the summer. To the south of the tundra is the taiga, or forest, belt. The largest of the four zones, being 600 to 1,300 miles wide and 4,600 miles long, it includes a fifth of the total forest area of the world.

In its northern reaches the forest is predominantly conifer and birch, while further south it is a mixture of elms, aspens, poplars, and maples. In these forests the Russians felt most at home, and they were able to advance across the whole of Eurasia without losing at any time the familiar protective covering.

On their southern edges the forests thin out, and the trees grow smaller until they give way completely to the open, treeless steppe. Here is to be found the fertile black earth formed by millennia of decayed grass. Today it is the breadbasket of Russia, but for centuries it was a source of misery and woe. The steppe was the home of the marauding horse nomads of Central Eurasia. A major theme of Russian history is this continued conflict between the Slavic peasant of the forest zone and the Asiatic nomad of the steppe. The fourth zone, the desert, is the smallest in area, starting in China but extending westward only to the Caspian Sea. We have seen that for various reasons—inaccessibility, severe climate, and the military prowess of the native peoples—the desert zone was not engulfed by the Russian tidal wave until the late nineteenth century.

II. CROSSING OF THE URALS

The early Slavs began their expansion in all directions about 1,500 years ago. As noted in Chapter 15, sections VI and VII, they fanned out over the great plains, north to the Arctic, south to the Black Sea, and east to the Volga. They organized a loose federation of principalities strung out along river routes with Kiev as the center. This state flourished until the Mongol conquest in 1237 began a period of foreign domination that lasted until the reign of Ivan III (1462–1505). A new national center now emerged—the principality of Moscow located deep in the forest zone away from the dangerous steppes. During the reign of Ivan IV (1533–1584) the scattered Russian principalities were united under Moscow's sway, and the entire Volga valley was freed from Mongol or Tatar rule. The way was now open for limitless Russian advance beyond the Urals.

The crossing of the Urals and the conquest of Siberia were largely the work of the rough-and-ready frontiersmen known as the Cossacks. These men resembled in many respects the frontiersmen of the American West. Most of them were former peasants who had fled from Russia or Poland to escape the bonds of serfdom. Their refuge was the wild steppe country to the south, where they became hunters, fishers, and pastoralists. Just as their counterparts in America became half-Indian, so they became half-Tatar. They were liberty-loving and equalitarian, but unruly and marauding, ever ready to turn bandit-freebooters if it seemed profitable to do so.

A typical product of this frontier environment was Yermak, horse thief and river pirate, who entered the service of Grigori Stroganov, a wealthy merchant-colonizer. Stroganov's efforts to develop his settlement in the upper Volga Valley were frustrated by nomad raids from across the Urals. The organizer of these raids was the militant Moslem leader of the Siberian Tatars, the blind Khan Kuchum. Hired to guard the settlements, Yermak decided that the best defense was offense. With the audacity of the conquistador and at the head of 840 men Yermak attacked Khan Kuchum in September, 1581, on his own territory. Like his Spanish counterparts, Yermak had the great advantage of superior weapons, being well equipped with firearms and cannon, which inspired terror in the natives. Kuchum fought desperately to save his capital, Sibir, but arrows could not stop the Cossacks. Sibir fell, and the Russians gave its name to the entire trans-Ural territory, Siberia being the Anglicized form of Sibir.

Kuchum continued to resist, and one of his raiding parties killed Yermak in 1584. But the Tatars were fighting a losing battle. The Russians were too strong to be pushed back across the Urals, and Kuchum finally surrendered. The way to the Pacific now lay open.

III. CONQUEST OF SIBERIA

The Russian conquest of Siberia was a remarkable achievement. Like the Spaniards in America, the Russians in Siberia won a great empire in a few years with incredibly small forces. The pace of the Russian advance was staggering. Yermak campaigned between 1581 and 1584. At the same time, in 1584, Sir Walter Raleigh landed on Roanoke Island in North Carolina. Within half a century, by 1637, the Russians reached Okhotsk on the Pacific Ocean, covering a distance half as much again as that between the Atlantic and the Pacific coasts of the United States. During that same period the English colonists had not crossed to the other side of the Allegheny Mountains.

Various factors explain the rapidity of the Russian advance. The climate, the terrain, the vegetation, and the river systems, were, as we have seen, all favorable to the invaders. The native peoples were handicapped by paucity of numbers, inferiority of armaments, and lack of unity and organization. Account should be taken also of the stamina and courage of the Cossacks who, like the *coureurs des bois* of French Canada, endured fantastic hardships and dangers in the wilderness. And the reason they did so may be summed up with one word—"fur." The sable lured them ever eastward, from river to portage and on to new rivers.

As the Cossacks advanced, they secured their communications by building fortified posts or *ostrogs,* which were like the blockhouses of the American frontier. The first ostrog in Siberia was at Tobolsk, near Sibir, at the junction of the Tobol and the Irtysh. Discovering both these rivers to be tributaries of the Ob, the Russians paddled down that river and found themselves within portage distance of the next great waterway, the Yenisei. By 1610 they were in the Yenisei valley in force and had built the Krasnoyarsk ostrog. At this point they encountered the Buriat, a warlike people who offered the first serious resistance since the struggle with Kuchum. The Russians avoided the Buriats by veering to the northeast where they discovered the Lena River. There they built the Yakutsk ostrog in 1632 and conducted a highly profitable trade with the natives, the mild Yakuts. But the Buriats continually attacked their communication lines, so the Russians waged a ferocious war of extermination. Finally the Russians prevailed and pushed on to Lake Baikal where they established the Irkutsk ostrog in 1651.

Meanwhile exploration parties had been going out from Yakutsk in all directions. In 1645 a band of Russians reached the Arctic coast. Two years later another group was on the shores of the Pacific where they built Okhotsk. The following year, 1648, the Cossack explorer, Semion Dezhnev, started out from Yakutsk on an extraordinary journey. He sailed down the Lena which he found to be at certain points so broad that he could see neither bank. The delta was filled with debris of a watershed of continental proportions. After passing the delta, Dezhnev sailed eastward along the Arctic coast until he reached the very tip of Asia. Then he sailed down a waterway to be known later as Bering Strait. After losing two boats in a storm he reached the Anadyr River, where he established the ostrog Anadyrsk, no less than 7,000 miles from Moscow! Dezhnev sent a report of his journey to the governor in Yakutsk who filed it away and forgot it. It was not recovered until after the official expedition by Vitus Bering, which was sent out in 1725 to determine whether America and Asia were joined—something that Dezhnev had brilliantly settled 77 years earlier.

Up to this point the Russians had not encountered any power capable of stopping them. But when they pushed down from Irkutsk into the Amur valley they more than met their match, for they came up against the outposts of the mighty Chinese Empire, then at the height of its strength.

It was hunger that drove the Russians to the Amur basin. The frozen north yielded furs but no food. And the granaries of European Russia might as well have been on another planet. So the Russians hopefully turned southward to the Amur valley, which, according to native lore, was a fabulous country with fertile soil and golden grain. They captured the town of Albazin, built a string of ostrogs, and killed and pillaged in typical Cossack fashion. The Chinese emperor finally was sufficiently exasperated by these outrages on the fringe of his empire to send an expedition northward in 1658. The Chinese recaptured Albazin and cleared the Russians out of the whole Amur basin. But as soon as they withdrew, the Russian adventurers flocked back. Another Chinese force was sent to the Amur, and at the same time the two governments opened negotiations for the settlement of the frontier question. After much wrangling, the Treaty of Nerchinsk was signed on August 27, 1689.

This treaty, the first between China and a European power, fixed the frontier along the Stanovoi mountain range north of the Amur River, so that the Russians were forced to withdraw completely from the valley in dispute. In return, the Russians were given commercial privileges by Article IV, which provided that the subjects of both empires be free to travel freely across the frontier and to buy and sell without hindrance. The trade that grew up in the following years was carried on by caravan, and consisted of gold and furs, which the Russians exchanged for tea. It was from the Chinese that the Russians obtained what was to become their national drink. With the signing of this treaty the first stage of the Russian expansion in Asia came to a halt. For the next 170 years the Russians stayed out of the Amur basin, not resuming their advance southward until the mid-nineteenth century, when they were much stronger and the Chinese relatively weaker.

IV. ADMINISTRATION AND DEVELOPMENT OF SIBERIA

Because Siberia was acquired within a short period in one continuous wave of expansion, it was natural that the Russian government should regard it as a unit and administer it as such. The office in charge of Siberian affairs was the *Sibirskii prikaz* or Siberian bureau, located first in Moscow and then in St. Petersburg, after Peter the Great transferred the capital there in 1703. The administrative center was at Tobolsk until 1763, when Catherine the Great divided Siberia into two districts with centers in Tobolsk and Irkutsk. This move was necessitated by the fact that western Siberia, adjoining the homeland, was developing faster than the distant eastern regions.

The fur trade dominated Siberia throughout the seventeenth century to an even greater extent than it did French Canada. The government was the chief fur trader; indeed, fur was one if its most important sources of revenue. The government acquired furs by various means: it collected tribute, or tax, from the natives in furs and a 10 per cent tax in the best furs from the Russian trappers and traders; in addition, it reserved the right to buy the best furs obtained by both the natives and the Russians. By 1586, the state treasury was receiving from these various sources 200,000 sables, 10,000 black foxes, and 500,000 squirrels, besides beavers and ermines. Furthermore, the government exercised a lucrative monopoly of the foreign trade in furs. Estimates of the revenue derived from Siberian furs in the mid-seventeenth century vary from 7 to 30 per cent of the total income of the state, the lower figure probably being closer to the truth. A leading student of this subject has concluded that "The government paid the administrative expenses in Siberia out of the fur trade, retained a large surplus, and added an immense region to the state."[1]

The impact of the Russian expansion on the Siberian tribes was as disastrous as the effect of the American expansion on the Red Indians. On the one hand, the Moscow government repeatedly instructed its officials to treat the natives with "clemency and kindness." On the other hand it ordered the same officials to "seek profit for the sovereign with zeal."[2] Since promotion was affected by the number of furs collected, it is understandable that the welfare of the natives did not receive primary consideration. One effect of this fur tribute system was that it checked the missionary activities of the Russian Orthodox Church. Since converts were not required to pay tribute, missionary work was for long discontinued as a luxury that the state treasury could not afford. As a result, Islam spread widely among the Tatar peoples on the southern fringes of the forest zone, and Buddhist Lamaism did likewise among the Mongol Buriat. Thus we see that a basic difference between the Russian expansion in Siberia and the Spanish in the Americas was the great discrepancy in the intensity of Catholic and Orthodox proselytizing zeal. It is inconceivable that the Catholic Church ever would have allowed another creed to be propagated amongst its New World charges.

In the eighteenth century, the traders and trappers began to give way to permanent colonists in the area west of the Yenisei. Some colonists were prisoners shipped off to Siberia in the same manner that prisoners from the Western European countries were shipped to America, Australia, and the French West Indies. Most of these prisoners were hardened criminals, but a considerable proportion were political offenders who comprised the most enlightened and cultivated strata of society. Other colonists were forced to go by official summons. Each region of European Russia was required to provide a certain number of peasants each year for the colonization of Siberia. These people were granted certain exemptions and state assistance to enable them to get started in their new surroundings.

Most of the permanent settlers in Siberia were neither prisoners nor compulsory colonists, but rather peasants who emigrated voluntarily in order to escape creditors, military service, religious persecution, and, above all else, the bonds of serfdom. It is of the utmost importance that serfdom, which developed and spread through European Russia in the sixteenth and seventeenth centuries, did not take root in Siberia at any time. The explanation seems to be that serfdom grew primarily to satisfy the needs of the nobility who were essential for the functioning of the state. But the nobles did not migrate to Siberia, which offered no attractions comparable to those of Moscow and of St. Petersburg. Consequently, Siberia escaped the nobility, and thus also escaped serfdom. Government decrees did stipulate that runaway serfs should be sent back to their owners. But local authorities in Siberia, impressed more by the need for obtaining settlers than for enforcing the law, often provided refuge to the fugitives.

The growth of population in Siberia to 1763 is given in Table 1.

TABLE 1   SIBERIAN POPULATION, 1622–1763 (in thousands)

	1622	1662	1709	1763
Natives	173	288	200	260
Russians and foreigners	23	105	229	420
Total	196	393	429	680

Source: Arved Schultz, *Siberien: eine Landeskunde,* as reprinted in W. Treadgold, *The Great Siberian* Migration (Princeton: Princeton University Press, 1957), p. 32.

It is significant that whereas only 420,000 Russians were living in Siberia by 1763, the population of the Thirteen Colonies had risen by the same date to between 1½ and 2 million, or about four times as many. In other words, the Russians, who had been much faster in exploring and conquering, were now much slower in colonizing. One reason was that Siberia could draw only upon Russia for immigrants, whereas the American colonies were receiving immigrants from several European countries. Even more important was the greater attractiveness of America for would-be colonists. One may visualize the drawbacks of the Siberian environment by imagining, as the counterpart to the Himalayan range, a lofty chain of mountains along the Gulf coast of the United States cutting off the warm moisture-laden southerly winds. The resulting cold and aridity is what the emigrants to Siberia had to face. Thus the climatic conditions in Siberia were more akin to those prevailing in Canada. It is not accidental that the populations of the two countries by 1914 were about the same—8 million for Canada and 9 million for Siberia. And the United States, smaller in area than either Canada or Siberia, had grown in population by 1914 to 100 million.

V. CONQUEST OF THE UKRAINE

Ivan the Terrible's mid-sixteenth-century conquest of the Volga valley left two independent khanates—that of the Crimean Tatars in the south, and of Kuchum's Tatars across the Urals. The latter were subdued in a few years by Yermak and his successors, but the Crimean Tatars held out until the end of the eighteenth century. One reason for their survival is that they enjoyed the powerful support of the Ottoman Empire. The khan at Bakhchi-sarai, the capital of the Crimean Horde, recognized the suzerainty of the Ottoman sultan in Constantinople, and supplied him with cavalry forces in time of war. In return the sultan went to the assistance of the khan whenever he was threatened by the Christian infidels. Furthermore, the khan usually could play off against each other the various infidels who had conflicting claims to the Ukrainian steppes—that is, the Russians, the Poles, and the Cossacks. Finally, the khan was greatly aided by the inaccessibility of his domain. The Perekop Isthmus guarding the approaches to the Crimean Peninsula was 700 miles direct from Moscow, and far more in actual riding miles. Thus, the Russians were not able to undertake serious campaigning against the Crimean Tatars until their line of settlement had advanced sufficiently far south to provide them with a base for striking across the steppes.

These various factors explain why the Crimean khanate survived until the time of Catherine the Great in the late eighteenth century. The 250 years between Ivan the Terrible and Catherine the Great were years of bloodshed and anarchy on the Ukrainian steppes north of the Black Sea. The Ukraine was a

wild no man's land in which Russians, Poles, Cossacks, and Tatars fought intermittently and in constantly changing combinations. Particularly devastating were
the incessant Tatar raids that were, in effect, slave-hunting expeditions. Riding
up their three main trails crouched "like monkeys on greyhounds," the Tatars
raided deep into the heart of Moscow in search of ablebodied men, women, and
children for the slave markets of the Middle East.

Finally Catherine the Great was able to remove the Tatar thorn from the side
of Russia. She succeeded where so many of her predecessors had failed because
several factors were operating in her favor. One was the rapid decline of both
Poland and Turkey, the two powers that hitherto had contested Russia's claims to
the Ukraine. Russia, by contrast, was growing steadily stronger, partly because
of her spectacular territorial expansion and also because of her strongly centralized government. Russia's power was particularly effective during Catherine's
reign because the empress was a superb diplomat and skillfully took advantage of
every opportunity afforded by the international situation. She concluded agreements with Joseph II of Austria and Frederick the Great of Prussia that enabled
her to wage war against Turkey without becoming embroiled with any major
European power. Furthermore, Catherine had the gift of selecting first-class advisers and generals. The most outstanding was General Aleksandr Suvorov, a
military genius comparable to Napoleon, and a matchless instrument for Catherine's policies. Moreover, in the eighty years since Peter the Great's campaigns,
the Russian peasantry had been unobtrusively and patiently advancing its line of
settlement southward so that Suvorov had a stronger base for operations than
Peter had had.

Catherine fought two wars against the Tatars and the Turks. The first, between 1768 and 1774, gave Russia effective control of the Crimean Peninsula.
The Treaty of Kuchuk-Kainarji in 1774 severed the ties between Bakhchi-sarai
and Constantinople, and gave Russia several strategic strongholds in the Crimea.
The second war, from 1787 to 1792, was marked, like the first, by spectacular
victories won by Suvorov. In fact, the magnitude of his triumphs created difficulties, because both Prussia and Austria became alarmed at the sweeping Russian advances toward the Mediterranean. Catherine, however, shrewdly took
advantage of the outbreak of the French Revolution by pointing out to the
Austrian and Prussian rulers that the revolutionary movement in Paris represented a far greater peril than Russian expansion in the Near East. Thus
Catherine was able to press her war against the Turks until, in 1792, they accepted the Treaty of Jassy. This settlement gave to Russia the entire north shore
of the Black Sea from the Kuban River in the east to the Dniester River in the
west.

The whole of the Ukraine now was under Russian rule. The forest at length had
triumphed over the steppe. The desert zone of Central Asia still held out, but it
also was destined to fall under Moscovy's sway during the following century.

SUGGESTED READING

T. ARMSTRONG, Russian Expansion in the North (Cambridge Univ., 1965); V. CHEN,
Sino-Russian Relations in the Seventeenth Century (Nijhoff, 1966); R. H. FISHER, The
Russian Fur Trade, 1550–1700 (Univ. California, 1943); F. A. GOLDER, Russian Expansion
on the Pacific, 1641–1850 (Clark, 1914); R. J. KERNER, The Urge to the Sea: The Course
of Russian History (Univ. California, 1942); L. H. NEATBY, Discovery in Russian and
Siberian Waters (Ohio Univ., 1973); D. W. TREADGOLD, The Great Siberian Migration
(Princeton Univ., 1957).

chapter twenty-three

Incipient Global Ecumene

The discovery of America . . . certainly made a most essential (change). By opening a new and inexhaustible market to all the commodities of Europe, it gave occasion to new divisions of labour and improvements of art, which, in the narrow sphere of ancient commerce, could never have taken place. . . . The silver of the new continent seems in this manner to be one of the principal commodities by which the commerce between the two extremities of the old one is carried on, and it is by means of it, in great measure, that those distant parts of the world are connected with one another.—Adam Smith

The early modern period from 1500 to 1763 is one of the more critical periods in the history of mankind. It was at this time that the great discoveries disclosed the existence of new continents and thereby heralded the global phase of world history. It was during this period also that the Europeans began their rise to world primacy by virtue of their leadership in overseas activities. The global interrelationships that developed during these centuries naturally became stronger with the passage of time. Hence the years from 1500 to 1763 constitute a period of incipient global ecumene—a period of transition from the regional isolationism of the pre-1500 era to the European global hegemony of the nineteenth century. The purpose of this chapter is to analyze the precise nature and extent of the global ties developed in various fields. (See Map XXIV, "World of the Emerging West, 1763.")

I. NEW GLOBAL HORIZONS

The first and most obvious result of Europe's expansion overseas and overland was an unprecedented widening of man's horizons. No longer was geographic knowledge limited to one region or continent or hemisphere. For the first time, the configuration of the globe as a whole was determined and charted. (See Map XXIII, "Western Man's Knowledge of the Globe, A.D. 1 to 1800.") This was largely the work of the Western Europeans who had taken the lead in transoceanic exploration. Before the Portuguese began feeling their way down the coast of Africa in the early fifteenth century, Europeans had accurate information only of North Africa and the Middle East. Their knowledge concerning India was vague; it was still vaguer regarding Central Asia, East Asia, and sub-Saharan Africa. The very existence of the Americas and of Australia—let alone Antarctica—was, of course, unsuspected.

293

By 1763 the picture was altogether different. The main coastline of most of the world had become known in varying degrees of detail, including the Atlantic coasts of the Americas, the Pacific coast of South America, the whole outline of Africa, and the coasts of South and East Asia. In certain areas European knowledge went beyond the coastlines. The Russians were reasonably familiar with Siberia, and the Spaniards and Portuguese with Mexico, Central America, and parts of South America. North of the Rio Grande the Spaniards had explored considerable areas in futile search for gold and fabled cities, while the French and English ranged widely further north, using the canoes and the river-lake routes known to the Indians.

On the other hand, the Pacific coast of North America was largely unknown, while Australia, though sighted on its west coast by Dutch navigators, was almost wholly uncharted. Likewise, the interior of sub-Saharan Africa remained largely a blank, as was the case also with Central Asia, about which the main source of information still was the thirteenth century account of Marco Polo. In general, then, the Europeans had gained knowledge of most of the coastlines of the world during this period to 1763. In the following period they were to penetrate into the interior of continents and also explore the polar regions.

II. GLOBAL DIFFUSION OF MAN, ANIMALS, AND PLANTS

The European discoveries led not only to new global horizons but also to a new global distribution of races. (See Map III, "Global Race Distribution.") Prior to 1500 there existed, in effect, worldwide racial segregation. The Negroids were concentrated in sub-Saharan Africa and a few Pacific islands, the Mongoloids in Central Asia, Siberia, East Asia, and the Americas, and the Caucasoids in Europe, North Africa, the Middle East and India. Today this pattern has been fundamentally altered to the point where half the people of European descent live outside Europe, and a third of the people of African descent live outside Africa. By 1763 this radically different race distribution was clearly discernible. The Russians had begun their slow migration across the Urals into Siberia. Much more substantial was the mass migration to the Americas, voluntary in the case of the Europeans, involuntary with the Africans. (See Table I.)

TABLE 1 Estimated Slave Imports into the Americas, by Importing Region, 1451–1870 (in thousands)

British North America	399
Spanish America	1,552
Caribbean (British, French, Dutch, and Danish)	3,793
Brazil	3,646
Total	9,390

Source: Adapted from P. D. Curtin, *The Atlantic Slave Trade: A Census* (Madison: Univ. of Wisconsin, 1969), p. 268.

This influx changed the Americas from purely Mongoloid continents to the most racially mixed regions of the globe. Negro immigration continued to the mid-nineteenth century, reaching a total of about ten million slaves, while European immigration steadily increased, reaching a high point at the beginning of the twentieth century when nearly one million arrived each year. The net result is that the New World today is peopled by a majority of whites, with substantial minorities of Negroes, Indians, mestizos, and mulattoes, in that order. (See Chapter 31, section I.)

(See Chapter 31, section I.)

The new global racial pattern that resulted from these depopulations and migrations has become so familiar that it is now taken for granted, and its extraordinary significance generally overlooked. What happened in this period to 1763 is that the Europeans staked out claims to vast new regions, and in the following century they peopled these territories—not only the Americas, but also Siberia and Australia. The meaning of this fundamental redrawing of the racial map of the world may be gauged if it be imagined that the Chinese rather than the Europeans had first reached and settled the under-populated continents. In that case the proportion of Chinese to the total world population now would probably be closer to three out of four rather than the present one out of four.

The intermixture of human races was accompanied inevitably by a corresponding intermixture of plants and animals. With a few insignificant exceptions, all plants and animals being utilized today were domesticated by prehistoric man in various parts of the world. Their diffusion from their respective locales had proceeded slowly until 1500, when globe-spanning man began transplanting them back and forth amongst continents. An important contribution of the Old World was the various stockyard animals, especially horses, cattle, and sheep. The New World had nothing comparable, the llama and alpaca being of relatively little value. Old World grains also were important, especially wheat, rye, oats, and barley. The Spaniards, being lovers of orchards, brought with them a large variety of fruits, as well as the olive and the European vine.

The American Indians in return contributed their remarkable store of food plants, particularly corn and potatoes, but also cassava, tomatoes, avocados, sweet potatoes, peanuts, and certain varieties of beans, pumpkins, and squashes. So important are these Indian plants that today they are responsible for at least a third of the world's total plant food production. In addition to these food plants, the American Indians were responsible for two major cash crops, tobacco and cotton, as well as several drugs that are prominent in modern pharmacology, especially coca in cocaine and novocaine, curare used in anesthetics, cinchona bark as the source of quinine, datura in pain relievers, and cascara in laxatives.

This interchange of animals and plants was not, of course, confined to Eurasia and the Americas. The entire globe was involved, as is illustrated strikingly in the case of Australia, now a leading world exporter of primary products such as wool, mutton, beef, and wheat, all commodities derived from transplanted species. The same is true of Indonesia with its great rubber, coffee, tea, and tobacco production, and of Hawaii with its sugar and pineapples.

III. GLOBAL ECONOMIC RELATIONS

By the latter part of the eighteenth century intercontinental trade of substantial proportions had developed for the first time in history. Before 1500, Arab and Italian merchants had transported from one part of Eurasia to another mostly luxuries—spices, silk, precious stones, and perfumes. By the late eighteenth century this limited luxury trade had been transformed into a mass trade because of the exchange of new bulky necessities. This was particularly true of Atlantic commerce, for the New World plantations produced for sale in Europe huge quantities of tobacco, sugar and, later, coffee, cotton, and other commodities. Because the plantations practiced monoculture, they imported all their needs, including grain, fish, cloth, and metal products. They also had to import their labor, and so a flourishing triangle trade resulted: rum, cloth, guns, and other metal products from Europe to Africa; slaves from Africa to the New World; sugar, tobacco, and bullion from the New World to Europe.

Another important aspect of the new mass global trade of this era was that between Western and Eastern Europe. Here again Western Europe received raw materials, especially the bread grains that were in great demand because of population increase and the conversion of much arable land into pasture. At Danzig, chief port for the Baltic grain trade, rye prices between 1550 and 1600 rose 247 per cent, barley 187 per cent, and oats 185 per cent. This stimulated a great increase in the export of grains and other raw materials, so that the value of Polish and Hungarian exports to the West during these decades usually was double that of imports. Poland, Hungary, Russia, and ultimately the Balkans received textiles, arms, metal products, and colonial goods, and in return provided grain, cattle, hides, ship stores, flax, and furs. The furs were obtained by the Russians in Siberia (see Chapter 22, section IV) in the same manner that the Spaniards obtained bullion in the New World, namely, by the exploitation of native labor.

Western Europe's trade with Asia did not equal the trade with the Americas or Eastern Europe for two principal reasons. One was the opposition of the long-established European textile industries to the importation of cotton goods from various Asiatic countries. These foreign cotton goods were immensely popular in Europe, being light, bright, inexpensive, and, above all, washable. They began to be imported in large quantities, whereupon objections were raised by native textile interests and by those who feared that national security was endangered by the loss of the bullion that was drained away to pay for them. Laws were passed forbidding the importation of Indian cottons, and though these laws were by no means universally observed, they did serve to cut down appreciably the volume of trade with Asia.

The other factor limiting European commerce with Asia was the difficulty of finding something that could sell in the Asiatic market. This problem dated back to classical times when the Roman Empire was drained of its gold to pay for Chinese silk and Indian textiles. So it was in the sixteenth, seventeenth, and eighteenth centuries, when Asia remained uninterested in European goods, while Europe was reluctant to send bullion to pay for the Asiatic produce she desired. Europe did not solve this problem of trade with Asia until she developed power machinery at the end of the eighteenth century. Then the situation was reversed, for it was Europe that was able to flood Asia with cheap, machine-made textiles. But until that time, East-West trade was hampered by the fact that Asia was willing to receive from Europe bullion and little else.

What was the significance of the new worldwide economic ties? First and foremost, international division of labor for the first time had been achieved on a significant scale. The world was on the way to becoming an economic unit. The Americas and Eastern Europe (with Siberia) produced raw materials, Africa provided manpower, Asia an assortment of luxury commodities, and Western Europe directed these global operations and increasingly concentrated on industrial output.

The requirements of the new global economy raised the question of labor supply in the raw material producing regions. The New World plantations met this by importing African slaves on a large scale. Negroid elements are most numerous today in precisely those areas that had been devoted to plantation agriculture—northern Brazil, the West Indies, and southern United States. This was to leave a bitter legacy, for these areas to the present day are wracked by basic problems dating back to the colonial period—the problems of race and of underdevelopment. The current race conflict in American ghettos and in Caribbean islands is the end result of over four centuries of transatlantic slave trade, and the underdevelopment of all of Latin America is simply a continuation of the economic dependency of the Spanish and Portuguese colonies (and of Spain and Portugal themselves) on northwestern Europe.

Whereas the price for the participation of the Americas in the new global economy was slavery, the price for Eastern Europe was serfdom. The basic reason was the same—the need for a plentiful and reliable supply of cheap labor to produce goods for the lucrative West European market. Heretofore the nobles in Poland and Hungary had required minimal labor from the peasants—three to six days a year—for there was no incentive to increase output. But when production for market became profitable, the nobles responded by drastically raising the labor obligation, first to one day a week, and by the end of the sixteenth century to six days a week. To make sure that the peasants would remain to perform this corvée, laws were passed progressively limiting their freedom of movement. Eventually they were completely bound to the soil, thereby becoming serfs, without freedom of movement, and subject to the exactions of the nobles.

A similar evolution occurred in the Balkan countries under Turkish rule, the peasants there being bound to private estates known as *chifliks*. It was not accidental that Balkan peasant revolts coincided with the spread of *chifliks*. Peasant jacqueries were the sequel to East European serfdom, just as slave revolts followed from New World plantation bondage.

Africa was also vitally affected, positively as well as negatively, by the new global economy. The slave trade was responsible for the loss of an estimated thirty-five to forty million Africans who were abducted for transportation to the Americas, though this figure has yet to be verified by adequate research. Only about ten million actually reached their destination, the remainder perishing in transit, either in Africa or on shipboard. The effect of the slave trade varied greatly from region to region. Angola and East Africa suffered severely because their populations were relatively sparse to begin with, and their economies often close to the subsistence level, so that even a small population loss was devastating. By contrast, West Africa was more advanced economically and hence more populous, so that the depredations of the slavers were not so ruinous. Considering the continent as a whole, the demographic repercussion was relatively slight because the slaves were taken over a period stretching from 1450 to 1870, and from a total sub-Saharan population estimated at seventy to eighty million. Nevertheless, the slave trade had a corrosive and unsettling effect on the entire African coast from Senegal to Angola, and for four to five hundred miles inland. The appearance of the European slavers with their cargoes of rum, guns, and hardware set off a chain reaction of slave-hunting raids into the interior, and of wars among assorted groups for control of the lucrative and militarily decisive trade. With some rising to ascendancy, such as the Ashanti Confederacy and the Dahomey Kingdom, and with others declining, such as the Yoruba and Benin civilizations and the Congo kingdom, the over-all effect was definitely disruptive.

And yet the slave trade did involve trade as well as slavery. In return for their fellow countrymen whom the Africans themselves sold to the Europeans, they received not only alcohol and firearms, but also certain useful and economically productive commodities, including textiles, tools, and raw materials for local smithies and workshops. A more important positive influence in the long run was the introduction of new food plants from the Americas. Corn, cassava, sweet potatoes, peppers, pineapples, and tobacco were brought in by the Portuguese and spread very rapidly from tribe to tribe. The substantially larger number of people that could be supported with these new foods probably outweighed the manpower lost to the slave trade.

Of the various continents, Asia was the least affected, being sufficiently strong militarily, politically, and economically to avoid direct or indirect subjugation. Most of Asia was quite unaware of the persistent and annoying European merchants who were appearing in the coastal regions. Only a few coastal areas in India, and some of the islands in the East Indies, felt significantly the impact of Europe's economic expansion. So far as Asia as a whole was concerned, its attitude was best expressed by the Emperor of China, Ch'ien–lung, who, in 1793, replied as follows to a message from King George III of Britain requesting the establishment of diplomatic and commercial relations: "Swaying the wide world, I have but one aim in view, namely, to maintain a perfect governance and to fulfill the duties of the State: strange and costly objects do not interest me. . . . As your Ambassador can see for himself, we possess all things. I set no value on objects strange or ingenious, and have no use for your country's manufactures."[1]

Europe also was affected by the new global economy, but the repercussions in this case were all positive. The Europeans were the pioneer middlemen of world trade. They had opened the new oceanic routes and supplied the necessary capital, shipping, and technical skills. So it was natural that they should have profited most from the slave trade, the sugar and tobacco plantations, and the eastern commerce. Some of the benefits trickled down to the European masses, as is indicated by the fact that tea cost about £10 a pound when introduced in England about 1650, but had become an article of common consumption one hundred years later. More important than the effect on living standards was the stimulating impact of the new global commerce upon Europe's economy. As will be noted later, the Industrial Revolution that got under way in the late eighteenth century owed much to the capital accumulated from overseas enterprises and to the growing demand for European manufactures in overseas markets.

It was during this period, then, that Europe forged ahead in the great ascent to global economic primacy. The overall results were positive, for global division of labor led to increased global productivity. The world of 1763 was richer than that of 1500, and the economic growth has continued to the present day. But from the beginning northwestern Europe, as the world's entrepreneur, derived most of the benefits at the expense of the other regions. What this expense involved is apparent in the current conflict of races, in the gross discrepancy between rich and poor nations, and in the still discernible scars left by serfdom throughout Eastern Europe.

IV. GLOBAL POLITICAL RELATIONS

Global political relations changed as fundamentally during this period to 1763 as did the economic. The Western Europeans no longer were fenced in on the western tip of Eurasia by an expanding Islam. Instead, they had outflanked the Moslem world in the south by winning control of the Indian Ocean, while the Russians had outflanked it in the north by their conquest of Siberia. At the same time, the Western Europeans, by their discovery of the New World, had opened vast territories for economic exploitation and colonization. In doing so, they acquired a tremendous reservoir of resources and power that further strengthened their position vis-à-vis Islam, and that was to prove increasingly decisive during the forthcoming century.

All this represented a basic and fateful change in the global balance of power—a change comparable to that which had occurred in the demographic balance. Hitherto the Moslem world had been the center of initiative, probing and pushing in all directions—into Southeast Europe, into sub-Saharan Africa, into Central and Southeast Asia. Now a new center had risen which was able to operate on a global, rather than merely Eurasian, scale. From this new center, first in the Iberian Peninsula and later in Northwest Europe, the routes of trade and of political influence radiated outward to envelop the entire world—westward to the Americas, south around Africa, and east to India and around Southeast Asia.

This did not mean actual control of all these territories by 1763. It did mean the effective domination of the underpopulated lands—the Americas, Siberia, and later Australia—even though their actual peopling on a continental scale had to wait till the nineteenth century. But in Africa and Asia the Western Europeans obtained only coastal footholds during this period, with the exception of the Dutch penetration of the Cape and of the East Indies. Elsewhere the native peoples were too strong and highly organized to allow a repetition of what happened in the Americas and in Siberia.

In West Africa, for example, the Europeans were prevented from penetrating inland by climatic difficulties and by the opposition of the coastal chiefs who jealously guarded their profitable position as middlemen between the interior tribes and the Europeans. Consequently, the latter had to content themselves with coastal stations from which they carried on their trade in slaves and in any other commodities that might yield profit.

In India the Europeans were kept at arm's length for 250 years following the arrival of Vasco da Gama in 1498. During those centuries they were allowed to trade in a few ports, but clearly and explicitly on the sufferance of the native rulers. It was not until the end of the eighteenth century that the British were strong enough to take advantage of the disintegration of the Mogul Empire to begin their territorial conquests in India.

In China and Japan there was no question whatsoever of European territorial encroachment, as the Russians discovered when they entered the Amur valley. Even trade with the Far East was quite precarious, being subject to unchallengeable arbitrary decrees. In 1763, more than two centuries after the arrival of the Portuguese in the Far East, Western merchants were allowed to trade only in Canton and Nagasaki. Even the Ottoman Empire had lost only its outlying provinces beyond the Danube River. And this despite the fact that it was in a moribund state and was vulnerable to aggression by both the land and naval powers of Europe.

We may conclude that in the political field, as in the economic, Europe in 1763 was at a halfway point. It was no longer a relatively isolated and unimportant peninsula of the Eurasian landmass. It had expanded overseas and overland, establishing its control over the relatively empty and militarily weak Americas and Siberia. But in Africa, the Middle East, and South and East Asia, the Europeans had to wait until the nineteenth century to assert their dominance. To underscore the transitional nature of these centuries, it should be emphasized that while the Western Europeans were executing their global flanking movement by sea, the Moslems still had sufficient impetus on land to continue their advances into Central Europe, where they besieged Vienna in 1683, and into sub-Saharan Africa and Southeast Asia, where they were winning new converts.

V. GLOBAL CULTURAL RELATIONS

The imposition of European culture, like that of European political rule, depended on the state of the indigenous societies. The English and the French, for example, were able to transport bodily their respective cultures to the Americas because the native peoples were either wiped out or pushed aside. Yet even in this case the Indians had an appreciable effect upon the white man's civilization, particularly in Latin America, where even the casual traveler cannot fail to notice evidence of Indian cultural survivals. There is, for example, the use of adobe for building purposes, and of unmilled pine logs as beams, or vigas. Likewise the blanket, or serape, that is draped over the shoulders is of Indian origin, as is also the poncho, consisting of two blankets sewn together with a slit left open for the head. The Roman Catholicism currently practiced in much of Latin America is a blend of Christian and Indian beliefs and practices. Perhaps the most conspicuous evidence of Indian influence is to be found in the Latin American cuisine. Tamales, tortillas, and the various chili dishes are based on the two great Indian staples, beans and corn.

European influence upon the indigenous cultures of Africa and Eurasia was negligible in the period prior to 1763, apart from the diffusion of new food plants, which, as noted, was of first importance. In West Africa the native chiefs confined the European traders largely to their coastal posts. In the old Middle Eastern, Indian, and Chinese centers of civilization, the native peoples, as might be expected, were not at all impressed by the culture of the European intruders. The Moslem Turks, who had the closest ties with the Christian Europeans, looked down upon them with the utmost contempt. Even in the seventeenth and eighteenth centuries, when the Turks were themselves on the downgrade, they did not hesitate to express their disdain for the Christian infidels. "Do I not know you," broke out the grand vizier to the French ambassador in 1666, "that you are a Giaour [nonbeliever], that you are a hogge, a dogge, a turde eater?"[2]

This contemptuous arrogance toward Europe and the Europeans may be explained in large part by the age-old feud between Christianity and Islam. The reaction to the Europeans in the rest of Eurasia was less contumelious, but at the same time there was no indication of respect, much less of awe. On the mainland of India, the native peoples reacted very negatively when the Portuguese, who were ensconced at Goa, introduced the Inquisition in 1560. Between 1600 and 1773, seventy-three victims were consigned to the flames because of their heretical views. The Indian population could not fail to note the incongruity of a religion that imprisoned, tortured, and condemned to the flames those whose only crime was unorthodoxy, while at the same time it prevented widows being burnt of their own free will as an act of sublime virtue.

The Chinese reaction to the Europeans was relatively favorable at the outset because of the exceptional ability and intellectual attainments of the Jesuit missionaries. The Jesuits succeeded in winning some converts, including a few scholars and some members of the imperial family. But even the capable Jesuits, with their knowledge of astronomy and mathematics and geography, did not unduly impress the Chinese. So far as the popular Chinese attitude to the Europeans at that time is concerned, it probably was reflected accurately in the proverb that they, the Chinese, alone possessed two eyes, the Europeans were one-eyed, and all the other inhabitants of the earth were blind. Given this atmosphere, it is understandable that, with the exception of certain specialized fields of learning such as astronomy, European influence on Chinese civilization prior to 1763 was negligible.

Although the Chinese, the Indians, and the Turks were unimpressed by the culture of the Europeans during this period, the Europeans, by contrast, were very much impressed by what they observed in Constantinople, in Delhi, and in Peking. They became familiar first with the Ottoman Empire, and their reaction was one of respect, admiration, and apprehension. As late as 1634, after the decline of the empire had set in, a thoughtful English traveler concluded that the Turks were "the only modern people great in action," and that "he who would behold these times in their greatest glory, could not find a better scene than Turkey."[3] During the seventeenth century the Ottoman Empire lost prestige among Europeans. Numerous symptoms of decay were becoming apparent, including dynastic degeneration, administrative corruption, and military impotence. But at the same time European intellectuals were being fascinated by numerous detailed accounts of the fabulous civilization of far-off Cathay. These accounts, based on the reports of the Jesuit missionaries, generated a tremendous enthusiasm for China and for things Chinese. Indeed the influence of China on Europe in the seventeenth and early eighteenth centuries was considerably greater than Europe's influence on China. The Westerners were entranced as they learned of China's history, art, philosophy, and government. China came to be held up as a model civilization because of its Confucian system of morals, its examination system for government service, its respect for learning rather than for military prowess, and its exquisite handicrafts, including porcelain, silk, and lacquer work. In the late eighteenth century European admiration of China began to wane, partly because the Catholic missionaries now were being persecuted, and also because the Europeans were beginning to be more interested in China's natural resources than in her culture. This shift of attitude is reflected in the sixteen volumes of the *Memoirs on the History, Sciences, Arts, etc., of the Chinese*, published in Paris between 1776 and 1814. The eleventh volume, which appeared in 1786, contained little but reports on resources that might interest traders—borax, lignite, quicksilver, ammoniac, horses, bamboo, and wool-bearing animals.

Just as European interest had shifted in the seventeenth century from the Ottoman Empire to China, so now in the late eighteenth century it shifted to Greece and, to a lesser extent, India. The classical Greeks became the great favorites among educated Europeans. "How can you believe," wrote a German scholar in 1778, "that uncultivated Oriental peoples produced annals and poetry and possessed a complete religion and morality, before the Greeks, who were the teachers of Europe, were able to read?"[4] Yet a few European intellectuals did become engrossed in Indian culture. The general European public had long before this time been aware of India, and had been thrilled by the reports of the riches and magnificence of the "Grand Mogul" of Delhi. This superficial concept of India and her civilization began to deepen as the Europeans gradually became aware of the ancient literature of the Hindus. The Hindu pandits were unwilling to impart their sacred lore to foreigners, but a few Europeans, mostly Jesuit fathers, acquired a knowledge of Sanskrit language, literature, and philosophy. An English scholar, Sir William Jones, proclaimed before the Asiatic Society of

Bengal in 1786 that "The *Sanskrit* Language, whatever be its antiquity, is of wonderful structure; more perfect than the Greek, more copious than the Latin, and more exquisitely refined than either."[5]

VI. EARLY MODERN PERIOD IN HISTORICAL PERSPECTIVE

The early modern period from 1500 to 1763 represents a halfway point between the regional isolationism of the preceding ages and the European world hegemony of the nineteenth century (See Map XXIV, "World of the Emerging West, 1763.") Economically, it was a time when the Europeans extended their trading operations to virtually all corners of the globe, though they were not yet able to exploit the interiors of the great landmasses. Intercontinental trade reached unprecedented proportions, but it was still far below the volume it was to attain in the following centuries.

Politically, the world was still far from being a single unit. The great Seven Years' War which convulsed Europe did not affect the Americas west of the Mississippi, the interior of Africa, most of the Middle East, and the whole of East Asia. The Europeans had secured a firm grip on Siberia, South America, and the eastern portion of North America, but they had as yet only a few territorial enclaves in Africa, India, and the East Indies, while in the Far East they could venture only as merchants. And even in that capacity they had to submit to the most restrictive and arbitrary regulations.

Culturally, it was a period of widening horizons. Throughout the globe peoples were becoming aware of other peoples and other cultures. By and large, the Europeans were more impressed and affected by the ancient civilizations of Eurasia than was the case in reverse. They felt a sense of wide-eyed wonder as they discovered new oceans and continents and civilizations. They exhibited a certain humility at the same time that they were scrambling greedily for booty and for trade. They even underwent on occasion an anxious searching of conscience, as in the case of the treatment of the Indians in Spanish America. But before this period had passed, Europe's attitude toward the rest of the world was noticeably changing. It was becoming coarser and harder and more intolerant. In the mid-nineteenth century the French sinologist Guillaume Pauthier complained that the Chinese civilization, which in the time of Leibniz had keenly interested European intellectuals, "now scarcely attracted the attention of a select few. . . . These people, whom we daily treat as barbarians, and who, nevertheless, had attained to a very high state of culture several centuries before our ancestors inhabited the forests of Gaul and Germany, now inspire in us only a deep contempt."[6] Part VII of this book will be concerned with why the Europeans came to feel themselves superior to the "lesser breeds," and how they were able to impose their rule upon them.

SUGGESTED READING

P. D. Curtin, *The Atlantic Slave Trade: A Census* (Univ. Wisconsin, 1969); L. S. S. O'Malley, ed., *Modern India and the West* (Oxford Univ., 1941); J. H. Parry, *The Age of Reconnaissance: Discovery, Exploration and Settlement 1450–1650* (World, 1963); A. G. Price, *The Western Invasions of the Pacific and Its Continents: A Study of Moving Frontiers and Changing Landscapes, 1513–1958* (Clarendon, 1963); A. Reichwein, *China and Europe: Intellectual and Artistic Contacts in the Eighteenth Century* (Knopf, 1925); S. J. and B. H. Stein, *The Colonial Heritage of Latin America* (Oxford Univ., 1970).

part seven

WORLD OF WESTERN DOMINANCE, 1763-1914

Basis of Dominance

Bring attention by italic

The century and a half between 1763 and 1914 stands out in the course of world history as the period of European hegemony over a large part of the globe. In 1763 Europe was still far from being the master of the world, having only coastal footholds in Africa and Asia. But by 1914 the European powers had annexed the whole of Africa and had effectively established their control over Asia, either directly, as in India and Southeast Asia, or indirectly, as in the Chinese and Ottoman empires. This unprecedented expansion of Europe was made possible by three great revolutions—scientific, industrial, and political—which gave Europe irresistible dynamism and power.

Two features of these revolutions might be noted at this point. One is that they were well under way before 1763. The English Civil War, a major phase of the political revolution, occurred in the 1640's. The scientific revolution took place primarily during the century and a half between the publication of Copernicus' *De revolutionibus orbium coelestium* (1534) and of Newton's *Principia* (1687). Likewise, the roots of the Industrial Revolution are to be found in the sixteenth and seventeenth centuries, when the countries of northwestern Europe "were seething with such genuinely capitalistic phenomena as systematic mechanical invention, company formation, and speculation in the shares of financial and trading concerns."[1] But the worldwide impact of none of these revolutions was fully felt until the nineteenth century. That is the principal reason for considering them here rather than earlier in this book.

The other point to note about these revolutions is that they did not run in parallel or independent lines. They were interdependent and reacted continuously one upon the other. Both Newton's discovery of the laws governing the movements of heavenly bodies and Darwin's theories of biological evolution had a

[1] E. J. Hamilton, "American Treasure and the Rise of Capitalism (1500–1700)," **Economica** (November, 1929), p. 356.

profound effect on political ideas. Likewise, modern nationalism is quite unthinkable without technological innovations such as printing and the telegraph. And contrariwise, politics affected science, as in the case of the French Revolution, which provided a powerful stimulus to scientific advance. Politics also affected economics, as was made clear by the English manufacturer John Wilkinson, who stated bluntly, "Manufacture and Commerce will always flourish most where Church and King interfere least."[2]

After analyzing the nature and the unfolding of these three European revolutions, we shall then, in the following chapters of Part VII of this volume, trace their effect on various parts of the globe. We shall see how they made possible the Europeanization of the Americas and of Australia, the partitioning of Africa, and the domination over Asia, culminating in a full-fledged global ecumene.

[2] *Cited by C. E. Robinson, "The English Philosophes and the French Revolution,"* History Today, *VI (February, 1956), 121.*

chapter twenty-four

Europe's Scientific and Industrial Revolutions

The so-called scientific revolution . . . outshines everything since the rise of Christianity and reduces the Renaissance and Reformation to the rank of mere episodes, mere internal displacements within the system of medieval Christendom. . . . It looms so large as the real origin both of the modern world and of the modern mentality that our customary periodisation of European history has become an anachronism and an encumbrance.—Herbert Butterfield

. . . A world thronged as never before with people hustling by each other on the sidewalks of huge cities, people brooding or daydreaming in uneasy seclusion in the cells of high apartment buildings; a world of streamlined automobiles, railway cars, and airplanes; sprayed by a din from microphones, bombarded by newspaper headlines and changing scenes of motion pictures and of television. This world is part of an economic regime unique in history—the regime of industrial civilization—now shared by Russians, Americans, and Japanese, even to some extent by Chinese and Indians, as well as by the peoples of Western Europe.—John U. Nef

Less than four hundred years, or about six average life spans, separate the work of Copernicus from that of Einstein. Yet in that short space of time science has grown from an esoteric avocation of a handful of devotees to what may be properly termed the dominant force of modern civilization. And the central characteristic of science today is its constantly accelerating rate of development. In 1899, the famous British naturalist Alfred Russell Wallace published a book entitled *The Wonderful Century*. He was referring to his own nineteenth century, which, in his opinion, had witnessed more scientific progress than all the preceding centuries of mankind. Yet today we can again boast that more scientific work has been done in the first half of the twentieth century than in the whole of previous history.

In the light of retrospect, it appears that this scientific revolution is of even greater significance than the agricultural revolution of Neolithic times. The agricultural revolution made civilization possible, but once this great step forward was taken, agriculture had no further contribution to make. Science, on the other hand, is by its very methodology cumulative. It contains within itself the possibilities of indefinite advance. If we bear in mind the achievements of science in the past few centuries and its present accelerating pace of development, we may appreciate, if not comprehend, its staggering potentiality and significance. Science, furthermore, is universal; being based on an objective methodology, it had secured general assent to its propositions. It is the one product of Western civilization that non-Western peoples generally respect and seek. In fact, it was science and its related technology that made possible Europe's domination of the world in the nineteenth century. And today the formerly subject peoples are striving to redress the balance by learning the mysteries of the West's great and unique contribution to mankind. Hence the basic significance of the scientific revolution for the study of world history.

I. ROOTS OF THE SCIENTIFIC REVOLUTION

The roots of science may be traced back to ancient Mesopotamia and Egypt, to classical Greece, and to the medieval Moslem world. Yet the scientific revolution is a unique product of Western civilization. The reason seems to be that only in the West did science become part and parcel of general society. Or, to put it another way, only in the West did the philosopher-scientist and the artisan effect a union and stimulate each other. And it was this union of science and society, of scientist and artisan, that contributed greatly to the unprecedented blossoming of science in the Western world.

In all human societies the artisans developed certain skills in hunting, fishing, farming, and in working with wood, stone, metal, grasses, fibers, roots, and hides. Yet the degree of progress achieved by all premodern societies was sharply restricted. The reason was that the artisans were interested only in making pots or building houses or constructing boats, and did not bother with underlying chemical or mechanical principles. They did not inquire regarding the relationship between antecedent and consequent phenomena. In short, the artisans by definition concerned themselves with technological know-how rather than with scientific know-why.

The significance of this is suggested by James Bryant Conant's definition of science as "an interconnected series of concepts and conceptual schemes that have developed as a result of experimentation and observation and are fruitful of further experimentation and observations."[1] It is apparent that artisans lacked the "conceptual schemes" that, according to Conant's definition, constitute the basis of science. Instead, such schemes traditionally have been the concern of philosophers, as intellectuals were generally termed in premodern times. But these philosophers were notoriously ignorant and impractical about questions of everyday life. They deemed themselves to be above mundane matters, and spent their time pondering the eternal verities or trying to reduce an incoherent universe into something comprehensible to the human mind. Until recent times the tendency was toward compartmentalization—toward the isolation of the thinker from the worker.

The great achievement of the West was to bring the two together. This fusion of know-how and know-why gave science the grounding and the impulse that was to make it the dominant force that it is today.

Why did this epochal development take place in the West? One reason was the humanistic scholarship of the Renaissance. Scholars and artists set themselves in opposition to the whole pattern of medieval life and strove to create a new pattern as similar as possible to that of classical antiquity. They went directly to the ancient sources, digging up the statues and reading the original texts for themselves. They gained access not only to Plato and Aristotle but also to Euclid and Archimedes, who stimulated the study of physics and mathematics. More important was the inspiration received in the biological sciences. Medical men studied the complete works of Hippocrates and Galen, and naturalists those of Aristotle, Dioscorides and Theophrastus.

These fruits of human scholarship could not by themselves have engendered the scientific revolution without a favorable social atmosphere in Western Europe, which narrowed the gulf between the artisans and the scholars. Artisans were not so despised during the Renaissance as they had been in classical and medieval times. Respect was given to the practical arts of spinning, weaving, ceramics, glass making, and, most of all, to the increasingly important mining and metallurgy. The enhancement of the status of the Renaissance craftsman made it possible to strengthen the tie between him and the scholar that had been so tenuous since the beginning of civilization. Each had an important contribution to make. The craftsman had the old techniques of antiquity, to which he added the new devices evolved during the Middle Ages. The scholar likewise provided the facts, speculations, and procedures of rediscovered antiquity and of medieval science. The two approaches fused slowly, but in the end they produced an explosive combination.

Science was stimulated also by the Discoveries and the opening up of overseas lands. New plants, new animals, new stars, even new human beings and new human societies were found, and all these challenged traditional ideas and assumptions. It is significant that in the writings of a great English exponent of science, Francis Bacon (1561–1626), much of the imagery is borrowed from the voyages of exploration. Bacon expressed himself as aspiring to be the Columbus of a new intellectual world, to sail through the Pillars of Hercules (symbol of the old knowledge) into the Atlantic Ocean in search of new and more useful knowledge. In fact, he explicitly stated that "by the distant voyages and travels which have become frequent in our times, many things in nature have been laid open and discovered which may let in new light upon philosophy."[2]

The scientific revolution in Europe owed much to the concurrent economic revolution. In early modern times Western Europe experienced rapid growth in both commerce and industry. This economic advance led to technological innovations, and the latter in turn stimulated, and were stimulated by, science. Oceanic commerce created an enormous demand for shipbuilding and navigation. A new class of intelligent, mathematically trained craftsmen appeared for compass, map, and instrument making. Navigation schools were founded in Portugal, Spain, Holland, and France, and astronomy was studied seriously because of its obvious utilitarian value. Likewise, the needs of the mining industry engendered advances in power transmission and pumps. This proved to be the starting point of a new interest in mechanical and hydraulic principles. In the same manner, metallurgy was responsible for notable progress in chemistry. The expanding mining operations brought to light new ores and even new metals, like bismuth, zinc, and cobalt. Techniques for separating and handling these had to be found by analogy and corrected by painful experience. But in doing so, a general theory of chemistry began to take form, involving oxidations and reductions, distillations and amalgamations.

These achievements gave the scientists, or philosophers, a self-assurance and a confidence that they were the harbingers of a new age. As early as 1530 Jean Fernel, physician to the king of France, wrote:

This age of ours sees art and science gloriously re-risen, after twelve centuries of swoon. . . . This age need not, in any respect, despise itself and sigh for the knowledge of the Ancients. . . . Our age today is doing things of which antiquity did not dream. . . . Ocean has been crossed by the prowess of our navigators, and new islands found. The far recesses of India lie revealed. The continent of the West, the so-called New World, unknown to our forefathers, has in great part become known. . . . A new globe has been given us by the navigators of our time.[3]

In 1662 Charles II of England granted a charter for the establishment of "The Royal Society of London for Promoting Natural Knowledge." Its members, sensing the advantage of cooperation between technicians and scientists, encouraged and coordinated efforts in every occupation throughout the country to gather data that might advance scientific knowledge. "All Places and Corners are now busy and warm about this Work: and we may find many noble Rarities to be every Day given in [to the Society] not only by the Hands of learned and professed Philosophers; but from the Shops of *Mechanicks;* from the Voyages of *Merchants;* from the Ploughs of *Husbandmen;* from The Sports, The Fishponds, The Parks, The Gardens of Gentlemen. . . ."[4]

At first, science received much more from the mine and the workshop than they received from science. During this early period science was not an integral part of economic life and was utilized sparingly and sporadically. This was true even in the early phases of the Industrial Revolution in the late eighteenth and early nineteenth centuries. But by the end of the nineteenth century the situation changed basically. Science no longer was in a subsidiary, consultative position; it had begun to transform old industries and even to create entirely new ones.

It is understandable that the first major advance of modern science occurred in the field of astronomy which was closely related to geography and to navigation. It is also understandable that Italy was the scene of this advance, since Italy in the fifteenth century was the most advanced country of Europe, economically and culturally. Thus we find that the great Mikolaj Kopernik (1473–1543), who became famous under his Latinized name of Copernicus, left his native Poland to enter the university at Bologna. After six years of studies, he returned to Poland and began an active career in the church. But he continued to work on the problems of astronomy that he had been engaged in in Italy, particularly because there was a general interest at the time in devising a more accurate calendar. He took up the idea of some ancient philosophers that the sun rather than the earth was the center of the universe, and then demonstrated that this provided a simpler explanation of the movements of the heavenly bodies than did the traditional Ptolemaic system.

Copernicus printed a short abstract of his work in 1530, and the complete book, *De revolutionibus orbium coelestium,* was published in 1543, the year of his death. Although Copernicus was a mathematician and astronomer of repute, his hypothesis at first was disregarded. In stating that the earth rotated diurnally on its axis and annually around the sun, he was uttering heresy, for according to scripture Joshua had caused the sun to stand still in the heavens. Furthermore, his hypothesis was repugnant to common sense. If the earth revolved, would not its motion produce a mighty wind? And would not objects thrown upward lag behind the surface of the whirling globe? Copernicus' new astronomy made necessary a new physics. The need was met by a well-to-do Florentine, Galileo Galilei (1564–1642).

Galileo's approach was strictly empirical. Against the traditional dicta of Aristotle and the schoolmen, he pitted experimental and verifiable facts. He was primarily a physicist interested in solving problems of military and civil engineering by working out laws of terrestrial motion. He conducted further experiments in dynamics, in which he devised more refined means for measuring small intervals of time, found means of estimating air resistance, friction, and other impediments occurring in nature, and conceived of pure or absolute motion, and of force and velocity, in abstract mathematical terms.

Galileo's work in astronomy made a greater impression at the time, though it was not as original or basic. He made use of the telescope, which had just been invented in Holland, to see what actually was in the heavens. Even in these days of fabulous scientific discoveries, one can sense the melodrama of Galileo discovering a whole new world and appreciating the significance of what he observed.

That which will excite the greatest astonishment by far, and which indeed especially moved me to call the attention of all astronomers and philosophers is this, namely, that I have discovered four planets, neither known nor observed by any one of the astronomers before my time. . . . By the aid of a telescope anyone may behold this in a manner which so distinctly appeals to the senses that all the disputes which have tormented philosophers through so many ages are exploded at once by the irrefragable evidence of our eyes, and we are freed from wordy disputes upon this subject, for the Galaxy is nothing else but a mass of innumerable stars planted together in clusters. Upon whatever part of it you direct the telescope straightway a vast crowd of stars presents itself to view; many of them are tolerably large and extremely bright, but the number of small ones is quite beyond determination.[5]

Galileo was particularly impressed by the discovery that Jupiter had satellites, moons moving around it like the moon around the earth. All this evidence assured him of the validity of the Copernican theory. This struck a shattering and frightening blow at philosophy and theology. Galileo was condemned by the Inquisition and forced to an ostensible recantation. But the impact of his findings on thoughtful minds was overwhelming. Poets repeatedly compared him to Columbus and other discoverers.

> Yield, Vespucci, and let Columbus yield. Each of these
> Holds, it is true, his way through the unknown sea. . . .
> But you, Galileo, alone gave to the human race the sequence of stars,
> New constellations of heaven.[6]

John Donne expressed the unsettling and disturbing effect of the new astronomy when he wrote "'Tis all in peeces, all cohaerence gone."[7] Two intellectual leaders of this period, however, were not upset by the seeming anarchy. They were René Descartes (1596–1650) and Francis Bacon, scientific thinkers who pointed out the potentialities of science and raised it to a status in polite circles comparable to that of literature. They were essentially prophets and publicists—men who had seen a vision of the possibilities of the new discipline and who made it their business to inform the world.

Descartes and Bacon approached problems in quite different fashions. Descartes was a great mathematician, the inventor of analytic geometry. In a sense it may be said that he unified the geometry received from the Greeks with the algebra learned from the Moslems. Henceforth it was possible to explain geometry algebraically and to develop new types of mathematics. Descartes was so carried away by the possibilities of the mathematical method that he made it the basis of his entire philosophy. He insisted that the only true way of knowing was by mathematical reasoning and abstraction. Experimentation was for him a mere auxiliary to deductive thought. Clear thinking, he believed, could discover anything that was rationally knowable.

Bacon, by contrast, employed the inductive method, which begins with facts and then proceeds to general principles. To arrive at the underlying causes, said Bacon, we must study the natural history of the phenomena, collect and tabulate all observations that bear on them, notice which phenomena are related in such a way as to vary together, and then, by a merely mechanical process of exclusion, discover the cause of a given phenomenon. As a corrective to medieval scholastic methods, Bacon's work was of the greatest value in the history of thought. It should be noted, however, that scientific discovery is seldom or never made by the pure Baconian method. Too many phenomena exist for any subject to be studied successfully without the aid of hypothesis conceived by scientific imagination. Facts are collected to prove or disprove the consequences deduced from the hypothesis, and thus the number of facts to be examined becomes manageable.

To derive maximum benefit from science, Bacon urged the founding of institutes to further scientific research. In fact, as early as 1560 there had been formed in Naples the *Accademia Secretorum Naturae.* In 1603 the *Accademia dei Lincei* appeared in Rome, and in 1661 the *Accademia del Cimento* in Florence. Meanwhile in England a scientific society that had been meeting sporadically under the name Philosophical or Invisible College was incorporated in 1662 as the Royal Society. In France a corresponding *Académie des Sciences* was founded by Louis XIV in 1666, and similar institutions followed in other lands. These bodies facilitated the growth of science, especially since most of them soon issued periodic publications which superseded the older method of correspondence between individuals.

By far the most outstanding figure of this early stage of science was Sir Isaac Newton (1642–1727). His contributions mark him as one of the very greatest figures in science, comparable to Euclid and Einstein. In mathematics Newton invented the infinitesimal calculus, established the binomial theorem, developed much of the theory of equations, and introduced literal indices. In mathematical physics he calculated tables by which the future position of the moon among the stars could be predicted—an achievement of the utmost value in navigation. He created hydrodynamics, including the theory of the propagation of waves, and made many improvements in hydrostatics. In optics he made important contributions toward the understanding of light beams, refraction of light, and the phenomenon of color. But it was in the field of physics that Newton did his most significant research. Here he built on Galileo, putting the grand copestone on the latter's work. Galileo had concerned himself largely with terrestrial motion; Newton discovered the laws pertaining to the universe itself.

Galileo's finding that moving bodies move uniformly in a straight line unless deflected by a definite force raised the question of why the planets, instead of flying off in straight lines, tend to fall toward the sun—the result being their elliptical orbits—and why the moon similarly tends to fall toward the earth.

Newton's answer was his law of gravitation, which he presented with a wealth of mathematical evidence in his famous book, *Mathematical Principles of Natural Philosophy* (1687), commonly called, after its Latin title, the *Principia.* According to this law, "every particle of matter in the universe attracts every other particle with a force varying inversely as the square of the distance between them and directly proportional to the product of their masses."

Here was a sensational and revolutionary explanation that tore the veils from the heavens. Newton had discovered a fundamental, cosmic law, susceptible of mathematical proof and applicable to the minutest object as to the universe at large. Nature indeed appeared to be a gigantic mechanical contrivance, operating according to certain natural laws that could be ascertained by observation, experiment, measurement, and calculation. All branches of human knowledge seemed to be reducible to a few, simple, uniform laws that rational man could discover. Thus the analytical method of Newtonian physics now began to be applied to the entire field of thought and knowledge, to human society as well as to the physical universe. As Voltaire put it, "It would be very singular that all nature, all the planets, should obey eternal laws, and that there should be a little animal, five feet high, who, in contempt of these laws, could act as he pleased, solely according to his caprice."[8] The search for these eternal laws determining human affairs is the essence of the so-called Enlightenment that preceded the French Revolution.

II. COURSE OF THE SCIENTIFIC REVOLUTION

No scientific discoveries comparable to those of the seventeenth century were made in the early eighteenth, the main interest being in the formulation of the social, political, and economic theories that comprised the Enlightenment. But noteworthy results were obtained in certain fields of science by the application of the new methodology of empirical research.

Experimentation was carried on, for example, with static electricity, and in 1746 two professors of the University of Leyden invented the so-called Leyden jar for the storage and sudden discharge of electric energy. Benjamin Franklin sensed the analogy between the electric spark in the jar and the lightning in the sky, and proved it with his kite experiment. In his typically practical manner Franklin in 1753 evolved the lightning conductor to prevent lightning strikes, which were particularly heavy and costly in the New World. He went further and evolved the first comprehensive theory of electricity, still used in practical circuitry today.

The early eighteenth century also witnessed a tremendous popular interest in nature, or, as it was called, natural history. Nature was regarded almost as a deity, as something of unlimited interest that could be forever studied and forever yield moral and factual instruction. Visible evidence of the natural history mania was to be found in the natural history cabinets that were assembled by all who could afford the investment of time and money. This collecting and cataloguing led to the more basic formulations of systematic botany and zoology. A pioneer in these fields was John Ray (1627–1705), author of a *History of Plants,* a *History of Insects,* and *Synopses* of animals, birds, reptiles, and fishes. In systematic botany Ray was followed by the Swedish professor Linnaeus (Carl von Linné, 1707–1778), who worked out the first acceptable method of classifying plants and who also divided animals into such classes as mammals, birds, fish, and insects. Another outstanding figure in natural history was the French nobleman Georges Louis Le Clerc, Comte de Buffon (1707–1788). In 1739 he was made keeper of the Jardin du Roi, now Jardin des Plantes, and he turned it into a great research institute where many of the famous scientists of France received their inspiration and training. He also wrote the monumental thirty-six-volume *Histoire Naturelle,* in which he sought to codify all available information on the natural sciences.

About this time also, great strides forward were being made in geography. Outstanding was the work of Captain James Cook, who was sent out in 1768 to observe a transit of Venus at Tahiti in the South Pacific. Cook's later voyages, undertaken to find an antarctic continent, failed in the object, but gave other information of scientific value, as well as new knowledge of the coasts of Australia, New Zealand, and the Pacific Ocean. It might be noted that in his first voyage Captain Cook lost over a third of his men to disease, mostly scurvy. By the time of his later voyages medical knowledge had advanced, so that citrus fruits were added to the sailors' diet and the dread scourge ended.

Revolution in Chemistry, 1770–1850

The science that made the most progress during the first half of the nineteenth century was chemistry—partly because of its close association with the textile industry, which experienced such rapid growth during those decades. Chemistry dates back to the earliest stages of human civilization, to the rise of the arts of cooking and metal working, the collection of medicinal plants and extraction of drugs. From the beginning it was sidetracked by the search for means to transmute cheap metals into gold and to discover an *elixir vitae* that would cure all human ills. If these attempts were doomed to failure, they nonetheless disclosed many chemical substances and reactions.

During the eighteenth century most attention was concentrated on the problem of combustion—what happened to materials when they burned? Since they disappeared in smoke and flame and left ash, it was concluded that in every case something escaped during the process of burning. This something, for long called sulphur, was given the name of phlogiston, or the principal of fire. This concept dominated chemical thought until the study of gases revealed that air was a much more complex substance than hitherto imagined. As early as 1755, Joseph Black of Edinburgh succeeded in isolating carbon dioxide by heating limestone. Then in 1781 Henry Cavendish demonstrated that water is composed of two parts hydrogen to one part oxygen. Important advances were next made by Joseph Priestly (1733–1804), who isolated oxygen and demonstrated that it was this element that was used up in burning and breathing. He further showed that in sunlight green plants produced oxygen from the carbon dioxide that they absorbed. Thus he solved the problem of the carbon cycle created by the balance of oxygen-producing plants and carbon dioxide-producing animals.

The full implications of this work with gases were brought out by the great chemist, Antoine Laurent Lavoisier (1743–1794), who fell victim to the guillotine during the French Revolution. Lavoisier's classic experiment with oxidation is very simple. He heated mercury in a sealed jar with air, and found that he obtained mercuric oxide, and that the volume of the air had been reduced by a fifth, that is, by its oxygen component. Lavoisier then heated the mercuric oxide, and obtained once again mercury plus oxygen. Having weighed all his substances most carefully, he found that the weight lost or gained after each step was the addition or subtraction of oxygen in the burning process. Thus he was able to discard the traditional phlogiston theory and replace it with his famous principle of balance, which reduced all the previously chaotic phenomena of chemistry into a law of combination of elements.

We may lay it down as an incontestable axiom, that, in all the operations of art and nature, nothing is created; an equal quantity of matter exists both before and after the experiment; the quality and quantity of the elements remain precisely the same; and nothing takes place beyond changes and modifications in the combination of these elements.[9]

Another important advance in the nineteenth century was the advent of organic chemistry. Originally chemists believed that organic compounds—the hydrocarbons produced by living organisms—were somehow controlled by a "vital force." But this notion was dropped as chemists discovered that organic compounds could be synthesized. One of the first successes was achieved in 1828 by Friedrich Wöhler, who produced the organic substance urea found in urine. He did this from inorganic compounds by ordinary chemical processes and without the means of a kidney. His friend Justus von Liebig (1803–1873) did invaluable work in showing that the food that plants draw from the ground consists of nitrogen, phosphates, and salts. Thus he was able to prepare chemical compounds with which he enriched a waste patch and made it into a fertile garden. The way was clear for the growth of the great fertilizer industry.

Another major contribution to industry was made by the English chemist W. H. Perkin (1838–1907). While seeking a substitute for quinine, he accidentally discovered in 1856 the first artificial aniline dye, magenta. His discovery was neglected in Britain, where chemistry was still the pursuit of only a few amateurs and the chemical industry boasted of being "practical." But the more scientifically minded directors of German industry saw that Perkin's discovery could provide a valuable outlet for the hitherto waste products of coal tar from the gas industry. The research they subsidized led to the preparation of numerous synthetic dyes, which yielded enormous profits. By the time of World War I the Germans had the most advanced chemical industry in the world and a virtual monopoly of synthetic dyes.

Equally significant for industry was the work of the great French chemist Louis Pasteur (1822–1895). While at the University of Lille, he was called upon to help local distillers who were having trouble extracting alcohol from beets—the pulp sometimes unaccountably spoiled. Finding no chemical explanation, Pasteur examined the mash with a microscope and found it swarming with strange, elongated growths in contrast to the spherical globules in unspoiled mash. By laboratory demonstration he showed how these harmful growths could be controlled and prevented from interfering with fermentation. This experience led Pasteur to further experiments that enabled him to disprove the traditional theory of spontaneous generation of life. In its place he propounded the now accepted doctrine of biogenesis—that life can come only from life. To demonstrate this he showed that by excluding the invisible microbes of the air, it is possible to keep animal and vegetable substances from putrefying. This later became the basis of the great canning industry. Pasteur also popularized the germ theory of disease, which led to the adoption of sanitary precautions that made possible the control of age-old scourges—typhoid, diphtheria, cholera, the plague, and malaria. These medical advances had profound repercussions, leading to a rapid increase of population, first in Europe and then throughout the world.

Revolution in Biology, 1850–1914

As Isaac Newton dominated seventeenth century science with his discovery of the laws governing the bodies of the universe, so Charles Darwin (1809–1882) dominated nineteenth, for he discovered the laws governing the evolution of man himself.

The concept of evolution, however, was by no means new with Darwin: it had been propounded and applied in various fields of science. Jean de Lamarck (1744–1829) had earlier challenged the traditional notion of the immutable fixity of species created at one time and existing ever since. Instead he envisioned a comprehensive evolution from worm to man, and sought to explain the process of evolution with the theory of acquired characteristics. Horses acquired their speedy legs from the need to run fast, giraffes their long necks from the need to feed on tall branches. And any such body changes are handed on by hereditary processes to be the starting point for the next generation.

Then came Charles Lyell with his classic three-volume *Principles of Geology* (1830–1833), which popularized the "uniformitarian" or evolutionary theory of the formation of the earth's surface. Hitherto it had been believed that the surface had been formed by past catastrophes such as volcanoes, earthquakes, and floods. The existence of seashells in high mountainous regions was conveniently attributed to Noah's flood. Lyell, by contrast, held that the present surface of the earth is the product of the operation during countless millennia of geologic forces such as glaciation, wind and water erosion, and freezing and thawing.

The concept of evolution was prominent at this time in the social sciences as well as the physical. From the 1840's, Karl Marx was writing that all social institutions were in constant process of change. Since the beginning of human history one type of society had given way to another—primitive tribalism to ancient slavery to feudal serfdom, to modern capitalism and, as he confidently predicted, to the socialism of the future. Much more influential was the all-embracing doctrine of evolution propounded by Herbert Spencer (1820–1903). He applied his doctrine to all things, material, biological, cultural, and social. In his *Progress, its Law and Cause,* published in 1857, Spencer wrote, "Whether it be in the development of Society, of Government, of Manufactures, of Commerce, of Language, Literature, Science, Art, this same evolution of the simple into the complex, through successive differentiations, holds throughout."[10]

This was the atmosphere in which Darwin worked out his epoch-making doctrine of evolution—that animal and vegetable species in their present diverse forms are not immutably fixed as results of separate special acts of creation but are different and changing natural outcomes of a common original source. Darwin believed that the chief manner in which variation took place was by "natural selection." He defined this process as follows:

As many more individuals of each species are born than can possibly survive, and as, consequently, there is a frequently recurring struggle for existence, it follows that any being, if it vary however slightly in any manner profitable to itself, under the complex and sometimes varying conditions of life, will have a better chance of surviving, and thus be *naturally selected*. From the strong principle of inheritance, any selected variety will tend to propagate its new and modified form.[11]

It may be hard to conceive of all the variety in nature as being the product of what appears to be such an inordinately slow process of change as that afforded by "natural selection." Yet statistical calculations show that even if a mutation resulted in only one per cent better chance of survival, it would establish itself in half the individuals of a species in a hundred generations. In other words, if a hundred and one individuals with this mutation survived for every hundred without it, it would spread through the species in what is, biologically speaking, a short time.

Darwin's theories have been modified in details on the basis of later research, but virtually all scientists now accept the essentials of the doctrine. During his lifetime, however, there was bitter opposition in certain quarters, particularly amongst the churchmen. This was understandable, because just as the Copernican system of astronomy had deposed the earth from its central place in the universe, so Darwinism seemed to dethrone man from his central place in the history of the earth. Such was the natural conclusion of the churchmen when Darwin published another book, *The Descent of Man,* in 1871. In this work he marshaled the evidence that man is related to all animal life, and concluded that "He who is not content to look, like a savage, at the phenomena of nature as disconnected, cannot any longer believe that man is the work of a separate act of creation."[12] Darwin, in other words, was denying the act of divine creation. He was denounced, with less than fairness, for undermining human dignity, morality, and religion, and for saying that men came from monkeys. Benjamin Diraeli solemnly declared that if it were a choice between apes and angels, he was on the side of the angels.

Despite this hostile reception in religious and other circles, Darwinism had profound repercussions upon Western society. The basic reason is that its emphasis on survival of the fittest and struggle for survival fitted in admirably with the temper of the times. In politics, for example, this was the period when Bismarck was unifying Germany by blood and iron. His nationalistic admirers in all countries believed that Darwinism offered them support and justification. They held that in politics, as in nature, the strongest are victorious, and that warlike qualities decide who will win in the international "struggle for survival." In economic life this was the period of free enterprise and rugged individualism. The upper and middle classes, comfortable and contented, stoutly opposed any state intervention for the promotion of greater social equality. They argued that they deserved their blessings and prosperity because they had proven themselves "fitter" than the shiftless poor, and, furthermore, the absorption of smaller concerns by big business was a part of the "struggle for survival." The late nineteenth century was also the golden age of colonial expansion, and Darwinism was used to justify imperialism. It was argued that colonies were necessary for the prosperity and survival of a Great Power, and also that native peoples, judged in terms of worldly success, were weak, inferior, and in need of the protection and guidance of the superior and stronger Europeans.

This application of Darwin's theories to the social scene is known as Social Darwinism. Darwin himself had never dreamt, let alone intended, that his findings would be exploited in this fashion. But the fact remains that they were, and the reason is that they seemed to offer scientific buttressing to the materialism, or *Realpolitik,* that came over Europe at this time from other causes. Darwinism, in short, fitted in conveniently with Kipling's dictum

> That they should take who have the power
> And they should keep who can.

Another English writer, Hilaire Belloc, expressed the same sentiment in reference to the position of the Europeans in Africa:

> Whatever happens we have got
> The Maxim gun, and they have not.

III. SIGNIFICANCE OF THE SCIENTIFIC REVOLUTION

As the nineteenth century passed, science became an increasingly important part of Western society. At the beginning of the century science still was on the periphery of economic and social life. But by the end it was making basic contributions to the old-established industries, it was creating entirely new industries, and it was affecting profoundly the way of thinking as well as the way of living of Western man. Furthermore, this metamorphosis wrought by the scientific revolution affected the entire world in myriad ways, direct and indirect. It made Europe's hegemony over the globe technologically possible, and it determined to a large extent the nature and effects of this hegemony. Also it provided the basis for the West's intellectual predominance in the nineteenth century. European art or religion or philosophy did not greatly affect non-Western peoples because they had made comparable contributions in these fields. But there was no such parity in science and technology. Only the West had mastered the secrets of nature and had exploited them for the material advancement of mankind. This was an undeniable and persuasive fact. Non-Westerners no longer looked down upon Europeans as uncouth barbarians who happened to have a certain superiority in sailing ships and firearms. Reluctantly they recognized the significance of Europe's scientific revolution. And today the primary aim of former colonial peoples is to experience for themselves this unique revolution which they missed because of fortuitous historical circumstances. Even before 1914 a native nationalist leader in far-off Uzbekistan exhorted his people to turn to science as the only means for regaining their freedom.

Science is the cause of the flourishing of a government. Science is the cause of the progress of a people. Science is that very potent means, the existence of which led the savage Americans to their present high status and power and whose . . . absence brought the Persians to their present lowly state and humiliation. Science is the means which made the British masters of India, Egypt, Baluchistan and parts of Arabia, and the Russians the rulers of the Tatar, Kirghiz, Turkestan and Caucasian Moslems. . . .

If you study contemporary science, you will be in a position to construct telegraphs, build railroads, transport hundreds of thousands of troops from one end of the earth to the other in twenty days. . . . to comprehend the secret meaning of the Koran, to prepare rifles and cannon for the defense of Islam, to liberate the fatherland from the hands of the foreigners . . . to free our nation from the yoke of the infidel and to restore Islam to its earlier heights.[13]

The distinguished British historian Herbert Butterfield has summarized this global significance of the scientific revolution as follows:

There does not seem to be any sign that the ancient world, before its heritage had been dispersed, was moving towards anything like the scientific revolution, or that the Byzantine Empire, in spite of the continuity of its classical tradition, would ever have taken hold of ancient thought and so remoulded it by a great transforming power. The scientific revolution, we must regard, therefore, as a creative product of the West. . . . And when we speak of Western civilization being carried to an oriental country like Japan in recent generations, we do not mean Graeco-Roman philosophy and humanist ideals, we do not mean the Christianising of Japan, we mean the science, the modes of thought and all that apparatus of civilisation which were beginning to change the face of the West in the latter half of the seventeenth century.[14]

IV. ROOTS OF THE INDUSTRIAL REVOLUTION

The material culture of mankind has changed more in the past two hundred years than it did in the preceding five thousand. In the eighteenth century man was living in essentially the same manner as the ancient Egyptians and Mesopotamians. He was still using the same materials to erect his buildings, the same animals to transport himself and his belongings, the same sails and oars to propel his ships, the same textiles to fashion his clothes, and the same candles and torches to provide light. But today metals and plastics supplement stone and wood; the railroad, the automobile, and the airplane have replaced the oxen, the horse, and the donkey; steam, diesel, and atom power drive ships in place of wind and manpower; a host of synthetic fabrics compete with the traditional cottons, woolens, and linens; and electricity has eclipsed the candle and has become a source of power available for a multitude of duties at the flick of a switch.

The origins of this epochal transformation are to be found partly in the scientific revolution noted in the preceding chapter, and partly in the so-called Industrial Revolution. The reason for the qualifying "so-called" is that there has been much uneasiness over the use of the term *Industrial Revolution*. It has been pointed out that, in certain respects, the Industrial Revolution had gotten under way before the eighteenth century, and that, for all practical purposes, it has continued to the present day. Obviously, then, this was not a revolution in the sense of a spectacular change that began and ended suddenly.

Yet the fact remains that during the 1780's a breakthrough did occur that was of prime importance for world history because it provided the economic and military basis for Europe's world hegemony in the nineteenth century, as well as the main goal for the underdeveloped world in the twentieth century. The aim of every new country today, having successfully "taken off" in the sense of independent political existence, is likewise to "take off" into a corresponding independent economic existence.

The first question that arises in considering the Industrial Revolution has to do with its timing. Why did it occur in the late eighteenth century rather than a hundred or a thousand years earlier? The answer is to be found in large part in the remarkable economic growth of Europe following the great expansion overseas. This growth, which we noted earlier, was so pronounced that it is commonly referred to as the Commercial Revolution.

The Commercial Revolution was characterized in the first place by a change in the articles of world trade. Before the sixteenth century the most important items were spices from East to West, and bullion in the opposite direction. But gradually new overseas products became staples of consumption in Europe and grew in commercial importance. These included new beverages (cocoa, tea, and coffee), new dyes (indigo, cochineal, and brazilwood), new flavors (allspice and vanilla), and new foodstuffs (guinea fowl and turkeys, and a greatly increased supply of Newfoundland cod). The other main feature of the Commercial Revolution was the marked increase in the volume of trade, the colonies accounting for a larger and larger portion of it. In 1698, for example, about 15 per cent of England's seaborne trade was with her colonies, but by 1775 this figure had risen to 33 per cent. Furthermore, the re-export of colonial goods was responsible for much of the increase of England's trade with other European countries.

This Commercial Revolution contributed to the Industrial Revolution in several important respects. First, it provided large and expanding markets for European industries, particularly those producing textiles, firearms, hardware, ships, and ships accessories, including lumber, rope, sails, anchors, pulleys, and nautical instruments. To meet the demands of these new markets, industries had to improve their organization and technology. A good example is afforded by the nail industry of the English Midlands. In response to the mounting need for nails in the colonies, it developed rolling and slitting mills that mechanized and increased output. The industry also evolved a putting-out system in which nail ironmongers, or ironmasters, sent out bundles of nailrod to be worked up by nailers in their homes and returned for sale. By 1775, the industry was using 10,000 tons of iron annually, and employing some 10,000 people.

The putting-out system employed by the nail industry, as well as other industries, was fundamentally different from the traditional craft guild arrangement in which the same man produced a commodity and sold it to the consumer at a fixed profit. Now a middleman—the capitalist entrepreneur—intervened between the producer and the consumer. He employed his capital to buy raw material which he "put out" to be processed on a piece-rate basis by artisans who were not guild members. Then he picked up the finished product and sold it to the consumer for as much profit as possible. Producers and consumers were now separated by the new entrepreneur, whose objective—in contrast to the fixed prices and profits of the guilds—was to buy cheap, sell dear, and make the maximum profit. It might be added that the putting-out system is also sometimes referred to as the domestic system, the reason being that the artisans normally did the piece work in their own homes, in contrast to the guildsmen who worked in the master's shop.

In any case, the significance of this putting-out system is that it was not bound by the innumerable guild restrictions and thus made possible a great increase in industrial output. Some of the entrepreneurs found it convenient and profitable to bring their craftsmen together under one roof and provide them with tools as well as raw materials. Once this step was taken, only labor-saving power machinery was needed to launch the Industrial Revolution.

The Commercial Revolution also contributed the large amounts of capital necessary to finance the construction of factories and machines for the Industrial Revolution. The capital, in the form of profits, poured into Europe from all parts of the world. In Siberia, the Russians sold iron pots to the natives in return for enough pelts to fill the pots. In North America, the price the Hudson's Bay Company traders charged the Indians for a rifle was a pile of beaver skins its height. In Mexico and Peru, the Spaniards used native labor to dig out vast stores of silver. Africa also yielded great profits for European adventurers in the form of the hundreds of thousands of slaves seized for labor in New World plantations. More profitable than the slave trade itself were the sugar plantations worked by slave labor. The West Indian sugar planters were the tycoons of the period, rivaled only by the "nabobs" who had made their fortunes in India. These individuals were spectacular in their lavish expenditures, but more significant in the long run were the lucrative earnings of the several East India Companies, West India Companies, Levant Companies, Africa Companies, and assorted others, including the Muscovy Company, the Hudson's Bay Company, and the various land settlement companies in the Americas.

It was this same Commercial Revolution that produced the dynamic and expansive type of society known as capitalism, where "the desire for profits is the driving motive and . . . large accumulations of capital are employed to make profits by various elaborate and often indirect methods."[15] During the Middle Ages it had been considered wrong for a man to try to earn more money than was necessary to keep him comfortably in the station of life to which he was born. But with the coming of the Commercial Revolution, the acquisitive spirit manifested itself in all fields of economic enterprise. In commerce the merchant guilds with their fixed prices and fixed profits were replaced by the joint stock companies seeking to make the highest profit possible for their shareholders. In industry the craft guilds with their numerous regulations concerning quality and mode of production and profits were swept away by the entrepreneurs with their putting-out system. In finance the injunctions of the medieval church against usury were ignored by large banking houses which loaned money, sold bills of exchange, and offered numerous other financial services.

All these manifestations were nascent in the late Middle Ages, but the Commercial Revolution stimulated them immensely. After 1500 the institutions and spirit of capitalism developed rapidly. Capitalism in those centuries was, of course, quite different from the capitalism of today. Because commercial enterprise was organized to a greater degree along capitalist lines than either industry or agriculture, the earlier form is commonly known as commercial capitalism. But whatever name is given to the economic system prevailing in Europe between the sixteenth and eighteenth centuries, the important point is that it was dynamic and expansive. The capitalist, in his increasing drive for profits, extended his operations to the four corners of the globe. In doing so he contributed in many ways to the coming of the Industrial Revolution and also to the establishment of European economic hegemony over the world.

The Industrial Revolution got under way first in England. This is a historical fact of the utmost significance, for it explains in large part England's primary role in world affairs in the nineteenth century. One reason for her head start was her flourishing commerce, especially after the great colonial acquisitions in 1763. Britain's trade also forged ahead during the French Revolutionary and Napoleonic wars when Continental rivals were blockaded by the English fleets.

Another important advantage enjoyed by Britain is that she had taken an early lead in the basic coal and iron industries. Because her forest reserves were being depleted, Britain early began using coal for fuel and for smelting iron. By the time of the French Revolution in 1789, Britain was producing about 10 million tons of coal per year, while France was producing 700,000 tons. England also pioneered in the development of the blast furnace which, in contrast to the old forges, could mass-produce iron. In 1780 Britain's iron output had been a third that of France; by 1840, it was three times more. All this meant that Britain was pushing ahead in the production of goods of mass consumption for which there was a large and steady demand, whereas France specialized more in luxury commodities of limited and fluctuating demand.

England also had more fluid capital available for the financing of the Industrial Revolution. More profits from commerce poured into England than into any other country. English court and military expenditures were less than French, so that English taxation was lighter and English government finances were in better condition. Futhermore, banking developed earlier and more efficiently in England, providing pooled funds for individual and corporate enterprise. By the end of the seventeenth century, London was competing with Amsterdam as the money-lending center of the world.

Noteworthy also is the impressive concentration of entrepreneurial talent in England. This is to be explained in part by the outstanding contributions of Nonconformists like the Darbys in the iron industry, Cookworthy in pottery, the Brights in cotton milling and in politics, and Dalton and Eddington in science. Freedom from convention and stress on personal responsibility produced a disproportionate quota of experimenters and inventors among the Nonconformists, while their frugality led them to plow profits back into business rather than to squander for luxurious living. The influence of the Nonconformists in England was enhanced by the influx of coreligionists from the continent. With the revocation of the Edict of Nantes in 1685, for example, France lost considerable entrepreneurial talent to England, especially in the textile industry.

Britain also had the advantage of a mobile and plentiful supply of labor made available by the earlier disintegration of the guilds and by the enclosing of the traditional strips of farmland. The passing of the guilds, with their manifold restrictions, made it easier to introduce both the putting-out system and the factories with power machinery. The land enclosures began in the sixteenth century and continued for three centuries, reaching their height in the late eighteenth and early nineteenth centuries. The earlier enclosures were impelled by the rising price of wool, so that the land was used mostly for grazing. In the later period the need to grow food-stuffs for the burgeoning cities was more important, so the enclosed land was cultivated according to the most up-to-date and efficient methods. These included crop rotation in place of the wasteful old system of allowing fields to lie fallow, development of superior seeds, improvement of cattle by scientific breeding, and development of some agricultural machinery, including a horse-driven hoeing machine and an automatic drill for planting seeds.

These innovations could not have been effected under the strip system of farming inherited from the Middle Ages. Now, with the enclosures, it was possible to implement them, and it was very profitable to do so for the market for agricultural products was expanding. The process of enclosing the land was unsettling and unpleasant, but so far as the Industrial Revolution was concerned it fulfilled two essential functions—it provided labor for the factories and food for the cities. For this reason the enclosures may be considered a prerequisite to England's industrial supremacy in the nineteenth century. Enclosures did occur in certain other European countries, but to a much lesser extent.

V. COURSE OF THE INDUSTRIAL REVOLUTION

The Industrial Revolution cannot be attributed merely to the genius of a small group of inventors. Genius doubtless played a part, but more significant was the combination of favorable forces operating in late eighteenth century England. Inventors seldom invent except under the stimulus of strong demand. Many of the principles on which the new inventions were based were known centuries before the Industrial Revolution, but they were not applied to industry because the incentive was lacking. This was the case, for example, with steam power. It was known, and even applied, in Hellenistic Egypt, but merely to open and close temple doors. In England, however, a new source of power was urgently needed to pump water out of mines and to turn the wheels of the new machinery. The result was a series of inventions and improvements until finally a commercially feasible steam engine was developed.

Industrial Revolution: First Stage, 1770–1870

This pattern of demand leading to invention is plainly evident in the development of the cotton industry. It was the first to be mechanized because cotton goods, which were originally imported from India, had become exceedingly popular with the British public. In fact, they were used so widely that the old and powerful woolen interests secured the passage of a law in 1700 prohibiting the importation of cotton cloth or goods. The law, however, did not ban the manufacture of cotton cloth. This created a unique opportunity for local industry, and enterprising middlemen soon were exploiting it to the hilt. The problem was how to speed up the spinning and weaving sufficiently to meet the demand of the large and protected home market. In 1754 there was founded in London the Society for the Encouragement of Arts, Manufacture and Commerce, and this society gave money, medals, and other rewards for specified achievements. In 1760, for example, it offered a prize for a spinning machine, explaining that "manufacturers of woolen, linen, and cotton find it extremely difficult in the summer season, when the spinners are at harvest work, to procure a sufficient number of hands."[16]

These favorable circumstances induced a series of inventions that made possible the complete mechanization of the cotton industry by 1830. Outstanding were Richard Arkwright's water frame (1769), which spun fine strong yarn between rollers, James Hargreaves spinning jenny (1770), on which one person could spin eight, then sixteen, and finally over a hundred threads of yarn at once, and Samuel Crompton's spinning mule (1779), so called because it combined features of the water frame and of the jenny. All these new spinning machines soon were producing far more thread than could be handled by the weavers. A clergyman, Edmund Cartwright, sought to redress the balance by patenting in 1785 a power loom operated first by horses and after 1789 by steam. By the 1820's the power loom had largely supplanted the handweavers in the cotton industry.

Just as inventions in spinning led to balancing inventions in weaving, so inventions in one industry stimulated balancing inventions in others. The new cotton machines created a demand for more plentiful and reliable power than that provided by the traditional waterwheels and horses. A primitive steam engine had been built by Thomas Newcomen about 1702, and was widely used to pump water out of coal mines. But it consumed so much fuel in proportion to power delivered that it was economically feasible only in the coal fields themselves. In 1763 James Watt, a technician at the University of Glasgow, began to make improvements on Newcomen's engine. He formed a business partnership with a manufacturer, Matthew Boulton, who financed the rather costly experiments and preliminary models. The enterprise proved eminently successful, and by 1800, when Watt's basic patent expired, some 500 Boulton and Watt engines were in service. Thirty-eight per cent were engaged in pumping water, and the remainder in supplying rotary power for textile mills, iron furnaces, flour mills, and other industries.

The historical significance of the steam engine can scarcely be exaggerated. It provided a means for harnessing and utilizing heat energy to furnish driving power for machines. Thus, it ended man's age-old dependance on animal, wind, and water power. A vast new source of energy now was available, and before long man was also to tap the other fossil fuels locked up in the earth—namely, oil and gas. In this manner began the trend that has led to the present situation in which Western Europe has 11.5, and North America has 29, times as much energy available per capita as Asia.

The new cotton machines and steam engines required an increased supply of iron, steel, and coal—the need was met by a series of improvements in mining and metallurgy. Outstanding were Abraham Darby's reduction of coal to coke, Henry Cort's "puddling" process for removing impurities from smelted iron, and Sir Humphry Davy's saftey lamp for use in mines. Thus Britain was producing by 1800 more coal and iron than the rest of the world together. More specifically, Britain's coal output rose from 6 million tons in 1770 to 12 million tons in 1800 to 57 million tons in 1861. Likewise, her iron output increased from 50,000 tons in 1770 to 130,000 tons in 1800 to 3,800,000 tons in 1861. Iron had become sufficiently plentiful and cheap to be used for general construction purposes, and man had entered the Age of Iron as well as the Age of Steam.

The expansion of the textile, mining, and metallurgical industries created a need for improved transportation facilities to move the bulky shipments of coal and ore. The first significant step in this direction was taken in 1761, when the Duke of Bridgewater built a seven-mile canal between Manchester and the coal mines at Worsley. The price of coal in Manchester fell by half, and the duke extended his canal to the Mersey, offering rates one-sixth those charged by land carriers. These spectacular results generated a canal-building fever that endowed England with 2,500 miles of canals by 1830.

The canal era was paralleled by a great period of road building. After 1750 a group of road engineers—John Metcalf, Thomas Telford, and John McAdam—evolved methods of building hard-surfaced roads that would bear traffic all through the year. Travel by coach increased from four miles an hour to six, eight, or even ten. Travel by night also became possible, so that the journey from Edinburgh to London, which had once taken fourteen days, now required only forty-four hours.

After 1830 both roads and waterways were challenged by the railroad. The chief figure here was a mining engineer, George Stephenson, who first used an engine to pull coal trucks from a mine to the River Tyne. In 1830 his *Rocket* pulled a train thirty-one miles from Liverpool to Manchester at an average speed of fourteen miles per hour. Within a few years the railroad dominated long-distance traffic, being able to move passengers and freight faster and cheaper than was possible on roads or canals. By 1838 Britain had 500 miles of railroad; by 1850, 6,600; and by 1870, 15,500.

The steam engine was applied also to water transportation. The first commercially successful steamship was built by an American, Robert Fulton, who went to England to study painting but turned to engineering after meeting James Watt. In 1807 he launched his *Clermont* on the Hudson River. Other inventors followed Fulton's example, notably Henry Bell of Glasgow, who laid the foundations of Scottish shipbuilding industry on the banks of the river Clyde. The early steamships were used only for river and coastal runs, but in 1833 the *Royal William* steamed from Nova Scotia to England. Five years later the *Sirius* and the *Great Western* crossed the Atlantic in the opposite direction, taking 16½ and 13½ days respectively, or about half the time required by the fastest sailships. In 1840 Samuel Cunard established a regular transatlantic service, announcing beforehand dates of arrival and departure. By 1850 the steamship had bested the sailship in carrying passengers and mails, and was beginning to compete successfully for freight traffic.

The Industrial Revolution produced a revolution in communication as well as transportation. Hitherto a message could be sent to a distant place only by wagon, postrider, or boat. But in the middle of the nineteenth century the electric telegraph was invented, the work chiefly of an Englishman, Charles Wheatstone, and of two Americans, Samuel F. B. Morse and Alfred Vail. In 1866 a transatlantic cable was laid, establishing instant communication between the Old and New Worlds.

Man thus conquered both time and space. Since time immemorial he had defined distances between places as involving so many hours travel by wagon, by horse, or by sailboat. But now he strode over the earth in seven-league boots. He could cross oceans and continents by steamship and railroad, and he could communicate with fellow-beings all over the world by telegraph. These achievements, and the others that enabled man to harness the energy in coal, to produce iron cheaply, and to spin one hundred threads of yarn at one time—all suggest the impact and significance of this first stage of the Industrial Revolution.

Industrial Revolution: Second Stage, 1870–1914

The Industrial Revolution which got under way in the late eighteenth century has continued steadily and relentlessly to the present day. Hence it is essentially artificial to divide its evolution into various periods. Yet a case can be made for considering 1870 as a transition date. It was about that time that two important developments occurred—science began to affect industry significantly, and mass-production techniques were perfected and applied.

We noted in the preceding chapter that science, at the outset, had little effect upon industry. Very few of the inventions that we have noted thus far in the textile, mining, metallurgical, and transportation industries were the work of scientists. Rather they were effected mostly by talented mechanics who responded to extraordinary economic incentives. After 1870, however, science began to play a more important role. Gradually it became an integral part of the operations of all large industries. The laboratories of industrial research, equipped with expensive apparatus and staffed by trained scientists who carried on systematic research on designated problems, supplanted the garrets or workshops of lone inventors. Whereas inventions previously were the result of individual response to opportunity, now they were planned and virtually made to order.

The impact of science was felt by all industries after 1870. In metallurgy, for example, a number of processes were developed (Bessemer, Siemens–Martin and Gilchrist–Thomas) that made possible the mass production of high-grade steel from low-grade iron ore. The power industry was revolutionized by the harnessing of electricity and by the invention of the internal combustion engine which uses chiefly oil and gasoline. Communications also were transformed by the invention of the wireless, or radio. In 1896, Guglielmo Marconi devised a machine for sending and receiving messages without wires, but his work was based on the researches of the Scottish physicist James Clerk Maxwell, and the German physicist Heinrich Hertz. The oil industry developed rapidly as a result of the work of geologists who located oilfields with remarkable accuracy, and of chemists who devised ways to refine crude oil into naphtha, gas, kerosene, and both light and heavy lubricating oils. One of the most spectacular examples of the effect of science on industry may be seen in the case of the coal derivatives. In addition to yielding coke and a valuable gas that was used for illumination, coal also gave a liquid, or coal tar. Chemists discovered in this substance a veritable treasure trove, the derivatives including hundreds of dyes and a host of other by-products such as aspirin, wintergreen, saccharin, disinfectants, laxatives, perfumes, photographic chemicals, high explosives, and essence of orange blossom.

The second stage of the Industrial Revolution was also characterized by the development of mass-production techniques. The United States led in this field as Germany did in the scientific. Certain obvious advantages explain U.S. primacy in mass production: the great storehouse of raw materials; the abundant supply of capital, both native and European; the constant influx of cheap immigrant labor; and the vast home market of continental proportions and with a rapidly growing population and a rising standard of living.

Two principal methods of mass production were developed in the United States. One was the making of standard interchangeable parts, and the assembling of these parts into the completed unit with a minimum of handicraft labor. The American inventor Eli Whitney employed this system at the very beginning of the nineteenth century in manufacturing muskets for the government. The next step, early in the twentieth century, was the working out of the assembly line. Henry Ford gained fame and fortune by devising the endless conveyor belt that carried car parts to the place where they were needed by the assembly workmen. The evolution of this conveyor-belt system has been graphically described as follows:

The idea of the belt was borrowed from the Chicago packers, who used an overhead trolley to swing carcasses of beef down a line of butchers. Ford tried the idea first in assembling the motor itself, and then in assembling the chassis.

A chassis was attached to a rope one day, and six workmen, picking up parts along the way and bolting them in place, travelled with it on an historic journey down a line two hundred and fifty feet in length as a windlass dragged it through the factory. The experiment worked, but developed one difficulty. God had not made men as accurately as Ford made piston rings. The line was too high for the short men and too low for the tall men, with a resultant waste in effort.

More experiments were tried. The line was raised; then lowered; then two lines were tried, to suit squads of different heights; the speed of the lines was increased; then lessened; various tests were made to determine how many men to put on one assembly line, how far to subdivide operations, whether to let one man who set a bolt in place put on the nut and the man who put on the nut to take time to tighten it. In the end, the time allotted for assembly on a chassis was cut from twelve hours and twenty-eight minutes to one hour and thirty-three minutes, the world was promised Model T's in new abundance, and mass production entered a new phase as men were made still more efficient cogs of their machines. . . .[17]

Next was perfected the manipulation of large masses of material by means of advanced mechanical devices. The prime example of this method of mass production—also perfected in the United States—is the iron and steel industry. What mass production in this industry meant in terms of dollars and cents is evident in the justifiable boast of the steel magnate Andrew Carnegie:

Two pounds of ironstone mined upon Lake Superior and transported nine hundred miles to Pittsburgh; one pound and one-half of coal, mined and manufactured into coke, and transported to Pittsburgh; one-half pound of lime, mined and transported to Pittsburgh; a small amount of manganese ore mined in Virginia and brought to Pittsburgh—and these four pounds of materials manufactured into one pound of steel, for which the consumer pays one cent.[18]

Science and mass-production methods affected agriculture as well as industry. Again it was Germany that led in the application of science, and the United States in mass production. German chemists discovered that to maintain the fertility of the soil it was necessary to replace the nitrogen, potassium, and phosphorus that was taken out by plants. At first guano was used for this purpose, but toward the end of the nineteenth century it gave way to purer forms of the necessary minerals. As a result, world production of the minerals increased between 1850 and 1913 from insignificant amounts to 899,800 net tons of nitrate (three-fourths of which was used for fertilizer), 1,348,000 metric tons of potash, and 16,251,213 tons of superphosphates.

In the United States the large size of the farms and the lack of sufficient rural labor stimulated the invention of agricultural machinery. The tractor which replaced the horse could pull a rotary plow that plowed as much as fifty acres a day. The combine could automatically cut, gather, thresh, and clean the grain, and even bundle it in sacks ready for the market. As important as these new machines were the grain elevators, the canning factories, the refrigerated cars and ships, and the rapid transportation facilities, which resulted in a world market for agricultural as well as for industrial products. The wheat of Canada, the mutton of Australia, the beef of Argentina, and the fruits of California were to be found in markets throughout the world. Agriculture, which traditionally had offered a means of independent livelihood, was becoming a large-scale business enterprise geared to production for national and international markets.

During the nineteenth century the Industrial Revolution spread gradually from England to the Continent of Europe, and even to the non-European portions of the globe. At first there were various obstacles in the way of diffusion. A British law forbade the exportation of machinery, and conditions on the Continent were not conducive to industrialization, particularly because of the strength of the guilds and the disturbances connected with the Revolutionary and Napoleonic Wars. But the wars ended in 1815, and the British law was repealed in 1825. Soon the railway-building fever, which got under way in England in the 1830's was affecting the Continent. Furthermore, British industrialists by this time were accumulating surplus capital and were on the look-out for investment opportunities on the continent. By 1830, fifteen to twenty thousand British workers were employed in France alone to man the new machines.

Once the Industrial Revolution began to spread, certain factors determined the pattern of diffusion. Most important were an adequate supply of natural resources, particularly iron and steel, and a free and mobile working population, unencumbered by either guild restrictions or feudal obligations. Belgium met both these requirements and hence was the first country on the Continent to be industrialized. The process began before 1830, and proceeded so rapidly that by 1870 the majority of Belgians lived in cities and were directly dependent upon industry or trade.

France followed after Belgium, though—for several reasons—at a much more leisurely pace. French coal and iron resources were located some distance from each other, and the cession of iron-rich Alsace-Lorraine to Germany in 1871 further weakened her position. French industry traditionally had specialized in luxury products that were not so suitable to mechanization and mass production. And the labor supply was limited because of the strength of the guilds and the unwillingness of the peasants to leave the soil, especially after the distribution of land during the revolution. Nevertheless, industrialization did gradually affect France, especially in the north of the country—in Alsace-Lorraine and in the regions about Lille, Rouen, and Paris. The number of steam engines increased from 15 in 1815 to 625 in 1830, 26,146 in 1871, and 82,238 in 1910. The most rapid tempo of industrialization came after 1870, when the value of manufactured products rose from 5 billion francs in that year to 15 billion in 1897. Yet the fact remains that by 1914 France was not so thoroughly industrialized as Belgium, England, or Germany.

The pattern of industrialization in Germany was very different from that in France. Because of the political disunity, the poor transportation facilities, the strong guilds, and other considerations, Germany started very slowly. But after 1871 German industry advanced in such giant strides that all the other economies of Europe, including that of Britain, were left behind. The formation of the German Empire in 1871 contributed to this remarkable progress. The acquisition of Alsace-Lorraine at the same time added valuable iron reserves to Germany's plentiful natural resources. Germany also had the advantage of starting off with new and up-to-date machinery which was more efficient than Britain's older equipment. And the German government aided substantially by building a network of canals and railroads, providing tariff protection and subsidies when they were needed, and establishing an efficient educational system which turned out a stream of well-trained scientists and technicians. These factors enabled Germany by 1914 to surpass all other European states in the iron, steel, chemical, and electrical industries, and to follow after Britain in coal and textiles.

Several other European countries had developed substantial industries by 1914, the most important being Russia, Austria-Hungary, and Italy. Among the overseas countries, the United States had advanced at a phenomenal rate, while Japan, Canada, and Australia had made appreciable progress. The United States, especially, with its unique advantages previously noted, by the beginning of the twentieth century had become the first industrial power in the world. In steel production, for example, the United States in 1910 was producing 26,512,000 metric tons as against 13,698,000 by Germany, her closest competitor, and in coal her output was 617 million metric tons as against 292 million tons by Great Britain, who was in second place.

We may conclude that by 1914 the Industrial Revolution had spread significantly from its original center in the British Isles. In fact, the diffusion reached such proportions that Britain now not only faced formidable competition, but had been surpassed by two other countries, Germany and the United States.

VI. EFFECT OF THE INDUSTRIAL REVOLUTION ON EUROPE

Rise of Industrial Capitalism

One effect of the Industrial Revolution on Europe was to alter the nature of capitalism. We noted earlier that the commercial revolution created commercial capitalism, so called because commerce was more affected by the capitalistic form of organization than agriculture or industry. In the same manner, the Industrial Revolution during its first stage between 1770 and 1870 created industrial capitalism. By this is meant that industry was organized increasingly upon a capitalistic base and was gradually dominating the economic life. After 1870, during the second stage of the Industrial Revolution, still another change occurred in the prevailing form of economic organization, this time to finance capitalism. The distinguishing feature of the new form was the investment banker, who came to be the controlling figure in economic enterprise. Or, to put it another way, finance capitalism took the place of industrial capitalism.

Increase of Population

Another effect of the Industrial Revolution on Europe was to make possible an unprecedented increase in population. In spite of the emigration overseas of millions of Europeans during the nineteenth century, the population of the Continent in 1914 was well over three times that of 1750. The reasons for this population explosion are economic and medical. The great increase of productivity in both agriculture and industry meant increased means of subsistence in terms of food, clothing, shelter, and other necessities of life. Famine in most parts of Europe west of Russia became a memory of the past. Even if crops failed, the new transportation facilities ensured adequate supply from outside. The population increase was due also to the advances of medical science and to the adoption of numerous public health measures. There was little or no increase in the birth rate, but the death rate was sharply reduced by preventing or curing disease. Vaccination, segregation of infected persons, safeguarding of water supplies, knowledge of antiseptics—all these reduced the death rate in northwestern Europe from at least 30 per 1,000 persons in 1800 to about 15 in 1914. Thus Europe's population climbed steeply from 100 million in 1650 (18.3 per cent of the world's total population), to 266 million in 1850 (22.7 per cent of world), and to 401 million in 1900 (24.9 per cent of world). Furthermore, by

1900 most of the population of the United States, Canada, Oceania, and at least half the population of Latin America were of European origin, thanks to the mass emigration from Europe. Thus between 1650 and 1900 the population of Europeans and people of European origin had risen from less than a fifth to about a third of the world's total.

Urbanization

The Industrial Revolution led also to an unprecedented urbanization of world society. Cities date back to the Neolithic period when the invention of agriculture produced a food surplus that could support urban centers. During the following millennia the size of cities depended on the amount of food that the surrounding land could produce. Thus the most populous cities were to be found in the valleys and flood plains, like the Nile, the Fertile Crescent, the Indus, and the Hwang Ho. With the development of large-scale river and sea transport, cities were able to specialize in trade and industry and thus to expand their populations beyond the limits of their agricultural hinterlands.

Far more significant, however, is the modern worldwide urbanization produced by the Industrial Revolution. The replacement of the putting-out system by the factory system led to a mass influx into the new centers of industry. The large new urban populations could be fed because food supplies now were available from all parts of the world. Technological and medical advances made it possible to eliminate the plagues that previously had decimated cities, and even to make city living relatively endurable and pleasant. The more important of these advances include ample provision of pure water, perfection of centralized sewerage and waste disposal systems, insurance of an adequate food supply, and prevention and control of contagious diseases. Thus cities all over the world grew at such a rate that by 1930 they included 415 million people or one-fifth of the human race. This represents one of the great social transformations in human history, for city-dwelling meant an entirely new way of life.

Increase of Wealth

The Industrial Revolution, with its efficient exploitation of human and natural resources on a worldwide scale, made possible an increase in productivity that is without precedent in all history. Great Britain, who first was affected in this respect, increased her capital from 500 million pounds sterling in 1750 to 1,500 million pounds in 1800, to 2,500 million pounds in 1833, and to 6,000 million in 1865. In the latter part of the nineteenth century the entire world felt the impact of the increasing productivity. The wool of New Zealand, the wheat of Canada, the rice of Burma, the rubber of Malaya, the jute of Bengal, and the humming factories of Western Europe and eastern United States—all these resources were enmeshed in a dynamic and constantly expanding global economy. The figures in Table 1 indicate the rate at which industrial production rose in the second half of the nineteenth century in Europe and throughout the world.

Distribution of Wealth

There has been much difference of opinion among authorities in recent years concerning the distribution of the wealth created during the Industrial Revolution. One group holds that all classes benefited to a greater or lesser extent, while

TABLE 1   RISE OF INDUSTRIAL PRODUCTION (1913 = 100)

	1860	1870	1880	1890	1900	1910	1913
Germany	14	18	25	40	65	89	100
Great Britain	34	44	53	62	79	85	100
France	26	34	43	56	66	89	100
Russia	8	13	17	27	61	84	100
Italy	—	17	23	40	56	99	100
U.S.A.	8	11	17	39	54	89	100
World	14	19	26	43	60	88	100

Source: F. Sternberg, *Capitalism and Socialism on Trial* (New York: Day, 1951), p. 21.

the other maintains that a few made huge fortunes while the many were ruthlessly exploited and suffered declining standards of living.

There is no doubt that there was much exploitation and social disruption in the early days of industrialization. The tenant farmers were dispossessed, and the weavers and other handicraftsmen were wiped out by the irresistible competition of the new machine-made goods. These people, and others like them, faced the strain of moving to the city, finding employment, and adjusting to an unfamiliar environment and to strange ways of living and of working. They were completely dependent on their employers, having no land, no cottage, no tools, and no capital. In short, they had become mere wage earners, having nothing to offer but their labor.

When they found employment, they discovered that the hours were long, a sixteen-hour day being by no means rare. When two twelve-hour shifts were finally won, the workers looked upon the change as a blessing. The long hours alone would have been tolerable, since they were no worse than the hours worked at home under the putting-out system. But the real hardship came in getting used to the discipline and monotony of tending machines in a factory. The workers came and went at the sound of the factory whistle. They had to keep pace with the movements of the machine, always under the strict supervision of an ever-present overseer. The work was monotonous—pulling a lever, brushing away dirt, mending broken threads. Employers naturally regarded their wage bill as an expense that should be kept as low as possible. Consequently, many of them, particularly in the textile industries, preferred to employ women and children, who were willing to accept smaller wages and were more amenable to orders. Exploitation of woman and child labor reached such proportions that a number of parliamentary committees conducted investigations and found shocking conditions.

There is, however, another side to this question of the effect of the Industrial Revolution on the working class. In the first place, the parliamentary committees investigated only those industries, such as mining and textiles, where conditions were worst. The shocking testimony of the witnesses who appeared before the committees was based on facts, but those facts were by no means applicable to English industry as a whole. Furthermore, the plight of the worker in early nineteenth century England must be viewed in the light of contemporary rather than present-day standards. The fact is that the villages from which these workers came were in many respects as squalid and stultifying as the cities. Rats and vermin infested the straw bedding, and the wind whistled through the thinly thatched roof and the poorly plastered walls. Day laborers in the countryside were so poorly paid that they kept crowding into the new industrial cities. Thousands of Irish also crossed over to fill the jobs opening up in the new factories. Furthermore, the population of England soared during these early days of the Industrial Revolution, a fact that does not jibe with the usual picture of unrelieved and debilitating misery.

Although we cannot be sure of the effect of the Industrial Revolution on working-class living standards in the late eighteenth and early nineteenth centuries, we are quite certain that the standards rose substantially in the second half of the nineteenth century. The great increases in productivity together with the profits made from the huge overseas investments gradually benefited even the lower classes in Western Europe. After the "Hungry Forties," when there was much suffering from unemployment, the workers of Western Europe enjoyed general prosperity and rising living standards until World War I. Between 1850 and 1913, *real* wages in Britain and France almost doubled.

This marked rise in national income did not mean, of course, that all classes benefited equally. The proceeds of the general prosperity did trickle down somewhat, but they were mostly absorbed at the top. In Great Britain, for example, 4.93 per cent of the persons over 25 years of age possessed over 60 per cent of the wealth in 1911–1913. Likewise, in Prussia in 1911, 3,425 individuals had an average wealth of 5,321,400 marks, whereas 1,608,050 individuals had an average of 23,295 marks. This discrepancy meant a corresponding discrepancy in manner of living. The poor no longer starved, but they did live in crowded tenements, they subsisted on monotonous diets, and they were restricted for their pleasure or relaxation to the churches or the drinking establishments. By contrast, the middle classes could afford better living quarters and food, attend the theater and concert, and educate their children adequately. At the top, the wealthy with their town and country houses, their art collections, and their well-advertised sports activities and foreign travels, lived in a style that was all but incomprehensible to the masses at the bottom.

This class differentiation based upon money influenced to a great degree the pattern of European politics. In the following chapter we shall consider the details of these politics, but it should be noted here that economic or class considerations explain why the wealthy, by and large, preferred to maintain the status quo, why the middle classes wanted only enough political reform so that they could participate in political life, and why the working classes wanted thoroughgoing political and social reform in order to secure a more equitable distribution of the fruits of the Industrial Revolution. To put it more specifically, the wealthy tended to be conservative; the middle classes, liberal; and the politically conscious workers, socialist. This working-class socialism, it should be added, was predominantly of the peaceful or revisionist variety: although the workers resented the class inequalities, they also appreciated the rising standard of living.

VII. EFFECT OF INDUSTRIAL REVOLUTION ON THE NON-EUROPEAN WORLD

Europeanization of the Earlier Empires

In the period before 1763 the European powers had only a few footholds in Asia and Africa, their major holdings being in the Americas. After 1763 they established their political control over large parts of Asia and almost all of Africa. In the Americas, however, they were able to do much more than this. Taking advantage of the relatively sparse population in the New World, they literally Europeanized North and South America. This could not be done in Asia and

Africa, where the indigenous populations were too numerous and highly developed. But in the Americas, and even more in Australia, the Europeans bodily transplanted their civilization in all its aspects—ethnic, economic, and cultural.

The Industrial Revolution was in large degree responsible for this Europeanization. We have seen that increased productivity together with the advances of medical science had led to a sharp increase in Europe's population in the nineteenth century. This created a population pressure that found an outlet in overseas migration. Railways and steamships were available to transport masses of people across oceans and continents, and persecution of one sort or another further stimulated emigration, the chief example of this being the flight of 1½ million Jews from Russia to the United States in the fifteen years preceding World War I. These various factors combined to produce a mass migration unequaled in human history. With every decade the tide of population movement increased in volume. In the 1820's a total of 145,000 left Europe, in the 1850's about 2,600,000, and between 1900 and 1910 the crest was reached with 9 million emigrants, or almost 1 million per year. Table 2 shows the sources of the European emigrants.

TABLE 2   PRINCIPAL SOURCES OF EUROPEAN EMIGRATION, 1846–1932

Great Britain and Ireland	18,000,000
Russia	14,250,000*
Italy	10,100,000
Austria-Hungary	5,200,000
Germany	4,900,000
Spain	4,700,000
Portugal	1,800,000
Sweden	1,200,000
Norway	850,000
Poland	640,000†
France	520,000
Denmark	390,000
Finland	370,000
Switzerland	330,000
Holland	220,000
Belgium	190,000
Total	63,660,000

* Consists of 2,250,000 who went overseas, 7,000,000 who migrated to Asiatic Russia by 1914, 3,000,000 who migrated to the Urals, Siberia, and the Far East from 1927 to 1939 and 2,000,000 who migrated to Central Asia from 1927 to 1939.
† 1920–1932 only.

Source: A. M. Carr-Saunders, *World Population* (Oxford: Clarendon, 1936), pp. 49, 56; and W. S. and E. S. Woytinsky, *World Population and Production* (New York, Twentieth Century Fund, 1953), pp. 69, 93.

Before 1885 most of the emigrants came from northern and western Europe; after that the majority were from southern and eastern Europe. By and large, the British emigrants went to the Dominions and to the United States, the Italians to the United States and Latin America, the Spaniards and Portuguese to Latin America, and the Germans to the United States and, in smaller numbers, to Argentina and Brazil. From the perspective of world history, the significance of this extraordinary migration is that it was all directed to the New World and

Oceania, with the exception of the large flow to Asiatic Russia and the trickle to South Africa. The result has been the almost complete ethnic Europeanization of North America and Australia. The Indian population in South America managed to survive but was left a minority. In other words, the colonial offshoots of the pre-1763 period now, during the course of the nineteenth century, became new Europes alongside the old.

The Americas and Australia were Europeanized economically as well as ethnically. Before 1763 the European settlements in these continents were confined largely to the coasts. But during the following century the interiors of the continents were traversed. The Industrial Revolution made this overland penetration possible by providing the necessary machines and techniques. The wilderness could not have been tamed without the roads leading inward from the coast, the canals connecting riverways, the railroads and telegraphs spanning continents, the steamers plying rivers and coastal waterways, the agricultural machines capable of cutting the prairie sod, and the repeating rifle that subdued the native peoples. These mechanical aids for the conquest of continental expanses were as essential to Latin Americans and Australians as to American frontiersmen. For example, an Argentinian writing in 1878 observed that "the military power of the [Indian] barbarians is wholly destroyed, because the Remington has taught them that an army battalion can cross the whole pampa, leaving the land strewn with the bodies of those who dared to oppose it."[19]

The peopling and economic development of the new continents led automatically to the transplanting of European culture as well. It is true that the culture changed in transit. It was adapted as well as adopted. Canada and Australia and the United States today are not identical to Great Britain, nor is Latin America an exact reproduction of the Iberian Peninsula. But the fact remains that the languages are essentially the same, even though Englishmen are intrigued by American slang and Frenchmen by the archaic French-Canadian patois. The religions also are the same, despite the campfire revival meetings and the Mormons. The literatures, the schools, the newspapers, the forms of government—all have roots extending back to England and Spain and France and other European countries.

There are, of course, certain cultural strains in the Americas and in Australia that are not European. The Negro element in the New World has retained a certain residue of its African background. The surviving native peoples, especially the Indians in Latin America, are responsible for a hybrid culture. Nor should one forget the impact of the wilderness, leaving its indelible imprint on the European immigrants and on their institutions. All these forces explain why New York, Melbourne, and Toronto are very different from London, and why Buenos Aires, Brasilia, and Mexico City differ from Madrid. Yet from a global viewpoint the similarities loom larger than the differences.

New Imperialism Conquers New Empires

The Industrial Revolution was largely responsible not only for the Europeanization of the New World and Australia, but also for the creation of huge European colonial structures in Asia and Africa. This empire building went on steadily during the decades following the great colonial settlement in 1763. Britain, for example, obtained the Cape Colony and Ceylon in 1815, New Zealand in 1840, Hong Kong in 1842, and Natal in 1843. France likewise conquered Algeria between 1830 and 1847, Cochin China between 1858 and 1867, and attempted unsuccessfully to get a foothold in Mexico in 1862. These acquisitions, however, were insignificant compared to the great wave of empire building after 1870, when the "New Imperialism" made a large part of the earth's surface into an appendage of a few European powers.

The close relationship between the New Imperialism and the Industrial Revolution may be seen in the growing desire to obtain colonies that might serve as markets for the rising volume of manufactured goods. The several European and overseas countries that became industrialized during the nineteenth century were soon competing with each other for markets, and in the process they raised tariffs to keep out each other's products. Soon it was being argued that each industrialized country must have colonies to provide "sheltered markets" for its manufactures.

The Industrial Revolution also produced surplus capital, which again led the Great Powers to seek colonies as investment outlets. The more capital piled up at home, the lower the returns fell and the greater the need was for more profitable investment markets abroad. Vast amounts of capital were, in fact, invested in foreign countries, especially by Britain, France, and Germany. Britain, for example, by 1914 had invested £4 billion abroad, a sum amounting to one fourth of her total national wealth. By the same date France had invested 45 billion francs, or one-sixth of her national wealth. Germany, a latecomer who was using most of her capital for domestic industrial expansion, had invested overseas between 22 and 25 billion marks or one fifteenth of her national wealth. Thus Europe by 1914 had become the banker of the world. In the first half of the nineteenth century most of these overseas investments were made in the Americas and Australia —in the white man's world. But in the second half of the century they were made mostly in the nonwhite and relatively unstable countries of Asia and Africa. Ten thousands of small private savers and the large banking combinations that provided the capital naturally were anxious about its safety. They preferred "civilized" administration, preferably by their own respective governments, in the regions in which their investments were situated. In this manner the need to invest surplus capital promoted the New Imperialism.

The Industrial Revolution also created a demand for raw materials to feed the machines. Many of these materials—jute, rubber, petroleum, and various metals —came from the "uncivilized" portions of the globe. In most cases heavy capital outlays were needed to secure adequate production of these commodities. Such investments, as we have seen, usually led to the imposition of political control.

The New Imperialism was not entirely economic in its origins; it was not related exclusively to the Industrial Revolution. A variety of other factors also were operative at this time. One was the desire to strengthen national security by strategic naval bases such as at Malta and Singapore. Another was the need to secure additional sources of manpower, as the French did in North Africa. Still another was the influence of the missionaries, who were particularly active during the nineteenth century. Finally, the vogue of Social Darwinism, with its doctrines of struggle for existence and survival of the fittest, led naturally to ideas of racial superiority and of the white man's "burden" of ruling over the "inferior" colored peoples of the earth. The great empire builder Cecil Rhodes was quite outspoken on this matter. "I contend that we are the first race in the world, and that the more of the world we inhabit the better it is for the human race . . . If there be a God, I think what He would like me to do is to paint as much of the map of Africa British red as possible."[20]

The net result of these economic, political, and intellectual-psychological factors was the greatest land-grab in the history of the world, unequaled even by the conquests of Genghis Khan. The extent of this empire building by 1914 is revealed by the figures in Table 3.

TABLE 3   OVERSEAS COLONIAL EMPIRES IN 1914 *

Countries having colonies	Number of colonies	Area (square miles)		Population	
		Mother country	Colonies	Mother country	Colonies
United Kingdom	55	120,953	12,043,806	46,052,741	391,582,528
France	29	207,076	4,110,409	39,602,258	62,350,000
Germany	10	208,830	1,230,989	64,925,993	13,074,950
Belgium	1	11,373	910,000	7,571,387	15,000,000
Portugal	8	35,500	804,440	5,960,056	9,680,000
Netherlands	8	12,761	762,863	6,102,399	37,410,000
Italy	4	110,623	591,250	35,238,997	1,396,176
Total	115	707,116	20,453,757	205,453,831	530,493,654

* Including colonies and other noncontiguous territories.

The industrialized European powers not only owned outright these vast colonial territories, but they also dominated those economically and militarily weak areas that, for one reason or another, were not actually annexed. Examples are China, the Ottoman Empire, and Persia, all of which were nominally independent but which, in fact, were constantly harried, humiliated, and controlled in various direct and indirect ways. Latin America also was an economic appendage of the Great Powers, though in this region military action by Europe was discouraged by the Monroe Doctrine. The latter, however, did not preclude repeated armed intervention by the United States Marine Corps to "restore law and order." The great Russian Empire also was dominated economically to a very large extent by Western Europe, though in this case the military strength of the Tsarist regime was great enough to prevent foreign economic influence from extending into other fields.

Thus we see that Europe's control extended not only over her farflung empires but also over the equally extensive dependent regions. In fact, more European capital was invested in the dependent countries than in the colonies. These investments were safeguarded through various devices and pressures such as military missions that trained the local armed forces, financial missions that supervised and usually controlled local finances, and extraterritorial and capitulatory arrangements that gave special privileges to Europeans residing or doing business in these areas. If necessary, as a last resort, there were always the Marines in the New World or the gunboats in the Old.

The details of these relationships between the Great Powers and the various colonial and dependent areas will be considered in later chapters. The purpose here is to present only the general pattern of the relationships. This pattern shows clearly that by 1914 most of the earth's surface and most of the world's population had come under the direct or indirect domination of a few European countries, including Russia and the United States. This was a development without precedence in the history of man. Today, in the mid-twentieth century, much of the global turmoil represents the inevitable reaction to this European hegemony.

Impact of the New Imperialism

Why should the great European expansion of the late nineteenth century be labeled the New Imperialism? Imperialism, after all, was not something new. If it be defined as "the rule or control, political or economic, direct or indirect, of one state, nation or people over other similar groups . . ." then imperialism is as old as human civilization. Certainly the Romans were imperialistic, having conquered, and for centuries ruled, large parts of Europe and the Near East. And many other empires, both before and after the Romans, were conquered in all parts of the globe by all types of peoples.

Yet the term "New Imperialism" is justified, because this late nineteenth century European expansion was quite unprecedented in its impact upon the colonial and dependent territories. Rome exploited its possessions simply and directly by plundering and by collecting tribute, chiefly in the form of foodstuffs, but its exploitation did not particularly affect the economic life and structure of the colonies. They continued to produce pretty much the same foodstuffs and handicrafts in the same ways as in the past. To compare this imperialism with the later version that overran and remade entire continents is like comparing a spade to a steam shovel. The traditional imperialism involved exploitation but no basic economic and social change. The tribute merely went to one ruling clique rather than another. The New Imperialism, by contrast, forced a thorough transformation of the conquered countries. This was not so much deliberate policy as it was the inevitable impact of the dynamic industrialism of Western Europe upon the static, self-contained agrarian regimes of Africa and Asia. In other words, Europe's industrial capitalism was far too complex and expansionist for a simple tribute relationship with the colonies.

At the outset, the European conquerors certainly did not hesitate to plunder and to levy tribute. The British did so in India, as the Spaniards had earlier in Mexico and in Peru. But after this initial phase, Europe's dynamic economy began in various ways to enfold and refashion the colonial economic and social structures. This happened because, as we have seen, industrialized Europe needed sources of raw materials and markets for its surplus capital and manufactures. England, for example, shipped to India vast quantities of textiles and capital, the latter principally for building railways. By 1890, approximately 17,000 miles of railroads had been built in India, which was about equal to the English railway system. But from 1890 to 1911 the Indian network was approximately doubled to 33,000 miles, while in the same period the increase in England was only a little over 300 miles.

It should be noted that the railways, and other large projects such as irrigation works and harbor installations, were paid for by British capital. In other words, India did not have to develop her economy and increase her exports until she accumulated sufficient capital. Thus India's economic development at this early stage was stimulated by the tie with Britain. But the important point is that it was not only stimulated but also revamped, and at a later stage, stultified. The British textiles, which were so cheap, and which now could be distributed throughout the country by the railroad system, ruined the native artisans as inexorably as they had the British artisans a century earlier. But there was one vital difference between the two situations. The British artisans went to work in the factories that were mushrooming in the cities; the Indian artisans had nowhere to go because no factories appeared in their cities. The British, not unnaturally, did not wish to build a rival industrial structure in India. They preferred that the Indian economy supplement rather than compete with their own. Thus, India supplied Britain with raw materials, and in return received manufactured goods and capital for construction projects.

This was a natural and understandable arrangement, but it affected the people of India in a profound fashion. They had earned their livelihood traditionally through agriculture and handicrafts. Now the artisans were undercut and had no alternative source of livelihood. Nor did the peasants escape untouched, for many of them became involved in producing jute and other commodities for the British factories. This meant that they no longer merely fed themselves and the people of nearby towns. Now they were part and parcel of the world economy, subject to its fluctuations and crises. Europe also affected India basically by introducing medical science and sanitary measures that resulted in a sharp population increase. This had occurred also in Europe, but Europe's millions went to the cities or overseas, while the Indians could do neither. The net result, therefore, was growing population and arrested economic development.

This, then, was the nature of the impact of the New Imperialism on the colonial and dependent areas. India has been used as an illustration of the impact, but the general pattern was the same in other areas, though naturally with local variations. This pattern should be kept in mind, because it explains why the globe today is divided into developed and underdeveloped worlds, why such a shocking discrepancy prevails in the living standards of the two worlds, and why the primary aim of the people of the underdeveloped world, after they have gained political independence, is to become developed—to reach Western economic levels as rapidly as possible.

New Imperialism in Retrospect

It should not be concluded that the New Imperialism was an unmitigated evil for the world, or even for the subject colonial peoples. In the light of historical perspective it undoubtedly will be viewed as a great step forward for the world, as the Industrial Revolution was a step forward for the Europeans. In fact, the historic role of the New Imperialism was to carry the Industrial Revolution to its logical conclusion—to enable the industrial nations, or industrial capitalism, to operate on a worldwide scale. This resulted in a much more extensive, coordinated, and efficient utilization of the material and human resources of the globe. Certainly world productivity rose immeasurably when European capital and skills were combined with the raw materials and labor power of the underdeveloped regions to produce, for the first time, an integrated global economy. In fact, world industrial production increased three times between 1860 and 1890, and seven times between 1860 and 1913. The value of world trade grew from 641 million pounds in 1851, to 3,024 million pounds in 1880, to 4,025 million pounds in 1900, and 7,840 million pounds in 1913.

There is no disagreement over the advantage of this increase in the size of the cake. The dispute rather centers on how the cake is sliced. The colonial peoples have felt that in the past they have received less than their due share. The total amount that they have received obviously has increased, otherwise their rising populations could not have been supported. For example, a British economist has shown that in 1949 European companies engaged in mining in mineral-rich Northern Rhodesia sold their output for a total of £36.7 million. Of this, they spent only £12.5 million in Northern Rhodesia, which meant that two-thirds of the money was transferred abroad. Moreover, of the £12.5 spent in Northern Rhodesia £4.1 million was paid to Europeans living and working there. Only £2 million out of the £36.7 million went to the Africans working in the mines. And yet these workers were receiving an average of £41 a year compared to an average income of £27 a year per adult African male in the colony.

Under these circumstances it is understandable that colonial peoples are not so impressed by increased productivity or by the wages paid by foreign companies. They are more impressed by the wretched level at which they subsist, especially in comparison with Western levels. They resent also their consignment to the role of hewers of wood and drawers of water, even in regions where human and material resources exist for industrial development.

There is apparent here a parallel between the reaction of Western workers to industrial capitalism and of colonial peoples to the New Imperialism. Both have been dissatisfied with their lot, and both have supported movements designed to bring about radical change. But a basic difference is that the colonial peoples are ranged not against employers of their own nationality but rather against foreign rulers. Accordingly their movement of protest, at least in the first stage, was not socialism, but rather a range of Western political doctrines—liberalism, democracy, and, above all, nationalism.

We now turn to consider these isms, which comprise Europe's political revolution. An understanding of this revolution is as essential for world history as an understanding of the Industrial Revolution. The world, as we shall see, was affected by Western ideas and slogans and political institutions as well as by Western cottons and railways and banks.

SUGGESTED READING

J. G. CROWTHER, *Scientists of the Industrial Revolution* (Cresset, 1962); W. C. DAMPIER, *A Shorter History of Science* (Harcourt, 1957); A. R. and M. B. HALL, *A Brief History of Science* (New Am. Lib., 1967); D. S. LANDES, *The Unbound Prometheus.* . . . (Cambridge Univ., 1969); A. G. R. SMITH, *Science and Society in the Sixteenth and Seventeenth Centuries* (Thames & Hudson, 1973); L. L. SNYDER, ed., *The Imperialism Reader* (Van Nostrand, 1962); A. THOMPSON, *The Dynamics of the Industrial Revolution* (Arnold, 1973); E. P. THOMPSON, *The Making of the English Working Class* (Gollancz, 1963).

chapter twenty-five

Europe's Political
Revolutions

*When individuals and nations have once got in their heads the abstract
concept of fullblown liberty, there is nothing like it in its
uncontrollable strength.*—G. W. F. Hegel

Europe's domination of the world in the nineteenth century was based
not only on its industrial and scientific revolutions, but also on its political revolution, the essence of which was the ending of the concept of a divinely ordained
division of humanity into rulers and ruled. No longer was government regarded
as something above the people, and the people as something below the government. The political revolution involved for the first time in history, on a scale
larger than the city-state, the identification of government and people—the
awakening and activization of the masses so that they not only participated in
government but also considered it their inherent right to do so. In this chapter
we shall consider the general pattern of this political revolution, its origins in
the English, American, and French Revolutions, and its varied manifestations
and worldwide impact during the nineteenth century.

I. PATTERN OF THE POLITICAL REVOLUTION

The political revolution, like the economic, developed in several stages. We noted
that the economic revolution began in England, then spread to the Continent
and to the United States, and later to other parts of the globe. Likewise, the
political revolution got under way with the English Revolution in the seventeenth century, developed much further with the American and French Revolutions that followed and then affected the whole of Europe during the nineteenth
century and the entire globe during the twentieth.

This parallelism in the diffusion of the two revolutions was not accidental; indeed, the two were intimately related. The economic revolution was in large
degree responsible for the political, because it created new classes with new
interests and new ideologies that rationalized their interests. This will become
clear if we trace briefly the general course of the economic and political revolutions.

During the early medieval period, three well-defined social groups were to be found in Western Europe: the nobility who constituted a military aristocracy, the clergy who formed an ecclesiastical and intellectual elite, and the peasants who labored to support the two upper classes. With the development of commerce, this profile of the medieval social order began to be changed by the appearance of a new element, the urban bourgeoisie. As this class grew in wealth and numbers, it became increasingly discontented with the special privileges of the feudal orders and with the numerous restrictions that hampered the development of a free market economy. Accordingly, the bourgeoisie made a mutually beneficial alliance with the national monarchies. The kings obtained financial support from the bourgeoisie and thereby were able to assert their authority over the feudal orders, and the bourgeoisie in return profited from the establishment of law and order throughout the royal domains. This alliance lasted until it became irksome for the constantly growing middle class, which turned against the kings to free itself from royal restrictions on commerce, from a growing burden of taxation, and from restraints on religious freedom. These objectives were important factors in the English, the American and the French Revolutions. The success of these revolutions meant also the success of liberalism—the new ideology that provided a rationalization for bourgeois interests and objectives. In this sense liberalism may be defined as the particular program by which the growing middle class proposed to secure for itself those benefits and that control at which it aimed.

The middle class, with its creed of liberalism, was challenged in turn by the urban workers, or proletariat. With the Industrial Revolution of the late eighteenth century, the workers in the crowded cities became increasingly class conscious. More and more they felt that their interests were not identical with those of their employers, and that their situation could be improved only by combined action on their part. Consequently the workers, or rather the intellectuals who led them, developed a new ideology, socialism. It directly challenged the liberalism of the bourgeoisie, calling for social and economic change as well as for political reform. We shall see that socialism was to become a major force in European affairs in the late nineteenth century, and in world affairs in the twentieth.

Europe's political revolution was powered not only by the dynamic creeds of liberalism and socialism, but also by nationalism—an ideology that cut across classes and activated great masses of people. Traditionally the first allegiance of these people had been to region or to church. In early modern times it had extended to the new national monarchs. But beginning with the English Revolution, and particularly during the French Revolution, increasing numbers of Europeans subordinated their loyalty to the new cause of the nation. The rise of national churches, national dynasties, national armies, and national educational systems, all combined to transform former ducal subjects and feudal serfs and town burghers into the all-inclusive nation. The new national ideology spread during the nineteenth century from Western Europe, where it originated, to all parts of the Continent, and today, in the twentieth century, it is the driving force behind the awakening of formerly subject colonial peoples throughout the world.

These three creeds—liberalism, socialism, and nationalism—are the principal components of Europe's political revolution. Together they galvanized into action broader and broader strata of the peoples of Europe, giving them a dynamism and a cohesiveness unequaled in any other portion of the globe. In this manner the political revolution, like the scientific and the economic, contributed vitally to

Europe's world hegemony. When the Europeans began to expand overseas, they encountered societies in which there was little rapport between rulers and ruled. The apathy of the masses—their lack of identification with their governments— explains why in region after region the Europeans were able to establish and to maintain their rule with little difficulty. India is perhaps the leading example of the vulnerability to European expansionism of societies that had remained disparate congeries of peoples, religions, and conflicting provincial loyalties. For over a century and a half, this great Indian subcontinent, with its teeming millions, its splendid civilization, and its ancient historical traditions, was ruled with little difficulty by a comparative handful of British officers and officials. When the mutiny against British rule broke out in 1857, it was put down not only by British troops but also Indian. The correspondent of the London *Times* reported this fact with astonishment. "I looked with ever-growing wonder on the vast tributary of the tide of war which was running around and before me. All these men, women and children, with high delight were pouring towards Lucknow to aid the Feringhee [Europeans] to overcome their brethren."[1]

But European political and economic domination inevitably meant the diffusion of European political ideas. Just as the entire globe felt the impact of Stephenson's locomotive, of Fulton's steamship, and Gatling's machine gun, so it felt the impact of the Declaration of Independence, of the Declaration of the Rights of Man and Citizen, and the Communist Manifesto. The worldwide convulsions that are the hallmark of our present age are the direct outcome of these heady documents.

II. ENGLISH REVOLUTION

The first phase of Europe's political revolution was the English Revolution of the seventeenth century. The roots of the upheaval in England are to be found in the conflict between Parliament and the Stuart dynasty, which degenerated to an open civil war from which Parliament emerged victorious. The Tudor dynasty which preceded the Stuart was generally popular, particularly with the middle class and the gentry. It brought the warring noble families under central control. It severed the ecclesiastical ties with Rome by establishing a national Anglican church, and in the process distributed extensive lands and other properties that had belonged to the Catholic institution. It also built up the navy and pursued an anti-Catholic foreign policy that met with popular approval.

The first Stuart king, James I (1603–1625), and his son and successor Charles I (1625–1649), soon dissipated this fund of goodwill. They sought to impose the doctrines and ritual of the Anglican church on all the people, thereby alienating their Nonconformist, or Puritan, subjects. They also tried to rule without Parliament, but encountered difficulties because Parliament controlled the national purse. They attempted to get around this obstacle by selling monopolies in the export and import trades, in domestic commerce, and in many fields of manufacturing. This produced considerable revenue, but it also antagonized the bourgeoisie, which demanded that "all free subjects be inheritable to the free exercise of their industry."[2]

The crisis came when the Scots rose in rebellion against Charles's attempt to impose Anglicanism upon them. In order to obtain funds to put down the uprising, Charles was forced to summon Parliament. And this Long Parliament, which met in 1640, ignored his requests for money and instead made a number of far-reaching demands, including the execution of the chief royal advisers and the complete reorganization of the Anglican church. Charles refused to submit, and in 1642 fighting broke out between the royalist Cavaliers and the Puritan Roundheads.

England was not to settle down again for almost half a century, until the so-called Glorious Revolution of 1688. The stirring events of those decades comprise the English Revolution, which went through five stages. The first, from 1642 to 1645, was the civil war, during which the royalists were routed by the famous New Model Army organized by Oliver Cromwell. During the second stage, from 1645 to 1649, a situation developed that was to be repeated with certain variations during the French Revolution in 1792 and the Russian Revolution in 1917. A split occurred between the moderate and radical elements among the victorious Puritans. The moderates, led by Cromwell, prevailed over the radicals, led by John Lilburne. When Charles was executed in 1649, Cromwell emerged as the head of an English republic known as the Commonwealth.

Cromwell and his Puritan followers ruled England with much efficiency and Godliness during the third stage from 1649 to 1660. This was the time when the various feudal rights were suppressed and the religious question settled. Cromwell died in 1658 and was succeeded as Lord Protector of the Commonwealth by his son Richard. The latter was a nonentity, and furthermore the country was weary of the restricted and austere life under the Puritans. Accordingly, the Stuarts were placed back on the throne, so that the fourth stage, from 1660 to 1688, is known as the Restoration.

The Stuart kings, Charles II (1660–1685) and James II (1685–1688), did not and could not undo the reforms of the republic. But they did try to revive personal rule, and this, together with their subservience to the French crown and their encouragement of Catholicism, made them increasingly unpopular. Finally James II was overthrown with the Glorious Revolution of 1688, which marks the fifth and last stage of the English Revolution. The new ruler was William of Orange, son-in-law of James I. In 1689 William accepted a Bill of Rights which enunciated the essential principles of parliamentary supremacy. The bill stipulated that no law could be suspended by the king, no taxes raised or army maintained except by Parliament's consent, and no subject arrested and detained without legal process. These provisions did not mean that England had become a democracy. Not until the establishment of universal suffrage in the late nineteenth century was this goal attained. But the settlement in 1689 did establish once and for all the supreme authority of Parliament, and in doing so it concluded the English Revolution that had begun almost half a century earlier.

From the viewpoint of world history, the major significance of the English Revolution is that it defined and implemented the principles of liberalism. This was to be expected, because the English Revolution was essentially a middle-class affair. The merchants and the lesser gentry who supported Parliament had two principal objectives in view—religious toleration and security of person and of property. But there was no unanimity of opinion on the Puritan side concerning these matters. Many conflicting views were expounded and passionately debated. In the case of religion, for example, a veritable torrent of heterodox opinion gushed forth, and numerous new sects appeared, including the Congregationalists, the Baptists, and the Quakers. At the same time, the Presbyterians strove to establish their church as a national organization exercising its discipline upon all citizens. These religious differences obviously had to be reconciled or else Parliament's victory would be undone and the state itself might founder. It was under these circumstances that the basic liberal doctrine of religious toleration was worked out and established. On grounds of principle as well as expedience it came to be generally agreed that it was both immoral and ineffective to attempt to coerce men into belief. It is true that the Anglican Church remained the official, state-supported church, and that its members were favored in the filling of government posts and in other respects. But, by and large, the principle was established that liberty of conscience should be granted to all Christians who did not threaten public order or interfere with other men's worship.

The question of the rights of person and property also aroused fierce controversy. This question divided the right- and left-wing elements among the Puritans even more sharply than did the religious issue. The split occurred gradually, as the common soldiers of the New Model Army came to feel that their interests were being ignored by their officers and by Parliament. These feelings were articulated by the Levellers, a name of opprobrium given to a mass movement drawn chiefly from the lower middle class and from agricultural tenants. It is true that legislation passed by the House of Commons for the establishment of the Commonwealth included basic Leveller doctrine: "The People are, under God, the Original of all just Power," and the Commons "being chosen by, and representing the People, have the supreme Power in this Nation."[3]

If Parliament was thus willing to accept the principle of the sovereignty of the people, then what was the issue dividing Parliament and the Levellers? The answer is to be found in the definition of the word "people." Cromwell and his followers held that the "people" who should participate in the election of the Commons were those with a "real or permanent interest in the kingdom"—that is, property owners—whereas the Levellers maintained that "any man that is born in England ought . . . to have his voice in election of burgesses [members of Parliament]."[4] Thus, the issue was between constitutional parliamentary government and democratic government. Many of those who favored democratic government did so with the intention of using their votes to bring about social reform, and fear of such reform motivated Cromwell and his followers in their resolute opposition to the Levellers.

The fact is that there were two revolutions under way in seventeenth century England. The first was the political revolution of the lesser gentry and the bourgeoise, who were interested in winning the civil and religious freedom necessary to make their way in the world. The second was the social revolution of the lower-middle class and the tenant farmers, who had a vision of a community of small-property owners, with complete religious and political equality, and with generous provisions for the poor. The social revolution failed in England in the seventeenth century, as it was to fail in France in the eighteenth. In both cases the protagonists lacked the numbers, the organization, and the maturity necessary for victory. Their time was to come in the late nineteenth century, by which time the Industrial Revolution had spawned a sufficiently large and class-conscious urban proletariat. And this proletariat was to evolve its own ideology—socialism—distinct from, and in opposition to, the liberalism of the bourgeoisie.

III. ENLIGHTENMENT

The next stage in Europe's political revolution, following the upheaval in seventeenth century England, was the so-called Enlightenment that manifested itself during the century before the French Revolution of 1789. The term *Enlightenment* owes its origin to the fact that the leaders of this movement were convinced that they lived in an enlightened age. They regarded the past largely as a time of superstition and ignorance, and believed that only in their day was mankind at last emerging from darkness into sunlight. Thus, one basic characteristic of this age of Enlightenment was the idea of progress, an idea that was to persist into the twentieth century. With the Enlightenment, it began to be generally assumed that the condition of man would steadily improve, so that each generation would be better off than that which came before.

How was this unceasing progress to be maintained? The answer was simple and confident: by the use of man's reasoning powers. This faith in reason was the other basic feature of the Enlightenment. Indeed, the two key concepts were progress and reason. And the exponents of these concepts were a highly articulate group known as the philosophes. Not to be confused with formal philosophers, the philosophes were not profound or systematic thinkers in any particular field. They were mostly literary men or popularizers—more journalists than philosophers. They were closer to H. G. Wells and G. B. Shaw than to G. E. Moore and A. N. Whitehead. Like Wells and Shaw, the philosophes were generally opposed to the existing order, and they wrote plays, novels, essays, and histories to popularize their ideas and to show the need for change.

Much influenced by the law of gravitation, the philosophes believed in the existence of natural laws that regulated not only the physical universe, as Newton had demonstrated, but also human society. Acting upon this assumption, they proceeded to apply reason to all fields in order to discover the operating natural laws. Thus the philosophes subjected the old regime in France, and throughout Europe, to a barrage of devastating criticism. More important, they evolved a set of revolutionary principles by which they proposed to effect a wholesale reorganization of society. Of particular interest to us are their specific proposals in three areas—economics, religion, and government.

Their key slogan in economics was laissez faire—let the people do what they will, let nature take its course. This opposition to government intervention was a reaction to the comprehensive and rigid regulation of economic life generally known as mercantilism. The classic formulation of laissez faire was made by the Scotsman Adam Smith in his famous work, *An Inquiry into the Nature and Causes of the Wealth of Nations* (1776). He argued that individuals are motivated by self-interest so far as their economic activities are concerned; that the national welfare is simply the sum of the individual interests operating in a nation; and that each man knows his own interest better than does any statesman.

In religion the key slogan was "Ecrasez l'infâme!"—crush the infamous thing, or stamp out religious fanaticism and intolerance. More specifically, the philosophes rejected the traditional belief that God controls the universe and determines arbitrarily the fate of man. Instead, they sought a natural religion that was in conformity with the dictates of reason. The outcome was a variety of radical departures from religious orthodoxy. Some became outright atheists, denying the existence of God and denouncing religion as a tool of priests and politicians. Others became agnostics, who neither affirmed nor denied the existence of God. The majority were deists, willing to go along with the proposition that God existed and had created the universe, but insisting that, after the act of creation, God allowed the universe to function according to certain natural laws and refrained from intervention. Thus the deists were able to have their cake and eat it too. They could accept God and the teachings of Christianity, and at the same time reject supernatural features such as the virgin birth, the resurrection, the divinity of Christ, and the divine inspiration of the Bible. The important point to note is that all these new dogmas—atheism, agnosticism, deism—reflected the unprecedented growth of rationalistic skepticism of "revealed" or "supernatural" religion. For the first time since the triumph of Christianity in Europe, a definite break had occurred with the Christian tradition.

In government, also, the philosophes had a key phrase—the "social contract." The contract theory of government was not new: the English political theorist John Locke had formulated it in his *Essay on Civil Government* in 1690. Locke stated in that work that if rulers misgoverned their subjects, "by this breach of trust they forfeit the power the people had put into their hands for quite contrary ends, and it devolves to the people, who have a right to resume their original liberty. . . ." In other words Locke viewed government as a political contract between rulers and ruled. But the French philosopher Jean-Jacques Rousseau transformed it into a social rather than a political contract. For him it involved an agreement amongst the people themselves. In his major political work, *The Social Contract* (1762), Rousseau stated that all citizens, in forming a government, fused their individual wills into a combined general will, and agreed to accept the findings of this general will as final. Rousseau's concept of the general will was abstruse and susceptible of various interpretations. Twentieth century dictators were to use this doctrine to justify their totalitarian regimes. But from the viewpoint of Europe's political revolution, the important consideration is Rousseau's emphasis on the sovereignty of the people. He viewed government as simply a "commission," and thus justified revolution as a restoration to the sovereign people of its rightful power. "The depositaries of the executive power are not the people's masters, but its officers; it [the people] can set them up and pull them down when it likes; for them there is no question of contract, but of obedience. . . ."

This brief survey suggests how the Enlightenment was subversive of traditional institutions and practices. Furthermore, it represented a challenge to the status quo not only in France, but throughout Europe, and even in overseas lands. In fact, the philosophes thought of themselves, not as Frenchmen or Europeans, but as members of the human race. They sought to discover laws of universal applicability, corresponding to Newton's laws of the physical world.

If the philosophes did not discover immutable laws governing the whole of mankind, their writings did influence thinking people in many parts of the world. Their greatest immediate success was in persuading a number of European monarchs to accept at least some of their doctrines. These monarchs still held to the theory that they ruled by divine right, but they changed their ideas about the purpose of their rule. Governmental authority was still to be the prerogative of the kings, but now it was to be used for the benefit of the people. Hence these rulers were known as benevolent despots, the best known of them being Frederick the Great of Prussia (1740–1786), Catherine the Great of Russia (1762–1796), and Joseph II of the Hapsburg Empire (1765–1790). They mouthed typical slogans of the Enlightenment, such as "All citizens ought to be equal before the law," and "Sovereigns are made to serve their people." They even made sporadic attempts at concrete reform, but, in spite of their royal authority, these rulers had very modest success. Their successors frequently undid their work, while the clergy and the aristocrats fought unrelentingly the reforms that menaced their vested interests.

IV. AMERICAN REVOLUTION

Britain decisively defeated France in the Seven Years' War and, by the Treaty of Paris of 1763, acquired France's colonies north to the Arctic and west to the

Mississippi. Both the British and the Americans felt considerable pride in the magnitude of their joint victory. But the victory created new problems at the same time that it settled old ones. One new problem was the growing spirit of independence in the Thirteen Colonies now that the danger of a French attack had been removed. Another was the decision of the British government, following its acquisition of vast new colonial territories, to tighten its imperial organization. This tightening might have been feasible at an earlier date, but now, after a long period of "salutary neglect," and after the elimination of the French danger, the colonists were convinced that they were able to take care of themselves and had every right to do so. Thus the American Revolution arose basically out of the conflicting claims of imperial authority and colonial self-government.

The steps leading to the Revolution are well-known and need not be related in detail. First there was the Proclamation of 1763 prohibiting settlement west of a line drawn along the crests of the Appalachians. This was intended as a temporary measure to preserve peace until an orderly land policy could be worked out, but the prospective settlers and speculators assumed that they were to be perpetually excluded for the benefit of a few British fur traders. Then there was a series of financial measures—the Sugar Act, Quartering Act, Stamp Act, and Townshend Duties—designed to shift a part of Britain's heavy tax load to the American colonists. These levies seemed reasonable to the British, especially in view of the expenditures incurred in defeating the French in the recent war, and the estimated expenditures necessary to protect the American frontiers in the future. But the colonists, being all affected by these imposts, unanimously opposed them. They called an intercontinental congress which organized a boycott of British goods until the financial measures were repealed. But then another series of ill-considered measures by the British government aroused a fresh storm that was to lead to revolution.

The sequence of the dramatic events is familiar—the East India Company's tea monopoly, the Boston Tea Party, and the Coercive, or Intolerable, Acts intended as punishment for the vandalism in Boston harbor. At the same time, in 1774, Parliament enacted the Quebec Act, providing a governmental system for the conquered French Canadians and drawing the boundaries of Quebec to include all the territories north of the Ohio River—that is, the present states of Wisconsin, Michigan, Illinois, Indiana, and Ohio. Much can be said in defense of the Quebec Act, but the American colonists denounced it as another Intolerable Act that blocked their westward expansion for the benefit of the Catholic French Canadians. The First Continental Congress met in Philadelphia in September, 1774, and organized another boycott on British goods. Fighting began the next year when British troops set out from Boston to seize unauthorized stores of weapons at Concord. It was during this operation that someone fired at Lexington Green the "shot heard round the world." The outcome was that the British troops found themselves besieged in Boston. When the Second Continental Congress met the following month, in May, 1775, it had a full-fledged war on its hands and proceeded to raise an American army.

Congress was still reluctant to make the final break with the mother country. But sentiment for independence grew with the spread of the fighting. In January, 1776, Thomas Paine published his incendiary pamphlet, *Common Sense,* which was read everywhere in the colonies, and which contributed substantially to Congress' decision on July 4, 1776, to adopt the Declaration of Independence. Once military operations got fully under way, the decisive factor proved to be France's aid to the revolutionaries. During the first two years of the war France was not officially involved, yet she poured munitions into the colonies. Nine-tenths of the arms used by the Americans in the crucial battle of Saratoga in 1777 were of French origin. The following year France signed an alliance with the insurgents and declared war on Britain. Holland and Spain joined France, while most of the other European powers formed an Armed Neutrality to protect their commerce from Britain's naval power. The help of the French navy and of a French expeditionary force of 6,000 men contributed substantially to the victories of George Washington's forces and to the final British surrender at Yorktown in 1781. The peace treaty signed at Paris in 1783 recognized the independence of the American republic, whose frontiers were to extend west to the Mississippi. But Canada remained British, and received an influx of 60,000 American Tories who remained loyal to Britain and who now balanced the original French population in the St. Lawrence Valley.

From the viewpoint of world history the American Revolution is significant not because it created an independent state but because it created a new and different type of state. The Declaration of Independence had declared, "We hold these truths to be self-evident: that all men are created equal." Now the American people, both during and after the Revolution, passed laws aimed at making this declaration true in life as well as on paper.

These laws, in the first place, abolished the Old World system of entail and primogeniture. Land that was entailed could not be sold outside the family, while the law of primogeniture required that lands be turned over to the eldest son. These were devices designed to maintain large estates intact under their traditional owners. But ten years after the Declaration of Independence every state but two had given up entails, and fifteen years after the Declaration, every single state had given up primogeniture. In other words, the new American Republic was to be based on small holdings worked by the farmer himself, rather than on large estates in the hands of a few. This process was furthered also by the seizure and distribution of the extensive estates owned by the Tories, such as that of the Fairfax family in Virginia, which covered six million acres. These estates were seized and sold in small lots, thus changing appreciably the landholding system in the new republic.

The American Revolution led also to a considerable extension of the franchise, though manhood suffrage was not attained until fifty years later. The Revolution also stimulated an antislavery movement. One state government after another passed laws forbidding the importation of slaves—Rhode Island and Connecticut in 1774, Delaware in 1776, Virginia in 1778, and Maryland in 1783. By 1784 laws had been passed in Pennsylvania, Massachusetts, Connecticut, and Rhode Island providing for the gradual and complete abolition of slavery. Even in the slaveholding center of Virginia, laws passed in 1782 made it easier to free Negroes, and within eight years over ten thousand slaves were freed in that state.

Greater religious freedom was another result. Previously there had been state churches in nine of the thirteen colonies. This meant that Congregationalists living in Maryland had to help support that state's Episcopal church; Episcopalians living in Massachusetts had to do the same for the local Congregationalist church; and even those with no church affiliations at all saw some of their tax money used to support a state church. But immediately after the Revolution began, the established churches in five states were abolished, thus beginning the freedom of religion that characterizes present-day United States.

Constitutionalism was also advanced by the Revolution. All thirteen of the states adopted constitutions based upon the principles of the Declaration of Independence. These constitutions were not fully democratic, giving special privileges to owners of property. But they limited government by a separation of governmental powers, and they appended Bills of Rights, which defined the natural rights of the citizens and the things that no government might justly do.

The Northwest Ordinance of 1787 ensured that western lands would share the hard-won benefits of the Revolution: it provided that new states, identical in all legal respects with the old, but excluding slavery, should be formed in the territories north of the Ohio River. Western lands were not to be subjected to a system of colonial subordination or of competitive expansion on the part of the original states. Instead, as they became eligible for statehood, by the principle of an elastic federalism they were to enjoy the rights and liberties won in war and revolution by the original thirteen states.

These changes were not so far-reaching and fundamental as those that were to be effected by the French and Russian Revolutions. These later revolutions, and particularly the Russian, involved much more social and economic reorganization. Nevertheless the American Revolution had a profound impact in its time. The establishment of an independent republic in the New World was widely interpreted in Europe as meaning that the ideas of the Enlightenment were practicable—that it was possible for a people to establish a state and to formulate a workable system of government based on the rights of the individual. America became a symbol of freedom and of opportunity. It was envied as a new land, free from the burdens and encrustations of past millennia. For example, the Irish nationalist leader Henry Grattan was inspired by the success of the American revolutionaries and he told his fellow countrymen, "Before you decide on the practicability of being slaves forever look to America."[5]

V. FRENCH REVOLUTION

Roots of Revolution

The French Revolution looms much larger on the stage of world history than the English or the American revolutions. It brought about more economic and social change, and influenced a larger portion of the globe, than did the earlier upheavals. The French Revolution marked not only the triumph of the bourgeoisie but also the full awakening of the hitherto dormant masses. Middle-class liberalism came to the fore, but so did nationalism with its appeal to people of all ranks. And these people, so long in the wings, now strode out to the front of the stage, and have remained there ever since. It was in France, in other words, that the world first felt strongly and unmistakably the earthquake that is still rumbling under our feet.

Why did this great transformation take place in France? The basic reason is to be found in the fact that France, the home of the Enlightenment, was not ruled by an enlightened despot until the advent of Napoleon. Consequently, France was a country of such gross inefficiency and inequity that the machinery of government creaked to a standstill. It was this breakdown that gave the ambitious and dissatisfied bourgeoisie a chance to make its successful bid for power.

This pattern is clearly evident in the financial crisis that was the immediate cause for the outbreak of the revolution. In 1789 the French government debt was only half as great as the national debt of Great Britain, and less than a fifth as heavy per capita. Yet France could not carry this debt load because its two privileged classes, the clergy and the nobles, were largely exempt from taxation. These two classes, or "estates," comprised only about 2 per cent of the total population, yet they owned about 35 per cent of the land and enjoyed most of the benefits of government patronage. And despite these disproportionate advantages they were exempted from almost all taxes, which, indeed, they deemed to be beneath their station.

The burden of taxation consequently fell upon the Third Estate, which included the merchants, artisans, and peasants. The latter comprised over 80 per cent of the population but owned only 30 per cent of the land. Furthermore, the peasants were required to pay to the church the tithe, to the nobles an assortment of feudal dues, and to the state a land tax, an income tax, a poll tax, and various other imposts. This tax load was particularly onerous because the general price level had risen 65 per cent between 1720 and 1789, while the prices of farm goods lagged far behind.

The artisans in the cities also were discontented, because their wages had risen only 22 per cent during those same decades. The bourgeoisie, by contrast, were not so badly off in the matter of taxes because they were better able to protect themselves than the artisans and the peasants. Furthermore, most businessmen profited from the rising prices and from the fivefold increase in French trade between 1713 and 1789. Yet the bourgeoisie were thoroughly dissatisfied with the old regime. They resented being snubbed by the nobility, treated as second-class subjects by the crown, and excluded from the higher posts in the bureaucracy, church, and army. In short, the bourgeoisie wanted political power and social prestige to match their growing economic importance.

Aristocratic Revolution

Such was the nature of the old regime in France when the great upheaval began. This French Revolution, like others before and after, started moderately and became progressively more radical. In fact, it began, not in 1789 as a bourgeois revolution, but in 1787 as an aristocratic revolution. Then it moved to the left through bourgeois and mass phases until a reaction occurred that brought Napoleon to power.

The aristocrats began the revolution because they wished to regain the political power they had lost to the crown during the sixteenth and seventeenth centuries. The king's intendants had replaced the noble governors, and the king's bureaucracy controlled all levels of government throughout the country. The power of the monarchs was reflected in the fact that they had not bothered to call the Estates-General, or national parliament, since 1614. It is understandable then, that when Louis XVI in 1787 attempted to levy a uniform tax on all landed property without regard to the social status of the holder, the privileged orders branded the new tax illegal and asserted that only the nation as a whole assembled in the Estates-General could institute so sweeping a change. The pinch for money became so acute that the king finally gave way and summoned the Estates-General to meet in the spring of 1789. The nobility assumed that they would be able to control this body, but the meeting of the Estates-General led rather to the loosing of an elemental revolutionary wave that was to sweep away established institutions in France and in much of Europe.

Bourgeois Revolution

The Estates-General that met in Versailles on May 5, 1789, did not represent the people of France; it rather represented the three estates into which they traditionally had been divided. From the beginning the Third Estate proved to be the most dynamic and decisive. It had the advantage of numbers, there being 600 representatives in the Third Estate as against 300 each in the other two. Actually, the Third Estate outnumbered the other two combined, because a certain number of clergy were ready to throw in their lots with the lower orders, as were also a few liberal-minded noblemen, like the Marquis de Lafayette, who already had fought for the revolutionary cause in America. The middle-class representatives also had the advantage of possessing ideas. They knew that they wanted to change the old regime, and, from their reading in the works of the philosophes, they had at least a general idea of how the change should be effected. They also had the ready cash that the government needed so desperately, and they did not hesitate to use this potent weapon to extract the concessions they desired.

The commoners won their first victory in pressuring King Louis on June 23 to transform the Estates-General into a National Assembly. This was a vital change because so long as decisions were made on the basis of estates, the Third Estate would be in a perpetual minority of one amongst three. But as soon as the representatives of all three estates combined to form a National Assembly, the commoners, with their allies in the other two camps, would possess a majority. The king's concession did not represent a change of heart. Indicative of the king's real intentions was his dismissal on July 11 of Jacques Necker, the minister who was regarded as most favorable to reform. At the same time several regiments of loyal troops were quietly transferred to Versailles. The rumor spread that the king was preparing to dissolve the Assembly by force, and it seemed that nothing could prevent him from doing so. But at this critical point the commoners in the National Assembly were saved by an uprising of the common people in Paris. The masses intervened decisively, initiating the third, or mass, phase of the revolution.

Mass Revolution

The masses that now saved the revolution in France were not the riffraff of the streets. In fact, they were the lesser bourgeoisie, comprising shopkeepers and heads of workshops. They were the ones who circulated news and organized demonstrations, while their illiterate journeymen and clerks followed their leadership. The revolutionary outburst occurred following the dismissal of Necker. Mobs roamed the streets, demanding cheaper bread and parading busts of Necker draped in mourning. On July 14, they stormed and razed the Bastille, an ancient royal castle in Paris used as a prison. The event was of little practical significance, since the Bastille by this time was little used. Nevertheless it stood in the eyes of the populace as a symbol of oppression, and now this symbol was destroyed. Thus the fall of the Bastille marks the appearance of the masses on the historical stage.

The mass revolution manifested itself in the countryside as well as in Paris. The peasants took up arms, incited by their long-standing grievances and by the stirring news of the storming of the Bastille. In many parts of the countryside they tore down fences, seized lands, and burned manor houses. Faced with this revolutionary situation, the nobles and the clergy in the National Assembly made a virtue of necessity and voted with the commoners to abolish feudalism. During the famous "August Days" of 1789, legislation was passed ending all feudal dues, the privilege of tax exemption, the right of the church to collect tithes, and the exclusive right of the nobility to hold office. Outstanding among the numerous other important measures decreed by the Assembly were the confiscation of church lands, the reorganization of the judicial and administrative systems, and the adoption of the Declaration of the Rights of Man and Citizen.

The Declaration set forth certain fundamental principles concerning liberty, property, and security—"Men are born, and always continue, free and equal, in respect of their rights. . . . The Nation is essentially the source of all sovereignty . . . law is an expression of the will of the community . . . liberty consists in the power of doing whatever does not injure another. . . ." The final clause showed that the bourgeoisie had not lost control of the direction of the revolution: "The right to property being inviolable and sacred, no one ought to be deprived of it, except in cases of evident public necessity, legally ascertained, and on condition of a previous just indemnity." This Declaration was the essential message of the revolution. In the words of a French historian, it represents the death certificate of the old regime. Printed in thousands of leaflets, pamphlets, and books, and translated into other languages, the Declaration carried the revolutionary slogan of "Liberty, Equality, Fraternity" throughout Europe, and eventually the world.

King Louis was by no means willing to accept either the sweeping reforms of the Fourth of August or the revolutionary principles of the Declaration. Once more it was the Paris mob that overcame the royal opposition. Early in October a hungry crowd, composed chiefly of women, raided bread stores in Paris and then marched on the royal palace in Versailles. Under the pressure of this mob, Louis agreed to move the court to Paris. The royal family took up residence in the Tuileries (a palace in Paris), where they became virtual prisoners, and the National Assembly settled down in a nearby riding school. These turbulent October days assured the ratification of the decrees of August. They also increased tremendously the influence of the Paris mob, with both the royal family and the Assembly now being vulnerable to mass action.

War and Terror

Although the king in Paris was virtually powerless, many of the clergy and nobles were determined to regain their lost estates and privileges. Some of them fled abroad, where they worked to embroil foreign powers against the revolutionary regime in France. They were successful, war beginning in April, 1792, with Austria and Prussia ranged against France. At first the poorly prepared French were routed, but thousands of volunteers flocked to the colors in a wave of national patriotism. At the same time the Paris mob swung into action against the unpopular Louis and his hated Austrian queen, Marie Antoinette. Under pressure from the mob, the Assembly suspended the king on August 10 and called for the election of a National Convention.

The Convention, elected by universal franchise, met on September 21, 1792, and was brilliantly successful in meeting its most pressing problem—the defense of the country against the Austro-Prussian invaders. The combination of revolutionary élan and popular support proved irresistible, and the Prussians and the Austrians were driven back across the frontier. In 1793 Britain, Holland, and Spain joined the coalition against France. The revolutionaries responded with their famous *levée en masse*. The people rose to the defense of their *patrie*. Fourteen armies were put into the field, under the command of young generals who had risen from the ranks. Inspired by the revolutionary slogan "Liberty, Equality, Fraternity," the French citizen armies swept everything before them. By 1795 the enemy coalition had been smashed.

Meanwhile, the Convention was shifting increasingly to the left, partly because it had been elected by universal franchise, and also because of the revolutionary fervor engendered by the war effort. By June, 1793, the Girondists had been displaced by the more radical Jacobins. The dominant organ of government now was the Committee of Public Safety. With revolutionary zeal and passionate patriotism, this Committee appointed and discharged generals, spurred the masses to heroic action, conducted foreign policy, legislated on countless matters, and crushed the opposition by means of a ruthless Reign of Terror. Thousands were charged with treason, or merely with insufficient patriotism, and were subjected to the "national razor," as the guillotine was called.

But the Terror got out of control, and the revolution began "devouring its own children." In the unceasing struggle for power, one after another of the revolutionary leaders followed Louis and Marie Antoinette to the guillotine. Equally disturbing for the bourgeoisie was the growing social radicalism of the revolution. The *sans-culottes* (literally, those who lacked the knee-breeches of genteel society) were pressing hard for a more egalitarian state. They corresponded to the Levellers of the English Revolution, and they demanded a more equitable division of the land, government regulation of prices and wages, and a social security system. Such measures were quite beyond the plans of the French bourgeoisie. So, like their counterparts in England, they worked to halt the leftward course of the revolution. In England, the outcome was the defeat of the Levellers and rule by Cromwell. In France, the *sans-culottes* were brought under control, first by a Directory of five in 1795, and then by Napoleon Bonaparte in 1799.

Napoleon

Napoleon, having won fame as a brilliantly successful general in Italy, used his reputation and popularity to overthrow the Directory. He governed France as First Consul from 1799 to 1804, and as Emperor from 1804 to 1814. Two features of his fifteen-year rule of France are noteworthy for our purposes: his domestic reforms, which consolidated the gains of the revolution, and his military campaigns, which provoked a nationalist reaction in neighboring countries and eventually brought about his downfall.

So far as domestic policies are concerned, Napoleon may be compared to the enlightened despots. He was interested in technical efficiency rather than abstract ideology. He ruled the country autocratically, but he ruled it efficiently. He codified the laws, centralized the administration, organized a system of national education, established the Bank of France, and reached an agreement with the Papacy concerning church-state relations in France. These solid achievements of Napoleon made him generally popular. There were irreconcilables who hankered for the restoration of the old regime or who thought that Napoleon had betrayed the revolution. But the majority hailed him for ending the turbulence and instituting an honest and energetic government.

Napoleon squandered this goodwill by waging war unceasingly. Being a military genius, he was fabulously successful. By 1810 he reached the height of his fortunes, having extended France's frontiers across the Rhine to Lübeck and across the Alps to Rome. The rest of Europe consisted of dependent satellites or allies. Britain alone remained independent and implacably hostile.

In all his conquered territories, Napoleon implemented some of the basic principles of the French Revolution. He abolished feudalism and serfdom, recognized the equality of all citizens, and instituted his famous law codes. These innovations represented progress, or at least modernization. If disturbed vested interests everywhere objected to these changes, there was also widespread support for them in many quarters. The bourgeoisie and many intellectuals responded favorably to them outside France as well as in the countries they occupied. French rule was progressive, but the fact remains that it was foreign rule and that, where necessary, it was imposed by force. His non-French subjects eventually grew tired of the requisitioning, the taxes, the conscription, and the wars and rumors of wars. French rule usually meant a raising of the quality of administration, but the time came when people were impressed more by the Frenchness of the administration than by its quality.

In other words, these people had become nationalistic, and their nationalism had developed as a movement of resistance against Napoleon's domination. This explains the unrest in Italy, the armed resistance in Spain, and the growing national unity in Germany. Most vital for Napoleon was the bitter resistance of Russians of all classes when he invaded their country in 1812. This resistance, as much as the ice and the snow, was responsible for the catastrophic destruction of his Grand Army. From the frozen plains of Russia, the course of Napoleon's career ended precipitously and inevitably on the island of Elba. Thus the ideology of the French Revolution boomeranged against its originators. The people Napoleon had "offended" were people who had first been awakened and enthused by the slogan "Liberty, Equality, Fraternity" and who then had turned against their teachers when they betrayed their own principles.

Vienna Settlement

The Congress of Vienna, which met in 1815 to redraw the map of Europe after Napoleon's downfall, was guided by three principles—legitimacy, containment, and compensation. By the principle of legitimacy, the monarchs of France, Spain, Holland, and the Italian states were restored to their thrones. By the principle of containment, the states bordering France were made as strong as possible. Holland was given Belgium; Austria received Lombardy and Venetia; and Prussia received lands along the Rhine as well as part of Saxony. The victorious allies compensated themselves with various territories—Norway to Sweden; Malta, Ceylon, and the Cape of Good Hope to Britain; Finland, Bessarabia, and most of Poland to Russia; and Dalmatia and Galicia (as well as Lombardy and Venetia) to Austria. In anticipation of later events it should be noted that Germany and Italy remained disunited: Germany as the loose Germanic Confederation of thirty-nine states, and Italy as a "geographic expression" comprising nine states, all of them dominated by Austria because of her commanding position in Lombardy and Venetia.

VI. NATIONALISM

What is the significance for world history of the three great revolutions we have studied—the English, the American, and the French? The best answer to this question was given by an illiterate Greek guerrilla chieftain who led his countrymen in revolt against the Turkish overlord in 1821. "According to my judgement," he declared, "the French Revolution and the doings of Napoleon opened the eyes of the world. The nations knew nothing before, and the people thought that kings were gods upon the earth and that they were bound to say that whatever they did was well done. Through this present change it is more difficult to rule the people."[6]

In this simple language the guerrilla leader summarized the essence of the English and the American, as well as the French Revolutions. We have seen how the eyes of the world were opened by the Levellers and the Minutemen and the *sans-culottes*. This opening of eyes represented a profound political revolution. It marked the beginning for the first time in history of active and institutionalized mass participation in government. This revolution expressed itself in numerous isms which flourished during the nineteenth century. In the remainder of this chapter we shall concern ourselves with three of them—nationalism, liberalism, and socialism—which have since exerted the most influence on the course of European and of world history.

Nationalism is a phenomenon of modern European history. It was not to be found in recognizable form in the Middle Ages. At that time the universalism of the Roman Empire persisted in the Catholic Church, to which all Western Christians belonged, in the Latin language, which all educated people used, and in the Holy Roman Empire, ramshackle structure though it was. Consequently, mass allegiance to a nation was, during those centuries, unknown. Instead, most men considered themselves to be first of all Christians, second, residents of a certain region such as Burgundy or Cornwall, and only last, if at all, Frenchmen or Englishmen.

Three developments gradually modified this scale of allegiances. One was the rise of vernacular languages and the use of these languages for literary expression. Another was the break-off from the Catholic Church of several national churches. Finally, the western European dynasties built and consolidated several large, homogeneous, independent states—England, France, Spain, Portugal, and Denmark. These developments laid the basis for the rise of nationalism, though it should be noted that until the late eighteenth century the nation was identified with the person of the sovereign. Luther, for example, regarded "the bishops and princes" as constituting Germany while Louis XIV stated that the French nation "resided wholly in the person of the king."

Nationalism did not assume its modern form until the eighteenth century, when the western European bourgeoisie came to share or obtain full power. They did so in the name of the nation, so that the nation no longer was the king, his territory, and his subjects. Rather it was now composed of citizens (only propertied citizens until the late nineteenth century) "who inhabited a common territory, possessed a voice in their common government, and were conscious of their common (imagined or real) heritage and their common interests."[7]

This modern form of nationalism received its greatest impetus during the French Revolutionary and Napoleonic period. In order to survive the onslaught of the *anciens régimes* of Europe, the revolutionary leaders were forced to mobilize national armies—armies of politically conscious citizens ready and eager to fight for *la patrie*. The French Revolution contributed to the development of nationalism in several other ways. It required all French citizens to speak French—"the central or national language"—in place of the numerous regional dialects. It established a network of public elementary schools for the purpose of teaching French and inculcating love of country. The French Revolution also stimulated the publication of newspapers, pamphlets, and periodicals that were cheap and popularly written, and therefore effective in leaving their imprint upon the whole nation. And it inaugurated such nationalist rites and symbols as the national flag, the national anthem, and national holidays. All these developments enabled nationalism to overcome the traditional commitments to religion and to region.

We noted earlier that this passionate identification with the nation spread from France to neighboring countries. It did so by the natural diffusion of nationalist ideology, and also as a reaction to French aggression and domination. Nationalism was further stimulated by the Industrial Revolution which, with its new media for mass communication, made possible a more effective and all-embracing indoctrination of citizens. Thus nationalism became a prime factor in European history in the nineteenth century, and in world history in the twentieth. But nationalism changed in character as the nineteenth century passed. It began as a humane and tolerant creed, based on the concept of the brotherhood rather than the rivalry of the various nationalist movements. But in the latter part of the century it became increasingly chauvinistic and militaristic because of the influence of Social Darwinism and the success of Bismarck in uniting Germany by Machiavellian diplomacy and war, or, as he put it, by "blood and iron."

Nationalism manifested itself strongly immediately after 1815 because the territorial settlement of that year left millions of peoples either disunited or under foreign rule. This was the case with the Germans, the Italians, the Belgians, the Norwegians, and the numerous nationalities of the Hapsburg and Ottoman empires. The inevitable result was a series of nationalist revolts that broke out in all parts of Europe after 1815. The Greeks revolted successfully in 1821, winning their independence from Turkish rule. The Belgians did likewise in 1830, breaking away from Dutch domination. The Italians, after futile uprisings in 1820, 1830, and 1848, established an independent and united state between 1859 and 1871. The Germans, under the leadership of Prussia, built their German Empire after defeating Austria in 1866 and France in 1870–1871.

The principle of nationalism had triumphed in western Europe by 1871. But in central and eastern Europe the Hapsburg, Tsarist, and Ottoman empires remained "prisons of nationalities." The inmates of these prisons, however, were becoming increasingly ungovernable as nationalist movements succeeded all around them. The rulers of the three empires were aware of the consequences of nationalism for their multinational states, and tried to check it by various restrictive measures and by deliberately playing one subject nationality against another. These measures were successful at first but could not prevail indefinitely. The first breaches in the imperial structures were made by the Balkan subjects of the Turks. By 1878 the Serbs, the Rumanians, and the Montenegrins had gained their independence, and in 1908 the Bulgarians did likewise. Much more significant was the assassination in June, 1914, of the Hapsburg Archduke Francis Ferdinand by a young Serbian patriot, Gavrilo Princip. This was the fateful event that precipitated World War I, whose outcome was the destruction of all the empires of central and eastern Europe—the German, Austro-Hungarian, Russian, and Turkish. The peace treaties that terminated the war (discussed in Chapter 33, section VII) were generally based on the principle of nationalism, so that several new states appeared—Poland, Czechoslovakia, Yugoslavia, and Albania— that embodied the independent existence of hitherto subject peoples. For better or worse, nationalism had triumphed throughout Europe with the conclusion of World War I. And in the following decades, as we shall see in later chapters, this idea of nationalism began to awaken and spur to action the hundreds of millions of subject peoples in Europe's overseas possessions.

VII. LIBERALISM

Liberalism, whose central feature is the emancipation of the individual from class or corporate or governmental restraint, was the second great European doctrine to affect the globe. Its rise was intimately related to the rise of the bourgeoisie, although in central and eastern Europe, where the bourgeoisie was weak, liberalism was espoused by enlightened members of the nobility. Yet the fact remains that liberalism developed in its classic form in western Europe, and has remained essentially a middle-class movement in both tenets and source of support.

Liberal doctrines were first clearly formulated and implemented during the English Revolution. These doctrines were, at that time, primarily religious toleration and security of person and of property against the arbitrariness of the crown. More specifically, this involved parliamentary control of government, the existence of independent political parties, and the recognition of the need for, and the rights of, opposition parties. On the other hand, the franchise was limited by property qualifications, so that the lower-middle class and the workers, who comprised the great majority of the population, were left voteless. Thus, liberalism in seventeenth century England safeguarded and advanced bourgeois interests.

Liberalism was further defined and applied with the American Revolution, when substantial advances were made in restricting slavery, extending religious toleration, broadening the franchise, and establishing constitutional government. The federal constitution adopted in 1791 was based on the principle of the separation of powers in order to prevent tyranny—by having the executive, legislative, and judicial powers check and balance each other. The Bill of Rights guaranteed freedom of religion, speech, press, and assembly. And the American constitution, like the English settlement, carefully safeguarded the interests of the propertied classes: by limiting the franchise and by providing for the indirect election of the president and the senators, and for the election of the various branches of the government for different periods of time. These arrangements were designed to prevent a radical popular movement from obtaining control of the entire government at any one time and introducing dangerous changes.

Even more advanced in its liberal tenets than the American Revolution was the French. Its Declaration of the Rights of Man and Citizen is the classic statement of eighteenth century liberalism, proclaiming in ringing phrases the liberties of the individual. But French liberalism, too, was primarily a bourgeois movement. The Declaration, like all of the several constitutions adopted by the French revolutionaries, stressed the rights of property as "inviolable and sacred." And Napoleon's famous codes, which proved to be the most durable and influential, specifically forbade the organization of trade unions and the waging of strikes.

We may conclude that the liberalism that emerged from the English, American, and French Revolutions took the institutional form of constitutional parliamentary government, and was concerned about equal civil rights, though not equal political and social rights. Even in this restricted sense liberalism was on the defensive during the years following the Congress of Vienna. This was a period of reaction against the excesses of the revolutionary years, and restored monarchs, with the assistance of the aristocracy and the clergy, sought to turn the clock back to 1789. In most cases the monarchs ruled autocratically with no constitutional checks. Where constitutions did operate, the franchise was so severely limited that most of the middle class, not to mention the workers, were left voteless. Consequently, the period after 1815 was one of liberal as well as nationalist agitation.

Where the ruling power was foreign, the revolutionary movements were nationalist in character, as in Greece against Turkey, in Poland against Russia, in Belgium against Holland, and in Hungary against Austria. Where the governments were native but unrepresentative, the revolutionary movements were liberal in character. One example is to be found in France, where the restored Bourbon dynasty was overthrown in 1830 and replaced by the self-styled "bourgeois king" Louis Philippe. Another example is the British Reform Bill of 1832, which extended the franchise somewhat, though so modestly that the number of voters increased only from about half a million to about 813,000.

As the nineteenth century passed, liberalism, like other historical movements, changed appreciably in character. It could not continue to concern itself primarily with bourgeois interests at a time when the masses were becoming more assertive as a result of increasing education and trade-union organization. Consequently, there was a shift from the early, classical liberalism to a more democratic variety. Equality before the law was supplemented by equality before the ballot box. By the end of the nineteenth century manhood suffrage was operative in most of the western European countries. Even the hallowed principle of laissez faire was gradually modified. Hitherto intervention by the government in economic and social matters had been regarded as mischievous and futile meddling with the operation of natural laws. This theoretical proposition, however, did not jibe with the facts of life so far as the workers were concerned. Civil liberties and the right to vote did not relieve them from poverty and insecurity produced by unemployment, sickness, disability, and old age. So they used their voting power and union organization to press for social reforms. Under this pressure a new democratic liberalism developed which recognized the responsibility of the state for the welfare of all its citizens. Thus the western European countries, led by Germany, adopted social reform programs, including old age pensions, minimum wage laws, sickness, accident, and unemployment insurance, and regulation of hours and conditions of work. These reforms of democratic liberalism were the prelude to the welfare state that has become the hallmark of our own age.

VIII. SOCIALISM

Despite its adjustment to a changing world, liberalism during the past century has lost ground steadily to socialism. In most respects socialism is the antithesis of the classical liberalism of the eighteenth and early nineteenth centuries. Liberalism emphasizes the individual and his rights, socialism the community and its collective welfare. Liberalism represents society as the product of natural laws and denies the possibility of advancing human welfare artificially by legislation. Socialism, by contrast, holds that man, by rational thought and action, can determine his own social system and social relationships. Furthermore, it maintains that human nature is primarily the product of social environment, and that, accordingly, contemporary evils may be eliminated by establishing a society specifically designed to promote collective well-being rather than individual profit. In short, socialism stresses society and planned social change rather than the individual and laissez faire.

Plans for the reorganization of society are by no means peculiar to our modern age. Ever since the rise of civilization, political and economic power has been concentrated in the hands of a few. This has led prophets and reformers of all periods to advocate plans promoting social justice and equality. In the classical world, for example, Plato in his *Republic* called for an aristocratic communism, a dictatorship of communist philosophers. In the medieval period the English peasant leader John Ball declared to his followers, "My good people,—things cannot go well in England, nor ever will, until all goods are held in common and until there will be neither serfs nor gentlemen, and we shall all be equal."[8] The turmoil and the passions of the English and French Revolutions naturally stimulated more schemes for the promotion of the common welfare but the final outcome, as we have seen, was the triumph of the relatively conservative Cromwell and Napoleon.

A vigorous new school of social reformers—the Utopian Socialists—appeared in the early nineteenth century. Outstanding were the two Frenchmen, Henri de Saint-Simon (1760–1825) and Charles Fourier (1772–1837), and the English industrialist Robert Owen (1771–1858). All had one basic characteristic in common. They concentrated their attention on the principles and on the precise workings of their projected model communities. But the problem of how these were to supplant the existing society they never seriously faced. They definitely did not think in terms of revolution or of class warfare. In fact, they scarcely thought at all about how their elaborate blueprints might be implemented. It is for this reason that they are known as Utopian Socialists.

Karl Marx (1818–1883), the father of modern socialism, differed fundamentally from the Utopian Socialists in almost every respect. He was as materialistic in his outlook as they were idealistic. He spent most of his life studying the historical evolution and the precise functioning of the existing capitalistic society while they prepared blueprints of model communities. He was firmly convinced from his study of history that class struggle offered the only means of social change, while they looked for the support of wealthy benefactors.

Marx summarized the materialist interpretation of history as follows in the Preface of his earlier work, the *Communist Manifesto,* which he wrote in 1848 with his lifelong friend and benefactor, Friedrich Engels: "In every historical epoch, the prevailing mode of economic production and exchange, and the social organization necessarily following from it, form the basis upon which is built up . . . the political and intellectual history of that epoch." The slave economy of the classical world, for example, explains its political conditions—democracy for the freemen and bondage for the slaves. It also explains the cultural attainments of the classical world—slave labor allowed a few to live in leisure and to devote themselves to cultural pursuits.

The doctrine of class struggle also is best summarized in the *Communist Manifesto.* "The history of all hitherto existing society is the history of class struggles. Freeman and slave, patrician and plebeian, lord and serf, guildmaster and journeyman, in a word, oppressor and oppressed, . . . carried on an uninterrupted . . . fight that each time ended, either in a revolutionary re-constitution of society at large, or in the common ruin of the contending classes." The idea of classes with conflicting interests was by no means new with Marx. But what *was* new, and immensely significant, was the proposition that it is through class struggle that mankind has passed from one type of social organization to another. Marxists state, for example, that the transition from feudalism to capitalism was made possible by the appearance of a middle class whose interests were antithetical to those of the feudal lords and who, therefore, led the revolutionary movement that eventually overthrew feudalism.

The materialist interpretation of history and the doctrine of class struggle form the basis of Marx's interpretation of past history. So far as the future was concerned, he was certain that capitalism would give way to socialism, and his conviction was based on his third major doctrine, the theory of surplus value. According to this theory, the workingman who provides the labor receives in the form of wages substantially less than the price charged the consumer. Marx argued that this represents the Achilles' heel of capitalism, because the workers as a class cannot purchase with their wages what they produce. In the long run this will lead to overproduction, or, as the Marxists put it, to underconsumption due to inadequate purchasing power because of inadequate wages. Thus, the result is the closing of factories, unemployment, a further decline of purchasing power, and at length, a full-scale depression. Furthermore, Marx believed that these depressions would become increasingly frequent and severe until finally the unemployed proletariat would be driven in desperation to revolution. In this way capitalism would be superseded by socialism as feudalism earlier had been by capitalism. And the new socialist society would be depression-proof because, with government ownership of the means of production, there could be no private employers, no profits, and hence no lack of purchasing power.

The course of events since the mid-nineteenth century, when Marx wrote his books, has not followed the precise pattern that he forecast. The poor have not become poorer in the advanced capitalist countries. Rather the workers have become increasingly affluent and hence increasingly satisfied with the *status quo*. Nevertheless, despite these facts, Marx's doctrines have exerted tremendous influence throughout the world, and today represent one of the most vital forces shaping the course of history. The reason is to be found in the nature and the appeal of his doctrines. In the first place they gave the workers everywhere a feeling of self-confidence, a conviction that time was on their side. For did not the theory of surplus value prove the inevitable collapse of capitalism? Marxism also made the workers active and militant, because the theory of class struggle demonstrated that the socialist millennium was to be won not by the assistance of philanthropic benefactors but rather by the efforts of the workers themselves. Finally, Marxism gave workers throughout the world a sense of brotherhood and cohesion by stressing international class ties rather than national allegiance. The last sentence of the *Communist Manifesto* reads "Workers of the world, unite!"

Marx played an important role in the establishment in 1864 of the International Workingmen's Association, or, as it is commonly called, the First International. This body was committed to Marx's program of the seizure of power by the workers for the purpose of reorganizing society along socialist lines. It attracted considerable attention with its propaganda and its participation in various strikes. But it disintegrated in 1873, largely because its membership comprised an undisciplined and constantly feuding assortment of romanticists, nationalists, and anarchists, as well as socialists.

In 1884 the Socialist, or Second, International was established in Paris. This was a loosely knit organization to which were affiliated the numerous Socialist parties that had appeared by this time in various countries. The Second International grew rapidly, so that by 1914 it comprised the Socialist parties of twenty-seven countries with a total membership of twelve million workers. This Second International was much more moderate in its doctrines and its actions than the First. The reason for this shift in emphasis is that the major constituent parties were themselves turning away from simon-pure Marxism to what was termed Revisionism. A number of factors explain this shift in emphasis. One was the gradual extension of the franchise in the western European countries, which meant that the workers could use ballots rather than bullets to attain their objectives. Another was the steady rise after 1850 in European living standards, which tended to make workers more willing to accept the *status quo*. The German revisionist leader Eduard Bernstein expressed the new viewpoint when he declared that socialists should "work less for the better future and more for the better present." Not all socialists were willing to go along with this revisionism. Some of them remained true to what they considered to be the teachings of Marx, so that most Socialist parties split into "orthodox" and "revisionist" factions. The revisionists, however, were more in tune with the temper of the times, and usually controlled their respective parties.

When World War I began in 1914, the Second International paid the price for its revisionism: the majority of its members proved to be nationalists first and socialists second. They responded to the exhortations of their respective national governments, with the result that millions of workers died fighting on both sides of the trenches. Thus the Second International was torn asunder, and although it was revived after the war, it never attained its former strength and prestige.

Socialism, however, did not peter out with the disintegration of the Second International. In fact, it was during World War I that the Russian socialists or Bolsheviks, as they were called, succeeded in seizing power and establishing the first proletarian government in history. Furthermore, the Bolsheviks organized the Third, or Communist, International to challenge the Second, or Socialist, International. We shall consider later the nature and the activities of the Communist regime in Russia and of the international Communist movement. Suffice it to note here that millions of people today live in avowedly socialist states, that many more millions live in communist states, and that the vast propaganda apparatuses of the communist states proclaim day in and day out that Marx's prophecies will soon be fulfilled—that the days of capitalism are numbered. Thus it is apparent that Marxism, in its socialist and communist varieties, is today a central force in world affairs, rivaling nationalism in its dynamism and in its universal appeal.

SUGGESTED READING

M. Ashley, *England in the Seventeenth Century* (Penguin, 1952); P. Gay, ed., *The Enlightenment: A Comprehensive Anthology* (Simon & Schuster, 1973); L. H. Gipson, *The Coming of the Revolution, 1763–1775* and J. R. Alden, *The American Revolution, 1775–1783,* both in the "New American Nation" series (Harper, 1954); C. Hill, *The World Turned Upside Down. Radical Ideas During the English Revolution* (Viking, 1972); G. Lefebvre, *The Coming of the French Revolution* (Random House, 1957); G. Lichtheim, *The Origins of Socialism* (Praeger, 1969); R. R. Palmer, *The Age of the Democratic Revolution: A Political History of Europe and America, 1760–1800* (Princeton Univ., 1959, 1964); J. R. Pennock, *Liberal Democracy: Its Merits and Prospects* (Holt, 1950); B. C. Shafer, *Nationalism: Myth and Reality* (Harcourt, 1955); J. Sigmann, *1848. The Romantic and Democratic Revolutions in Europe* (Harper, 1973).

Impact of Dominance

Having considered the three revolutions that made possible Europe's domination of the globe in the nineteenth century, we turn now to the domination process itself. We shall examine precisely how this domination manifested itself in the various parts of the world. Considering first the Eurasion lands, there is evident a certain pattern in both the timing and the unfolding of Europe's impact.

The timing was determined by three principal factors. The first was geographic location, which explains why Russia, for example, felt Europe's dynamism long before China or Japan. The second was the attitude of the local population, and particularly the local ruling class, toward what the West had to offer. Peter the Great's ardent westernism, for example, ensured the early penetration of Western thought and technology into Russia, while the rigid seclusion policies of China and Japan contributed to the exclusion of Western influence from those countries until the second half of the nineteenth century. The third factor was the strength and cohesion of the local societies. Where there was weakness and disunity, Western penetration and control came early, as in the case of India; where there was strength and unity, the West was for long kept at arm's length, as in the case of China.

As regards the nature of the actual impact itself, it is reminiscent of a pebble falling in a pool and stimulating a series of ever expanding circles. Western intrusion was at first usually confined to some single specific area, but invariably it had repercussions in other fields, which in turn induced further impulses until the entire society was affected. Precisely this point has been made by Sir Henry Maine, the English jurist and historian who served in India between 1862 and 1869:

It is by indirect and for the most part unintended influence that the British power [in India] metamorphoses and dissolves the ideas and social forms underneath it, nor is

359

there any expedient by which it can escape the duty of rebuilding upon its own principles that which it unwillingly destroyed . . . we do not innovate or destroy in mere arrogance. We rather change because we cannot help it. Whatever be the nature and value of that bundle of influences which we call Progress, nothing can be more certain than that, when a society is once touched by it, it spreads like a contagion.[1]

More specifically, the contagion from the West usually began in the military field. Non-Europeans were most impressed and alarmed by the West's superior military technology, and strove to learn the secrets of this technology as soon as possible. This happened in region after region—in Russia, in the Middle East, in China and in Japan. But Western arms required the development of certain industries, so that the original military objectives led to new objectives in the economic field. We shall see that for various reasons there was substantial industrialization in the nineteenth century in Russia and Japan, but comparatively little in the Middle East, in India, and in China. Modernization in tools led inevitably to modernization in ideas and values. Arms and factories required schools and science, as one Western borrowing continued inexorably to necessitate another. Military and economic change produced intellectual change, and also social and political. A new merchant and industrial class appeared which challenged the traditional society and ruling groups, and eventually also challenged Western domination. This explains the intellectual ferment and the revolutionary movements that opposed Tsardom in Russia, British control in India, and Manchu rule in China.

This general pattern overlooks innumerable nuances and exceptions—the virtual absence of a native Moslem middle class amongst the Turks, the fateful disparity in the Japanese and Chinese responses to the West, the significance of total European political domination in India, compared to the semi-control in China, and the relative lack of political control in Russia and Japan. The details of these individual developments we shall now analyze in the following chapters on each of the regions of Eurasia. Succeeding chapters will analyze the even greater influence that the West had beyond Eurasia—in sub-Saharan Africa, the Americas, and Australia.

[1] *H. S. Maine,* Village-Communities in the East and West *(New York, Henry Holt, 1880), pp. 237, 238.*

chapter twenty-six

Russia

For three hundred years Russia has aspired to consort with Occidental Europe; for three hundred years she has taken her most serious ideas, her most fruitful teachings, and her most vivid delights from there.—
Peter Y. Chaadayev

It is paradoxical to be considering Europe's impact upon Russia, for Russia, after all, is a part of Europe, and the Russian people are a European people. But Russia lies on the fringe of Europe and comprises a great buffer zone between that continent and Asia. Because of this location the historical experience of the Russian people has been quite different from that of other Europeans, and the culture they have developed is correspondingly different. As a result, Russian thinkers have tormented themselves generation after generation with the basic issue of national orientation and national goals.

Russia's relationship with the West has generally been that of passive recipient. Only in the past century and a half has Russia been able to repay the West, at first with the creations of her great writers and composers, and later with the economic planning techniques and the social stimuli generated by the Bolshevik Revolution. But until the twentieth century, Europe's impact on Russia was much greater than the reverse, and this influence has been a central factor in the development of the country.

I. RUSSIA AND EUROPE TO 1856

The first Russian state that developed around the principality of Kiev in the ninth century after Christ had numerous ties with the rest of Europe. (See Chapter 15, sections VI and VII.) During the following centuries two crucial developments effectively isolated Russia: Prince Vladimir's decision about A.D. 990 to adopt the Byzantine Orthodox form of Christianity rather than the Roman Catholic, and the Mongol conquest of the country in 1237. When the Russians rid themselves of the Mongols in the fifteenth century, the Muscovite civilization that came to light was quite different from anything in Western Europe. It was a homogeneous civilization in the sense that Orthodoxy shaped and colored men's outlook and actions. But it was also a civilization largely devoid of the commerce, the industry, and the science that had made the West so dynamic and expansionist. The more emancipated and far-seeing Russian leaders soon perceived that their economic and technological backwardness represented an intolerable threat to their national security. Thus it was that the Russians in the sixteenth century, like the Turks and the Japanese and the Chinese in later centuries, began to borrow from the West as a measure of self-defense. And primarily they were interested in military technology.

There was nothing academic or abstract about this policy. Rather, it was a matter of life or death, for Russia was surrounded by the powerful Swedes, Lithuanians, and Poles in the west, and by the Turks and Crimean Tatars in the south. It is significant that when Tsar Ivan IV (1533–1584) proposed to Queen Elizabeth of England a military and even a marriage alliance, the King of Poland hastily wrote to Elizabeth begging her to reject the proposition. "Up to now," he wrote, "we could conquer him [the Russian] only because he was a stranger to education and did not know the arts."[1]

Thus the neighbors of Russia were deliberately seeking to prevent that country from acquiring Western arms and techniques. The Russians, on their part, naturally sought to break the isolating encirclement, and they did so with increasing success. During the seventeenth century they employed many foreign officers to train and lead their armed forces, especially after the end of the Thirty Years' War in 1648, which left many professional soldiers unemployed. Tsar Peter the Great (1682–1725) accelerated tremendously this process of westernization. With his iron will and herculean energy he issued over 3,000 decrees, many in his own hand, and almost all inspired by him. He reorganized his administration and armed forces along Western lines, established industries to support his armies, imported thousands of foreign experts of various types, sent droves of young Russians to study abroad, and set up a number of schools, all of them utilitarian in character: schools of mathematics and navigation, admiralty schools, war department schools, ciphering schools, and, at the summit, the Academy of Sciences. By all these means Peter realized in large part his expressed aim of opening a "window to the West." Furthermore, he opened this window in a literal sense by defeating Sweden and acquiring frontage on the Baltic Sea, where he built his new capital of St. Petersburg—the symbol of the new Russia, as Moscow was of the old.

Peter's work was continued by the gifted and colorful Catherine the Great (1762–1796). Catherine regarded herself and her court as media for the Europeanization of Russia. Being much more intellectual than the pragmatic Peter, she energetically patronized literature, art, the theater, and the press. She was not an original thinker, but she readily absorbed the ideas of others, especially of the philosophes. In fact, she prided herself on being an Enlightened Despot, and often quoted the maxims of the Enlightenment. During her reign the higher Russian nobility became Europeanized to the point of deracination. The nobles who had worn beards and flowing Oriental robes during Peter's reign now aped the court of Versailles in their speech, clothes, dwellings, and social functions. This was the time when the children of the nobility, brought up by French governesses, learned French as their mother tongue, and then picked up only enough Russian to manage the servants. Thus the Europeanization of Russia no longer was confined to technical matters, though it continued to be limited to the upper class. Indeed, the gulf between the Europeanized upper crust and the peasant masses who were bound to the estates as serfs was becoming wider and more provocative.

This inequity in Russian society scarcely jibed with the principles of the Enlightenment that Catherine ostentatiously propounded. But Catherine was too much a realist to be unduly concerned about the discrepancy between theory and reality. Knowing that she was dependent upon the nobles for her position, she never seriously challenged their interests and privileges. On the contrary, she turned violently against the teachings of the philosophes when the French Revolution broke out. She denounced the revolution as "an irreligious, immoral, anarchical, abominable, and diabolical plague, the enemy of God and of Thrones." "The National Assembly," she added, "should burn all the best French authors, and all that has carried their language over Europe, for all that declares against the abominable mess that they have made. . . . As for the people and its opinion, that is of no great consequence."[2]

Catherine could afford to dismiss so lightly the views of "the people," but it was to be different with her successors. This was especially true after the great Russian victory over Napoleon's Grand Army. Between 1815 and 1818 a Russian army of occupation was stationed in France, and many of its officers were much impressed by the relatively free Western society in which they had lived. They absorbed the liberal and radical ideas in contemporary France and were profoundly influenced by them. When they returned to Russia in 1818, they found the Tsarist autocracy to be intolerable.

They were responsible for the so-called Decembrist Revolt that broke out in December, 1825, upon the death of Alexander I, and that sought to westernize Russia by abolishing serfdom and the autocracy. The revolt failed miserably because there was no mass support. The Russians at this time lived under conditions so utterly different from those prevailing in Western Europe that they simply were not ready for western political ideas and institutions. More specifically, Russia lacked the commerce, the industry, and the middle class that had played so decisive a role in the political evolution of the West. Instead, there were at the bottom the bound and inert serf masses—the "dark people," as they were called—and at the top the nobility and the court. Consequently, there was no mass support for the reforms and for the Western type of society desired by the Decembrists.

The meaning of these basic differences between Russia and the West divided Russian thinkers into two groups, the Westerners and the Slavophils. The Westerners deplored the differences, interpreting them as a product of Russia's slower rate of development. Accordingly, their hero was Peter the Great, and they urged that other rulers match Peter's heroic efforts to goad Russia to catch up with the West. The Slavophils, on the other hand, rejected the Westerners' basic assumption of the unity of human civilization. They maintained that every state embodies and expresses the peculiar spirit of its people, and that if an attempt is made to model one state after another, the inevitable result will be contradiction and discord. They held the differences between Russia and the West to be fundamental and inherent, reflecting profound dissimilarities in national spirit rather than degrees of advance. Accordingly these Slavophils idealized the homogeneous Muscovite society of the pre-Petrine period, and regarded Peter as the archenemy of Russian civilization and national unity. Far from considering Western society as superior, they rejected it as being materialistic, faithless, and torn by dissension and revolution.

II. RUSSIA AND EUROPE, 1856–1905

The issue between the Slavophils and the Westerners was settled not by persuasion of one side by the other, but rather by the irresistible pressure of the rapidly developing and expanding Western society. This pressure was dramatically illustrated by the Crimean War (1854–1856) between Russia and a number of Western powers, of which the most important were Britain and France. The war was fought on Russian soil—in the Crimean Peninsula—and yet Russia was defeated and forced to accept the humiliating Treaty of Paris. This treaty required Russia to scrap her naval units in the Black Sea and her fortifications along the Black Sea coast, and also forced her to surrender certain small but strategic territories along the Danube.

The Crimean defeat was a severe shock for the Russian nationalists and Slavophils. They had confidently predicted that the superiority of Russia's autocratic institutions would lead to a victory comparable to that of 1812 over Napoleon. But Russia was defeated, and the defeat served to unveil the corruption and backwardness of the old regime. Russia's soldiers had fought as gallantly in 1855 as in 1812. But the odds were hopelessly against them: They had rifles that shot only a third as far as those of the Western armies. They had only sailing ships to use against the steamships of the British and the French. They had no medical or commissariat services that were worthy of the name. And the lack of railways in the Crimean Peninsula forced them to haul military supplies in carts, and to march on foot for hundreds of miles before reaching the front. In short, the war was lost because, as the Westerners had perceived, "Europe has been steadily advancing on the road of progress while we have been standing still."

The revelation of the bankruptcy of the old regime led to its modification. The first change was the emancipation of the serfs, who had been intensely restless even before the war. In fact, over 500 peasant disturbances had broken out during the three decades of Nicholas I's reign between 1825 and 1855. With the disaster in the Crimea, the mounting pressure of the serfs became irresistible, and Nicholas' successor, Alexander II, accepted emancipation as the only alternative to revolution. Alexander's decision was encouraged also by many nobles, who favored emancipation in order to take advantage of the growing demand for grain in a Europe that was becoming increasingly industrialized and urbanized. They discovered that they could not produce a substantial surplus for export so long as all the land was divided among the serfs, who grew only enough for their own needs, and a little extra for the noble proprietors. So the more forward-looking nobles were all in favor of freeing the serfs from the bonds that hitherto had bound them to their plots. In this way the nobles planned to consolidate the small plots, introduce efficient, large-scale agricultural techniques, and employ as day laborers only those former serfs whose labor they actually needed, instead of being required to support the whole of a rapidly growing serf population.

These circumstances combined to make possible the Emancipation Decree issued on March 1, 1861. By its term all serfs were declared free, and the land that they tilled was divided between themselves and the noble proprietors. The latter were paid with government treasury bonds for the land that was distributed among the peasants. In return, the peasants were required to compensate the government by paying redemption dues for forty-nine years. This was a great turning point in Russian history, even greater than the 1863 Emancipation Proclamation in American history. Emancipation in the United States concerned only the Negro minority, whereas in Russia it involved the overwhelming majority of the population. So far-reaching were the repercussions of the freeing of the serfs that a series of other reforms proved unavoidable, including the reorganization of the judiciary and of the local government.

During the decades following the Crimean War, Western Europe further undermined the old regime in Russia by contributing decisively to the industrialization of the country. The number of factory workers rose from 381,000 in 1865 to 1,620,000 in 1890, and to 3,000,000 in 1898. By 1913, Russia was producing as much iron and three-fourths as much coal as France. The significance of the West's contribution is evident in the fact that of the total of £500 million invested in Russian industry in 1917, just over one-third comprised foreign investments. Foreign capital controlled 50 per cent of coal and oil output, 60 per cent of copper and iron ore, and 80 per cent of coke.

These developments meant that the Russia of 1914 was much more similar to Europe than had been the Russia of the Decembrists of 1825. But the growing similarity generated, as the Slavophils had warned, certain divisions and conflicts within Russian society. One of these was the growing unrest and political consciousness of the peasant masses. They had been far from satisfied with the terms of the Emancipation Decree which, they felt, had left too large a proportion of the land to the nobles. During the following decades, as the peasants grew rapidly in numbers, their land hunger grew correspondingly, and they became increasingly dissatisfied with the *status quo*. Another source of grievance for the peasants was the intolerably heavy tax load. They paid not only the redemption dues for the land they had received in 1861 but also an assortment of local taxes. In addition, they bore much of the cost of Russia's industrialization, because the high protective tariffs forced up the cost of the manufactured goods they bought. The extent and the intensity of peasant discontent became apparent with the increasing frequency of violent peasant outbreaks against landlords and unpopular government officials.

This peasant disaffection found political expression in the Socialist Revolutionary party which was organized in 1898. Since no political parties were allowed in Russia prior to the 1905 Revolution, the Socialist Revolutionaries had to operate as an illegal underground group. The main plank of their platform was the distribution of state and noble lands amongst the peasantry. In two important respects they differed from the various types of Marxist socialists. In the first place, they regarded the peasantry rather than the urban proletariat as the main revolutionary force in Russia. In the second place, they advocated and practiced individual acts of terrorism, rather than relying on mass organization and pressure. Within the Socialist Revolutionary party was the highly secret Fighting Organization which directed the terroristic activities. Its success may be gauged from its long list of illustrious victims, including governors of provinces, ministers of state, and even the Tsar's uncle, Grand Duke Sergei.

The unrest of the peasants was matched by that of the urban proletariat who had appeared with the growth of industry. The early days of industrialization in Russia, as elsewhere in Europe, involved gross exploitation of labor: sixteen-hour working days, low wages, child labor, and abominable working and living conditions. Under these conditions the Russian workers, like those of Central and Western Europe, came under the influence of Marxist doctrines. Thus a Social Democratic party was organized in 1898 as similar socialist parties had been established elsewhere in Europe. And like the other socialist parties, that of Russia split into revisionist and orthodox factions, or, as they were called in this instance, the Mensheviks and the Bolsheviks.

The split occurred during the second party congress held in London in 1903. The issues concerned party membership and party discipline. Nikolai Lenin, the leader of the orthodox faction, maintained that because of the repressive Tsarist autocracy, the Social Democratic party had to operate very differently from other socialist parties. Membership should be open not to any sympathizer who paid his dues, but only to a small group of full-time professional revolutionaries. And this select membership was to function according to the principle of "democratic centralism." Any major issue facing the party was to be discussed freely by the members until a decision was reached democratically by a vote. But then the "centralism" part of the principle became operative. Every party member, regardless of his personal inclinations, was required on pain of expulsion to support undeviatingly what was now the "party line."

Only with such rigid discipline, Lenin maintained, could Russian socialists carry on effectively their underground operations. Lenin won the support of most of the delegates to the 1903 congress, so that his followers henceforth were known as Bolsheviks, after the Russian word for "majority," and his opponents as Mensheviks, or "minority." It should be noted, however, that the Bolsheviks remained an infinitesimally small group until the outbreak of World War I. Then the chaos and misery produced by the defeats at the front gave the Bolsheviks the opportunity to use their superior organization to mobilize and lead the disaffected masses.

In addition to the peasants and the urban workers, there was in Russia at the turn of the century a middle class that also was becoming increasingly discontented with the Tsarist regime. The political organization reflecting the views of this group was the Constitutional Democratic party, commonly known under the abbreviated title of Cadets. The program of this party, founded in 1905, resembled that of the English Liberals: a constitutional monarchy balanced by a parliamentary body similar to Britain's House of Commons. The Cadets included many of Russia's outstanding intellectuals and businessmen. When the Tsar was forced to accept an elected assembly (Duma) following the 1905 Revolution, the Cadets played a leading role in its deliberations because of their articulateness and their knowledge of parliamentary procedures. And yet the Cadets never won a mass following comparable to that of the Social Democrats or the Socialist Revolutionaries. One reason was that the middle class was relatively small in Russia, thanks to the retarded development of commerce and industry. The middle class was further weakened because so much of the national economy was controlled by foreign interests. And the Cadets were peculiarly vulnerable to the pressures of the Tsarist autocracy, because, with their middle-class background, they were less willing to meet force with force.

Such, then, was the West's impact upon Russia by the turn of the century. The intrusion of the West had undermined a distinctive and homogeneous society; and the repercussions of the resulting stresses and dissensions were to culminate in the great revolutions of 1905 and 1917. Before considering these upheavals, we shall survey Russian policies in Asia to the Russo-Japanese War, which set the stage for the 1905 revolution.

III. RUSSIA AND ASIA TO 1905

Just as the relations between Russia and Europe were determined largely by the economic and technological superiority of Europe, so the relations between Russia and Asia were determined by the superiority of Russia. This superiority had enabled Russia between the sixteenth and the eighteenth centuries to overcome the tribespeople of Siberia and to expand eastward to the Pacific. But in the southeast the Russians had been halted by the strong and populous Chinese Empire and forced to accept the Nerchinsk Treaty (1689) confining them to the territory north of the Amur Valley. (See Chapter 22, section III.).

During the eighteenth and nineteenth centuries the Russians resumed their advance to the east and the south, rounding out their empire by acquiring Alaska, the Amur Valley, and Central Asia. These successes were made possible by Russia's steady technological progress. Inadequate vis-à-vis the West—indeed, it was derived from the West—it was nonetheless sufficient to give the Russians a decisive advantage in their relations with the Chinese in East Asia and with the Moslems in Central Asia. Thus, the Russians continued to extend their imperial frontiers until stopped by powers that were technologically equal or superior—that is, by the Americans in Alaska, by the British in India and Persia, and by the Japanese in Manchuria.

Alaska

The Russian advance to Alaska got under way during the reign of Peter the Great. The westernizing tsar was as much interested in the Far East as in Europe, so he selected Captain Vitus Bering to lead an expedition to determine whether Siberia and America were separate or joined. Bering conducted two expeditions, in 1728 and 1740. He did not settle the question of the junction of Siberia and America, because he sailed eastward across the Bering Sea before reaching the strait that also bears his name and that separates the two continents. But Bering and his associates did explore the Aleutian Islands and also landed on the coast of Alaska. Russian merchants followed on the heels of the explorers, attracted by the profitable trade in sea-otter skins. The merchants first exploited the Aleutian Islanders and then established posts along the Alaskan coast. In 1799 the various private trading companies combined to form the Russo-American Company. The outstanding Russian leader in Alaska was Alexander Baranov, who directed operations energetically and autocratically for a generation. His chief problem was transporting supplies from Siberia across one of the world's stormiest and foggiest seas. Accordingly, Baranov sent expeditions down the American coast to establish settlements where fresh supplies could be grown for the Alaskan posts. In November, 1811, Fort Ross was established on the Russian River north of San Francisco, and by 1819 the Russians had a chain of nineteen settlements on the American coast.

This expansion led to friction with Spain and with the United States. In fact, the presence of the Russians in the northwest Pacific contributed appreciably to the enunciation of the Monroe Doctrine in 1823. In the end, the Russians decided to give up their American holdings. The decline in the fur trade had brought the Russo-American Company to the point of bankruptcy. And the Russians feared that Alaska was too distant to be defended against American expansionism. Anticipating that they would lose the territory sooner or later, they sold it to the United States in 1867 for $7 million, or less than two cents per acre.

Amur Valley

Meanwhile, this Russian activity in North America had reawakened Russian interest in the Amur Valley. The Russians needed an outlet on the Pacific Ocean to serve as a base for supplying their American settlements. They did have the port of Okhotsk, but this was altogether inadequate, being frozen every year until June, and almost continually fogbound. Consequently, the Russians once more looked longingly toward the broad and navigable Amur River from which they had been ousted by the Nerchinsk Treaty in 1689.

Russian interest was further whetted by the so-called Opium War of 1839–1842 between Britain and China. (See Chapter 29, section I.) As a result of the war, Britain annexed Hong Kong and acquired a predominant influence in the Yangtze Valley. The Russians now resolved to establish themselves in the Amur Valley lest the British next gain control of the mouth of the river and thus block their natural outlet to the Pacific. In little more than a decade, the Russians gained all their objectives in this vital region. One reason for their success was the ambition and energy of young Count Nikolai Muraviev, who was appointed governor general of Eastern Siberia in 1847 at the age of 38. Another reason was the weakness of China, by that time a hollow shell compared to the powerful empire that had expelled the Russians from the Amur Valley in the seventeenth century.

Count Muraviev was given extensive viceregal powers, but he exceeded them in sending out exploratory expeditions that planted the Russian flag on foreign soil. One of his officers, Captain (later Admiral) Nevelskoi, established the fortress of Petropavlovsk on the Kamchatka Peninsula, explored and occupied Sakhalin Island after ousting Japanese settlers, launched steamships on the Amur River, encouraged Russian colonists to settle in the Amur Valley, and founded a number of posts along the coast between the mouth of the Amur and the Korean frontier. The entire region was a no man's land over which the Chinese had only a vague suzerainty and no control whatsoever. In fact, the Chinese court was quite unaware of the Russian measures, and it was the Russian government itself which, in May, 1851, informed the Chinese of what had taken place.

Five years later, in 1856, hostilities broke out once more between China and Britain. The Chinese again were badly beaten and forced by the Tientsin Treaties (1858) to open more ports to Western merchants and to make other concessions. Muraviev seized the opportunity to warn the Chinese of the danger of British control of the Amur and to propose joint Russo-Chinese defense of the region. The outcome was the Aigun Treaty (1858) by which Russia obtained the left bank of the Amur to the Ussuri River, beyond which Russia and China were to exercise joint sovereignty over both banks of the river to the ocean.

Muraviev now explored carefully the newly won territories and discovered that the formation of ice on the lower Amur was such that control of both banks was essential for navigation purposes. He also found a magnificent harbor on the coast near the Korean frontier. Despite the provisions of the Aigun Treaty, he founded there a city (1860) which he significantly named Vladivostok, or Queen of the East. Meanwhile, China had become embroiled in further trouble with the Western powers, and in 1860 Peking was occupied by an Anglo-French force. The Russian minister in Peking, Count Nikolai Ignatiev, offered his services as an intermediary and succeeded in getting the allies to evacuate the capital under not too onerous conditions. In return for this service the Chinese government negotiated the Treaty of Peking (1860) giving Russia both banks of the Amur from the Ussuri to the sea, and also the entire coastal area from the mouth of the Amur to the Korean border. With the winning of these new farflung frontiers (which exist to the present day), Russian expansion in the Far East came to a halt. It was not resumed again until the beginning of the twentieth century, when Tsar Nicholas II attempted to penetrate south into Korea and Manchuria, and thereby precipitated a disastrous war with Japan.

Central Asia

In the meantime, the Russians had been penetrating also into Central Asia, although their advance in this region did not begin until the second quarter of the nineteenth century. The delay was due in part to the absence of economic incentives comparable to the profitable fur trade in the north. But there were other reasons: The climate and vegetation of Central Asia were quite different to what the Russians were accustomed. Immediately to the south of Siberia was the steppe country in which lived the Kazakh nomads. Still further south began the great desert, dotted with rich oases that supported the ancient Moslem khanates of Bukhara, Khiva, and Kokand. Much stronger militarily than the scattered Siberian tribes, these khanates were able to keep the Russians at arm's length until the late nineteenth century.

During the three decades between 1824 and 1854 the Russians made their first advance into Central Asia by conquering the Kazakh steppes to the Syr Darya River. They hoped that the river would serve as a permanent natural frontier, but this did not prove to be the case. The ambition of local commanders, remote from the capital and eager for glory and promotion, frequently forced the hand of the government by presenting it with a *fait accompli*. The constant harassment of marauding bands also led the Rusians to press further in spite of misgivings in St. Petersburg and protests from Britain. One after another, the legendary centers of Central Asian Moslem civilization fell to the advancing Russians—Tashkent in 1865, Bukhara in 1868, Khiva in 1873, Geok-Tepe in 1881, and Merv in 1884. These thrusts greatly alarmed the British in India, and there were recurring crises and rumors of war. But the century passed without open conflict, primarily because the distances were so immense and the means of transport so limited. Instead of a test of arms, the Anglo-Russian struggle was fought over the control of intervening states, particularly Persia and Afghanistan.

Russian rule changed Central Asia significantly, though not so much as British rule changed India. On the positive side the Russians abolished the widespread slavery and slave trade, freeing 10,000 slaves in Samarkand and its environs alone. The Russians also built railways—notably the Orenburg-Tashkent line—which helped them both for subjugating and modernizing. Thanks to the cheap transportation and the growing demands of the Russian textile industry, cotton cultivation increased spectacularly. In 1884, 300 desiatinas (1 desiatina = 2.7 acres) were planted to cotton on Russian initiative; by 1899, cotton acreage had jumped to 90,000 desiatinas. The Russians also introduced certain agrarian reforms, including a reduction of peasant tax and labor obligations to the state and to landlords.

On the other hand, the Russians' systematic expropriation of Kazakh grazing lands led to a decrease in the size of herds and to widespread famine. The Russians did nothing for the education of the natives, leaving this almost entirely to the Moslem mullahs. In other areas, such as the judiciary and local government, they were less active than the British were in India. The net result was that prior to the Bolshevik Revolution, which brought as many changes to Central Asia as to other regions of the Tsarist empire, the mass of Kazakhs, Kirghizes, Turkomans, Uzbeks, and Tajik were little affected by the coming of the Russians. Despite the railway building and the spreading cotton cultivation, conquerors and conquered lived in different worlds, separated by barriers of language, religion, and customs.

Manchuria and Russo-Japanese War

In the 1890's Russian interest was shifting from Central Asia to the Far East. The Trans-Siberian railway, which was slowly nearing completion, presented new opportunities for Russian economic and political expansion. Count Sergei Witte, the newly appointed Minister of Finance, presented a report to Tsar Alexander III (November 6, 1892) in which he stated that the Trans-Siberian line would supersede the Suez Canal as the principal trade route to China. He foresaw Russia in the position of arbiter between Asia and the Western world, and advocated a Russo-Chinese alliance as the best means for attaining that position.

The outbreak of the Sino-Japanese War in 1895 (see Chapter 29, section I) paved the way for the alliance that Witte favored. China again was easily defeated, and repeatedly requested Britain and the United States to mediate. Their refusal forced China to accept the Treaty of Shimonoseki (April 17, 1895), by which she ceded to Japan the Formosa and Pescadores Islands, and the Liaotung Peninsula. But Russia, together with Germany and France, now intervened and compelled the Japanese to restore the peninsula.

This assistance impressed the Chinese who, in the following year, signed a secret treaty with Russia. It provided for mutual assistance in case of Japanese aggression, and it also granted a joint Russo-Chinese Bank a concession for the construction of the Chinese Eastern Railway across Manchuria to Vladivostok. The bank, nominally a private concern, was actually owned and operated by the Russian government. By the outbreak of the Russo-Japanese War in 1904, it had built a total of 1,596 miles of railway in Manchuria.

Russia's next advance in the Far East was in 1898, with the negotiation of a twenty-five year lease of the Liaotung Peninsula, including strategic Port Arthur. And two years later the Russians took advantage of the disturbances attendant upon the Boxer Rebellion to occupy the entire province of Manchuria. This steady encroachment of Russia alarmed the Japanese, who had ambitions of their own on the mainland of Asia. Being in no position to stop the Russians singlehanded, they decided to strengthen themselves by securing an ally. On January 30, 1902, they concluded a military alliance with Britain (details in Chapter 29, section VII) and, fortified with this backing, they resolved to settle accounts with Russia. In July, 1903, the Japanese proposed that Russia should recognize their "preponderant interests" in Korea, and in return they would recognize Russia's "special interests in railway enterprises in Manchuria."

The Russians were divided concerning this Japanese offer. The finance minister, Count Witte, favored acceptance because he was interested in economic penetration rather than in political annexation with its dangers of war. But influential Russian adventurers with vast timber concessions in northern Korea wished to involve their government to advance their personal fortunes. Russian military circles wanted to obtain a base along the Korean coast because of the great distance between their existing bases at Port Arthur and Vladivostok. And certain Russian politicians, concerned by the mounting revolutionary wave in the country, favored a "little victorious war" that would serve as a lightning rod for the popular unrest. There was no doubt in their minds, or in those of the military, that Russia would prevail in a war with Japan.

This group of adventurers, militarists, and politicians had their way, securing the dismissal of Witte and the virtual rejection of the Japanese offer. Assured by their British alliance and apprehensive about the near-completion of the Trans-Siberian railway, the Japanese struck promptly and decisively. On February 5, 1904, they terminated the negotiations, and three days later they attacked the Russian fleet at Port Arthur without a formal declaration of war.

In the campaigns that followed, the Japanese David consistently defeated the Russian Goliath. The single-track Trans-Siberian railway proved quite inadequate to meet the supply needs of Russian armies fighting several thousand miles distant from their industrial centers in European Russia. In the first stage of the war, the Japanese surrounded Port Arthur and, after a siege of 148 days, captured the fortress on December 19, 1904. The second stage consisted of a series of battles on the plains of Manchuria. The Japanese were victorious here also, driving the Russians north of Mukden. These campaigns, however, were not decisive, because the Russian armies remained intact, and were reinforced and strengthened as communications improved. But on the sea the Japanese won an overwhelming triumph that led to the beginning of peace negotiations. On May 27, 1905, the Russian-Baltic fleet finally arrived at the Tsushima Straits between Japan and Korea, after sailing a distance equivalent to more than two-thirds the circumference of the globe. At once it was attacked by a Japanese fleet superior in both numbers and efficiency. Within a few hours virtually all the Russian units had been sunk or captured, while the Japanese lost merely a few destroyers.

With this debacle the Russians were ready to discuss peace, especially since the war was very unpopular at home and the 1905 Revolution had started. The Japanese also wanted peace negotiations because, although they had won the victories, their still-meager resources had been strained by the burden of the war. On September 5, 1905, the Treaty of Portsmouth was signed, by which Russia acknowledged Japan's "paramount political, military, and economic interests" in Korea, surrendered all preferential or exclusive concessions in Manchuria, and ceded to Japan the southern half of Sakhalin Island and the lease of the Liaotung Peninsula.

In this manner the Japanese halted Russia's expansion in the Far East. Not until four decades later, when the Japanese were disastrously defeated in World War II, was Russia able to recover the territories lost at Portsmouth. Nevertheless, Russia had yielded in 1905 only a few square miles of her periphery. She still remained, as she does today, a great Asiatic power, with territories stretching across the heart of Asia—from Korea on the Yellow Sea to Turkey on the Black Sea. Russia alone, of the European powers, is today inside Asia looking out, rather than, as in the case of the Western powers, being left only with imperial remnants such as Macao and Hong Kong. This is the significance, for our own age, of this overland expansion of Russia during the three centuries between Yermak's crossing of the Urals and the Russo-Japanese battles on the plains of Manchuria. (See Map XXV, "Russian Expansion in Europe and Asia.")

IV. FIRST RUSSIAN REVOLUTION AND AFTERMATH, 1905–1914

While the Russo-Japanese War was being fought in the Far East, revolution was spreading behind the lines within Russia. The roots of the revolution are to be found in the chronic disaffection of the peasants, the urban workers, and the middle class. This disaffection was aggravated by the war with Japan, which was unpopular to begin with and became increasingly so after the string of defeats. Finally there occurred the so-called "Bloody Sunday" of January 22, 1905, when the Imperial Guard fired on a crowd of several thousand persons marching peacefully toward the Winter Palace in St. Petersburg. Between 75 and 1000 were killed, and 200 to 2000 wounded, the discrepancy in the figures being due to the fact that some eyewitnesses reported only the Sunday casualties, whereas the disturbance continued in the capital another two days.

Bloody Sunday irreparably smashed the benevolent "Little Father" image of the Tsar that so many Russians had traditionally cherished. Citizens throughout the Empire turned against the regime, precipitating the great Russian Revolution of 1905. This elemental upheaval passed through three stages before the imperial government was able to reassert its authority. The first, between January and October, 1905, was the rising wave of revolution. All classes and interests came out against the autocracy: the subject nationalities demanded autonomy, peasants pillaged manor houses and seized estates, city workers organized councils, or soviets, for revolutionary action, university students everywhere walked out of their classrooms, and the sailors of the Black Sea fleet mutinied and seized their ships. The world witnessed the extraordinary spectacle of an entire nation on strike. The Tsar had no alternative but to yield, so he issued his famous October Manifesto (October 30). This read like a confession of sin by the government. It promised freedom of speech, press, and assembly, and also granted Russia a constitution and an elective national assembly, or Duma.

During the second stage of the revolution, between October, 1905, and January, 1906, the uprising continued at high pitch, but the revolutionaries no longer were united. The moderates, consisting mostly of middle-class elements, accepted the October Manifesto, while the radicals, including the Social Democrats and the Socialist Revolutionaries, demanded that a constituent assembly rather than the Tsar's ministers prepare the new constitution. In order to gain their ends the radicals sought to prolong the revolution by organizing more strikes and disturbances. By this time, however, the government was getting stronger and was able to hit back. The signing of the Portsmouth Treaty with Japan on September 5, 1905, freed many troops that were sent home to restore order; and a timely loan of $400 million from Paris and London greatly strengthened the faltering Tsarist government. Consequently, it was able to crush a dangerous workers' revolt that raged in Moscow between December 22 and January 1. Meanwhile, the moderates, alienated by the prolonged violence, were swinging over to the government's side. Thus by the beginning of 1906 the crest of the revolutionary wave had passed.

The third stage of the revolution, from January to July 21, 1906, was that of Tsarist consolidation of power. Government forces hunted down radicals and rebellious peasants, in some cases burning whole villages. On May 6, the government issued the so-called Fundamental Laws by which the Tsar was proclaimed autocrat and retained complete control over the executive, the armed forces, and foreign policy. The elective Duma was to share legislative power with an upper chamber, while its budgetary power was closely restricted. When the Duma did meet on May 10, it refused to accept the Fundamental Laws and criticized the government violently. A deadlock ensued, and the Tsar dissolved the Duma on July 21. The liberal Duma members retaliated by calling on the country to refuse to pay taxes, but the response was feeble. The fact is that by this time the revolutionary tide had ebbed and the First Russian Revolution had run its course.

Although the Revolution failed, it left its imprint on the course of Russia's history. Russia now had a constitutional regime, even though the Duma was emasculated. A second Duma was elected in February, 1907, but it proved to be even more defiant than the first. The government then reduced the franchise so drastically that the third and fourth Dumas elected in 1907 and 1912 were acceptably conservative and subservient. Nevertheless, the absolutist Tsarist autocracy did end with the October Manifesto, and, after World War I began, the Duma came increasingly into its own until it was swept away with the Bolshevik Revolution.

The events of 1905 are important also because of their contribution to Russian revolutionary experience and tradition. Soviets had been organized in the cities and had proven their value as organs for revolutionary action. It is true that after 1906 a lull seemed to set in, but it proved to be a brief respite. The number of workers on strike declined from 1,000,000 in 1905 to 4,000 in 1910. But by 1912, the number had risen again to 1,000,000, and remained at that level during the next two years. Then all discord ceased abruptly with the outbreak of World War I. But with the catastrophic defeats at the front, new storm clouds gathered, and the Tsarist regime entered a new time of troubles from which it never emerged. Thus, the Russian Revolution of 1905 stands out as a dress rehearsal for the world-shaking revolutions of 1917.

SUGGESTED READING

E. E. ALLWORTH, *Central Asia: A Century of Russian Rule* (Columbia Univ., 1966); E. E. BACON, *Central Asia under Russian Rule: A Study in Culture Change* (Cornell Univ., 1966); W. L. BLACKWELL, *The Beginnings of Russian Industrialization, 1800–1860* (Princeton Univ., 1968); M. MALIA, *Russia under Western Eyes: From Peter the Great to Khrushchev* (Wiley, 1964); R. A. PIERCE, *Russian Central Asia, 1867–1917: A Study in Colonial Rule* (Univ. California, 1960); D. W. TREADGOLD, *The West in Russia and China. Vol. I, Russia 1472–1917* (Cambridge Univ., 1973).

chapter twenty-seven

The Middle East

It is not open to question that all social changes in the Near East during the past century or so have arisen, directly or indirectly, from the impact of our Western society and the penetration of Western techniques and ideas.—H. A. R. Gibb

The West's influence on the Middle East was quite different from its influence on Russia, and the response of the Middle Eastern peoples was as dissimilar. Different peoples, religions, and cultures were involved, to be sure, but there was also a different political and social organization. The Ottoman Empire, which embraced most of the Middle East during the nineteenth century, remained a congeries of peoples and religions` and conflicting loyalties. It was organized as a theocracy on the basis of ecclesiastical communities rather than ethnic groups. These communities, the most important after the Moslem being the Greek Orthodox, Roman Catholic, and Jewish, were allowed full autonomy under their respective ecclesiastical leaders. Thus for centuries the various Moslem peoples (e.g., Turks, Arabs, Albanians, and Kurds) and the various Christian peoples (e.g., Serbs, Greeks, Bulgars, and Rumanians) lived side by side in autonomous and self-sufficient communities. Each community was allowed its own church, language, schools, and local government, so long as it accepted the sultan's authority and paid taxes to the imperial treasury.

The significance of this flaccid imperial organization is that Western ideas and pressure encountered a variety of cultures and conditions. Consequently, the West did not have a uniform impact on the Ottoman lands. In analyzing the nature of that impact it is therefore essential to take into account the marked variations in regional conditions and responses. For this reason, after analyzing the Ottoman Empire at its height, we shall consider the Western impact on its three main regions in turn—the Balkan Peninsula with its predominantly Christian population, Asia Minor with its ruling Moslem Turkish population, and the provinces south of Asia Minor with their Moslem Arab peoples. Finally we shall consider also certain significant developments in the Persian kingdom, which comprised an important element in the Middle East, though not a part of the Ottoman Empire.

I. OTTOMAN EMPIRE AT ITS HEIGHT

When the Turks overran the Byzantine Empire, and then captured Constantinople in 1453, they laid the solid foundation of their empire that was to endure to the twentieth century. (See Chapter 14, section VI, and Chapter 15, section IV.) Up to this point their expansion had been westward at the expense of the Christian infidels. But now, with Constantinople as their new capital, they turned southward against the rich Moslem states of Syria and Egypt. In a whirlwind campaign, they overran the first in 1516 and the second in the following year. The final phase of Ottoman conquest took place in Central Europe. Under their famous Sultan Suleiman the Magnificent, the Turks crossed the Danube River and in one stroke crushed the Hungarian state in the Mohács battle in 1526. Three years later, Suleiman laid siege to Vienna but was repulsed, partly because of torrential rains that prevented him from bringing up his heavy artillery. Despite this setback, the Turks continued to make minor gains: Cyprus in 1570, Crete in 1669, and the Polish Ukraine in the following decade.

At its height, the Ottoman Empire was indeed a formidable imperial structure. It sprawled over three continents and comprised some fifty million people, compared to the five million of contemporary England. Its ever-victorious armed forces won the respect of the Europeans, as did also its administration composed of slaves that were carefully selected, thoroughly trained, and promoted on the basis of merit. Little wonder that Christians of the time looked upon the ever-expanding Ottoman Empire with awe and described it as "a daily increasing flame, catching hold of whatsoever comes next, still to proceed further."[1]

This empire was at its height in the sixteenth century, but thereafter it declined precipitously, so that it soon became generally known in the West as the "Sick Man of Europe." One reason for this decline was the moribund state of the Islamic faith, which had degenerated to the point where it meant little more than a series of rituals to be performed and a Heaven-sent book to be memorized. This in turn had its effect upon education, which regressed to superficial, hair-splitting concentration on Moslem sacred studies. (See Chapter 14, section VII.) Yet this decadence was accompanied by a blindly invincible superiority complex that let down an iron curtain between the Moslem world and the West. Officials and scholars of the Ottoman Empire looked down with contempt and arrogance on anything relating to Christian Europe. In the fifteenth and sixteenth centuries this attitude was perhaps understandable; in the eighteenth and nineteenth it was grotesque and suicidal.

A more basic explanation for the decline of the Ottoman Empire was that, like all the other non-Western civilizations, it did not experience the scientific, industrial, and political revolutions that had transformed and modernized the West. Thus the Ottoman Empire was doomed for the same reason that the Byzantine Empire had been doomed. At the outset a combination of religious élan, capable rulers, and efficient bureaucracy ensured success and expansion. But the new West leapfrogged overseas and gained control of world trade, which in turn further stimulated Western strength and dynamism. The Ottoman Empire, by contrast, though in command of the traditional Middle Eastern trade routes, now was excluded from the new global economy. Remaining static, it became an anachronism in the modern world.

This was why the hitherto invincible Turks were stopped at Vienna and then pushed back across the Danube in the late seventeenth century. From then on, the Ottoman Empire was on the defensive, vulnerable to Western armies and diplomats and financiers. The nature and course of the ensuing Western penetration is the subject of the following sections.

II. BALKAN CHRISTIANS

The Balkan peoples were affected earlier and more profoundly by the West than any of the other ethnic groups of the Ottoman Empire. Mostly Christians, they were more receptive to the Christian West than were the Moslem Turks and Arabs. The territorial contiguity of the Balkan lands to the rest of Europe made it easier for persons and goods and ideas to converge upon the Balkan Peninsula from across the Danube and the Adriatic, Mediterranean, and Black Seas. And with the growth of commerce, of industry, and of a middle class during the eighteenth and nineteenth centuries, the growing demand for food imports in Western Europe stimulated agriculture in the Balkans, especially the cultivation of the new colonial products, cotton and maize. The export of these commodities in turn contributed to the growth of a class of native Balkan merchants and mariners. The expansion of trade also stimulated the demand and output of handicraft products. Important manufacturing centers appeared in various parts of the peninsula, frequently in isolated mountain areas where the artisans could practice their crafts with a minimum of Turkish interference. And the rise of commerce and industry had still another effect: it promoted the growth of a merchant marine along the Dalmatian, Albanian, and Epirote coasts, and amongst the Aegean Islands. The new Balkan marine exported products such as cotton, maize, dyeing materials, wine, oil, and fruits, and brought back mostly colonial products and manufactured goods—spices, sugar, woolens, glass, watches, guns, and gunpowder.

The significance of this economic renaissance is that it created a middle class of merchants, artisans, shipowners, and mariners that was particularly susceptible and sympathetic to Western ideas and institutions. These people, by their very nature, were dissatisfied with Ottoman rule, which by this time had become ineffective and corrupt. Merchants and seamen who journeyed to foreign lands, and frequently resided there, could not help contrasting the security and enlightenment they witnessed abroad with the deplorable conditions at home. Very naturally they would conclude that their own future, and that of their fellow countrymen, depended upon the earliest possible removal of the Turkish incubus.

Serbian merchants in southern Hungary, Bulgarian merchants in southern Russia, and Greek merchants scattered widely in the main cities of Europe, all contributed to the awakening of their fellow countrymen. They did so by publishing books and newspapers in their native languages, by establishing schools and libraries in their home towns and villages, and by financing the education of young men of their race in foreign universities. All this meant not only more education but a new type of education. It was no longer primarily religious. Instead, it was profoundly influenced by the current Enlightenment in Western Europe.

Western influence in the Balkans became more directly political and inflammatory during the French Revolutionary and Napoleonic era. Politically conscious elements were much impressed by the uprisings in Paris, by the slogan "Liberty, Equality, Fraternity," and by the spectacle of Napoleon toppling over one dynasty after another. A contemporary Greek revolutionary testified: "The

French Revolution in general awakened the minds of all men. . . . All the Christians of the Near East prayed to God that France should wage war against the Turks, and they believed that they would be freed. . . . But when Napoleon made no move, they began to take measures for freeing themselves."[2]

The tempo of national awakening varied greatly from one Balkan people to another. The Greeks came first because of certain favorable circumstances: their numerous contacts with the West, their glorious classical and Byzantine heritage which stimulated national pride, and their Greek Orthodox Church which embodied and preserved national consciousness. After the Greeks came the Serbs, who enjoyed a high degree of local self-government as well as the stimulating influence of the large Serbian settlements in southern Hungary. These advantages of the Greeks and the Serbs suggest the reasons for the slower rate of national revival among the other Balkan peoples. The Bulgars had no direct ties with the West and were located near the Ottoman capital and the solid Turkish settlements in Thrace and eastern Macedonia. The Rumanians suffered from a sharp social stratification which was unique in the Balkans and which produced a cultivated upper class and an inert peasant mass. The Albanians were the worst off, with their primitive tribal organization and their division among three creeds, Orthodoxy, Catholicism, and Islam.

These factors explain why in place of a common Balkan revolution against Ottoman rule, there occurred separate uprisings ranging from the early nineteenth century to the early twentieth. The Greeks won complete independence from the Turks following a protracted War of Independence between 1821 and 1829. The Serbs had revolted earlier in 1804, but only gained an autonomous status within the Ottoman Empire in 1815. It was not until 1878 that the Serbian Principality gained full independence and became the Kingdom of Serbia. The Rumanians came next, winning autonomy in 1859 and full independence in 1878. The Bulgarians followed later, gaining autonomy in 1878 and independence in 1908. Three of these Balkan peoples, the Serbs, Greeks, and Bulgarians, combined forces in 1912 to drive the Turks completely out of the peninsula. They were successful on the battlefield, and, despite a fratricidal war amongst the victors, the Turks were compelled in 1913 to surrender all their remaining territories in the Balkans with the exception of an enclave stretching around the Straits from Constantinople to Adrianople.

In this manner the imperial Ottoman frontiers shrank from the walls of Vienna in 1683 to the Danube in 1815, to the mid-Balkans in 1878, and to the environs of Constantinople in 1913. As the empire receded, independent Balkan states took its place—Greece, Serbia, Rumania, Bulgaria, and, in 1912, Albania. The West contributed decisively to this resurgence of the Balkan peoples by providing a revolutionary nationalist ideology, by stimulating the growth of a middle class that was ready to act on the basis of that ideology, and by sporadically helping the Balkan revolutionaries in their struggle against Turkish rule.

III. TURKS

The West affected the Turks much less and much later than it did the Balkan Christians. Various factors explain this difference, of which the most important probably were the Moslem religion of the Turks, and their lack of a native middle class.

If the Christian faith of the Balkan peoples constituted a bond with the West, the Moslem faith of the Turks was a barrier. And it was a most formidable barrier because of the long history of antagonism and conflict between Christianity and Islam. The Turks also were little affected by the West because they never developed their own middle class. They had no interest in, or respect for, commercial pursuits, so that the Ottoman bourgeoisie was largely Greek, Armenian, and Jewish. By contrast, the Turks were either peasants (who were generally apathetic), or teachers and judges in the Moslem ecclesiastical organization (which almost always meant that they were bitterly anti-Western), or else they were officeholders in the imperial bureaucracy (in which case they usually were interested only in retaining their posts and advancing in rank). The significance of this situation is apparent in view of the vital role played by Greek, Serbian, and Bulgarian merchants in their respective countries. But no comparable group existed among the Turks, so that their rare advocates of reform found themselves without any following. They found themselves, in other words, in the same plight as did the Decembrists in Russia in 1825, and for the same reason.

This lack of mass support for reform was strikingly illustrated by the fate of Sultan Selim III. Selim ascended the Ottoman throne in 1789—a symbolically appropriate year, given the revolutionary nature of his ideas and aspirations. Selim was not the first sultan to recognize the need for reform in the empire, but he was the first to realize that the reform measures must look forward rather than backward. He was the first to consider reforms in terms of borrowing from the West rather than returning to the days of Suleiman the Magnificent. His plans included the reorganization of administration, the revamping of education, and the complete transformation of the janissary corps.

The janissaries, who had once been the elite of the Ottoman infantry, by this time had degenerated to a worthless and insubordinate Praetorian Guard. Several sultans had attempted in the past to curb or destroy this pernicious body. They all failed because the heads of law and religion, known collectively as the ulema, had sided with the janissaries. Important economic interests also supported the *status quo,* because of the large sums obtained from the imperial treasury over many decades in the guise of pay for janissary units that actually did not exist.

This powerful combination of military, religious, and economic vested interests explains why earlier sultans had failed to reform the janissary corps, and why Selim also was destined to fail, and to forfeit his throne and his life. In 1793, he took the decisive step of establishing a military force known as the New Regulations Army, a Western-type army with common uniforms, specified enlistment and recruitment procedures, European methods of training, and modern armaments. The New Army demonstrated its worth in several engagements, but this only intensified the apprehension and opposition of the janissaries and their allies. They spread rumors that the New Army was an invention of the Christian infidels and that Selim sponsored it precisely because he no longer was the true defender of the Faith. Sufficient unrest was fomented to enable the janissaries to force Selim to abdicate in May, 1808. Two months later he was strangled when his supporters attempted to rescue him from his palace quarters where he was held captive.

In retrospect it is clear that Selim had tried to do what Peter the Great of Russia had accomplished a century earlier. He failed partly because he was not so forceful or decisive a personality as the Russian Tsar. But his failure was due even more to the fact that the janissaries, together with their allies in the ulema and the bureaucracy and the court, comprised a much more powerful opposition bloc than any that Peter had faced. And Selim had no middle class, no mass party or movement, to fall back upon. Thus, the Ottoman Empire seemed at the end of 1808 to be as unchanging and as unchangeable as ever.

Yet during the course of the nineteenth century the Ottoman Empire, like the Russian, was penetrated and influenced and controlled by the West in numerous direct and indirect ways. Of the several channels of penetration, the earliest and in some respects the most effective, was the military. The Turks, like the Russians, found it necessary to adopt European military techniques for self-preservation. But of the considerable number of young men who were sent abroad to study in foreign military academies, some inevitably imbibed Western ideologies as well as Western military techniques. Thus, of all Ottoman institutions, the army became the most westernized in outlook as well as in organization. It is not surprising that when the old regime was finally overthrown in the Ottoman Empire in 1908, the coup was executed not by a political party or a mass movment, but by an army clique.

In the field of religion, also, the West impinged upon the Moslem Middle East. Missionaries were preaching and founding schools throughout the empire. By 1875 the American missionaries alone had 240 schools with 8,000 pupils. Most of the latter were Armenians and other Christians, since proselytism amongst Moslems was forbidden. But a fair number of Turkish students were to be found in the foreign colleges scattered throughout the empire, such as the American-operated Constantinople Women's College and Robert College (also in Constantinople), and the French Jesuit University of St. Joseph at Beirut. The Turks themselves by this time had established several institutions of higher learning, including the School of Medicine (1867), the Imperial Lycée (1868), the University of Constantinople (1869), the School of Law (1870), and the School of Political Science (1878). The Turkish press, too, was developing rapidly during these years. In 1859 there was only one official and one semiofficial weekly in the empire. By 1872 there were three daily papers and several weeklies.

At least as significant as this cultural impact was the West's economic penetration of the Ottoman Empire. In 1869 the Suez Canal was opened after ten years of construction by a European syndicate headed by a French diplomat and promoter, Ferdinand de Lesseps. The effect of the canal was to place the Ottoman Empire once more on the main trade route between Europe and Asia. At the same time the Ottoman government was falling hopelessly into debt to European governments and to private financiers. They contracted their first loan in 1854, and by 1875 their debts totaled £200 million sterling. Some £12 million sterling a year was required to meet annuities, interest, and sinking fund, a sum that amounted to a little more than half the total revenues of the empire. The load proved too heavy, and some of the interest payments were defaulted, whereupon the European powers imposed in 1881 the Ottoman Public Debt Administration. This body consisted mostly of foreign representatives and was entrusted with the revenues from various monopolies and customs duties for the service of the imperial debts.

In addition to this hold over Ottoman public finances, foreign interests had control over the Turkish banking and railway systems, irrigation works, mining enterprises, and municipal public utilities. The empire, besides, was still subject to the capitulations, or extraterritorial privileges, that foreigners had enjoyed in the Ottoman Empire since the fifteenth century. These privileges included exemption from the jurisdiction of Ottoman courts and from certain taxes, including personal imposts and customs tariffs. The latter were set at a very low level and could not be raised by the Ottoman government without the consent of the European powers, which, needless to say, was not forthcoming. Thus we may conclude that the Ottoman Empire, much more than the Russian, was in a semicolonial economic relationship with Europe.

The effect of all these Western pressures and controls cannot be measured precisely. But there can be no doubt that they gradually cracked the hitherto impregnable and monolithic Islamic structure. Canals, railways, banks, missionaries, schools, and newspapers constitute the background and also the explanation for a literary and intellectual awakening that occurred amongst the Turks in the latter half of the nineteenth century.

The best-known leaders of this awakening were Ibrahim Shinassi, Namik Kemal, and Abdul Hamid Ziya. These men did not agree on all issues, but they all had lived in Western Europe, and they all had been tremendously impressed by the thought and literature as well as the material achievements of the West. So they began with cultural activities, such as linguistic reform and translation of foreign authors. They did not organize a political party, the only real parties in the Ottoman Empire at this time being the "ins" and the "outs" gathered about individual political leaders. But by 1865 a fairly well-defined group of young Western-minded writers had formed about the newspaper *Mushbir,* or *Herald of Glad Tidings.* The paper championed, among other things, the introduction of some form of constitutional representative government. This was too much for the imperial regime, which suppressed the paper in 1867. The editor and his colleagues now found themselves in the same position as Selim III in the beginning of the century. Lacking mass support, they were forced to flee to Paris and London, where they continued their journalistic attacks on the imperial regime.

Meanwhile, a few Turkish statesmen had realized that a comprehensive reform program along Western lines was essential for the survival of the empire. Outstanding were Reshid Pasha (1802–1858) and Midhat Pasha (1822–1884), both of whom served as grand vizirs and issued numerous reform decrees. In May, 1876, Midhat took advantage of a financial crisis at home and a revolution in the Balkan provinces to force Sultan Abdul Aziz to abdicate. He then prepared a constitution providing for an elected parliament, a bill of rights, and an independent judiciary. The new sultan, Abdul Hamid II, was forced to accept the constitution, but he had no intention of abiding by it. In January, 1877, he dismissed Midhat from office and banished him from Constantinople. The only signs of protest were a few placards on walls. Turkish reformers still were faced with a mass inertia comparable to that which had doomed the Russian Decembrists in 1825. Consequently, Abdul Hamid was able to rule as the unchallenged master of his empire for the rest of the century.

During those decades Abdul Hamid kept himself in power by relentlessly combatting the disruptive forces of nationalism and constitutionalism. To this end he discouraged travel and study abroad, maintained a great host of informers, and enforced a strict censorship of the press. Periodically his agents flushed out small groups of disaffected elements, mostly intellectuals and officeholders, who usually fled to Paris for refuge. There they published periodicals and pamphlets criticizing the Hamidian autocracy, and thus became popularly known in Western Europe as the Young Turks. These Turkish exiles were joined by revolutionary leaders of the various subject peoples under Abdul Hamid, including Arabs, Greeks, Armenians, Albanians, Kurds, and Jews. Representatives of all these nationalities held a congress in Paris in February, 1902, with the aim of organizing a common front against the autocracy. But they quickly discovered that they agreed on nothing except that they all disliked the sultan. One group wanted Turkish predominance and centralized rule, while another favored a decentralized empire with full autonomy for the subject peoples.

While the exiled intellectuals were quarreling in Paris, reform-minded Turkish army leaders were taking decisive measures to break the Sultan's grip on the empire. Most of them had studied in the West or had contact with Western military missions within the empire, so that they had come to realize that the Sultan's rigid *status quo* policy was obsolete and dangerous. They organized the Ottoman Society of Liberty with headquarters in Saloniki. Army officers were the backbone of this body, though they were greatly aided by other groups, and particularly by the Jews who were the most numerous and wealthy element in Saloniki. The Society of Liberty was organized into cells of five, so that no one knew more than four fellow members.

This organization, later known as the Committee of Union and Progress, revolted in July, 1908, when it telegraphed an ultimatum to the sultan, threatening to march upon Constantinople unless the 1876 constitution was restored within twenty-four hours. Abdul Hamid was advised by his State Council to comply to the ultimatum. And the Sheik-ul-Islam, the highest religious and legal authority of the Empire, refused to issue a *fetva* authorizing suppression of the rebels. So on July 24, Abdul Hamid proclaimed the restoration of the constitution. Making the best of the situation, he added that he had always favored constitutional government but had been misled by evil councillors.

The news of the Sultan's capitulation was greeted with wild rejoicing. Christians and Turks embraced one another in the streets. The young Turk leader Enver Pasha exclaimed, "There are no longer Bulgars, Greeks, Romans, Jews, Mussulmans. We are all brothers beneath the same blue sky. We are all equal, we glory in being Ottoman."[3] This euphoric atmosphere did not last long. The issue of centralization versus decentralization that had divided the exiles in Paris now had to be faced as an urgent matter of policy rather than of theory. There were also conservative elements who distrusted all Young Turks, as the new leaders were generally called. The dissension came to a head on April 12, 1909, when the conservatives staged a counterrevolution in Constantinople and seized control of the capital. The Young Turks gathered their forces in Macedonia, marched on Constantinople, captured the city after a few hours' fighting, and then compelled Abdul Hamid to abdicate, although his complicity in the coup was not proven. The new sultan, Mohammed V, according to his own account had not read a newspaper in ten years. Accordingly, he served as a compliant figurehead for the Young Turks who now were the undisputed masters in Constantinople.

During the few years before the outbreak of World War I they tried to strengthen and modernize their empire but with little success. They attempted a policy of centralization and Turkification, but the more they persisted the more opposition they aroused. It was too late to deny the inexorable awakening of Albanians, Arabs, Greeks, Bulgarians, and other subject peoples. Thus the result was a vicious circle of repression and revolt. The Albanians took up arms in 1910, and two years later the Balkan states formed a league and turned upon the Turks. Meanwhile, Italy also had invaded the African province of Tripolitania in 1911. The Young Turks thus found themselves almost continually at war until 1914, when they decided to throw in their lot with that of the Central Powers.

It is apparent, then, that the efforts of the Turks to adjust to the West had proven singularly ineffective. Because of religious and historical traditions they had been more impervious to the West than the Russians, and for that very reason ended up much more vulnerable to the West. They did not develop their own industry, so that their armed forces remained dependent on Western arms as well as Western instructors. Indeed, the Ottoman Empire survived to World War I because of the conflicting interests and policies of the Great Powers rather than because of its own strength.

IV. ARABS

The Arab peoples, during most of the four centuries that they were under Turkish rule, did not regard it as an onerous foreign yoke. In the first place, Ottoman administration in the early period was efficient and generally acceptable. The Arabs, who as Moslems thought in theocratic rather than secular, Western terms, regarded the Turks more as fellow Moslems than as foreigners, and consequently felt a genuine affinity with the Moslem Ottoman Empire of which they were a part. In modern times this feeling was enhanced as a result of the aggressiveness of the Europeans who conquered ancient Moslem kingdoms in North Africa and Central and South Asia. Faced with such a formidable threat, the Arabs very naturally regarded the Turks as protectors who, though becoming increasingly corrupt and oppressive in the later period, nevertheless were still much preferable to the infidels. These considerations explain why the Arabs lagged far behind the Balkan Christians in receptivity to Western influences and in development of nationalist aspirations.

The West's impact upon the modern Arab world may be said to have begun on that day in 1798 when Napoleon landed in Egypt with his army of invasion. Napoleon's real objective was to strike at Britain's position in the East, but after Admiral Nelson destroyed his fleet near Alexandria, Napoleon gave up his objective and returned home. Yet his expedition had a lasting effect on Egypt, for it was more than a military affair. It was also a cultural incursion by the West into the heart of the Arab world. Napoleon brought with him the first printing press to reach Egypt, as well as scientists who deciphered the ancient hieroglyphic writing, and engineers who prepared plans for joining the Mediterranean and Red Seas.

Napoleon also smashed the power of the established ruling class in Egypt during his brief campaigning in that country. This paved the way for the rise to power of an Albanian adventurer of genius, Mehemet Ali. The historical significance of Mehemet Ali is that he was the first Middle Eastern potentate who sensed the significance of Western technology and utilized it efficiently to serve his purposes. His achievements were numerous and revolutionary. He started the modern system of irrigation; introduced the cultivation of cotton, which quickly became the country's greatest resource; reopened the harbor of Alexandria; encouraged foreign trade; sent students to study abroad; opened schools of all varieties, though he himself was illiterate; and established a School of Translation which translated into Arabic about two thousand European books between 1835 and 1848. Mehemet Ali also engaged foreign experts who helped him build the first modern army and navy in the Middle East. He even tried valiantly to build a modern industrial structure in Egypt, and did erect a considerable number of factories in Cairo and Alexandria. These enterprises, however, eventually failed because of domestic deficiencies and the opposition of the European powers.

These accomplishments transformed Egypt into a formidable power. With little difficulty Mehemet overran Arabia, the Sudan, the island of Crete, and the entire Levant coast comprising present-day Israel, Lebanon, and Syria. These conquests raised the question of his relations with Sultan Mahmud, his nominal overlord in Constantinople. Mahmud had attempted to prevent Mehemet from expanding up the Levant coast but had been trounced quickly and decisively. In fact, it was only foreign intervention that prevented the Egyptian armies from entering Constantinople and putting an end to the five-hundred-year-old Ottoman dynasty. It was foreign intervention, also, that prevented Mehemet from realizing an alternate scheme that he seemed to have in mind. This was a plan for creating an Arab Empire out of the Ottoman provinces south of Asia Minor. Mehemet already was well on the way, since he controlled most of the Arab lands, including the Holy Cities. But a strong Arab Empire in command of the routes to India was contrary to British imperial interests, and Lord Palmerston took the lead in compelling Mehemet to surrender all his possessions except Egypt, where he remained the hereditary and autonomous ruler. Great Power interests had postponed the realization of Arab unity and independence for over a century.

Thanks to Napoleon's expedition and to Mehemet Ali's herculean efforts, Egypt became by far the most significant bridgehead for Westernism in the Arab world. After 1870 Syria, which included the entire Levant coast at that time, rivaled Egypt as a center of Western influence. One reason was the flourishing commerce between Syria and Europe, and the large number of Syrian merchants who engaged in business activities abroad and then exerted the same catalytic effect upon their countrymen at home, as the Balkan merchants had done in earlier decades. Another reason was the extensive missionary-educational activity carried on mostly by the French Jesuits and the American Presbyterians. They established schools in Syria that trained Arab students, and also printed and distributed Arab books. In this manner the Syrian Arabs were helped to rediscover their past and to learn about Western literature, ideology, and technology.

This stimulus from the outside was responsible for the earliest manifestations of Arab nationalism. The leaders at the outset were mostly Christian Arabs, since the Moslems did not enroll in the missionary schools until a later date. In 1860 Butros el Bustani, a convert to Protestantism, began publication of his newspaper, *Nafir Suriya* (*Syrian Trumpet*). Ten years later he founded a political, literary, and scientific journal, *El Jenan* (*The Shield*). Its motto was "Love of our country is an article of faith"—a sentiment hitherto unknown in the Arab world.

Bustani and the other pioneer nationalists could not carry on political agitation openly because of the repressive measures of the Ottoman authorities. Consequently, the first avowedly political activity was the organization of a secret revolutionary society in 1875 by five students at the Protestant College. They drew up a national program which included demands for self-government, freedom of the press, and the adoption of Arabic as an official language. Turkish officials conducted an investigation and attempted to unearth the secret society's leadership. The latter became alarmed and dissolved their society in 1878. Then they made their way to Egypt, where the imperial agents had little control and where conditions were more promising for modern-minded Arabs.

The Western-educated Syrian intellectuals published newspapers and magazines which acquainted Egyptians with liberal and scientific French and British currents of thought. At the same time the deciphering of the hieroglyphs, the establishment of museums, and the development of Egyptology stimulated an awareness of Egypt's ancient history and a pride in her achievements. This embryonic nationalism was further aroused by the growing Western domination of the country. This domination was imposed because Khedive Ismail's heavy borrowings on the European money markets had led to bankruptcy and ultimately to foreign military intervention and rule. By 1876 Ismail was bankrupt and was forced to accept an international Public Debt Commission. This body saw to it that all obligations were promptly met, but the country was bled white in the process. The total revenue in 1877 amounted to £9,543,000, of which £7,473,000 had to be paid out for the service of the debt, and other amounts for fixed obligations such as the annual tribute to the Sultan. Only a little over £1 million was left for the administration of the country, a sum that was patently inadequate.

Under these circumstances a nationalist revolt broke out in 1882 under the leadership of an Egyptian army officer, Ahmed Arabi. It was directed partly against foreign intervention in Egyptian affairs and partly against the khedive and the Turkish oligarchy that monopolized all the senior posts in both the army and the bureaucracy. After some rioting and loss of life in Alexandria, a British fleet bombarded the city in July, 1882, and two months later an expeditionary force landed in Egypt and defeated Arabi. Prime Minister Gladstone declared at the time that he opposed an indefinite occupation, but the expeditionary force remained to become an army of occupation. Egypt was still nominally a Turkish province, but Britain now controlled the country in every respect—economically, politically, and militarily.

These events naturally provoked strong xenophobic sentiments in Egypt, but they were directed more against the Westerners than against the Turks. Only a handful of Christian Arab leaders wished at this time to break away from Constantinople. The Moslem masses were still largely apathetic, while the small minority of politically conscious Moslems wanted nothing more than autonomy within the Ottoman imperial structure.

With the Young Turk revolt of 1908 it appeared that this desire would be satisfied. The Arabs, like the other peoples of the empire, welcomed the revolt with unrestrained enthusiasm. But their hopes were quickly dashed. The Young Turk leaders soon were resorting to severe Turkification measures in a desperate attempt to hold the empire together against foreign military aggression and internal nationalist subversion. The Arabs resented this repression, as did the Balkan Christians. Yet the great majority of Arabs still aspired to autonomy rather than independence. For example, Moslem Arab students in Paris founded on November 14, 1909, a secret body, the Young Arab Society, better known as *al-Fatat* (Youth), which played a leading role in the Arab nationalist movement. Its goal was Arab autonomy within the framework of a biracial Turko-Arab Ottoman Empire organized along the lines of the Austro-Hungarian Empire.

Such were the sentiments of the great majority of Arabs until the outbreak of World War I. Then the decision of the Young Turk leaders to throw in their lot with the Central Powers changed the situation overnight and precipitated a chain reaction of events that culminated in the great Arab Revolt of 1916 against the centuries-old Turkish imperium.

V. PERSIANS

While these events were taking place in the Arab world, equally significant developments were occurring in neighboring Persia. Under Shah Abbas I, in the early seventeenth century, Persia reached a pinnacle of greatness comparable to that of the Ottoman Empire under Suleiman the Magnificent. Then followed a decline, again similar to that of the Turks, the country sinking into a state of impotence and obscurity. Nor did Persia have a Napoleonic expedition or wide-ranging Syrian merchants or large numbers of foreign missionaries to allow outside influences to freshen the stagnant atmosphere. Yet by the late nineteenth century the impact of the ubiquitous West was beginning to be felt appreciably in Persia. The roots and nature of the impact were generally similar to those amongst the Turks. There was first an attempt to borrow Western military techniques, which in turn required greater centralization and a new bureaucracy. Students were sent abroad, while a variety of new Western-type schools were established within the country. Gradually a group of intellectuals appeared who were impressed by the material advances of the West and who wished to introduce Western institutions and practices in their homeland.

In the late nineteenth century this small group of intellectuals was able to arouse considerable mass support in the cities because of growing economic intrusion and exploitation by the West. As early as 1828, the Russians had obtained capitulatory rights similar to the extraterritoriality imposed later upon China. Most European powers quickly followed Russia in securing special rights for their nationals. The process was facilitated by the readiness of the shahs to grant monopoly concessions to foreigners in order to raise funds to pay for their extravagant excesses.

Such were the conditions in Persia when news arrived in 1905 of the Russian defeats in Manchuria, and then of the great revolutionary upsurge within Russia itself. These dramatic developments had important repercussions in Persia because of the considerable number of Persian students in Russian universities and the much larger number of Persian workers employed in the oil fields and factories of the Transcaucasus. The Persian consul in St. Petersburg estimated in 1910 that no less than 200,000 migratory workers were crossing over into Russia each year. These laborers inevitably were affected by the revolutionary movements convulsing the Russian working class of the period. Consequently, the stirring events of 1905 aroused a response in Persia among many workers and intellectuals, as well as among religious leaders alarmed by Western encroachment.

A wave of strikes and riots swept the country until the Shah agreed in July, 1906, to dismiss his unpopular prime minister and to convoke a national assembly or *majlis*. The first majlis met at Teheran in October, 1906, and drew up a liberal constitution which the Shah signed two months later, just before he died. The new ruler, reactionary Mohammed Ali Shah, was determined to suppress the constitution, but he had an aroused populace on his hands. For the first time in the modern period, Persia was being shaken by a reform movement with genuine mass following. This movement was strongly nationalistic and anti-Western because of the humiliation and exploitation suffered at the hands of foreigners.

It was when they became convinced that their country was despised abroad, that their interests were betrayed for a vile price, and that their religion and their independent existence as a nation were alike threatened with destruction, that they began to demand a share in the government of the country. Many European journalists and other writers have made merry over the idea of a Persian Parliament, repeating like so many parrots the expression "comic opera" on almost every page. . . . Yet the Persians have consciously been fighting for their very existence as a Nation, and in this sense the popular or constitutional party may very properly be termed "Nationalists." . . . it is essentially the patriotic party, which stands for progress, freedom, tolerance, and above all for national independence. . . .[4]

The reformers were doomed to failure because the *status-quo* forces were too powerful during this pre-World War I period. Tsarist Russia was adamantly opposed to the reformers for obvious reasons, and strongly supported the Shah against the majlis. Britain was ambivalent, being favorably disposed toward the moderate reformers but frowning upon revolutionary or antidynastic activities. If the two powers had neutralized each other, the reformers might have had a fighting chance. But this faint possibility evaporated when Russia and Britain concluded their 1907 entente. One of its provisions designated northern and central Persia as a Russian sphere of influence, southeastern Persia as a British sphere, and the intervening territory as a neutral buffer zone.

The chief military force in Persia at this time was the Cossack brigade, trained and officered by Russians. In June, 1908, this body, on the Shah's orders, dispersed the majlis and routed its supporters in Teheran. But the following year Bakhtiari tribesmen marched on Teheran, captured the capital, and deposed the Shah, who was succeeded by his twelve-year-old son. The majlis, now the real ruler of the country, invited an American financial adviser, W. Morgan Shuster, to help repair the economic ravages. Shuster organized a treasury gendarmerie to collect taxes and planned a series of comprehensive reforms, but he aroused the antagonism of influential Persian elements and of the Russians. The latter demanded his ouster, and after a show of force, compelled the majlis in November, 1911, to dismiss him. The following month the majlis was suddenly disbanded, and from then until the outbreak of World War I, Persia was pretty much dominated by Russia.

SUGGESTED READING

F. AHMAD, *The Young Turks* (Oxford Univ., 1970); R. H. DAVISON, *Reform in the Ottoman Empire, 1856–1876* (Princeton Univ., 1964); C. E. DAWN, *From Ottomanism to Arabism. Essays on the Origins of Arab Nationalism* (Univ. Illinois, 1973); A. HOURANI, *Arabic Thought in the Liberal Age, 1798–1939* (Oxford Univ., 1962); C. ISSAWI, ed., *The Economic History of the Middle East 1800–1914* (Univ. Chicago, 1966); F. KAZEMZADEH, *Russia and Britain in Persia, 1864–1914: A Study in Imperialism* (Yale Univ., 1967); B. LEWIS, *The Middle East and the West* (Univ. Indiana, 1964); L. S. STAVRIANOS, *The Balkans Since 1453* (Holt, 1958).

chapter twenty-eight

India

India is the one great non-Western society that has been, not merely attacked and hit, but overrun and conquered outright by Western arms, and not merely conquered by Western arms but ruled, after that, by Western administrators. . . . India's experience of the West has thus been more painful and more humiliating than China's or Turkey's, and much more so than Russia's or Japan's. . . .—Arnold J. Toynbee

Prior to the appearance of the British, India had been invaded time and time again—by the Aryans, Persians, Greeks, Scythians, and a succession of Moslem peoples. The first of these were the Arabs who invaded the Sind region in 712; then came the Turks who began raiding India from Afghanistan about A.D. 1000 (see Chapter 14, section I); and finally the Moguls, another Turkish people, who captured Delhi in 1526. The outstanding Mogul ruler was Akbar (1542–1605), who extended his empire to encompass most of the peninsula. Perhaps his main achievement was his reconciliation of his Hindu subjects, who were relieved of a discriminatory poll tax and given access to high imperial posts. Yet Mogul India remained Hindu in its base despite its Moslem superstructure. The mass of the people in the villages were left basically unchanged, still faithful to their inchoate, polytheistic Hinduism that was so different from the austerely monotheistic Islam.

Very different was the impact of the last of the invaders of India; the British. Whereas their predecessors had wrought changes mostly at the top, the British impact was much more pervasive and disruptive. It was felt down to the level of the village. The reason for this difference in influence is to be found in the dynamic and expansive nature of British society, which consequently undermined the comparatively static and self-sufficient society of India. To understand this process of penetration and transformation it is necessary first to study the character of the traditional Indian society. Then we shall consider the nature of the British impact and the Indian reaction to it.

I. INDIA'S TRADITIONAL SOCIETY

The basic unit of traditional Indian society was the village, as it was in most of the rest of the world, including Europe, in the pre-industrial period. Within the village it was not the individual that mattered, but rather the joint family and the caste. This group form of organization was a source of social stability but also of national weakness. Loyalty to the family, to the caste, and to the village was the primary consideration, and this prevented the formation of a national spirit.

The land was regarded by immemorial custom as the property of the sovereign, who was entitled to a share of the gross produce or its equivalent. This constituted the land tax that was the main source of state revenue and the main burden of the cultivator. The share paid to the state varied from period to period from a sixth to a third or even half. Usually the responsibility for making this payment, whether in produce or in money, was collective, resting upon the village as a unit. The peasant had hereditary right to the use of the land so long as he paid his share of the taxes.

Transportation and communication facilities were primitive, so the villages tended to become economically and socially self-sufficient. Each village had its potter, who turned out on his wheel the simple utensils needed by the peasants; its carpenter, who constructed and repaired the buildings and ploughs; its blacksmith, who made axes and other necessary tools; its clerk, who attended to legal documents and wrote out correspondence between people of different villages; its town herdsman, who looked after the cattle and returned them at night to their various owners; its priest and its teacher, who frequently were combined in the same person; and its everpresent astrologer, who indicated the auspicious time for planting, for harvesting, for marriages, and other important events. These artisans and professional men served their villages on something akin to a barter basis. They were paid for their services by receiving grain from the cultivating households or by receiving tax-free village land for their own use. These hereditary and traditional divisions of occupation and function were given the stamp of obligation by the caste system.

The political structure of the village consisted of an annually elected council of five or more, known to this day as the Panchayat ("Pancha" meaning "five"). The Panchayat, which normally consisted of caste leaders and village elders, met periodically to dispense local justice, to collect taxes, to keep in repair the village wells, roads, and irrigation systems, to see that the craftsmen and other professionals were provided for, and to extend hospitality to travelers passing through the village and furnish them with guides. The village had little contact with the outside world apart from the payment of the land tax and the irregular demand for forced labor. The combination of agriculture and hand industry made each village largely independent of the rest of the country except for a few indispensables like salt and iron. Consequently, the towns that existed in traditional India were not industrial in character. Rather, they were religious centers such as Benares, Puri, and Allahabad, political centers such as Poona, Tanjore, and Delhi, or commercial centers such as Mirzapur on the trade route from Central India to Bengal.

Indian writers have tended to romanticize this traditional society, painting an idyllic picture of village life, continuing peacefully generation after generation in its slow and satisfying rhythm. It is true that the existence of group organizations such as the joint family, the caste, and the village council provided the peasants with both psychological and economic security. Each individual had recognized duties, rights, and status in his native village. If the central government was sufficiently strong to maintain order and to keep the land tax down to the customary sixth of the harvest, then the peasant masses did lead a peaceful and contented existence. But as often as not the central government was too weak to keep order, and the villagers were mercilessly fleeced by rapacious tax collectors and by robber bands. This was the case in the seventeenth century when the Mogul imperial structure was disintegrating. Yet even in such trying periods the Indian village was not transformed in any basic respect. Individual regions were ravaged, but eventually the cultivators returned to resume their traditional institutions and their traditional ways of life.

II. BRITISH CONQUEST

The Indian village was relatively unchanging and self-sufficient until the coming of the British. But before examining the impact of these Western intruders we shall consider the reasons why they were able with comparatively little difficulty to conquer the whole of India during the late eighteenth and nineteenth centuries. This is a real question, because for 250 years after Albuquerque had captured Goa early in the sixteenth century, the Europeans in India had been able only to cling to a few stations along the coasts. Then within a few decades the balance of power shifted decisively and the whole of the Indian subcontinent fell under British rule.

This denouement may be explained in part by the growing economic and military strength of the Western nations. But this is not the only factor, for it does not explain why India succumbed to the West so much earlier than did China. It is necessary, therefore, to take into account the conditions prevailing within India itself. First and foremost there was the decline of Mogul power, especially after the reign of Emperor Aurangzeb (1658–1707), who alienated his Hindu subjects with his forceful proselytizing. The weakness of Delhi enabled Moslem warlords and provincial governors to declare their independence and establish personal dynasties in various regions. In this fashion the Nizam of Hyderabad came to power in 1724, and Hyder Ali and his son Tipu Sultan ensconced themselves in Mysore in 1761. At the same time the Hindus asserted themselves by organizing the powerful Maratha confederacy with its center in the city of Poona. The Marathas won control of the entire Deccan and then, about 1740, began to invade northern India with the intention of displacing the declining Moguls. Thus India was in an anarchical state in the eighteenth century, with various officials seeking to convert their posts into hereditary princedoms and intriguing with any power, whether Indian or foreign, in order to realize their ambitions. The British consequently were able to play off one Indian prince against another until they became the masters of the entire peninsula.

Another important factor that contributed substantially to the vulnerability of India was the rise of a powerful merchant class whose economic interests were bound up with those of the Western companies. These companies were allowed to trade relatively freely in India (they were almost entirely excluded in China). During the sixteenth century India's economy was little affected by the trade because it was confined largely to spices and textiles. But in the seventeenth century various commercial crops such as indigo, mustard seed, and hemp, as well as saltpeter, were exported in large quantities. Bengal was the center of this trade, and in that province there now arose wealthy native merchants who dominated the local economy and who were becoming increasingly restless under the corrupt and inefficient rule of the Mogul officials. It was one of these merchants, Jagat Seth, who bought the allegiance of the generals who supposedly were under the orders of the nawab, or governor, of Bengal. At the Battle of Plassey (1757) these generals refrained from fighting against the British, who lost only sixty-five men in that fateful encounter. As one Indian historian has put it, Plassey was "a transaction, not a battle."

The British now were the actual rulers of Bengal, though they continued to recognize puppet nawabs as a matter of form. In 1764, after defeating the Mogul's forces, the English East India Company was granted the *Diwani,* or the right of tax collection, in the rich provinces of Bengal, Bihar, and Orissa. This opened up manifold opportunities for profit making and outright extortion, which the English agents exploited to the full. By raising the taxes, controlling the trade, and accepting numerous "gifts" from native officials, they amassed fortunes for themselves and their superiors in London.

The foothold in Bengal gave the British the base and the resources necessary for further expansion in India. At that time there were four other contenders for the Mogul domains—the French, the Moslem rulers of Mysore and of Hyderabad, and the Maratha Confederacy. The French were eliminated during the course of the Seven Years' War, being forced to surrender virtually all their posts in India by the Treaty of Paris of 1763. (See Chapter 21, section V.) Then during the American Revolution the British were challenged in India also by a coalition of the three principal native powers. The governor-general, Warren Hastings, managed to hold out and later took the offensive. By 1800 only the British and the Marathas were left, and during the following years the British gradually prevailed because of dissension within the Maratha Confederacy. By 1818 the back of the Marathas had been broken, though some fighting continued with them as well as with the Sikhs in the Punjab.

After having established themselves in the heart of the subcontinent, the British began pushing northward in a search for natural frontiers. To the northeast, in Himalayan Nepal, they defeated the Gurkhas who henceforth fought on the side of the British. Likewise to the northwest they finally defeated the proud Sikhs of the Punjab. Thus by the middle of the nineteenth century the British were the masters of all India, from the Indus to the Brahmaputra, and from the Himalayas to Cape Comorin. A few major kingdoms still survived, including Kashmir, Hyderabad, Baroda, and Travancore, but these were now dependent territories, isolated from each other, and powerless against the might of Britain.

With their authority firmly established in India, the British now overran neighboring states. First they acquired strategic Singapore (1819), giving them control of the route to China, and then they conquered Burma in three campaigns—1824, 1852, and 1886. In addition to these outright annexations, the British surrounded India with a defensive network of alliances and spheres of influence. With an eye on expansionist Russia in Central Asia, the British invaded Afghanistan in 1839 and 1879, and eventually recognized the independence of this state and granted it a subsidy in return for the right to control its foreign relations. Likewise, rumors of Russian penetration in Tibet caused the British to send an expedition to that country in 1904. An agreement followed whereby Tibet undertook not to admit any foreign agents. Further to the west the British clashed repeatedly with the Russians for paramount influence in Persia. The struggle veered back and forth until the two rivals agreed, in the Anglo-Russian Entente of 1907, to divide Persia into a British sphere of influence in the south, a Russian sphere in the north, and a buffer zone in the center.

It might be added that at the same time that the British were establishing themselves in India and the surrounding territories, the French were conquering Indochina. They compelled the Chinese government to relinquish its claims to suzerainty in Indochina in 1883. Siam escaped foreign domination because of the desire of the British to preserve a buffer state between British Burma and

French Indochina. The East Indies remained under the rule of the Dutch, who had conquered them from the Portuguese in the seventeenth century.

III. BRITISH RULE

We have seen that the East India Company was at first outrageously exploitive in its administration of the Indian territories it controlled. The excesses aroused public opinion in Britain, and this, together with political considerations, prompted Parliament to pass acts in 1773 and 1784 that placed the company under the supervision of the London government. The company continued to trade, and its servants and soldiers continued to govern and fight in India, but it functioned under the watchful eye of Parliament and the British government. The next change came in 1833, when the company lost its commercial monopoly and served henceforth as a largely administrative body under the Crown. The main privilege and justification for the existence of the company now was the appointment of civil servants, which constituted very substantial and influential patronage. But an act of 1853 took away this patronage by instituting an open competitive examination for the recruitment of civil servants. The continued existence of the company could scarcely be justified, and, in fact, its demise was precipitated by the Indian Mutiny of 1857.

The Mutiny was not the national movement or war of independence that some Indian writers have called it. Rather it was primarily a military outbreak that was exploited by certain discontented princes and landlords whose interests had been harmed by the British. Lord Dalhousie, the governor-general between 1848 and 1856, had dispossessed many princes and aroused uneasiness and suspicion amongst those who remained. Other groups, too, were dissatisfied: Conservative elements of the Indian population were deeply disturbed by the introduction of the railway and telegraph, the opening of Western-type schools, the aggressive activities of certain Christian missionaries, the legalization of widow remarriage, and the abolition of practices such as infanticide and suttee, or the self-cremation of widows on their husbands' funeral pyres. The Sepoys, as the Indian soldiers serving in the British forces were called, were disaffected because of prolonged campaigning in distant lands and the refusal of extra allowances for such service. The spark that set off the uprising was the introduction of cartridges that were greased with cow and pig fat, obnoxious to both the Hindus and the Moslems. All these factors combined to make the Mutiny assume the proportions of a popular uprising in certain scattered regions.

When the Mutiny began on May 10, 1857, the British were caught by surprise and forced to the defensive. But the revolt did not spread throughout the country, being confined largely to the north. Even there most of the important native states remained loyal to the British and gave invaluable assistance. Thus after about four months, the British were able to counterattack, and by July, 1858, the Mutiny had been crushed. Both sides were guilty of brutality, the Indians murdering many captives, and the English burning down villages and indiscriminately killing the inhabitants.

A month after the suppression of the Mutiny, Parliament passed the India Act ending the rule of the East India Company and substituting that of the Crown. Henceforth India was ruled by a vast hierarchy with its base in India and its apex in London in the person of the Secretary of State for India. This official was a member of the cabinet and generally was allowed a free hand by his colleagues. The top official in India was the governor-general, or viceroy, acting as the direct representative of the Crown, and usually appointed for a five-year term. The viceroy was assisted by an executive council of five members, none of them Indian until 1909. Beneath these top officials was the famous Indian Civil Service which collected the revenues, maintained law and order, and supervised the judicial system. Prior to 1919 almost all the members of this small but elite group consisted of British graduates of Oxford and Cambridge. The Civil Service in turn supervised a subordinate provincial service that was exclusively Indian in personnel. It was through these Indian officials in the lower ranks of the bureaucracy that the authority of the government penetrated to the masses.

The efficiency of British rule in India is reflected in the fact that in 1900 there were a total of 4,000 British civilian administrators in the country compared to 500,000 Indian. And in 1910 the Indian army comprised 69,000 Britishers and 130,000 Indians. It should be noted that Britain's position in India was based not only on the army and the bureaucracy but also on the surviving Indian princes. Prior to the Mutiny the British often had no compunction about taking over principalities when it suited them to do so. But this policy was reversed following the Mutiny, so that India remained thenceforth a crazy-quilt pattern of some 550 native states intermingled with British Indian provinces. The reason for this change of policy was made clear in 1860 by Lord Canning, the first viceroy following the Mutiny: "if we could keep up a number of Native States without political power, but as royal instruments, we should exist in India as long as our naval supremacy was maintained."[1]

IV. BRITISH IMPACT

The British impact upon India was felt first in the economic field, and naturally so since the British arrived in India in search of markets and commodities. Particularly after they became masters of the country, the British affected India's economy decisively, especially by their taxation and trade policies. Being unfamiliar with the Mogul revenue system and lacking experienced personnel, the British decided with their Permanent Settlement of 1793 to recognize the former imperial tax farmers and district revenue officers as English-type landlords, or zamindars. The "permanent" feature of this arrangement was that the annual sum expected of the zamindars was frozen at £3 million, while they were free, as landlords, to raise the rents they collected from the peasants. This was easy to do as land values were rising and the peasants now were tenants-at-will rather than hereditary cultivators of village lands. By World War II the landlords were collecting 12 to 20 million pounds annually, leaving them a huge surplus which, unlike their English counterparts, they did not use to improve their holdings. Nevertheless the British preserved this arrangement because, as Governor-General William Bentinck observed, it "created a vast body of rich landed proprietors deeply interested in the continuance of British Dominion and having complete command over the mass of the people."[2] This Permanent Settlement was confined to the Ganges basin. Elsewhere the British either collected the land taxes directly or from village communities. Their levies were not heavier than those of the Mogul period, but they had to be paid in cash, and there was less chance now of evading payment.

As regards trade, there was a strong demand in the nineteenth century for Indian raw materials such as jute, oilseeds, wheat and cotton. These commodities were transported to the seaports by a newly built railroad network totalling

4,000 miles by 1870 and 41,000 miles by 1939. The opening of the Suez Canal also facilitated the export of Indian raw materials by reducing the distance traversed by freighters between London and Karachi from 10,800 to 6,100 miles. Thus India became one of the world's most important sources of raw materials. And because of the high prices commanded by these materials, India was left with a favorable balance of trade throughout the nineteenth century.

The resulting capital surplus could have been used to develop modern industry. The fact that this was not done doomed India to her present critical state of underdevelopedness. Britain made no attempt to encourage manufacturing in India, and in certain crucial areas such as textiles, actively discouraged it. Thus there was no chance to erect tariffs to protect Indian infant industries against the tidal wave of cheap machine-made products from British factories. Indian economic historians describe this as a case of "aborted modernization." India had entered the world market and earned large sums of capital with no structural change in the archaic national economy. In place of the economic modernization that had occurred in Europe, the British and their associates "skimmed cash crops off the surface of an immobilized agrarian society."[3]

Meanwhile, thanks to Western medical science, health measures, and famine relief arrangements, India's population rose from 255 million in 1872 to 305 million in 1921. Similar population growth had occurred earlier in Europe but had been absorbed by new factories in the cities. Since no such industrialization occurred in India, the new extra millions could only fall back on agriculture. This produced the terrible overpressure on land that remains to the present day one of the most acute problems of the Indian economy—and indeed of most Third World economies which also suffer from "aborted modernization" and for the same reason.

British rule affected India profoundly in intellectual matters, as well as economic. For about half a century after their conquest of India, the British made no attempt to impose their culture upon the country, being too busy with immediate pressing problems. They left the existing system of education undisturbed but also unsupported. Elementary education continued to be given in village schools, both Hindu and Moslem. But higher learning declined because it no longer received the customary patronage from the native princes and nobles.

Nothing effective was done by the government until 1823, when a Committee on Public Instruction was appointed. This body decided that it should encourage not an English but an Oriental type of education based on Sanskrit, Arabic, and Persian. This is not surprising, for English scholars had discovered India's cultural heritage and were tremendously impressed, especially by the common origin of the Aryans of India and Europe. On the other hand, some Indians objected to this decision because they wished to learn English in order to get jobs with the new government. The more farseeing of these objectors favored an English-type of education in order to make available to their countrymen the whole corpus of Western learning. Most outstanding was the distinguished Bengali scholar Ram Mohan Roy, whose career we shall consider shortly.

The controversy split the Committee on Public Instruction into two factions, the "Anglicists" and the "Orientalists." The deadlock persisted until Thomas Babington Macauley was appointed president of the Committee in 1834. The following year he prepared his famous Minute on Education in which he adopted wholeheartedly Roy's viewpoint and concluded "that English is better worth knowing than Sanskrit or Arabic. . . ." Macauley added that "it is impossible for us, with our limited means, to attempt to educate the body of the people.

We must at present do our best to form a class who may be interpreters between us and the millions whom we govern; a class of persons, Indian in blood and color, but English in taste, in opinions, in morals, and in intellect."[4]

Macauley worked hard to implement his recommendation as soon as it was officially adopted. During the following decades, a national system of education was worked out, consisting of universities, training colleges for teachers, high schools, and vernacular elementary schools designed for the masses. Between 1885 and 1900 the number of students in colleges and universities rose from 11,000 to 23,000, and those in secondary schools from 429,000 to 633,000. At the same time the introduction of the printing press greatly stimulated intellectual life in India. Sanskrit works became public property rather than the jealously guarded monopoly of Brahmins. And newspapers appeared published in the various modern Indian languages as well as in English.

These developments affected the intellectual climate of India profoundly. They did not touch the masses, which remained completely illiterate. Nor, at first, did they reach the Moslems, who remained generally hostile to the new schools and books. Thus, English education became almost the exclusive possession of a small Hindu upper class. But this was enough to start off a chain reaction that has continued to the present day. English education created a new class of Indians familiar with foreign languages and cultures, and committed to liberal and rational ideologies. It was precisely this class that used European ideology to attack British domination and to organize a nationalist movement that eventually culminated in an independent India.

V. INDIAN RENAISSANCE

Britain's intellectual impact stimulated an upsurge and a creativity in Indian thought and culture that is commonly known as the Indian Renaissance. To appreciate the significance of this movement, it should be noted that when the British arrived upon the scene, Hinduism was for the most part in a depressed and demoralized state. During the preceding 700 years of Moslem domination, Hinduism had been looked down upon as the idolatrous religion of a subject race. It lacked prestige, organization, and active leadership. But when the British overthrew Mogul rule, Hinduism for the first time in seven centuries stood on a plane of equality with Islam. And when the British opened their schools, the Hindus, in contrast to the Moslems, flocked to them eagerly. By so doing, they benefited in two ways: they filled the posts in the new bureaucracy, and they experienced an intellectual revival by virtue of their Western contacts.

The stimulus of the West provoked three types of reaction or three schools of thought amongst the Hindus, although the lines were by no means clearcut, and there was much overlapping. The first was wholeheartedly and uncritically pro-Western and antitraditional: everything Western was accepted as *ipso facto* superior and preferable.

The second reaction was one of complete rejection. The West was admittedly stronger, but its ideas were subversive and its customs repugnant. No true Indian, Hindu or Moslem, should compromise with the evil thing. Rather he should withdraw so far as possible from contact with the foreigner and live his own life in the traditional way. Proponents of this view regarded caste rule as immutable, accepted textual authority without reservations, and opposed such reforms as the abolition of suttee or of infanticide.

The third and most common reaction to the West represented a compromise between blind worship and outright rejection. It accepted the essence of Western secularism and learning, but it also sought to reform Hinduism from within and to preserve its basic truths while ridding it of corruption and gross encrustations. The outstanding leader of this school of thought was Ram Mohan Roy, widely venerated as "The Father of Modern India." Born in 1772 in a devout Brahman family of Bengal, he broke with his parents over the spectacle of his sister's torture on the funeral pyre of her husband. An insatiable student, he mastered Persian, Arabic, and Sanskrit, and then learned English and entered the service of the government. He was fascinated by Western thought and religions, and studied Greek and Hebrew in order to read the Scriptures in the original. Roy also reinterpreted Hinduism in his *Brahmo Samaj,* or Society of God, a new reformed sect of Hinduism which he founded. The Samaj was not a Christian dilution of Hinduism, as is often stated, but rather a synthesis of the doctrines of the European Enlightenment with the philosophical views of the Upanishads. Roy was above all a rationalist who believed that Hinduism rested squarely upon reason. This principle established, he proceeded both to prune current Hindu practices and to borrow freely from the West. Thus he left his followers a creed that enabled them to face the West without losing their identity or their self-respect.

The Brahmo Samaj remained for two generations after Roy's death in 1833 the focus of efforts to purify Hinduism. Then the initiative passed to Swami Dayananda (1824–1883), who rejected the "Brahmos" of his day as being too much under Western influence and ignorant of their own Hindu culture and traditions. Dayananda founded the *Arya Samaj,* or Aryan Society. The name emphasized that the new organization stood for Indian as against "foreign" principles. The Arya Samaj program stressed Sanskrit education and the authority of the Vedas. Dayananda was by no means a reactionary, for he used the Vedas as his authority in attacking untouchability, child marriage, sex inequality, and idol worship.

Two other outstanding leaders of India's renaissance were Sri Ramakrishna (1836–1886) and Swami Vivekananda (1863–1902). Ramakrishna was a saintly mystic whose natural purity and selfless devotion to God attracted disciples throughout India and even abroad. His most famous disciple was Vivekananda, who attracted international attention when he addressed the First World Parliament of Religions at Chicago in 1893. After four years of lecturing in the United States and Europe, he returned to India a national hero. His success in preaching to the world the principles of Hinduism had given his countrymen a sense of dignity and of pride. The Hindu response to the Western challenge had thus made a full circle from rejection and imitation to critical reevaluation and confident assertiveness.

VI. INDIAN NATIONALISM

Ram Mohan Roy was the pioneer leader not only of India's religious renaissance but also of her political awakening, or nationalist movement. This was a new phenomenon in India, where hitherto there had been cultural unity and regional loyalties but no all-Indian feeling of patriotism. Nationalism developed under British rule for several reasons. One was the "superiority complex" of the English —their conviction that they were a racial elite and divinely ordained to rule India permanently. This racism, which was particularly strong following the Mutiny, manifested itself in all fields—in the army and the bureaucracy, where

Indians could not rise above certain ranks regardless of their qualifications, and in social life, where Indians were excluded from certain hotels, clubs, and parks. In these circumstances it was perhaps inevitable that an opposing sense of cultural and national consciousness should have gradually developed.

The British also stimulated nationalism by virtue of the unprecedented unity that they imposed on the Indian Peninsula. For the first time the whole of India was under one rule, and throughout the land Pax Britannica prevailed. The British also forged a physical unity with their railways and telegraph and postal services. Equally important was the unprecedented linguistic unity that followed the adoption of English as the common speech of the educated.

The British system of education, which introduced into the country the whole body of Western literature and political thought, also furthered Indian nationalism. The principles of liberalism and nationalism, of personal freedom and self-determination, inevitably were turned against the foreign British rule. The Indian leaders used not only Western political principles but also Western political techniques. Newspapers, platform oratory, pamphleteering, mass meetings, and monster petitions—all were used as grist for the nationalist mill.

Among the early Indian nationalist leaders, three are especially noteworthy. The first is Dadabhai Naoroji (1825–1917), an Indian businessman who resided many years in London and who, in fact, was elected in 1892 to the House of Commons on the Liberal ticket. Naoroji emphasized the drain of India's wealth to Britain, and secured the appointment of a parliamentary commission to investigate the financial administration of British India. M. G. Ranade (1842–1901), another distinguished leader, was disqualified from entering active politics because he was a judge, so he concentrated on social and economic reform. After careful study of India's problems, he concluded that the greatest need was for rapid industrialization under British auspices, and he bent his efforts towards the realization of this goal. Ranade's disciple was G. K. Gokhale (1866–1915), who also was interested primarily in economic problems. As a member of the Legislative Council he raised the cry "No taxation without representation," and his annual speeches on the imperial budget forced many tax reductions and financial reforms.

All these men were "moderates," in the sense that they accepted British rule and sought merely to secure certain concessions. Accordingly, they cooperated in supporting the Indian National Congress founded in 1885. The aim of this body was to secure some popular representation under British rule, which was cheerfully accepted and even extolled. This first generation of Indian nationalists, then, were admirers of Great Britain and apostles of cooperation. But after 1890 these "moderates" were challenged by the extremists led by Bal Gangadhar Tilak (1856–1920), the "father of Indian unrest." Tilak was a militant crusader who sought to transform the nationalist cause from an upper-class to a popular mass movement. This may explain his dogmatic support of many Hindu social customs, going so far as to organize a cow-protection society and to support child marriage. Yet at the same time he fought for a minimum wage for labor, freedom for trade union organization, creation of a citizen army, universal franchise, and free and compulsory education without distinction as to sex. Tilak won followers throughout the country with slogans such as "Educate, Agitate, and Organize," "Militancy, not mendicancy," and "Freedom is my birthright and I will have it."

Tilak was aided in his crusade by a series of famines and plagues in the 1890's that gave impetus to the growing sense of grievance. Indian militancy was also aroused by the revolution in Russia in 1905 and by Japan's defeat of Russia in the same year. The latter event was particularly exciting, being taken as a practical and signal refutation of the claim of Western superiority. At this point the Indian government passed in 1905 an act for the partition of Bengal into two provinces: the new East Bengal with 18 million Moslems and 12 million Hindus, and the remaining Bengal with 42 million Hindus and 12 million Moslems. The government's professed aim was to improve administration, for the original province had been too large and the area east of the Ganges had been neglected. But to the Indian nationalists it appeared that by dividing Bengal into predominantly Moslem and predominantly Hindu sections, the British were following a policy of divide and rule. This issue united the nationalists throughout the country to an unprecedented degree. They fought the government very effectively with the slogans *"Swaraj,"* or self-government within the British Empire, and *"Swadeshi,"* or boycott of British goods. The strong feelings aroused by the Bengal issue enabled the Extremists to control the 1906 meeting of the Indian Congress, and to secure a majority vote in favor of Swaraj and Swadeshi. Some of the nationalists went further, and, following the example and methods of the underground in Ireland and Russia, resorted to acts of terrorism.

Widespread though it was, this nationalist movement was predominantly Hindu. Under the leadership of Sir Sayyid Ahmad Khan, the Moslems had for the most part stayed out of the Indian Congress. They foresaw that if the Congress' demand for representative government were satisfied, the Moslems would suffer as a permanent minority. The Moslems also were alarmed by the increasing strength and militancy of Hindu nationalism, particularly since some of the most ardent Hindu patriots referred to the Moslems as "foreigners." In self-protection the Moslems organized the Moslem League, which, like the Indian Congress, held annual meetings. The British naturally welcomed and supported the League as a makeweight against the Congress. But the existence of the League was due basically not to British machinations but rather to the error of many nationalist leaders, such as Tilak, in basing their campaign on a revival of Hinduism. The formation of cow-protection societies, for example, undoubtedly aided the nationalist movement, but it also alienated Moslem Indians who naturally felt apprehensive about their future in a Hindu-controlled India.

Meanwhile, the spread of terrorism and the growing dissatisfaction of even the "moderates" convinced the British government that some concession was necessary. Accordingly, in 1909 the Secretary of State for India, Lord Morley, and the Viceroy, Lord Minto, presented the so-called Morley-Minto Reforms. These provided that a very small group of Indian voters, selected on the basis of high property, income, or education qualifications, should elect a majority of the members in the Legislative Councils of the provincial Governors, and a minority of members in the Viceroy's Legislative Council. A specified proportion of the legislative seats were reserved for Hindus and Moslems, and Moslem representation was weighted very considerably. For example, to become an elector, the Moslem had to pay income tax on an income of 3,000 rupees a year, the non-Moslem on an income of 300,000 rupees. Furthermore, even where an elective majority existed, as in the provincial councils, the British government could, and was prepared to, override any opposition. Thus the Reforms were in no way designed to introduce responsible government. Rather they were intended to split the opposition by permitting an element of representative government while leaving full power and final decisions in British hands.

This strategy succeeded in large part. The moderate nationalists, who had regained control of the Congress, passed a resolution expressing "deep and general satisfaction at the Reform proposals." They were further placated when the British made several more concessions in 1911, including the annulment of the unpopular partition of Bengal, the release of certain political prisoners, and the granting of substantial sums for educational purposes. Thus although individual acts of terrorism continued sporadically, India was relatively tranquil between 1910 and 1914.

Throughout this period, the nationalist movement was confined largely to the intellectuals. It is true that the National Congress had grown remarkably during the quarter-century following its establishment in 1885. Its membership was drawn from all parts of British India rather than from Bengal and a few cities on the west coast, as was originally the case. Yet the fact remains that it was almost exclusively a middle-class movement of lawyers, journalists, teachers, and merchants. These people were more familiar with John Stuart Mill, Herbert Spencer, and Charles Darwin than with the misery and grievances and aspirations of the masses of their own countrymen in the villages. Not unnaturally, there was little rapport between the nationalist leaders and the illiterate peasants. The gulf persisted until bridged by Mohandas Gandhi in the postwar period. And Gandhi succeeded because he sensed the essentially religious outlook of his people, and preached, not political abstractions, but religious concepts to which he gave a political meaning.

In conclusion, the impact of the West on India was quite different from its impact on Russia or the Middle East. In the case of Russia, the West exerted decisive cultural and economic influence, but Russia remained politically and militarily strong and independent. The Near East, on the other hand, was dominated economically and militarily by the West, yet, because of strategic considerations, the Ottoman Empire managed to retain its independence until World War I. India, by contrast, was conquered outright by Britain during the late eighteenth and nineteenth centuries. British rule lasted for nearly two centuries in Bengal and for more than one century in the Punjab. Consequently, India did not have the privilege of picking and choosing those features of European civilization that were most appealing. She was subjected to the Western impact more indiscriminately than any other major region of Asia.

SUGGESTED READING

See bibliography for Chapter 9. Also see the following: P. Griffiths, *The British Impact on India* (Macdonald, 1952); M. D. Lewis, ed., *The British in India: Imperialism or Trusteeship* (Health, 1962); R. P. Masani, *Britain in India* (Oxford Univ., 1961); L. S. S. O'Malley, *Modern India and the West* (Oxford Univ., 1941); A. Seal, *The Emergence of Indian Nationalism* (Cambridge Univ., 1968); S. A. Wolpert, *Tilak and Gokhale: Revolution and Reform in the Making of Modern India* (Univ. California, 1962); P. Woodruff, *The Men Who Ruled India,* 2 vols. (J. Cape, 1954–1955).

chapter twenty-nine

China and Japan

The historian who grasps the true secret of Japan's success in rapid Westernization has a key to modern Far Eastern history.—John K. Fairbank

The Far East was the last major region of Eurasia to feel the impact of expanding Europe. Various factors explain why China and Japan, in this respect, followed behind Russia, the Near East, and India. First, and most obvious, is the fact that the Far East, by definition, is that portion of the Eurasian continent that is farthest removed from Europe. China and Japan are not contiguous to Europe, as were the Russian and Ottoman Empires; and they are much further to the east and north than India. Probably more significant than geographic isolation was the political unity of the two Far Eastern countries. The European intruders were not able to employ in China and Japan the divide-and-rule policy that had proven so effective in India. There were no independent local potentates who could be enlisted against the central governments in Peking and Tokyo. And, thanks to the rigid seclusion policies of both these governments, there were no potential fifth column elements that could be exploited by the Europeans. Consequently, the Far Eastern countries were able to limit their contact with Europe to a mere trickle of closely supervised trade. But in the mid-nineteenth century this situation changed suddenly and drastically. First China and then Japan were forced open and compelled to accept Western merchants and missionaries and consuls and gunboats. The two Far Eastern countries were fundamentally affected, though in very different ways. Japan was able to adopt and to utilize the principles of Western power and to exploit them for self-defense and, later, for aggrandizement. China, by contrast, proved incapable of reorganizing herself along modified Western lines. On the other hand, she was too large and cohesive to be conquered outright, like India and the countries of Southeast Asia. Thus China remained in uncomfortable and unstable limbo until World War I, and even for some decades thereafter.

I. OPENING OF CHINA

Over a period of 4,000 years the Chinese people developed a unique and self-contained society at the extreme eastern end of the Eurasian landmass. This society, like others in Asia, was based on agriculture rather than trade and was governed by landlords and bureaucrats rather than by merchants and politicians. It was a distinctly self-centered and self-assured society that regarded the rest of the world as inferior and subordinate.

The Chinese first came into direct contact with the West when the Portuguese appeared in 1514 and were allowed to trade at the port of Canton. By the mid-eighteenth century the Chinese opened the trade to all European nations, though confining it to Canton and Macao. Meanwhile the Russians had come overland to the Amur Valley, and the Chinese reacted in the same way when, by the Nerchinsk Treaty (1689), they restricted Russian trade to three border points. (See Chapter 22, section III.) The Western intruders were kept at arms length in cultural matters as well as economic. Jesuit missionaries did win respect with their knowledge of astronomy and mathematics, but when the Pope in 1745 pronounced ancestor worship incompatible with Christianity, the missionaries were forbidden further proselytizing. Intellectual contact between China and the West ceased, and the Chinese remained profoundly uninterested in the outside world and convinced of their superiority over the "long-nosed barbarians."

The Chinese were forcefully jarred out of their seclusion and complacency by three disastrous wars: the first with Britain in 1839–1842, the second with Britain and France in 1856–1858, and the third with Japan in 1895. Britain was able to take the lead in opening up China because she had a powerful base in India as well as control of the seas. Britain's main objective was to remove the innumerable obstacles that the Chinese placed in the way of trading operations. The immediate issue that provoked hostilities was the trade in opium. European sailors had introduced opium smoking into China in the seventeenth century, and the habit spread rapidly from the ports. The demand for opium solved the British problem of paying for Chinese products. Hitherto the British had been forced to pay mostly in gold and silver, because the Chinese were little interested in Western goods. But now the market for opium reversed the balance of trade in favor of the British. The Peking government issued decrees in 1729 and 1799 prohibiting the importation of opium, but the trade was so profitable that Chinese officials could be bribed to permit smuggling.

The first Anglo-Chinese War, or Opium War, as it is frequently called, broke out when the Chinese attempted to enforce their prohibition of the opium traffic. The Emperor appointed as special Imperial Commissioner a man of proven integrity and firmness, Lin Tse-hsu. Lin seized 20,000 chests of opium worth $6 million, and destroyed them at a public ceremony. Complications following this action led to a clash between Chinese war junks and British frigates, and war began in November, 1839. The course of the following hostilities made clear the hopeless military inferiority of the Chinese. With a squadron of ships and a few thousand men, the British were able to seize port after port at will. The Chinese fought valiantly, their garrisons often resisting to the last man. But the odds were much more uneven than they had been between the Conquistadors and the Aztecs. European warships and artillery had been developed immeasurably between the sixteenth and nineteenth centuries, while Chinese military technology had stagnated at a level little above that of the Aztecs. In 1842, the Peking government capitulated and accepted the Treaty of Nanking, the first of a long series of unequal treaties that were to nibble away much of China's sovereignty.

By the Nanking Treaty China ceded the island of Hong Kong and opened five ports to foreign trade—Canton, Foochow, Ningpo, Amoy, and Shanghai. At these ports British consuls could be stationed and British merchants could lease land for residential and business uses. China also agreed to a uniform tariff fixed at 5 per cent ad valorem, to be changed only by mutual agreement. This provision deprived China of tariff autonomy and hence of control over her national revenue. Furthermore, a supplementary treaty concluded the following year granted Britain extraterritoriality in criminal cases, and also included a most-favored nation clause assuring Britain any additional privileges that China might grant other powers in the future.

The Nanking Treaty did not end the friction between the Chinese and the Europeans. The latter were disappointed because the opening of the treaty ports did not lead to so great an expansion of trade as they had anticipated. The remedy, they believed, was to secure even more concessions. The Chinese, on the other hand, felt that the treaties had granted too many privleges and constantly evaded fulfillment of the treaty obligations. Furthermore, the European merchants and the numerous adventurers of unsavory character who now flocked to the treaty ports aroused strong antiforeign feelings amongst the Chinese populace.

With such sentiments prevailing on both sides it is not surprising that hostilities began again in 1856. The occasion this time was the imprisonment by Chinese officials of the Chinese crew on board a Chinese ship flying the British flag. When the Peking government refused to release the crew, the British bombarded Canton. The French also entered the war, using the murder of a French priest as a pretext. The Anglo-French forces proved as irresistible as in the first war. In June, 1858, the Chinese were compelled to sign the Tientsin Treaties, but they refused to carry out the provisions and delayed formal ratification. The Anglo-French forces renewed the attack, capturing the capital and forcing China to sign the Peking Conventions in 1860. The Tientsin and Peking agreements opened several more ports on the coast and in the interior, redefined and extended extraterritoriality, and permitted the establishment of foreign legations in Peking and of Christian missions throughout the country. It should be recalled that it was at this time that the Russians took advantage of China's difficulties to secure by diplomatic means large areas in the Amur Valley and along the Pacific coast. (See Chapter 26, section III.)

The third defeat suffered by China was the most humiliating, for it was at the hands of the small neighboring kingdom of Japan. We shall see later in this chapter that the Japanese, in contrast to the Chinese, had been able to adapt Western technology to their needs and to build an efficient military establishment. Having accomplished what no other Oriental state had been able to achieve thus far, Japan now pressed certain shadowy claims in Korea. Traditionally, the Koreans had recognized the suzerainty of China, but they also had periodically submitted tribute to Japan. Thus when China sent a small force to Korea in 1894 in response to an appeal for aid in suppressing a revolt, the Japanese also landed a detachment of marines. The two forces clashed, and war was formally declared by China and Japan in August, 1894. The Chinese armies again were easily routed, and in April, 1895, Peking was forced to accept the Treaty of Shimonoseki. Its terms required China to pay an indemnity, recognize the independence of Korea, cede to Japan the island of Formosa, the Pescadores

Islands, and the Liaotung Peninsula, and open four more ports to foreign commerce. Some of the European powers were not at all pleased with the appearance of a new rival for concessions in China. Accordingly, Russia, France, and Germany joined in a demand that the strategic Liaotung Peninsula be returned to China, a demand to which Japan yielded reluctantly.

The Japanese war was a shattering blow to the pride and complacency of China. The great empire had been shown up to be completely helpless before a despised neighbor equipped with modern instruments of war. Furthermore, the European powers during the preceding years had been taking advantage of China's weakness and annexing outlying territories that traditionally had recognized Peking's suzerainty. Russia took the Amur Valley, the Maritime Provinces, and for a while occupied the Ili region in Central Asia. France seized Indochina, Britain took Burma, and Japan, having established her predominance in Korea by defeating China, proceeded to annex the country outright in 1910. In addition to these territorial acquisitions, the Western states divided China proper into spheres of influence in which were recognized the political and economic primacy of the respective powers concerned. Thus Yunnan and the area bordering on Indochina became a French sphere, Canton and the Yangtze Valley and the large area in between was a British sphere, Manchuria was Russian, Shantung was German, and Fukien Japanese. The humiliations and disasters that China experienced in the latter half of the nineteenth century forced the traditionally self-centered Middle Kingdom to undertake a painful self-searching, reappraisal, and reorganization. We will now trace the course of this process, noting how the Chinese slowly and grudgingly tried to follow the Western model, first in the military field, then in the economic, later in the social and intellectual, and finally in the political.

II. MILITARY AND ECONOMIC IMPACT

Lin Tse-hsu, the Chinese commissioner who had tried to stem the flow of opium and who had borne the brunt of the first British attack, realized the superiority of foreign arms. In a letter to a friend he described the impossibility of coping with British warships, and concluded that "ships, guns, and a water force are absolutely indispensable." But Lin was by no means willing to broadcast these views. "I only beg you to keep them confidential," he requested his friend. "By all means, please do not tell other persons."[1]

His aversion to publicity indicated that he feared a hostile reaction among his colleagues and superiors. This fear was by no means unjustified. The scholar-officials who ruled China remained, with a few exceptions, profoundly antipathetic and scornful of everything Western. The shock of defeat compelled them to take certain measures toward imitating Western arms and techniques. But in actual practice they did little more than go through the motions. The mandarins were hopelessly incompetent in mechanical matters even if they were sincerely desirous of imitating the West, which fundamentally they were not. Thus China did little during the interwar years of 1842 to 1858 to face the challenge of European expansionism.

The second defeat at the hands of the Western powers forced a few forward-looking Chinese intellectuals again to reconsider their traditional values and policies. Their response was what they called the "self-strengthening" movement. The phrase itself is from the Confucian classics, and was used in the 1860's to mean the preservation of Chinese civilization by grafting on Western mechanisms. In this regard the leaders of China now were ready to go beyond purely military matters to include railroads, steamship lines, machine factories, and applied science generally. This "self-strengthening" movement was doomed to failure because the basic assumption on which it rested was fallacious. Westernization could not be a halfway process; it was all or nothing. Westernization in tools led inevitably to westernization in ideas and institutions. So Western science could not be used to preserve a Confucian civilization; rather it was bound to undermine that civilization.

The fallacy of half-way modernization was apparent to the conservative Chinese scholar-bureaucrats, who consequently rejected westernization outright. Since they comprised a large majority of China's ruling class, they effectively blocked the attempt to modernize China in economic matters, as they had checked the earlier attempt at military modernization. For example, the China Merchants Steam Navigation Company was established in 1872 to build steamships for transporting rice from the Yangtze Delta to the capital in the north. The steamer fleet needed coal, so the Kaiping coal mines were opened north of Tientsin in 1878. To transport this coal, China's first permanent railroad began operations in 1881. This integrated complex of enterprises had a sound economic basis and should have prospered. But its directors were motivated, in the traditional Chinese fashion, more by family than by corporate considerations. They appointed needy relatives and greedy henchmen to the various posts, with the result that the entire undertaking fell heavily into debt and eventually passed under foreign control.

China's failure to build up her economy and her armed forces led inevitably to increasing Western penetration and control. Numerous loans were made to the Peking government, frequently under pressure and on conditions that gave the creditors control over segments of China's economy. Another means of economic influence was the concessions held by the European powers in various Chinese ports. Most important was the "international settlement" of Shanghai which developed into a sovereign city-state in which Chinese laws did not apply and Chinese courts and police had no jurisdiction. These concessions profoundly affected China's economy, which traditionally had been self-sufficient and land-based. But now it was becoming increasingly dependent upon the foreign-controlled coastal cities, and particularly upon Shanghai. The Western powers also dominated the great inland waterways as well as the coastal ports. They maintained fleets of gunboats that patrolled the Yangtze River between Shanghai and Chunking, a distance of 1,500 miles across the heart of China. In fact, Britain maintained an officer with the revealing title of Rear-Admiral Yangtze!

III. SOCIAL AND INTELLECTUAL IMPACT

In the late nineteenth and early twentieth centuries, the Chinese response to the West's challenge broadened from the military and economic spheres to the social and intellectual. One reason for this shift in interest was the defeat by Japan in 1894–1895, a crushing blow to the pride and complacency of the ruling scholar-official class. The other reason was the massive and seemingly irresistible intrusion of the West. In the years following the war with Japan, this intrusion reached such proportions in every field that the very existence of the Chinese state seemed endangered. As a result, a growing number of Chinese leaders were being forced to the conclusion that drastic change was essential for survival, and that this change could not be limited to military and economic matters. Furthermore, the very process of Western penetration created forces and conditions that were propitious to change.

The extension of foreign business into the interior of the country stimulated the growth of a Chinese merchant class, which soon took over the distribution of Western goods. Later, Chinese manufacturers began to establish match factories, flour mills, cotton mills, and silk-spinning factories. These new economic leaders tended to be an independent political force. They disliked European domination because of the privileges it conferred upon foreign business competitors. But they also had little use for the reactionary imperial court in Peking, which neither offered effective resistance to the foreigners nor showed any understanding of the nature and needs of a modern economy. Thus, these Chinese merchants felt no more loyalty toward the Manchu regime in Peking than the Indian merchants had felt earlier for the Mogul regime in Delhi. Consequently it was they who provided the dynamism behind the revolutionary nationalist movement that developed at the turn of the century. It was not accidental that the first antiforeign boycotts were organized in the coastal cities, and that the 1911 revolution that overthrew the Manchu dynasty also broke out in those cities.

The perilous situation of China also affected the ruling scholar-bureaucrats, though they were impelled in the direction of reform rather than revolution. Because of their official positions and vested interests, they wanted only "change within tradition." They still held that China's Confucian civilization could be renovated to meet modern needs. An outstanding exponent of this view was the fiery Cantonese scholar K'ang Yu-wei (1858–1927), who startled his colleagues with his study of *Confucius as a Reformer*. This iconoclastic work depicted Confucius as a champion of the rights of the people, rather than imperial authority.

This advocacy of people's rights and of their participation in government was something new for China. Hitherto the Western concepts of democracy and nationalism had been conspicuously absent. Instead, the emphasis had been on the family, and, so far as a broader allegiance was concerned, it took the form of "culturalism" rather than nationalism. By culturalism is meant identification with the native cultural tradition, which was viewed simply as the alternative to foreign barbarism. China's ruling scholar-bureaucracy was steeped in this tradition, and many of its members still avowed that it was "better to see the nation die than its way of life change."[2] But against the standpatism of this traditional culturalism the reform leaders now affirmed revolutionary Western concepts. "What does nationalism mean?" asked one of these reformers. "It is that in all places people of the same race, the same language, the same religion, and the same customs, regard each other as brothers and work for independence and self-government, and organize a more perfect government to work for the public welfare and to oppose the infringement of other races. . . . If we wish to promote nationalism in China, there is no other means of doing it except through the renovation of the people."[3]

IV. POLITICAL IMPACT

The new reform spokesmen in China were able to win a hearing following the defeat at the hands of the Japanese in 1895. They gained the ear of the young emperor, Kuang-hsü, who momentarily broke away from the influence of the empress dowager, Tz'u-hsi. So impressed was he by their oral and written presentations that he issued in the summer of 1898 a series of sweeping reform decrees that are collectively called the Hundred Days Reform. Numerous sinecures were to be eliminated, the provincial governments were to be more centralized under Peking, new schools were to disseminate European learning, Western-style production methods were to be encouraged, and a national conscript army was to be organized along Western lines. But these measures never got beyond the paper stage. The empress dowager, with the support of the military, effected a coup and deposed the unfortunate emperor. Then she declared herself regent, rescinded all the reform decrees, and executed six of the reform leaders.

The collapse of the Hundred Days Reform gave the reactionaries full power. In their zeal they actively channeled social and political discontent against the foreigners. Antiforeign secret societies, incited by court reactionaries and provincial governors, organized local militias to combat foreign aggression. Chief among these societies was the I Ho T'uan, or Righteous Harmony Fists, popularly termed Boxers. With official connivance the Boxers began to attack foreigners, and by 1900 numerous Chinese Christians and foreigners had been killed in North China. When European naval detachments began to land at Tientsin, the Boxers declared war on all foreigners and besieged the foreign legations in Peking. Within a few months, international armies relieved the legations, and the Imperial Court fled from the capital. Once more China was forced to accept a peace with humiliating terms, including further commercial concessions and payment of an indemnity of $333 million.

The fiascos of the Hundred Days Reform and of the Boxer Rebellion dramatically demonstrated the futility of trying to modernize China by reform from above. The alternative was revolution from below, and this did take place in 1911, when the Manchu dynasty finally was overthrown and its place taken by a republic.

The leader and ideologist of the revolutionists was Dr. Sun Yat-sen (1866–1925). Compared to the reform leaders who had hitherto been prominent, Sun was a strange and anomalous figure. He was not one of the upper-class literati; in fact, his training was as much Western as Chinese, and his knowledge of the traditional classics was far from secure. He was born in the Canton Delta, which had been subject to foreign influence longer than any other area in China. At the age of thirteen he joined his brother in Honolulu where he remained five years and completed a high-school course in a Church of England boarding school. Then he went to Queen's College in Hong Kong, and after graduation he enrolled in the Hong Kong Medical College and received his medical degree in 1892. Thus Sun acquired an excellent scientific education that he could have used to acquire wealth and status; instead he identified with the poor and always felt a passionate concern for their welfare.

With such sentiments, he did not remain long in professional practice. The defeat by Japan in 1895 convinced him that the government of his country was rotten to the core and that nothing short of a revolution would provide the remedy. So he embarked on the career of a revolutionary and went first to Japan, then to America, and later to Europe. It was at this time that Sun became definitely republican in his thinking. He had for long been a revolutionary in the sense that he wished to overthrow the Manchu dynasty. But hitherto his constructive proposals had been limited to training competent personnel and carrying out technological improvements. Now he decided that the aim of revolution should be the establishment of a democratic republic. At a conference held in Tokyo in 1905 Sun founded the T'ung-meng-hui, or League of Common Alliance. Its program called for a republican government elected by "the people of the country" and also for the division of the land amongst the peasantry. It is significant that no one had earlier raised the issue of land distribution as a possible element in self-strengthening or reform. The explanation is that no one had seriously considered the idea of a fundamental revolution in the Chinese way of life. No one, before Sun, had proposed the notion that the peasant masses might be transformed into literate, property-owning, and politically active citizens.

When the revolution came in 1911, it was partly the work of landlord gentry and commercial interests in the provinces which were opposed to the belated efforts of the Manchu regime to nationalize railway construction. The provincial leaders fomented strikes and riots, ostensibly on the ground that nationalization would lead to foreign control, but actually because they feared it would exclude them from profit possibilities. In any case, the revolutionists exploited the discontent and worked effectively amongst students and soldiers. A small-scale republican uprising in Canton was suppressed, but on October 10, 1911, an accidental explosion in a revolutionist bomb factory at Hankow led to mutiny among nearby imperial troops. Despite lack of coordination, the revolutionary movement spread rapidly throughout the country. Sun Yat-sen, who was in the United States at the time, hurried back and on December 30, 1911, was elected President of the United Provinces of China by a provisional revolutionary assembly.

The movement that overthrew the Manchus obviously represented a good deal more than the revolutionary leadership supplied by Sun Yat-sen. Consequently, Sun was unable to control the country even though he was the nominal leader. Actual power was in the hands of an able and ambitious imperial official, Yüan Shih-k'ai (1859–1916), who commanded the most effective army in China. Rather than risk a civil war that would invite foreign intervention, Sun, in February, 1912, yielded the presidency to Yuan, and the latter agreed to work with a parliament and a responsible cabinet. This arrangement, however, did not really settle the basic question of what form of government would replace the fallen Manchu regime. Yuan was all for Western military technology and administrative methods, but Western political institutions, including control of the executive by representatives of the people, he regarded as antithetical to China's traditions and certainly antithetical to his personal ambitions.

The issue was joined with little delay. Sun Yat-sen founded a new political party, the Kuomintang, or National Peoples' party. To organize his own followers, Yuan formed the Chinputang, or Progressive party. When the National Assembly was elected in April, 1913, the majority of seats was held by the Kuomintang. But this setback did not unduly restrict Yuan, for he had the backing of the army, the bureaucracy, and the foreign powers. In fact, the showdown came over a loan of £25 million, which Yuan borrowed from a group of five powers. Realizing that Yuan would use some of this money to strengthen his hold on the government, the Kuomintang leaders warned the governments that the constitution required parliamentary approval of loans, and since the Assembly would never approve this particular loan, it would not be legally binding. But the Powers preferred to back the strongman Yuan, as they had backed the Manchu dynasty in earlier years. So Yuan received the money, and, as the Kuomintang had feared, he used it to consolidate his position. The measures that he now took, including the assassination of a top Kuomintang leader, led Sun Yat-sen to resort to an armed uprising in the summer of 1913. The move was premature and Yuan suppressed the revolt with ease.

Sun fled to Japan with his principal followers, and Yuan made preparations to fulfill his ill-concealed ambition to establish himself as emperor. In October, 1913, he had himself elected permanent president. Then he ordered the dissolution of both the Kuomintang and the Parliament. With the opposition out of the way, he engineered "spontaneous" requests that he fulfill his duty to his country and become emperor. In December, 1915, Yuan announced that he would assume the title of emperor on January 1, 1916. But the popular response was unexpectedly negative. A revolt broke out in Yunnan in December, 1915, and quickly spread. Yuan found it necessary first to postpone and finally, in March, 1916, to abandon the restoration of the monarchy. Humiliated and embittered, Yuan died in June of the same year. After his death the army commanders who had served under him divided the country amongst themselves. Until 1926, these warlords paid little attention to the republican government that nominally ruled from Peking. Rather, they pillaged the countryside mercilessly and dragged China down to a brutalizing anarchy. The early years of the republic marked one of the worst periods in the history of China.

Several factors account for this wretched outcome of several decades of response to the West. First there is the sheer size of China, which for many years left the interior of the country unaffected by Western contact. This interior functioned as a vast reservoir, out of which tradition-minded civil service candidates continued to appear for several decades. The bureaucracy that they formed consisted of intellectuals who were steeped in the Confucian classics and who consequently placed much greater emphasis upon ethical principles than upon the manual arts or the technology of warfare. This ruling class was further inhibited by the fact that, apart from Buddhism, China had little or no tradition of borrowing from abroad. Thus it is not surprising that although China did change in the second half of the nineteenth century, the tempo of her change was far below that of other countries responding to the West.

However, the bureaucracy cannot be shouldered with the entire responsibility for China's failure. The young Western-trained Chinese also were partly to blame. Some of them played leading roles in the early days of the republic, but they tried to set up in China carbon copies of the institutions they had observed and studied abroad, and especially in the United States. What they established naturally had no meaning for the Chinese people and quickly crumbled before the realities of Chinese politics.

V. JAPAN IN SECLUSION

Historians have proffered several factors in explanation of the difference between the Chinese and the Japanese responses to the challenge of the West. The physical compactness of the Japanese islands facilitated both the forging of national unity and the spread of new values and new learning throughout the country. It also made the country vulnerable to, and aware of, foreign pressure. Perry's ships sailed within sight of the capital, Edo, and within a few weeks all of Japan knew of this fateful event. By contrast, the vast, densely populated, interior provinces of China were for long inaccessible and impervious to Western influences, and served instead as reservoirs of traditional attitudes and forces. Furthermore, Japan's long tradition of borrowing from the great Chinese cultural world made similar borrowing from the Western world in the nineteenth century less jarring and painful. Japan had adapted selected aspects of Chinese culture with the slogan "Japanese spirit and Chinese knowledge." Now she borrowed what she wished from the West with the slogan "Eastern morale and Western arts." And Japanese government and society were pluralistic in structure in comparison with the monolithic features of the Chinese Empire. The clan tradition and regional particularism of Japan were reinforced by geographic compartmentalization—by the broken mountainous terrain. The merchant class in Japan had more autonomy and economic strength, and, as we shall see, was rapidly extending its power at the critical moment of the West's intrusion. The military elements in Japan were at the top of the social ladder, rather than at the bottom, as was the case in China. This meant that Japan had a ruling class that was much more sensitive and responsive to Western military technology than were the Chinese literati. In sum, geography, cultural traditions, and pluralistic organization combined to make Japan more vulnerable to Western intrusion than China, and more quick to respond to that intrusion.

Despite these basic differences, Japan, like China, remained in seclusion until the mid-nineteenth century. It is true that the Japanese welcomed the Portuguese in the sixteenth century and embraced Christianity in large numbers. (See Chapter 16, section VIII.) But the Tokugawa shoguns perceived that Western religion and trade represented an unsettling force that threatened their authority. For this reason they severed one by one the ties between Japan and the Western world. By the mid-seventeenth century the sole remaining contact was the handful of Dutch traders who were confined to the islet of Deshima, and even they were subjected to the most restricting and humiliating regulations.

The aim of the Tokugawa leaders was to keep Japan isolated and unchanging in order to perpetuate their regime. But despite their efforts, certain developments did occur that gradually altered the balance of forces in the country and undermined the *status quo*. The long peace enforced by Tokugawa rule stimulated population growth, economic expansion, and the strengthening of the merchant class. The population jumped from 18 million in 1600 to 26 million in 1725. Cities grew disproportionately, Edo approaching the million mark by 1700, and Osaka and Kyoto each reaching 300,000. The population spurt increased the demand for commodities and encouraged merchants and rich peasants to invest surplus capital in new forms of production, including the domestic, or putting-out, system. They provided materials and equipment for peasants and craftsmen, and marketed the finished products. It appears that in certain areas this industrial development had reached the level of factory organization by the end of the Tokugawa period. Regional specialization based on available raw materials and local skills became widespread, so that particular areas were noted for their lacquerware, pottery, textiles, or rice wine.

The rising production led to wide-scale exchange of goods, which in turn led to the development of money economy. At first money was imported from China and Korea, but in the seventeenth century a gold mint was established. The aristocrats became dependent on brokers to convert their rice into money, and upon merchants to satisfy their consumption needs. In these transactions the aristocrats lost out because of merchant manipulation of prices through monopolies, and because the price of rice failed to keep up with the soaring costs of other commodities. The aristocrats, besides, had acquired a taste for luxuries and tended to compete with each other in ostentatious living. The net result was that they generally became indebted to the merchants, even though the latter ranked far below in the social scale. In time the merchant families bought their way into the aristocracy by intermarriage or adoption. These families dominated not only the economy but also the art and literature of the eighteenth and early nineteenth centuries.

These changes, it should be noted, affected not only the top levels of the aristocracy, but also the samurai, whose services were not so much in demand during this long period of peace. The mass of the peasants also suffered severely with the lag of the price of rice. Many of them migrated to the cities, but not all were able to find employment, for the growth of the national economy was not keeping pace with the growth of population.

Thus, Japanese society was in a state of transition. It was experiencing profound economic and social change, and this engendered political tensions that were reaching the breaking point when Admiral Perry forced Japan's doors open to trade. One reason the Japanese proved so ready to reorganize their society under the impact of the West was precisely that many of them were all too aware that this society needed reorganizing. On July 8, 1853, Commodore Matthew Perry cast anchor in Edo Bay and delivered a letter from President Fillmore asking for trading privileges, coaling stations, and protection for shipwrecked Americans. Within a week he sailed away after warning that he would be back for an answer the following spring. When he returned in February, 1854, he made it clear that the alternative was a treaty or war. The Japanese yielded and on March 31 signed the Treaty of Kanagawa. Its terms opened the ports of Shimoda and Hakodate for the repair and provisioning of American ships, provided for proper treatment and repatriation of shipwrecked Americans, permitted the appointment of consular representatives if either nation considered it necessary, and promised most-favored-nation treatment for the United States.

In accordance with the provisions of this treaty, the United States sent Townsend Harris, an unusually able man, as the first consul to Japan. With his extraordinary tact and patience, Harris gradually won the confidence of the Japanese and secured the Commercial Treaty of 1858. This opened four more ports to trade, provided for mutual diplomatic representation, gave to Americans both civil and criminal extraterritoriality, prohibited the opium trade, and gave freedom of religion to foreigners. Soon after signing these two treaties with the United States, Japan concluded similar pacts with Holland, Russia, Britain, and France. Thus Japan, like China before her, now had to suffer the intrusion of the West. But her response to that intrusion was altogether different from that of the Middle Kingdom.

VI. MODERNIZATION OF JAPAN

The first effect of the Western encroachment was to produce a crisis that precipitated the downfall of the Tokugawa Shogunate. With the signing of the treaties the shogun was subject to conflicting pressures: on the one hand from the foreign powers, which demanded implementation of all the provisions, and on the other from the Japanese population, which was strongly antiforeign. This popular sentiment was exploited by the anti-Tokugawa clans, especially the Satsuma, Choshu, Hizen, and Tosa, often referred to as the Satcho Hito group. Between 1858 and 1865, attacks were made upon Europeans and their employers with the slogan "Honor the Emperor! Expel the barbarians!" With the death in 1867 of both the emperor and the Tokugawa Shogun, the way was clear for the so-called Meiji Restoration. The Tokugawa clansmen were shorn of their power and fiefs, and their place was taken by the Satcho Hito clans, which henceforth controlled the government in the name of the new Meiji Emperor. It was young samurai in the service of these clans who now provided Japan with extraordinary leadership that made possible successful modernization.

It should be noted that Japan at this point had fallen fully as much under Western control as China. Foreign settlements were being established in the ports, and these settlements were utilizing their extraterritoriality privileges to set up municipal organizations along the lines of those in the Chinese treaty ports. The foreign communities fully expected that, with dissension rampant in the country, Japan would speedily fall under Western domination as had the other Asian countries. But in contrast to China's literati, Japan's young new leaders realized that they were retarded in certain fields, and were willing and able to do something about it.

This is not altogether surprising if it is noted that even during their centuries of seclusion the Japanese leaders had gone out of their way to keep informed of developments in Europe. In fact, the Dutch were allowed to continue trading primarily so that they could be questioned concerning the outside world. Both the Shogunate and the clans promoted military industry and maintained schools for the study of foreign languages and foreign texts. The general level of knowledge rose to the point where, in the natural sciences, physics was separated from chemistry, and, in medicine, students were trained in special fields such as surgery, pediatrics, obstetrics, and internal medicine. In the Nagasaki naval school, instruction was given in navigation and gunnery only after a solid base had been laid in mathematics, astronomy, and physics. In other words, the Japanese all along had been much more appreciative of, and responsive to, Western culture.

In the light of this background, it is understandable why the Japanese acted differently from the Chinese once the Westerners forced their way in. In 1868 the emperor promulgated an imperial oath (known as the Charter Oath) that was designed to quiet the general unrest and to clarify the objectives of the new regime. This document emphasized two general points: that "all matters shall be decided by public discussion," and that "the evil customs of the past shall be broken off. . . . Knowledge shall be sought throughout the world."[4] In fact, Western ideas and Western material objects became the craze of the 1870's. It became fashionable to eat beef, to wear trousers, to carry an umbrella, and to sport a watch and diamond rings.

Japan's new leaders disapproved of this indiscriminate adulation of all things Western. They were interested not in Western civilization per se, but only in those features that enhanced national power. In the field of religion, for example, the Meiji statesmen supported Shinto as the state cult because it identified the national character with the emperor, and held that the emperor was descended from the Sun Goddess. In other words, Shinto stimulated national unity and patriotism, and these attributes were properly deemed necessary if Japan were to hold her own in the modern world. In education, it was explicitly stated that the objective was the furtherance of state interests rather than the development of the individual. Compulsory elementary education was decreed because the state needed a literate citizenry. Large numbers of foreign educators were brought to Japan to found schools and universities, and thousands of Japanese studied abroad and returned to teach in the new institutions. But the entire educational system was kept under close state supervision to ensure uniformity of thought as well as of administration.

In military affairs the Japanese abolished the old feudal levies and organized modern armed forces based on the latest European models. They built a conscript army with the aid of a German military mission, and a small navy under the guidance of the British. The Meiji leaders foresaw that the new military forces required a modern economy to supply their needs. Accordingly, they secured the establishment of the needed industries by granting subsidies, purchasing stock, or forming government corporations. The government leaders were careful to support not only light industries such as textile, but also heavy industries such as mining, steel, and shipbuilding, which were necessary to fill military needs. Once these enterprises were founded, the government generally sold them to various favored private interests at extremely low prices. It was in this manner that a few wealthy families, collectively known as the Zaibatsu, gained a stranglehold on the national economy that has persisted to the present. It might be added that the capital for this industrial expansion was obtained largely from agriculture. A substantial increase in agricultural yield was attained at relatively low cost by introducing better seed strains, improving land use, and expanding irrigation and drainage. Between 1878 and 1892 the area under cultivation increased by 7 per cent, the yield by 21 per cent, and the population by 15 per cent. The resulting agricultural surplus was siphoned off by taxes which furnished the capital for industrialization.

The Japanese also overhauled their legal system. This was in such a state when the Westerners appeared that their demand for extraterritoriality was at least understandable. The laws were chaotic and harsh, individual rights were disregarded, the police were arbitrary and all-powerful, and prison conditions were revolting. In 1871 a judicial department was organized, and in the following years new codes were adopted and a distinction made between judicial and administrative powers.

At the same time various political innovations were made in order to provide Japan with at least the trappings of parliamentary government. A cabinet and a privy council were first established, and then a constitution was promulgated with due ceremony in 1889. This document promised the citizens freedom from arbitrary arrest, protection of property rights, and freedom of religion, speech, and association. But in each instance the government was given authority to curb these rights when it so desired. Hence the constitution provided Japan with a parliamentary façade while preserving oligarchic rule and emperor worship. Indeed, the first article of the constitution provided that "The Empire of Japan shall be reigned over and governed by a line of Emperors unbroken for ages eternal," and the third article likewise stipulated that "The Emperor is sacred and inviolable."

With the adoption of the constitution and of the legal reforms, the Japanese were in a position to press for the abolition of the unequal treaties. They could fairly argue that Japan now had taken her place in the comity of civilized nations and that there was no longer any need for extraterritoriality and for the other infringements on their sovereignty. After prolonged diplomatic efforts they were able in 1894 to persuade Britain and the United States to terminate extraterritoriality and consular jurisdiction in five years. In the same year the Japanese won their unexpected and spectacular victory over the Chinese Empire. Henceforth there could be no more question of treating Japan as an inferior country, and the other powers soon followed Britain and the United States in yielding their special privileges. By 1899 Japan had gained legal jurisdiction over all foreigners on her soil, and in doing so, she became the first Asian nation to break the chains of Western control.

VII. EXPANSION OF JAPAN

Having modernized herself, Japan embarked on a career of expansion on the mainland. This is not surprising in view of Japan's warlike tradition and the immense prestige that her military leaders enjoyed from earliest times. Furthermore, the Far East was then most patently an area of international rivalry and of jostling for position. The practical-minded leaders of Japan drew the obvious conclusion that each people must grab for themselves and so they turned their attention to Korea. At first they were interested in ensuring Korea's independence, particularly as against China. As noted earlier in this chapter, this policy led to an armed clash in 1894 that precipitated the Sino-Japanese War. The course of the hostilities revealed to a startled world how far Japan had progressed in two decades. The Chinese troops fought bravely but hopelessly against a modern military machine. By the Treaty of Shimoneseki of 1895, Japan acquired Formosa, the Pescadores, and the Liaotung Peninsula, though the latter had to be restored on the insistence of France, Russia, and Germany.

After defeating China, the Japanese were faced by a much more serious adversary, Russia. Not only had Russia acted with France and Germany to force Japan to restore the Liaotung Peninsula, but in addition Russia now encroached upon both Korea and Manchuria. During the Sino-Japanese War, Korea signed a treaty agreeing to accept Japanese guidance and capital. Immediately after the war, the Japanese minister to Korea began a comprehensive reform program and placed Japanese officials in strategic positions. But the Korean queen, who led the conservative faction, opposed the Japanese minister. The latter organized a conspiracy resulting in the murder of the queen, but the coup was short-lived. The king now turned to Russia, replacing Japanese advisers with Russians, and granting a timber-cutting concession to a Russian company.

At the same time that the Russians were supplanting the Japanese in Korea, they were also winning concessions in Manchuria. We noted earlier the secret Chinese-Russian treaty of 1896 that allowed Russia to construct a railroad across Manchuria to Vladivostok. We also noted that in 1898 Russia obtained a twenty-five year lease of the Liaotung Peninsula, and two years later occupied the entire province of Manchuria during the Boxer Rebellion. These Russian advances engendered warm debates among the ruling group in Tokyo. Some favored trying to reach an accord with Russia that would be based on a division of the spoils. Others preferred an alliance with Great Britain as the country with which Japan most nearly had common cause. With such an alliance to back her up, Japan would then be able to stand up to Russian expansionism.

Feelers were sent out to both the British and the Russian capitals, and it was soon evident that London was as receptive as St. Petersburg was intractable. On January 30, 1902, the Anglo-Japanese alliance was signed, providing for the independence of China and Korea, and recognizing Britain's special interests in Central China and Japan's special interests in Korea. If either Japan or Britain became involved in war with a third power, the other party would remain neutral, but if another power intervened, then the other party was bound to aid its ally. Since Russia and France had been allied for the past eight years, the Anglo-Japanese alliance obviously was designed to keep France from aiding Russia in the event of war.

Japan was now in a position to force the issue with Russia. In mid-1903 Japan offered to recognize Russia's primacy in Manchuria if Russia would reciprocate concerning Japan's position in Korea. The negotiations dragged on, with the over-confident Russians temporizing and evading. The Japanese concluded, with good reason, that the Russians were not negotiating in good faith, and severed diplomatic relations on February 6, 1904. Two days later, without an ultimatum or declaration of war, the Japanese attacked the Russian base at Port Arthur on the Liaotung Peninsula.

As noted above, the Japanese won an even more unexpected victory over the Russians than they had won a decade earlier over the Chinese. By the Treaty of Portsmouth (September 5, 1905) Japan acquired the southern half of Sakhalin

Island and Russia's Liaotung leasehold, and secured recognition of her special interests in Korea. In retrospect this war stands out as a major turning point in the history of the Far East, and even of the world. Certainly it established Japan as a major power and altered the balance of forces in the Far East. But much more significant is the fact that for the first time an Asian state defeated a European state, and a great empire at that. This had an electrifying effect on all Asia. It demonstrated to millions of colonial peoples that European domination was not divinely ordained. For the first time since the days of the conquistadors the white man had been beaten, and a thrill of hope ran through the nonwhite races of the globe. In this sense the Russo-Japanese War stands out as a landmark in modern history; it represents the prelude to the great awakening of the non-European peoples that today is convulsing the entire world.

SUGGESTED READING

See bibliographies for Chapters 10 and 16. See also the following: W. FRANKE, *China and the West* (Blackwell, 1967); W. W. LOCKWOOD, *"Japan's Response to the West,"* *World Politics*, IX (October, 1956); G. B. SANSOM, *The Western World and Japan* (Knopf, 1950); H. Z. SCHIFFRIN, *Sun Yat-Sen and the Origins of the 1911 Revolution* (Univ. California, 1969); SSU-YU TENG and J. K. FAIRBANK, *China's Response to the West: A Documentary Survey, 1839–1923* (Harvard Univ., 1954); Y. C. WANG, *Chinese Intellectuals and the West, 1872–1949* (Univ. North Carolina, 1966); M. C. WRIGHT, ed., *China in Revolution: The First Phase 1900–1913* (Yale Univ., 1968).

chapter thirty

Africa

For better or for worse the old Africa is gone and the white races must face the new situation which they have themselves created.—
Jan Christiann Smuts

Europe's impact on sub-Saharan Africa was felt considerably later than that upon Eurasia. The European powers fastened their rule upon India, the East Indies, and much of North Africa, before they expanded south of the Sahara. France acquired Algeria in 1830 and Tunisia in 1881, while England occupied Egypt in 1882. European penetration southward came generally later because of various reasons, including adverse climate, prevalence of disease, geographic inaccessibility, and the superior organization and resistance of the Africans compared to the American Indians or the Australian aborigines. (See Chapter 18, section I.) Also there was a lack of exploitable riches to entice Europeans into the interior, as was the case with the bullion of Mexico and Peru. Thus sub-Saharan Africa, apart from certain coastal regions, remained largely unaffected by Europe until the late nineteenth century. In the last two decades of that century, however, the European powers made up for lost time, partitioning virtually the entire continent and exploiting its material and human resources. By 1914 the African peoples had, in many respects, come under European influence even more than had the Asians, though many villagers in the interior regions continued to live largely unaffected by the European intruder.

I. SLAVE TRADE

For centuries the most valuable of African resources for Europeans were the slaves, but these were obtainable at coastal ports, without any need for penetration inland. Although the slave stations were restricted to the coast, the slave trade nevertheless had profound repercussions upon considerable areas of sub-Saharan Africa. The trade began in 1442 when two captains of Prince Henry the Navigator took twelve African slaves to Lisbon. It is true that slavery already was an established and widespread institution in Africa. Prisoners of war were enslaved, as were also debtors or individuals guilty of serious crimes. But these slaves usually were treated as part of the family; they had clearly defined rights, and their status was not necessarily hereditary. In Europe, by contrast, slavery was a very different institution and had a very different history. From the beginning it was primarily economic, so that slaves were being worked to death in mines during classical times. This impersonalism was reinforced by racism when the Europeans became involved in the African slave trade on a large scale. Perhaps as a subconscious rationalization they gradually came to look down upon Negroes as inherently inferior savages, and therefore preordained to serve their white masters. Rationalization also may have been involved in the Europeans' resort to religion to justify the traffic in human beings. Enslavement, it was argued, assured the conversion of the African heathen to the true faith as well as to civilization.

In this self-satisfying spirit the Portuguese shipped thousands of African slaves to their homeland. But this was a petty prelude to the new and fateful phase of the slave trade that began in 1510 when the first shipload of African slaves was shipped to the New World. The venture proved highly successful, for there was urgent need for labor in the Americas, especially on the sugar plantations. The market for slaves was almost limitless, and several other countries entered the slave trade to share in the rich profits. Portugal dominated the trade in the sixteenth century, Holland during most of the seventeenth, and Britain in the eighteenth. The west African coast was dotted with about forty European forts which were used for defense against the rival trading nations and for storing the slaves who were awaiting shipment across the Atlantic.

Thanks to the prevailing trade winds, the "middle passage" was normally swift and brief. Nevertheless, the death rate during the trip ranged from 10 to 55 per cent, depending on the length of the voyage, the treatment accorded the slaves, and the chance occurrence of epidemics. Even greater casualties were suffered earlier, during the overland march to the coast. Native raiding parties rounded up captives in the interior and drove them from dawn to dusk until they reached the coastal markets, where they were branded with the name of the buyer and herded into the forts to await shipment across the ocean. Thus in supplying American plantations with some 10 million slaves, Africa suffered an estimated total loss of 35 to 40 million people. (See Chapter 23, section III for the overall effects on Africa.)

Despite these horrors, the slave trade persisted for over four centuries. The profits were so great that powerful vested interests—African, European, and American—resolutely opposed any proposals for control or abolition. The Africans who conducted the raids into the interior reaped handsome profits and went so far as to organize riots on African soil against abolition proposals. The plantation owners in the Americas likewise supported the slave trade, especially the Barbados planters who held an important bloc of seats in the British Parliament in the eighteenth century. There were European vested interests also that championed the slave trade, both amongst the traders and the various merchants at home who provided the rum and the manufactured goods. According to one estimate, Britain shipped to Africa manufactures valued at one million pounds a year, and the other European countries sent an equal amount for the same purpose. The return on this outlay was so extraordinarily high that in the eighteenth century the prosperity of cities such as Liverpool and Bristol depended heavily on this traffic. Finally the champions of the slave trade used military as well as economic arguments to support their case. The large number of vessels involved not only supported shipyards but also provided jobs for thousands of seamen. So it was maintained that any country that took the lead in abolition would weaken itself as a naval power.

Despite these formidable obstacles, a small group of reformers campaigned vigorously for abolition. In 1787 they established in England the Society for the Abolition of the Slave Trade. In 1823 they founded the Anti-Slavery Society to end the institution of slavery as well as the slave trade. These abolitionists were aided by the progress of the Industrial Revolution, which was rendering slavery obsolete. Advancing technology called for overseas markets rather than for a cheap supply of human power.

The first success of the abolitionists was a law in 1807 providing that no British ships could participate in the slave trade, and prohibiting the landing of slaves in British colonies. Finally, in 1833 Parliament passed a decree completely abolishing slavery on British territory, and providing 20 million pounds as compensation for the slaveholders. The British government went further and persuaded other European countries to follow its example in allowing British warships to seize slave ships flying other flags. At one period, a fourth of the whole British navy was patrolling the coasts of Africa, Cuba, and Brazil with a force of 56 vessels manned by 9,000 sailors. In twenty years these patrol ships captured over 1,000 slavers and set free their human cargoes. Needless to say, many traders continued to slip through the blockade, lured on by the fortunes awaiting them in the Americas. Complete success was not possible until the various countries in the New World gradually abolished slavery as an institution —as did Haiti in 1803, the United States in 1863, Brazil in 1888, Cuba at about the same time, and so forth.

While the slave trade was being stamped out on the west coast of Africa, it continued to be carried on by the Arabs in Central and East Africa. The Arabs had been engaged in this trade long before the appearance of the Europeans, and they continued through the nineteenth century and even into the twentieth. The captives were marched across the Sahara to North African fairs, or they were taken to east coast ports and then shipped to Zanzibar, Madagascar, Arabia, Turkey, Persia, and even India. This traffic was much more difficult to suppress than that on the west coast. Despite British naval patrols in the Red Sea and the Indian Ocean, it persisted until World War I and later.

II. EXPLORATION OF AFRICA

The agitation for the abolition of slavery contributed directly to the exploration and opening up of the "Dark Continent." The abolitionists hoped to curtail the slave trade by pushing into the interior where the slaves were captured and they sought to develop "legitimate" or regular commerce that would replace the traffic in slaves. At the same time, a growing scientific fad for geography made Europeans intensely curious about unexplored lands. These factors all combined to bring to Africa in the nineteenth century a number of remarkable and colorful explorers.

The systematic exploration of the continent began with the founding of the African Association in 1788. Its purpose was "to promote the cause of science and humanity, to explore the mysterious geography, to ascertain the resources, and to improve the conditions of that ill-fated continent."[1] The Association's attention was directed first to the problem of the Niger. No one knew where it rose or where it ended. To solve the mystery, the Association in 1795 sent out a Scottish physician, Mungo Park. After enduring blistering heat, sickness, captivity, and hunger, he succeeded in reaching the Niger, but illness compelled him to return to the coast instead of following the river to its mouth. In 1805 Park returned at the head of a sizeable expedition, but he and most of his companions died of disease, as did his eighteen-year-old son who set out to find his father. Many others tried to unlock the mystery of the Niger until finally Richard Lander followed it to its mouth in 1830. The exploration of West Africa was furthered the most during the 1850's by Dr. Heinrich Barth. This remarkable German visited the most important cities of the western Sudan and then crossed the Sahara and returned to England in 1855. His journey is one of the greatest feats in the history of African travel. Barth's account of his travels is equally outstanding because of his thorough exposition of the geography, history, and ethnology of the lands he visited.

Interest shifted to East Africa after a disastrous trading expedition up the Niger proved that commercial opportunities were scanty there. The big question in East Africa was the source of the Nile. Hostile natives, vast marshes, and innumerable rapids had defeated all attempts to follow the river upstream to its headwaters. In 1856 two Englishmen John Speke and Richard Burton started inland from the African east coast. They discovered Lake Tanganyika, and with Burton ill, Speke pushed on another two hundred miles to discover Lake Victoria. On a second trip (1860–1863) Speke saw the White Nile pouring from Lake Victoria at Ripon Falls, and then followed the great river to Khartoum and on through Egypt to the Mediterranean.

Head and shoulders above all the other explorers stands the figure of the great David Livingstone. He had trained himself originally to become a medical missionary in China, but the outbreak of the Opium War diverted him to Africa where he landed at Capetown and worked his way northward. In 1849 Livingstone crossed the Kalahari River to see what fields for missionary enterprise lay beyond. He discovered Lake Ngami where he heard that the country ahead was populous and well-watered, in contrast to the desert he had just crossed. In 1852 he set forth on the great journey that was to take him first to the Atlantic and then back across the continent to the Indian Ocean, which he reached in 1856. Between 1857 and 1863 Livingstone headed an expedition that explored the Zambesi region, and in 1866 he set forth again to settle various questions concerning the source of the Nile. Disappearing in the African bush, he was not heard from until found in 1871 on Lake Tanganyika by a foreign correspondent, Henry M. Stanley. Although Livingstone was weak and emaciated, he continued his explorations until May 1, 1873, when his followers found him dead in a praying position beside his cot.

Stanley was so inspired by Livingstone's character and career that he returned to Africa to solve some of the problems left by "the Good Doctor." He discovered that the Lualaba River, thought by Livingstone to flow into the Nile, instead became the Congo, which flowed westward to the Atlantic. Stanley arrived in Boma on the west coast on November 26, 1877, exactly 999 days after leaving Zanzibar. The last of the four great African rivers had at last been traced from source to mouth. Two years later, in 1879, Stanley was again on the Congo River, but this time he was functioning as the agent for King Leopold of Belgium rather than as an explorer. The age of African exploration had given way to the age of African partition.

III. PARTITION OF AFRICA

Prior to 1870 the European powers had insignificant holdings in Africa. They consisted mostly of seaports and fortified trading stations, together with bits of adjacent territory acquired as adjuncts to trade rather than as bases for territorial expansion. With the termination of the European slave trade, most of these coastal footholds were virtually abandoned since the legitimate trade was insufficient to support them. The only significant exceptions to this general picture were at the opposite ends of the continent, in French Algeria and British South Africa, where actual colonization was taking place. But even there the activities were haphazard, with no definite plans for expansion and annexation.

After 1870 a combination of factors (see Chapter 24, section VII) produced a reversal of this anticolonial attitude. Colonies now were regarded as assets for the mother country, and the continent of Africa, being unoccupied and defenseless, became the vortex of imperialist aspirations. A typical expression of the new colonialism was that of the French economist Paul Leroy-Beaulieu, who wrote in 1874, "Colonization is for France a question of life and death: either France will become a great African power, or in a century or two she will be no more than a secondary European power; she will count for about as much in the world as Greece and Roumania in Europe."[2]

The leader of the imperialistic drive in Africa was King Leopold of Belgium. A shrewd monarch, he sensed the opportunities offered by the great interior plateaus that were being opened up by the explorers. At the outset Leopold was interested primarily in East Africa. But with Stanley's exploration of the Congo Basin in 1876–1877, he at once perceived the potentialities of this great central region. In fact Stanley himself saw the opportunity but he was unable to enlist support in England. So in 1878 Stanley entered Leopold's service, and the following year he returned to the Congo. Between 1879 and 1880 Stanley signed numerous treaties with chiefs, handing over no less than 900,000 square miles to the International Association of the Congo, a new organization set up under Leopold's direction. The chiefs had no way of knowing that signing the pieces of paper and accepting token payments meant permanent loss of their tribal lands. An African chief traditionally was entrusted with his people's land. His selling was like a mayor's selling "his" city hall. Yet this was the standard procedure all over the continent, and repercussions are being felt to the present day.

The immediate effect of Leopold's machinations was to jolt the other European leaders to action. The French already had sent their famous explorer, Count de Brazza, to the lower Congo, and he was able to acquire for his country the lands to the north of the river. The Germans also entered the race, obtaining in 1884 South-West Africa, Togoland, and the Cameroons. Now the Portuguese joined in, especially since they had been claiming for some time the west coast as far north as 5° 12′ S., that is, both sides of the Congo mouth and inland indefinitely. Britain never had been willing to recognize these Portuguese claims but she now changed her mind in hopes of checking the aggressive Belgians and French. So an Anglo-Portuguese Convention was signed on February 26, 1884 recognizing Portuguese sovereignty over the mouth of the Congo and providing for Anglo-Portuguese control of navigation on the river.

The treaty was furiously denounced by the other powers, so an international conference was held in Berlin in 1884–1885 to prepare rules for the further acquisition of African territories. It was agreed that no power should annex land or establish a protectorate without first giving notice of intent; that recognition of territorial claims must depend on effective occupation; and that disputes were to be settled by arbitration. The conference also recognized the rights of Leopold's International Association of the Congo to much of the Congo Basin, to be known as the Congo Free State. Finally, high-sounding declarations were made about uplifting the natives, spreading the Gospel, and stamping out slavery. All these were to be conspicuous by their absence in the so-called Free State.

Now that an international code for territorial aggrandizement was agreed upon, the entire continent was partitioned in less than two decades. In the Congo, Leopold bought out in 1887 all non-Belgian interests in order to eliminate possible criticism of his enterprise. Then he reimbursed himself by reserving a crown district of the richest rubber lands, ten times the size of Belgium. Here, as elsewhere in the Congo, special monopolies for the exploitation of natural products, including rights of native labor, were awarded to commercial concerns in most of which Leopold was a heavy stockholder. His profits, therefore, were derived both from the stipends paid to the state by the concessionaires and from the dividends earned in the course of their immensely successful operations. In the final analysis, the fortunes that were made in the Congo were extracted by ruthless exploitation of the native peoples. So unbelievably brutal were the various methods of forced labor that the population of the Congo declined by one-half (from 20 to 10 million) between 1885 and 1908 when it was ruled by Leopold.

News of the atrocities leaked out and Leopold was forced to hand over his Congo possessions to the Belgian government in 1908. What had been private property now became a Belgian colony. The government took measures to end the atrocities, though a modified form of forced labor did continue. Leopold, the mercenary promoter to the end, induced the Belgian parliament to compensate him handsomely for his "sacrifice" of the Congo.

In the rest of West Africa the French were the most active. Starting from their old trading posts on the Ivory Coast, in Dahomey, and on the north bank of the Congo, they conceived a grand plan for pushing inward and founding a French West African Empire that would stretch from Algeria to the Congo and from the Senegal to the Nile or even the Red Sea. Since the Germans and the British also had footholds along the west coast, the French had to outflank their rivals in a race for the hinterland. By and large they were successful. Only the British in Nigeria and the Germans in the Cameroons were able to expand significantly into the interior. All the rest of West Africa, together with the vast Sahara, became a great French domain ruled from Paris.

In order to extend their holdings eastward across the whole of Africa, the French sent Colonel Marchand on a perilous expedition. It took him from the French Congo to Fashoda on the Nile, which he reached in July 1898. A few weeks later, General Kitchener arrived at the head of an expedition that had ascended the Nile from Egypt. In the name of Britain, Kitchener demanded that Marchand withdraw from Fashoda. The two men then sensibly decided to refer the dispute to their respective governments. For some months Britain and France were on the brink of war, but in the spring of 1899 France gave way, leaving Britain in possession of the Upper Nile.

In East Africa the Portuguese had held Mozambique since the sixteenth century and France had claims to Madagascar. The chief rivals for the remaining territory were the Germans and the British. At the end of 1884, while the Berlin Conference was in session, a young German colonial enthusiast, Dr. Carl Peters, landed secretly in East Africa. Within ten days he had persuaded the local chiefs to sign away more than 60,000 square miles, an area almost one-third the size of his own homeland. The following year the German government proclaimed a protectorate over the region obtained by Carl Peters.

The German activities aroused the British who proceeded to sign treaties giving them the territory in the Kenya area. This land grabbing drew repeated protests from the Sultan of Zanzibar who for long had held sovereignty over the East African coast opposite his island. Both the British and the Germans ignored his protests and signed two agreements in 1886 and 1890 settling their respective territorial disputes. The Germans retained the huge area known as the German East Africa Protectorate, to be named Tanganyika after 1919; the British were allotted their East Africa Protectorate, later to be known as Kenya Colony, together with a protectorate over Uganda. The Sultan of Zanzibar retained possession of his island, but had to recognize Britain as his suzerain.

Meanwhile, the Italians had belatedly joined the scramble for African territory. They managed to obtain two barren colonies on the Red Sea coast, Eritrea and Somaliland, and later, in 1896, they gambled for higher stakes by sending an army to conquer the kingdom of Ethiopia. The Christian Ethiopians were not a primitive tribal people like those in most other parts of Africa. Their Emperor Menelik had an army of 80,000 men trained by French officers and armed with French weapons. He was able to defeat the small Italian army of 10,000, and his kingdom remained free from European rule. Except for the small republic of Liberia on the west coast, by 1914 Ethiopia was the only independent state on the whole continent. And even Liberia, set up in 1822 as a settlement for freed American Negroes (named from the Latin *liber,* meaning "free"), became a virtual United States protectorate in 1911 because of bankruptcy and internal disorders.

Meanwhile, on the southern tip of the continent the British were roused to action by the establishment of a German protectorate in South-West Africa and by Portuguese plans for the linking of Angola on the west coast to Mozambique on the east. The British took control of three areas—Basutoland, Bechuanaland, and Swaziland—all of which were made into native reservations and placed under British commissioners. North of the Limpopo River the British were attracted by rich goldfields and healthy plateau lands that were suitable for white colonization. In 1889 the British government granted a charter to the British South Africa Company whose field of operations was defined as "to the north and west of the South African Republic, and to the west of the Portuguese dominions." Settlers began to move in and in 1890 the town of Salisbury was laid out on the beautiful and salubrious plateau between the Limpopo and the Zambesi. After World War I the British company gave up its charter and its lands were organized as the two colonies of Northern and Southern Rhodesia.

The British also had difficulties in South Africa proper, where a long smoldering feud with the Boer settlers flared up into full-scale war in 1899. After the war the British granted self-government to the Boers in the Orange Free State and the Transvaal, and in 1907 these two colonies joined with Natal and Cape Colony to form the Dominion of the Union of South Africa.

The net result of this unprecedented territorial aggrandizement was the partitioning of the entire continent of Africa among the European powers. The only exceptions, as noted above, were the precarious states of Liberia and Ethiopia.

IV. EUROPE'S IMPACT

Economic

Since economic motives were prominent in the partitioning of Africa, it is not surprising that drastic economic changes followed the partitioning. Europe no longer was content with boatloads of slaves at the coastal ports. The industrialized West no longer needed human slaves; technology had provided an abundance of the mechanical variety. Instead the West had need for the raw materials found in the interior of Africa, and it now had the technological means to extract these materials.

The first important step in the exploitation of Africa's resources came with the discovery of diamonds in Kimberley (1867) and gold in the Witwatersrand (1884). Equally great mineral wealth was discovered in the Rhodesias (gold and copper) and in the Congo (gold, copper, and diamonds). Many portions of the west coast yielded rich supplies of such tropical forest products as palm oil, rubber, and ivory. European and American companies bought vast plantations in such regions as the Congo, the Cameroons, and French Equatorial Africa. Not only did foreign companies lease large tracts of land, but foreign settlers took over much of the good agricultural land. Explorers had reported that some of the interior plateaus had fertile soil as well as a pleasant climate. Consequently, European settlers flocked in, particularly to Southern Rhodesia and East Africa. Before long they had gained possession of the most desirable agricultural properties in these regions.

In order to transport the minerals and the agricultural commodities now being produced, the Europeans proceeded to build a network of railways in Africa as they already had done in Asia. The expansion of production and the construction of transportation facilities stimulated trade to the point where the traditional barter gave way to a monetary system. No longer did the Africans exchange slaves, gold dust, feathers, and ivory for the Europeans' salt, glassware, cloth, rum, and gin. By the end of the nineteenth century there was fairly widespread use of English silver coins and of Austrian and American dollars.

All of these economic developments naturally had profound effects upon the native peoples. The inhabitants of the temperate plateau areas were affected most by the loss of the lands taken by white settlers. In some cases whole districts were reserved for exclusive white use, and the land could not be tilled by the Africans, even though it sometimes lay fallow. Consequently, the Africans were forced to work for wages on the white man's plantations, while some even "squatted" on the land of the white farmers for whom they worked to gain the privilege of tilling a small plot for themselves. In other regions the Africans found it necessary to leave their families and go to work in the mines. If the Africans refused to provide the labor needed for the plantations and mines, various types of forced labor were used. The most common was the levying of a head tax compelling the African to work in order to earn the money to pay the tax. These various developments reduced the traditional economic self-sufficiency of the African. For example, a depression in the industrialized countries immediately affected the operation of copper mines, while a slump in the world price for palm oil immediately lowered the income of a large number of individual producers in West Africa. Thus the effect of Europe's economic impact was twofold: to entangle the Africans in a world-wide money economy, and to subordinate them, directly or indirectly, to the white man who was everywhere the "boss."

Cultural

Together with the trader, the investor, and the settler from Europe came the European missionary. He had a profound effect upon African culture because he was the first European who consciously sought to change it. The others affected it indirectly and incidentally, as when they forced Africans to leave their ancestral villages to work in cities or mines. But the missionary came with the avowed purpose of changing the African way of life, and he used three instruments to carry this out: education, medicine, and religion.

Schools offering a Western education and Western ideals were an integral part of every mission station. These schools were particularly influential since most colonial governments left education to the missionaries. In many respects the mission schools were constructive in their influence, teaching the pupils new agricultural methods and the rudiments of hygiene and sanitation, as well as skills in reading and writing African and European languages.

On the other hand, these schools inevitably had a subversive influence on the African people; they often taught that the traditional way of life was primitive and wrong. In time the students listened less to their parents and elders and more to their European teachers whom they learned to respect. The mission schools used European books that taught more about Europe than about Africa. Missionary education encouraged individualism, which was contrary to the communal African way of life. The missions also brought medical knowledge and facilities that saved the lives of many Africans, but also forced Africans to question their traditional ideas of what caused illness and death. The White man had the power to make people well even after the proper petitioning of spirits had not worked. So traditional religion no longer could be counted upon to meet all emergencies and to provide all the answers. Even though the majority of Africans clung to their old faiths, traditional religion no longer was as effective a cement in holding together the African's whole way of life as it previously had been.

Political

Europe's imprint was as marked in the political field as it was in the economic and cultural fields. In drawing the boundaries of the various colonies, no attention was paid to the indigenous people concerned, so that they often found themselves under the rule of two or even three European powers. Some of the Somali, for example, were ruled by the French, others by the British, still others by the Italians, and a number even found themselves within the boundaries of Ethiopia.

Once the boundaries had been settled, the problem of organizing some administrative system arose. The European governments did not have enough manpower to rule directly all the peoples of the vast African continent, so they resorted to various forms of indirect rule; administration was conducted through tribal chiefs who were allowed to retain some of their authority. On the surface the Africans retained their traditional political institutions. They still had their councils of elders, their laws, their courts, and their chiefs. But in practice this political structure was undermined. The chiefs could be appointed or removed by the local European administrators, and their decisions no longer had the force of law since tribesmen could go over their heads to the European officials whose word was final.

Perhaps the most important factors undermining the traditional political systems were the economic and cultural changes brought about by European rule. Chiefs often were believed to have been given their authority by the tribal gods, so that their religious leadership buttressed their political power. Obviously both their religious leadership and political power were weakened where the people were converted to a new religion or where their faith was shaken in the old. Likewise, people who gained money wealth by working in cities or mines acquired a status and independence that would have been inconceivable had they remained in their villages. In some cases these newly rich people actually had more prestige and power than the old chiefs. The most serious and direct challenge to the traditional tribal authorities came from the class of Western educated Africans that gradually developed in almost all the colonies. They tended to challenge not only the native chiefs but also the European officials. They usually were the first to demand that educated Africans should be allowed to participate in the administration of their countries. These people were the first nationalists; they laid the foundations for the powerful nationalist movement of today.

V. CONCLUSION

The above survey indicates that in many basic respects Europe had a much deeper imprint on Africa than on Eurasia. There was no parallel in the latter area to the draining of African manpower through the slave trade. With the exception of Southeast Asia, there was also no parallel to the alienation of agricultural lands, even though this was limited to East Africa and South Africa. Likewise, there was no parallel in Eurasia to the virtually total European domination of transport, finance, foreign trade, mining and manufacturing. Finally, there was no parallel, with the exception of the Philippines, to the widespread diffusion of European Christianity and European languages, and to the proliferating cultural influence of the European missionaries with their schools and their medical facilities.

The basic reason for this contrast in degree of European influence is to be found in the coresponding contrast in the level of general development that had been attained in Africa and in Eurasia. This contrast prevailed in all fields—in the sophistication of cultures, in the development of economies and technologies, and, consequently, in the density of populations. It was this contrast that made sub-Saharan Africa infinitely more vulnerable to European missionaries, entrepreneurs, and settlers.

And yet this very underdevelopedness of sub-Saharan Africa provided a natural resistance at the village level (as distinct from the European-influenced urban centers). In most parts of the continent prior to 1914, the interior villages retained their economic self-sufficiency and their integrated traditional cultures, which made them largely impervious to the West. While acknowledging the decisive impact of Europe in certain basic respects, one must still realize that even to the present day, many of the villages of sub-Saharan Africa remain relatively unchanged in their traditional patterns of life.

SUGGESTED READING

P. D. CURTIN, ed., *Africa and the West: Intellectual Responses to European Culture* (Univ. Wisconsin, 1972); B. DAVIDSON, *Black Mother: The Years of the African Slave Trade* (Little, 1963); T. HODGKIN, *Nationalism in Colonial Africa* (New York Univ., 1957); M. PERHAM and J. SIMMONS, *African Discovery: An Anthology of Exploration* (Faber, 1942); H. SCHIFFERS, *The Quest for Africa: Two Thousand Years of Exploration* (Odhams, 1957); H. A. WIESCHOFF, *Colonial Policies in Africa* (Univ. Pennsylvania, 1944).

chapter thirty-one

The Americas and
the British Dominions

*After the Spaniards resolved to go and hunt the Indians who were in
the mountains [of Cuba] where they perpetrated marvellous massacres.
Thus they ruined and depopulated all this island which we beheld
not long ago; and it excites pity, and great anguish to see it deserted,
and reduced to a solitude.*—Bartolome De Las Casas, 1552

*The disappearance of these people [Australian aborigines] before the
white invaders is just as certain as the disappearance of wolves in a
country becoming civilized and populous.*—James Stephen, 1841

Even more far-reaching than Europe's impact upon Asia and Africa
during the nineteenth century were its effects upon the Americas and the British
Dominions. The section titles of this chapter, then, refer not to "impact," but to
outright Europeanization.

Europeanization involves more than just political domination or cultural penetration. It involves actual biological replacement, the physical substitution of
one people by another—as happened in the relatively empty territories of the
Western Hemisphere and the South Pacific. The scanty indigenous populations
were either wiped out or pushed aside, and tens of millions of European emigrants swarmed in and occupied their lands, bringing with them their political
institutions, their ways of earning a living, and their cultural traditions. Thus the
ethnic Europeanization of overseas territories was followed inevitably by political,
economic, and cultural Europeanization.

I. ETHNIC EUROPEANIZATION

An earlier chapter explained why Europe was able to supply so many emigrants,
and why these millions of people were willing to leave their ancestral homes
and brave unknown dangers in far-off continents. The thin ribbons of European
settlement that existed in 1763 had stretched by 1914 to cover entire continents,
including Australia and New Zealand, which had still been untouched at the
earlier date.

Tables 1, 2, and 3 show that the majority of European emigrants went to the
Americas. This is understandable, because the earliest European colonies were
established in the Americas, and also because those continents offered much
greater natural resources and economic opportunities. However, since the first
European settlements were in Central and South America, it is surprising that so
many more of these emigrants settled in North America.

TABLE 1   RACIAL DISTRIBUTION IN THE AMERICAS (in millions)

	White		Negro		Indian
	1835	1935	1835	1935	1935
North America	13.8	124.3	2.6	12.4	1.8
Central America	1.9	6.9	2.7	8.4	21.4
South America	2.9	40.9	4.5	18.7	29.2
Total	18.6	172.1	9.8	39.5	52.4

Source: See Table 3.

The basically different character of the Spanish and Portuguese colonies, compared to the English explains it. The Spaniards and the Portuguese settled in territories with relatively dense Indian populations. Although estimates of the number of Indians in the Americas before the coming of the Europeans vary tremendously, it is agreed that the Indian populations were concentrated in what came to be Latin America. These native peoples supplied all the labor that was needed, so European settlers were not required for that purpose. Accordingly, emigrants to the Spanish and Portuguese colonies in the Americas were mostly soldiers, members of the clergy, government officials, and a few necessary craftsmen.

TABLE 2   RACIAL DISTRIBUTION IN AFRICA

	Whites		Africans
	1835	1935	1935
Mediterranean countries*	20,000	1,660,000†	30,000,000
Union of South Africa	66,000	1,950,000	6,600,000
Rest of South Africa‡	3,000	190,000	12,200,000
Rest of continent	1,000	100,000	87,700,000
Islands	45,000	100,000	4,500,000
Total	135,000	4,000,000	141,000,000

Source: See Table 3.
* Egypt, Libya, Tunis, Algeria, Moroccos, Spanish North Africa, Tangier.
† Includes only the settlers of European origin.
‡ Angola, S.W. Africa, Rhodesias, Nyasaland, Bechuanaland, Basutoland, Swaziland, Mozambique.

TABLE 3   RACIAL DISTRIBUTION IN OCEANIA

	Date	Whites	Natives
Australia	June, 1935	6,674,000	81,000
New Zealand	Dec., 1935	1,486,000	76,000
Papua (Australia)	June, 1933	1,000	275,000
Fiji Islands (Br.)	Dec., 1934	5,000	107,000
New Guinea (Austr.)	June, 1935	4,000	679,000
Other islands (15)	1930's	109,756	464,525
Total (of 19 areas)		8,279,756	1,682,525

Source: R. R. Kuczynski, *Population Movements* (Oxford: Clarendon, 1936), pp. 91, 95, 102–3, 109–10, 118. By permission of The Clarendon Press, Oxford.

North of the Rio Grande, by contrast, the Indian population was relatively sparse and provided no reservoir of labor power. The English along the Atlantic Seaboard and the French on the banks of the St. Lawrence had to do their own work, whether it was cutting the forests, plowing the cleared land, or fishing the coastal waters. Under these circumstances North America wanted all the settlers it could get, and so the British North American colonies were opened to immigrants of all races, languages, and faiths. By 1835 there were 4.8 million European settlers in all of Central and South America as against 13.8 million in North America.

In the second half of the nineteenth century European emigration steadily increased, reaching its height between 1900 and 1910 when almost one million people left each year. This unprecedented flood poured into every continent, so that Australia, South Africa, and South America now were peopled by substantial numbers of Europeans, although North America continued to be the main beneficiary.

So far as the specific sources of immigration were concerned (see tables in Chapter 24, section VII), the Latin American countries were peopled, as might be expected, mostly by emigrants from the Iberian Peninsula, though considerable numbers also came in the late nineteenth century from Italy and Germany. The great majority of the emigrants to North America were, until 1890, from northwestern Europe. After that date, approximately one-third came from northwestern Europe, and the remaining two-thirds came from eastern and southern Europe. In the case of the British Dominions, immigration restrictions limited the supply largely to the British Isles. After World War I, and especially after World War II, the Dominions liberalized their immigration policies in order to get more people into their wide open spaces.

The net result of these migrations has been the ethnic Europeanization of the Americas and the British Dominions. These areas have become largely European in population, although there are certain important exceptions such as the native Indian strain remaining predominant (58 per cent of the total population) in Central America, and comprising one-third of the total population of South America. The substantial Negro element introduced into the Americas as a result of the slave trade is another exception to ethnic Europeanization. It is estimated that approximately 10 million slaves survived the transatlantic passage and reached the New World. Their descendants today comprise about 10 per cent of the total population in North America, 30 per cent in Central America, and 21 per cent in South America. South Africa represents the third exception to ethnic Europeanization; there the native Africans outnumber the whites (whether of Boer or British origin) by more than three to one.

II. POLITICAL EUROPEANIZATION

Colonial and Revolutionary Periods

From the beginning, Europe's colonies had a wide variety of political institutions. Such a variety arose from the different political backgrounds of the mother countries. For example, Spain was ruled autocratically by the Madrid court, so naturally the Spanish colonies were ruled in the same manner. The officials that were sent to the colonies had virtually absolute authority, so that the colonists had little choice but to take orders. Very rarely was a colonist given a government post. The French colonies were also ruled autocratically, with power concentrated in the hands of the governors, who were responsible for the defense of each colony, and the intendants who handled economic affairs.

By contrast, the English colonies had popularly elected representative institutions that reflected the flourishing parliamentary government of the mother country. The precise nature of these institutions varied somewhat from colony to colony. In Virginia the settlers were granted permission to elect a local legislature as early as 1619. This body gradually grew in power until by the time of the American Revolution it had more influence than the royal governor. In New England, instead of individual settlers braving the wilderness, groups of people migrated to the frontier to set up new towns. There they developed a type of town government with regular "town meetings" at which decisions were made and various officials were elected. Despite these differences in the precise forms of government, the Thirteen Colonies had one thing in common: popular participation in public affairs, which led to constant friction between the elected representatives and the royal officials. This friction prompted the call to arms in 1776 that led to the establishment of the independent United States of America. (See Chapter 25, section IV.) Furthermore, the revolution of the Thirteen Colonies triggered a chain reaction of similar uprisings that swept all the colonies in the New World during the six decades between 1776 and 1837.

Various factors contributed to the revolts in Latin America, one of which was the example of the Thirteen Colonies whose successful revolution was followed closely and sympathetically. Latin Americans were as well acquainted with what they called the philosophy of Philadelphia, as they were with the teachings of the French *philosophes*. The writings of the latter were smuggled in large quantities across the Atlantic in what were called "the ships of the Enlightenment." Spain's colonial policy, especially the economic exploitation and the lack of self-government, was another obvious factor promoting revolution. The concentration of power in the hands of officials from Spain alienated the creoles (Spaniards born in America) and the mestizos (people of Spanish and Indian blood). The long years of the French Revolution and the Napoleonic Wars, when Spain was preoccupied in Europe and her colonies were left to shift for themselves, also stimulated revolutionary ideas. The Spanish colonies were unwilling to give up the new freedom they had tasted and enjoyed, and they were backed up by foreign powers interested in liquidating Spain's colonial empire.

Napoleon Bonaparte's domination of Spain and the establishment of his brother, Joseph, on the Madrid throne was the immediate cause of revolution in Latin America. The Spanish colonials refused to recognize Joseph and proclaimed allegiance to the deposed Ferdinand VII. Their professions of loyalty did not convince the Spanish authorities, and widespread fighting broke out in 1809 between the patriots and the loyalists. The wars of independence dragged on until 1825, with the British giving help as decisive to Latin American victory as French aid had been to that of the Thirteen Colonies. Almost all Latin America won its independence from European rule. The only exceptions were British, Dutch, and French Guiana to the north of Brazil, certain Caribbean islands such as Jamaica, which remained British until the winning of independence in 1962, the Virgin Islands, which were under Denmark until 1917, and Cuba, which was under Spanish rule until 1898.

The Latin American wars of independence were over by 1825, but revolution in the Americas was not. In 1837, a little over a decade later, insurrection broke out in two British colonies, Upper and Lower Canada. The roots of this uprising go back to 1763 when Britain acquired the colony of New France on the banks of the St. Lawrence, and to 1774 when the Quebec Act of that year extended the boundaries of Quebec to the Ohio and Mississippi rivers, and forbade frontiersmen to cross over the Alleghenies into the Ohio Valley. We have already seen that this restriction contributed to the outbreak of the American Revolution in 1776. But the Revolution, paradoxically enough, was responsible for making French Canada British territory. Thousands of Tories—or United Empire Loyalists, as they are known in the Empire—emigrated during and after the Revolution. Some returned to Britain, others fled to various British islands in the Caribbean, but many headed northward to the Maritime Provinces (Nova Scotia, New Brunswick, and Prince Edward Island) and to the wilderness that is now Ontario. These loyalists proved to be Canada's Pilgrim Fathers. Their settlements, together with those of the earlier French, created the basis of the great Dominion of Canada.

These loyalists who settled in what is now Ontario were dissatisfied because according to the terms of the Quebec Act, they did not have the representative type of government they had enjoyed in the Thirteen Colonies. Accordingly, the British Parliament passed the Constitutional Act of 1791, dividing Quebec into Upper and Lower Canada, and setting up elective assemblies in both parts. But now the same conflict recurred between imperial authority and colonial self-government that had convulsed the Thirteen Colonies. In both Canadas a constitutional struggle developed between the governors and the appointed councils on the one hand and the popular elective assemblies on the other. The specific points of conflict were such issues as patronage abuses, control of revenue and of the judiciary, and the allocation of public lands exclusively for the established Anglican Church, even though the Methodists and Presbyterians claimed to have more members.

By 1837 affairs had reached a bitter deadlock and the popular leaders (William Lyon Mackenzie in Upper Canada and Louis Joseph Papineau in Lower Canada) decided to use force. Although some fighting took place around Montreal and Toronto, the mass of the people remained passive. The rebels were easily defeated and the leaders fled to the United States. The British government responded by sending out Lord Durham as governor-general of all the Canadian provinces, with sweeping powers for administration and investigation. Apart from his recommendation that the two Canadas be reunited once more, his great contribution was the radical proposal for granting "responsible government" to the colonies. Lord Durham meant by responsible or representative government that the traditional conflict between imperial authority and colonial self-government be resolved in favor of the latter. He was ready to grant colonial assemblies as much authority as was enjoyed by the British parliament, though with certain reservations: The imperial government would retain control of foreign relations, regulation of trade, disposal of public lands, and determination of colonial constitutions.

If this daring and unprecedented recommendation had been proposed and adopted earlier, the American colonies probably would never have revolted. Even in 1839, when the report was submitted, it was widely attacked as a utopian document that would surely undermine the Empire. But the pressure of further events soon forced British statesmen to try out Lord Durham's novel principle. The test was made cautiously and tentatively, but it proved an immediate success in British North America. Responsible government was then extended to other colonies, with equal benefit. And so Lord Durham's concept provided the basis on which the British Commonwealth was to be organized during the decades following the ill-fated Canadian rebellions.

National Period

Once the former European colonies had won independence or autonomy, they proceeded to develop individual political institutions and practices that varied widely, depending on such factors as geographic background and past experiences during the colonial period.

UNITED STATES. The Articles of Confederation of 1777 constituted the first document prepared for the governing of the new United States. It was the work of liberals who were convinced that tyranny and centralization were indissolubly linked, and that popular liberties could best be preserved by dispersing power. Accordingly, the creators of the Confederation allowed the central government jurisdiction over purely national affairs, and left all other matters to state control. Such an arrangement did not give the national government enough authority over the states or individuals to keep them under control. This became clear during the depression of 1785–1787, when the federal government found there was little it could do to help. In some regions the unemployed organized marches on the state capitals to secure relief by force (Shay's Rebellion of 1787 in Massachusetts). In other states, where the lower classes gained control of the legislatures, laws were passed to ease debtors' burdens. These developments convinced the conservative men of property that a strong central government was needed to keep "mobocracy" in check. All this provided the background for the Constitutional Convention that met in Independence Hall, Philadelphia, on May 25, 1787.

The document that emerged from Constitution Hall was carefully designed to curb popular democracy. Its chief characteristic was an elaborate system of checks and balances. There were to be four separate units of government—a House of Representatives, a Senate, a President, and a Supreme Court—chosen by distinct methods, serving different terms of office. The elective House of Representatives was controlled by several devices: suffrage restrictions, a bicameral system that provided a Senate to check an over-impetuous House, a presidential veto that Congress could override with only a two-thirds veto of each house, and a Supreme Court with judicial review power over Congress. This Constitution welded together thirteen states to form the first durable federal government in the world's history.

The framers provided that the new Constitution would go into operation as soon as conventions in nine of the states acted favorably upon it. The choice of delegates to these conventions occasioned the first national political campaign in American history. On one side were the so-called Federalists: the wealthy merchants, lawyers, and landowners who stood to gain the most from the new frame of government. On the other side were the opponents of the Constitution—small farmers, workers, and artisans who wanted nothing to do with a document that left them little political power. The latter constituted the majority of the population but were defeated because they were scattered, disorganized, and unprepared. The Constitution was ratified after a bitter contest, and the first President and Congress were elected in the fall of 1788.

Not until April 30, 1789 did enough congressmen straggle into New York to inaugurate George Washington, the unanimous choice of the electoral college for first President of the United States. Staggering problems faced these pioneering officeholders: no bureaucracy, no funds or revenue system, and no precedents on which to base the new government were available. Yet stabilization took a surprisingly short time, and the federal government was soon functioning. The able leadership of President Washington, the lifting of the depression that had plagued the country during the postwar years, and the Constitution itself all aided in making the system work. Although the Constitution provided for strong national leadership, it was, at the same time, elastic enough to adjust to changing times and conditions. An early example of this was the adoption in 1791 of a Bill of Rights, despite the opposition of most of the well-to-do. A number of privileges for citizens were spelled out by the Bill, including free speech, freedom of religion and assembly, freedom of the press, and right to counsel.

The overland expansion of the new United States was foreseen by the Northwest Ordinance of 1787. This provided that new states, identical in all legal respects with the old, except for the exclusion of slavery, should be formed in the territories north of the Ohio River. This ensured that the western lands, as they qualified for statehood, would join the federal union under the same principle and conditions. Under these circumstances the United States steadily extended its frontiers westward from the Alleghenies to the Pacific. Vast territories were acquired by various means: the Mississippi Valley by the Louisiana Purchase, from France; the Southwest by conquest and purchase, from Mexico; the Northwest by negotiation with Britain; and Alaska by purchase, from Russia. Out of these new lands were carved a succession of states, mounting finally to the fifty that comprise the present-day United States of America.

LATIN AMERICA. Political developments in Latin America during the national period were very different from those in the United States. The trend in Latin America was toward political fragmentation rather than unification. Mountain and jungle barriers separated one region from another, and lack of communication facilities meant that the regions often had closer contact with Europe than they did with each other. Fragmentation was also promoted by the centuries of isolation under Spain, which fostered separatist tendencies. And the personal ambitions of individual leaders who preferred prominence in a small state to obscurity in a large union must also be taken into account. The original eight Spanish colonies have now become no fewer than eighteen separate countries: The old Viceroyalty of the United Provinces of the Rio de la Plata has become the separate republics of Argentina, Paraguay, Bolivia, and Uruguay; the former Viceroyalty of New Granada has become the countries of Colombia, Ecuador, Venezuela, and Panama; the Captaincy-General of Guatemala has been divided into the separate states of Guatemala, Costa Rica, El Salvador, Honduras, and Nicaragua.

The chronic instability reflected in the frequent overthrow of governments by military coup is another characteristic of Latin American politics in the national period. By contrast, the United States has retained the Constitution of 1787 to the present day, albeit with numerous amendments. In addition, the United States has enjoyed relative political stability during most of its history; usually two parties have succeeded each other in office on the basis of the returns of regular elections. In Latin America, on the other hand, 20 republics have adopted since independence a total of 186 constitutions, or an average of 9.3 each. The rise and fall of governments has been much more frequent. However, almost all these Latin American "revolutions" are revolutions in name only. A true revolution is one that produces a fundamental change in a system, a basic reorganization of the social and political order. Most of the so-called "revolutions" in Latin America simply involve the replacement of one military dictator by another without fundamental changes in the existing order. This intervention of the military in political affairs arises partly from the sharp class distinctions and the political apathy or exclusion of the masses in many of the Latin American states, and has enabled a handful of wealthy landowners and high military officers to conduct politics like a game. A procession of military and civilian leaders have succeeded each other, with little attention being paid to the wishes of the people or to the needs of the countries involved.

CANADA. In contrast to Latin America and the United States, the British possessions during the nineteenth century gradually won self-government while preserving the imperial tie. The basis of this unique evolution, as noted earlier, was the principle of responsible government propounded by Lord Durham in 1839. After a few years of administration by responsible government, the governor of Canada concluded: "I have been possessed with the idea that it is possible to maintain on this soil of North America, and in the face of Republican America, British connection and British institutions, if you give the latter freely and trustingly. Faith, when it is sincere, is always catching. . . ."[1] In this manner a complete revolution was inaugurated in the relations between England and her North American colonies. And because the principle of responsible government was extended to other colonies, the British Empire was transformed into the durable Commonwealth that is still flourishing today.

Further major political development in Canada—the achievement of Confederation in 1867—was necessary because the Maritime Provinces, and even the reunited province of Canada, were too sparsely populated to effectively stand alone. Furthermore, the vast Canadian West, with its unexplored resources, was waiting to be developed, and this was Canada's responsibility. The conclusion of the Civil War in the United States was followed by spread-eagle oratory on the part of American super-patriots who covetously eyed the British colonies to the north, so unity promised military security as well as economic advantages. After surprisingly short discussion the Canadian statesmen agreed on the terms of union, and the Dominion of Canada was created by the passage of the British North America Act on July 1, 1867. During the following decades the Dominion extended its domain westward to the Pacific after the manner of the United States. Manitoba became a province in 1870, British Columbia in 1871, and Alberta and Saskatchewan in 1905.

AUSTRALIA AND NEW ZEALAND. Meanwhile, similar developments were taking place in other parts of the Empire settled by Europeans. The colonization of Australia began in 1787 when an expedition arrived from England with 750 convicts and 250 guards. With the loss of the Thirteen Colonies, Australia had been selected as the new dumping ground for convicts. By 1793 free settlers began to arrive, and colonies were established in what are now Queensland, Victoria, South Australia, Tasmania, and even distant Western Australia.

At the same time bands of whalers, sealers, and traders made their way even further afield to the islands of New Zealand, and by 1792 they were arriving frequently, despite the native Maoris, a Polynesian people who were much more advanced and militant than the primitive Australian aborigines. By 1839 there were 2,000 settlers, and London formally proclaimed New Zealand as British territory.

By the middle of the nineteenth century a string of settlements had taken root along much of the coast line of Australia and New Zealand, and as they grew more populous and stable, they began to demand control of their own affairs. Agitation for self-government became increasingly frequent, as it had earlier in Canada, but the Canadian precedent now served as a model that eased the way for the Pacific colonies. In 1850 the British parliament passed the Australian

Colonies Government Act granting the colonies the right to constitute their own legislatures, fix the franchise, alter their constitutions, and determine their own tariffs, all subject to royal confirmation. But confirmation was forthcoming, in accordance with the procedure tested and proven in Canada. Likewise, in New Zealand a constitution was granted in 1852 that set up six provinces with larger powers of local government, and a general assembly for local purposes. Four years later responsible government was formally sanctioned in New Zealand.

The final task of unifying the six widely separated Australian settlements into a federation was carried out more leisurely in Australia than it had been in Canada because the pressure of an expansionist neighbor was missing. But by the end of the century even isolated Australia was feeling the pull of outside influences. Foreign nations were annexing Pacific islands that Australians regarded as being within their security zone. In addition, the problem of Asiatic immigration was considered a threat to white supremacy in Australia; consequently, a referendum in 1899 returned a majority in every colony in favor of federation. A bill was passed by the British Parliament in 1900, and on January 1, 1901 the Commonwealth of Australia formally took its place in the family of nations.

SOUTH AFRICA. The colony of South Africa, as noted earlier, was established by the Dutch but came under British rule in 1814. The Dutch farmers, or Boers as they called themselves, were a hard-bitten, intractable lot who wanted only to be left alone to pasture their herds on vast interior tracts, and to rule over their families and native slaves like patriarchs of old. When the British interfered with their treatment of the natives the Boers started on their Great Trek of 1836. Some settled in the country beyond the Orange River while others pushed on beyond the Vaal. But the British continued to claim dominion over them, and planted a colony of English settlers at Natal on the east coast.

Cape Colony obtained representative institutions in 1853, although responsible government was withheld until 1872; Natal did not reach the same stage until 1893. In both cases the delay was largely due to the preponderance of natives, whose treatment was a matter of concern to the imperial government. In addition, continual friction existed between the two white peoples, the Boers and the English. At one point it seemed that the problem had been solved by the Convention of Bloemfontein (1854) by which the British accepted the Orange River as their northern frontier, and recognized the independence of the Boer republics of the Orange Free State and the Transvaal. But in 1871 diamonds were found at Kimberley to the north of the Orange River, and by 1890 some six tons of diamonds were mined, valued at £39 million. Equally important was the discovery of gold in southern Transvaal in 1886.

Such great wealth naturally attracted hordes of miners from all over the world, and this in turn caused complications that rendered obsolete the Bloemfontein Convention. On the one hand the Boers resented the intruders and sought to restrict their privileges, while on the other hand the British government was being strongly pressured to annex the rich mineral territories despite the Bloemfontein commitment. The most vigorous advocate of expansionism was the legendary Cecil Rhodes who began his career as a sickly immigrant and then amassed great wealth, first in the diamond fields and then in the gold mines. But wealth for Rhodes was not an end in itself; it was the means to a greater goal—the aggrandizement of the British Empire. He entered politics, became premier of Cape Colony, and then proceeded to scheme and work for the realization of his dream. Because the London governments vacillated, Rhodes decided to force the issue by violent methods. In 1895 he financed a revolution against Paul Kruger, President of the Transvaal, and organized a raid into the Transvaal under his friend Dr. L. S. Jameson. Both the revolution and the raid failed, and Rhodes was forced to resign as premier. But these incidents further embittered British-Boer relations until finally, in 1899, full-scale war broke out.

The Boers resorted to guerrilla tactics, which prolonged the war for three years and compelled the British to mobilize 300,000 troops against the 60,000 to 75,000 Boers. Eventually the Boers had to sign the Treaty of Vereeniging (1902) accepting British sovereignty, but in return they were promised representative institutions as soon as circumstances should permit. At first the British hesitated to confer full responsibility on a people who had so recently been fighting for full independence, but the new Liberal government that took office in 1905 decided on a policy of conciliation and equality. Accordingly, in 1907 both the Transvaal and the Orange River Colony were granted constitutions providing for full responsible government. The following year these two colonies, together with Cape Colony and Natal, began negotiations for a union. A draft constitution was agreed upon, and the British parliament incorporated it into the South Africa Act of 1909. The following year the Act came into effect and the Union of South Africa became a member of the self-governing British communities.

CONCLUSION. It is apparent that a great variety of political institutions and practices were developed by Europeans in their overseas settlements. The differences are so marked that a Canadian or Australian or New Zealand political leader would have been quite lost if he had found himself at the head of an American political party with its precarious balance of sectional interests, nationality blocs, and big city machines. He would have been even more bewildered by Latin American politics and their unceasing succession of constitutions and caudillos. Yet beneath these obvious differences certain underlying similarities stem from the common European origin of all these political systems. This common origin explains the similarity in law codes: Anglo-Saxon law in the United States and the British Dominions, Roman law in Latin America and Quebec—and it also explains the commitment to constitutionalism, despite the diversity in the methods of observing or evading the commitment.

III. ECONOMIC EUROPEANIZATION

Colonial Period

Europeanization prevailed as much in the economic as in the political field. So far as the European powers were concerned, their economic objectives and methods were basically the same at the outset. All believed in the mercantilist doctrine of subordinating colonial economies to those of the mother countries. Despite this common mercantilist background, the various European settlements soon developed distinctive economies that differed in many respects from each other as well as from those in Europe. We shall see that this diversity was produced by several factors, including differences in the economic development of the mother countries and in the natural and human resources in the colonies.

LATIN AMERICA. The economic development of Latin America was determined by the availability of abundant bullion and native labor, both of which were lacking in British and French America, by the development of monoculture plantations based on African slave labor, and by the economic backwardness of the Iberian states, which was transmitted to their colonies. The result was that

Latin America never achieved the balanced economic growth characteristic of the lands north of the Rio Grande. Instead there was chronic subservience to northwestern Europe and later to the United States.

THIRTEEN COLONIES AND NEW FRANCE. The economic history of the Thirteen Colonies and of New France was basically different from that of Latin America because a native labor supply and precious metals were lacking. This situation compelled the English and French settlers to do their own work and to develop from the available natural resources some type of viable economy. Both the Paris and London governments attempted from the beginning to mold the economic growth of their colonies along traditional lines.

But regulations and restrictions proved unenforceable in both the French and English colonies, and the reason in both cases was the abundance of land to which a dissatisfied settler could turn. These colonies could not depend upon the mother country for the award of feudal *encomienda* with an abundant supply of native labor, as did Latin America. The habitant did pay dues to the seignior, but they were much lighter than those customary in France. The church tried to collect as tithe one-thirteenth of the habitant's produce, but had to settle for only half of that proportion. And every effort of the authorities to prevent young men from running off and becoming coureurs de bois failed before the lure of the wilderness and the lucrative fur trade. So New France developed along its own lines, with most of the population engaged in self-sufficient agriculture, and a minority carrying on the fur trade, which produced the only important export commodity.

Similarly, in the Thirteen Colonies the companies were not able for long to keep control over their settlers. Strengthened by the fact that land was more plentiful than labor, the English colonists worked out their own economic institutions and practices. In the warm, rich, southern colonies, settlers found their best crops were tobacco, rice, and indigo. In the middle colonies—Pennsylvania, New Jersey, Delaware—grain grew well and this area quickly became the bread-basket of the colonies. Most of New England also turned to agriculture, but the long winters and rocky soil were a severe handicap. So they resorted to other occupations, mainly fishing, shipping, and manufacturing.

We see, then, that the economy of the Thirteen Colonies was much more diversified than that of Latin America, and it was more dynamic because native laborers, held down to a level of bare subsistence, did not form its basis. In place of Indian serfs and African slaves who toiled century after century, using the same tools and techniques, there were in the Thirteen Colonies clipper ships sailing the seven seas, a string of factories along the river fall line, and individual frontiersmen who, with rifle and ax, won homesteads in the wilderness and steadily pushed westward the line of settlement.

Revolutionary Period

THIRTEEN COLONIES. Precisely because the economy of the Thirteen Colonies was so dynamic, it created difficulties with the mother country, making it hard to control and to subordinate to England's own economic interests. New England's manufacturing and shipping ran afoul of mercantilist legislation such as the Navigation Laws, and after the liquidation of the French colonies in 1763, the British government began to crack down on infractions of their decrees. In order to avoid trouble with the Indians, they forbade settlers to cross the Appalachians into the Ohio Valley. The colonists protested loudly and repeatedly against these restrictions, and eventually they resorted to arms. The American Revolution was a struggle for economic as well as political independence.

The war itself caused colonial manufacturing to grow tremendously in order to meet the needs of the American armies as well as of the civilians who formerly had been supplied by the British. American shipping, expanded and converted into a make-shift navy during the Revolution, continued in its expanded form after the winning of independence. Yankee sea captains opened a highly profitable trade with California and with China only a few years after the peace treaty. The Revolution profoundly affected agriculture, in which the great majority were still engaged. State legislation now abolished obsolete systems of land tenure embodied in the laws of primogeniture and entail that were designed to perpetuate a landed aristocracy. Large estates, especially in the South, were divided amongst the farmers, and the lands west of the Appalachians were opened to the frontiersmen for settlement. The dynamic American economy was freed in these various ways for rapid expansion overland and overseas.

LATIN AMERICA. Economic grievances contributed to the revolutions in the Spanish as well as the English colonies. Conflict existed between the Spaniards born in the colonies (the creoles) and those born in Spain (the peninsulares); the latter were favored in appointments to government positions and in the right to enter certain professions. Consequently, the revolutionary movements in many colonies were organized and led by creoles who wished to end this discrimination. Equally important in stimulating revolution was Spain's mercantilist legislation limiting colonial trade with the mother country. This was especially burdensome because Spain could neither absorb the new materials produced in the colonies, nor provide in return the needed manufactured goods as cheaply and as well made as could England and other European countries. And so an immense contraband trade developed, particularly during the years when Spain was locked in desperate struggle with Napoleonic France and could not maintain normal economic relations with her colonies. When the war ended and Spain attempted to reimpose her trade restrictions, the colonists finally took up arms in protest. They were encouraged and assisted by the British, who had built up a lucrative trade with Spanish America.

The winning of independence did not stimulate economic growth in Latin America as it did in the United States, basically because the Latin American economy continued to be dominated by mines, plantations, and haciendas manned by Indians and African slaves laboring at subsistence level. Free trade did bring greater economic activity along the coasts, but this had little impact on the static interior. Lacking capital, technological skills, and a healthy socio-economic structure, independent Latin America held a stagnant position in the world economy.

BRITISH COLONIES. Economic grievances contributed to the outbreak of the Canadian Rebellions in 1837, an outstanding factor of which was the popular resentment against the Crown and Clergy Reserves, each amounting to one-seventh of the total lands of the province. These huge tracts were set aside to defray the expenses of the government and of the established Anglican Church. They were bitterly resented because they blocked the progress of settlement and because only a minority of the population adhered to the endowed church. In addition, a small privileged group known as the Family Compact enjoyed the same official favors in Canada as the peninsulares did in Latin America. Furthermore, the Canadian provinces were not as prosperous as the American states across the border, and many held British rule responsible for the economic discrepancy.

Such was the sentiment that culminated in the Rebellions of 1837. Since these proved futile, no radical reform took place in Canada during the following years. Instead, the country developed modestly and quietly: Population grew steadily and new districts were opened for settlement; roads and canals were built; a few industries were started to meet local needs—sawmills to supply lumber for building, gristmills to provide flour, carding and woolen mills to prepare the wool for spinning and to weave it into cloth, and cheese factories to process the farmers' surplus milk. Yet Canada did not have the rich and varied resources of the republic to the south, so that the disparity in the rate of economic development continued after 1837 as it had before.

National Period

The process of economic Europeanization was most thorough and most spectacular during this national period when most of the overseas colonies settled by Europeans had won their independence. The unprecedented economic growth and expansionism of Europe during those years basically explains this paradox. As noted earlier, this was the period of mass migration from Europe, and this migration meant not only ethnic Europeanization but also stronger economic ties between Europe and overseas settlements. Scientific and technological advances made it possible for Europe to provide the railways, steamships, machine guns, and agricultural machinery that were essential for the conquest and effective exploitation of vast continents. In addition to exporting the capital necessary to finance these costly operations, Europe afforded a market for the flood of foodstuffs and industrial raw materials from overseas. These developments all added up to an unparalleled economic impact by Europe upon the rest of the globe, and especially upon those areas settled by European emigrants.

UNITED STATES. The American economy expanded at a fast rate between the Revolution and the Civil War. This was especially true of industry following the adoption of a protective tariff in 1816. But it was during the decades following the Civil War that the United States experienced its most spectacular economic growth. The Civil War itself stimulated a vast industrial expansion, and this continued after the War with the opening of the West and the building of transcontinental railroads. Great quantities of foodstuffs and various raw materials were hauled by railroads and steamships to the burgeoning urban centers of eastern United States and western Europe. At the same time, the millions of immigrants provided an abundant supply of cheap labor and further expanded the domestic market for American industrialists and farmers. The net result was that the United States economy spurted ahead in the second half of the nineteenth century at a rate unequaled to that time: In 1860 the United States was ranked fourth in the industrial nations of the world; by 1894 it was the first. Between 1860 and 1900 the number of industrial establishments increased three times, the number of industrial wage earners four times, the value of manufactured products seven times, and the amount of capital invested in industry nine times.

LATIN AMERICA. For several decades after the winning of its independence, Latin America, as noted above, remained economically stagnant; however, after the mid-nineteenth century, rapid strides began to be made. Europe's mounting demand for foodstuffs such as grains, meat, coffee, sugar, and cocoa, and for industrial commodities such as minerals, lumber, wool, and hides was as important as its role in building railroads, steamships, and refrigerated ships, and in providing the capital necessary for such equipment. And so Latin America entered the world economy as it had never done before. On the other hand, this economic growth was in many respects one-sided and unhealthy. Most Latin American countries experienced booms in one or two commodities, while the rest of their economies remained static. The semifeudal hacienda system of land tenure and labor relations remained virtually unchanged, so the mass of people continued to exist as peons at subsistence level. And foreign economies penetrated and controlled most of the profitable enterprises, whether railways, public utilities, or mining properties. The benefits of this economic expansion, instead of being widely diffused as they were in the United States, accrued to a small number of foreign and native landlords, merchants, and concessionaires, producing a social friction and political instability that has persisted to the present.

BRITISH DOMINIONS. Like Latin America, the British Dominions also lagged behind the United States in rate of economic growth. The cause in this case, however, was not a semifeudal social system but rather inferior natural resources compared to those of the United States. The dominions do possess abundant resources, but it was not profitable to exploit them until the mid-twentieth century when air transportation made them accessible and when more readily available resources in other countries had been depleted. This happened after World War II, with the result that manufactures and extractive industries have been booming in the dominions in recent decades. But during the nineteenth century their economic development was modest, being based mostly on the export of foodstuffs and minerals, usually to the mother country.

CONCLUSION. The national period to 1914 was a time of rapid economic growth in the Americas and the British Dominions, but one should bear in mind that this was the product of economic Europeanization. It was Europe that provided in large part the manpower, the capital, the technology, and the markets. Europe's contributions were as vital for the independent countries as for the dominions that retained their ties with the mother country. It is perhaps understandable that British capital should have financed the building of Canada's transcontinental railroads and the development of South Africa's mines. But British capital, and commerce as well, were fully as active in lands where the Union Jack did not fly. After the Thirteen Colonies won their independence, for example, trade with Britain rose steeply instead of declining. In 1765, the last year of normal trade before the Revolution, Britain exported £1,944,114 of goods to the Thirteen Colonies; the corresponding figure for 1784, the first normal postwar year, was £3,679,467. Between 1820 and 1830, 36 per cent of all American exports went to Britain, and 43 per cent of all American imports came from Britain. European capital—mostly British, Dutch, and German—poured into the United States during the nineteenth century, especially in the building of railways. By 1914 total foreign investments amounted to no less than 7.2 billion dollars. And in the comparatively underdeveloped Latin American countries, European investments dominated the national economies to a much greater degree than they did the American.

IV. CULTURAL EUROPEANIZATION

Latin America

Cultural Europeanization inevitably accompanied the ethnic, political, and economic Europeanization, and this was true almost as much of the regions that won independence as of those that remained within the British Commonwealth. In Latin America the predominant cultural pattern is Spanish, with the exception of Portuguese Brazil; this pattern is evident in the Spanish language spoken by the majority of the people, and in the Roman Catholicism they profess. One sees it also in architectural forms such as the patio or courtyard, the barred window, and the house front that is flush with the sidewalk. Town planning, based on the central plaza rather than on the main street, is equally revealing. Much of the clothing is Spanish, including the men's broad-rimmed hats of felt or straw, and the women's cloth head coverings—mantilla, head shawl, or decorative towel. In family organization the typical Spanish pattern of male dominance and close supervision of girls, including chaperoned dates, is followed, as is the tendency to regard physical labor as undignified and unsuitable for gentlemen.

Although Latin American culture is basically Spanish or Portuguese, a strong Indian influence prevails, especially in Mexico, Central America, and the northwestern part of South America where the Indians comprise a large percentage of the total population. This influence (see Chapter 23, section V), is evident in cooking, clothing, building materials, and religious practices.

Latin American culture also has a considerable African element, brought over by the millions of slaves imported to work on plantations. This African influence is strongest in the Caribbean area where most of the slaves settled, although examples of their influence, especially music, can be found in most parts of Latin America; here the Negroes contributed their traditional drums.

United States

The culture that developed in the United States was less influenced by the native Indian population than was Latin American culture, the main reason being that the Indians were fewer in number and less advanced. Nevertheless, Indian influence was not altogether negligible: 25 states bear Indian names; at least 300 Indian words are now part of the English language; and many Indian inventions are commonly used, including moccasins, canoes, toboggans, and snowshoes.

Likewise, the United States has been less influenced by African culture than have certain Latin American states in the Caribbean area. Still, the influence here has been considerable; Negroes comprise over 10 per cent of the total population of the country compared to the one-half of one per cent comprised of Indians. The chief impact of the Negroes has been in the field of folk culture. One example is their folk music, including so-called spirituals or religious songs, and secular songs such as work songs, prison songs, railroad and steamboat songs, narrative ballads like "Frankie and Johnny" and "John Henry," and the world famous jazz.

Despite these Indian and African elements, American culture is overwhelmingly European in origin, although its European characteristics were drastically modified during the process of transplantation and adaptation. In a country where unceasing labor had been necessary first to establish the colonies and then to conquer the continent, it was natural for Americans to believe that toil was virtuous and idleness sinful. President Theodore Roosevelt expressed this national sentiment when he said, "I pity the creature who doesn't work—at whichever end of the social scale he may be."[2] Closely related to the American's belief in social equality was his belief in social mobility. He considered himself as good as the next man, and insisted that all men should be free to rise on the basis of ability and effort rather than of class origin. Reflecting his farm and frontier background, the American was an inveterate tinkerer, constantly engaged in devising gadgets to speed up the work that had to be done. And where his future was concerned, the American was an optimist: he had a sturdy faith in the inevitability of progress. Living in a country of great resources and equally great opportunities, he found it natural to glorify the future and to talk as though it had already materialized. Frontier humor was based on "tall tales," and the folk heroes were supermen like Paul Bunyan and Pecos Bill.

In the more sophisticated realm of formal arts and letters, the nineteenth century American felt distinctly inferior to his European contemporary—and for very good reasons. He had been too busy taming the wilderness to find time for gentility and aesthetics. Besides, the Puritan tradition placed greater value on hard work and saving of souls than it did on cultivation of the arts. As late as 1820, fully 80 per cent of all books in the United States were imported from Britain, and by 1830 the figure was still as high as 70 per cent. Accordingly, the nineteenth century Americans earnestly strove to imitate European culture. They went to school in London, Paris, Vienna, and Rome, built Greek temples for public buildings and churches, and imported European musicians and singers to help establish opera houses and orchestras. Toward the end of the nineteenth century some change in this attitude began to be noticeable. Walt Whitman and Mark Twain were fully and truly American. European intellectuals were becoming increasingly aware of a growing galaxy of American stars: John Dewey, William James, Oliver Wendell Holmes, Thorstein Veblen, and William Dean Howells. Yet Europe's tutelage remained hard to shake. At the end of the century, Henry Cabot Lodge still could write, "The first step of an American entering upon a literary career was to pretend to be an Englishman in order that he might win the approval, not of Englishmen, but of his own countrymen."[3]

British Dominions

Europe's cultural influence was stronger in the Dominions than in the United States or Latin America. One reason was the preservation of the imperial bonds, which occasioned more interaction with the mother country. Also, with the exception of South Africa, a much larger percentage of the peoples of the Dominions were of European origin than was the case in the United States and Latin America with their substantial Negro and Indian elements. This does not mean, however, that the Dominions all developed a uniform culture; distinctive local environments created distinctive local cultures.

Canada's cultural development, for example, has been molded by two overruling factors: a French Canadian bloc comprising one-third of the total population, and geographic proximity to the United States. The large French Canadian minority has made Canada officially bilingual, as can be seen in the coinage, the paper money, government proclamations, and inscriptions on nationally distributed commodities. More important is the outlook and national role of the French Canadians. In a very real sense they are a people without a mother country. Abandoned by France in 1763, they have been taught by their all-powerful Catholic Church to turn their backs on republican and secular France, and to scorn what they consider to be the commercialism and materialism of the English-speaking Canadians and the Americans. Consequently, their main desire is to be left alone and to preserve their identity in a predominantly Protestant, Anglo-Saxon continent.

Perhaps even more important for Canada is the overwhelming impact of the colossus to the south, whose influence has led not only to the wholesale draining of Canadian manpower and to the control of Canadian industries and natural resources, but also to a decisive molding of Canadian ways of living and thinking. American periodicals, movies, radio and television programs, and consumer goods, all leave an indelible imprint on the Dominion. In 1949 the Canadian government appointed a "Royal Commission on National Development in the Arts, Letters and Sciences." The report of this Commission included the following passage:

American influences on Canadian life to say the least are impressive. There should be no thought of interfering with the liberty of all Canadians to enjoy them. Cultural exchanges are excellent in themselves. They widen the choice of the consumer and provide stimulating competition for the producer. It cannot be denied, however, that a vast and disproportionate amount of material coming from a single alien source may stifle rather than stimulate our own creative effort; and, passively accepted without any standard of comparison, this may weaken critical faculties. We are now spending millions to maintain a national independence which would be nothing but an empty shell without a vigorous and distinctive cultural life.[4]

The cultural development of Australia and New Zealand has been greatly affected by their ethnic homogeneity. These dominions have neither a one-tenth Negro minority, as does the United States, nor a one-third French Catholic minority, as does Canada. Despite considerable non-British immigration since World War II, the population of Australia remains 90 per cent British in origin, and that of New Zealand, 98 per cent. As a result, both dominions maintained exceptionally close cultural ties with the mother country. New Zealanders commonly regarded England as "home" and New Zealand as a place in which to make a living.

It is perhaps worth noting that since World War II, Australians and New Zealanders have expressed the same concern about American cultural penetration as Canadians did. The impact of the United States has extended as far as the South Pacific, partly because of heavy American investments made in recent years, and also as an aftermath of the stationing of American troops there during World War II. A young Australian writer Robin Boyd has expressed the alarm of many of his countrymen: "Australia is sinking [culturally] into the Pacific, and a new state is rising which we might call Austerica. . . . Austerica's chief industry is the imitation of the froth on the top of the American soda-fountain drink. Its religion is 'glamor' and the devotees are psychologically displaced persons who picture Heaven as a pool terrace of a Las Vegas hotel."[5]

Conclusion

We have seen that in culture, as in politics and economics, wholesale transplanting of European civilization took place, though with a good deal of modification. This cultural diffusion and adaptation is most strikingly evident in the field of language. An Englishman who visits Australia, the United States, or Canada can easily understand the variations of his language spoken in those countries, although it is true that in Australia he would be mystified by such words as "aboes" (aborigines), "sheilas" (girls), "galahs" (chatterboxes), and "dills" (fools), and in both Canada and the United States he would soon learn that his petrol, silencer, boot, and demister, have become gas, muffler, trunk, and windshield wiper. He would also find instances where the Canadians have maintained their individuality against both English and American influences. If he asked for a "chesterfield," he would receive a man's coat in England, a pack of cigarettes in the United States, and an over-stuffed sofa in Canada.

Such miscellaneous differences, however, are too often exaggerated at the expense of the underlying, basic similarities. Actually, very few words would cause trouble to the Englishman traveling throughout the widely scattered English speaking world. The same would be true of a Frenchman in Quebec, a Portuguese in Brazil, or a Spaniard in the rest of Latin America. Most of the peculiar usages that are found overseas can be traced back to provincial dialects in the mother country. A Spaniard could find in his own country most of the variations he would encounter abroad, and the same would hold true for an Englishman or a Frenchman.

We may conclude, then, that the cultural Europeanization of the Americas and the British Dominions has been both pervasive and enduring. A European need only visit New York, Mexico City, Montreal, or Melbourne, and then visit Cairo, Delhi, Tokyo, or Peking to sense the reality and the extent of the overseas diffusion of his culture.

SUGGESTED READING

E. Fisher, *The Passing of the European Age* (Harvard Univ., 1948); W. B. Hamilton, ed., *The Transfer of Institutions* (Duke Univ., 1964); L. Hanke, ed., *Do the Americans Have a Common History?* (Columbia Univ., 1964); L. Hartz, *The Founding of New Societies* (Harcourt, 1964); P. Sharp, "Three Frontiers: Some Comparative Studies of Canadian, American and Australian Settlements," *Pacific Historical Review*, XXIV (1955), 369–77; W. P. Webb, *The Great Frontier* (Houghton, 1952); W. F. Wilcox, *et al.*, *International Migrations*, 2 vols. (National Bureau of Economic Research, 1929, 1931).

chapter thirty-two

Global Ecumene

Above all I wish to urge upon you once again the immense vista of difficulty and possibility of danger opened up by the newly awakened ambitions and aspirations of the Eastern races. What may be the final outcome of the collision . . . it is impossible to foretell. This, however, is certain—that contact with Western thought and Western ideals has exercised a revivifying influence upon all the races of the East. Those that have come into sharpest contact with it have exhibited most markedly its effects.—Lord Ronaldshay, 1909

The period between 1763 and 1914 stands out in world history as the period when Europe became master of the entire globe, whether directly or indirectly. Europe's hegemony was evident not only in the political sphere—in the form of great colonial empires—but also in the economic and cultural spheres. This hegemony meant the forging for the first time of a full-fledged global ecumene, in contrast to the pre-1763 period when the global bonds were still in the formative stage. On the other hand, the decade before 1914 also witnessed the first serious challenges to Europe's predominance, the most significant one being Japan's defeat of Russia. The contemporary revolutions in Turkey and Persia, and the underground rumblings in various colonial or semicolonial regions were also noteworthy. Let us now consider Europe's political, economic, and cultural predominance, and then the early challenges to this predominance.

I. EUROPE'S POLITICAL DOMINANCE

Between 1500 and 1763 Europe had emerged from obscurity by gaining control of the oceans and the relatively empty spaces of Siberia and the Americas. But so far as Asia and Africa were concerned, Europe's impact still remained negligible at the end of the eighteenth century. In Africa there were only a string of slave-trading stations along the coasts and an insignificant settlement of Boers on the southern tip of the continent. Likewise, in India the Europeans were confined to their few coastal trading posts and had not yet begun to affect substantially the vast hinterland. In East Asia the Westerners were rigidly restricted to Canton and Deshima despite their pleas for further contacts. If by some miracle the relations between Europe on the one hand and Africa and Asia on the other had been suddenly severed in the late eighteenth century, there would have been little left to show for the three centuries of interaction. A few ruined forts and churches would have been almost the only reminders of the intruders who had come across the sea. Everyday life would have continued along traditional lines as in the past millennia.

By 1914 this situation had changed fundamentally. Europe's impact had grown immeasurably, both in extent and in depth; vast portions of the globe—the United States, Latin America, Siberia, and the British Dominions—had been Europeanized. Europeans had migrated to those territories en masse, displacing to a greater or lesser degree the indigenous peoples. It is true that by 1914 the United States and Latin America had won political independence, while the British Dominions were self-governing. Nevertheless, as we have seen, these had become Europeanized lands; they were intimately related to Europe as regards ethnic composition, economic ties, and cultural institutions.

Vast territories, including the entire continent of Africa, with the exception of Liberia and Ethiopia, and the greater part of Asia, had become outright colonial possessions of the European powers. Of the 16,819,000 square miles comprising Asia, no less than 9,443,000 square miles were under European rule. These included 6,496,000 square miles under Russia, 1,998,000 under Britain, 587,000 under Holland, 248,000 under France, 114,000 under the United States, and a paltry 193 for Germany. In contrast to these tremendous colonial territories, Japan, the only truly independent Asian nation in 1914, accounted for a mere 161,000 square miles.

The remaining portion of the globe, apart from these colonial possessions and the Europeanized territories, consisted of countries that were nominally independent but actually semicolonial. These included the great Chinese and Ottoman empires as well as such smaller states as Iran, Afghanistan, and Nepal. All these countries were dominated by European economic and military power; they were allowed to retain a nominal political independence simply because the European powers could not agree on the details of their dismemberment.

In this manner the entire globe had come under Europe's hegemony by 1914. It was the extraordinary climax of the long process started half a millennium earlier when Portuguese captains began to feel their way down the coast of Africa. One peninsula of the Eurasian landmass now was the center of the world, with a concentration of power altogether unprecedented in past history. (See map, "World of Western Dominance, 1914.")

II. EUROPE'S ECONOMIC DOMINANCE

That Europe's hegemony in 1914 was unprecedented not only in extent but also in depth was evident in the economic control that Europe exercised. Europe had become the banker of the world, providing the capital needed for building transcontinental railroads, digging interoceanic canals, opening mines, and establishing plantations. Europe had become also the industrial workshop of the world. By 1870 Europe was responsible for 64.7 per cent of the world's total industrial output, the only rival being the United States with 23.3 per cent. Even though the United States had forged ahead by 1913 to 35.8 per cent, Europe's factories in that year still turned out 47.7 per cent of the world's total production.

The effect of Europe's great outpouring of capital and technology was an unprecedented global economic unity: By 1914 over 516,000 kilometers of cables had been laid on ocean beds, as well as a vast network of telegraph and telephone lines on the land surface of the globe. By 1914 over 30,000 ships with a total tonnage of 50 millions carried goods from one part of the world to another. Several canals were built to facilitate world commerce, the most important being the Suez (1869), which shortened the route between Western Europe and India by 4,000 miles, and the Panama (1914), which reduced the distance between New York and San Francisco by almost 8,000 miles. Continents were opened for economic exploitation by the construction of several transcontinental rail-roads, the first in the United States being completed in 1869, the first in Canada in 1885, the trans-Siberian in 1905; the Berlin to Bagdad and the Cape to Cairo railroads were almost completed by 1914.

This economic integration of the continents led to a spectacular increase in overall global productivity. World industrial production multiplied no less than six times between 1860 and 1913, while the value of world trade increased twelve times between 1851 and 1913. Europe, as might be expected, benefited the most from this economic leap forward. Statistics are not available for conditions all over the globe, but it is estimated that the difference in per capita income be-tween colonial or semicolonial regions and the European metropolitan countries was roughly three to one in 1800, and by 1914 had increased to about seven to one.

III. EUROPE'S CULTURAL DOMINANCE

The everyday life of the peasant masses in colonial territories had been drastically affected by the shift from a traditional natural economy to a money economy. Money had been used in the earlier period but only in a peripheral manner, and production had been carried on by the peasant households primarily to satisfy family needs. A few commodities might have been sold in the local market, but not for the purpose of making a profit. Rather the aim was to secure a little money to meet any tax obligations and to buy a few essentials such as salt and a little iron. Frequently the transactions and obligations were met by simple barter, and no money at all changed hands. But a new market economy was introduced when the Europeans appeared with their railroads, their machine-made goods, and their insatiable demands for foodstuffs and industrial raw materials. The peasants affected by this intrusion found themselves producing for an inter-national market rather than for themselves and their neighbors, which in turn meant that they became subject to the vagaries of economic fluctuations as well as to the mercies of merchants and moneylenders who now flourished in this new economy. The transition from a closed and static natural economy to a dynamic money and market economy was beneficial so far as productive capacity was concerned, but certainly its initial effects were disruptive and uncomfortable.

The way of thinking as well as the way of life was affected by Europe's intru-sion. However, this intellectual change involved primarily the small upper class in the colonial world rather than the peasant masses; it was the few members of the thin upper crust who knew some Western language, who read Western news-papers and books, and who were familiar with European history and current politics. The initial response to this exposure to the alien culture was often an enthusiastic, uncritical admiration of everything Western, but was usually followed by a reaction against the West and an attempt to preserve and foster at least some elements of the traditional culture. This ambivalent response to Western culture is clearly expressed in the following reminiscence written in 1925 by a prominent Indian:

Our forefathers, the first fruits of English education, were violently pro-British. They could see no flaw in the civilization or the culture of the West. They were charmed by its novelty and its strangeness. The enfranchisement of the individual, the substitution of the right of private judgement in the place of traditional authority, the exaltation of duty over custom, all came with a force and suddenness of a revelation to an Oriental people who knew no more binding obligation than the mandate of immemorial usage and of venerable tradition. . . . Everything English was good—even the drinking of brandy was a virtue; everything not English was to be viewed with suspicion. . . . In due time came the reaction, and with a sudden rush. And from the adoration of all things Western, we are now in a whirlpool that would recall us back to our ancient civilization and our time-honored ways and customs untempered by the impact of the ages that have rolled by and the forces of modern life.[1]

IV. WHITE MAN'S BURDEN

The political, economic, and cultural dominance of Europe at the turn of the century naturally led Europeans to assume that their primacy arose from the superiority of their civilization, and that this in turn reflected the superiority of themselves as a race. It was confidently believed that God had created man unequal. He had made the Whites more intelligent so that they could direct the labor and guide the development of the inferior races who had broad backs and weak minds. Hence the concept of the White Man's Burden, to use the well-known phrase of Rudyard Kipling.

On all continents the European masters accepted the homage of the "lesser breeds" as part of the divine nature of things—as the inevitable outcome of the "survival of the fittest." In India they were addressed respectfully as "sahib," in the Middle East as "effendi," in Africa as "bwana," and in Latin America as "patron." Under these circumstances it is scarcely surprising that Europeans came to view the world with a myopia and a self-centeredness that today seems incredible. Americans also shared this attitude. President Theodore Roosevelt in a message to Congress in 1904 warned Latin America that ". . . chronic wrong doing, or an impotency which results in a general loosening of the ties of civilized society, may in America, as elsewhere, ultimately require intervention by some civilized nation."[2] Likewise an American missionary, Henry W. Luce, father of the well-known publisher, reported from China in 1904 that conditions were favorable for their activities, and that "We may work together for God, for China and for Yale."[3] Most spectacular was the supreme self-confidence and aggressiveness of Cecil Rhodes who was ahead of his time in dreaming of other planets to conquer: "The world is nearly parcelled out and what there is left of it is being divided up, conquered, and colonized. To think of these stars that you see overhead at night, these vast worlds which we can never reach. I would annex the planets if I could; I often think of that. It makes me sad to see them so clear and yet so far."[4]

V. FIRST CHALLENGES TO EUROPE'S DOMINANCE

Europe's global hegemony seemed in 1914 to be unassailable and eternal, but in the clearer light of retrospect one can easily perceive the lurking nemesis of a colonial world slowly awakening and striking the first blows against the Western imperium.

Throughout history, whenever a weaker society has been threatened by one more vigorous and aggressive, there have been two contradictory types of reactions: One severs all contact with the intruding forces, withdraws into isolation, and seeks refuge in traditional beliefs and practices. The other tries instead to adopt as many features of the alien society as are necessary to meet it on equal terms and thus to resist it effectively. The first reaction represents retreat and escapism; the other, adjustment and adaptation. The slogan of the first is "Back to the good old days"; that of the second is, "Learn from the West in order to fight the West."

There were many cases during the nineteenth century of both types of reaction to the Western intrusion, classic examples of the escapist variety being the Indian Mutiny in 1857–1858 and the Boxer Rebellion in 1900. (See Chapter 28, section III, and Chapter 29, section IV for details.) Both the Mutiny and the Rebellion were bitter, bloody affairs, yet neither of them seriously challenged Europe's supremacy because they were essentially negative revolts, seeking to oust the hated Europeans by force in order to restore the good old days. But it was an entirely different matter when native peoples began to adopt Western ideas and technology in order to use them against the West.

The Japanese were the first Asian people to successfully carry out this policy of resistance by adaptation. They defeated the weak Chinese Empire in 1894–1895, and then the mighty Russian Empire in 1904–1905. (See Chapter 29, sections VI and VII for details.)

The triumph of a small Asian kingdom over a giant European power marks a turning point in recent world history. It was an event that sent a tremor of hope and excitement throughout the colonial world. As influential as the outcome of the Russo-Japanese War was the great Russian Revolution, stimulated in part by the war. (See Chapter 26, section IV.) The news that the Tsarist autocracy was on the verge of downfall was as exciting to oppressed peoples everywhere as the reports from the battlefields of Manchuria. A Britisher who was in Persia at this time sensed an undercurrent of aroused emotions and expectations in all the colonial lands. In a letter of August 1906 he reported:

It seems to me that a change must be coming over the East. The victory of Japan has, it would appear, had a remarkable influence all over the East. Even here in Persia it has not been without effect. . . . Moreover, the Russian Revolution has had a most astounding effect here. Events in Russia have been watched with great attention, and a new spirit would seem to have come over the people. They are tired of their rulers, and, taking example of Russia, have come to think that it is possible to have another and better form of government . . . it almost seems that the East is stirring in its sleep. In China there is a marked movement against the foreigners, and a tendency towards the ideal of "China for the Chinese." In Persia, owing to its proximity to Russia, the awakening would appear to take the form of a movement towards democratic reform. In Egypt and North Africa it is signalized by a remarkable increase in fanaticism, coupled with the spread of the Pan-Islamic movement. The simultaneousness of these symptoms of unrest is too remarkable to be attributed solely to coincidence. Who knows? Perhaps the East is really awakening from its secular slumber, and we are about to witness the rising of these patient millions against the exploitation of an unscrupulous West.[5]

This analysis proved prophetic. It was borne out by the 1905 Persian Revolution, the 1908 Young Turk Revolution, the 1911 Chinese Revolution, and by the heightened unrest and terrorism in India. We may conclude that although Europe's global hegemony in 1914 seemed irresistible and everlasting, it actually was being challenged at many points and in many ways. In some cases the challenge was direct, as in India and in Central Asia where a few pioneer nationalists were beginning to demand independence from Britain and Russia. In other cases the challenge was indirect, being aimed against the weak Ottoman, Kajar, and Manchu dynasties because of their failure to resist Western aggression. In this pre-1914 period the European Powers were able to suppress the opposition, either by direct force or by supporting the Shah against the *majlis* or the conservative Yüan Shih-k'ai against the radical Sun Yat-sen. Yet this early opposition did represent a beginning—the genesis of the nationalist movements that, after World War I, and especially after World War II, were to sweep everything before them.

SUGGESTED READING

H. C. d'Encausse and S. R. Schram, *Marxism and Asia* (Lane, 1969); E. Fischer, "Rebellion Against the European Man in the Nineteenth Century," *Journal of World Affairs,* II (1954), 363–80; C. J. H. Hayes, *A Generation of Materialism, 1871–1900* (Harper, 1941); I. Spector, *The First Russian Revolution: Its Impact on Asia* (Prentice-Hall, 1962).

part eight

WORLD OF
WESTERN DECLINE
AND TRIUMPH, 1914

The decades since 1914 have witnessed at one and the same time the decline and triumph of the West. Indeed these two seemingly antithetical trends were mutually reinforcing. Thanks to the unprecedented integration of the globe, Western technology, ideas, and institutions have been proliferating at an accelerating pace, thus raising to a new level the intensity of their impact. But it was precisely this new triumph that served to undermine the Western global hegemony that had appeared so invulnerable prior to 1914. Colonial peoples reacted by selectively adopting Western civilization to better resist the West.

The Turkish leader Kemal Atatürk paid in 1925 this glowing tribute to the West, which he flatly equated with "civilization."

Resistance to the flood-tide of civilization is vain; she is quite merciless to those who ignore or disobey her. Civilization pierces the mountains, soars in the skies, sees and illuminates and studies all things, from the invisible atoms to the stars. Nations which try to function with medieval minds, with primitive superstitions, in the presence of her sublime might and her sublime majesty, are doomed to annihilation or, at best, to servitude or ignominy.[1]

The significance of this statement is that it was Kemal Atatürk, who saw most clearly the power and dynamism of the new "civilization," who was also the most successful in coping with it. His Turkish republic, which became the most Westernized state in the Middle East, was for that very reason able to be the most independent of the West. "Decline" and "triumph" were indeed two sides of the same coin.

[1] G. Lewis, "Modern Turkish Attitudes to Europe," in The Glass Curtain Between Asia and Europe, ed. R. Iyer (London: Oxford Univ., 1965), pp. 169–70.

chapter thirty-three

World War I: Global Repercussions

There is no doubt that Mankind is once more on the move. The very foundations have been shaken and loosened, and things are again fluid. The tents have been struck, and the great caravan of Humanity is once more on the march.—J. C. Smuts (1918)

The great war of 1914–1918 was from the Asian point of view a civil war within the European community of nations.—K. M. Panikkar, *Indian diplomat and historian*

In the autumn of 1914, as one European country after another was being dragged into the holocaust of World War I, the British Foreign Secretary, Earl Grey, remarked, "The lamps are going out all over Europe." His comment was indeed fully justified, and to a much greater degree than he could have foreseen at the time. World War I was destined to bring down in ruins the Europe with which Earl Grey was familiar. It wiped out the centuries-old Hapsburg, Hohenzollern, Romanoff, and Ottoman dynasties. In their places appeared new leaders, new institutions, and new ideologies that aristocrats such as Earl Grey only dimly comprehended. The Europe of 1918 was as different from that of 1914 as the Europe of 1815 had been different from that of 1789.

World War I also marked the end of the Europe that had dominated the globe so completely and abnormally during the nineteenth century. By the end of the war Europe's control had manifestly weakened and was everywhere being challenged. In one way or another the challenges were successfully resisted in most parts of the world. But the respite lasted only two decades, for the Second World War completed the undermining process begun by the First, and left the European empires everywhere in shambles.

From the viewpoint of world history as well as European, World War I stands out as a historic turning point. The purpose of this chapter is to analyze the roots, the course, and the global repercussions of this fateful episode.

I. ROOTS OF WAR

Historians distinguish between background causes that had been operative for some decades, and immediate causes that came into play during the hectic weeks following the assassination of the Archduke Francis Ferdinand on June 28, 1914. The most important of the background factors are four in number: economic rivalries, colonial disputes, conflicting alliance systems and irreconcilable nationalist aspirations.

Most of the major European powers became involved in tariff wars and in competition for foreign markets. For example, Italy and France waged a tariff war between 1888 and 1899, Russia and Germany between 1879 and 1894, and Austria and Serbia between 1906 and 1910. The most serious economic rivalry developed between Britain and Germany because of the latter's extraordinarily rapid rate of industrialization in the late nineteenth century. In 1870 Britain produced 31.8 per cent of the world's total industrial output, compared to Germany's 13.2 per cent. By 1914 Britain's share had dropped to 14 per cent, due largely to the spectacular upsurge of the United States from 23.3 to 35.8 per cent. Germany's production, however, had risen sufficiently so that her share rose slightly to 14.3 per cent, or a shade greater than that of Britain.

Germany's spurt in industrial production meant stiff competition for Britain in overseas markets. Britain was able to retain her economic predominance in her own colonies, but in Latin America, the Middle East, and the Far East, she lost heavily to the aggressive German businessmen. It is impossible to define precisely the political repercussions of this economic rivalry, but it manifestly strained the relations between the two countries. It further contributed to international tension by stimulating competition in naval armaments. In both countries it was argued vociferously that it was essential to build up naval strength in order to safeguard trade routes and merchant shipping.

Economic rivalries also fomented colonial disputes, for additional colonies were eagerly sought after in order to be assured of protected overseas markets for surplus capital and manufactures. Since the Germans did not enter the colonial race until after their national unification in 1871, they were particularly aggressive in their demands for an empire commensurate with their growing economic strength. The Pan-German League pointed to the substantial colonial possessions of small countries like Portugal, Holland, and Belgium, and insisted that Germany also must have her "place in the sun." But in almost every part of the globe the Germans found themselves blocked by the farflung possessions of the British, whom they bitterly accused of "dog in the manger" selfishness.

The competition for colonies, however, was by no means restricted to Britain and Germany. Almost all the major powers were involved in the scramble for empire in the late nineteenth century, so they repeatedly clashed in one region or another: Britain and Germany clashed in East Africa and Southwest Africa; Britain and France, in Siam and the Nile Valley; Britain and Russia, in Persia and Afghanistan; and Germany and France, in Morocco and West Africa.

These colonial rivalries in turn contributed to the forging of conflicting alliance systems that were in large part responsible for the coming of war. The systems began in 1879 when the German chancellor, Otto von Bismarck, concluded the Dual Alliance with Austria-Hungary. This was a defensive pact, designed to protect Germany against the French, who aspired to recover the Alsace-Lorraine provinces lost in 1871, and also to protect Austria-Hungary against the Russians, with whom they continually clashed in the Balkans. In 1882 the Dual Alliance became the Triple Alliance with the adhesion of Italy. Again the objective was defensive: to protect Italy against France because of sharp conflict over Tunis. The Triple Alliance, then, was definitely not aggressive in intention or in its provisions. Germany and Austria-Hungary were both satiated powers interested primarily in preserving the *status quo* on the Continent.

But from the other side of the fence the Triple Alliance appeared quite differently. For France and Russia it meant an overwhelming bloc that dominated Europe and left them isolated and vulnerable. Furthermore, France and Russia both had serious difficulties with Britain over colonial issues in several regions. The result was the Franco-Russian Alliance, concluded in 1894 with the double purpose of countering the Triple Alliance and resisting Britain in colonial disputes. The Franco-Russian Alliance became the Triple Entente with the signing of the Anglo-French Entente in 1904 and the Anglo-Russian Entente in 1907. Both of these arrangements were essentially colonial in nature. Britain and France, for example, agreed to recognize their respective interests in the Nile Valley and Morocco, while Britain and Russia likewise agreed to divide Persia into spheres of influence.

Thus all the major powers now were aligned in rival alliance systems, with disastrous results for international relations. Whenever any dispute of consequence arose, the members of both blocs felt compelled to support their respective allies who were directly involved, even if they entertained doubts regarding the issues. Otherwise they feared that their alliances would disintegrate, leaving them alone and exposed. Each dispute consequently tended to be magnified into a major crisis involving, willy-nilly, all the members of both alliances. In the middle of the 1914 crisis, for example, the Austro-Hungarian foreign minister, Count Berchtold, declared, ". . . we are playing a great game, in which there are serious difficulties to overcome, and in which we might fail, unless the Powers of the Triple Alliance hold firmly together." This attitude explains why crises became increasingly frequent during the decade prior to 1914, and why they became increasingly difficult to resolve as the bloc members fearfully and compulsively supported each other.

The fourth and final background cause was the rising nationalist aspirations of Europe's subject minorities. This was difficult enough in Alsace-Lorraine, where the French remained unreconciled to German rule. But it was a nightmare in Central and Eastern Europe, where the multinational empires were in danger of being literally torn to pieces by the growing demand for self-determination. In the Hapsburg Empire, for example, the ruling Austrians and Hungarians were confronted by the resurgent Italians and Rumanians as well as the great Slavic multitude: Czechs, Slovaks, Ruthenians, Poles, Slovenes, Croats, and Serbs. Very understandably the Hapsburg officials decided that firm measures were necessary if the empire was to survive. This was especially true regarding the militant Serbs who were clamoring for unification with the independent Serbia across the Danube. Hence the stiff terms sent to Belgrade when the Archduke was murdered by a Serb patriot at Sarajevo. But behind Serbia was Russia, and behind Russia were France and Britain. Austria-Hungary, likewise, was backed by Germany and, theoretically, by Italy. Thus this combination of national self-determination and conflicting alliance systems brought Europe to Armageddon.

II. SARAJEVO

On June 28, 1914, Archduke Francis Ferdinand and his wife were assassinated in Sarajevo, the capital of the recently annexed province of Bosnia. The murder was committed by a young Bosnian Serb student named Gavrilo Princip. He was not alone in carrying out the murder. Behind him was the secret Serbian organization *Ujedinjenje ili Smrt,* or "Union or Death," popularly known as the Black Hand. Founded in Belgrade in 1911, the Black Hand set out to unify all Serbs by conspiracy and terror. The Serbian government was not behind this society, which indeed it regarded as dangerously radical and militant. But this did not prevent the Black Hand from organizing an underground revolutionary organization that conducted an effective campaign of agitation and terrorism. A Serbian diplomat stationed in Vienna at this time testified: "The year 1913 in Bosnia was the year of revolutionary organization. . . . 'Action, action, enough of words' was the cry on all lips. The young dreamed of nothing but bombs, assassinations, explosives to blow up and destroy everything."[1]

The unfortunate Francis Ferdinand played into the hands of these Serb revolutionaries by agreeing to pay an official visit to the Bosnian capital. When the archduke and his duchess paid their visit on the radiant Sunday morning of June 28, no less than six assassins, armed with bombs and revolvers, were waiting along the designated route. As fate would have it, the procession stopped at the very corner where Princip was stationed. He drew his revolver and fired two shots, one at Francis Ferdinand and the other at General Potiorek, the Governor of Bosnia. The second shot went wild and hit the duchess instead. Before medical aid arrived, both the archduke and his wife were dead.

Now the system of alliances began to operate relentlessly and fatally. First Germany assured Austria-Hungary of full support regardless of what course she decided upon. This famous "blank check" from Berlin did not signify that the Germans wanted war. Rather they assumed that Russia would not dare support Serbia against both Germany and Austria, and that it was therefore in the interest of peace to make this common front perfectly clear at the outset. The assumption was understandable in view of the fact that this is precisely what had happened in 1908 when Austria annexed the province of Bosnia from the Turks. The Serbs, who for long had eyed this Slavic province, reacted violently against the annexation and were backed by Russia. But when Germany supported Austria, the Russians decided they were in no condition to risk war and backed down.

This sequence was not to be repeated in 1914, however, because Russia was now in a stronger position than she had been in 1908. She had recovered from the defeat of 1904–1905 in the Far East. She now had firm support from France, as she had not had in 1908, when France had been lukewarm to make an issue of Bosnia. Thus, the German assumption that the Sarajevo crisis could be localized proved a miscalculation, and the stage was set for the great catastrophe.

On July 23, Austria presented Serbia a stiff ultimatum, which included demands for explanations and apologies, suppression of anti-Austrian publications and organizations, participation of Austrian officials in the inquiry regarding responsibility for the crime, and judicial proceedings against those accessory to the plot. The Serbian reply on July 25 appeared conciliatory at first glance, but actually was so hedged with qualifications as to be evasive and unsatisfactory. Austria promptly broke off diplomatic relations, and on July 28 declared war on Serbia.

Russia now retaliated by ordering full mobilization on July 30. The next day Germany sent a twelve-hour ultimatum to Russia demanding that mobilization be stopped. When no reply was received, Germany declared war against Russia on August 1 and against Russia's ally, France, on August 3. On the same day Germany began actual hostilities by invading Belgium. This aggression provided a welcome pretext for Britain's declaration of war on Germany on August 4. Thus the great powers of Europe were at each others' throats five weeks after the murder at Sarajevo.

III. EUROPEAN PHASE OF THE WAR, 1914–1917

1914: War of Attrition in the West

World War I began with cheering crowds and marching soldiers singing the "Marseillaise," or "In der Heimat," or "Tipperary." Troop trains on both sides bore the chalked inscription "Home by Christmas." All peoples confidently expected a brief and victorious war. Instead, they soon found themselves embroiled in a prolonged and brutalizing ordeal that was unprecedented in its toll of material wealth, human lives, social institutions and political structures.

The explanation for the bloody stalemate that gutted European civilization is to be found in the failure of traditional war strategy. The General Staffs of all the European armies had for years been carefully preparing for war against any neighbor or combination of neighbors. The Germans had a plan devised in 1905 by their Chief of Staff, Count Alfred von Schlieffen. This Schlieffen Plan called for a speedy and overwhelming attack upon France before turning against the slow-moving Russians in the East. The bulk of the German forces were to be concentrated in the north and were to attack through Belgium and Luxembourg in a vast wheeling movement that would roll up the French army to the east of Paris and thus end the war in thirty days.

On August 4 this plan went into operation when German forces crossed the frontier of Belgium, of whose neutrality Germany was herself a guarantor, and rushed through Belgium and northern France. They reached the Marne River, and by September 2 were at Chantilly, only 25 miles from Paris. Now the tide unexpectedly began to turn, when the French counterattacked through a thirty-mile gap between the advancing armies. Outnumbered 4 to 3, and exhausted by their long advance, the Germans retreated to the natural defense line of the Aisne River. The opposing armies now began a series of flanking and counterflanking movements that ended only when the battle front extended from the coast of Flanders to the frontier of Switzerland.

This line did not shift by more than ten miles in either direction during the next three years despite offensives that took a ghastly toll in lives. The reason for the bloody deadlock was that from the beginning of the war defensive weapons proved superior over offensive. The traditional mode of attack was the massed infantry charge supported by a preliminary artillery barrage. But this was of no avail against the combination of deep trenches, barbed wire entanglements, ingenious land mines, and machine-gun nests. Thus the casualties on the western front during the first four months were 700,000 Germans, 850,000 French, and 90,000 British. Contrary to the plans of all General Staffs, the struggle in the west now became a war of position and attrition.

This was not the case on the Russian and Balkan fronts, where vast distances and scanty transportation facilities necessitated a fluid war of movement. The Russians led off with a surprisingly fast and powerful offensive into East Prussia, designed to relieve the pressure on the French in the west. The strategy worked, for the Germans transferred four divisions from Belgium to the east. Before they reached their destination, the issue had been decided by smashing victories over two Russian armies advancing into East Prussia. The German commanders, Hindenburg and Ludendorff, used their superior railway network to concentrate their forces against first one Russian army and then the other. By the middle of September, East Prussia was cleared of her invaders.

On the Balkan front the Austrians meanwhile were suffering humiliating setbacks. General Potiorek, who had barely escaped Princip's bullet in Sarajevo, was impatient to destroy "the viper's nest." On August 12 he crossed the Drina River into Serbia with 250,000 men. But he was met by a Serbian army of 350,000, of whom 90 per cent were seasoned veterans of the Balkan Wars of 1912–13. In less than two weeks these Serbs had forced the Austrians back across the river with a loss of one-third of their numbers. Potiorek returned to the attack in September and succeeded in taking Belgrade on December 2. But again the Serbians counterattacked and by the end of the same month had cleared their country of the invaders.

1915: Russian Retreat in the East

The 1915 campaigns were dominated by the decision of the new German Commander in Chief, Erich von Falkenhayn, to reverse the Schlieffen Plan. In view of the stalemate on the western front he concentrated his forces on the east in an effort to knock out the Russians. Combined German and Austrian armies attacked with stunning effect on May 1, advancing by the end of the summer an average of 200 miles. In addition to military casualties totalling 2,500,000 men, Russia had lost 15 per cent of her territories, 10 per cent of her railways, 30 per cent of her industries, and 20 per cent of her civilian population. The Tsarist regime had suffered a blow from which it never was able to recover.

The Western Powers sought to help by attempting to force the Straits in order to knock out Turkey and open a supply route to Russia. When Turkey joined the Central Powers on November 2, 1914, the Straits automatically were closed to the Allies, thus making it difficult to ship much-needed supplies to Russia. Accordingly, on March 18, 1915, a squadron of fourteen British and four French battleships steamed into the Straits with guns blazing. Heavy losses from mines and coastal artillery forced the Allied ships to withdraw. An attempt then was made to take the Straits by landings on the Gallipoli beaches, but only shallow footholds were secured in the face of withering machine-gun fire. The Turks held on to the heights above the beaches until the Allies finally faced facts and withdrew permanently in January, 1916.

The failure at the Straits together with the disaster on the Russian front persuaded Bulgaria to join the Central Powers on October 14, 1915. This intervention spelled the end for the gallant Serbs. An overwhelming number of German, Austrian, and Bulgarian divisions attacked Serbia on October 6 from three sides. By the end of the year the entire country was occupied.

To counterbalance these setbacks in the Balkans, the Allies were strengthened by the decision of Italy to join their cause. Although the Italians technically had been allies of the Central Powers, they decided at the outset of the war to remain neutral. The bulk of the Italian people favored this course, especially since it was Austria that held the "unredeemed" lands across the Adriatic. The Allies now freely offered these lands to Italy, together with additional territories at the expense of Turkey. The bait proved effective, and on April 29 Italy signed the Treaty of London agreeing to enter the war in one month in return for these territorial promises. Actually Italy's intervention scarcely affected the course of the war, apart from compelling the Austrians to divert a few divisions from the eastern front.

1916: Verdun and the Somme

By 1916 the Central Powers had reached the height of their military fortunes. But even though they controlled the continent of Europe from Hamburg to the Persian Gulf, they still were not able to force a peace settlement on the Allies. At Christmas of 1915 General Falkenhayn submitted a memorandum to His Majesty the Kaiser in which he analyzed this dilemma and proposed a way out. After a survey of the situation on the various fronts, he pointed out that, with Russia on the ropes, France now was the most vulnerable Allied Power. Accordingly, he proposed an all-out attack on Verdun, a key French fortress that was easy to attack but hard to defend. The French High Command, he reasoned, would be forced to throw in every reserve to hold Verdun, and thus France would be bled white and her will to resist would be broken.

The battle for Verdun began on February 21, 1916. The Germans continued their attacks until July, when they went over to the defensive. The net result was French casualties totaling 350,000 men, and German casualties almost as great. The Verdun bloodbath did not bring the decision that Falkenhayn had hoped for. Indeed, the French counterattacked toward the end of the year and regained the positions lost in the spring. Meanwhile the British on July 1 launched a great offensive to the northwest at the Somme. The slaughter continued until November, when operations bogged down in rain and mud. The maximum advance was about seven miles, and the total cost was 400,000 British lives, 200,000 French, and 500,000 German.

To everyone's surprise, the Russians mounted a successful offensive on the eastern front in 1916. The Austrians had thinned their lines in Galicia in order to reinforce an attack against Italy. Consequently, when General Brusilov started what was intended at first to be merely a feint to relieve the pressure on Verdun, the Austrian front "broke like a pie crust" for a distance of 200 miles. The surprised Russians poured all reserves into the gap and overran the province of Galicia.

The failure of the Germans at Verdun and the unexpected success of the Brusilov offensive encouraged Rumania to intervene in the war on the side of the Allies on August 27, 1916. The Central Powers now decided to make an object lesson of Rumania as a warning to other neutrals contemplating following her course. German, Austrian, Bulgarian, and Turkish forces descended in full speed and overwhelming force. By the end of the year the Rumanians had lost two-thirds of their country, including their capital.

The involvement of Rumania in the war left Greece as the only neutral in the Balkans. That country was fairly evenly divided on the issue of neutrality or intervention. The most prominent statesman, Eleutherios Venizelos, was all for joining the Allies, but King Constantine, who was the Kaiser's brother-in-law, insisted on neutrality. The deadlock was broken in 1917 when the Allies decided that Greek assistance was essential to succeed in Macedonia, where they had been fighting inconclusively against the Bulgars. Accordingly, the Allies resorted to various extralegal measures, such as seizing the Greek fleet, blockading Greek ports, and even landing troops at Piraeus. Finally, on June 27, 1917, Greece entered the war on the Allied side, thereby paving the way for the 1918 offensives in Macedonia that knocked Bulgaria out of the war.

1917: Bloodletting and Defeatism

Meanwhile, the terrible bloodletting was continuing unabated on the western front. Whereas in 1916 the Germans had assumed the offensive at Verdun, now in 1917 the Allies took the lead. The cautious General Joffre was replaced by the audacious General Nivelle who had distinguished himself in the Verdun fighting. Nivelle preached with persuasive fervor a new type of lightning offensive that would bring victory with few casualties. Despite the opposition of many military leaders, both French and British, Nivelle's aggressive strategy was accepted.

The Germans at the same time had replaced Falkenhayn with their eastern front team of Hindenburg and Ludendorff. After the shattering experience of the previous year at Verdun and the Somme, they decided to go on the defensive on the western front while opening unrestricted submarine warfare at sea. They hoped thereby to starve England into submission, leaving France isolated on the Continent. They were well aware that submarine warfare involved the risk of American intervention, but they gambled that England would be broken before American aid became effective.

We shall see shortly that this gamble came within an ace of being won, though in the end it brought disaster. But the defensive strategy on land paid off handsomely. In order to consolidate and strengthen his front lines, Hindenburg withdrew his forces to a new fortified position, the Siegfried Line, or as it was more commonly called, the Hindenburg Line. This was straighter, shorter, and more heavily fortified. The withdrawal badly upset Nivelle's offensive plans, but he persisted in going through with them. French, British, and Canadian troops went over the top as scheduled, but they suffered one of the bloodiest repulses of the war. Hindenburg's defensive strategy had served the Germans well. They inflicted 400,000 casualties on the Allies, while incurring only 250,000 themselves.

By this time the peoples of Europe were enduring the fourth year of the most devastating and murderous war in history. Despite all the sacrifices and grief, no end was yet in sight. War weariness and defeatism appeared not only in the trenches but also amongst the civilians in both camps. One of the most spectacular manifestations was the passage of a Peace Resolution by the German Reichstag on July 19, 1917, by a vote of 212 to 126. In Austria-Hungary the death of the respected old Emperor Francis Joseph on November 21, 1917, removed a venerable symbol of loyalty and discipline. The subject nationalities, always restive under Hapsburg rule, now began to take concrete measures for independent statehood. The young new Emperor Charles doubted that the ramshackle imperial structure would hold together through another winter, and sent his brother-in-law, Prince Sixtus, to France to make peace overtures. Likewise in England, a former Foreign Secretary, Lord Lansdowne, wrote an open letter prophesying the collapse of Western civilization unless some way was found to end the conflict.

IV. GLOBAL PHASE OF THE WAR: 1917 RUSSIAN REVOLUTIONS

From European to Global Phase

1917 proved to be the year of decision because of two fateful developments—the Russian Revolutions and the intervention of the United States. These events changed the character of the war—from an essentially European affair fought over primarily European issues, to a war of global proportions. It is true that Japan had entered the war on August 23, 1914, but she had done little more than help herself to scattered German colonial possessions in the Pacific. But now the entry of the United States involved a great non-European power that quickly decided the outcome of the war.

The American intervention and the Russian Revolutions also introduced a new ideological element that immediately had worldwide repercussions. Wilson's Fourteen Points and Lenin's revolutionary slogans were universal and disruptive in their impact, in contrast to parochial European issues such as the fate of Alsace-Lorraine or of the Hapsburg subject nationalities. It was in 1917, then, that the transition occurred from the European to the global phase of World War I.

Roots of Russian Revolution

Russians of all classes rallied behind their government when war with Germany began on August 1, 1914. In contrast to the Japanese War of 1904–1905, this conflict was popular with the masses of the people, who were convinced it was a war of defense against the aggression of their traditional Teutonic enemies. The only exception to this closing of ranks came from the extreme left-wing Bolsheviks. Their leader, Lenin, branded the war as an imperialist struggle over markets and colonies. There was no reason, therefore, why the workers of the world should sacrifice themselves in such a conflict. Tirelessly he repeated the slogan "Turn the imperialist war into a class war!" This, however, was the only discordant note in 1914, and at that time it was unnoticed and insignificant. The Bolsheviks were a tiny faction within Russia, and their outstanding leaders were in exile abroad, including Lenin who was in Switzerland and Trotsky in New York. Consequently, Bolshevik agitation did not mar the impressive national unity behind the Tsarist regime.

The Russians not only were united against the Germans but they also were confident that they would win the war in short order. But instead of quick victory, Russia suffered disastrous defeats. The two Russian armies that penetrated into East Prussia in 1914 eventually suffered crushing defeats. In the following year came the great rout, when Russian armies reeled back before a great German-Austrian attack. The most densely populated and highly industrialized provinces of the empire were lost to the Central Powers. The disasters of 1915 proved to be the beginning of the end of the Tsarist regime.

One reason why Russia never recovered from the military setbacks is that she simply lacked the economic strength to wage modern warfare against first-class industrial powers. This economic weakness became much worse with the loss of the industrialized portions of the empire in 1915. In addition, Russia's war effort was handicapped by incompetent military leadership. When hostilities began, Tsar Nicholas selected as Commander in Chief his uncle, Grand Duke Nicholas, who was considered eminently unqualified by his own staff.

The Russians were handicapped also by political dissension on the home front. The Duma and the imperial bureaucracy were constantly feuding over their respective jurisdictions and prerogatives. Both of them, in turn, clashed with the military in assigning responsibility for the shortage of war supplies and, ultimately, for the defeats at the front. This discord might have been minimized and controlled if there had been strong leadership at the top. Unfortunately, Tsar Nicholas was a well-meaning but weak and vacillating ruler with limited intelligence and imagination. His strong-willed but highstrung and unstable wife constantly urged him to assert his authority and crack the whip. But Nicholas remained an irresolute and pathetic figure, usually following the advice of who-ever spoke to him last. His crowning error was his decision in August, 1915, in the midst of disaster at the front, to dismiss Grand Duke Nicholas and to assume personal command of military operations. He was even less qualified to do so than his uncle, and proved to be a nuisance at General Headquarters. Yet he had a mystical belief that his self-sacrifice might save the situation. "Perhaps a sin offering is needed to save Russia. I shall be the victim. God's will be done." Ultimately he was indeed the victim, for henceforth he was held personally re-sponsible for military defeats. Thus, the final outcome was the destruction of his family, the ending of the Tsarist regime, and the advent of the Bolsheviks.

March Revolution

Two revolutions occurred in Russia in 1917: the first, in March, ended Tsarism and created a Provisional Government, while the second, in November, toppled the Provisional Government and substituted Soviet rule. The first revolution was an unplanned affair that took everyone by surprise. Strikes and riots broke out in Petrograd on March 8 because of the desperate shortage of food and fuel arising from inadequate transportation facilities. The authorities ordered the army to restore order, but, instead, the soldiers mutinied and fraternized with the demon-strators. The Tsar, always distrustful of the Duma, suspected it of complicity and ordered its dissolution on March 11. The Duma leaders refused to comply with the order, and the Tsar discovered that he no longer could enforce obedience. This realization of powerlessness was to all intents and purposes the revolution itself. Russia no longer had a functioning government. This was the situation legally as well as factually when Tsar Nicholas abdicated on March 15 in favor of his brother Michael, and when Michael in turn gave up the throne the follow-ing day.

Some new structure had to be erected quickly lest the radical elements in the streets take over. On March 12 a Provisional Government was organized to ad-minister the country until a Constituent Assembly could be elected. The new government was headed by the liberal Prince Georgi Lvov and included the Cadet leader, Professor Paul Miliukov, as minister for foreign affairs, and Alex-ander Kerensky, the only socialist, as minister of justice. This was a bourgeois, liberal, middle-of-the-road cabinet, which favored reform up to a certain point. In fact, it did proclaim freedom of speech, press, and assembly; it declared an amnesty for political and religious offenses; recognized the legal equality of all citizens without social, religious, or racial discrimination; and passed labor legis-lation, including the eight-hour day. Despite this reform record the Provisional Government never sank roots in the country. For eight months it strove desper-ately but in vain to provide an adequate administration. At the end of that time the new government was not overthrown; rather, it collapsed as helplessly and ignominiously as the Tsarist regime had in March.

Between Revolutions

The period between March and November, 1917, was one of struggle for power between the Provisional Government and the soviets. In this struggle the Provi-

sional Government was fatally handicapped because from the beginning it refused to consider the two things that most Russians wanted—peace and land.
Prince Lvov and his ministers insisted that such a fundamental reform as redistribution of land must wait for a Constituent Assembly that would be truly
representative of the people and would have the authority to decide on such a
basic issue. Likewise, the government refused to end the war, because Russia had
certain commitments to her allies that could not be violated. These arguments
were sensible and understandable, but politically suicidal. While the government
was temporizing and pleading for patience, the soviets were winning over the
masses by demanding immediate peace and immediate distribution of land.

The origin of the soviets goes back to the 1905 Revolution when the workers
elected councils, or soviets, to coordinate their struggle against Tsarism. Although
suppressed at that time, the soviets had proven their value as organs for agitation
and direct action. They had precisely that quality which the Provisional Government conspicuously lacked—intimate rapport with the masses. Very naturally,
soviets reappeared with the crisis precipitated by the World War. Because of
their origin and composition, they had none of the Provisional Government's
squeamishness about waiting for elections before proceeding with peace negotiations and land distribution. Thus the Soviet movement mushroomed throughout
the country, developing virtually into a grass-roots government that continually
challenged that in Petrograd. Village soviets were organizing seizures of nobles'
estates; city soviets were behind the unceasing demonstrations and riots in the
streets; while the soldiers' soviets were gradually usurping the authority of the
officers to the point where they had control of all weapons and countersigned all
orders before they could be executed.

At the beginning, the delegates elected to the soviets were predominantly
Socialist Revolutionaries and Mensheviks. The Bolsheviks remained relatively
insignificant until the return of their leaders from Switzerland. On April 16,
Lenin and several of his lieutenants arrived in Petrograd, having been transported through Germany in a sealed carriage. The German High Command calculated that these revolutionaries would undermine the pro-Allied Provisional
Government, and their calculation proved correct. Lenin promptly issued his
famous "April Theses" demanding immediate peace, land to the peasants, and
all power to the soviets.

Lenin was almost alone in thus calling for a second revolution at once. Time,
however, was on his side, for the longer the war continued, the more the public
discontent mounted, and the more popular his demands became. Slogans that
seemed bizarre in April were to sound perfectly reasonable half a year later. By
late 1917 many were ready to fight for "all power to the soviets" in order to be
rid of the Provisional Government that stood in the way of the much-desired
peace and land and bread.

An early indication of shifting public opinion was the forced resignation of
Foreign Minister Miliukov on May 17. His insistence that Russia remain in the
war made him so unpopular that he was dropped, and a new Provisional Government formed under Lvov and Kerensky. It remained in office until July 20,
when Kerensky, who had been steadily emerging as the strongman, organized a
new government with himself as premier. By this time the temper of the country
had swung so far to the left that the new ministers were mostly Socialist Revolutionaries and Mensheviks. Gone were the days when the Cadets were regarded as
the radicals of Russian politics. Now Kerensky was cooperating with the Mensheviks and the Socialist Revolutionaries in order to withstand Lenin and his
Bolsheviks.

Bolshevik Revolution and Brest-Litovsk Treaty

Kerensky declared that his main objective was "to save the revolution from the extremists." In an effort to halt the growing seizure of estates he warned that the future Constituent Assembly would not recognize land transfers made after July 25. He also tried to restore some semblance of discipline in the armed forces by reintroducing the death penalty for certain offenses. These measures naturally made Kerensky very unpopular with the Bolsheviks and other radicals. Unfortunately for him, he did not thereby attract the support of the military men and other conservatives. They regarded him as a weak, loud-mouthed politician, and demanded that he take immediate steps to crush the soviets. When he refused to do so, a certain General Lavr Kornilov staged an army revolt against Kerensky with the avowed aim of freeing the government from soviet domination.

The soviets took the lead in organizing resistance against Kornilov and in conducting propaganda amongst his troops until many deserted. Thus Kornilov was defeated primarily by the soviets, and Kerensky consequently found himself under their domination. Furthermore, the Bolsheviks by this time were becoming increasingly influential within the soviets as public opinion veered more and more to the left. By October they had a majority in both the Petrograd and Moscow soviets. Lenin now decided that the time had come to overthrow Kerensky and effect the socialist revolution. But his own party still was not ready for the final plunge, fearing that they would not be able to retain power even if they were able to topple the Provisional Government. Lenin replied that 240,000 Bolshevik party members could govern Russia in the interest of the poor against the rich as easily as 130,000 landlords previously had governed in the interest of the rich against the poor. Finally, after threatening to resign, Lenin persuaded the Central Committee of his party to vote for revolution, and the date was set for November 7.

The actual revolution was anticlimactic. With almost no resistance the Bolshevik forces seized key positions in Petrograd—railway stations, bridges, banks, and government buildings. Blood was shed only at the Winter Palace, and casualties there totaled one Red soldier and five Red sailors. Kerensky managed to escape, and after a futile attempt to organize resistance, fled to exile abroad. Thus fell the Provisional Government with a humiliating casualness reminiscent of the end of Tsarism. There was no fighting, because Kerensky had as few dedicated supporters in November as Nicholas had had in March.

The easy victory of the Bolsheviks did not mean that they commanded the support of all the Russian people, or even the majority. This was demonstrated by the composition of the Constituent Assembly that was finally elected on November 25: Socialist Revolutionaries, 370; Bolsheviks, 175; Left Socialist Revolutionaries, 40; Cadets, 17; Mensheviks, 16; national groups, 86. The Assembly met in Petrograd on January 18, 1918, and, after holding one session, was dispersed by the Bolsheviks, who now had military power. Nevertheless, the make-up of the Assembly is revealing of the relative following enjoyed by the various parties at that time.

One of the first measures of the new Bolshevik government was to fulfill the promise of peace by signing with Germany the Brest-Litovsk Treaty on March 3, 1918. Its Draconian terms required the surrender by Russia of Poland, the Baltic provinces, Finland, the Ukraine, and parts of the Caucasus. These cessions involved 62 million people and 1¼ million square miles of territory producing three-fourths of Russia's iron and coal, and including half of her industrial plants and a third of her crop area.

In this manner Russia dropped out of World War I, and the new Bolshevik rulers proceeded to organize the Union of Soviet Socialist Republics with repercussions still being felt in all parts of the globe.

V. GLOBAL PHASE OF THE WAR: AMERICAN INTERVENTION

When World War I began, President Wilson immediately called upon his fellow countrymen to observe strict neutrality. This met with general approval, for the great majority of Americans wished to avoid involvement in the war. And yet, by 1917, Wilson himself was leading the country into war. Why the intervention in the face of this strong proneutrality sentiment?

One factor was the campaign for military preparedness. The National Security League, founded on December 1, 1914, was vigorously supported by military men, munitions makers, and politicians seeking an issue. They publicized the possibility of war with Germany and demanded compulsory military training and very substantial increases in the standing army and the navy. Wilson at first opposed this agitation, but for political reasons he sponsored the National Defense Act of June 3, 1916, which doubled the standing army, reorganized the National Guard, and provided for the training of officers in colleges and summer camps. Two months later another bill authorized a three-year program for major expansion of the navy. The intensive agitation and publicity connected with this military preparedness helped to prepare the nation psychologically for intervention in the war.

Very similar was the effect of the armed American incursion into Mexico between March, 1916, and February, 1917. This was precipitated when Francisco (Pancho) Villa, a half revolutionary and half bandit, raided the border town of Columbus in New Mexico, leaving behind nineteen dead. Villa's aim was to provoke American intervention and thereby to discredit and overthrow President Carranza. Wilson did respond by promptly ordering a punitive expedition of over 100,000 men under General John Pershing. Both Carranza and Wilson, however, wished to avoid full war, and arrangements finally were worked out making possible the withdrawal of American troops. Nevertheless, this strange interlude contributed to the building up of a war spirit in the United States by providing the thrills of military action without the grief and sacrifice.

Another factor operating in favor of intervention was the American financial and industrial commitment to the Allied cause. Bryan foresaw this pressure and urged from the beginning a "moral embargo" on loans to belligerents. This was rejected by Wilson, so that by the end of 1914 the House of Morgan was already "coordinating" Allied purchases of war material in the United States. To pay for these purchases the Allied powers first gave cash, then sold the bonds and stocks they held in the United States, and finally had to resort to large-scale borrowing. This situation inevitably generated pressures for American involvement in the war. Booming industries in the United States were dependent upon continued Allied orders, while American bankers had safes full of British and French paper that would become worthless if Germany emerged victorious.

Also noteworthy are the propaganda campaigns conducted by both sets of belligerents to influence American thinking. The Allies on the whole were more successful, partly because of superior skill and communication facilities, but also because their case was easier to justify and defend. British highandedness on the seas paled before the German invasion and occupation of Belgium. The alleged starvation in Germany resulting from England's blockade was soon forgotten when the U-boats began taking their toll of American lives.

This leads to what proved to be the most important single factor responsible for American intervention—Germany's submarine campaign against merchant ships. Germany refrained from waging unrestricted submarine warfare until 1917 for a simple military reason—there were not enough submarines available to guarantee Britain's defeat before the military strength of the United States could be brought to bear. But the number of U-boats rose rapidly—from 27 in February, 1915, to 74 in August, 1916, and to 103 in February, 1917. Thus by the beginning of 1917 the German military believed that if they were given a free hand, England could be brought to her knees within six months. This was the basic reason why the German government ordered unrestricted submarine warfare beginning on February 1, 1917. The order was issued with full realization that it would lead almost inevitably to American intervention. But it was logically calculated that the United States as a belligerent could not give more economic support to the Entente than it was already providing as a neutral, and that its armies would arrive too late in Europe to save Britain from being forced to surrender.

On March 1, 1917, the American press made public the notorious Zimmermann telegram sent by the then German foreign secretary to his minister in Mexico City. In case of war with the United States, the minister was to propose to the Carranza government an alliance whereby Mexico would intervene on Germany's side and would receive in return "generous financial aid" and also the restitution of the "lost territory in Texas, New Mexico, and Arizona." American public opinion was deeply shocked, especially in the Middle and Far West, where there had been relative apathy. At the same time the Germans were torpedoing American ships and American lives were being lost. To cap it all, the Tsarist regime was now overthrown, and the United States recognized the new Russian Provincial Government on March 20. Without reservations the United States now could join a league of democratic powers battling the autocracies of Central Europe.

Early in April the United States entered the war. Wilson's enunciation of objectives in his War Message of April 2 was necessarily couched in abstract and general terms. But in his address to the joint session of Congress on January 8, 1918, he set forth specific and detailed war aims in the form of his famous Fourteen Points. Outstanding among these were "open covenants of peace" as against secret diplomacy, freedom of the seas, removal of barriers to international trade, reduction of armaments, impartial adjustment of all colonial claims on the principle that the interests of the colonial peoples must have equal weight with the claims of colonial powers, and the application of the principle of self-determination in dealing with the various subject minorities in Central and Eastern Europe.

VI. ALLIED VICTORY

Eminent British and American naval experts are agreed that only a few more submarines would have enabled Germany to win the war. But in the end the Allies won out by stepping up ship construction and also by cutting down on ship sinkings. The latter was achieved by a variety of methods, including the development of an efficient convoy system, the camouflaging of merchantmen, the use of depth bombs containing large charges of high explosives, and the invention of hydrophones, which made possible the detection of nearby submarines. Thanks to this variety of devices the Allies passed the danger point early in 1918, when the construction of new ships for the first time surpassed the tonnage destroyed.

Once the U-boat threat was overcome, the United States was able to make effective use of her enormous economic potential. How decisive this was is made clear in the statistics concerning the productivity of the belligerents shown in Table 1.

The intervention of the United States gave the Allies decisive superiority in manpower as well as in war supplies. In the month of March, 1918, a total of 84,889 American soldiers reached the western front, and in July the number rose to 306,350. Thus a fresh new army was made available to the Allied commanders each month. The German High Command made a final desperate effort to avoid defeat by launching an all-out drive on Paris in the spring of 1918. Their effort was aided by the Brest-Litovsk Treaty which enabled them to transfer divisions from the eastern to the western front. In the greatest offensive of the war to that date, the Germans managed to reach within forty miles of the capital, but then were stopped. The turning point came when the Allies on July 18 launched a counterattack supported by fleets of tanks. The attack not only proved the value of the tank as an instrument for trench warfare, but also disclosed for the first time widespread defeatism in the German ranks. Whole battalions of Germans surrendered, sometimes to single infantrymen, while retiring German troops greeted fresh units going up to the line with shouts of *"Streikbrecher," "Kriegsverlängerer"* ("Strike breakers" and "War prolongers").

Meanwhile, Germany's allies were in even worse straits. The Bulgarian front crumbled when General Franchet d'Esperey, commander of the Allied forces in Saloniki, attacked in mid-September. On September 29, 1918, Bulgarian representatives signed an armistice, and on October 3 King Ferdinand abdicated in favor of his son Boris. Likewise in Turkey, British imperial forces were advancing victoriously in a two-pronged drive—one from Egypt up the Levant coast, and the other from the Persian Gulf up the Mesopotamian valley. At the same time an Allied force from Saloniki was marching upon Constantinople. Staggered by these setbacks and isolated by Bulgaria's surrender, the Turks accepted an armistice on October 30, 1918.

Most desperate was the position of Austria-Hungary. The numerous minorities were organizing national assemblies and proclaiming their independence. Even German-Austrians and Hungarians, who hitherto had ruled the empire, now were talking in terms of independent states of their own. At the same time the Italians were breaking through on the Piave, while Franchet d'Esperey was advancing up the Danube. On November 3 an Austro-Hungarian Armistice Com-

TABLE 1 PRODUCTION OF THE BELLIGERENT POWERS (In Millions of Tons)

	August 1, 1914		September 15, 1914		1917	
	Allies	*Central Powers*	*Allies*	*Central Powers*	*Allies*	*Central Powers*
Pig Iron	22	22	16	25	50	15
Steel	19	21	16	25	58	16
Coal	394	331	346	355	851	340

Source: F. Sternberg, *Capitalism and Socialism on Trial* (New York: Day, 1951), pp. 166–67. By permission of The John Day Company, Inc., publisher.

mission accepted the terms of the Italian High Command, and on November 6 Count Michael Karolyi, a liberal Hungarian leader, signed a separate armistice at Belgrade in behalf of Hungary. The ancient Hapsburg Empire finally reached its end on November 11, when Emperor Charles renounced his sovereign rights.

Meanwhile, the German position on the western front had steadily deteriorated. With American soldiers pouring in, Marshal Foch, the Allied commander in chief, was able to strike where and as he pleased. German casualties were outstripping replacements, and deserters were crowding into depots and railroad stations. General Ludendorff, in something of a panic, demanded on September 29 that the government initiate armistice negotiations "without delay" while the army was still reasonably intact. In preparation for the negotiations the Kaiser appointed his cousin, Prince Max of Baden, as the new chancellor. Prince Max, who had the reputation of a liberal and pacifist, requested President Wilson for negotiations on the basis of the Fourteen Points. There followed an exchange of notes between Berlin and Washington that extended over several weeks. A principal stumbling block was the Kaiser's adamant refusal to abdicate. His hand was forced, however, by mutiny in the German fleet at Kiel on November 3. The mutiny spread rapidly from port to port and then into the interior. Prince Max forced the issue by announcing the abdication of the emperor November 9. Two days later the armistice was signed and fighting ceased on the western front.

Thus ended the First World War—a war that lasted four years and three months, involved thirty sovereign states, overthrew four empires, gave birth to seven new nations, took approximately 8,500,000 combatant lives and 10,000,000 noncombatant, and cost $180.5 billion directly and $151.6 billion indirectly.

VII. PEACE SETTLEMENT

Separate peace treaties were signed with each of the Central Powers: the Versailles Treaty with Germany, June 28, 1919; the St. Germain Treaty with Austria, September 10, 1919; the Trianon Treaty with Hungary, March 22, 1919; the Neuilly Treaty with Bulgaria, November 27, 1919; and the Sèvres Treaty with Turkey, August 20, 1920. Three features of this over-all peace settlement are of significance for world history: the establishment of the League of Nations, the application of the principle of self-determination in Europe, and the failure to apply this principle outside Europe.

The League of Nations stands out in world history as the first worldwide association of nations pledged to mutual protection against aggression and to resolution of disputes by nonviolent methods. The idea of a league of this sort had been frequently proposed during the course of the war, so that this was one of the few features of the peace to which serious thought had been given before hostilities ended. The League Covenant, which was an integral part of the Versailles Treaty, came into effect in January, 1920. In a world made safe for democracy—as was then hoped—it was natural that the Covenant should provide the standard democratic pattern of parliament, cabinet, and civil service. The Assembly was the League's parliament, and each of the forty-two original member states had one vote in the Assembly. The Council was the League's cabinet, and consisted of the representatives of the five "Principal Allied and Associated Powers," each with a permanent seat, and in addition the representatives of four other powers "selected by the Assembly from time to time in its discretion." The original permanent members were England, the United States, France, Japan, and Italy, but the United States did not join the League. Subsequently, Germany and Russia were given permanent seats, and the number of nonpermanent members was increased to ten. Finally, there was the Secretariat, which functioned as the League's civil service, and consisted of a Secretary General and a staff.

The primary purpose of the League was to preserve the peace. Its members were to afford each other mutual protection against aggression, to submit disputes to arbitration or inquiry, and to abstain from war until three months after an award. The secondary purpose of the League was to concern itself with health, social, economic, and humanitarian problems of international scope. For this purpose there were established specialized League bodies such as the Health Organization, the Committee on Intellectual Cooperation, and the International Labor Organization, as well as numerous temporary advisory commissions. By and large, the League succeeded brilliantly in its secondary functions. It proved invaluable in improving international labor conditions, promoting world health, combatting the narcotic and slave traffics, and coping with economic crises. But we shall see that the League was not able to keep the peace, and since this was its *raison d'être,* the failure spelled the end of the entire organization.

The post-World War I settlement was characterized also by the redrawing of European frontiers on the basis of the principle of self-determination. This had been propounded fairly explicitly in the Fourteen Points, and was then officially implemented in the various peace treaties. The net result was a drastic revision of the map of Europe. Alsace-Lorraine was returned to France without question. Russia was deprived of most of her Baltic coastline by the establishment of the independent states of Finland, Latvia, Estonia, and Lithuania. An independent Poland was created, carved out of former Russian, German, and Hapsburg provinces; and likewise, Czechoslovakia emerged from the former Hapsburg Empire. The new state of Yugoslavia also appeared, comprising prewar Serbia and Montenegro together with various former Hapsburg territories inhabited by South Slavs. Rumania more than doubled in size as a result of her acquisitions from Austria-Hungary, Russia, and Bulgaria. Finally, from the remains of the old Hapsburg Empire also, there emerged the two rump states of Austria and Hungary.

It does not follow that the principle of self-determination was invariably respected in the drawing of the new frontiers. Indeed, there were bitter protests concerning the sizable German minorities in Poland and Czechoslovakia, and the Russian minorities in Poland, Czechoslovakia, and Rumania. The explanation is to be found partly in the fact that the numerous ethnic groups in Central and Eastern Europe were so inextricably mixed that no frontiers could be drawn without creating considerable minorities on one side or the other. The inevitable minorities, however, were substantially increased because frontiers sometimes were drawn to comply with strategic considerations as well as to satisfy nationalist aspirations. This was why the Sudeten Germans were left in Czechoslovakia, why the Tyrol Germans were left in Italy, and why the union of Austria and Germany was specifically forbidden by the St. Germain Treaty even though it would have been in accord with popular will, at least in the immediate postwar years. Yet despite these deviations, the new frontiers were infinitely more in accord with nationalist aspirations than the old. The number of the minority peoples was much smaller after World War I than before.

Although the peacemakers generally applied self-determination in Europe, they definitely did not do so outside Europe. This discrimination was clearly evident in Wilson's Fourteen Points, which specifically spelled out how the aspirations of the various European minorities were to be satisfied. By contrast, Point 5 declared that in the colonies "the interests of the populations concerned must have equal weight with the equitable claims of the government whose title is to be determined." The significant point here is the reference to the "interests" rather than to the "wishes" of the colonial peoples. Needless to say, it was the Europeans themselves who decided what these "interests" were, and the outcome was a modified form of imperial rule known as the mandate system.

Article 22 of the League Covenant referred to the inhabitants of the colonies taken from the Central Powers as "peoples not yet able to stand by themselves under the strenuous conditions of the modern world." The article accordingly provided that the "tutelage of such peoples should be entrusted to advanced nations who, by reason of their resources, their experience, or their geographical position, can best undertake this responsibility . . . and that this tutelage should be exercised by them as Mandatories on behalf of the League." It is significant that this provision for "tutelage" under "Mandatories" was not extended to the colonies of the victorious Allies, whose inhabitants in many cases were at a similar level of development or lack of development.

The Mandates article divided the foreign and overseas territories of Germany and the Ottoman Empire into Class A, B, and C mandates. The category varied according to the level of development of the territory concerned. On this basis the former Ottoman possessions were put in Class A, and the German colonies in B and C. Of the Ottoman territories, Mesopotamia and Palestine were allotted to Britain as the Mandatory Power, and Syria and Lebanon to France. Of the German colonies, the greater part of Tanganyika went to Britain and the remainder to Belgium; Togoland and the Cameroons were divided between Britain and France; South-West Africa was allotted to the Union of South Africa; and Germany's Pacific islands north of the equator went to Japan, and those south of the equator to Australia and New Zealand.

The Mandatory Powers assumed specific obligations toward the inhabitants of the mandated territories. For fulfillment of these obligations they were accountable to the Permanent Mandates Commission, and were required to report annually to the Council of the League of Nations. Though neither the Commission nor the League itself had authority to coerce a recalcitrant Mandatory Power, yet it is significant that European states for the first time accepted certain specified procedures. The procedures varied according to the type of mandate. In the case of Class A, the Mandates article looked forward specifically to the granting of independence as soon as feasible. The duty of the Mandatory Power was merely "the rendering of administrative advice and assistance . . . until such time as they [the people of the territory] are able to stand alone. The wishes of these communities must be a principal consideration in the selection of the Mandatory." But for B and C Class mandates, there was no reference to eventual independence. The obligation rather was to provide administration in accord with the interests of the inhabitants.

Although the mandate system represented a certain improvement over the traditional division of colonial booty by the victors in a war, nevertheless it is strongly reminiscent of the 1815 settlement in its ignoring of national aspirations. We shall see that the inhabitants of the Ottoman territories did not want mandated status, and were violently opposed to France as Mandatory Power. Their wishes were directly flouted when Syria and Lebanon were allotted to France. Even in the case of some of the Class B mandates in Africa, there was acute dissatisfaction with the arrangements made. It is not surprising, then, that just as the ignoring of nationalist wishes in 1815 led to a long series of revolutions in Europe during the nineteenth century, so this mandate system was to lead to uprisings in the colonial world during the post-war years.

VIII. WORLD WAR I IN WORLD HISTORY

The overriding significance of World War I from a global viewpoint is that it began the undermining of Europe's supremacy—a process that was completed following World War II. The undermining was evident in at least three regards: the economic decline, the political crisis, and the weakening hold over the colonies.

Before 1914, Europe's economy was dependent to a considerable degree upon massive overseas investments, yielding massive annual returns. During World War I, however, Britain lost a quarter of her foreign investments, France a third, and Germany lost all. The reverse of this trend may be seen in the new financial strength of the United States. In 1914 the United States owed about $4 billion to European investors, but the war reversed this relationship, for the Allied governments were forced to sell their American holdings to pay for war materials, and then to borrow in the United States from both the government and from private sources. Thus, by 1919 the United States had become a creditor nation to the tune of $3.7 billion; by 1930 this had risen to $8.8 billion. The same pattern is evident in industry, for many European industrial areas were devastated, while American factories mushroomed spectacularly under the impetus of unlimited wartime demand. By 1929 the United States was responsible for no less than 42.2 per cent of world industrial output, an amount greater than that of all the countries of Europe, including Russia. Thus, the economic relationships between Europe and the United States were reversed as a result of World War I. Europe no longer was the banker and the workshop of the world, as she had been during the nineteenth century. Leadership in both areas had crossed the Atlantic.

The war gutted Europe politically as well as economically. Prior to 1914 Europe had been the source of the basic political ideas and institutions of modern times. Their impact, as we have seen, had been felt in all corners of the globe. The holocaust of war, however, left Europeans demoralized and unbelieving. In all parts of the Continent the old order was being questioned and challenged. In a confidential memorandum of March, 1919, the British premier, David Lloyd George, wrote, "There is a deep sense not only of discontent, but of anger and revolt, amongst the workmen against pre-war conditions. The whole existing order in its political, social and economic aspects is questioned by the masses of the people from one end of Europe to the other."[2]

In this revolutionary crisis, many Europeans looked for guidance to two non-Europeans, the American Wilson and the Russian Lenin. Wilson's Fourteen Points had stirred up a ferment of democratic hope and expectancy. When he stepped on the bloodsoaked soil of Europe in December, 1918, huge crowds greeted Wilson with delirious enthusiasm as "King of Humanity," "Savior," "Prince of Peace." At the same time large masses were receptive to Lenin's call for revolution and for a new social order. In imitation of the Bolshevik Revolution, soviets were set up in Berlin, Hamburg, and Budapest. Demonstrations were staged in the streets of London, Paris, and Rome. Wilson's confidante, Colonel House, wrote in his diary on March 22, 1919: "Rumblings of discontent every day. The people want peace. Bolshevism is gaining ground everywhere. Hungary has just succumbed. We are sitting upon an open powder magazine and some day a spark may ignite it."[3]

Finally, Europe's hegemony was undermined by World War I because of the repercussions in the overseas colonies. The spectacle of one bloc of European powers fighting another to the bitter end damaged the prestige of the white master irreparably. No longer was he regarded as almost divinely ordained to rule over colored multitudes. Equally disruptive was the participation in the war of millions of colonials as soldiers or as laborers. Indian divisions fought on the western front and in Mesopotamia; many Africans in French uniform fought in northern France; and large numbers of Chinese and Indochinese served in labor battalions behind the lines. Needless to say, the colonials who returned home after such experiences were not likely to be as deferential to European overlords as before. For example, a French Governor-General of Indochina wrote in 1926: "The war which covered Europe with blood has . . . awakened in lands far distant from us a feeling of independence. . . . All has changed in the past few years. Both men and ideas and Asia herself are being transformed."[4]

Revolutionary ideas in the colonies were also spread by propaganda associated with the conduct of the war. It is true that Wilson's Fourteen Points had referred only to the "interest" rather than to the desires of the colonial peoples. But this was an overfine distinction in a time of war, and the revolutionary phrase "self-determination of peoples" left its imprint upon the colonial world as well as upon Europe. Equally influential were the ideologies of socialism and communism. Before World War I, Asian intellectuals had been inspired by Western liberalism and nationalism. They had quoted Voltaire, Mazzini, and John Stuart Mill. But their sons now were likely to quote Marx, Lenin, or Harold Laski. Dr. Sun Yat-sen, on July 25, 1919, gave evidence of this shift when he declared, "If the people of China wish to be free . . . its only ally and brother in the struggle for national freedom are the Russian workers and peasants of the Red Army."[5]

All these repercussions of World War I on the colonial world inevitably had profound political consequences. One of the few who saw this clearly was the American black leader W. E. B. DuBois, who in 1918 wrote the following remarkable forecast of the world to come.

This war is an end and, also, a beginning. Never again will darker people of the world occupy just the place they had before. Out of this place will rise, soon or late, an independent China, a self-governing India, an Egypt with representative institutions, an Africa for the Africans, and not merely for business exploitation. Out of this war will rise, too, an American Negro with the right to vote and the right to work and the right to live without insult.[6]

SUGGESTED READING

L. ALBERTINI, *The Origins of the War of 1914,* 2 vols., trans. and ed. I. M. MASSEY (Oxford Univ., 1953); H. W. BALDWIN, *World War I: An Outline History* (Harper, 1962); E. H. CARR, *The Bolshevik Revolution, 1917–1923,* 3 vols. (Macmillan, 1951–1953); R. W. LEOPOLD, "The Problem of American Intervention, 1917: An Historical Restrospect" *World Politics,* II (1950), 405–25; A. J. MAYER, *Politics and Diplomacy of Peace-making. Containment and Counterrevolution at Versailles 1918–1919* (Knopf, 1967).

chapter thirty-four

Nationalist Uprisings in the Colonial World

Since the day of Japan's victory over Russia, the peoples of Asia have cherished the hope of shaking off the yoke of European oppression, a hope which has given rise to a series of independence movements—in Egypt, Persia, Turkey, Afghanistan, and finally in India. . . . If we want to regain our rights, we must resort to force.—Sun Yat-Sen, 1924

World War I was followed by a wave of revolutions in the colonial territories. The roots of these revolutions go back to the pre-1914 years, but it was the war itself that provided the immediate stimulus. The final outcomes varied, with the Turks at one extreme winning most of their objectives, the Rif tribesmen at the other going down to bloody defeat, and, in between, the Egyptians, Iraqis, Indians, and others winning modest constitutional concessions. In the light of retrospect, these uprisings represent the prelude to the elemental upheavals that finally ended the European empires during the two decades following World War II.

I. TURKEY

The most spectacular and successful of all the post-World War I colonial revolts against European domination was that of the Turks. They had suffered disastrous defeat during the war, and had then been compelled to accept humiliating armistice and peace terms. Yet they bounced back, defeating their enemies in armed conflict, and winning a new treaty with more favorable terms. Thus, of all the Central Powers, only primitive and despised Turkey proved capable of turning upon the victorious Allies and forcing them to accept a revision of the peace settlement. To understand this extraordinary outcome it is necessary to review the tangled wartime diplomacy concerning the Ottoman Empire.

Wartime Diplomacy

Britain was the prime mover behind most of the diplomacy involving the Middle East during the war years. She was responsible for three sets of often-conflicting agreements—with her own allies, with Arab representatives, and with the Zionists.

The agreements among the Allies consisted of four secret treaties providing for the partitioning of the Ottoman Empire: The Treaty of Constantinople (March-April, 1915), the Treaty of London (April 26, 1915), the Sykes-Picot Agreement (April 26, 1916), and the Saint-Jean-de-Maurienne Treaty (April, 1917). These treaties provided for the postwar partitioning of the Ottoman Empire as follows: Syria to France, southwest Asia Minor to Italy, Mesopotamia and the Haifa and Acre enclaves on the Mediterranean to Britain, and finally, Constantinople, the Straits, and northeast Asia Minor to Russia. Thus the Turks were to lose not only their Arab provinces but also most of their own Asia Minor homeland.

These secret treaties were in direct conflict with certain agreements that Britain was concluding at this time with the leading dignitary among the Arabs, Emir Hussein of the Hashimite family, Keeper of the Holy Places and Prince of Mecca. Early in 1914 Hussein's second son, Abdullah, in passing through Cairo, sounded out the British about possible aid for an Arab uprising against the Turks. As soon as Turkey joined the Central Powers in November, 1914, the British eagerly renewed these contacts. Protracted negotiations between Hussein and Sir Henry McMahon, British High Commissioner in Egypt, culminated in a military alliance and in an ambiguous political understanding that was to cause endless troubles in later years. In return for an Arab revolt against the Turks, the British agreed to recognize the independence of the Arab countries south of the 37th latitude, including the Arabian Peninsula. In the course of the correspondence, which dragged on between July, 1915, and March, 1916, McMahon stipulated that the agreement could not infringe upon unspecified French interests in Syria. Hussein replied that he would not consent to any Arab land becoming the possession of any power, meaning France. In order to avoid delay of the Arab revolt, this disputed point remained unclarified, with unfortunate results a few years later.

While the British Foreign Office was dealing with Hussein, the India Office was negotiating with Ibn-Saud, Sultan of the Nejd, whose territories were nearer the Persian Gulf. On December 26, 1915, an agreement was reached by which the India Office recognized Ibn-Saud's independence in return for his benevolent neutrality during the war. That a different British government agency was involved did not alter the fact that contradictory commitments had been made to Ibn-Saud and to Hussein.

More ominous for the future was another conflicting commitment, this one to Lord Rothschild of the World Zionist Organization. Zionism was a nationalist movement that had developed among European Jews in the last quarter of the nineteenth century as a reaction against mounting anti-Semitism. The World Zionist Organization, established in Basel in 1897, had vainly sought permission from the Ottoman government to set up a Jewish settlement company in Palestine. With Turkey's involvement in World War I, Zionist leaders in England and the United States seized the opportunity to press for an Allied commitment to create a Jewish commonwealth in Palestine upon the demise of the Ottoman Empire. Government leaders in Britain were won over to the Zionist position, influenced partly by the desire to earn for the Allied cause the support of numerous and influential Zionist organizations in Russia and the United States. Also it was feared, with some justification, that Germany and Turkey were ready to make concessions to attract international Zionist support. Consequently, on November 2, 1917, Lord Balfour wrote to Lord Rothschild that the British Government favored the establishment in Palestine of a "national home for the Jewish people

. . . it being clearly understood that nothing shall be done which may prejudice the civil and religious rights of existing non-Jewish communities in Palestine. . . ." It is evident that this Balfour Declaration conflicted with both the secret treaties and the Hussein-McMahon agreement.

In the end it was Britain and France who determined the settlement, for the United States was withdrawing into isolation, Russia was convulsed by civil war and intervention, while Italy was immobilized by internal dissension. The Treaty of Sèvres (August 10, 1920), then, was essentially of Anglo-French origin, and its provisions reflected its origin. France secured Syria as a mandate, while Britain obtained Mesopotamia and Palestine, in addition to a protectorate over Egypt. The Dodecanese Islands were ceded to Italy, while Greece, thanks to the artful diplomacy of her Premier Venizelos, obtained several Aegean islands, Eastern Thrace, and the right to administer the Smyrna region for five years, after which its final disposition was to be determined by a plebiscite. Armenia and the Kingdom of Hejaz were recognized as independent. Finally, Soviet Russia, in armed conflict with Allied interventionist forces and having published and repudiated the secret treaties that the Tsarist ministers had signed, did not obtain Constantinople and the Straits. Instead, this strategic territory was left under Turkish sovereignty, though the Straits were to be demilitarized and placed under international control.

These provisions, so contrary to the promises made to the Arabs and to the professed Allied principle of self-determination, aroused a wave of armed resistance throughout the Middle East. A combination of factors enabled the Turks to scrap the Sèvres Treaty altogether, while the Arabs won piecemeal concessions after years of stubborn struggle.

Republican Victory

The George Washington of modern Turkey is Mustafa Kemal, later known as Atatürk, or Foremost Turk. He won fame for his successful defense of the Dardanelles during the war, and now he led the opposition to the Sèvres Treaty. He was perfectly willing to surrender the Arab provinces of the old empire, but he refused to accept the cession of parts of Asia Minor, and the relegation of other parts to spheres of influence. He traveled about in the Turkish hinterland, organizing resistance to the Allies and their puppet sultan in the capital. By September, 1919, Kemal had summoned a nationalist congress which adopted a National Pact consisting of six principles. These included self-determination, abolition of capitulations, security for Constantinople, and a new Straits settlement. In the elections of October, 1919, Kemal's followers won a majority, and when Parliament met in January, 1920, it adopted the National Pact. Kemal now made the final break by summoning his nationalist deputies to Angora in central Asia Minor. There, on April 23, 1920, they denounced the Sultan's regime and established a provisional government with Kemal as president.

The nationalists triumphed over seemingly overwhelming odds. One reason was the courageous and inspired leadership of Kemal. Another was the loyal support of the mass of the Turkish people, who were united to an unprecedented degree by the highhandedness of the Allies in Constantinople, and even more by the landing of Greek troops in Smyrna in the spring of 1919. Finally, Kemal exploited serious differences amongst the Allies and concluded separate treaties with the French and Italians, thereby isolating the Greeks in Smyrna and paving the way for their defeat. Even with the Russians, the traditional enemies of the

Turks, Kemal was now able to reach an agreement, because both were at war with Britain.

This series of treaties fundamentally transformed the balance of power in the Middle East. Turkey and Russia now presented a united front, while the Allies were so divided that only Britain and Greece were left to enforce the terms of the Sèvres Treaty. And Britain, because of her worldwide commitments and the state of public opinion at home, could do no more than maintain her ships in Constantinople and the Straits. In other words, the Greeks now were left alone in Smyrna to face the Turkish nationalist upsurge in Asia Minor.

Fighting between the Greeks and the Turks began at the end of March, 1921. At first the Greeks met with weak resistance, because the opposition consisted of little more than guerrilla bands. But the population was so hostile that fully two-thirds of Greek manpower had to be used to guard transportation lines. The turning point came when the invaders reached the Sakarya River in the heart of Asia Minor. Kemal struck back, and the overextended Greeks were stopped dead and then pushed back. Retreat brought demoralization and eventually a stampede. By September 9, 1922, Kemal was riding triumphantly into Smyrna. Not only the Greek army, but also Greek civilians who had lived for centuries in the Smyrna region, were evacuated.

Kemal now was in a position to demand revision of the Sèvres Treaty. After protracted negotiations the Lausanne Treaty was signed on July 24, 1923. This returned to Turkey Eastern Thrace and some of the Aegean Islands. Also Turkey was to pay no reparations, and the capitulations were abolished in return for a promise of judicial reform. The Straits remained demilitarized, and open to ships of all nations in time of peace or war if Turkey remained neutral. If Turkey was at war, enemy ships, but not neutrals, might be excluded. Finally, a separate agreement provided for the compulsory exchange of the Greek minority in Constantinople for the Turkish minority in Western Thrace and Macedonia.

New Turkey

The Lausanne Treaty represented a great personal triumph for Kemal. The decrepit Ottoman Empire at long last was dead after half a millennium of checkered history. On October 29, 1923, the Turkish Republic was formally proclaimed with Kemal as president. Having created the new Turkey, Kemal now turned to the equally difficult task of creating new Turks. He ruthlessly swept away the outdated institutions of the past, as reform followed reform in a great torrent of change.

October 14, 1923—Capital of the Turkish state moved from Constantinople to Angora in the heart of Turkish Anatolia.

March 3, 1924—Caliphate abolished, and all members of the Ottoman dynasty banished from Turkey.

April 20, 1924—Adoption of a constitution providing for a president, premier, cabinet, and a grand national assembly elected quadrennially by indirect vote.

September 2, 1925—All religious orders and houses suppressed, and individuals prohibited from living as members of orders and from wearing the costumes or bearing the titles associated therewith.

January–February, 1926—Introduction of new civil, criminal, and commercial law codes, based respectively on Swiss, Italian, and German systems.

August 17, 1926—Polygamy abolished.

November 3, 1928—Latin alphabet introduced in place of intricate Arabic script, the change being applied first to newspapers and then to books.

March 28, 1930—Place names changed: Constantinople to Istanbul; Angora to Ankara;
Smyrna to Izmir; Adrianople to Edirne, and so forth.
December 14, 1934—Women given the right to vote and sit in the assembly.

By the time of Kemal's death on November 10, 1938, the New Turkey was
definitely established. It is true that the newness was more horizontal than verti-
cal. A large proportion of the peasantry, which constituted the great majority of
the population, still clung to their age-old Moslem ideas and customs. On the
other hand, the new elite that governed the country had been Europeanized in its
way of life and way of thought. Many of the peasants also had changed sufficiently
to have established rapport with the government unprecedented in past centuries.
To a much greater degree than any other Moslem country, Turkey had become,
as Kemal had planned, a modern nation.

II. ARAB MIDDLE EAST

While the Turks were successfully scrapping the Sèvres Treaty, the Arabs were
stubbornly resisting the Mandatory Powers to which they had been assigned.
Contrary to the Hussein-McMahon Agreement, Syria-Lebanon had been given as
a mandate to France, Mesopotamia and Palestine had been made British mandates, and full British control had been established in Egypt. This high-handed
parceling out of Arab lands was bound to lead to trouble, because the war itself
had stimulated tremendous national sentiment among the Arabs. Allied propaganda concerning national self-determination inevitably had its effect on Arab
opinion. The successful operations of Arab military units also aroused national
consciousness and pride. Equally significant was the widespread suffering and
outright starvation caused by the disruption of trade during the war. Finally
there was the all-important religious consideration, especially for the fellahin in
the villages. This is borne out by the fact that Arab nationalist leaders in the
cities often were surprised by the degree of support they received from the peasantry with whom they had little contact. The inference is that the village uprisings were spontaneous movements motivated by religious feelings against the
infidel foreign rulers.

This combination of factors explains the postwar Arab struggle for independence. A common pattern is discernible in the evolution of the struggle. First, an
explosion of defiance and armed revolt occurred during the years immediately
following the peace treaties. Then Britain and France gradually restored order
and reasserted their authority. Finally they granted varying degrees of autonomy,
which did not entirely satisfy the nationalists, but which did preserve an uneasy
peace until World War II.

In Egypt, the mandatory relationship, strictly speaking, did not exist. But the
situation was essentially similar because Britain at the beginning of the war had
repudiated the nominal Ottoman suzerainty and had declared the country a
British protectorate. Immediately, the nationalist Wafd party organized violent
opposition. In 1922 Britain proclaimed Egypt "an independent sovereign state"
but reserved for herself control of foreign affairs and of external security, as well
as protection of minorities and of foreign interests. The nationalists rejected this
illusory independence and continued the struggle. One of their weapons was terrorism, and they succeeded in 1924 in assassinating the British head of the Egyptian army, Sir Lee Stack. The nationalists also could count on popular support,
which was manifested in the repeated electoral victories they won. Finally in 1936

a compromise settlement was reached with the signing of a twenty-year alliance treaty. Britain undertook to end her military occupation of the country and to arrange for Egypt's admission to the League of Nations. In return, Egypt agreed to stand by Britain in time of war; to accept the British garrison stationed for the defense of the Suez Canal; and also to continue the joint British-Egyptian administration of the Sudan. Nationalist leaders were far from satisfied with this settlement. But they accepted it as the best available under the circumstances and they waited for the first opportunity to abolish the obnoxious vestiges of foreign control.

Nationalist opposition in Iraq followed much the same course as in Egypt. A widespread armed revolt broke out in 1920. The British first restored order and then attempted to conciliate nationalist feeling by enthroning as king the third son of Hussein, Prince Faisal. The following year, in 1922, the British negotiated a treaty of alliance in which they retained such controls as they deemed necessary to protect their interests. The nationalists remained dissatisfied and continued their agitation. Finally an alliance treaty was concluded in 1930, by which Britain agreed to terminate the mandate and to support Iraq's application for admission to the League of Nations. In return, Iraq agreed that Britain should maintain three air bases in the country and also should have full use of railways, rivers, and ports in time of war. In 1932 Iraq became a member of the League of Nations, the first Arab country to gain that distinction. As in the case of Egypt, however, nationalist circles remained dissatisfied.

In Syria and Lebanon, the French proved less flexible than the British and therefore less successful. Nationalist outbreaks occurred periodically, the most serious being in 1925, when the French were forced to shell Damascus in order to retain control. Finally in 1936 the French government negotiated treaties with Syria and Lebanon modeled after the Anglo-Iraqi treaty of 1930. Neither of these treaties, however, was ratified by the French Chamber of Deputies, so that the conflict remained unresolved when World War II began.

In Palestine the situation was unique because it quickly deteriorated into a bitter three-way struggle involving Britain, Arabs, and Jews. The Arabs maintained that the Balfour Declaration concerning a Jewish "nationalist home" was in flagrant contravention of prior commitments made to the Arabs in the Mc-Mahon correspondence. Britain attempted to appease the Arabs by setting apart in 1921 the interior portion of the country as the independent state of Transjordan. This was exempt from all the clauses of the mandate concerning the establishment of a Jewish home. Furthermore, the British installed Faisal's elder brother, Abdullah, as ruler of Transjordan. This tactic proved eminently satisfactory so far as Transjordan itself was concerned. Abdullah always cooperated loyally with the British, particularly since the poverty of his country made him dependent on subsidies from London. Probably the most effective military unit in the Arab world was Transjordan's Arab legion, supported by British funds and led by the British General John Glubb.

In Palestine proper, however, the triangle conflict became increasingly fierce as Jewish immigrants poured in and the apprehensive Arabs struck back against both the Jews and the British. Article 6 of the mandate required Britain to "facilitate" Jewish immigration and to "encourage close settlement by Jews on the land." But the same article also provided that "the rights and position of other sections of the population" were to be safeguarded. The British apparently felt at the time that the two orders were not necessarily contradictory. They expected that Jewish immigrants would never reach such proportions as to impinge upon "the rights and position" of the Arabs. They could not have foreseen the repercussions of Hitler's rise to power in 1933. Jewish immigration jumped from 9,553 in 1932 to 30,327 in 1933, 42,359 in 1934 and 61,854 in 1935. The total Jewish population in Palestine rose from 65,000 in 1919 to 450,000 in 1939.

So long as the Jewish influx had been modest, the Arabs had not raised serious objections. In fact they had welcomed the Jews with their money and energy and skills. They themselves had benefited substantially from the miracles the Jews had performed in restoring exhausted land, founding industries, and checking diseases. But when the stream of immigration became a torrent, the Arabs reacted violently, and understandably so. Arab attacks against the Jews became increasingly frequent and serious. Highlights were the Wailing Wall disorders in 1929, the Arab "National Political Strike" in 1936, and the Arab Rebellion of 1938. The British response was to send out Royal Commissions following the major outbreaks. By the time of World War II several commissions had investigated the situation and had vacillated in their recommendations as they sought to satisfy three distinct and conflicting interests—Jewish Zionist aspirations, Arab nationalist demands, and British imperial interests. The White Paper of May, 1939, for example, proposed that Palestine become an independent state in ten years, and that definite limits be placed on Jewish immigration and land purchases. Both Arabs and Jews rejected this proposal, and the Palestine controversy remained as far from settlement as ever when World War II began.

III. NORTH AFRICA

The territory west of Egypt, known as the Maghreb, had gradually fallen under European rule during the nineteenth century. France conquered Algeria in the 1830s, Tunisia in 1881, and Morocco in 1912, while Italy invaded Libya in 1911. The latter invasion provoked a stubborn resistance that lasted into the postwar period and that represented the beginning of the Maghreb's general struggle for liberation.

The Italians had little difficulty in defeating the small Turkish garrisons in Libya in 1911. But the native Arab and Berber population continued the struggle with arms left by the departing Turks. The Senussi religious order organized and led the resistance so effectively that by the summer of 1915 the Italians were confined to half a dozen points along the coast. After World War I the Italians again tried to impose their authority over the entire country, but with little success. They held the coast, but much of the interior remained under Arab control.

The Italian failure in Libya was a serious blow to European prestige, but it was soon overshadowed by the spectacular defeats inflicted on the Spaniards by the Rif mountaineers of Morocco. For centuries the Spanish possessions in Morocco had been limited to four tiny enclaves along the Mediterranean coast. Meanwhile, France had been pushing out from Algeria, establishing a protectorate over Tunisia in 1881, and beginning the occupation of Morocco after the Algeciras Conference of 1906. This stimulated the Spaniards to similar action, so they reached an agreement with the French for the division of Morocco between them, and began in 1909 to advance into the interior. Their pace was slow, so that for several years there was little resistance. Then suddenly, in the summer of 1921, they suffered a disastrous defeat—the worst inflicted on a Western army since the Ethiopians defeated the Italians at Adowa in 1896.

Abd-el-Krim, leader of the Rif tribesmen, was responsible for the unexpected blow. Having been well educated in Spain, he knew the value of Western technology and how to use it. The startled Spaniards poured in 150,000 men, but failed to recover much ground. In the summer of 1923 they offered Krim autonomy, but, flushed with victory, he demanded full independence. By 1924 the Spaniards again were confined to the coast, except for a few interior garrisons, which were usually encircled by the Rif. For all practical purposes Krim now was the master of virtually all of Spanish Morocco.

The following year Krim challenged the French as well as the Spaniards—a move that led directly to his downfall. Krim began his offensive on April 13, 1925, and was so successful that Spain and France concluded a pact for joint action against the Rif, including a land and sea blockade of Rif territory in order to stop gunrunning.

Krim's failure to win complete victory in his initial offensive meant the beginning of the end. The combined Franco-Spanish resources were so overwhelmingly superior that eventual defeat of the Rif was inevitable. By the fall of 1925, the 60,000 Rif troops were facing Franco-Spanish forces totaling 280,000 men. The odds were too great, especially since Krim did not succeed in raising a general revolt in the French rear. During the winter and spring he suffered a succession of defeats, until he surrendered on May 27, 1926. Krim's exploits, although they had failed to drive out the French, had aroused the entire Maghreb and inspired the various nationalist parties that were organized in the 1930's and that successfully fought for freedom after World War II.

IV. PERSIA

Shortly before World War I, Persia had been divided into British and Russian spheres of influence. (See Chapter 27, section V.) When the war began, the shah announced an official policy of neutrality; because he lacked the power to enforce this policy, the northern sections of the country were soon overrun by Turkish and Russian troops, and the southern by British. The end of the war found the British in control of most of the country, thanks to the revolution and civil war that occupied the Russians. The British were determined to maintain this control both because of the importance of Persia for India's defense and because of the oil properties of the Anglo-Persian Oil Company, whose crucial significance for the imperial navy had been amply demonstrated during the war.

Meanwhile, the Russians had not been idle. On January 14, 1918, they denounced the 1907 Anglo-Russian convention, and on June 26, 1918, they announced the nullification of all Russian concessions and special privileges in Persia and all Persian debts to Tsarist Russia. Being faced with civil war and intervention, the Bolsheviks presumably made these sweeping concessions in the hope of placating their Persian neighbors and stimulating anti-Western popular uprisings in the colonial world. Pursuing their policy further, the Russians signed a formal Persian-Soviet Treaty of Friendship on February 26, 1921. Of benefit to the Persians were the official cancellation of all outstanding debts, surrender of all physical commercial installations in Persia, and the nullification of all concessions, extraterritorial rights, and other special privileges. On the other hand, certain provisions favored the Russians, including the denial to Persia of the right to grant the surrendered concessions in the five northern provinces to any other power, and the right of the Russians to send troops into Persia if any foreign power were using Persian territory as a base of operations against Russia.

While this treaty was under negotiation, Persian political life was becoming ever more anarchical. One prime minister, for example, resigned on January 19, 1921, resumed office four days later, formed on February 3 a cabinet which resigned on the 6th, and formed another cabinet on the 16th, which was overthrown by a coup d'état on the 21st. The coup was engineered by Reza Khan, a colonel in the Persian Cossack Brigade that had been organized by the Russians before World War I. For the next two decades the story of Persia is the story of this dominating personality who rose to become the great reforming shah of his country.

Reza was an austere, single-minded military man of exceptional courage and determination. Through sheer ability and concentration on military duties he rose from the ranks and won the respect and loyalty of his men. His chance came when the British compelled the Russian officers of the Cossack Division to resign their commissions in the fall of 1920. Reza moved into the power vacuum, and by February, 1921, he was strong enough to lead the coup that overthrew the government. From now on his rise was rapid. Immediately after the coup he became commander in chief of the Persian army. A few weeks later he was appointed Minister of War. After making and unmaking several ministries, he became Prime Minister himself on October 28, 1923. The ruler, Ahmad Shah of the Kajar dynasty, now left Persia for the Riviera, and two years later, on December 15, 1925, Reza assumed the throne, founding the Pahlevi dynasty which has survived to the present.

Despite his eccentricities and excesses, Reza Shah's reign was like a breath of fresh air in the prevailing atmosphere of corruption, incompetence, and obscurantism. Indeed, the Shah is reminiscent of Kemal, whom he admired and imitated. His first move was to modernize and strengthen the army, which enabled him to resist undue foreign pressures and also to assert the central government's authority over tribal chieftains who had been *de facto* independent since the mid-nineteenth century.

Reza Shah also sought to modernize his country's economy. The most spectacular manifestation was the building of the trans-Iranian railroad. It was impressive, if not economically practical, requiring over 4,000 bridges and 200 tunnels in its course of 870 miles. Completed in 1939, it was destined to play a key role in transporting military supplies to the Soviet Union during World War II. The railroad was typical of the Shah's economic ventures. There was no coordinated plan, and individual projects were not conceived in the light of the over-all economic needs of the nation. By the time of the Shah's abdication in 1941, a considerable number of factories had been built, including textile mills, cement plants, sugar refineries, and cigarette factories; yet despite high protective tariffs, almost all operated at a loss.

Like Kemal, Reza Shah attacked various symbols of the past. He forbade the use of honorary titles, abolished the veil for women, and ordered men to wear European hats or caps. Above all else, nationalism was emphasized, and foreign influences were rooted out wherever possible. Arabic words were purged from the Persian language, and modern buildings were modeled after the Achaemenid style of architecture found in the ruins of the magnificent palaces of old. Typical of this nationalism was the adoption in 1934, in place of "Persia," of the name "Iran," harking back to Indo-European ancestors three millennia removed.

Reza Shah's reign ended abruptly with his abdication on September 16, 1941. During the preceding years he had been leaning increasingly toward Nazi Germany. Trade with Germany rose to number one place, while German technicians, teachers, merchants, and tourists increased steadily in numbers. With Hitler's attack on the U.S.S.R. in June, 1941, the Shah received several joint Soviet-British notes requesting him to expel the Germans from Iran. His replies were considered unsatisfactory, and on August 25, 1941, Soviet and British forces occupied the country. On September 16 Reza Shah abdicated in favor of his son, Mohammed Reza Pahlevi, the present ruler.

In retrospect, Reza Shah did not have so profound an impact on his country as Kemal did on Turkey. Kemal profited from a preceding military disaster of such magnitude that it made it easier to abolish outmoded institutions and practices. And the Turks, having been subject to Western influences longer, were more receptive to them. Nevertheless, Reza Shah stands head and shoulders above his predecessors, and his reign represents a major turning point in modern Iranian history.

V. INDIA

At the turn of the century British rule in India seemed perfectly secure for the foreseeable future. In 1912, a great imperial durbar was held in Delhi to celebrate the coronation of King George V. Amidst pageantry and splendor, King George received the homage of India's princes and potentates without a voice being raised in dissent. In 1914, India rallied solidly behind Britain at war. The princes contributed generous financial aid, while no less than 900,000 Indians served in the British army as combatants and another 300,000 as laborers.

Only three decades after World War 1 British rule in India came to an end. One reason for this extraordinary outcome was the impact of the war itself—the influence of slogans about self-determination, and the unsettling effect of overseas service upon hundreds of thousands of soldiers who returned with new ideas and attitudes. Unrest was stimulated also by a series of disasters in the immediate postwar years. The failure of the monsoon in 1918 brought famine to many parts of India. A year earlier the bubonic plague left a trail of death, but it was trifling compared to the influenza epidemic of 1918–1919, which killed no less than 13 million people! Another factor contributing to unrest was the repressive policy followed by Britain after the war. The Rowlatt Acts of March, 1919, authorized the government to intern agitators without trial and entitled judges to try cases without juries. Gandhi struck back by organizing a campaign of passive resistance and noncooperation. During the riots that followed, the British General Dyer perpetrated the infamous Amritsar Massacre of April 13, 1919, when he ordered his troops to fire without warning on a crowded political meeting of unarmed civilians. Nearly 400 were killed and 1,000 wounded. A committee of the House of Commons censured the general, who was relieved of his command. But the House of Lords supported Dyer, and a solatium of £26,000 was raised for him by public subscription. A wave of bitter protest swept the nation, and Gandhi denounced the government as "satanic."

Gandhi was by all odds the outstanding figure in this postwar anti-British movement. The Indian Congress, organized in 1885, did not seriously threaten the British prior to 1914. (See Chapter 28, section VI.) It had remained essentially a middle-class movement with negligible support from village masses. Gandhi's great contribution was that he managed to break through to the villagers, establish rapport with them, and involve them in the struggle for independence. His message was simple and appealing. He pointed out that in 1914 the British were ruling 300 million Indians with a mere 4,000 administrators and 69,000 soldiers. This was possible only because all classes of the population were cooperating with the British in one way or another. If this cooperation were withdrawn,

British rule inevitably would collapse. The task, then, was to educate and prepare the people for *satyagraha,* or nonviolent passive resistance. Gandhi also called on the people to practice *hartal,* or boycott of British goods. In place of imported machine-made goods, Gandhi preached the wearing of homespun cloth. This would undermine the economic basis of British rule and also revive village industries. He himself wore a loin cloth of homespun material, and publicly worked at his spinning wheel. The combination of *satyagraha* and *hartal,* Gandhi taught, would make possible the realization of *swaraj,* or home rule.

In an effort to forestall the gathering storm, the London government introduced on December 23, 1919, the Montagu-Chelmsford reforms establishing an administrative system known as "dyarchy." This left the central government in Delhi much the same as before, with an appointed viceroy and executive council, and a legislative assembly of 140 members, of whom 100 were elected by a very restricted suffrage. The dyarchy principle operated in the provincial governments, each of which consisted of an appointed governor and executive council, and a legislative council which was 70 per cent elective by a rigidly limited suffrage. Important matters were "reserved" for the governor and his executive council; the less important, such as sanitation, agriculture, medical relief, and education, were to be "transferred" to the Indian ministers. The theory was that more matters would be transferred from the "reserved" to the "transferred" list if this "dyarchy," or division of responsibility, proved workable.

The National Congress, led by Gandhi, rejected the British reform proposal. In September, 1920, an all-out noncooperation campaign was launched. The response was impressive, but it gradually got out of hand. Gandhi insisted on strict nonviolence, yet strikes and riots broke out in the cities, while in the countryside the peasants rose against landlords and moneylenders. The shocked Gandhi promptly ordered suspension of the noncooperation campaign, but he was nevertheless arrested and sentenced to six years' imprisonment. He was released after two years because of his precarious health, but the nationalist campaign had largely petered out by then.

For several years after his release from prison, Gandhi stayed out of politics. During this period new and more radical nationalist leaders were emerging. Up to this time the leadership of the National Congress had been largely upper and middle class in its origins and views. By the mid-1920's workers groups began to appear, with a socialist or communist political orientation. This trend resulted in the growth of a left-wing element within the National Congress, and in the organization of an All-India Independence League with Jawaharlal Nehru as president. The distinguishing feature of the League is that it demanded not only complete independence from Britain but also basic social change within India along socialist lines.

Nehru himself provides a good illustration of the new trend. The son of a wealthy lawyer, he was educated at Harrow and Cambridge, and was admitted to the bar in 1912. On his return, he plunged into the nationalist struggle for freedom, becoming a follower and admirer of Gandhi. Nehru, however, was very different from his mystical and ascetic leader. He was a socialist and a firm believer in science and technology as the means for liberating mankind from its age-old misery and ignorance. He parted company with Gandhi when the latter rejected the modern world in his mystical teachings, and yet Nehru recognized Gandhi's extraordinary service in arousing India's peasantry. Even the National Congress, rent with personal rivalries and doctrinal disputes, was dependent on Gandhi. He returned to political life in December, 1928, and persuaded Congress to accept a compromise resolution acceptable to both the radical and conservative elements. A few months later the British Labour Party defeated the Conservatives and formed a new government. The outlook seemed promising, for the Labourites consistently had criticized the Conservatives for tardiness in extending self-government to India. The promise, however, was not realized; the decade 1930–1939 proved a disappointment.

One reason was the increasing dissension between warring Hindu and Moslem blocs. As early as 1919 the All-India Moslem League had been founded, but for many years it had little following. Not only were the Moslems less than a quarter of the total population of the subcontinent, but the National Congress claimed it represented all Indians, regardless of religion. Indeed, the Congress did have a Moslem wing headed by the distinguished Abdul Kalam Azad. Thus the Moslem League was of little significance until after 1935, when it came under the leadership of a Bombay lawyer, Mohammed Ali Jinnah. He offered to cooperate with the Congress on a coalition basis, but Congress rejected this and would deal only with Moslems who joined the party as individuals. Jinnah retaliated by appealing to the Moslem masses with the cry "Islam is in danger." The response was enthusiastic, for many Indian Moslems felt they had more in common with the rest of the Moslem world than with their Hindu neighbors. Jinnah's electoral successes made possible the future establishment of the independent Moslem Pakistan.

Meanwhile Gandhi had started another civil disobedience campaign to force the British to get out of India. His tactic was the great salt march to the sea, 170 miles away. There he dipped up sea water and placed it on a fire, a symbolic act of defiance against the government's salt tax, which he denounced as iniquitous. It was a shrewd, as well as a highly dramatic and well publicized move, for the peasant mass bitterly resented this tax and actively supported Gandhi. Widespread disorders broke out, including attacks on government salt works, terrorist assaults on officials, and rioting by unemployed factory workers who were hard hit by the worldwide depression. On May 5, 1930, Gandhi was again arrested and imprisoned, along with some 60,000 of his followers.

Lord Irwin was aware that force alone offered no solution. After order had been somewhat restored, he released Gandhi on January 26, 1931, and resumed negotiations. Finally on August 2, 1935, the British Parliament passed the Government of India Act as the constructive half of the dual policy of repression of violence and advance toward self-government. It provided that Burma and Aden were to be separated from India and to become crown colonies. India itself was to become a federal union of the provinces and the princely states, subject to the latter's concurrence. Since this was not forthcoming, the projected federal union did not materialize. But the Act also provided for new provincial arrangements that were implemented with the election of provincial legislatures in 1937. The Nationalists gained control in seven of the eleven provinces, and promptly proceeded to liberate political prisoners, restore civil liberties, and prepare agrarian reform.

In 1939 all this abruptly ended when the viceroy proclaimed that India was a party to the new World War. Since the Indians were in no way consulted, the Nationalist ministries in the seven provinces resigned. British governors then took over and governed by decree. Once again the Nationalists raised the cry for complete independence, while the Moslems under Jinnah demanded that the subcontinent be partitioned into two states, one Hindu, and the other Moslem and to be called Pakistan.

VI. CHINA

Although nominally independent, China experienced an anti-Western movement after World War I comparable to that of India. China entered the war in 1917 in hope of recovering Shantung province, which Japan had occupied in 1914. When the lost province was not restored by the peacemakers at Versailles, wild demonstrations broke out among the students and intellectuals in Peking. The protests soon spread to other cities, and the merchants joined by closing their shops. Newly organized labor unions also participated in the protest movement by staging strikes. Japan and the Western powers were the targets of this violent outburst, but Soviet Russia, by contrast, was regarded with sympathy and admiration. One reason was the understandable appeal of Lenin's anti-imperialistic teachings. Another was that the Soviet government had renounced Tsarist special privileges in China, as it also did at this time in Turkey and Persia. It is understandable that Chinese nationalists now looked increasingly to the Soviet Union as against the Japanese and the Westerners.

These changes gave Dr. Sun Yat-sen the opportunity to make a fresh start with new policies and methods. He had come on hard times following the 1911 revolution that established the republic. (See Chapter 29, section IV.) Yüan Shih-k'ai had shunted him aside, while the provincial warlords ignored the central government and ruled as independent potentates. Sun now decided that his Kuomintang Party had to be strengthened to defeat the warlords and to create a unified and modernized state. He appealed for international aid but was turned down by the Western governments. The Soviets, however, responded positively, and thus began the Kuomintang-Communist Entente that lasted to 1927.

In January, 1923, Dr. Sun and the Soviet representative, Adolf Joffe, agreed that the purpose of the entente was not to establish communism in China but rather "to achieve national unification and attain full national independence." The Russians followed up by sending their able Mikhail Borodin to Canton, where he became Sun's right-hand man. Together they were able to bring about three basic changes: they remodeled the Kuomintang Party along communist lines, organized an efficient modern army, and developed a more effective and appealing political ideology.

In the reorganization of the Kuomintang, Sun came to exercise control through a Central Executive Committee elected by a Party Congress. For the first time the party was now able to function as a disciplined unit from headquarters to the smallest subdivision. At the same time a new army was being organized with the help of Russian arms and officers led by General Vasili Blücher. Finally, Sun recast the ideology of his party into the form of his famous Three Principles of the People: Nationalism, Democracy, and Livelihood. The Principle of Democracy looked toward the achievement of democratic government, though a period of tutelage under one-party rule was deemed necessary. The Principle of Livelihood sought economic betterment for the people through equitable distribution of the land, and state management or control of industry.

Sun Yat-sen died in 1925, at the very time when the instruments had been forged to fulfill his ambitions. Although he did not live to see the warlords humbled and the country united, he is today recognized, both by the mainland Communists and the Taiwan Nationalists, as one of the creators of modern China. Dr. Sun's death made it possible for the army leader, Chiang Kai-shek, to become the leading figure in the Kuomintang. In May, 1926, he assumed command of the "Northern Expedition," a campaign to unify China by crushing the warlords in the north. The Kuomintang forces, preceded by propaganda corps, swept everything before them, reaching the Yangtze by October. The capital was now moved to Hankow, which was dominated by left-wing and communist elements.

This pointed up a growing split within the Kuomintang between the left wing ensconced in Hankow and the right wing under General Chiang. The latter favored nationalism but not social revolution. He had become alarmed by the activities of the leftist propaganda corps that had been operating ahead of his divisions. Working among the peasantry and the city workers, these propagandists whipped up a revolutionary movement against the landed gentry, the urban bourgeoisie, and the Western business interests. Although Chiang had worked closely with his Russian advisers, he was definitely anti-communist and determined to prevent the leftists from getting control of the Kuomintang.

The showdown came when Nanking fell on March 24, 1927. As had happened in other cities, worker and student battalions were organized as the Kuomintang army approached. They waged a general strike and were able to take over control of the city during the interval between the departure of the warlord forces and the arrival of Chiang. The latter was not at all happy to be greeted by a revolutionary committee, so with the backing of conservative elements in the Kuomintang and of financial interests in Shanghai, he carried out a bloody purge of communists and their leftist allies. Borodin returned to Russia, and Chiang reorganized the Kuomintang so that he was the undisputed head. In June, 1928, his armies took Peking, destroying the power of the northern warlords and completing the official unification of the country. The capital of the new China was moved to Nanking.

During the following decade the country made appreciable progress under Chiang's guidance. Railway mileage almost doubled, and that of modern roads quadrupled. Internal tariff barriers, of which there had been about 500, were abolished in 1932. Likewise, a unified currency was created for the first time. Significant progress was also made in governmental procedures, in public health, in education, and in industrialization. Equally striking were the government's successes in the diplomatic field. Control of the tariff was regained, some of the territories ceded to foreign nations were recovered, and many of the special privileges wrested by the Western powers were returned. By 1943 extra-territorial rights had been surrendered by all foreign nations.

But there were serious gaps in Chiang's reform program, and these ultimately proved fatal. Badly needed land reform was neglected because the Kuomintang Party in the rural areas was dominated by landlords who opposed any change. And Chiang's authoritarian, one-party government prevented the growth of democracy, so that opposition groups could not assert themselves by constitutional means; revolution was the sole alternative. Finally, the Kuomintang failed to develop ideas that could attract the support of the people. Nationalist appeals had little attraction for land-hungry peasants and poverty-stricken city workers.

These weaknesses of the Kuomintang regime might have been gradually overcome if it had been given a long period of peace. But it did not have this opportunity because of two mortal enemies, the Communists at home and the Japanese abroad. The Chinese Communist party was organized in Shanghai in May, 1921, and in the following years branches appeared in all parts of the country. Many students and intellectuals joined the ranks, attracted by the call for action and the assurances of a classless and equitable society for the future. As we have seen, the Communists first cooperated with Sun Yat-sen and then broke with Chiang Kai-shek in 1927. Most of the Communist leaders were killed off by Chiang, but a number managed to escape to the mountainous interior of South China. One of their leaders was Mao Tse-tung, who now worked out a new revolutionary strategy in defiance of the Communist International in Moscow. He rejected the traditional Marxist doctrine that only the city proletariat could be depended upon to carry through a revolution. From firsthand observation in the countryside he concluded that the poor peasants, who comprised 70 per cent of the population, were "the vanguard of the revolution. . . . Without the poor peasant there can be no revolution." This was pure heresy in Moscow, but Mao went his way, organizing the peasants and building up a separate army and government in the south.

Chiang responded by launching five "bandit extermination campaigns," as they were called. The Communists managed to survive, thanks to the support of the peasants who were won over by the Communist policy of dividing large estates without compensation to the owners. The fifth campaign did succeed in dislodging the Communists, who were completely surrounded by the Kuomintang armies. Finally 90,000 managed to break through, and of these, less than 7,000 survived a 6,000 mile trek of incredible hardship. During this historic "Long March" of 368 days (October 16, 1934 to October 25, 1935) they fought an average of almost a skirmish a day with Kuomintang forces totaling more than 300,000. Finally the Communist survivors reached the northwest provinces, where they dug in and established a base. Their land reform policies again won them peasant support, so that they were able to build up their strength to the point where they became serious rivals of the Kuomintang regime in Nanking.

While Chiang was involved in this domestic struggle with the Communists, he was being attacked from the outside by the Japanese. We shall see later (Chapter 37, section I) that this aggression began with the occupation of Manchuria in 1931, and continued until the Japanese were in control of the entire eastern seaboard by the beginning of World War II. This combination of Communist subversion and Japanese aggression culminated in 1949 in Chiang's flight to Taiwan (Formosa), leaving Mao to rule the mainland from his new capital in Peking.

SUGGESTED READING

P. Avery, *Modern Iran* (Praeger, 1965); P. Balfour, *Ataturk: The Rebirth of a Nation* (Weidenfeld, 1964); N. S. Fatemi, *Diplomatic History of Persia, 1917–1923* (Moore, 1952); M. K. Gandhi, *An Autobiography: The Story of My Experiments with Truth* (Beacon, 1957); A. Hourani, *Arabic Thought in the Liberal Age 1798–1939* (Oxford Univ., 1962); G. Lenczowski, ed., *The Political Awakening in the Middle East* (Prentice-Hall, 1970); H. M. Sachar, *The Emergence of the Middle East 1914–1924* (Knopf, 1969); H. Z. Schiffrin, *Sun Yat-sen and the Origins of the 1911 Revolution* (Univ. California, 1969); *Toward Freedom: The Autobiography of Jawaharlal Nehru* (Day, 1941); C. Tse-tsung, *The May Fourth Movement: Intellectual Revolution in Modern China* (Harvard Univ., 1964).

chapter thirty-five

Revolution and Settlement in Europe to 1929

The failure to strangle Bolshevism at its birth and to bring Russia, then prostrate, by one means or another, into the general democratic system, lies heavy upon us today.—Winston Churchill, *April 1, 1949*

At the same time that the colonial world was in the throes of national revolution, Europe itself was seething with social revolution. All over the Continent the old order was being questioned, partly because of the trauma of the World War, and partly because of the impact of the great Russian Revolution. Thus, European history during the decade to 1929 was largely a history of struggle between revolutionary and counterrevolutionary forces. In Russia, communism emerged triumphant after years of civil war and intervention. In Central Europe the extremist revolutionary forces were crushed and a variety of non-Communist regimes appeared, ranging from the liberal Weimar Republic in Germany to the rightist Horthy government in Hungary and to the fascist Mussolini state in Italy. Western Europe was spared such violent upheavals, but even here, the authority of traditional parliamentary institutions was being strained by economic difficulties, mass unemployment, and cabinet instability. By the late 1920's, some measure of order seemed to be returning to Europe. Prosperity was growing, unemployment was on the decline, and various international issues appeared to be resolved by the Dawes Plan, the Locarno Pacts, the Kellogg-Briand Pact, and the commitment of the Soviet Union to Five Year Plans rather than to world revolution. Europe was returning to a normal state, or so it seemed, until the Great Depression precipitated the series of domestic and international crises that were to culminate in World War II.

I. COMMUNISM TRIUMPHS IN RUSSIA

Origins of Counterrevolution and Intervention

By signing the harsh Brest-Litovsk Treaty on March 3, 1918 (see Chapter 33, section IV), the Bolsheviks hoped that at last they would be able to turn from war to the more congenial task of building a new social order. Instead, they were destined to fight on for three more years against counterrevolution and foreign intervention. The counterrevolution was in part the work of members of the propertied classes—army officers, government officials, landowners, and businessmen—who for obvious reasons wished to be rid of the Bolsheviks. Equally ardent in their counterrevolutionary activities, however, were the various elements of the non-Bolshevik Left, of whom the Socialist Revolutionaries were by far the most numerous. They agreed with the Bolsheviks on the need for social revolution, but they bitterly resented the Bolshevik monopolization of the revolution. They regarded the Bolshevik coup of November 7, 1917, as a gross betrayal, particularly because the Constituent Assembly elected on November 25, 1917, included only 175 Bolsheviks as against 370 Socialist Revolutionaries and 159 other assorted representatives. Accordingly, the non-Bolshevik Left took the lead in organizing underground opposition, while the rightist elements led armed forces in open revolt, beginning in the Cossack territories.

These anti-Bolshevik groups were encouraged and assisted by the Western powers, the latter being motivated by various considerations such as the strident Bolshevik campaign for world revolution. Both in Europe and in the colonial regions the Bolsheviks called on the "toiling masses" to "convert the imperialist war into a class war." Many Western leaders naturally responded by seeking to crush these Marxist incendiaries before they could ignite the smoldering tinder of revolution scattered throughout the world. Also, certain British and French statesmen erroneously regarded the Bolsheviks as tools of the German general staff, and wished to be rid of them in order to bring Russia back into the war. And there were economic motives behind the Allied intervention: Bolshevik nationalization of foreign properties and repudiation of foreign debts naturally alienated powerful vested interests, which used their influence in behalf of intervention.

Course of Civil War

Under these circumstances several counterrevolutionary governments were set up soon after the Brest-Litovsk Treaty all along the borders of Russia—in the northern Archangel-Murmansk region, the Baltic provinces, the Ukraine, the Don territories, Transcaucasia, and Siberia. These governments were generously provided with funds and war materials, as well as with military advisers and small detachments of troops on certain fronts. Soon after operations had gotten under way, the war ended in the West, raising the question of whether the Allied intervention should be pressed further. The original argument about bringing Russia back into the war was now irrelevant since the war was over.

The issue of whether to continue the intervention was debated by the Allied leaders in conference at Paris. Both President Wilson and Prime Minister Lloyd George favored immediate cessation of hostilities. Georges Clemenceau, however, maintained that the whole of Europe was menaced by the threat of revolution and that Bolshevism must be crushed in its place of origin. Having to leave the conference in order to attend to political duties at home, Wilson and Lloyd George were unable to back up their views. The deputies they left behind, Secretary of State Robert Lansing and Secretary of War Winston Churchill, held positions closer to Clemenceau's. Hence a decision was reached for continued intervention, a fateful choice that was to mean three more years of war and a bitter legacy of international mistrust for the postwar years.

At first the Bolsheviks suffered one reverse after another, simply because the old Russian army had disintegrated and there was nothing else to take its place.

The Commissar for Defense, Leon Trotsky, gradually built up a new Red Army, which numbered about 500,000 men by the end of 1918. At times this force had to fight on two dozen different fronts, as revolts broke out in all parts of the country and Allied forces landed in coastal areas.

The chief opponents of the Bolsheviks in 1919 were Admiral Kolchak in Siberia, General Denikin in the Crimea and the Ukraine, and General Yudenich in Estonia. A common pattern is evident in their campaigns. Beginning with sudden attacks from their bases, they gained easy initial victories, came within reach of full victory, then were stopped, gradually pushed back, and finally routed and "liquidated," to use a favorite Bolshevik expression. In March, 1919, Kolchak captured the city of Ufa to the west of the Urals; in August, Denikin had advanced north to Kiev, and by October, Yudenich had penetrated to the very suburbs of Petrograd. Lenin's regime now was limited to the Petrograd-Moscow regions, an area about equal to the fifteenth century Muscovite principality. However, by the end of 1919 the tides had turned: Denikin had been driven back to the Crimea, Yudenich to the Baltic, and Kolchak was not only forced back over the Urals, but was captured and shot.

It appeared early in 1920 that the ordeal was finally over. But another full year of fighting lay ahead, owing to the appearance of the Poles and renewed large-scale intervention by the French. The Poles, determined to extend their frontiers as far eastward as possible, took advantage of the confusion and exhaustion to invade the Ukraine in April, 1920. The pattern of the previous year's operations was now repeated. The Poles advanced rapidly and took Kiev on May 7, but five weeks later they were driven out of the city, and by mid-July were back in their own territory. The triumphant Bolsheviks pressed on, reaching the outskirts of Warsaw on August 14. But the Poles, strongly supported by the French, stopped the advancing Russians and managed to push them back. The campaign ended in mid-October, and on March 18, 1921, the treaty of Riga defined the Polish-Russian frontier that prevailed until World War II.

Meanwhile, General Wrangel, who had replaced Denikin, had overrun much of southern Russia with the generous assistance of the French. But after the Bolsheviks were through with the Poles, they turned their forces against Wrangel, driving him south to the Crimea. This peninsula, once the playground of tsars and grand dukes, was now crowded with a motley host of refugees—high ecclesiastics, tsarist officials, aristocratic landowners, and the remnants of White armies. As many as possible were evacuated in French warships and scattered in ports from Constantinople to Marseilles; the remainder were left to the mercy of the victorious Red Army.

The only foreign troops now left on Russian soil were the Japanese operating from Vladivostok. Originally there had been American and British as well as Japanese contingents in eastern Siberia, but the first two were withdrawn in 1920. The Japanese stayed on, hoping to retain control of these vast but sparsely populated regions through the medium of a puppet regime. The United States repeatedly brought diplomatic pressure on the Japanese to leave, and finally persuaded them to do so at the Washington Naval Disarmament Conference in 1922.

Roots of Bolshevik Victory

One reason for the victory of the Bolsheviks was the dissension and vacillation amongst the Western powers. Aside from certain passionately dedicated anti-Bolsheviks who occupied subordinate posts, the Allied leaders regarded the intervention as little more than a sideshow, and they supported it fitfully with varied and conflicting motives. Even more disunity prevailed amongst the White Russians, partly because of the conflicting ambitions of individual leaders, but also because of the basic incompatibility of the leftist Socialist Revolutionaries and the assorted right-wing elements.

The Communists, by contrast, enjoyed certain advantages that proved decisive in the end. Their monolithic party organization imposed a cohesion and discipline that was unmatched on the other side. The Communist party was effectively supported by an efficient secret police organization, the Cheka, that ruthlessly ferreted out opposition groups. The Commissar of War, Leon Trotsky, skillfully combined the enthusiasm of proletarian volunteers with the indispensable technical knowledge of former Tsarist officers to forge a formidable new Red Army. Futhermore, this army enjoyed the substantial advantage of having internal lines of communication, in contrast to the tremendous distances separating the White forces from each other and from their sources of supplies in Western Europe and the United States. Finally, the Bolsheviks were generally more successful in winning the support of the peasant masses. This does not mean that the Russian peasants were won over to Marxist ideology; indeed, most of them were fed up with both the Reds and the Whites, and would rather have been left alone. But when forced to make a choice, they more frequently decided in favor of the Reds who, they thought, were on their side and would allow them to keep the plots they had seized from the landlords.

In retrospect, the protracted civil war and intervention was a disaster for all parties concerned. It left the Russian countryside devastated from the Baltic to the Pacific, and the Russian people decimated by casualties, starvation, and disease. Equally serious was the poisoning of relations between the new Soviet state and the Western world. The Soviet leaders were confirmed in their Marxist fears of "capitalist encirclement," while Western statesmen took all too seriously the futile manifestoes of the Communist International established in 1919. So deep and lasting was this mutual distrust that it envenomed international relations during the following decade and contributed significantly to the coming of World War II.

II. COMMUNISM FAILS IN CENTRAL EUROPE

Balance of Power in Germany

While civil war was raging in Russia, the crucial question for Europe was whether communism would spread westward. Lenin and his fellow Bolsheviks assumed that if this did not occur, their cause would be doomed. Accordingly, they followed closely and hopefully the course of events in Central Europe —especially Germany. If it went communist, the combination of German industrial strength and Russian natural resources would be unbeatable, and the future of the revolution would be assured.

At first it appeared that these Bolshevik hopes might be realized. The Kaiser was forced to abdicate on November 9, 1918, following a mutiny in the navy and the spread of revolution from the Baltic ports into the interior. (See Chapter 33, section VI.) Workers' and Soldiers' Councils, similar to the Russian Soviets, appeared in all the major cities, including Berlin. So strong was the revolutionary movement that it seemed probable that communism would engulf the Continent, at least to the Rhine. The final outcome, however, was not a Soviet Germany but the bourgeois German Republic.

Several factors that escaped attention at the time explain this fateful outcome, one being the prosperity of prewar Germany, which left the working class relatively contented and in no mood for revolution. Equally important was the prosperity of the German peasants, who were infinitely better off than those of Russia. They had not fared too badly during the war years, so that the Bolshevik slogan "Land to the Peasants," which had been so effective in Russia, made very little impact on Germany. Also, the war had already ended at the time of the German revolution, again in contrast to the situation in Russia. The demand for peace, which probably helped the Bolsheviks more than anything else, was irrelevant in Germany. Furthermore, although the German army was defeated, it was far from being as demoralized and mutinous as the Russian army of 1917. The opponents of revolution in Germany were able to call upon reliable military forces when the showdown came.

A final factor of major significance was the split in the ranks of the German socialists. The Majority Social Democrats, led by Friedrich Ebert and Philipp Scheidemann, had supported the German war effort from the beginning. Being relatively conservative, they now strenuously opposed the revolutionary Workers' and Soldiers' Councils. "I hate the social revolution," Ebert declared candidly, "I hate it like sin." At the other end of the spectrum was the Spartacist League, the counterpart of Lenin's Bolsheviks, led by two able and outstanding revolutionaries, Karl Liebknecht, of a well-known German socialist family, and Rosa Luxemburg, of Polish-Jewish origin. The Spartacists, as might be expected, supported the Workers' and Soldiers' Councils and wished to establish a Soviet-type regime in Germany. Between the Majority Socialists and the Spartacists was the Independent Socialist party; it also favored a Soviet Germany but in addition wished to cooperate with the Majority Socialists.

Establishment of Weimar Republic

When Prince Max announced the abdication of the Kaiser, he himself resigned the chancellorship and handed the government over to Friedrich Ebert. The latter formed a cabinet, or council, of "Six Commissars," composed of three Majority Social Democrats and three Independent Socialists. The Spartacists chose to remain outside for the simple reason that they were interested only in forcing the revolution further to the Left. Philipp Scheidemann had proclaimed the establishment of the German Republic from the balcony of the parliament building, but Liebknecht at the same time had proclaimed a Soviet Germany from the balcony of the Imperial Palace a mile away. The great question now was which side would prevail.

The situation was comparable to that in Russia when the Provisional Government was established in March, 1917. Ebert was very much aware of the outcome in that country, and had no desire to be another Kerensky. Accordingly, on November 10, the day after the Kaiser's abdication, he formed a secret alliance with General Wilhelm Groener, Chief of the General Staff, for the suppression of the Spartacists and the Workers' and Soldiers' Councils. Every night between 11:00 P.M. and 1:00 A.M., the two men talked on a special telephone linking the chancellory at Berlin and headquarters at Spa. With this powerful support, Ebert moved aggressively against the extreme Left. The Independent Social Democrats refused to go along and resigned from the cabinet, but this made little difference. On December 30, the Spartacists renamed themselves the Communist Labor

Party of Germany and made plans for revolt, but before these were completed, Karl Liebknecht and Rosa Luxemburg were arrested and shot "while trying to escape." Over a thousand of their followers were killed during the ruthless street fighting that followed. The critical turning point had been passed, and on January 19, 1919, elections were held throughout Germany for a National Assembly rather than for a Congress of Soviets. The delegates, overwhelmingly of the moderate Left, met in Weimar, and elected Ebert the first president of the Republic, and Scheidemann the first chancellor.

The constitution adopted in July, 1919, was unimpeachably democratic, at least in principle. It embodied all the devices then favored by the democracies, including universal suffrage, proportional representation, a bill of rights, and separation of church and state, and church and school. Behind this new constitutional facade, much of the old Germany remained unchanged. The bureaucracy, the judiciary, and the police survived intact. The new *Reichswehr* was the old imperial army in miniature. Except for the legal eight-hour day, virtually no social reforms were introduced. The industrial cartels and monopolies continued as before; the Junkers of East Prussia retained their landed estates, as did the Kaiser and the various local rulers. In short, the German revolution had preserved more than it had changed. Power was left largely in the hands of the old ruling elements, which never accepted the new order. At first the Weimar Republic did succeed in stabilizing itself with foreign financial aid. But when the Great Depression undermined the foundations of the state, most of these unreconciled bureaucrats, army officers, and landed gentry turned upon the Republic and helped in its destruction.

Revolution and Reaction in Central Europe

The suppression of the Spartacists and the establishment of the Weimar Republic ensured that the rest of Central Europe would not go communist. Nevertheless, for a number of years this part of Europe seethed with unrest and revolt. The peasant masses between the Baltic and the Aegean were politically awake and active to an unprecedented degree, one reason being that millions of peasant army recruits had widened their horizons immeasurably as a result of their war experiences. They had observed not only the differences between city and village life, but also the differences in living standards and social institutions among various countries. The peasants were also profoundly affected by the overthrow of the Hapsburg, Hohenzollern, and Romanoff dynasties. In the light of centuries-old traditions, this was a seismic shock that aroused nationalist aspirations and class consciousness. Finally, the unprecedented destructiveness and suffering that took place during the long years of war aggravated the revolutionary situation, especially in the countries that had suffered defeat.

The precise manifestation of this revolutionary ferment varied from country to country according to local circumstances. The Communist parties did not play an outstanding role except in the case of Hungary, where in March 1919 a Soviet republic was established under the leadership of Bela Kun. It lasted less than a year, because of the hostility of the peasants and the invasion of the country by Rumanian troops. When the Rumanians departed in February, 1920, a right-wing government headed by Admiral Miklós Horthy was established with Allied support. Horthy remained in power for the whole interwar period, during which time Hungary was unique in Central Europe for the almost complete absence of agrarian or other reforms.

In most of the other Central European countries, agrarian or peasant parties were giving voice to popular discontent. The following peasant leaders assumed office in the postwar years: Aleksandr Stamboliski in Bulgaria in 1919, Stefan Radich in Yugoslavia in 1925, Wincenty Witos in Poland in 1926, and Iuliu Maniu in Rumania in 1928. Owing to their pacifism and distaste for violence, however, none of them was able to retain power for long. They were left vulnerable to the entrenched military and bureaucratic elements that did not hesitate to forcefully seize power when their interests were threatened. Another reason for their failure was the increasing control that lawyers and urban intellectuals, who were attracted by the political opportunities, gained over the peasant parties. Under this leadership, the parties usually represented the interests of the wealthy peasants and had little contact with the great mass of poor peasants.

One after another the peasant leaders were ousted from office. Stamboliski was assassinated in 1923, and a dictatorship was established by King Boris. Radich was assassinated in 1928, and the following year King Alexander set up his dictatorship. In Poland, Witos lasted only a few days before he was removed by General Joseph Pilsudski, who dominated the country until his death in 1935. Maniu was eased out of office in 1930 by King Carol II, who made and unmade governments until forced to flee Rumania a decade later.

The same pattern prevailed in Austria and Greece where, for various reasons, agrarian parties never took hold. Yet Austria ended up with an authoritarian government under Chancellor Dollfuss in 1934, and Greece with an avowedly fascist regime under General Metaxas in 1936. Thus, by World War II the whole of Central Europe was under dictatorial rule, with one exception—Czechoslovakia. This country possessed certain advantages that explain its uniqueness: a high level of literacy; a trained bureaucracy inherited from the Hapsburg empire; the capable leadership of Jan Masaryk and Eduard Benes; and a balanced economy that provided higher living standards and greater security than was possible in the predominantly agrarian countries to the east.

III. ITALY GOES FASCIST

While bolshevism, agrarianism, and traditional parliamentarianism battled for primacy in Eastern and Central Europe, an entirely new *ism* was coming to the fore in Italy—fascism, the outstanding political innovation in Europe in the postwar years. Bolshevism had a history going back at least to the Communist Manifesto of 1848, while agrarianism was taking political form with the appearance of peasant parties at the turn of the century. Fascism, by contrast, appeared unexpectedly and dramatically with Mussolini's march on Rome in October, 1922.

Postwar conditions in Italy provided fertile soil for a violent, melodramatic, and anti-intellectual movement such as fascism. The Italy of 1919 had behind it only two generations of national independence and unity. Parliamentary government was, in practice, a morass of corruption in which party "bosses" manipulated shortlived coalition blocs. This unstable political structure was further weakened in the postwar years by serious economic dislocation, which left many of the demobilized millions unable to find jobs. The popular unrest engendered by this economic stress was aggravated by the slighting of Italian claims at the Paris peace conference. The expenditure of blood and treasure appeared to have been in vain, and the resulting frustration and injured pride produced an inflammable situation.

This became evident with the November, 1919, elections, which returned 160 for the Socialist party and 103 for the Catholic Popular party as against 93 and 58 respectively for the traditional Liberal and Radical parties. The climax came in September, 1920, when workers throughout north Italy began taking over factories. Giovanni Giolitti, the old prewar political manipulator who had formed a cabinet in June, 1920, decided to leave the "campers" in possession, partly because he did not know whether the soldiers would obey orders or join the workers. All the classical conditions for a revolution were present—except for the will to start one. The Socialist watchword at this time was "the revolution is not made. The revolution comes." Within two years this slogan was proven wrong by one who was ready to make revolution.

Benito Mussolini had first attracted attention during the Tripolitan War of 1911 when he referred to the Italian flag as "a rag fit only to be planted on a dung heap." The following year he became editor of the official Socialist paper *Avanti!* When World War I began in August, 1914, he was still a revolutionary and a pacifist, but the following month his great transformation took place, facilitated by funds from the French government, which was desperately anxious at this point to secure Italy as an ally. Mussolini was enabled to start his own newspaper, *Il Popolo d'Italia,* in which he conducted a passionate interventionist campaign.

Called to battle in September, 1915, Mussolini fought in the trenches for a few weeks until he was wounded and invalided out of the army. He languished in obscurity until 1919, when he formed his first "combat troops," or *fasci di combattimento.* The *fasces,* a bundle of rods tied around the haft of an ax, was the emblem carried by the Roman lictors who attended the magistrates. Thus it was a symbol for unity and authority, which became Mussolini's watchwords against the political anarchy and social strife of the period. In the November, 1919 elections he polled a mere 4,795 votes as against 180,000 for his Socialist opponent, but in the elections of May 15, 1921, the Fascist party won 22 seats, while the Socialist representation declined from 160 to 122.

Mussolini was still far from a position of authority, but at least his party had a nationwide organization with about 250,000 members at election time. From then on it forged rapidly ahead, partly because the passivity of the Socialists had created a vacuum that Mussolini promptly filled. Equally important was the substantial support that Mussolini was now receiving from industrialists, landowners, and other members of the propertied classes. Terrified by the widespread seizure of factories and estates, they now looked hopefully to the Fascist *squadristi,* or armed bands, as a bulwark against the dreaded social revolution. Actually, the danger of revolution had passed with the evacuation of the factories in late September, 1920. Now it was the Fascist bands, aided by the benevolent neutrality of the police, that were disturbing the peace. With impunity they attacked trade union offices and Socialist party headquarters, raided working-class districts, drove out mayors and other officials who were Socialists, and wrecked opposition newspaper offices.

In the fall of 1922, Mussolini prepared for a coup by winning over both the monarchy and the Church with specific assurance that their interests would be respected. Since the regular army and the police already had manifested their benevolent neutrality, Mussolini proceeded with assurance to mobilize his Blackshirts for a widely publicized march on Rome. Prime Minister Luigi Facta asked King Victor Emmanuel to proclaim martial law, but the King refused and instead called on Mussolini to form a government. Thus only a token march on Rome by the Blackshirts was necessary, while Mussolini arrived anticlimactically in Rome on October 27 in a sleeping-car.

Parliament and the King gave Mussolini dictatorial powers until December 31, 1923, to restore order and introduce reforms. During this period he allowed a degree of liberty to the press, to the trade unions, and to the parliamentary parties. But at the same time he was gaining control of the state machinery by appointing prefects and judges of Fascist sympathies and organizing a voluntary Fascist militia. The showdown came with the elections of April 6, 1924. Through liberal use of the *squadristi,* the Fascist party polled 65 per cent of the votes and won 375 seats, compared to the 35 they had previously held. Two months later a prominent Socialist deputy, Giacomo Matteotti, was found murdered. He had written a book, *The Fascisti Exposed,* presenting detailed case histories of hundreds of illegal acts of Fascist violence. It was widely suspected, and later proven, that Matteotti had been killed on orders from Mussolini himself. Most of the non-Fascist deputies walked out of the chamber, vowing not to return until the Matteotti affair had been cleared up. Mussolini faced a major crisis but managed to survive, thanks to the indecisiveness of the opposition and the unwavering support of the king.

By the fall of 1926, Mussolini felt strong enough to take the offensive. He declared the seats of the absent deputies vacant, disbanded the old political parties, tightened censorship of the press, and established an organization of secret police. Italy had become a one-party state, with the Chamber functioning as a rubber-stamp body for passing Fascist bills.

The new Fascist regime gradually evolved certain distinctive features. One was the corporative state in which deputies were elected as representatives not of geographical constituencies but rather of trades and professions. Theoretically it eliminated class conflict by bringing capital and labor together under the benevolent auspices of the state. Actually, only capital enjoyed true self-government, while labor was denied the right to strike or to select its own leaders. Neither the position of the workers nor that of the peasants was basically improved under the corporative state.

Another feature of Mussolini's Italy was the elaborate public works program designed to provide employment and to erect impressive structures for the glorification of fascism. Monuments of the past were restored, and many cities were adorned with large new buildings, workers' tenements, and stadiums. Certain marshlands were drained and made available for cultivation. Tourists were particularly impressed by trains that ran on time and extensive new highways or *autostrade.*

IV. PROBLEMS OF DEMOCRACY IN WESTERN EUROPE

In Western Europe there were no upheavals comparable to the civil war in Russia or to the bitter clash between Right and Left in Central Europe. Democratic institutions had deeper roots in the West, and the prevailing social structures were healthier and enjoyed more popular support. In addition, the Western powers had been the victors rather than the losers in the war, a fact that further contributed to political and social stability. It does not follow, however, that Western Europe experienced no difficulties in the postwar years. There were many problems, the most serious being economic in nature, though with far-reaching social and political repercussions. The experiences of the two leading Western countries, Great Britain and France, illustrate this.

Great Britain

The chief problem in Britain was, by all odds, the severe and chronic unemployment. There was a short-lived boom immediately after the war when factories operated overtime to meet long pent-up consumer demands. But the bust came in 1920, and by March of 1921, over 2,000,000 people were out of work. Unemployment persisted through the 1920's, and the situation grew worse in the 1930's. Thus the depression actually began in Britain in 1920 rather than in 1929, and continued without significant respite to World War II.

These economic difficulties stemmed in part from World War I which, by stimulating the industrialization of such countries as the United States, Japan, and the British Dominions, meant reduced overseas markets, especially in the case of textiles where Britain faced stiff Japanese competition. The destruction of much of Britain's merchant marine also caused the invisible revenues to be reduced, as did the fact that Britain was no longer the world's financial center. The Bolshevik revolution further hurt the British economy, wiping out an important market for manufactured goods as well as substantial investments. Finally there was the failure of the British themselves to keep up with the rest of the world in industrial efficiency. Initially, they had led the world in the Industrial Revolution, but now they lagged behind in modernizing their equipment. Because they tended to keep machines until they were worn out rather than until they had become obsolete, productivity per man-hour lagged in comparison with other countries. For example, taking the year 1913 as 100, the output per man-shift in British mines rose by 1938 to a mere 113, compared to 164 in the German mines, and 201 in the Dutch.

This combination of circumstances was responsible for the almost unrelieved depression that gripped Britain during the interwar period. Millions of families subsisted on state relief, or the "dole" as it was popularly called. A whole generation grew up without an opportunity to work. Inevitably this had political repercussions. Most important was the decline of the Liberal party as the workers turned increasingly to the Labor party in the hope of finding relief. Thus the economic crisis tended to polarize British politics, with the propertied classes generally voting Conservative, the workers supporting Labor and the middle class fluctuating between the two. Each party had its panacea for the country's ills: the Conservatives called for protection; the declining Liberals, for free trade; and Labour for a capital levy and for the nationalization of heavy industry. The net result was a succession of alternating Conservative and Labour ministries, under Stanley Baldwin and Ramsey MacDonald, respectively, none of which was able to improve significantly the national fortunes. In the May 1929 elections, the Labourites won a plurality of the seats, and MacDonald formed his second government with the backing of the Liberals. He could not have known that within half a year the country would be hit by the Great Depression that was to cripple Britain's economy still more, ultimately sweeping away MacDonald's new administration.

France

France, too, was plagued by economic difficulties in the postwar years, although in certain respects she was better off than most of her neighbors. France had a well-balanced economy, so that she was not as vulnerable as the predominantly agrarian or industrial countries. The peace settlement strengthened her economy by adding the Saar Basin with its coal mines, and the Alsace-Lorraine region with its textile industry and rich potash and iron ore deposits. Conversely, France had been weakened by the loss of 1.4 million men who had been in the prime of life, and by unprecedented destruction of property. The war on the western front had been waged mostly on French soil, causing 23 billion dollars worth of damage to villages, towns, factories, mines, and railways. Also France had financed the war by loans rather than taxes, and this now meant that further loans would be needed for reconstruction purposes. The government resorted to printing more money, which led to the depreciation of the franc, which, in turn, resulted in political repercussions.

In contrast to Britain's two or three parties, France had several, so that a government's life depended on its ability to muster a large enough coalition or bloc of these parties to secure majority support. This explains the relatively rapid turnover of governments in France compared to that in Britain. The leading parties, from Left to Right, were the Communists and Socialists, who represented mostly urban and rural workers; the Radical Socialists, who were in the center and were supported by the lower middle class; and various parties on the Right, such as the Republican Democratic Union and the Democratic Alliance, which were usually strongly Catholic and represented big business and high finance.

As had happened in Britain, elections in 1919 returned a predominantly conservative and nationalistic parliament in France. For the next five years France was ruled by National Bloc ministries based mostly on the parties of the Right. The dominant personality during this period was Raymond Poincaré, who was determined to make the Germans pay the costs of reconstruction. His policy culminated in the French occupation of the Ruhr in 1923, an expensive operation that yielded little revenue. By early 1924 the franc had fallen from its prewar value of 19.3 cents to little more than 3 cents. The French public was alienated by this financial instability and by the Ruhr adventure, which aroused fears of renewed warfare. Accordingly, the May, 1924, elections returned a majority for the Cartel des Gauches, or Left Bloc. Edouard Herriot, leader of the Radical Socialists, became premier with the support of the Socialists. In foreign affairs he ended the Ruhr occupation, agreed to a settlement of the reparations issue, and recognized the Soviet Union. But the financial dilemma remained unsolved, and the franc fell to two cents—one-tenth of its prewar value.

France now turned once more to the Right. In July, 1926 Poincaré formed a National Union ministry of all parties except the Socialist and Communist and adopted stringent measures to reduce expenditures and increase revenues. By the end of 1926, the franc stood at 4 cents, and was stabilized at that level. Since this was only one-fifth of its prewar value, the government had relieved itself of four-fifths of its debts, though this was achieved at the expense of French bondholders. The devaluation attracted many tourists, especially the Americans, and also facilitated the exportation of French goods. Poincaré's success enabled him to remain premier for three years, an interwar record. He retired in the summer of 1929, just in time to escape the economic cyclone that was to destroy the precarious stability he had achieved.

V. STABILIZATION AND SETTLEMENT IN EUROPE

Reparations Settlement: Dawes Plan

The period from 1924 to 1929 was one of peace and settlement in Europe. The negotiation in 1924 of the Dawes Plan, an agreement concerning reparations payments, was the first phase of this process of stabilization. Germany had been required by the Versailles Treaty to accept responsibility for the war and to promise to make payments for the losses sustained. No agreement was reached at Versailles concerning the amount and the schedule of payments, and during the following years this issue was a perennial source of discord amongst the Allies as well as between them and Germany.

The Reparations Commission, a body that had been appointed to work out the details, decided in 1920 that the payments from Germany should be divided as follows: 52 per cent to France, 22 per cent to Britain, 10 per cent to Italy, 8 per cent to Belgium, and the remaining 8 per cent to the allied powers. The following year the Commission set the total German indemnity at $32 billion, to be paid both in cash and in kind. Some payments were made in 1921 and 1922, but at the same time Germany was undergoing a disastrous inflation. The mark, worth 25 cents in 1914, had fallen to 2 cents by July, 1922, and a year later it was worthless—two and one-half trillion to the dollar. Under these circumstances the Germans requested a two-year moratorium on payments. The British, suffering from unemployment and being anxious to hasten the revival of international trade, responded favorably to the request. The French, however, having suffered the heaviest damages, were convinced that the Germans could pay if they wished to, and proceeded to use force. In the face of British criticism, a French army, with Italian and Belgian contingents, occupied the Ruhr industrial region in January, 1923.

The Germans responded with a general strike, so that the French were forced to spend more on the occupation than they got out of it. With the German economy prostrate and the French stymied, the reparations issue was deadlocked, and so a commission of economic experts, headed by an American banker, Charles Dawes, was called in. On September 1, 1924, the so-called Dawes Plan was approved by both sides and went into effect. Based on the slogan, "Business, not politics," the plan called for annual payments beginning at $238 million and reaching a maximum of $595 million. Also, Germany was to receive a foreign loan of $200 million, and France was required to evacuate the Ruhr.

However, this arrangement, like so many others, was to be swept away by the onslaught of the Great Depression. Even during the four years that it operated, up to September, 1928, the Germans paid in cash and in kind only about half of what they borrowed from foreign markets, mostly American. Nevertheless, the Dawes Plan did ease tensions in Europe and prepare the way for the settlement of political issues.

Quest for Peace: Locarno Pacts

Theoretically, the League of Nations assured peace and security with Article 10 of the Covenant, which required member states "to respect and preserve against external aggression the territorial integrity and existing political independence of all members of the League." The difficulty rested in the League's lacking the power necessary to enforce this article. The Council could invite members to bring to bear an economic boycott, or even armed reprisal, against an aggressor, but any such measures of economic or military restraint could be applied only by the governments of individual states. The League itself possessed no weapons and no armed force; a French proposal to place an international police corps at its disposal was voted down.

Having experienced two German invasions in less than 50 years, France refused to entrust her security to a League without authority. First she proposed a

British-French-American triple alliance that would guarantee Anglo-American aid to France in case of German aggression. When this plan failed because the United States Senate refused to ratify the Treaty, France turned to the smaller European states that shared her interest in supporting the peace settlement and opposing treaty revision. She negotiated a formal military alliance with Belgium in September, 1920, with Poland in 1921, and with Czechoslovakia in 1924. Czechoslovakia had already organized the so-called "Little Entente" with Rumania and Yugoslavia in 1920–1921 for the purpose of providing mutual aid in case of either an attack by Hungary or the restoration of the Hapsburg dynasty. Poland was attached to the Little Entente in 1921 through an alliance with Rumania in which the two guaranteed reciprocal help in the event of attack by Russia. France's relationship with the Little Entente enabled her, then, to extend her own alliance system to include Rumania in 1926 and Yugoslavia in 1927.

This alliance system was basically anti-German, its primary purpose being to protect France and her allies by isolating Germany. About 1925, however, Franco-German relations improved, thanks to the temporarily successful operation of the Dawes Plan, and also to the mutually conciliatory attitudes of the foreign ministers of the two countries, Aristide Briand of France and Gustav Stresemann of Germany, who decided that the security of their respective countries could be enhanced by direct negotiations and agreements. They were encouraged by the British foreign minister, Sir Austen Chamberlain, who also brought the Italians around to this view. The outcome was a series of agreements known as the Locarno Pacts, signed in October, 1925.

These provided that Germany should enter the League of Nations and become a permanent Council member. In return, Germany agreed not to seek treaty revision by force and to settle peacefully every dispute with France, Belgium, Czechoslovakia, and Poland. Germany did reserve the right to seek modification of her eastern frontiers by peaceful means, but she recognized the permanence of her western frontiers. Germany, France, and Belgium undertook to respect for all time their mutual borders, and Britain and Italy guaranteed observance of this provision.

The Locarno Pacts led many to believe that peace at last was assured. In the afterglow of this optimism, the American Secretary of State, Frank Kellogg, acting on a suggestion of Briand, proposed that nations pledge themselves to renounce war as "an instrument of national policy." The proposal was implemented, and on August 27, 1928, the Kellogg-Briand Pact was signed. Since the pact only involved renunciation of war and made no provision for sanctions, it was quickly signed by over 60 countries. Although it depended exclusively on the moral pressure of world public opinion, the mere fact that so many countries signed contributed to a further lessening of international tension.

Equally promising were the improved relations with Germany. That country was admitted into the League of Nations in 1926, and was made a permanent member of the Council. Also, a further settlement was reached with Germany concerning the payment of reparations. The Dawes Plan had not stipulated the sum total of reparations that Germany should pay, so in 1929, a second commission of economic experts, under the chairmanship of another American financier, Owen Young, met in Paris and prepared a new payment schedule that was adopted early in 1930. The total amount to be paid by Germany was set at $8 billion, and the installments were to be extended over 58 years. In return for Germany's acceptance of the Young Plan, France evacuated the Rhineland in 1930, four years earlier than was required by the Versailles Treaty.

At the same time, a series of disarmament conferences was being held, partly because of the pressure of international public opinion, but also because the Allies had forced Germany to disarm with the expressed intention of initiating "a general limitation in the armaments of all nations." The conferences, however, failed to limit armaments. The countries with conscript armies did not wish to include trained reserves as effectives, while those with volunteer armies insisted that they should be included. Some countries wanted armaments to be limited on the basis of financial expenditures, but Britain and the United States were strongly opposed, because their expenditures were much higher per soldier. In addition, France and her allies insisted on international control and supervision of armaments, while Britain and the United States preferred reliance on good faith. The basic difficulty was that, given the absence of an international security system, each country sought security in its own armed forces.

Despite the failure in disarmament, there was a general feeling in the late Twenties that Europe had at last returned to normalcy: Germany and her former enemies appeared to be reconciled; French troops were out of the Rhineland and the Germans were in the League; the problem of reparations appeared to be finally resolved; over 60 nations had renounced war "as an instrument of national policy"; prosperity was on the rise, and unemployment was correspondingly declining. Even the news from the Soviet was encouraging, for that country had launched in 1928 a novel and grandiose Five Year Plan. Most authorities in the West regarded the Plan as impractical and doomed to failure, but at least it diverted the Russians from international adventures to internal economic development. Thus it was assumed that Europe now could settle back to enjoy decades of peace and prosperity as it had in the nineteenth century.

SUGGESTED READING

W. T. Angress, *Stillborn Revolution: The Communist Bid for Power in Germany, 1921–1923* (Princeton Univ., 1964); E. H. Carr, *The Bolshevik Revolution, 1917–1923* (Macmillan, 1951–1953), and also his *International Relations between the Two World Wars* (Macmillan, 1947); F. L. Carsten, *Revolution in Central Europe 1918–1919* (Univ. California, 1972); C. L. Mowat, *Britain Between the Wars, 1918–1940* (Univ. Chicago, 1955); H. Seton-Watson, *Eastern Europe Between the Wars, 1918–1941* (Cambridge Univ., 1946); D. Thomson, *Democracy in France* (Oxford Univ., 1952); E. Wiskemann, *Fascism in Italy: Its Development and Influence* (Macmillan, 1969).

chapter thirty-six

The Five Year Plans
and the
Great Depression

*The year 1931 was distinguished from previous years in the "post-war"
and in the "pre-war" age alike—by one outstanding feature. In 1931,
men and women all over the world were seriously contemplating and
frankly discussing the possibility that the Western system of Society
might break down and cease to work.*—Arnold J. Toynbee

As the 1920's drew to a close, Europe seemed to be settling down to an era of peace, security, and relative prosperity. This comfortable prospect was, however, destroyed completely by the onset of the Great Depression. The resulting economic dislocation and mass unemployment undermined the foundations of the settlement that had been reached in the preceding years. Everywhere governments rose and fell under the pressure of mounting distress and discontent. Such political instability affected directly—and disastrously—the international situation; some governments resorted to foreign adventures as a means for diverting domestic tension, while others ignored the acts of aggression because of their own pressing problems at home. Thus the Depression represents the Great Divide of the interwar period. The years before 1929 were years of hope, as Europe gradually resolved the various issues created by World War I. By contrast, the years after 1929 were filled with anxiety and disillusionment, as crisis followed crisis, culminating finally in World War II.

The impact and significance of the Great Depression was heightened by Russia's Five Year Plans. At a time when the West's economy was in a shambles, the Soviet Union was proceeding with its unique experiment in economic development. Although accompanied by rigid repression and mass privation, the Five Year Plans were substantially successful. The Soviet Union rose rapidly from a predominantly agrarian state to the second greatest industrial power in the world. This unprecedented achievement had international repercussions, particularly because of the economic difficulties besetting the West at the time.

And so the Five Year plans and the Great Depression stand out in the interwar period, the one accentuating the other, and each having repercussions that are being felt to the present day.

I. FIVE YEAR PLANS

War Communism

When the Bolsheviks found themselves the masters of Russia, they faced the challenge of creating the millennium about which they had preached so long. They soon discovered it a challenge they were quite unprepared to meet. There was no model in past history to follow. Lenin himself admitted, "We knew when we took power into our hands, that there were no ready forms of concrete reorganization of the capitalist system into a socialist one. . . . I do not know of any socialist who has dealt with these problems. . . . We must go by experiments."[1]

At first there was little opportunity for experimenting because the struggle for survival took precedence over everything else. The so-called "War Communism" that prevailed between 1917 and 1921 evolved out of the desperate measures taken to supply the battle front with needed materials and manpower. One feature of War Communism was the nationalization of land, banks, foreign trade, and heavy industry. Another was the forcible requisitioning of surplus agricultural produce needed to feed the soldiers and the city dwellers. The original plan was to compensate the peasants with manufactured goods, but this proved impossible because almost all factories were producing for the front.

The ending of the civil war meant that this stopgap system of War Communism was no longer needed, so it was promptly dropped. The peasants were up in arms against confiscation without compensation. At the same time, the economy of the country was paralyzed, owing largely to the uninterrupted fighting between 1914 and 1921. Industry had fallen to 10 per cent of prewar levels, while the grain crop declined from 74 million tons in 1916 to 30 million tons in 1919. The crowning disaster was the widespread drought of 1920 and 1921, which contributed to the worst famine in Russia's history. Millions of people died of starvation, and millions more were kept alive only by the shipments of the American Relief Administration.

New Economic Policy to Gosplan

The practical-minded Lenin realized that concessions were unavoidable—hence the adoption in 1921 of the New Economic Policy, or NEP as it was commonly known, which allowed a partial restoration of capitalism, especially in agriculture and trade. Peasants were permitted to sell their produce on the open market after paying to the state a tax in kind that consisted of about 12 per cent of their output. Private individuals were allowed to operate small stores and factories. Both the peasants and the new businessmen, or Nepmen as they were called, could employ labor and retain what profits they made from their operations. Lenin, however, saw to it that the state kept control of title to the land and of what he termed "the commanding heights" (banking, foreign trade, heavy industry, and transportation). So far as Lenin was concerned, the NEP did not mean the end of socialism in Russia; rather it was a temporary retreat, "one step backward in order to take two steps forward."

The great question in the following years was how these "two steps forward" should be made. By 1926, industrial and agricultural production had reached pre-1914 levels; but the population had increased by eight million since 1914, so the prewar per capita standards had not been reached. Even more disturbing was the growing strength of the well-to-do peasants, or kulaks (*kulak* means "the fist"), and their supporters. They were openly hostile to the Soviet regime because agricultural prices had fallen to just over half what they had been in 1913, while the prices for manufactured goods had nearly doubled. The kulaks, who produced most of the surplus foodstuffs, retaliated by reducing their output or keeping it from the market in order to force prices upward. Thus the hostile kulaks were in a position to starve the cities at will. Such was the unpleasant state of affairs more than a decade after the great revolution that was to have heralded the new socialist society.

Lenin died in 1924, and the economic issue concerning the replacement of the NEP was tied up with the political issue of Lenin's successor. Stalin eventually emerged as the Party leader, and after consolidating his position, he launched in 1928 the first of a series of Five Year Plans. These Plans were without precedent in that they provided a blueprint and a mechanism for the reorganization and operation of a nation's entire economy. At the center was the State Planning Commission (Gosplan), appointed by the Council of Peoples Commissars, the Soviet counterpart of a Western cabinet. The function of the Gosplan to the present day is to prepare the plans on the basis of the general directives received from the government and the statistical data received from all parts of the country.

The government (actually the Communist party leadership) makes the basic decisions, such as whether a particular Plan should concentrate on producing armaments or building up heavy industry or turning out more consumer goods or reducing grain crops in favor of industrial crops. With these directives as a guide, the Gosplan sets to work on the huge mass of statistical information that is constantly pouring into headquarters. All Soviet organizations—whether agricultural, industrial, military, or cultural—are required by law to provide the Gosplan with specified data concerning resources and operations. This mass of information is processed by a highly trained staff of statisticians, economists, and technical experts, who proceed to work out a provisional Five Year Plan. After consultation and counter-suggestions from the organizations concerned, a final Plan is drafted. The first of these Five Year plans, though primitive when compared with the current computer-prepared ones, comprised a three-volume text of 1,600 pages, including tables and statistics that ranged over heavy industries, light industries, finance, cooperatives, agriculture, transportation, communications, labor, wages, schools, literature, public health, and social insurance.

Collectivization of Agriculture

Stalin once stated that the kulak resistance to collectivization of the land was the most dangerous challenge he ever encountered. The kulaks naturally opposed the collective farms that they had to enter on the same terms as the poor peasants who brought little with them. In some cases, the kulaks burned the buildings of the collectives, poisoned the cattle, and spread rumors to frighten away other peasants. The Soviet government crushed such resistance without mercy. The police uprooted hundreds of thousands of kulak families from their villages, putting them in prisons and in Siberian labor camps. In the end, the government had its way, so that by 1938 almost all peasant holdings had been amalgamated into 242,400 collective farms, or *kolkhozy*, and 4,000 state farms, or *sovkhozy*.

The *kolkhozy* are cooperatives, whose members divide the profits at the end of the year on the basis of the amount and the skill of the work contributed. The *sovkhozy*, by contrast, are operated by the government, and its members are paid set wages as though they were factory hands.

The Soviet agricultural system has not worked well, as indicated by the fact that the 38 million workers on Russian farms produce only about 80 per cent as much as do the 4 million workers on American farms. One reason for this disparity is that the climate of the Soviet Union is much less favorable for agriculture than that of the United States. Another reason is that the Soviet government has been more interested in developing industry and therefore has starved agriculture. This has meant less machinery and fertilizers on Russian farms than American. It also has meant high state taxes and low agriculture prices, so that little was left for the collective members at the end of the year. Lack of incentive affected productivity so adversely that it contributed significantly to Khrushchev's fall from power in October, 1964, and to the continued failure of agriculture under Khrushchev's successors.

Although collectivization has not been successful from the viewpoint of production, it has nevertheless provided the essential basis for the Five Year Plans. It has eliminated the kulaks who at one time threatened the very existence of the Soviet regime. The peasants are no longer an independent political force, and Soviet authority is firmly established in the countryside. This, in turn, has enabled the Soviet government to foist much of the cost of industrialization upon the peasantry. Surplus produce has been siphoned off by the state in the form of tax levies, and then exported in order to finance the cost of industrialization. Even though the peasants have been dragging their heels, the collectivist system of agriculture has enabled the government to squeeze enough out of them to feed the city dwellers and to help pay for the new industrial centers.

Growth of Industry

Whereas most of the farms are run as cooperatives, most factories are owned and operated by the government. Besides providing industry with the necessary capital, the government also employs a combination of the "carrot" and the "stick" to stimulate maximum production. Both workers and managers are required to meet certain quotas on pain of fine or dismissal. On the other hand, if they surpass their quotas, they are rewarded with bonuses. Trade unions are allowed and recognized, but are denied the basic right to strike—for strikes would be incompatible with the goals and functioning of the Soviet-planned economy. The purpose of a strike is to secure for the workers, in the form of higher wages, a larger proportion of what is produced; but the Gosplan has already decided how much will go to workers and how much to the government for reinvestment in industry.

In actuality, Soviet industry has grown as rapidly as it has because the government withdraws about a third of the national income for reinvestment; in comparison, the United States withdraws about half that proportion. Furthermore, in a planned economy the government is able to allocate investment capital as it wishes. Thus about 70 per cent of the total Soviet industrial output consists of capital goods, and 30 per cent of consumer goods, whereas in the United States, the ratio is roughly the reverse. By the end of the first Five Year Plan, in 1932, the Soviet Union had risen in industrial output from fifth to second place in the world. Soviet gross national product, which included the lagging agricultural as well as the industrial output, increased three and a half times during the quarter century between 1928 and 1952—a rate of growth surpassing that of any other country during this period.

It should be emphasized that Soviet economic growth has been achieved at the expense of the Soviet citizens, who have been forced to work hard for the future and to endure privation in the present, regardless of what their wishes might be. Consumer goods are scarce, expensive, and of poor quality. The gross national product (total output of goods and services) of the Soviet Union has remained for the past several years at 46 to 48 per cent of the GNP of the United States. And in per capita terms, the Soviet GNP is about 20 per cent of that of the United States.

Significance for World History

From the point of view of global impact, it is likely that the Gosplan will prove to be of greater significance than the Communist International. The Five Year Plans attracted worldwide attention, particularly because of the concurrent breakdown of the West's economy. Socialism was no longer a dream of visionaries; it was a going concern.

The Five Year Plans did not impress the Western countries as much as the underdeveloped nations, one reason being that by Western standards, Soviet citizens were grossly exploited. Western visitors to Russia were struck by the shabby clothing, the monotonous diet, the wretched housing, and the scarcity of consumer goods. They were also appalled by the lack of individual freedom as reflected in the one-party political structure, the hobbling of trade unions, the regimentation of education, and the rigid control of all communications media. Soviet society, despite the achievements of the Five Year Plans, did not seem to most Westerners a Socialist paradise worthy of emulation.

Former colonial peoples in the underdeveloped world reacted very differently. Although most of them had recently won political independence, they were still far from economic independence. And so they regarded Soviet living standards with envy rather than commiseration. Less attention was paid to the absence of individual liberties in the Soviet Union because these people had not customarily enjoyed such liberties in their own countries. This was noted by an American correspondent who travelled extensively in Central Asia in 1953.

What is it that gives Asian visitors to Tashkent such [favorable] impressions? It is the sight of a . . . huge Asian city with excellent health standards, education, sanitation, clean streets, rapidly improving housing, electric facilities, substantial if not fancy consumers' goods, an abundance of food, an abundance of work, a rapidly widening industrialization program and constantly improving agricultural productivity.

Along with this they see equality of races under the law and the participation of large numbers of Uzbeks and other Central Asian peoples in government, industry and education.

Against this background the Asian visitor is not likely to be too much influenced by Western arguments about democracy nor does the individual human factor impress the Asian visitor so strongly since he is more likely to know the mortality tables of his own country.

While the European visitor to Tashkent might reach one set of conclusions based on comparisons with Europe and on a lack of facilities to which he has been accustomed, an Asian might arrive at directly the opposite conclusions. It is the Asian's conclusions that are important, since Tashkent has prime importance as a symbol for Asia rather than for Europe.[2]

On the other hand it should be emphasized that Soviet policies in Central Asia have not met with unanimous approval. Between 100,000 and 200,000 Kazaks fled into Chinese Sinkiang to escape the repression of the early days of the Plans. Many of the older generation have been bitterly opposed to the growing Russification of their republics—a result of deliberate government policy and mass Slavic immigration. Finally, Communist China in recent years has attracted increasing attention and sympathy at the expense of the white, and now affluent, Soviet Union.

II. THE GREAT DEPRESSION

Origins of the Crash

With the opening of the year 1929, the United States appeared to be flourishing. Businessmen, academic economists, and government leaders were all expressing confidence in the future. Their optimism proved unjustified; in the fall of 1929, the bottom fell out of the stock market, and a worldwide depression, unprecedented in its intensity and longevity, followed. The serious international economic imbalance that developed when the United States became a creditor nation on a large scale (following World War I) seems to have been one reason for this unexpected denouement. Britain had been a creditor nation before the war, but she had used the proceeds from her overseas investments and loans to pay for her chronic excess of imports over exports. The United States, by contrast, normally had a favorable trade balance, accentuated by tariffs that were kept at high levels for reasons of domestic politics. In addition, money poured into the country in the 1920's in payment of war debts, and the American gold hoard rose between 1913 and 1924 from $1.924 to $4.499 billion, or half the world's total gold supply.

This imbalance was neutralized for several years by large-scale American loans and investments abroad: between 1925 and 1928, the average annual total for American foreign investments amounted to $1.1 billion. In the long run, this, of course, intensified the imbalance and could not be, continued indefinitely. As payments came due, debtor countries were forced to curtail imports from the United States, and certain branches of the American economy, especially agriculture, were hurt. In addition, some countries found it necessary to default on their debts, which shook certain financial firms in the United States.

As serious as the imbalance of the international economy was that of the American economy, the basic reason being that wages lagged behind the rising productivity. Between 1920 and 1929, hourly industrial wages rose only 2 per cent, while the productivity of workers in factories jumped 55 per cent. At the same time, the real income of the farmers was shrinking because agricultural prices were falling while taxes and living costs were rising. Whereas in 1910 the income per farm worker had been slightly less than 40 per cent that of the non-farm worker, by 1930, it was just under 30 per cent. Such poverty in the countryside was a serious matter, because the rural population then comprised one-fifth of the total population.

The combination of stationary factory wages and falling farm income resulted in severe maldistribution of national income. In 1929, 5 per cent of the American people received one-third of all personal incomes (compared to one-sixth by the end of World War II). This meant inadequate purchasing power for the masses, combined with a high level of capital investment by those who were receiving the high salaries and dividends. Production of capital goods during the 1920's rose at an average annual rate of 6.4 per cent, compared to 2.8 per cent for consumer goods. Eventually this led to the clogging of the economy; the low purchasing power was unable to support such a high rate of capital investment. As a result, the index of industrial production dropped from 126 to 117 between June and October, 1929, creating a slump that contributed to the stock market crash that autumn.

The weakness of the American banking system was a final factor contributing to the crash of 1929. A great number of independent banking firms were operating, and some of these lacked sufficient resources to weather financial storms. When one closed its doors, panic spread, and depositors rushed to withdraw their savings from other banks, thus setting in motion a chain reaction that undermined the entire banking structure.

Worldwide Depression

The stock market crash in the United States began in September, 1929. Within one month, stock values dropped 40 per cent, and apart from a few brief recoveries, the decline continued for three years. During those three years, 5,000 banks closed their doors. General Motors had produced 5.5 million automobiles in 1929, but in 1931, they produced only 2.5 million. The steel industry in July, 1932 was operating at 12 per cent of capacity. By 1933, both general industrial production and national income had slumped by nearly one-half, wholesale prices, by almost one-third, and merchandise trade, by more than two-thirds.

The Great Depression was unique not only in its intensity but also in its worldwide impact. American financial houses were forced to call in their short-term loans abroad; naturally, there were repercussions. In May, 1931, the Credit-Anstalt, the largest and most reputable bank in Vienna, declared itself insolvent, setting off a wave of panic throughout the Continent. In September, 1931, Britain went off the gold standard, to be followed two years later by the United States and nearly all the major countries.

The breakdown of the financial world had its counterpart in industry and commerce: the index of world industrial production, excluding the Soviet Union, fell from 100 in 1929 to 86.5 in 1930, 74.8 in 1931, and 63.8 in 1932, a drop of 36.2 per cent. The maximum decline in previous crises had been 7 per cent. Even more drastic was the shrinking of world international trade, from $68.6 billion in 1929 to 55.6 in 1930, 39.7 in 1931, 26.9 in 1932, and 24.2 in 1933. Again it might be noted that the maximum drop in international trade in the past had been 7 per cent, during the 1907–1908 crisis.

Social and Political Repercussions

These economic cataclysms gave rise to social problems of corresponding magnitude. Most serious and intractable was the problem of mass unemployment, which reached tragic proportions. In March, 1933, the number of people out of work in the United States was estimated conservatively at over 14 million, or a fourth of the total labor force. In Britain, the jobless were numbered at nearly 3 million, representing about the same proportion of the workers as in the United States. Germany was the worst off with no less than 6 million out of work: trade-union executives estimated that more than two-fifths of their members were wholly unemployed, and another fifth had only part-time work.

Unemployment on this scale drastically lowered living standards in all countries. Even in the wealthy United States there was wholesale misery and privation, especially in the beginning, when relief was left to private and to local agencies with inadequate funds. These were years of bread lines, of soup kitchens, and of veterans selling apples on street corners. In England, where unemployment had been chronic throughout the 1920's, the situation now became even worse. A substantial proportion of a whole generation was growing up with little opportunity or prospect of finding employment. Some bitterly referred to their purposeless existence as a "living death." In Germany, with its higher percentage of jobless people, the frustrations and tensions were more acute; they eventually made possible the triumph of Hitler.

Social dislocation on such a large scale inevitably had profound political repercussions. Even in the United States, with its superior resources and its tradition of political stability, these were years of strange ideas and agitations: a Bonus Army composed of uprooted war veterans; technocracy, an anti-capitalist movement for rule by engineers; a Farm Holiday amounting to a sit-down strike in agriculture; and various proposals for income redistribution, including the Townshend Plan for munificent old-age pensions, and the Share-Our-Wealth movement of Senator Huey Long of Louisiana. Another manifestation of the political turbulence was Franklin Roosevelt's sweeping electoral victory in 1932. The New Deal that followed served as an escape valve for the political discontent, and effectively neutralized the extremist movements.

Political developments in Britain and France during these years were generally the same as in the United States. Both countries were hit by political storms but managed to ride them out within the framework of their traditional institutions. The British Labour party, which had come into office in June, 1929, was faced almost at once with the problem of paying "dole" to ever greater numbers of unemployed. In August, 1931, Prime Minister Ramsay MacDonald disbanded his Labour government and formed a new National government. This proved to be a mere façade for Tory rule, with the Conservatives comprising the majority of the cabinet. Three years later, the aging and ailing MacDonald resigned in favor of Stanley Baldwin, and so Britain passed under virtual Conservative rule, though the coalition still existed nominally.

In France, too, the Left was forced out of office by the pressures of the Depression. It won the 1932 elections, and the Radical Édouard Herriot formed a government with Socialist support as had been done in 1924. On this occasion also, the Left ministry was undermined by mounting financial difficulties. The Radicals and the Socialists were hopelessly divided on the question of how to cope with the economic crisis. Herriot held office for only six months, and four other premiers followed in rapid succession. The showdown came in December, 1933, with the Stavisky scandal, involving a Russian-born promoter and a provincial pawnshop in a fraudulent bond issue; according to rumors, various important officials and politicians were implicated. Extreme rightist groups took advantage of the opportunity to stage street riots in an effort to overthrow the republic itself. Although they failed to do so, they did force the government to resign in February, 1934. A number of conservative ministries followed, none of which proved capable of coping with the country's basic ills.

Much more dramatic and fateful was the rise of Hitler to power in Germany. When the Depression hit the country, its government was a Left-Center coalition led by the Socialist Chancellor Herman Müller, while the conservative old war hero Paul von Hindenburg was functioning as president. Like Socialist ministries elsewhere, the Müller ministry in Germany was undermined by dissension over how to cope with unemployment and other problems created by the Depression.

The Left favored increased unemployment relief, while the Right insisted on retrenchment and a balanced budget. The Müller cabinet was forced to resign in March, 1930, and from then on, Germany was ruled by parties of the Center and Right.

At first a coalition government was organized by Heinrich Brüning, an intelligent and upright, though cold and rigid, Centrist, who commanded more respect than friendship. It was the tragedy of this well-meaning patriot that he dug the grave of German democracy. Lacking a parliamentary majority, he fell back upon Article 48 of the constitution, which empowered the president, in case of emergency, to issue decrees that would have the force of law unless specifically rejected by majority vote of the Reichstag. The Reichstag did, in fact, vote against the first emergency decrees, but Brüning countered by persuading Hindenburg to dissolve the Reichstag and order new elections for September, 1930. Brüning expected that a majority for the various Center and Right parties would be returned, enabling him to govern the country in regular parliamentary fashion. Instead, the elections marked the emergence of Hitler's National Socialist party as a national force.

The son of a minor Austrian customs official, Adolf Hitler went to Vienna early in life, aspiring to be a painter. Lacking talent, he spent, according to his own account—which seems to be greatly exaggerated—five miserable years working at the most menial jobs to keep body and soul together. His misery, real or fancied, together with his undoubted professional failure, help to explain the passionate convictions he now acquired: a hatred of Marxists and Jews, a detestation of parliamentary government, and a contempt for the affluent bourgeoisie and its "decadent" culture. From Vienna, Hitler drifted to Munich, where in 1914 he enlisted in a Bavarian regiment. Although he fought bravely through the war, was thrice wounded, and was awarded the coveted Iron Cross, he apparently displayed no particular aptitude, because he rose no higher than a corporal despite his devoted service. Yet his army years were among the happiest of his life, the military discipline providing a sense of direction he had hitherto lacked.

At the end of the war, Hitler turned violently against the new Weimar Republic. In 1919, he joined a struggling group called the National Socialist German Workers' party, of which he soon became the leader, or Führer. After making rabble-rousing speeches on nationalist and anti-Semitic themes, he joined Field Marshal Ludendorff in an *opéra-bouffe* uprising in Munich in 1923. It was easily put down by the police, and Hitler was imprisoned for nine months. There, at the age of thirty-five, he wrote *Mein Kampf*—"My Battle"—a long and turgid autobiographical reflection into which he poured his hatred of democracy, Marxism, and Jews, and which specified how a defeated Germany could become "the lord of the earth." "Racial purity" was the key to this mastery: "A State, which in the age of racial poisoning devotes itself to the fostering of its best racial elements, must one day become the lord of the earth."

Upon release from prison, Hitler resumed his agitation but with disappointing results. In the December, 1924, elections, his Nazi party won only 14 seats and a mere 908,000 votes, and in May, 1928, won even fewer—12 seats and 810,000 votes, or 2.6 per cent of the total number. The turning point came with the September, 1930, elections when the Nazis won 107 seats and 6,407,000 votes, or 18.3 per cent of the total. This avalanche of ballots did not come from the workers; the Socialist and Communist parties between them gained 13 more seats in 1930 than in 1928. Hitler was getting his new-found support from the middle-class elements that were looking desperately for safety in the fierce economic storm (This is evident in Table 1, which shows the marked drop in the votes received from

TABLE 1 REICHSTAG ELECTIONS, 1919–1933 (Number of Deputies and Percentage of Total Votes*)

Party	1/19	6/20	5/24	12/24	5/28	9/30	7/32	11/32	3/33
Communist									
No. dep.	0	4	62	45	54	77	89	100	81
% vote		2.1	12.6	9.0	10.6	13.1	14.6	16.9	12.3
Social Democratic									
No. dep.			100	131	153	143	133	121	120
% vote			20.5	26.0	29.8	24.5	21.6	20.4	18.3
Ind.									
No. dep.	22	84							
% vote	7.6	17.9							
Maj.									
No. dep.	165	102							
% vote	37.9	21.6							
Democratic									
No. dep.	75	39	28	32	25	20	4	2	5
% vote	18.6	8.3	5.7	6.3	4.9	3.8	1.0	1.0	0.8
Centrum									
No. dep.	91	64	65	69	62	68	75	70	74
% vote	19.7	13.6	13.4	13.6	12.1	11.8	12.5	11.9	11.7
Bavarian People's									
No. dep.	0	21	16	19	16	19	22	20	18
% vote		4.4	3.2	3.7	3.0	3.0	3.2	3.1	2.7
Economic									
No. dep.	4	4	10	17	23	23	2	1	0
% vote	0.9	0.8	2.4	3.3	4.5	3.9	0.4	0.3	0
German People's									
No. dep.	19	65	45	51	45	30	7	11	2
% vote	4.4	13.9	9.2	10.1	8.7	4.5	1.2	1.9	1.1
National People's									
No. dep.	44	71	95	103	73	41	37	52	52
% vote	10.3	14.9	19.5	20.5	14.2	7.0	5.9	8.8	8.0
National Socialist									
No. dep.	0	0	32	14	12	107	230	196	288
% vote			6.5	3.0	2.6	18.3	37.4	33.1	43.9

* Under the electoral system provided for in the Weimar Constitution each party received approximately one representative for every 60,000 popular votes cast for its candidates. Various small parties, not listed here, were underrepresented in the Reichstag.

1930 onward by all the Center and Right parties except the Catholic Centrum). To the minor functionaries and bankrupt tradesmen, the Nazi platform offered comfort and hope. It called for abolition of unearned income and "interest slavery," nationalization of all trusts, profit sharing in large concerns, and the death penalty for usurers and profiteers. At the same time, all patriotic Germans were promised the smashing of the Versailles chains and the persecution of the Jews, who were branded as being both exploiting financiers and materialistic Communists. It should be emphasized that Hitler had been campaigning on this platform for years, with little response. The Depression was directly and primarily responsible for the change in his political fortunes. Before its full effects were felt, he had been regarded by most Germans as a loud-mouthed but quite harmless fanatic; when almost half the labor force was unemployed, he became for increasing numbers the beloved Führer who supplied scapegoats for their misery, and a program of action for individual and national fulfillment.

With the September, 1930, elections, the Nazis increased their Reichstag representation from 12 to 107, thus becoming the second largest party in the country. This unexpected outcome undermined parliamentary government in Germany because it denied a majority to both a Center-Right coalition desired by Brüning and a Center-Left coalition that had functioned under Müller. Consequently, Brüning had to rely for over two years on presidential decrees for all necessary legislation. The extent of his dependence on Hindenburg was demonstrated when he proposed legislation for the breakup of East Prussian estates; President Hindenburg, himself a Junker landowner, was strongly opposed, and forced Brüning to resign in May, 1932.

The new chancellor was Franz von Papen, nominally a member of the Center. Actually he was a reactionary aristocrat, well described as "an elegant, gracious, suave nonentity, clever to the point of stupidity." Papen headed a weak coalition government with negligible Reichstag support, so he held new elections in July, 1932, in the hope of strengthening his position. Instead, the Nazis were the big winners: their votes jumped to 13,799,000, or 37.4 per cent of the total number, and their seats to 230. Again, these gains were made at the expense of the Right and Center parties, because, compared to 1930, the combined Socialist and Communist seats actually increased by two. Parliamentary government was now impossible; since neither the Nazis nor the Communists would enter a coalition, no majority support could be organized.

In November, 1932, Papen held still another election in an attempt to break the deadlock. This time the Nazis lost 2 million votes and 34 seats in the Reichstag, reducing them to 196 deputies. They were still the strongest party in the country, but they could no longer pose as the irresistible wave of the future. Indeed, panic seized the party leaders, but they were saved by large-scale financial support from German businessmen who were worried that millions of votes might shift to the Left if the Nazi party disintegrated. Hitler was also helped by the morass of intrigues and cabals that passed for government in Berlin at the time. The aged Hindenburg was now senile and could function lucidly only a few hours each day. Persuaded to get rid of Papen, he appointed in his place General Kurt von Schleicher, who was even more devious than his predecessor. After proposing reforms that antagonized both landowners and businessmen, Schleicher was forced to resign on January 23, 1933. Two days later, Hitler became chancellor with a coalition cabinet of Nationalists and Nazis.

Within six months Hitler had regimented Germany, on the basis of his ideas concerning race and leadership. A new Reichstag was elected on March 5 following a campaign of unprecedented propaganda and terrorism. The Nazis received 288 seats and five and a half million votes, but they still comprised only 44 per cent of the total cast. When the representatives met, Hitler declared the Communist seats null and void, and then made a deal with the Catholic Center that gave him enough votes to pass the Enabling Act on March 23, 1933. This gave him authority to rule by decree for four years. But by the summer of 1933, he had eliminated or leashed virtually all independent elements in German life—trade unions, schools, churches, political parties, communications media, the judiciary, and the states of the federation.

Thus Hitler became master of Germany, and by technically legal methods, as he never ceased to boast. The Depression had made his triumph possible, though by no means inevitable; the possibility was translated into actuality by a combination of other factors, including Hitler's own talents, the support afforded by assorted vested interests, and the myopia of his opponents who underestimated him and failed to unite in opposition.

International Repercussions

The British Foreign Minister, Sir Austen Chamberlain, comparing the international situation in 1932 with that of the Locarno era, observed:

I look at the world to-day and I contrast the conditions now with the conditions at that time, and I am forced to acknowledge that for some reason or other, owing to something upon which it is difficult to put one's finger, in these last two years the world is moving backward. Instead of approaching nearer to one another, instead of increasing the measure of goodwill, instead of progressing to a stable peace, it has fallen back into an attitude of suspicion, of fear, of danger, which imperils the peace of the world.[3]

That "something" that Chamberlain could not identify was the Depression and its manifold repercussions, international as well as national. Various international agreements 'of the Locarno era were rendered unworkable, particularly those concerning reparations and war debts. It soon became obvious that governments, pushed to the brink of bankruptcy by their slumping economies and mounting unemployment, would not be able to meet commitments undertaken a few years earlier. In July, 1931, on the initiative of President Hoover, the powers agreed to a moratorium on all intergovernmental debts. The following summer, at the Lausanne Conference, the powers in fact, if not in theory, cancelled German reparations entirely. Simultaneously, the payment of war debts to the United States came to an end, though a few token payments were made in the following years. And so the sticky old issue of reparations and war debts was finally swept away by the economic storms let loose by the Depression.

Another effect of the storms was to accentuate the endemic economic nationalism to the point where it disturbed international relations. In the general spirit of *sauve qui peut,* self-protective measures by individual nations took such forms as higher tariffs, more rigid import quotas, clearing agreements, currency control regulations, and bilateral trade pacts. These measures inevitably fomented economic friction and political tensions among states. Various attempts were made to reverse the trend but without success. The World Economic Conference that met in London in 1933 was a dismal fiasco, and "autarchy," or economic self-sufficiency, gradually became a commonly accepted national goal.

Closely related was the petering out of disarmament efforts, which gave way to massive rearmament programs. The Disarmament Conference that met intermittently for twenty months, beginning in February, 1932, was as futile as the Economic Conference. As the 1930's progressed, countries devoted more and more of their energies to rearming. The trend proved impossible to stop because armament manufacturing provided jobs as well as imagined security. Unemployment in the United States, for example, was not substantially reduced until the country began to rearm on the eve of World War II. Likewise, Hitler quickly disposed of the unprecedented unemployment he faced by launching a gigantic rearmament program.

The armaments now being accumulated were bound sooner or later to be used, and their use required some justification; the most obvious was that of *Lebensraum,* or living space. This was the term coined by Hitler, but similar expressions and arguments were employed by Mussolini in Italy and by the military leaders in Japan. The unemployment and general misery, according to this doctrine, arose from the lack of *Lebensraum.* A few fortunate countries had seized all the colonies and underpopulated lands overseas, leaving the other nations without the natural resources needed to support their people. The obvious way out was to expand, by force if necessary, to remedy the injustices inflicted in the past. Such were the arguments used by the so-called "have-not" countries against the "haves."

The reasoning was manifestly specious in view of the fact that the Depression had devastated equally and impartially the United States, Canada, and Britain, along with Germany, Italy, and Japan. Nevertheless, the *Lebensraum* ideology served to unite the people of the "have-not" countries in support of the expansionist policies of their respective governments. It also gave a superficial moral justification to aggression committed for the avowed purpose of providing food for the needy and work for the jobless. Indeed, certain elements even within the "have" countries accepted these rationalizations and defended the aggressions that followed.

Such, then, was the combination of forces behind the "suspicion," the "fear," and the "moving backward" that Chamberlain had observed in 1932. During the following years, these forces undermined completely the settlement that had been reached in the Twenties and precipitated one crisis after another, culminating finally in World War II.

SUGGESTED READING

A. BULLOCH, *Hitler: A Study in Tyranny* (Harper, 1952); J. K. GALBRAITH, *The Great Crash, 1929* (Houghton, 1955); H. HOLBORN, ed., *Republic to Reich: The Making of the Nazi Revolution* (Pantheon, 1972); A. NOVE, *An Economic History of the U.S.S.R.* (Lane, 1969); W. L. SHIRER, *The Rise and Fall of the Third Reich* (Simon and Schuster, 1960); C. K. WILBER, *The Soviet Model and Underdeveloped Countries* (Univ. North Carolina, 1970).

chapter thirty-seven

Drift to War,
1929-1939

This is not peace. It is an armistice for twenty years.—Marshall
Foch, 1919

The late 1920's were years of prosperity, stabilization, and settlement;
the 1930's were years of depression, crises, and war. In Europe, the settlement of
the Twenties was based on the French system of alliances, and in the Far East,
on the Washington Conference agreements, the objective in each case being to
preserve the *status quo* in the two regions. This objective was realized in the
1920's, but during the next decade, everything was suddenly and decisively upset.
New leaders appeared in Germany and Japan who were determined to revise
the territorial settlement of World War I and who possessed the means and the
will to do so. Their massive rearming programs and their breath-taking aggressions drastically altered the balance of power. No longer was the relatively weak
Italy the only revisionist state attempting ineffectually to challenge the *status
quo;* the Third Reich and Imperial Japan also gave strength to the revisionist
drive, resulting in an entirely new power configuration. A triangle situation developed, with Britain, France, and their Continental allies supporting the *status
quo,* Germany, Italy, and Japan driving for revision; and the Soviet Union,
strengthened by the Five Year Plans, playing an increasingly important role. The
interplay of these three forces explains the recurring crises of the 1930's and the
final outbreak of World War II.

I. JAPAN INVADES MANCHURIA

The first major act of aggression was made by Japan, in pursuance of long-
cherished territorial ambitions on the mainland. The Japanese had entered
World War I promptly in order to exploit what appeared to be a golden opportunity. They took over with little difficulty the German islands in the Pacific and
the German holdings on the Shantung Peninsula. The full extent of their ambitions, however, was manifested by the Twenty-one Demands made upon China

in January, 1915. If implemented, these would have transformed China into a Japanese protectorate. The maintenance of the Japanese expeditionary force in Siberia after the British and American troops had been withdrawn in 1920 was another indication of their continental ambitions.

These Japanese aspirations were, for the most part, unsatisfied. At the Paris Peace Conference Japan did retain control of the former German islands, but as Class C mandates rather than as outright possessions. President Wilson strenuously opposed Japanese claims to the indisputably Chinese territory of Shantung. As a compromise, Japan was confirmed in "temporary" possession of the peninsula, but she conceded that it was her "policy" to restore the territory to China at an unspecified date, "retaining only the economic privileges [hitherto] granted to Germany."

At the Washington Naval Conference Japan formally renounced any territorial ambitions she may still have cherished. The nine powers at the conference signed a Nine-Power Treaty (February 6, 1922) guaranteeing the territorial integrity of China and reiterating the principle of the Open Door. At the same conference the United States, Britain, France, and Japan signed the Four-Power Treaty (December 13, 1921) by which they agreed to respect one another's rights in "insular possessions" in the Pacific and to settle any future differences by consultation. In addition, Japan, after energetic American mediation, agreed to restore Shantung to China and to evacuate her troops from Siberia; both commitments were fulfilled in 1922.

Having finished with foreign adventures, at least for the time being, Japan now turned to domestic problems: the aftermath of the disastrous 1923 earthquake, which destroyed three quarters of Tokyo and inflicted 160,000 casualties and $2 billion worth of property loss; and the troublous suffrage issue, which provoked riots and political upheavals until the acceptance of universal male suffrage in 1925 increasing the number of voters from 3 to 14 million.

Most acute was the economic problem, particularly that of the impoverished peasantry. Japan, like the United States, had prospered greatly during World War I, supplying munitions and merchant shipping. The prosperity, however, was poorly distributed, because of the unprecedented concentration of economic power in the so-called Zaibatsu (*Zai* means wealth, *batsu,* clique). This was the general name given to four giant family corporations (Mitsui, Mitsubishi, Sumitomo, and Yasuda) that by World War II controlled three-fourths of the combined capitalization of all Japanese firms, and held one-third of all deposits in Japan's private banks, three-fourths of all trust deposits, and one-fifth of all life insurance policies. The peasants, comprising one-half the total population, were impoverished by high rents and heavy debts. Only 7 per cent of these families owned five acres or more of land; the average holding was less than three acres. City workers suffered from high food prices, low wages, and lack of trade-union freedom.

The depressed living standards of the workers and peasants meant a severely restricted domestic market. Consequently, Japanese industry was particularly dependent upon foreign markets for the disposal of its products; this dependence spelled disaster with the coming of the Depression. Between 1929 and 1931, foreign trade decreased by almost 50 per cent. The peasants, who had supplemented their meager incomes by silk cultivation, were badly hurt by the sharp slump in silk exports to depression-ridden America. City workers suffered correspondingly from unemployment.

Army leaders and other champions of territorial aggrandizement were now able to argue persuasively that the source of Japan's trouble was her dependence upon foreign markets. Japan should conquer an empire that would make her self-sufficient and economically independent of the rest of the world. Military spokesmen had been preaching this doctrine for years, but the ravages of the Depression now provided them with a responsive audience, as had happened in the case of Hitler in Germany.

The Japanese expansionists were not only motivated by economic considerations. They were also concerned about the growing strength of the Soviet Union and the increasing success of Chiang Kai-shek in unifying China. In addition, they were fully aware of the unemployment situation and other problems that were then engrossing the attention of Western statesmen. These considerations explain the decision of the Japanese military to strike in the Chinese province of Manchuria. This province in the northeast corner of China had the double advantage of being loosely connected with the central Nanking government and possessing abundant natural resources, including iron, coal, and extensive fertile plains. Furthermore, Japan had obtained through past treaty arrangements certain special privileges in Manchuria; these could be used to find pretexts for justifying aggressive measures. This was precisely what was done when the Japanese military decided in the fall of 1931 that the time had come to move.

On the evening of September 18, 1931, an explosion wrecked a small section of track on the Japanese-controlled South Manchuria railway to the north of Mukden. In testimony before the International War Crimes Tribunal in Tokyo in June, 1946, Baron Shidehara, who was Foreign Minister in 1931, admitted that army officers had staged the incident that he had vainly tried to stop. His testimony is supported by the speed and precision with which the Japanese army quartered in the Kwantung Peninsula swung immediately into action. Without declaring war, it captured Mukden and Changchun in the space of twenty-four hours, and then fanned out in all directions. The taking of Harbin in late January, 1932, signified the end of all organized resistance in Manchuria. In March, 1932, the victors renamed their conquest Manchukuo, the "State of Manchu." Needing a puppet emperor, they dragged out of retirement Henry P'u Yi, the surviving head of the old Manchu dynasty that had fallen in 1911, and solemnly installed him as Regent.

Meanwhile, the Chinese government had appealed to the League of Nations under Article 11, and to the United States under the Paris Pact (Kellogg–Briand Pact). The result was much deliberation but no practical aid. Secretary of State Henry L. Stimson expressed "wholehearted sympathy" yet declined to invoke the Paris Pact. The League Council convened on September 19, October 13, and again on November 16, to discuss the Manchurian situation; the sessions were marked by delay and confusion as well as by courtesies and compliments. On November 21, the Japanese delegation accepted the original Chinese proposal for an impartial commission of inquiry, but the members were not chosen until January 14, 1932, and they did not actually reach Mukden until April 21; by that time, Manchuria had become Manchukuo.

The League Commission, known as the Lytton Commission after its chairman, Lord Lytton, collected evidence in Japan, China, and Manchuria. Its report, submitted in October, 1932, was carefully worded to avoid offending the Japanese. It denied that the Japanese aggression could be justified as a defensive measure and branded the new Manchukuo state a Japanese puppet regime. On the other hand, it refrained from ordering Japan to get out. Instead, the report proposed a settlement recognizing Japan's special interest in Manchuria and making that province an autonomous state under Chinese sovereignty but under Japanese control. On February 25, 1933, the League adopted the report, and the following month, Japan withdrew from the body.

In retrospect, the Manchurian affair stands out as the first serious blow leveled at the League of Nations and at the entire diplomatic structure designed to maintain the *status quo*—the Versailles settlement, the Washington Conference agreements, and the Paris Pact. The ease with which Japan had acquired its vast and rich new possession was not lost upon the revisionist leaders of Italy and Germany; Manchuria set off a chain reaction of aggressions that ultimately led to World War II.

II. DIPLOMATIC REACTIONS TO HITLER

The Japanese conquest of Manchuria was a rude challenge to the *status quo* in the Far East, but even more upsetting was Hitler's threat to the *status quo* in Europe. Hitherto, the French system of alliances had dominated the Continent with little difficulty. Mussolini had tried to organize a counter bloc, but his agreements with third-rate revisionist states such as Austria, Hungary, Bulgaria, and Albania were of little value. Likewise, the Soviet Union was cut off by the *"cordon sanitaire"* and, in any case, was engrossed in "building socialism in one country." Only Germany was left, and under Stresemann, this country had made peace with its wartime enemies when it accepted the Locarno Pacts and entered the League of Nations.

This comfortable situation was drastically altered when Hitler became chancellor in 1933. The Nazi leader from the beginning had demanded more *Lebensraum* for the German people. It is scarcely surprising that there were immediate diplomatic repercussions when Hitler became the master of Germany, the first being the revitalization of the Little Entente, which had been dormant for several years. In February, 1933, Czechoslovakia, Yugoslavia, and Rumania established a permanent council of their foreign ministers to facilitate the coordination and implementation of their diplomatic policies. Likewise, in that spring, the French foreign minister, Louis Barthou, toured the Little Entente capitals and also Warsaw, strengthening the bonds between France and her eastern allies.

Even Mussolini, who later was to form the Rome-Berlin Axis with Hitler, at first reacted strongly against his fellow dictator. In view of the substantial German minority in the South Tyrol, Mussolini was apprehensive of an expansionist Nazi regime with its slogan of *"Ein Volk, ein Reich, ein Führer."* Accordingly, he took the initiative in concluding the Four-Power Pact on July 15, 1933 with Britain, France, and Germany. The agreement reiterated the adherence of the signatories to the League Covenant, the Locarno Treaties, and the Kellogg–Briand Pact, and also prohibited any changes in the Versailles Treaty without the consent of all four powers. This proved to be a futile exercise, for Hitler repeatedly violated these commitments—without even a reference to his fellow signatories. In October, 1933, he announced Germany's withdrawal from the Disarmament Conference and from the League of Nations. Although he did not immediately reveal his rearming program, its existence, if not its pace and magnitude, became generally known.

These developments stimulated the formation of another regional bloc comprised of Turkey, Greece, Rumania, and Yugoslavia, the last two having considerable German minorities. On February 9, 1934, the four countries signed the Balkan Pact which provided for cooperation to preserve the *status quo* in southeastern Europe.

More significant than the formation of the Balkan Entente was the basic shift now occurring in Soviet foreign policy. Traditionally, the Soviet leaders had regarded the League as a concert of predatory imperialist powers. But the rise of Hitler led them to view the League as a possible instrument for organizing collective resistance to ward off the anticipated German aggression. This new attitude was encouraged by the French foreign minister, Louis Barthou. A conservative in domestic matters, Barthou's simple and consistent objective in foreign affairs was to build up a coalition that would be strong enough to dissuade Hitler from expansionist ventures. In addition to cementing the ties between France, the Little Entente, and Poland, Barthou now sought to add the Soviet Union to the *status quo* bloc. It was due largely to his efforts that the League of Nations invited the Soviet Union to join its ranks, and that the invitation was accepted on September 19, 1934.

The following month, an assassin's bullets killed Barthou, along with King Alexander of Yugoslavia, in Marseilles. It was a turning point in European diplomacy, for Barthou's successors followed a relatively devious and ambivalent policy vis-à-vis Germany. This was particularly true of Pierre Laval, who reached an agreement with Mussolini on January 7, 1935, in which the two agreed to cooperate in case of action by Hitler; they also settled various differences concerning their African possessions. France ceded to Italy certain desert territories adjoining the Italian colonies of Libya and Eritrea, and Mussolini, in turn, gave up claims in Tunis, where there was a considerable Italian population. However, a verbal understanding regarding Ethiopia was to lead to much controversy: Mussolini claimed that he had been promised a completely free hand in that country, while Laval insisted that the understanding had been limited to economic matters.

Two months later, on March 16, 1935, Germany formally renounced the clauses of the Versailles Treaty concerning her disarmament, reintroduced conscription, and announced that her army would be increased to 36 divisions. Britain, France, and Italy responded on April 11 at the Stresa Conference where they agreed on common action against the German menace. The "Stresa front" proved as futile as the Four-Power Pact two years earlier. Each of the signatories promptly proceeded to go its own way: Italy busied herself preparing to invade Ethiopia; Britain made a separate naval agreement with Germany on June 18 permitting the latter to build up to 35 per cent of British strength; France concluded on May 2 a five-year alliance with Russia, each promising to aid the other in case of unprovoked attack. On May 16, Czechoslovakia signed a similar pact with Russia, though Russian aid to Czechoslovakia was made contingent upon France also providing aid as required by the 1924 alliance.

In conclusion, Hitler's accession to power had stimulated within two years several new diplomatic groupings—the Balkan Entente, the revived Little Entente, the French-Russian alliance and the Czech-Russian alliance—all designed to block any aggressive moves on the Führer's part. On the other hand, there were serious fissures in this diplomatic lineup, such as the British-German Naval Pact, which was resented in Paris, the German-Polish Nonaggression Pact of January, 1934, which also was not appreciated in Paris, and the unpredictability of Laval who basically distrusted his Soviet ally and preferred to make his own private deals on the side. With the outbreak of the Ethiopian crisis, these fissures became gaping chasms that completely undermined the League of Nations and the entire postwar diplomatic structure.

III. ITALY CONQUERS ETHIOPIA

On October 3, 1935, Mussolini's legions invaded the independent African kingdom of Ethiopia. Behind this naked aggression were several motivations; the fascist yen for imperial glory, the hope that colonial expansion would relieve unemployment at home, and Mussolini's conviction that Laval had given him the green light, and that the opposition from other quarters would not be sufficiently resolute to stop him—an assumption that proved quite justified.

The pretext for the Italian aggression was reminiscent of the incident staged by the Japanese in Manchuria. On December 5, 1934, Ethiopian and Italian troops clashed at Walwal near the border between Italian Somaliland and Ethiopia. Emperor Haile Selassie offered to leave to an arbitration commission the question of whether Walwal was on Italian or Ethiopian territory. Mussolini refused to accept this and instead made various demands while preparing for invasion, which was started on October 3, 1935.

A little more than a week later, the League Council declared Italy the aggressor, and the Assembly voted for economic sanctions under Article 16 of the Covenant. These sanctions, which went into effect on November 18, 1935, included embargoes on arms, credits, and certain raw materials, but did not include the key ones—oil, coal, iron, and steel. Despite such limitations, the sanctions did represent a significant beginning toward stopping the Italian advance. Also, world public opinion expressed itself overwhelmingly against Mussolini's aggression, and the Ethiopians were resisting stoutly.

At this point, the wily Laval squandered what little chance there was of stopping the Italians. Early in December, 1935, he persuaded the British Foreign Secretary, Sir Samuel Hoare, to accept a plan by which Italy would be given outright about half of Ethiopia, and would control the remaining half of the country as a "zone of economic expansion and settlement." The two negotiators agreed to maintain secrecy until the plan had been submitted to the interested parties: Italy, Ethiopia, and the League. Laval, however, anticipated difficulties in Britain, so he permitted the plan to come to the attention of the French press. To his astonishment, the news of the deal aroused a storm of indignation in both London and Paris. Hoare was forced to resign, and was succeeded by Anthony Eden. The following month, Laval also had to go, after a drubbing at the hands of the Chamber.

For a while it seemed like a clean sweep for the supporters of the League against aggression, but the basic issue still was whether the sanctions would be made effective by adding the key materials, particularly oil. Eden was in favor of doing so, but the new French foreign minister, Pierre Flandin, persisted in dragging his feet. Flandin's chief argument was that Mussolini would quit the League if oil sanctions were voted; he insisted that another attempt be made to reach a settlement. Since the British cabinet was not united behind Eden, Flandin had his way and effective sanctions were never enforced.

The death blow to any remaining hope of effective sanctions came with Hitler's occupation of the Rhineland on March 7, 1936. A fateful move that had far-reaching repercussions (see the following section), it made the British and French governments even more sensitive to the German threat and more determined to placate Mussolini in order to keep him on their side and within the League of

Nations. Consequently, the League Council voted on April 20, 1936 to continue the sanctions without oil, thus spelling the doom of the Ethiopian armies.

The victories of the Rif in Morocco had demonstrated the effectiveness of guerrilla tactics against superior European armies, but the Ethiopian tribal leaders, in their suicidal pride and ignorance, scorned guerrilla warfare as unworthy and demeaning. Instead, they attempted to wage a war of position, and were mercilessly bombarded, strafed, and even sprayed with mustard gas. After a campaign of seven months, the Italians triumphantly entered Addis Ababa on May 5, 1936. The same day, Mussolini proclaimed "a Roman peace, which is expressed in this simple, irrevocable, definite phrase—'Ethiopia is Italian.'" Four days later, the King of Italy assumed the title "Emperor of Ethiopia." And so, at a cost of 3,000 men and $1 billion, Mussolini had won an empire of 350,000 square miles, ten million inhabitants, and rich natural resources.

So far as Europe and the rest of the world were concerned, the significance of the Ethiopian affair was that it undermined the League of Nations. Many small countries such as Greece, Rumania, and Yugoslavia had loyally supported the League during the crisis and enforced the sanctions against Italy, but their only rewards were heavy economic losses and exposing themselves to the wrath of the triumphant Duce. The obvious moral was that, given the pusillanimity of the leading Western powers, collective security was a snare and a delusion. Accordingly, the small countries henceforth followed a policy of *sauve qui peut* and turned their backs on the League of Nations. Ironically, the sacrifice of the League did not keep Italy on the side of the Western powers against Germany, which had been the great objective of those who insisted on placating Mussolini. Instead, the appeasement had precisely the opposite effect; both Mussolini and Hitler were impressed by their striking victories in Ethiopia and the Rhineland, and perceived the vast possibilities to which coordinated, aggressive activities could give rise. The final outcome was not the isolation of Nazi Germany but the formation of the Rome-Berlin Axis.

IV. ROME-BERLIN AXIS

At the beginning of the Ethiopian crisis Hitler played a wait-and-see game. If Mussolini failed, a rival in Central Europe would be eliminated; if he won, then the collective security system would be undermined, and Hitler's *Lebensraum* plans would be correspondingly enhanced. On March 7, 1936, Hitler dramatically ended this passive policy by sending a force of 35,000 marching into the Rhineland. The Versailles Treaty had stipulated that Germany should have no fortifications or armed forces on the left bank of the Rhine, nor in a zone of 50 kilometers from the right bank. Hitler's violation of this provision was a move of first-rate strategic significance: The French system of alliances was based on the accessibility of Central Europe to the French army; with the reoccupation of the Rhineland and the building of the Siegfried Line fortifications, which was immediately started, the French no longer had this accessibility. France was cut off from her allies while Germany's strength was immeasurably increased because her vitals were no longer left vulnerable by a demilitarized Rhineland. In short, Hitler's Rhineland coup represented a tremendous upset in Europe's military and diplomatic balance of power. Hitler had decided on the Rhineland move against the advice of nearly all his generals. The German armed forces were not yet ready to wage serious war, so with only two exceptions, the German military leaders opposed the reoccupation, which they naturally assumed would lead to conflict with France. Accordingly, Hitler ordered that his divisions should retire without firing a shot if France mobilized and sent her army across the frontier. Hitler, like Mussolini, was bluffing, and the tactics worked for both men.

Premier Sarraut and Foreign Minister Flandin refrained from action partly because their military advisers opposed any moves that involved the risk of war, but also because the British government held back as much as the French government had done during the Ethiopian crisis. When Flandin consulted Prime Minister Baldwin, the latter refused to have anything to do with the proposal to mobilize the French army and send it into the Rhineland. The French government, being itself divided, was incapable of decisive action without Britain's support, and since this was not forthcoming, Hitler won a majority victory with no opposition.

One result of this triumph was the beginning of the end of the French system of alliances. Not only did the Siegfried Line cut off France from Central and Eastern Europe, but at the same time, Germany conducted an economic offensive in southeastern Europe that made that region virtually an economic dependency. By 1936, Germany was taking 51 per cent of Turkey's total exports, 48 per cent of Bulgaria's, 36 per cent of Greece's, 24 per cent of Yugoslavia's, and 23 per cent of Hungary's. Such close economic ties inevitably resulted in political repercussions, especially since the dictatorial regimes now appearing in southeastern Europe felt a certain ideological predilection for the German and Italian fascist regimes as against the Western democracies. Certainly the foreign policies of General Metaxas, King Carol, and Prince Paul were quite different from those of Venizelos, Titulescu, and King Alexander.

The Rhineland coup also served to bring together the hitherto antagonistic Führer and Duce. Mussolini deeply appreciated Hitler's role in distracting the attention of the League at a time when oil sanctions were still a possibility. Within a short time, the two dictators had formed a working partnership that quickly made a shambles of the existing diplomatic structure. With the Austro-German accord of July 11, 1936, Hitler undertook to respect the integrity of Austria, thus removing the main source of discord between Rome and Berlin. A week later, civil war broke out in Spain, a tragic episode (see the following section) that was to drag on for three years, during which time Hitler and Mussolini worked together to encompass the downfall of the Spanish Republic. On October 24, 1936, the Rome-Berlin Axis was formally constituted; Italy and Germany agreed on general cooperation as well as on such specific issues as German recognition of Italian Ethiopia in return for economic concessions. The following month Japan associated herself with the Axis by concluding anti-Communist pacts with Germany and then with Italy.

By the end of 1936, the diplomatic balance was entirely different from what it had been when Hitler came into office. Italy and Germany now had a working partnership. France had lost her former hegemony and declined into relative isolation. Her old allies in Central Europe were drifting away, while the new alliance with the Soviet Union remained largely a paper creation. The French governments distrusted the Soviet regime to the point of refusing to conclude the military convention needed to make their alliance fully effective. Likewise, the relations of the French and the British were far from being close or trustful. Such disarray of the *status quo* bloc, together with the crippling of the League of Nations, as a result of Manchuria and Ethiopia, enabled the Rome-Berlin Axis to seize the initiative during the next three years and to score triumph after triumph with virtually no opposition.

V. SPANISH CIVIL WAR

The Spanish Civil War was of more than ordinary significance because it was essentially two wars in one—a deep-rooted social conflict generated by the decay and tensions of Spanish society, and a dress rehearsal for World War II arising from the clash of ideologies and of Great Power interests. Three principal elements made up Spain's traditional oligarchy: the large landowners, the army, and the church. The large landowners consisted of the old aristocracy and the wealthy upper middle class that had bought many estates. About 35,000 of these landowners possessed approximately 50 per cent of the total arable land. Agricultural productivity in the country as a whole was very low, and the peasants, comprising 70 per cent of the entire population, were as depressed as any in Europe. The landowners contributed nothing, being of the absentee type who squandered their incomes in Madrid or in foreign capitals.

The Spanish army was noteworthy for two reasons: the extraordinarily large number of officers in proportion to the number of rank and file, and the constant intervention of the military in the politics of the country. Indeed, the officers felt they had a right to supervise political affairs and they acted accordingly; specifically, this meant the safeguarding of the *status quo* against all challengers, whether of the Republican Center or the parties of the Left.

The established Roman Catholic Church, an enormously wealthy and influential institution, had lost its landed property in the early and mid-nineteenth century, but in compensation, it had acquired industrial stocks and had received a substantial subsidy from the government, amounting to 2 per cent of the annual budget in the 1920's. The bishops were nominees of the king, and some of them were members of the Senate; but most important of all, the church controlled most of the education of the country. In addition, the church exerted much influence through certain important newspapers, labor groups, and a variety of lay organizations. As had occurred in other countries where Catholicism played a similar role, this formidable power engendered a strong anticlerical movement in Spain. The widespread attacks on priests and nuns, and the wholesale destruction of church property during the Civil War were by no means unique in Spanish history.

Such was the Spain that Alfonso XIII was called upon to rule when he ascended the throne in 1902. Between that date and the establishment of the Rivera dictatorship in 1923, there were 33 different cabinets as well as a liberal number of strikes, mutinies, and assassinations. Spain's neutrality during World War I brought relative prosperity, but this lasted only for the duration of the war; with the peace, the chronic ailments and disorders returned. These were accentuated during the 1920's by the disasters suffered by the Spanish armies in Morocco at the hands of the Rif. The resulting discontent paved the way for the military coup d'état of General Primo de Rivera in September, 1923.

The new "strong man" admired Mussolini and imitated him in destroying the remnants of constitutional government, censoring the press and restricting the universities. He also followed the Duce's example in building highways and staging international exhibitions. But these were merely surface gestures, for underneath, traditional Spanish society creaked on with its inequities and anachronisms. Finally, Primo de Rivera lost the support of the army and the King, and was forced to resign in January, 1930.

With the dictator gone, popular discontent was turned against the King himself. The Depression made the situation still more precarious, until at last Alfonso decided to restore the constitution and to hold municipal elections in April, 1931. The vote went heavily against the regime, the Republicans carrying 46 of the 50 provincial capitals. The state of public opinion was evident, and Alfonso prudently left the country, as four of his predecessors had done since 1789.

A republic was proclaimed on April 14, 1931, and elections were held for a constituent assembly, or cortes. When this body assembled in July, its members fell into three broad groupings: a conservative Right, a republican Center, and a left comprising Socialists, Stalinist and Trotskyite Communists, and Anarcho-Syndicalists. The Center and the Left, which together comprised a large majority, combined to adopt a markedly liberal constitution that proclaimed complete religious freedom, separated church and state, secularized education, and nationalized church property.

The first prime minister under the new constitution, the able Republican, Manuel Azaña, was supported also by the moderate socialists, and laws were promptly passed to implement the provisions of the constitution: Government subsidies to the church were abolished, certain monastic orders were banned, the pay of farm laborers was raised above the usual $.20 per day, a few large estates were divided among the peasants with partial compensation for the owners, hundreds of army officers were retired, and home rule was granted to the province of Catalonia. These typical middle-of-the-road reforms satisfied neither the Right nor the Left, so that the November, 1933, elections for a regular cortes returned a conservative majority. The *bienio negro,* the "black" two years of clerical reaction, followed. Autonomy for Catalonia was revoked and much of the legislation concerning the church and land distribution was either repealed or not enforced.

In preparation for the elections of February, 1936, the parties of the Left and the Left-Center now banded together to form a Popular Front similar to that which had just appeared in France. The coalition won a narrow victory and Azaña formed a new Republican cabinet which the Left parties supported but did not enter. Catalan autonomy was restored and anticlerical measures along with mild social reform were resumed. In retrospect, the Republicans appear to have blundered in emphasizing anticlericalism rather than Agrarian reform, which most Spaniards accepted. This policy alienated the fervent Catholics and much of the middle class. At the same time, the Great Depression, with its widespread unemployment, strengthened the extremist and weakened the moderate parties. To hold the desperate workers, the Socialists had to move steadily to the extreme Left; reacting to this, much of the middle class allied itself with the extreme Right—hence the mounting ideological passions and the polarization of political life to the point where parliamentary government became increasingly tenuous.

At this juncture, the Spanish rightists, with the connivance of Germany and Italy, and under the leadership of General Francisco Franco, raised the standard of counterrevolution. On July 17, 1936, the army in Morocco revolted, and the next day a number of mainland generals took up arms. The rebels, or self-styled Nationalists, quickly overran the southern and the western regions, and these sections of the country remained their main bases throughout the protracted struggle. Franco had hoped that with the advantage of surprise, he would be able to capture quickly the main cities and fortresses and so gain control of the entire country. Instead, the struggle dragged on for almost three years with a savagery reminiscent of the sixteenth century Wars of Religion.

After losing about one-half the country in the first few weeks of the revolt, the Loyalists rallied and managed to retain control of Madrid in the center, the Basque provinces in the north, and the highly developed east coast with the large cities of Barcelona and Valencia. The Loyalists were now in a strong position, for they had behind them the industrial centers, the most densely populated regions, and the capital, with its exceptionally large gold reserve. Despite these advantages, the Loyalists were eventually beaten, the main reason being that they were unable to obtain arms from abroad in quantities approaching those received by the Nationalists.

That such a turn of events should take place was paradoxical, because the Loyalists had both the money to import arms and the right to do so under international law, since they constituted the legal government of the country. The British and French governments, however, refused to allow the sale of arms to the Republican regime. They were inhibited by the sharp division of public opinion in their respective countries concerning the civil war, and they feared that an unrestricted flow of arms to the contending parties might escalate into a European war. Accordingly, Britain and France took the lead in sponsoring a nonintervention agreement, which was accepted by Germany, Italy, and the Soviet Union, as well as by several smaller countries.

The agreement provided that the signatories should refrain from shipping arms to Spain, but Germany and Italy violated their pledge from the beginning, and the Soviet Union soon was doing likewise. Italy sent not only arms but also regular army units, which rapidly increased in numbers as the war continued. According to official Italian sources, during the four months between December, 1936 and April, 1937, Mussolini despatched 100,000 men along with 40,000 tons of munitions and 750 cannon. Russia, like Germany, sent no ground troops but did provide war materials of all types in addition to technical advisers and pilots. The Loyalists were also aided by the International Brigades, which first went into action in November, 1936 in the defense of Madrid. The Brigades consisted of volunteers—mostly young idealists from Britain, France, and the United States—as well as antifascist émigrés from Italy and Germany.

Foreign intervention affected the Civil War in two important respects: it favored by all odds the Nationalists and was the decisive factor behind their victory; it also served to bring the Nationalists closer to fascism and the Republicans closer to communism, the latter trend being the more pronounced. At the outset, the Anarchists and the Socialists were predominant on the Republican side, with moderate Socialists filling the leading posts in the Loyalist administration throughout the Civil War. But the Communists became increasingly dominant with the Loyalist dependence on Soviet war materials, and by late 1937, the Russian-controlled International Brigades, Russian aircraft, and Spanish Communist generals were leading the Loyalist armies and dictating policy.

If the Loyalists had won, a new civil war might well have followed, with the Communists ranged against the Socialists, Anarchists and Trotskyites. As it turned out, the Axis supplies of both ground troops and war materials proved irresistible, especially when Stalin decided to abandon the Spanish Republic. For two years there had been a stalemate, with the Nationalists controlling the Agrarian western and southern regions, and the Loyalists, the more developed northern and eastern sections, together with the Madrid salient. But in mid-1938, the Soviet government decided to cut its losses and stop the aid to Spain, in view of the continued refusal of the Western democracies to end the nonintervention farce, thus enabling Franco's armies to break the stalemate. In late December, 1938, the Nationalists began their great offensive against Catalonia; within a month they had taken Barcelona. Madrid and Valencia were now helpless, but they held out for two more months. With their fall in late March, the Civil War ended.

For Spain, the long ordeal involved three-fourths of one million casualties out of a population of 25 million, and one of every seven of the uninjured was left without shelter. For the Western powers, the Civil War represented another stunning defeat. As in the case of Ethiopia, they had again shown themselves weak and vacillating in the face of Axis aggression, a pattern that had also manifested itself during the German annexation of Austria, which had occurred in the course of the Spanish Civil War.

VI. ANNEXATION OF AUSTRIA

1938 was the year of the great bloodless victories of the Axis powers. At the center of these fateful developments was Neville Chamberlain, who succeeded Stanley Baldwin as Prime Minister in May, 1937, and who was taking over little by little the direction of British foreign policy even though Anthony Eden was his Foreign Secretary.

"The truth," wrote Eden, "was that some of my seniors in the Cabinet . . . could not believe that Mussolini and Hitler were as untrustworthy as I painted them. After all, had not Mussolini defeated the reds and made the trains in Italy run on time? Moreover, as old-fashioned Conservatives they felt little sympathy with Roosevelt whom they instinctively regarded as something of a demagogue."[1] This outlook explains in large measure the stunning Axis victories of these years. The Conservatives felt that they could do business with the dictators, and that this was preferable to "wooly" and "idealistic" projects based on the principle of collective security. Their counterparts in France likewise preferred to deal with Mussolini and Hitler rather than to turn to the Russians with whom they were nominally allied. The direct outcome of this way of thinking was the sacrifice of the independent states of Austria, Albania, and Czechoslovakia—a sacrifice that led not to "peace in our time" as was fondly imagined, but to World War II.

On February 12, 1938, Hitler invited Austria's Chancellor, Kurt von Schuschnigg, to his Bavarian mountain retreat at Berchtesgaden. There the scholarly, modest, and pious Schuschnigg was subjected to long hours of table-pounding and invective. When Hitler had finished, the softening-up process was resumed by German generals and Nazi leaders, Austrian as well as German. Thus Schuschnigg was bullied into accepting various demands, such as an amnesty for imprisoned Austrian Nazis, and the appointment of Nazis to various posts, including the key Ministry of Interior. On his return to Vienna, Schuschnigg delivered a radio speech in which he made clear his determination to preserve Austria's independence. "We know exactly that we were able to go, and did go, to that boundary line beyond which, clearly and unequivocally appear the words: 'So far and no further.'" Then he forbade the display of swastikas, the wearing of brown shirts, or the holding of Nazi demonstrations. These firm measures aroused sufficient popular support so that Schuschnigg was emboldened to schedule a plebiscite on March 13 on the following question: "Are you for a free and independent, German and Christian Austria?"[2]

This defiance infuriated Hitler, who began to concentrate troops on the frontier. In the ensuing crisis, he was proven justified in his calculation that no Great Power would lift a finger to help Austria. France had no government at all, being caught between two ministries. Chamberlain had already proclaimed his hands-off policy in a speech to the Commons on February 22. Mussolini was unhappy and resentful, especially since he had not been forewarned by his fellow dictator, but his hands were tied by the Rome-Berlin Axis, so he had to inform Schuschnigg that he could offer "no advice under the circumstances."

On March 11, Schuschnigg, in the face of two ultimatums, was compelled first to cancel the plebiscite and then to hand over the chancellorship to the Nazi Ministry of Interior, Dr. Artur von Seyss-Inquart. The latter, who had been in continual telephonic communication with Berlin, now issued a statement that had been dictated from Berlin and that requested the German government "to send in German troops as soon as possible . . . to restore peace and order . . . and to prevent bloodshed." On March 13, decrees from Berlin and Vienna declared Austria a part of Germany, and the next day Hitler made his triumphant entry into the land of his birth. Thus Austria was taken over by telephone; the event was not mentioned in the League of Nations.

VII. END OF CZECHOSLOVAKIA

With Austria safely annexed, Hitler turned against the neighboring state of Czechoslovakia, a larger and much stronger country, with an efficient modern army and a considerable industrial establishment, as well as the only surviving democratic institutions in East-Central Europe. But the presence of a three-million German minority in the Sudeten borderlands made Czechoslovakia vulnerable to Nazi propaganda and subversion. The fact is that the Sudeten Germans had been treated far more liberally than other minorities in Europe, so that they had remained relatively contented and quiet. After Hitler came to power, Nazi agents set to work, and their agitation, combined with the discontent arising from heavy unemployment due to the Depression, turned most of the German minority against Prague.

With the *Anschluss,* the Sudeten problem suddenly became a serious menace for Czechoslovakia. The country was now surrounded on three sides by the enlarged Reich. Even more serious were certain indications that the British and French governments were ready to abandon Czechoslovakia as they had Austria. This soon became apparent when Hitler precipitated the Czechoslovak crisis on September 12 with an inflammatory speech in which he violently attacked President Beneš for his "persecution" of the Sudeten Germans, and warned that, "if these tortured creatures can find no rights and no help themselves, they will get both from us." This speech set off a chain reaction: the Sudeten Germans rioted, the Prague government proclaimed martial law, Nazi leaders fled to Germany, and Hitler concentrated troops along Czechoslovakia's frontier. Chamberlain feared that if Hitler actually invaded, France and ultimately Britain might be embroiled in the war. To avert this danger, Chamberlain, in agreement with Premier Daladier, proposed to Hitler a personal conference. The latter accepted, and Chamberlain arrived at Berchtesgaden on September 15.

Hitler baldly set forth his demand for annexation of the Sudeten areas on the basis of self-determination, and indicated his readiness "to risk a world war" to attain his end. Chamberlain returned home and persuaded first his own cabinet, and then the French, to accept Hitler's terms. The two governments in turn urged acceptance upon the Czechoslovak government; when the latter resisted, they brought every pressure to bear, including the threat of desertion. Prague finally capitulated on September 21, in return for an Anglo-French guarantee for the new frontier.

The next day Chamberlain flew to Godesberg in the belief that he only needed to work out with Hitler the technical details for the transfer of the territories. Instead, the Führer made new demands: immediate surrender of the predominantly German areas without waiting for plebiscites and without any removal or destruction of military or economic establishments. In addition, Hitler now supported territorial claims on Czechoslovakia made by Poland and Hungary.

These new demands precipitated an acute international crisis. Czechoslovakia ordered full mobilization, France called up 600,000 reservists, while the Soviet foreign minister, Maxim Litvinov, declared on September 21 before the League Assembly: "We intend to fulfill our obligations under the Pact, and together with France to afford assistance to Czechoslovakia by the ways open to us."

"This public and unqualified declaration," as Churchill pointed out, was treated by the Western powers with "indifference—not to say disdain." Instead, they acted on Mussolini's suggestion for a four-power conference of Britain, France, Germany, and Italy. The meetings were held in Munich on September 29, and without either Czech or Soviet participation, it was decided that Hitler should be granted all his demands, the only modifications being the face-saving provisions that the Sudeten lands should be occupied in stages and that the final delimitation of the frontier should be determined by an international commission.

The Munich surrender was popular with the masses in both Britain and France. Chamberlain and Daladier were hailed as peacemakers by enthusiastic crowds. Loud cheers greeted Chamberlain when he declared "I believe it is peace in our time." Hitler was gratefully believed when he avowed, "This is the last territorial claim I have to make in Europe." The events of the next year were to demonstrate the worth of such statements.

In accordance with the provisions reached at Munich, an international commission was appointed to determine the new frontiers. It soon became apparent that, despite their commitments, Britain and France had no interest in the proceedings of the commission. Accordingly, no plebiscites were held, and the decisions were made by two German generals who were members of the commission. In the end, Germany acquired 10,000 square miles of Czechoslovak territory with a population of 3,500,000, of whom about one-fifth were Czechs. At the same time, Poland seized the Teschen area with its rich coal fields, while Hungary occupied generous portions of Slovakia and Ruthenia. The truncated Czechoslovak state now disintegrated, with Germany's help, into three fragments: an autonomous Slovakia, an autonomous Ruthenia, and the Czech provinces of Bohemia and Moravia.

The finale came in March, 1939, when the puppet heads of the Czech and Slovak lands were summoned to Berlin to hear from Hitler the dissolution of their respective states; on March 15, German troops entered Prague. Bohemia and Moravia were declared a protectorate of the Reich, and Slovakia was also placed under German protection. Simultaneously, the Hungarians were allowed by Hitler to invade and annex Ruthenia in the east. So ended the state of Czechoslovakia, as well as the illusion that Hitler's objective was simply the redemption of German-populated lands. The partitioning of Czechoslovakia with its predominantly Slavic population was a rude awakening for those who had taken the Führer at his word. Chamberlain was particularly shocked, for as an orthodox British businessman, he had assumed that Hitler would keep his pledge that he had no further territorial ambitions in Europe. The breaking of this promise forced Chamberlain, as well as Daladier, to painfully reappraise their policy and to take a firmer stand when Hitler now turned upon Poland.

VIII. COMING OF WAR

With Austria and Czechoslovakia taken, and with Spain and Hungary in the Axis camp, it was becoming apparent that the Western powers and the Soviet Union needed to work together in order to stem further aggression. "The key to a Grand Alliance," wrote Churchill, "was an understanding with Russia." The Russian government, on its part, was more than ready for such an "understanding." On March 18, it informed Berlin that it refused to recognize the partitioning of Czechoslovakia. Three days later, the Soviet government proposed a six-power conference (Britain, France, Russia, Poland, Rumania, and Turkey) to consider measures against future aggression. London replied that the proposal was "premature," and so it was not pursued further.

In the same month of March, however, Hitler forced Lithuania to hand over the city of Memel, and he sent stiff demands to Warsaw concerning Danzig and the Polish Corridor. Faced by the prospect of limitless German expansion, Chamberlain, on March 31, pledged Anglo-French aid to the Poles in the case of "any action which clearly threatened Polish independence." A week later this was expanded into a pact of mutual assistance. The next move of the Axis was Italy's invasion and conquest of Albania, which began on April 7. Again Britain and France countered by pledging on April 13 full support to Rumania and Greece in the event that their independence was clearly threatened. The following month, Anglo-Turkish and Franco-Turkish mutual assistance pacts were signed.

These commitments to various East European countries represented a revolutionary departure in British foreign policy. Half a year earlier, Chamberlain had refused to lift a finger in behalf of Czechoslovakia because it was a "faraway country" and no vital British interests were involved. Now he was promising to go to the aid of countries that were even more remote and inaccessible, and where no greater British interests were at stake. In fact, their very inaccessibility made his promises worthless unless Britain acted in concert with the Soviet Union. As Churchill declared in the Commons on May 19, "Without an effective eastern front, there can be no satisfactory defense of our interests in the West, and without Russia there can be no effective eastern front."[3] Chamberlain finally opened negotiations with the Russians on April 15.

By this time, there was so much distrust on both sides that little headway was made. The Western leaders were beset by doubts and fears concerning the effectiveness of the Red army, the motives of the Soviet leaders, and the reactions of Russia's neighbors. Likewise, Stalin's doubts had been steadily mounting with the successive Axis triumphs in Spain, Austria, and Czechoslovakia. More and more, he suspected that the basic aim of Western diplomacy was to divert German expansion eastward against the Soviet Union, a suspicion that manifested itself in his abandonment of the Spanish Republic in mid-1938 and in his replacement on May 3, 1939 of Litvinov, the indefatigable supporter of the League of Nations, with Vyacheslav M. Molotov, the grimly impassive Party veteran.

On the surface, both Russia and the Western powers favored the organization of a "Peace Front." However, given the current atmosphere, this was easier said than done. For example, on May 31, Molotov declared that no Peace Front was possible unless Britain and France accepted the elementary principle of reciprocity and equal obligations. Specifically, he demanded that the border states of the Soviet Union—Finland and the three Baltic countries—must be given the same guarantees as had been extended to Poland, Greece, Rumania, and Turkey. But the Baltic states had concluded nonaggression pacts with Germany and refused any Soviet-Western guarantees. London took the position that this ended the possibility of guarantees, whereas the Russians interpreted it as legalistic quibbling and evading of the issue. Likewise, the Poles refused to agree to allow the Red army to operate on Polish territory in case of war. Soviet aid, they insisted, should be limited to the providing of war materials. From the Polish viewpoint this was understandable, but the Soviet Marshal Voroshilov retorted, "Just as the British and American troops in the past World War would have been unable to participate in military collaboration with the French armed forces if they had no possibility of operating in French territory, the Soviet armed forces could not participate in military collaboration with armed forces of France and Great Britain if they are not allowed access to Polish territory."[4]

Behind this sparring was the gnawing suspicion in London that the real objective of the Soviets was to obtain legal justification for marching into Poland and the Baltic states at their pleasure. The Russians, on their part, feared that if they agreed to go to war in the event of an attack on Poland, and could not send their army into Polish territory to meet the advancing Germans, the latter would quickly overrun Poland and reach the Soviet frontier. Would Britain and France then wage serious war against Germany, or would they sit back and leave the Soviet Union to face the onslaught alone? Their apprehension was strengthened when, in July, two representatives of Chamberlain, acting on his instructions, broached to a German official in London the possibility of a British-German nonaggression pact that would enable Britain to rid herself of her commitments to Poland. Thus Chamberlain, who was not very happy about the guarantee to Poland, and was even less happy about the negotiations with the Soviet Union, was feeling out the Germans with a view to reviving his appeasement policy.

All of this was behind Stalin's fateful decision to turn to his hitherto mortal Axis enemies. In mid-August, he informed the Führer that he was ready for negotiations. Molotov talked with the German foreign minister, Joachim von Ribbentrop, as one realist to another. On August 23, they announced the diplomatic revolution that shook the world. The sworn enemies had signed a nonaggression pact and agreed to remain neutral if either were attacked by a third power. Significantly enough, the pact did not contain the so-called "escape clause," characteristic of Soviet nonaggression pacts with other countries, that would render the agreement inoperative if either party committed aggression against a third state. Perhaps this omission was related to a secret protocol in the pact stipulating that in the event of "a territorial or political rearrangement," Lithuania and western Poland were to come under the German sphere of influence, and the remainder of Poland, together with Finland, Estonia, Latvia, and Bessarabia, were to fall to the Russian sphere.

Now that he was protected on his eastern flank, Hitler felt free to strike. On August 25, he ordered his army to begin the invasion of Poland at 5:45 the next morning. In doing so, Hitler hoped that the Western powers, deprived of Russian support, would refrain from attempting to go to the help of Poland. But on the contrary, on the very same day that Hitler issued his orders, British government representatives officially signed the alliance pact with Poland. At the same time, Hitler heard that Mussolini had decided he would not fight, at least for the time being. These two setbacks persuaded Hitler that a temporary retreat was necessary, and during the evening of August 25, he countermanded his invasion order.

The Nazi leader now waited hopefully for another diplomatic Munich. During the following days, proposals for a variety of compromises, mediations, and plebiscites emanated from the Foreign Offices of Europe; none of these last minute efforts produced concrete results. Meanwhile, the German generals were reminding Hitler that only one month remained before the autumn rains would make tank maneuvers impossible on the Polish plains. Accordingly the Führer issued the final orders to march. Early in the morning of September 1, 1939, without a declaration of war, German troops, tanks, and planes crossed Poland's frontier all along the line. On September 3, both Britain and France declared war on Germany. Mussolini, despite his oratory about the Axis "pact of steel," remained neutral. World War II had begun.

SUGGESTED READING

D. BERGAMINI, *Japan's Imperial Conspiracy* (Morrow, 1971); D. F. FLEMING, *The Cold War and its Origins, 1917–1960,* 2 vols. (Doubleday, 1961); M. GILBERT, *The Roots of Appeasement* (Weidenfeld, 1966); G. F. KENNAN, *Russia and the West* (Little, 1960); L. LAFORE, *The End of Glory: An Interpretation of the Origins of World War II* (Lippincott, 1970); A. J. P. TAYLOR, *The Origins of the Second World War* (Hamilton, 1961); C. THORNE, *The Approach of War 1938–1939* (St. Martin's, 1968); G. L. WEINBERG, *Diplomatic Revolution in Europe 1933–36* (Univ. Chicago, 1970).

chapter thirty-eight

World War II:
Global
Repercussions

The next world war will be fought with stones.—Albert Einstein

When World War II began, Hitler had a definite schedule of conquest: first Poland, then the West, and finally Russia. He adhered to this schedule, and in doing so determined the course of World War II until Russia and the West became strong enough to seize the initiative.

World War II, like World War I, began as a European conflict precipitated by the issue of minorities in Eastern Europe. During the first two years the campaigns were waged on European battlefields. Then just as World War I was made global in 1917 by the Russian Revolution and the intervention of the United States, so World War II likewise was transformed in 1941 by Hitler's invasion of the Soviet Union and Japan's attack on Pearl Harbor. At this point, however, the similarity between the two wars ends. With Japan's lightning conquest of all of East and Southeast Asia, World War II came to involve much more of the globe than the preceding war had involved. Also the two wars differed fundamentally in the strategy and weapons employed. During the first war, the defense, based on trenches and machine-gun nests, proved superior to the offense; during the second war the offense, based on tanks and planes, proved stronger than the defense. This explains the extraordinary fluidity of battle lines that characterized the later struggle. Whole countries, and even continents, changed hands back and forth in striking contrast to the bloody stalemate on the western front between 1914 and 1918.

I. EUROPEAN PHASE OF THE WAR

Partitioning of Poland

In Poland the Germans demonstrated for the first time the deadly effectiveness of their new type of *Blitzkrieg,* or "lightning war." First came waves of dive bombers, or *Stukas,* blasting communication lines and spreading terror and confusion.

Then followed the armored tank divisions, or *Panzers*, smashing holes in the enemy lines, penetrating deeply into the rear, destroying transportation and communication facilities, and cutting the opposing forces into ribbons. Finally the lighter motorized divisions and the infantry moved in for the "mopping up" of the splintered and battered enemy forces, supported where necessary by air and artillery cover.

Unfortunate Poland, with its flat plains and obsolete army, was a "set-up" for this type of warfare. Within ten days the campaign had been virtually decided. The German tank-plane teams raced through the Polish countryside against declining resistance. The speed of the German advance forced Stalin to move in order to take over the territories he had staked out in his pact with Hitler. On September 17, the Red Army crossed over into Eastern Poland, and two days later established contact with the triumphant Germans. On September 27, Warsaw fell, the Polish government leaders fleeing to Rumania and thence to France. Their country was partitioned two days later, the Germans taking 37,000 square miles with 22 million people, and the Russians 77,000 square miles with a population of 13 million. Within less than a month one of the largest countries of Europe had disappeared completely from the map.

The Soviet government now took advantage of the secret protocol of the Moscow Pact to strengthen its strategic position in the Baltic area. In September and October, 1939, it compelled Estonia, Latvia, and Lithuania to accept Russian military bases on their territories. Lithuania, by way of compensation, received the long-desired district and city of Vilna, hitherto a part of Poland. The Soviets next demanded from Finland certain territorial cessions in the Karelian Isthmus and around Petsamo on the Arctic Ocean. Although the Russians offered substantial territorial compensation elsewhere, the Finns refused, for it would have meant the loss of their Mannerheim Line, a formidable fortification system in the Karelian region. Since these fortifications were within artillery range of Leningrad, the Russians pressed their demands, and finally on November 30, they attacked. The Finns resisted with unexpected success, but finally the Russians cracked the Mannerheim Line with heavy artillery bombardment, and by mid-March had forced the Finns to sue for peace. The ensuing treaty yielded the Russians somewhat more territory than they originally demanded, including the Petsamo region, the port of Viipuri, several islands in the Gulf of Finland, and a naval base at Hanko.

Poland to France

Meanwhile, the western front had been disconcertingly quiet. The British and the French had stood helplessly by while Poland was being partitioned. They could not enter the Baltic Sea which the Germans had sealed tight; their air forces were unable to operate across the breadth of the Reich; while their ground troops were confronted by the elaborate fortifications built by Hitler following his 1936 occupation of the Rhineland. Thus the French were forced to sit tight behind their Maginot Line, while the Germans made no move from behind their Siegfried Line or West Wall.

This surface calm proved deceptive. On April 9, 1940, the *Wehrmacht* suddenly erupted into action, sweeping through Denmark and making landings on the coast of Norway. The main objective was to gain control of the Norwegian fiords which could provide invaluable bases for German submarines and also safeguard the shipment of Swedish iron ore down the coast to Germany. The Danes could offer no resistance, but the Norwegians, with British support, fought back stubbornly. But by early June France herself was in mortal peril, so the Allied expeditionary forces sailed away, accompanied by the Norwegian government, which took refuge in London. The Germans set up their own administration in Norway under the collaborationist Quisling, whose name became a synonym for the self-seeking traitor.

The Allied setback in Norway was soon dwarfed by the stunning *Blitzkrieg* that overran France and the Low Countries in seven weeks. On May 10 the Germans attacked Holland and Belgium, and two days later France. The Dutch defense collapsed in five days. The Belgians held out longer, but by May 28 King Leopold surrendered in person, and the Belgian army capitulated. Meanwhile the Germans had skirted the northern end of the Maginot Line, which had never been extended to the sea, and drove through the Ardennes Forest, smashing a fifty-mile breach in the French lines at Sedan. The *Panzer* divisions now raced westward to Abbéville on the English Channel, and from there fanned out along the coast. The Allied armies in Flanders, mostly British, retreated to Dunkirk, the only port still free of the enemy. The prospects for evacuation appeared hopeless, with the harbor half destroyed and only a few miles of open beach. In fact, 366,000 were ferried back to Britain, though 13,000 dead and 40,000 prisoners were left behind, along with all the equipment.

With the completion of the Dunkirk evacuation on June 4, the agony of France began. On the following day the German forces resumed their advance southward. By June 13 Paris was occupied, undefended and abandoned by the government. The French Premier, Paul Reynaud, who had succeeded Daladier in late March, was thoroughly demoralized and under the influence of appeasers within his cabinet. Originally he had planned to move his government to North Africa, but on June 16 he wearily resigned the premiership to Marshal Pétain. It was this "hero of Verdun" who, ironically, now sued for peace. On June 22, at Compiègne, the site of the signing of the 1918 German armistice, the French accepted the severe armistice terms, including release of all German prisoners of war, disbandment of French military forces, surrender of French warships, and occupation by Germany of slightly over half of France, including the principal industrial and food-producing areas and the entire French coastline down to the Spanish border.

The staggering impact of the German *Blitzkrieg* is reflected in the incredibly low casualty figures. During the entire campaign the French lost about 100,000 men, the other Allies 20,000, and the Germans 45,000. These losses were less than half those sustained in single offensives during World War I. This speedy collapse by what was considered to be the strongest Western power came naturally as a most painful shock. Charges of treason and cowardice were leveled in explanation for the great disaster. Though these charges were not altogether unwarranted, other factors appear to have been more decisive. One was the effect of the Russo-German pact, which enabled Hitler to concentrate his forces on a single front. Perhaps most important was the German superiority in several fields, especially in the number of planes and tanks, and in the development of the new *Blitzkrieg* technique. The French High Command was handicapped not only by inadequate equipment, but even more by obsolete plans for waging World War II with World War I strategic concepts.

Battle of Britain

After Dunkirk and after the fall of France, Hitler not unnaturally assumed that Britain would see reason and would come to terms. But he failed to reckon with the British people and with Winston Churchill. A born fighter and maverick, Churchill was the descendant of Marlborough and the son of Lord Randolph Churchill and of Jennie Jerome, daughter of a former proprietor of *The New York Times.* As a soldier and as a correspondent he had seen action in several wars, and in the late 1930's had conducted almost singlehanded a campaign for rearmament, even though this was an unpopular cause at the time. Later he took the lead in demanding a firm stand against Axis aggression during the years of appeasement under Chamberlain.

This record of courage and forthrightness made him the natural successor to Chamberlain when the latter was forced to resign on May 10, 1940, because of the bungling of aid to Norway and the general failure to mobilize the country for a war of survival. Churchill formed an all-party cabinet, including the Labour party leaders, Clement Attlee and Ernest Bevin, as well as the Conservative Anthony Eden, who had resigned as Foreign Minister in 1938 in protest against the current appeasement policies. From the beginning, Churchill proved himself an incomparable war leader. With characteristic resoluteness and audacity he told his people—and the world: "We shall fight on the beaches. We shall fight on the landing grounds. We shall fight on the fields and in the streets. We shall fight in the hills; we shall never surrender."

Meanwhile Hitler was marking time, unsure what the next step should be. The unexpectedly rapid fall of France had caught him by surprise. First he tried to make a deal with the British, for whom he always had genuine respect. When his overtures were ignored, he issued on July 16, 1940, his directive "Sea Lion" for the invasion of the island. Reichmarshal Hermann Göring unleashed his *Luftwaffe,* confident that it could subdue Britain by air attack alone, without resort to a hazardous sea crossing.

The ensuing air assault developed into the critical Battle of Britain, one of the major turning points of World War II. In this epic struggle in the skies, the *Luftwaffe* had the advantage of numbers—2,670 planes against the Royal Air Force's 1,475. But the RAF Spitfires and Hurricanes were more advanced planes, because Britain had gone into mass production a couple of years later than Germany. The British also had the use of radar, a new invention that enabled enemy aircraft to be "sighted" fifty to a hundred miles before reaching their targets. Even so, the almost 2 to 1 numerical superiority of the *Luftwaffe* might have proven decisive if it had concentrated on the RAF fields and fighter forces. Instead, Göring kept shifting his targets: first the southeast ports and Channel shipping, then the RAF fields and radar stations, and finally, in September, 1940, London, Coventry, and other industrial centers. For a month these cities were bombed daily, but loss of life was surprisingly light, and industrial production was not seriously affected. Furthermore, Göring's switch to the cities was tacit admission that he was unable to destroy the RAF fighter strength. On September 17, Hitler gave orders that "Sea Lion" was to be postponed until the following spring. In actual fact, the plan for the invasion of Britain had been shelved forever. A few thousand British and Dominion fighter pilots, with a scattering of Poles, Czechs, French, and Belgians, had successfully repulsed the *Luftwaffe.* "Never in the field of human conflict," said Churchill at the height of the battle, "was so much owed by so many to so few."

Conquest of the Balkans

On July 31, 1940, two weeks before the Battle of Britain, Hitler held a conference with his top army and navy commanders. He was advised that a successful invasion of Britain that fall was highly improbable. Hitler thereupon made his momentous decision to invade Russia the following spring. Preparing for the invasion, Hitler sent troops into Rumania in October, 1940. He informed Moscow that these were "training troops" dispatched to "instruct" the Rumanian army. But at the same time a secret German order stated that the "real task" of the troops was to prepare the Rumanian army to participate in the forthcoming invasion of the Soviet Union.

At this point, when Hitler was occupying Rumania, Mussolini launched his blundering invasion of Greece. *Il Duce,* who for long had fancied himself the dean of the dictators, had become jealous of the spectacularly successful *Führer.* Although formally allied by the Axis Pact, Hitler had gone on from triumph to triumph without consulting or notifying his Italian partner. "Hitler always faces me with a *fait accompli,*" complained Mussolini to his son-in-law and foreign minister, Count Ciano. "This time I am going to pay him back in his own coin. He will find out from the papers that I have occupied Greece."[1]

What Mussolini assumed would be an effortless occupation proved in fact to be a humiliating fiasco. On October 28, 1940, Italian troops crossed over from Albania into Greece, expecting a triumphal procession to Athens. But taking advantage of the difficulties of the ponderous Italian armored divisions in the mountains of Epirus, the Greeks invariably made for the high ground and from there cut off and surrounded the enemy below. By mid-November they had driven the Italians back across the frontier into Albania. In the following weeks they captured the large Albanian towns of Koritsa, Argyrokastron, and Porto Edda. For a while it appeared that Mussolini might even have to endure a Dunkirk in the Adriatic.

At this point Mussolini was rescued from his mortifying predicament by the intervention of his Axis ally. Hitler was not motivated by sentiments of loyalty to his partner; in fact, he was furious that the war had been extended to the Balkans. But he could not sit back and watch the Italians flounder, particularly because the British were landing air units in Greece. So Hitler in January 1941 forced Bulgaria to accept the entry of German troops that had been massed across the Danube on Rumanian soil. Then on April 6 he invaded Yugoslavia and Greece.

The mountainous terrain of the Balkan Peninsula did not prove an effective obstacle, as had been hoped, while the British ground and air units were too weak to halt the tide. By April 13, the Germans had entered Belgrade, and ten days later the British were evacuating their forces from southern Greece to Crete. The Germans then launched an airborne invasion of Crete, catching by surprise the British who did not expect an air attack from the Greek mainland 180 miles to the north. Though they suffered heavy losses, the Germans finally gained complete control of the island by the beginning of June. Thus, with the Balkan Peninsula completely subjugated, the *Wehrmacht* on June 22, 1941, smashed across the frontier into the Soviet Union.

II. GLOBAL PHASE OF THE WAR

Invasion of Russia

Stalin signed the pact with Hitler in August, 1939, for a variety of reasons, including deep distrust of the Western leaders and desire to gain time to strengthen his military and industrial establishments. He also calculated that sooner or later Germany and the Western powers would clash in a war of attrition, while Russia, thanks to the pact, would be free to remain aloof until it was profitable for her to intervene. "If war begins," he told his comrades, "we cannot simply sit back. *We will have to get into the fighting, but we must be the last to join in.* And we shall join so as to cast the decisive weight on to the scales, the weight that will tip the balance."[2] This strategy was shrewd, yet it boomeranged and came very close to destroying the Soviet state. It was based on the assumption that the German and Western forces were evenly matched and would decimate each other, leaving the Red Army the dominant force on the Continent. Instead, the *Wehrmacht* crushed all opposition with incredible ease, leaving Germany the master of the Continent and the Soviet Union isolated and imperiled.

At first it seemed that Russia would collapse as ignominiously as had Poland and France. The *Panzer* divisions, in their now familiar fashion, smashed through the frontier defenses and drove deeply into the rear, encircling entire Soviet armies and taking hundreds of thousands of prisoners. By the end of the year the *Wehrmacht* had penetrated 600 miles eastward, overrunning the most industrialized and populous regions of the Soviet Union.

One reason for the German triumph, apart from the important factor of surprise, was numerical preponderance at the outset. Hitler struck with an army of about three million as against approximately two million on the other side. The Russians, of course, had huge reserves to draw upon, but the *Luftwaffe* bombing made it difficult to utilize them promptly and efficiently. The German forces also had the telling advantage of battle experience under varied conditions in Poland, France, and the Balkans. In addition, recent Russian publications have revealed hitherto unsuspected weaknesses in the Soviet armed forces. A large part of the Red air fleet had been concentrated on small fields near the frontier, where most of it was destroyed on the very first day. The Red Army lacked sufficient antitank guns to cope with the massive *Panzer* onslaught that sometimes reached 100 tanks per kilometer. And whereas in 1941 most German infantrymen had Tommy guns, the Russians had only rifles. Finally it should be recalled that this was not a struggle between the Soviet Union and Germany, but rather between the Soviet Union and the European continent. This meant that the Red Army had to cope with substantial Finnish, Rumanian, and Hungarian forces as well as German, and that Soviet armament plants were in competition with those of France and Czechoslovakia as well as Germany. Thus whereas Soviet steel output in 1941 was almost equal to Germany's, it was considerably less than half that of Germany and the rest of the Continent.

Hitler's strategy was to advance all along the thousand-mile front from Finland to Rumania, and to push eastward to a line running from Leningrad to Moscow to Kharkov to Rostov. The Red Army was to be encircled and destroyed to the west of this line, so that the *Wehrmacht* would not need to overextend its lines to the Urals and beyond. Thanks to the factors indicated above, the Germans attained almost all their territorial objectives. They captured both Kharkov and Rostov, and almost completely encircled Moscow and Leningrad.

Despite these impressive gains, the 1941 German campaign failed in its basic strategic objectives. Neither Moscow nor Leningrad was taken, while the Red Army, though badly mauled, remained intact. In fact, it was able on December 10 to launch a counteroffensive that broke the German pincers around Moscow and Leningrad, and also recaptured Rostov—the first city of any size that the *Wehrmacht* had taken and then been forced to surrender. Thus, despite its severe losses, the Red Army had done much better than expected.

Pearl Harbor

At the beginning of the war, almost all Americans were determined to remain neutral. President Roosevelt, like Woodrow Wilson, publicly expressed this determination; "there will be no blackout of peace," he declared to the nation on September 3, 1939. But Hitler's unexpected victories, and particularly the fall of France, compelled American policy makers to question whether neutrality automatically afforded protection against involvement. If Hitler were to conquer England and then gain control of the Atlantic—eventualities that seemed by no means improbable at the time—might not the New World be next on the schedule of conquest?

These considerations led Washington to conclude that the best way to avoid involvement in the war was to give all aid short of war to those still fighting Germany. This explains the steady drift of the United States from neutrality to nonbelligerency with the Destroyers-Bases Agreement (September 2, 1940), and from nonbelligerency to undeclared war with the Lend-Lease Act (March 11, 1941), the signing of the Atlantic Charter (August 12, 1941), and the orders (August-September, 1941) to provide naval escorts for all belligerent and neutral merchantmen between Newfoundland and Iceland, and to shoot on sight any Axis warships in those waters.

While striving to limit Axis expansion in the West, President Roosevelt also had attempted to restrain Japan from aggression in the Pacific. Successive Tokyo governments, however, became increasingly bellicose in response to what appeared to be golden opportunities provided by the course of events in Europe. Hitler's victories had left almost undefended the rich French, British, and Dutch possessions in East and Southeast Asia. Accordingly, on September 27, 1940, Japan signed the Tripartite Pact with Germany and Italy. This recognized the hegemony of Germany and Italy in Europe and of Japan in Asia, and called for full mutual aid if any of the signatories were attacked by the United States.

The Japanese, however, had no direct interest in the war in Europe. In pursuit of their own advantage, they concluded a treaty with Russia on April 13, 1941, in which each power pledged neutrality should the other "become the object of hostilities on the part of one or several third powers." When Hitler invaded Russia in June, 1941, he pressed Japan to join him and to attack from the east. The Japanese refused to oblige, distrusting German intentions in Asia. Furthermore, they perceived greener fields in Southeast Asia, which was seething with unrest and which offered obvious opportunity for them. By the summer of 1941 they had occupied bases in French Indochina, signed an alliance treaty with Thailand, and were demanding the oil and rubber output of the Dutch East Indies. The British were so hard-pressed in Europe that they had withdrawn from Shanghai, and maintained only feeble forces in Hong Kong and Singapore. Thus the entire East and Southeast Asia appeared ripe for plucking if only the United States would not intervene.

Japan's leaders were divided on the question of relations with the United States. The army was ready to challenge Britain, France, and the United States directly, but the navy, the diplomats, and the industrialists mostly held back. The turning point came with the resignation in October, 1941, of the Premier, Prince Fumimaro Konoye, who favored a settlement with the United States. He was succeeded by General Hideki Tojo, "Razor Brain," at the head of a cabinet of army and navy officers—a cabinet, it was said, that "smelled of gunpowder." Tojo decided to settle accounts with the United States, by diplomacy or by force, before the end of the year. The Japanese ambassador in Washington, Admiral Kichisaburo Nomura, joined by a special envoy, Saburo Kurusu, held an eleventh hour series of conversations with Secretary of State Cordell Hull. The positions taken by the two sides were so far apart that a compromise was out of the question.

Hull at this time knew of the day-to-day decisions of the Tokyo government because the Japanese radio code had been cracked. Accordingly, repeated "alert" warnings were sent to Pearl Harbor and to General Douglas MacArthur, commander of the United States armed forces in the Far East, stationed in the Philippines. The last warning was sent on December 7 from Washington to Pearl Harbor by General George C. Marshall, Chief of Staff. Static difficulties barred the use of the Army radio, so the message was sent instead through commercial channels. In Honolulu the telegram was given to a messenger boy who pedaled off on his bicycle. While he was on his way, a little after 7 A.M., Japanese bombs began to fall on the island. Within a few hours five of the eight battleships in Pearl Harbor had been destroyed, as well as three cruisers and three destroyers. At the same time another Japanese task force destroyed most of the United States Army's planes in the Philippines.

In conformity with the terms of the Tripartite Pact, Germany and Italy declared war on the United States. Thus America was fully involved in the war, both in Europe and in Asia. Her great contribution was to function as "the arsenal of the democracies." At the peak of output in 1943–44 this "arsenal" was producing one ship a day and one plane every five minutes; and during the six years of war it produced 87,000 tanks, 296,000 planes, and 53,000,000 tons of shipping.

1942: Year of Axis Triumphs

During the year 1942, Germany, Italy, and Japan were almost everywhere victorious. Great offensives overran large parts of Russia, North Africa, and the Pacific, like a huge three-taloned claw grasping the Eurasian hemisphere. At the same time, German submarines and surface craft were threatening Allied communication lines, their toll averaging about 400,000 tons a month in 1942.

The most spectacular triumphs were won by the Japanese, who quickly conquered a vast Pacific empire, stretching from the Aleutians to Australia, and from Guam to India. The Japanese were successful partly because they struck at a time when opposition was virtually impossible. France and Holland were occupied, Britain was struggling desperately for sheer survival, and the United States was only starting to convert from a peace to a war economy. Thus, the Japanese moved into a vacuum and filled it rapidly and easily. The Western powers' traditional treatment of their colonial subjects as providers of raw materials and consumers of manufactured goods also contributed to Japan's success. Profitable though this arrangement may have been for the mother countries, it left the colonial territories economically stunted. This meant that all basic war materials had to be transported several thousand miles from Europe or the United States. The traditional political policies of the colonial powers also boomeranged at this time of showdown: the average Indian or Burmese or Indonesian saw no reason why he should fight in defense of regimes that he regarded as alien and oppressive. Instead, he took a plague-on-both-your-houses attitude, when he did not actively welcome and assist the Japanese invaders. The latter shrewdly exploited this sentiment with slogans such as "Asia for the Asians." By Christmas, little more than two weeks after Pearl Harbor, the Japanese already had captured Guam,

Wake, and Hong Kong. They invaded the jungles of the Malay Peninsula, hitherto considered to be impregnable. Thanks to years of experience against guerrilla forces in China, the Japanese had trained their men to infiltrate around enemy positions and to attack on the flanks and the rear. These tactics proved so successful that by February 15, 1942, the great Singapore fortress fell, with a demoralized army of 80,000 British, Australian, and Indian troops surrendering to 50,000 Japanese.

Essentially the same pattern was repeated in Burma and Indonesia. Japanese troops crossed the Burmese frontier on December 10, 1941. By April they had taken Rangoon and Mandalay, and mixed British, Indian, and Chinese forces were fleeing to India along obscure jungle trails. In Indonesia the Dutch commander in chief capitulated with his army at Bandung on March 8. Nor had the Japanese more trouble landing in the Philippines and capturing Manila on January 2. But a mixed American-Filipino army under MacArthur, and later under General Wainwright, held out in the mountainous Bataan Peninsula until May 6. Further afield, the Japanese took the Andaman Islands in the Indian Ocean and the Attu and Kiska islets in the Aleutian chain. Thus, in five months, at a cost of only 15,000 killed and wounded, the Japanese had won an empire that had a population of over 100 million and that had supplied 95 per cent of the world's raw rubber, 90 per cent of the hemp, and two-thirds of the tin.

Meanwhile, on the Russian front, Hitler had launched another massive offensive in June, 1942. Since Moscow and Leningrad had proven impregnable the previous year, he now directed his armies southward. His objective was to reach the Volga and the Caspian, thereby cutting the Soviet Union in two and depriving the Red Army of its oil supplies from the Caucasus. As in 1941, the *Panzer* divisions at first rolled swiftly across the flat steppe country. In early July they took the great Sevastopol fortress in the Crimea, and at the end of the month they recaptured Rostov. Then they crossed the Don River and fanned out southeast toward the Caucasus oil fields and northeast toward Stalingrad on the Volga. By August 22, Nazi tanks had taken the Maikop oil center, though they fell short of the major oil fields at Grozny. About the same time, other Germans had fought their way through to the Volga slightly to the north of Stalingrad. In Berlin, Hitler proclaimed that his troops had reached the banks of the Volga in the heart of Russia and would never be dislodged.

In North Africa also, 1942 was a year of victory for the Germans. Under the dashing General Rommel, the Afrika Korps in March 1941 had driven the British back across Libya to the Egyptian border. In May 1942 Rommel resumed the attack, crossed into Egypt and reached El Alamein, a scant fifty miles from Alexandria.

On every front the Axis powers were at the height of their fortunes in 1942. In North Africa Rommel was preparing to strike for Cairo, in Russia the *Wehrmacht* had reached the Volga, in the Pacific the Japanese appeared to be ready to spring on Australia and India, while the shipping battle on the high seas remained close until the end of the year.

1943: Turning of the Tide

During the first three years of the war the Axis powers had everything their own way. The turning point began at the end of 1942 with the epic Russian victory at Stalingrad, the British breakthrough in Egypt, the Allied landings in French North Africa, the fall of Mussolini, the mounting serial bombardment of Germany, and the defeat of Japanese fleets in the Pacific.

At Stalingrad the Russians had dug in with orders to defend the city to the last man. The battle for the city began on August 22. By mid-September the Germans had fought their way into the center, and there they bogged down. Their planes had reduced the city to a great sea of rubble. This, paradoxically, prevented the Germans from exploiting their tank superiority that had proven so effective in the open steppe. Instead of mobile warfare, the battle of Stalingrad became the *Rattenkrieg* (War of the Rats), as men fought hand to hand in cellars, on rooftops, in alleys and courtyards and sewers. Then on November 19, 1942, two Russian armies crossed the Volga from the east, one attacking to the north of the city and the other to the south. The besiegers were in danger of becoming the besieged. The German commander, General Friedrich Paulus, wished to fight his way out of the threatening trap, but Hitler ordered him to hold on. Meanwhile, the Russian armies drove forward and closed around the Germans in a gigantic pincers movement. Paulus and his men now were hopelessly stranded. Thanks to Hitler's obstinacy, they were to endure a martyrdom of starvation, disease, and freezing. The end came on February 2, 1943, when Paulus surrendered with 120,000 men, the miserable survivors of the original army of 334,000.

At the same time that the Russians were destroying the German army at Stalingrad, they launched a series of offensives at other points along the front. By the end of March, they had regained all the territory they had lost in 1942. In a desperate effort to check the relentless advance of the Red Army, the Germans made an all-out attack on a Soviet salient at Kursk. Though they concentrated 160 tanks per mile, they gained only 20 miles, and this at a cost of 40,000 men, 1,400 planes and 3,000 tanks. On July 12 the Russians counterattacked, quickly rewon their positions, and then rolled on until logistic difficulties forced them to halt. The Kursk battle marks the turning point in the Russo-German War. It was the last major Nazi offensive on the eastern front. Henceforth the Russians had the initiative, and the Germans fought defensive actions to prevent their retreat from becoming a rout.

While the Germans were being forced back in Russia, they and their Italian allies were being driven out completely from North Africa. In late August, 1942, Rommel attempted to resume his offensive into Egypt but was heavily repulsed. With the aid of new and heavier tanks from the United States, the British commander, Sir Bernard Montgomery, unleashed his own offensive on October 23. After twelve days' hard fighting, the Germans and Italians were routed. As they fell back along the coastal road, they were harried by air and naval bombardment. By January 24, 1943, Montgomery had captured Tripoli, and the road to Tunisia lay open.

Meanwhile Anglo-American troops had landed on November 7–8, 1942, at the other end of North Africa, in Morocco and Algeria. The strategy was to squeeze the Axis forces in a great pincers operation from east and west, and thus remove them once and for all from this theater. On the night of November 7, 1942, some 850 ships in three great convoys, one from the United States and two from England, arrived at Casablanca, Oran, and Algiers. In three weeks 185,000 men landed against token resistance by Vichy French forces. The Anglo-American forces drove toward Tunisia, which was to be subdued by Christmas. This plan was upset, however, as Hitler rushed reinforcements across the Mediterranean. The fighting in Tunisia was hard, with the Anglo-American forces from the west supported by Montgomery advancing from the east and by a Fighting French unit from the south. Eventually, by the middle of May, 1943, Tunisia was subdued by the Allied forces.

Following their conquest of North Africa, the Anglo-Americans pressed on to Sicily, which they invaded on July 10. The German troops fought hard, but the Italians, discouraged by constant defeats and alienated by their domineering partners, offered only token resistance. The Sicilian capital, Palermo, fell on July 22, and by mid-August, allied troops were following the retreating enemy across the Messina Straits to the mainland.

Mussolini paid for these disasters with his office and eventually with his life. King Victor Emmanuel III was persuaded by monarchists and Fascist dissidents to dismiss Mussolini and to place him in prison. This was done on July 25, three days after the fall of Palermo. Supreme authority was now vested in the king and in Marshal Pietro Badoglio, the conqueror of Ethiopia. The latter concluded an armistice agreement with the Allies on September 3. At the same time, British troops landed at Calabria on the toe of the Italian Peninsula, while Americans attacked at Salerno, south of Naples. The Germans responded promptly by seizing Rome and occupying the central and northern parts of the country. In a bold raid, Nazi parachutists rescued Mussolini from prison. The shopworn *Duce* established a "Fascist Republic" in northern Italy and proclaimed his intention of fighting to the bitter end. For the next year and a half Italy was to be a divided and war-racked country; the Germans with their puppet Mussolini in the north, and the Allies with Badoglio's provisional government in the south.

Meanwhile, the soil of the Third Reich itself was being subjected to steadily increasing aerial bombardment. By 1943, round-the-clock bombing became possible, the British raiding by night and the Americans by day. Civilian deaths from air raids in Germany throughout the war have been estimated at 305,000. This unprecedented aerial assault was used by the Western powers as a partial answer to the growing Soviet demand for a second front in France. Yet the effectiveness of all this bombing remains a matter of dispute. Factories and railroads usually were in full operation within days after a major raid. The German munitions output, according to German figures, reached its highest point in 1944, the year when the bombing also was at its heaviest.

Meanwhile, the Japanese were suffering reverses comparable to those of their Axis partners in Europe. After their spectacular victories in the first six months, the Japanese finally were stopped and then were pushed back at an accelerating pace. The basic reason for this shift in the course of the war was the overwhelming superiority of American resources and productivity. When the war began, the Japanese economy was roughly comparable to the French in productivity. But compared to the American it was paltry. The Japanese could not even begin to match the flood from American factories. The empire they had conquered had an abundant supply of raw materials, but they could not convert these into war goods. One reason was the decimation of their merchant marine by American planes and submarines, so that the Japanese found it increasingly difficult to keep supplies flowing to their factories at home as well as to their armed forces abroad. Equally serious was the weakness of Japanese heavy industry. Even if raw materials had been available in adequate quantities, Japan lacked the industrial resources to utilize them. Manpower also was in short supply, despite the 73 million people who were then crowded on the home islands. No less than 40 per cent of this population was engaged in intensive rice cultivation, leaving no surplus for substantial expansion of industry. If Japan could have had a decade or two of peace to exploit her newly won territories, she might well have become a great world empire. But instead of peace, she was to suffer catastrophic defeat.

The first step on the long road to Tokyo was taken at Guadalcanal, where United States Marines landed on August 7, 1942. Slowly, and at heavy cost,

American and Australian forces captured vital bases in New Britain and New Guinea. Very few Japanese were taken prisoners, for capture was considered a disgrace and was rarely accepted. Suicidal *banzai* charges by officers and soldiers refusing to surrender became almost a routine climax to the taking of Japanese positions. In the face of such resistance, the American counteroffensive advanced northward, overwhelming Saipan and Guam in the Marianas by mid-1944. This brought the Japanese home islands within range of the new B-29 superfortresses and spelled the beginning of the end of Japan's brief hour of glory.

Liberation of Europe

Europe was liberated in 1944–1945 primarily by the Red Army advancing from the east and by Anglo-American forces invading from the Normandy landing beaches in the west. Fighting also continued in Italy during this period, but it was peripheral compared to the campaigns in the north. In an attempt to end the Italian war quickly, the Allies in January, 1944, made a landing at Anzio, only 30 miles from Rome, and also attacked the German stronghold at the Monte Cassino monastery. Both operations failed, and the Italian campaign bogged down to a dreary stalemate. Not until mid-May was Cassino captured, thanks largely to Free French mountain troops from North Africa. The way to Rome now lay open, and American and French troops pushed up the western flank of the peninsula while Britishers and Poles advanced on the eastern. On June 5, the Fifth American Army of General Mark Clark entered Rome, tempestuously welcomed by its inhabitants. Rome was the first of the Continental capitals to be freed from Nazi rule, but this triumph was overshadowed by the Allied landings in Normandy on the following day.

The vast armada, comprising 4,000 merchant vessels and 700 warships, began landings on June 6 at 6:30 A.M. By the end of the day, 326,000 men and 20,000 vehicles reached the shore. Fortunately for the Allies, the German High Command suspected that the Normandy landings were only a feint and that the main attack would come at Calais, where the Channel was narrowest. Accordingly, the German armored forces were kept in reserve until it was too late to dislodge the invaders. By D-Day plus five, the beachheads had been merged along a front of sixty miles. From the beginning, it should be noted, the Allied forces received invaluable aid from the French underground bands (*maquis*), which wrecked bridges, cut communication lines, and derailed German troop trains.

The Allied plan of campaign was for the British and Canadian forces on the left to repel the main enemy attacks, while the American forces on the right, trained and equipped for mobility, broke out of the bridgehead and took the Germans in the rear. On July 25, the Americans, aided by 1,500 heavy bombers that blasted a gap in the enemy lines, fought their way into open country at Saint-Lô. As they advanced, they trapped 100,000 of the enemy in the Cherbourg Peninsula. By early August the dashing tank commander General George Patton was rushing headlong across northern France toward Paris. On August 15, a new American army under General Alexander M. Patch, with strong French reinforcements, landed on the Riviera beaches and advanced rapidly up the Rhone valley. Meanwhile, central France was being liberated by the *maquis* who descended from the hills and attacked enemy garrisons and communication lines. Belabored from all sides, the Germans now made a general withdrawal toward their own frontiers. On August 19, resistance forces began open insurrection in Paris, and six days later a French armored division and an American infantry division completed the liberation of the capital. General de Gaulle, now universally recognized as the leader of the French people, drove in triumph to Notre Dame for the *Te Deum* of thanksgiving.

These sweeping victories raised hopes for an end to the war by Christmas. The German armies had pulled back behind the Siegfried Line and in front of the Rhine River for a desperate last stand. But Patton's tank army was running short of fuel, while the French and Americans advancing from the south were meeting stiff resistance in Alsace. By October it was apparent that victory was out of reach for that year.

While the Western powers were liberating France, the Red Army was advancing rapidly from the East. Having driven the *Wehrmacht* from the Crimea and the Ukraine by the spring of 1944, it then began a general offensive against approximately two million Germans (compared to the one million facing the Allies in France and Italy). In the north the Russians knocked Finland out of the war by September; in the center they crossed both the old and new frontiers of Poland and drove to the gates of Warsaw; in the south they reached the mouth of the Danube in the heart of Rumania. Young King Michael of Rumania seized the opportunity to pull his country out of the war in September, thus opening the Balkan Peninsula to the Red Army. Bulgaria followed this example by suing for peace and re-entering the war on the side of the Soviet Union. The German armies in the Balkans were now in danger of being trapped and began to pull out as fast as possible. Aided by the local Communist-led guerrillas, the Red Army drove up the Danube Valley until it was stopped in Hungary by stiffening German resistance.

At this point the Allies were caught off guard by a sudden offensive launched by the Germans on December 16, 1944, in the Ardennes in Belgium. Using much heavy armor and helped by foggy weather that hampered Allied aerial counterattacks, the Germans carved out a salient or "bulge" fifty miles in depth and as broad at the base. Finally the weather cleared on December 24, and 5,000 Allied planes pounded German supply lines, while Patton counterattacked from the south and Montgomery from the north. By the end of January, 1945, the Germans had been forced back to their original positions, and thereafter they were forced steadily backward under relentless Allied pressure.

While the "Battle of the Bulge" was raging in the west, the Russians were advancing steadily in Poland and Hungary. Both Warsaw and Hungary were taken by February, 1945, though only after bitter fighting that left the two capitals in ruins. Thanks to an exceptionally mild winter, the Red Army soldiers were able to press on into Austria and Germany. On April 13, they took Vienna, while to the north they overran East Prussia and Silesia. By late March, they were fighting their way across the Oder, only forty miles from Berlin.

Meanwhile, the American, British, Canadian, and French armies were making corresponding progress on the western front. After recovering from the shock at Ardennes they cracked the West Wall and fought their way through to the Rhine. There they discovered to their astonishment that the retreating Germans had neglected to blow up the Ludendorff railway bridge at Remagen, south of Bonn. The Allies swarmed over, and within a month they had conquered the Rhineland and taken a quarter-million prisoners. Seven Allied armies now raced eastward through the collapsing Reich. On April 25, an American patrol linked up with the Soviet vanguard at the village of Torgau on the Elbe, cutting Germany in two.

At the same time General Mark Clark was cleaning the Germans out of Italy with the noteworthy assistance of Italian guerrillas, who harassed the enemy as the *maquis* did in France. A final offensive was launched on April 10, and within a fortnight the German lines had crumpled and the Allies streamed down into the Po valley and beyond to the Alps. On May 2, the German commanders in Italy signed terms of unconditional surrender. Five days earlier Mussolini had been apprehended by guerrillas while attempting to escape to Switzerland and was summarily shot.

Hitler meanwhile was still holding out, even though both his eastern and western fronts had caved in. He clung to the hope that total disaster could be averted by playing off Russia against the Western powers. But on April 16, Marshal Zhukov opened his final offensive upon the German capital. Nine days later he had the city surrounded, and shells were thudding around Hitler's concrete bunker in the chancellery garden. On the last day of the month Hitler and his companion, Eva Braun, whom he had married a few days earlier, committed suicide. On May 2, Berlin surrendered to the Russians, and during the next week Nazi emissaries surrendered unconditionally to the Western powers at Rheims and to the Soviet Union in Berlin.

Surrender of Japan

The surrender of Germany made even bleaker the prospects for the Japanese in the Pacific. Already by mid-1944 their home islands were being bombed by superfortresses based on the Marianas. At the end of the year American forces landed in the Philippines, and by late February, 1945, they had forced the Japanese garrisons to surrender. More serious for the enemy was the loss of Iwo Jima, which was only 750 miles away from the Japanese homeland and Okinawa, which was only 350 miles distant. Using these two islands as bases, American airmen now subjected Japan's crowded cities to the same storm of explosives that had racked Germany. The Japanese were even more vulnerable, for their flimsy wood and paper structures went up in flames like so much kindling. In nine months from November, 1944, to the surrender in September, 1945, B-29 super-fortresses made 32,000 sorties against Japan, or more than a hundred a day. The toll of dead or homeless Japanese soared beyond eight million.

Now a series of unprecedented cataclysms forced the Japanese to surrender. On August 6, 1945, an American superfortress dropped an atomic bomb on Hiroshima, demolishing three-fifths of the city and killing 78,150 inhabitants. Two days later Russia declared war on Japan, and the Red Army promptly drove across the frontier into Manchuria. Russia's invasion came exactly three months after Germany's surrender, fulfilling an obligation assumed by Stalin during his meeting with Roosevelt and Churchill at Yalta in February, 1945. The final blow was the dropping of a second atomic bomb on August 9 upon the city of Nagasaki, with results as devastating as at Hiroshima. The extreme Japanese militarists still opposed a general surrender, but the Emperor, on the advice of the Cabinet and the Elder Statesmen, decided to capitulate. On August 14 the Allied ultimatum was accepted, the formal ceremony of surrender taking place on board the U.S.S. Missouri in Tokyo Bay on September 2 in the presence of General MacArthur, Admiral Nimitz, and ranking Allied officers.

III. WORLD WAR II IN WORLD HISTORY

World War II completed the undermining of Europe's global hegemony that had been started by World War I. Thus, in a general sense the two wars had a similar significance for world history. There were variations in detail, however, that are of prime significance for the contemporary scene. The Nazis and the Japanese militarists were infinitely more destructive of the old orders in Europe and Asia than the Hohenzollerns and the Hapsburgs had ever been. The Germans had overrun the entire continent of Europe; and the Japanese, the whole of East and Southeast Asia. But these vast empires proved short-lived. They disappeared in 1945, leaving behind two great power vacuums embracing territories of primary economic and strategic significance. It was the existence of these vacuums, as much as any ideological considerations, that was responsible for the outbreak of the Cold War and the inability to conclude a general peace settlement immediately after 1945.

Another difference between the two postwar periods was the successful upsurge of colonial subjects after 1945, in contrast to the enforcement of imperial authority after 1918. Within a period of two decades the farflung European empires had all but disappeared. In this sense, these were decades of European decline, political and military. Yet at the same time, thanks to the accelerating unification of the globe, Western ideas and institutions and technology were spreading throughout the globe at an unprecedented pace. Thus the post-World War II years constitute, paradoxically, a period of European triumph as well as decline.

SUGGESTED READING

R. A. Divine, *Causes and Consequences of World War II* (Quadrangle, 1969); B. Liddell Hart, *History of the Second World War* (Cassell, 1970); M. B. Hoyle, *A World in Flames: A History of World War II* (Atheneum, 1970); J. Toland, *The Rising Sun: The Decline and Fall of the Japanese Empire* (Bantam, 1970); G. Wright, *The Ordeal of Total War 1939–1945* (Harper, 1969); B. Whaley, *Codeword Barbarossa* (MIT Press, 1973).

chapter thirty-nine

End of Empires

Hereafter, perhaps, the natives of those [overseas] countries may grow stronger, or those of Europe may grow weaker, and the inhabitants of all the different quarters of the world may arrive at that equality of courage and force which, by inspiring mutual fear, can alone overawe the injustice of independent nations into some sort of respect for the rights of one another. But nothing seems more likely to establish this equality of force than that mutual communication of knowledge and of all sorts of improvements which an extensive commerce from all countries to all countries naturally, or rather necessarily, carries along with it.—Adam Smith

A major difference between World War I and World War II lay in their colonial aftermaths. Europe's hold over the colonial empires was weakened but not broken by World War I; indeed, the colonial holdings were expanded by the acquisition of Arab lands as mandates. After World War II, by contrast, an irrepressible revolutionary wave swept the colonial empires and ended European domination with dramatic dispatch. In 1939, the only independent states in sub-Saharan Africa were Liberia and South Africa, and they owed their independence to their atypical historical backgrounds. The one had been settled in the early nineteenth century by freed slaves, and the other was controlled by a resident European minority. Twenty-five years later, the only significant colonies left in sub-Saharan Africa were Portuguese Angola and Mozambique, and the cluster under South Africa's shadow: Southern Rhodesia, South-West Africa, Bechuanaland, Swaziland, and Basutoland. Just as most of Europe's colonies had been swiftly acquired in the last two decades of the nineteenth century, so most of them now were lost in an equally short period following World War II. Between 1944 and 1974, a total of 78 countries had won their independence (see Table 1). These countries had a population of over one billion people, or about a third of the world's total. After so many epoch-making triumphs and achievements overseas, the Europeans appeared in the mid-twentieth century to be retreating back to the small Eurasian peninsula whence they had set forth half a millennium earlier. (See map XXVII, "World of New Global Relationships.")

I. ROOTS OF COLONIAL REVOLUTION

The unexpected success of the colonial revolutions was the product of the exceptionally favorable international situation at the end of World War II and of certain historical forces within the colonial world that had been gathering momentum for several decades. An unprecedented weakening of the foremost colonial powers took place during World War II. France and Holland were overrun and occupied, while Britain was debilitated economically and militarily. Equally important was the growth of democratic, anti-imperialist sentiment within the imperial countries themselves. Mussolini's attack on Ethiopia in 1935 was widely regarded in Western Europe as a deplorable throwback, while the Anglo-French assault on the Suez in 1956 aroused vehement popular opposition in both Britain and France. The end of the West's global hegemony was due as much to the lack of will to rule as it was to lack of strength.

TABLE 1   AFRICAN-ASIAN MARCH TO INDEPENDENCE

	Became independent of	Year		Became independent of	Year
Syria	France	1944	Central African		
Lebanon	France	1944	Republic	France	1960
Jordan	Britain	1946	Chad	France	1960
Philippines	United States	1946	Gabon	France	1960
India	Britain	1947	Mauritania	France	1960
Pakistan	Britain	1947	Sierra Leone	Britain	1961
Burma	Britain	1948	Tanganyika†	Britain	1961
N. Korea	Japan	1948	Algeria	France	1962
S. Korea	Japan	1948	Burundi	Belgium	1962
Israel	Britain	1948	Rwanda	Belgium	1962
Sri Lanka			Uganda	Britain	1962
(Ceylon)	Britain	1948	Western Samoa	Britain	1962
Indonesia	Netherlands	1949	Kenya	Britain	1963
Libya	Italy	1952	Zanzibar†	Britain	1963
Cambodia	France	1954	Malta	Britain	1964
Laos	France	1954	Malawi	Britain	1964
N. Vietnam	France	1954	Zambia	Britain	1964
S. Vietnam	France	1954	Gambia	Britain	1965
Sudan	Britain-Egypt	1956	Maldive Islands	Britain	1965
Morocco	France	1956	Singapore	Britain	1965
Tunisia	France	1956	Guyana	Britain	1966
Ghana	Britain	1957	Botswana	Britain	1966
Malaya*	Britain	1957	Lesotho	Britain	1966
Guinea	France	1958	Barbados	Britain	1966
Republic of			South Yemen	Britain	1967
the Congo	Belgium	1960	Mauritius	Britain	1968
Somalia	Italy	1960	Swaziland	Britain	1968
Nigeria	Britain	1960	Equatorial Guinea	Spain	1968
Cameroon	France	1960	Nauru	Britain	1968
Mali	France	1960	Fiji	Britain	1970
Senegal	France	1960	Tonga	Britain	1970
Malagasy	France	1960	Bahrein	Britain	1971
Togo	France	1960	Bangladesh	Pakistan	1971
Cyprus	Britain	1960	Bhutan	Britain	1971
Ivory Coast	France	1960	Oman	Britain	1971
Upper Volta	France	1960	Qatar	Britain	1971
Niger	France	1960	United Arab		
Dahomey	France	1960	Emirates	Britain	1971
Congo Republic	France	1960	Guinea-Bissau	Portugal	1974

* Combined in 1963 with Singapore, Sarawak, and Sabah (British North Borneo), to form the state of Malaysia with a population of 10 million.
† Tanganyika and Zanzibar combined in 1964 to form the United Republic of Tanganyika and Zanzibar, or Tanzania.

In addition, the colonial revolution was helped along by the fact that the two dominant postwar powers, the United States and the Soviet Union, were not interested in acquiring overseas possessions at the expense of their defeated enemies or their weakened allies. They did gain control, directly or indirectly, over strategic islands and satellite states in the Pacific Ocean and in Eastern Europe, but they did not follow the example of Britain and France who eagerly divided German and Turkish colonies following World War I. Instead, by a curious paradox, the opposite occurred: The colonials exploited the Cold War to play off the Soviet Union against the United States and to use both powers in winning their independence and in obtaining economic assistance.

The short-lived Japanese Empire in Asia also contributed substantially to the colonial revolution. Western military prestige was shattered by the ease with which the Japanese drove the British out of Malaya and Burma, the French out of Indochina, the Dutch out of Indonesia, and the Americans out of the Philippines. The political foundations of Western imperialism were undermined by Japanese propaganda based on the slogan "Asia for the Asians."

It should be noted, however, that the Africans who escaped Japanese invasion also won freedom along with the Asians, thus pointing up the fact that, important as the Japanese impact was, it merely intensified the great unrest and awakening that had been gathering momentum since the beginning of the century. The series of colonial uprisings following World War I reflected this burgeoning movement. (See Chapter 34.) In the intervening years it had gained strength and purpose, with the growth of a Western-educated native intelligentsia. It was not accidental that the successful nationalist leaders were not un-reconstructed Malayan sultans or Nigerian chiefs or Indian princes, but rather men who had studied in Western universities and observed Western institutions in operation— men like Gandhi, Nehru, Sukarno, Nkrumah. This worldwide colonial awakening was further stimulated during World War II with the service of millions of colonials in both Allied and Japanese armies and labor battalions. Many Africans fought under the British, French, and Italian flags, over two million Indians volunteered for the British forces, and an additional 40,000 Indian prisoners captured in Hong Kong, Singapore, and Burma signed up for the Japanese-sponsored Indian National army. When all these men returned to their homes, they inevitably regarded the local colonial officials and native leaders in a new light.

II. INDIA AND PAKISTAN

By far the most important single event in the colonial revolution was the winning of independence by India and Pakistan. More than a century of British rule had prepared India better than any other colony for self-rule. The Civil Service had been largely Indianized; the universities had turned out generations of Western-educated leaders; and the Congress party had voiced and directed into the proper channels nationalist aspirations. (See Chapter 28, sections IV to VI.) When Britain declared war on Germany on September 3, 1939, the viceroy, the Marquis of Linlithgow, on the same day proclaimed India also to be at war. The Congress party protested bitterly but the viceroy announced that basic changes were not feasible during the war. He did promise postwar dominion status, but Congress promptly rejected this offer and the deadlock continued.

With Japan's precipitous conquest of Southeast Asia in early 1942, Churchill sent to India on March 22 a cabinet member, Sir Stafford Cripps. Again major change was excluded for the duration of the war, but as soon as it was over, India could become fully autonomous, with the right to secede from the Commonwealth. Congress turned down Cripp's offer and on August 7, 1942, passed a "Quit India Resolution" demanding immediate freedom, "both for the sake of India and for the success of the cause of the UN." Congress further threatened, if its demand was not met, to wage "a mass struggle on nonviolent lines." Britain's response was wholesale repression: Over 60,000 people were arrested, including all the Congress leaders; 14,000 were detained without trial; 940 were killed; and 1,630 were injured in clashes with the police and military.

It was a most critical moment for the Allies as well as for India. The Germans had by then reached the Volga and were only thirty miles from Alexandria, while the Japanese had overrun Burma. The gigantic German and Japanese pincers were separated only by India, which was seething with disaffection, and by the Arab countries, which sided more with the Axis than with the Allies. Britain's position in the subcontinent would have been precarious, if not impossible, had Congress made any preparations for armed revolt. Instead, under Gandhi's influence, only nonviolent resistance was offered.

During the remaining years of the war, the British stood firm in refusing to release the Congress leaders unless they modified their "Quit India" demand, which they refused to do. Meanwhile, Mohammed Jinnah, head of the Moslem League, took advantage of this hobbling of Congress to win India's Moslems to his organization and thus prepare the ground for an independent postwar Moslem state. A new and decisive turn in Indian affairs was taken with the Labour party victory in the British elections of July, 1945. Labour traditionally had championed Indian freedom, and now Prime Minister Attlee acted swiftly for its materialization. Apart from his party's commitments and sympathies, the fact is that Attlee had little choice but to accept independence. Indian nationalism, inflamed by the wartime experiences, no longer could be repressed by sheer physical force, as became apparent when the government brought to trial at the end of 1945 some officers of the Japanese-sponsored Indian National army. These men immediately became national heroes, not because they had cooperated with the Japanese, but because their aim had been to oust the hated British. So strong was the feeling throughout the country that the trial had to be dropped. The truth was that Britain could no longer rule the country against the wishes of its people. Nor was there much inclination any longer to attempt to do so. The Indian Civil Service had become even more Indianized during the war, while British investments in India had shrunk drastically; and the British public had become weary of the never-ending Indian problem. Thus Attlee was now able to sever ties with the former jewel of the empire with relatively little opposition at home.

Admiral Lord Louis Mountbatten, who was sent as the new viceroy, concluded that no plan for preserving Indian political unity was feasible because of enmity between Congress and the Moslem League. He recommended partition, with the two governments each to have dominion status. By this time the Congress leaders had realized that partition was inevitable, so they accepted the plan. In July, 1947, the British Parliament passed the Indian Independence Act, and on August 15, both Pakistan and the Union of India became free nations in the British Commonwealth. The elasticity of the Commonwealth was stretched one degree further to permit the two newcomers to participate as republics in an institution that necessarily maintained a monarch as its symbolic head.

III. SOUTHEAST ASIA

Southeast Asia, in contrast to India, was occupied by the Japanese during the war. A common pattern is discernible throughout the area during this brief occupation period between 1942 and 1945. In almost every country, widespread disaffection against Western rule had contributed substantially to the swift conquests of the Japanese. (See Chapter 38, section II.) The latter then proclaimed, like the Germans, that their conquests inaugurated the beginning of a "New Order." The watchwords of this "New Order" were "Asia for the Asians," "Greater East Asia Co-Prosperity Sphere," and "no conquests, no oppression and no exploitation."

If these principles had been applied, the Japanese could have mobilized solid popular support in most of Southeast Asia, especially since they had been welcomed generally by the local populations as liberators. The Japanese military, however, had other plans, so that the principles remained propagandist slogans which soon sounded hollow and unconvincing. These military leaders viewed Greater East Asia not as a "Co-Prosperity Sphere" but as a region consisting of satellite states held under varying degrees of control. The Japanese armed forces everywhere lived off the land as much as possible, frequently creating severe local shortages of food and supplies; and they expropriated ruthlessly whatever foodstuffs and industrial raw materials were needed for the home islands. In return, the Japanese were able to offer little, since their economy was not strong enough to produce both war materials and consumer goods.

It is understandable that after the initial honeymoon period, relations between the Japanese and the local nationalists rapidly deteriorated. If the occupation had been prolonged, the Japanese undoubtedly would have been faced with serious uprisings. Fortunately for them, they were forced to pull out during 1945. In doing so, they did everything possible to create obstacles in the way of a restoration of Western rule. In Indochina they overthrew the Vichy regime and recognized Ho Chi Minh's provisional government; in Indonesia they handed over the administration to the nationalist leader Sukarno; and in many regions they distributed arms to local revolutionary groups.

It is not surprising that within ten years of the Japanese withdrawal, all Southeast Asia was independent. The manner in which the various countries won their freedom varied, depending upon the imperial rulers involved. The British, having been forced to face facts in India, were the most realistic in coping with Southeast Asian nationalism. In January, 1948, they recognized Burma as an independent republic outside the Commonwealth, and in the next month they granted Ceylon full Dominion status within the Commonwealth. Malayan independence, however, was delayed until February, 1957, one reason being the country's mosaic-like ethnic composition, including Malayans and Chinese—each a little over 40 per cent of the total population—as well as Indians, Pakistanis, and a few Europeans. The Chinese were the prime movers behind a Communist uprising that began in 1948; the ensuing jungle warfare was very costly and dragged on until 1955. In 1963, Malaya combined with Singapore, Sarawak, and Sabah (British North Borneo) to constitute the new state of Malaysia. Tension between Malaya and the predominantly Chinese Singapore led in 1965 to the secession of Singapore, which became an independent state in the Commonwealth.

The French and the Dutch, whose subjects also demanded independence, proved less adjustable and fared much worse. When the Dutch returned to Indonesia in 1946, they were willing to grant some measure of self-government but not enough to satisfy the nationalists under Sukarno. The negotiations broke down and the Dutch resorted to armed force to reassert their authority. The war dragged on until 1947 when the Dutch finally recognized the independent United States of Indonesia. A Dutch-Indonesian Union with a common crown existed for a few years, but it ended when Sukarno withdrew in 1954. Relations became more strained in the following years because the Dutch refused to yield Netherlands New Guinea to the new republic. In 1957, in retaliation, Indonesia seized more than $1 billion worth of Dutch assets and, in 1960, severed diplomatic relations with The Hague. Three years later Sukarno gained control over West Irian, thus liquidating the last remnant of an empire older than most of the British Empire.

The French in Indochina fought longer and more stubbornly to retain their colony, but in the end they, too, were forced out. Indochina consisted of three nations: Vietnam, Laos, and Cambodia. Resistance against the restoration of French rule was led by the Vietminh, or League for the Independence of Vietnam. Though comprising many elements, the Vietminh was led by a Communist, Ho Chi Minh, who had lived in Paris, Moscow, and China. In 1945 he proclaimed the provisional Republic of Vietnam, but the French refused recognition and war ensued. Laos and Cambodia were easily reoccupied by the French, but an exhausting struggle dragged on in Vietnam.

With the advent of the Cold War, the United States backed up the French financially as a part of the policy of "containment." By 1954, most of northern Vietnam was in the hands of the Vietminh, and in the same year, the French suffered a major defeat at Dien Bien Phu. The ensuing Geneva settlement recognized the independence of all Vietnam, divided the country temporarily at the 17th parallel, and called for supervised elections to be held in 1956 to reunify the country. This settlement in effect gave Ho Chi Minh half the country, and the expectation of the other half within two years because his resistance record had made him a national hero.

To avert this outcome the United States supported in the south the anti-Communist Catholic leader Ngo Dinh Diem. His policies aroused such fierce opposition amongst the peasants and the powerful Buddhist monks that in 1963 his regime was overthrown and a succession of coups followed until the rise to power, with Washington's support, of Nguyen Cao Ky and then of Nguyen Van Thieu. They were able to hold out in Saigon only because of accelerating American intervention, beginning with money and arms, and progressing to "advisers," combat troops, and, after the Tonkin Bay incident (August, 1964), the bombing of North Vietnam. The bombing was designed to coerce Hanoi, which had been sending troops southward, to disengage and to recognize South Vietnam as a separate state. Although the bombing far surpassed World War II and Korean War levels, and although over a half million American troops were committed, victory remained elusive, as the enemy's January, 1968, Tet offensive painfully demonstrated. Hence President Johnson's decision to end the bombing of North Vietnam and to begin peace talks in Paris.

His successor, President Nixon, had been elected on the promise of a plan to end the war. This plan involved the withdrawal of American troops, a move which in any case had become unavoidable because of the growing disaffection of both the troops and the home population. But the Nixon plan also involved continued support to President Thieu, whose regime was deemed to be essential for American interests. Accordingly it was buttressed with United States funds, arms, non combative military personnel and supportive bombing on a scale surpassing that of the Johnson administration. Despite the magnitude of this American assistance, the position of the Thieu government remained so precarious that Nixon felt it necessary to launch incursions, supported by American troops and airpower into Cambodia (April-June 1970) and into Laos (February-March 1971).

These moves provoked intense dissension and mass demonstrations in the United States. But at the same time Nixon was conducting secret diplomacy with China and the Soviet Union, culminating in his well-publicized visits to Peking (February 1972) and to Moscow (May 1972). In October 1972, on the eve of the presidential election, Nixon announced an American-North Vietnamese agreement for a cease fire. But the announcement proved premature, as Nixon ordered the heaviest bombing of the entire war directed against North Vietnam's industrial heartland on December 18-30, 1972. Finally a ceasefire was signed in Paris on January 27, 1973 with terms essentially similar to those of the 1954 Geneva accords. Both agreements called for a temporary partition of Vietnam into a Communist North and a non-Communist South, for the determination of the future of South Vietnam by an election, for the neutralization of Laos and Cambodia, for the withdrawal from all Indochina of all foreign troops—French in 1954, American in 1973—and for the supervision of both settlements by a small and largely powerless international committee.

The cost of obtaining in 1973 what the United States had opposed in 1954 was the longest war in American history, 45,933 American deaths, 600,000 civilian and military deaths in South Vietnam, an estimated 900,000 deaths in North Vietnam, and incalculable damage to the American social fabric from GI drug addiction, bitter domestic discord, and festering national problems neglected with the financial drain of Vietnam war expenditures. Nor did the 1973 Paris agreement finally end the fighting and America's involvement. During the first year after the agreement, combat deaths from the continued fighting in Vietnam totalled well over 50,000, and the United States government found it necessary to spend three billion dollars to maintain the Thieu regime in power.

IV. TROPICAL AFRICA

In Africa the colonial revolution was even more dramatic than it was in Asia. The triumph of nationalism in the latter area was not altogether unexpected, given the ancient indigenous cultures and the local political organizations that had been agitating for some decades. In Africa, by contrast, the nationalist movements were much younger and weaker, and in addition the continent had not been jarred and aroused by Japanese occupation. And yet, just as the first postwar decade witnessed the liberation of Asia, so the second witnessed the liberation of Africa. During that decade, no less than 31 African countries won their independence; the few remaining colonies stood out painfully as obsolete hangovers from the past. The course of this nationalist awakening differed fundamentally from region to region because of the varying historical backgrounds and contemporary developments. Accordingly, the colonial revolution will be considered not on a continentwide basis, but individually in tropical Africa, South Africa, and North Africa.

Nationalist movements of any significance did not appear in tropical Africa until after World War I. The form they assumed depended on the policies and administrative institutions established by the colonial powers. In British West Africa, authority was vested in the hands of governors who were appointed from London and who were advised by executive and legislative councils. The executive councils consisted entirely of British officials, but the legislative councils included a few African nominees. The African leaders in these colonies sought to convert the legislative councils into African parliaments, and then to convert the executive councils into African ministries responsible to such parliaments. In the French colonies, by contrast, authority was wielded to a much greater degree from Paris, and the French Africans tried to affiliate with the metropolitan parties in order to be in a position to influence decisions in the capital.

These strategies had little impact prior to World War II. Only a few western-educated leaders were awake and active; the mass of the people were largely apathetic. The few nationalist organizations were more like debating societies than political parties, and they devoted more energy to sniping at the European administrators than to communicating with their own peoples. World War II drastically altered this traditional African pattern. In the first place, a tremendous economic expansion occurred during the war years because of the pressing demand for African raw materials and foodstuffs. This general economic upsurge led to a boom in the building of schools, the construction of roads, and the improvement of housing, sanitation, and medical services. At the same time, the Africans, observing a host of Asian peoples gaining their independence, naturally asked why they, too, should not be rid of the bonds of colonialism. The question became acute with the return of the war veterans, large numbers of whom had served for the French in Europe and for the British in Burma and the Middle East. All these factors combined to shake up and awaken tropical Africa out of her traditional lethargy.

The first outburst occurred on the Gold Coast in 1948, where the small farmers now had more income than ever before, but consumer goods were in short supply and very expensive. They suspected the European traders of profiteering, and organized a widespread boycott of their concerns. This was followed by rioting in the towns and general ferment in the countryside. A new leader now appeared who exploited this disaffection with startling success: Kwame Nkrumah had studied in American and English universities, where he had become converted to the Marxist socialism current among colonial students. Nkrumah quickly overshadowed the older West African nationalists by demanding immediate independence and organizing in 1949 the Convention People's party on a genuine mass basis.

In a general election held in 1951 under a new constitution, this party won an overwhelming majority. Nkrumah was in prison on election day, charged with sedition, but the British governor, sensing the trend of events, released Nkrumah and gave him and his colleagues leading posts in the administration. In the next few years the cabinet became all-African and was entrusted with full authority except for defense and foreign affairs. With this apprenticeship in self-government, it proved possible to make the transition to full independence without violence or dislocation. By 1957, thanks to the initiative of Nkrumah and the statesmanship of the British, the Gold Coast became the independent Commonwealth country of Ghana.

Once the colonial dam had been broken in Ghana, it was impossible to keep it from breaking elsewhere. Most decisive was the course of events in Nigeria, the most populous country in Africa, with its 35 million people. The three regions of the country—the North, the West, and the South—differed basically from each other in ethnic composition, cultural traditions, and economic development; this diversity led to serious interregional conflicts that delayed the winning of independence to 1960. The other British West African colonies, Sierra Leone and Gambia, followed in 1961 and 1963 respectively, their delay being due primarily to poverty and small size.

The British did not foresee how quickly their new colonial policy would affect the rest of tropical Africa. Repercussions were felt first in the surrounding French holdings where, in 1956, a "framework law" granted representative institutions to the twelve West African territories and to the island of Madagascar. Two years later the new de Gaulle regime, brought into power by the crisis in Algeria (see section VI, this chapter) decided to avoid a similar ordeal in tropical Africa. The sub-Saharan colonies were given the option of voting either for full independence or for autonomy as separate republics in the French "Community" that was to replace the Empire. At first this strategy appeared to be successful; in the ensuing referendum, all the territories except Guinea, which was under the influence of the trade-union leader Sékou Touré, voted for autonomy. The arrangement, however, proved transitory. In 1959, Senegal and the French Sudan asked for full independence within the Community as the Federation of Mali. When this was granted, four other territories—the Ivory Coast, Niger, Dahomey, and Upper Volta—went a step further and secured independence outside the Community. By the end of 1960, all the former colonies of both French West Africa and French Equatorial Africa had won their independence.

In contrast to the smooth transition to independence in French and British West Africa, the Belgian Congo endured a bitter and costly struggle involving the Great Powers as well as Belgium and assorted Congolese factions. One source of this trouble was the rigid paternalistic character of Belgian rule. The educated native elite were few in number and inexperienced, while tribal alliances and rivalries remained prominent. Such was the situation when the French colonies across the Congo were given self-rule, thus stimulating latent hostility to European rule, and bringing to the fore Patrice Lumumba, the only Congolese leader with any pretence to more than a regional following. His radical and nationwide approach to the problem of Congo independence won him a substantial following within his country as well as among pan-Africanists everywhere.

Early in 1959, after the Congo capital had been shaken by nationalist riots, the Belgians hastily decided that they could best protect their vast economic interests by allowing free elections and immediate independence. The predictable outcome was conflict and chaos. Lumumba became the first Premier, but he found he could govern only with the help of Belgian army officers and Civil Service officials. Some of the soldiers mutinied against the remaining officers, and attacks upon whites occurred in various parts of the country. At the same time, fighting broke out between tribes taking advantage of the opportunity to repay old scores. Most serious was the virtual secession of the rich mining province of Katanga, owing to an unholy alliance of local African politicians and Belgian mining interests. The Cold War now intruded when the Soviet Union threatened unilateral intervention under the guise of supporting the Congolese against a restoration of imperialist rule. Faced with the prospect of a Korea-like situation in Africa, the United Nations assumed the responsibility of policing the Congo with an international force consisting largely of Africans. After months of confused violence some semblance of order was restored, though not without the sacrifice of Lumumba, who was murdered by Katanga secessionists, and of the UN Secretary-General, Dag Hammarskjöld, who died in an airplane crash during a mediatory mission in the Congo.

Meanwhile, across the continent in East Africa, the nationalist cause was encountering much stiffer resistance because of the presence of white settlers in the salubrious highlands. In Kenya, the conflict between African and settler was particularly acute because of the settler's appropriation of much of the best farming land. This contributed to the uprising of the Mau Mau, a secret terrorist society made up of members of the Kikuyu tribe. Before the fighting was over, nearly 7,000 Mau Mau had been killed, over 83,000 were in prison, and many more were held in temporary detention camps. The uprising, though it led to sickening excesses on both sides, did force the British to recognize the futility of attempting to follow a conciliatory policy in West Africa and a rigid one in the East. Accordingly, they released from prison the outstanding Kikuyu leader, Jomo Kenyatta. Like Nkrumah, he won a majority vote in an election and was allowed in 1963 to become Premier. In the same year, Kenya became an independent state amidst wild rejoicing in Nairobi for the cherished *Uruhu*, or Freedom.

In neighboring Uganda, where the whites had not been allowed to take land, the issues were simpler and independence had been granted peaceably in 1962. Tanganyika, a German possession before World War I, had become a British mandate in 1922, with two segments, Ruanda and Urundi, becoming Belgian mandates. All three territories were granted independence in 1962, with Julius K. Nyerere of Tanganyika playing a key role in the transition. Under his leadership, Tanganyika and Zanzibar combined in 1964 to form the republic of Tanzania.

The Central African Federation, comprising Southern Rhodesia, Northern Rhodesia, and Nyasaland, was organized to the south of Tanganyika in 1953. Though it was created with the declared objective of "racial partnership," the Federation was beset by crises and violence, the root cause being the political and economic domination of more than 9,000,000 Africans by 300,000 Europeans, most of whom were living in Southern Rhodesia, a self-governing territory on the northern border of the Republic of South Africa. The nationalist movement made strong gains in Northern Rhodesia and Nyasaland, and in 1962, both were given self-rule under African prime ministers. Because Southern Rhodesia refused to follow suit and give Africans the vote, the Federation became impossible and was dissolved on January 1, 1964. Later in the year, Northern Rhodesia became fully independent as Zambia, and Nyasaland as Malawi. The center of strife then shifted to Southern Rhodesia, now known as Rhodesia, where the black majority demanded the vote. The London government sought a compromise settlement looking towards gradual enfranchisement of the Africans. The white minority was adamantly opposed to this, and under the leadership of Prime Minister Ian Smith it declared the independence of Rhodesia in 1965, followed by complete and official independence in 1970. By 1975, however, the black majority was becoming militant in its resistance to white domination. They were organizing increasingly successful guerrilla strikes from Zambia across the Zambezi into Rhodesia, and, more alarming, were receiving support from rural Africans in the border areas.

Portugal attempted to stem the tide of colonial revolution in Angola, Mozambique, and Guinea-Bissau, the remaining tropical African territories, by holding to the obsolete fiction that there were no Portuguese colonies—only overseas provinces of Portugal herself. Lisbon received strong support from South Africa, a country interested in preserving the *status quo* in Angola and Mozambique as a barrier against the spreading African nationalism. Yet, despite Portuguese attempts to isolate their colonies from outside contamination, insurrection broke out in all these colonies, most successfully in Guinea-Bissau, where, under the leadership of Amilcar Cabral, three-fourths of the colony was liberated. Despite the assassination of Cabral on January 20, 1973, the revolutionaries proclaimed the independence of Guinea-Bissau in September, 1973, and within one month were recognized by fifty-four countries.

The burden of unending colonial campaigns finally proved too much for Portugal to bear. Forty per cent of the budget was being spent on defense, and army recruits were deserting and fleeing abroad like their American counterparts during the Vietnam war. On April 25, 1974 Portugal's dictatorship was overthrown by a military coup headed by General Antonio de Spínola, former governor general of Guinea-Bissau. The new regime on August 26 recognized the independence of Guinea-Bissau. A month later, on September 20, 1974, the Mozambique Liberation Front (Frelino) took over power in an interim government in which it held six of the nine cabinet posts. Full independence for Mozambique was scheduled for July 25, 1975. Negotiations also were conducted in Angola, but a settlement there was more difficult because of the much greater Portuguese interests involved.

V. SOUTH AFRICA

The basic difference between tropical Africa on the one hand and North Africa and South Africa on the other is the relative absence of European settlers in the former region and their presence in large numbers in the latter two. This difference explains the brutal armed struggle that ravaged Algeria between 1954 and 1962, and the tense undercover conflict racking South Africa in the seventies. South Africa became a self-governing dominion of the British Commonwealth in 1909, following the Boer War (see Chapter 31, section II). A little more than half a century later, in May, 1961, South Africa left the Commonwealth to become an independent republic. The main reason for the separation was the clash between South Africa and new African and Asian Commonwealth members, such as Nigeria and India, over the issue of apartheid.

Apartheid involves two basic policies: the exclusion of all non-whites from any share in political life; and the relegation of the Africans to separate areas (Bantustans, or preserves for the "Bantu," as the Africans have been known), where it is vaguely theorized that they will some day form separate nations. Paradoxically, the whites comprised only 3.8 million of the 22.5 million total population of South Africa in 1973, the other elements being 16 million Africans, 2 million Coloreds or mixed race, and .7 million Indians. The Afrikaners (Boers), who have controlled South African politics and were responsible for apartheid, were themselves a minority of two-fifths within the white minority. The Afrikaners were able to have their own way partly because parliamentary representation was weighted in favor of the predominantly Afrikaner rural areas, but also because many English-speaking whites supported apartheid for economic reasons. This was especially true of Labour, which feared competition in employment from non-whites in the event that the latter be given equal opportunities. In fact, the first Afrikaner (Nationalist) government was able to take office in 1924 because of support from the South African Labour party.

It has been generally agreed that apartheid is not a viable program, either economically or politically. If the Africans were in fact segregated on the proposed Bantustans, the entire economy of South Africa would collapse. Their labor, as well as that of the 2,000,000 Coloreds and the 600,000 Indians, has been essential for the conduct of agriculture and commerce as well as mining and other industries. In addition, Bantustans have not been able to support even a third of the African population, and the government has been unwilling to spend the large sums needed to increase their absorptive capacity. Most important of all, the great majority of Africans have had no desire to be isolated as separate "tribal" entities. Instead, they have demanded a fair share in the united South Africa of which they are an integral part, and in this demand they have been backed by the growing power of African nationalism in the rest of the continent.

The outstanding development of the 1970s in South Africa has been a growing sense of "black consciousness" on the part of the Africans, Coloreds, and Indians. They have forced newspapers and other publications to drop the designation "non-white" hitherto applied to all of them. They reject this label as negatively defining blacks in terms of white culture. In place of "non-white", the term "black" is now proclaimed as a positive assertion of worth.

Three main organizations are active in fostering the new black-consciousness: the black South African Students Organization which originally launched the black consciousness campaign; the Black People's Convention, a nascent political movement; and Black Community Programs, a coordinating organization fostering the efforts of blacks to help themselves. The outstanding example of blacks helping themselves was the strike of black workers in about 150 industries in Natal Province in January-March 1973. The strike movement spread to the great Johannesburg industrial center, where strikes became chronic. Instead of responding with mass arrests, as was the case in the past, the government passed a bill granting African workers the hitherto denied right to organize unions and a qualified right to strike.

On fundamentals, however, the Afrikaner leaders refused to budge. At the same time that they made the trade union concessions in May 1973, they also announced their refusal to increase the 14 per cent of South Africa's land set aside for the Bantustans (even though Africans comprise 70 per cent of the population), and also their refusal to give permanent residence and other rights to the majority of Africans working and living in "white areas." Even the relatively conservative "chiefs" of the Bantustans have warned of a "bloodbath" if the discrimination and exploitation continue, while the more radical student and trade union leaders are concluding that meaningful change within the legal framework is impossible, and are planning accordingly.

The overthrow of Portugal's dictatorship in April 1974 also has affected South Africa which always has sought to preserve a "white belt" between its frontiers and the black African states of Zambia, Zaire and Tanzania. The principal buffers hitherto have been Angola, Mozambique and Rhodesia. The black nationalist victory in Mozambique, threatens the railway running from Johannesburg and Salisbury to the Mozambique ports of Laurenco Marques and Beira respectively.

VI. NORTH AFRICA

The course of colonial revolution in North Africa was molded not only by the existence of large European settlements but also by two other factors that were not to be found in the rest of the continent: the military campaigns fought on North African soil during World War II; and more important, the upsurge of Arab nationalism over the whole area.

Between 1940 and 1943, British, French, and American armies had fought against Italian and German forces in the North African coastlands and in Northeast Africa. At the war's end, Ethiopia regained its status as an independent state, with the addition of former Italian Eritrea. By contrast, Italian Somaliland remained under the administration of Italy for ten years, and was then combined with British Somaliland to form the independent Somali Republic. The Italian colony of Libya remained under British military administration until December 24, 1951, when it became independent under King Idris el Senussi, spiritual leader of the Senussi Muslim sect that had spearheaded the opposition to Italian rule. The granting of self-rule to Libya undermined Anglo-French imperial authority in the rest of North Africa. Since Libya was the least developed region of North Africa, its independence made British influence in Egypt and the Sudan, and French rule in Tunis, Algeria, and Morocco, appear particularly anachronistic and intolerable to Arab nationalists. (For the nationalist struggle in Egypt and Sudan, see section VII of this chapter.)

In North Africa, as in Indochina, the French fought long and stubbornly to retain their possessions, a principal reason being the substantial number of French settlers in this region—250,000 in Tunisia, 400,000 in Morocco, and 1,000,000 in Algeria. These colons, in league with powerful French economic interests in North Africa, bitterly opposed all proposals for self-rule, and sabotaged a number of provisional moves in this direction made by certain Paris cabinets.

Tunisia and Morocco had the legal status of protectorates, which France claimed to administer in behalf of their traditional rulers. Both territories were governed autocratically—not even the resident Europeans were allowed political rights. This foreign domination stimulated movements for national liberation: in Tunisia, the Neo-Destour party, established in 1934 and led by Habib Bourguiba; and in Morocco, the Istiqlal party, founded in 1944 and given some support by Sultan Mohamed Ben Youssef.

Tunisia and Morocco won their freedom relatively easily following World War II. The French were determined to hang on to Algeria, and were willing to accept losses elsewhere in order to concentrate on this prime objective. Accordingly, when armed resistance began in Tunisia in 1952, the French, after two years of guerrilla warfare, agreed to grant it autonomous status; and having made this concession in Tunisia, they were ready to do likewise in Morocco. Sultan Mohamed, who had been exiled for his pro-Istiqlal sympathies, was allowed to return to his throne; he then demanded complete independence, which the French conceded on March 2, 1956. In the same month, Tunisia also became fully independent, with Bourguiba as President of the new republic.

The French now were able to deal with the crucial Algerian problem without distractions. Legally, Algeria was not a colony but an integral part of France, with representatives in the National Assembly in Paris. In practice, a double standard of citizenship prevailed in Algeria, so that the country was dominated economically and politically by the Europeans who comprised only one-tenth of the ten million total population. On the other hand, the colons, like the Afrikaners at the other tip of the continent, did not regard themselves as mere colonists. Algeria was their homeland as much as that of the native Algerians. Their fathers and grandfathers had worked and died there, and they were resolved to defend their patrimony. This meant unalterable opposition to any concessions to the Algerian nationalists.

Armed revolt against French rule began in the fall of 1954. Having been ousted from Indochina only four months earlier, the French were in no mood for compromise. With the enthusiastic approval of the colons and of the army officers, who were still smarting from the Indochina humiliation, the Paris government resolved to crush the uprising. The result was an exhausting, brutalizing struggle that dragged on until 1962. At its height, the French were forced to send 500,000 men into Algeria, and to spend nearly $1 billion annually. The Algerians paid much more heavily in human terms, including one million dead, or one-ninth of of their total numbers.

Although the French suffered little by comparison—apart from the financial drain—they also paid much more heavily than they had anticipated. The bestialities of a repressive war so divided the country that the Fourth Republic was overthrown. In May, 1958, a North African "Committee of Public Safety" seized power in Algeria in order to replace the Republic with an authoritarian regime that presumably would be more successful in holding the empire together. The demoralized National Assembly bowed to this show of force, especially since most of the armed forces were in Algeria. In June, 1958, the Assembly voted full power to de Gaulle to rule France in whatever manner he wished for six months, and to prepare a new constitution for the country. Before the end of the year the Fourth Republic had given way to the Fifth, and political power had been shifted decisively from the legislative to the executive branch—specifically to the President.

President de Gaulle now used his unprecedented popularity to end the Algerian bloodshed, despite the opposition of the colons and the military who had made possible his rise to power. In March, 1962, after a referendum in France had approved such a move, de Gaulle agreed to a cease-fire and to a plebiscite to determine Algeria's future. On July 3, 1962, he proclaimed the independence of Algeria after its people had voted overwhelmingly in favor of it. All of North Africa was now free for the first time since French soldiers had landed in Algeria in 1830. The granting of independence to Algeria marked the end of a French African empire that once covered nearly 4,000,000 square miles and contained more than 41,000,000 people.

VII. MIDDLE EAST

Meanwhile, Arab nationalism had been as militant in the Middle East as it had been in North Africa. During the interwar years the British had relinquished their hold on Egypt and Iraq, and both countries had entered the League of Nations. Arab nationalists, however, were far from appeased, since the British still reserved various privileges, including the right to maintain a garrison along the Suez Canal, to maintain three air bases in Iraq, and to administer the Sudan together with Egypt. More galling had been the stiff-necked attitude of the French, who continued to hold Syria and Lebanon as mandates. Above all, Arab nationalism had been aroused by large-scale Jewish immigration into the British-held Palestine mandate during the 1930's. (See Chapter 34, section II.) During World War II most politically conscious Arabs were either neutral or openly hostile to the Western powers. This explains the pro-Axis uprising in Iraq in May, 1941, and the extremely reluctant assistance that King Farouk I of Egypt gave to the British despite his treaty obligations.

Although the Arab nationalists had been unable to satisfy their aspirations during World War II, the new postwar balance of power offered them a unique opportunity which they promptly exploited. Britain and France, who had dominated the Middle East before the War, now emerged drastically weakened. A power vacuum was created, which the United States and the Soviet Union attempted to fill. The Arabs skillfully took advantage of the Anglo-French weakness and the American-Russian rivalry to play off one side against the other, thus enabling them to win concessions that would have seemed preposterous only a few years earlier. The Arabs were further aided by their control over vast Middle East oil reserves, which appeared particularly indispensable to the fuel-hungry West during the postwar years.

In October, 1944, the Arabs organized a League of Arab states to coordinate their policies and maximize their effectiveness. The Arab League won its first success against the French in Syria and Lebanon. In May, 1945, a French expeditionary force landed in Beirut and proceeded to bombard Damascus in an attempt to cow the local nationalists. The Arab League Council promptly met and passed a resolution demanding the evacuation of all French forces. Churchill supported the Arabs, especially since the War was not yet over; and he had no desire to cope with an aroused Arab nationalism in the Middle East. Under British pressure the French withdrew their troops, and in July, 1945, they accepted the end of their rule in the Middle East.

In Egypt, the aim of the nationalist leaders after the war was to end or modify the 1936 treaty, which was the legal basis for Britain's control of the Canal Zone and of the Sudan. Direct negotiations and an appeal to the UN both failed, so the Egyptians in 1951 resorted to guerrilla attacks against the British garrison in the Canal Zone. This proved ineffective, and the resulting frustration, together with the general resentment against the disastrous failure in the Palestine War, culminated in an army revolt in July, 1952. General Muhammad Naguib assumed power and forced King Farouk to abdicate.

Naguib removed one of the sources of friction between Egypt and Britain when he concluded an agreement with Britain on February 12, 1953, by which the Sudanese were to be given a choice of independence, union with Egypt, or some other course. The decision was for independence, and in 1956, the Sudan joined the ranks of free nations. The remaining Egyptian grievance—the British presence at the Suez—was ended by Gamal Abdel Nasser, who displaced Naguib as head of the new Egyptian regime. After prolonged negotiations, Nasser signed an agreement with Britain on October 19, 1954, by which under certain stipulated conditions, the British garrison was to be removed and the British installations transferred to Egypt.

Arab nationalism was successful in Syria and Lebanon, and in Egypt and the Sudan, but it failed disastrously in Palestine. The mass extermination of Jews in Hitler-controlled Europe engendered strong pressures for opening up Palestine to the desperate survivors. In August, 1945, President Truman proposed that 100,000 Jews be allowed to enter the mandate; in April, 1946, an Anglo-American investigating committee reported in favor of the President's proposal. The Arab League responded by warning that it was unalterably opposed to such an influx, and that it was prepared, if necessary, to use force to stop it. The United Nations then sent a fact-finding commission to Palestine, and the General Assembly, after receiving the commission's report, voted on November 29, 1947 in favor of partitioning the mandate. On May 14 of the following year, the Jews invoked the partition resolution and proclaimed the establishment of a Jewish state to be called Israel; on the same day, President Truman extended recognition to the new state. On the following day, the Arabs carried out their long-standing threat and sent their armies across the Israeli border.

The course of the war went contrary to expectations. The Arab armies lacked discipline, unity, and effective leadership; the Israelis, fighting literally with their backs to the sea, possessed all three qualities to a high degree. They not only repulsed the Arab attacks from all sides, but advanced and occupied more territory than had been awarded to them by the UN Assembly's resolution. After two abortive truces, the Israelis finally signed armistice agreements with the various Arab states between February and July, 1949.

A peaceful settlement did not follow the cessation of fighting. Two big issues have continued to divide Israel from the surrounding Arab states, one being the question of what to do with the almost 1,000,000 Arab refugees who fled from Israel in the course of the fighting and who have been living miserably in camps near the Israeli borders. The Arab states have insisted that the refugees be allowed to return to their former homes; Israel has rejected this, partly because the refugees, being violently anti-Israel, would destroy the state if they were allowed to return, but also because Jewish refugees, some from Arab countries, have in the meantime occupied the areas vacated by the Arabs. In addition to the refugee question, there has existed the problem of the frontiers: The armistice agreements left Israel with more territory than had been allotted by the UN; the Arabs have been demanding that this extra territory be surrendered, while Israel has maintained that it was won in a war that the Arabs themselves started, and that the extra land has been needed for the Jewish immigrants constantly pouring in from all parts of the world.

These two issues resulted in renewed warfare in 1956, 1967, and 1973. Israel attacked Egypt in 1956 to stop repeated border raids, and Britain and France joined in the attack because Nasser had nationalized the Suez Canal. Both the United States and the Soviet Union strongly opposed the invasion and forced the three aggressors to withdraw. Quite different was the outcome of the six-day Israeli blitz of June 5–10, 1967. Claiming that the surrounding Arab states were planning invasion, the Israeli forces quickly advanced to the Suez Canal and the Jordan River, and also occupied Jerusalem, the Gaza Strip, the Golan Heights, and Sharm el-Shaikh on the Tiran Strait. The UN Security Council on November 22, 1967 passed a resolution requiring withdrawal of the Israeli armed forces from the overrun territories, and acknowledgement of the independence and integrity of Israel. The resolution remained inoperative because Israel demanded direct peace negotiations with the Arab states, while the latter demanded Israeli withdrawal before negotiations.

The deadlock persisted for six years, marked by an unending succession of terrorist acts by both sides: the massacre of Israeli athletes at the Munich Olympic games in the fall of 1972; the Libyan airliner shot down with 106 casualties by Israeli fighters when it strayed over Sinai in February 1973; the predawn raid by Israeli commandos into Beirut in April 1973; and the sporadic attacks on Israeli settlements by Arab guerrillas. On October 6, 1973, the fourth round in the protracted Arab-Israeli struggle exploded with the Egyptians attacking across the Suez Canal and the Syrians into the Golan Heights.

In successfully crossing the Suez canal and occupying a wide strip in the Sinai along the northern half of the Canal, the Egyptians destroyed the myth of Israeli invincibility, even though the Israelis counterattacked and occupied an equally wide strip of Egyptian territory along the southern half of the canal. On January 17, 1974 Egypt and Israel agreed that Israeli forces should withdraw to a north-south line roughly twenty miles east of the Canal, and that a UN buffer force should be installed between the two armies. On May 31, a comparable agreement was signed by Israel and Syria concerning the Golan Heights, thanks to Secretary of State Henry Kissinger who shuttled between Jerusalem and Damascus for 32 days to arrange the settlement. It was hoped that these agreements would clear the way for a stable peace in the Middle East, but two great obstacles remained. One was the status of Jerusalem which now is the capital of Israel. But Jerusalem is as sacred a city for Moslems as it is for Jews and Christians, so that most Arabs, and especially the devout and powerful King Feisal of Saudi Arabia, are determined to regain the city. The other obstacle to lasting peace is the fate of the Palestinians, whose guerrilla organizations are demanding the establishment of a Palestine state at the expense of Israel and Jordan. The specific demands range from varying degrees of autonomy to full independence, depending on the guerrilla group involved.

This fourth round changed the balance of power in the Middle East because of Kissinger's leading role in the negotiations. He succeeded in restoring American influence in that region at the expense of the Soviets who had gained a strong position during the Nasser era. Even more significant was the unprecedented Arab unity against Israel and the supporters of Israel, especially the United States. The oil-exporting Arab states declared an embargo on oil shipments to most Western countries. The embargo exposed the degree of Western dependence on Arab oil supplies, as the various Western states scrambled to negotiate bilateral oil deals to meet their needs. Before the embargo was lifted the price of oil had soared from two dollars per barrel delivered to Western Europe in 1965 to six dollars by the end of the war. The fifty billion dollars *additional* income that the oil exporting nations received in 1974 represented a major shift in global economic relationships.

SUGGESTED READING

S. C. Easton, *The Rise and Fall of Western Colonialism* (Praeger, 1964); R. Emerson, *From Empire to Nation: The Rise to Self-Assertion of Asian and African Peoples* (Harvard Univ., 1960); R. Emerson and M. Kilson, eds., *The Political Awakening of Africa* (Prentice-Hall, 1965); R. Gibson, *African Liberation Movements* (Oxford Univ., 1972); W. Laqueur, ed., *The Israeli-Arab Reader* (Bantam, 1969); L. L. Snyder, *The New Nationalism* (Cornell Univ., 1969).

chapter forty

Grand Alliance, Cold War, and Aftermath

It is not so difficult to keep unity in time of war since there is a joint aim to defeat the common enemy, which is clear to everyone. The difficult task will come after the war when diverse interests tend to divide the Allies.—Stalin, at Yalta

World War I was followed by revolution in Central and Eastern Europe and by the threat of revolution in Western Europe. World War II stimulated no comparable disturbances. Revolutions did not convulse the Continent, despite the fact that the second war inflicted greater material damage and political dislocation than the first. One reason was the occupation of all Europe by the forces of the victorious Allies. The Red Army, no less than the British and the American, stamped out opposition and disorder. A revolution in the social structure did occur in Eastern Europe, but it was an imposed revolution directed from Moscow. The Communist parties throughout Europe were obedient instruments of Soviet foreign policy rather than fomenters of indigenous revolutions. Thus, Russia and Britain and the United States effectively controlled developments in Europe after the downfall of Hitler.

During the postwar years, these powers, which had fought against Hitler during their wartime Grand Alliance, pursued policies that brought on the Cold War. The effect of the Cold War was to polarize the globe into two hostile camps led by the United States and the Soviet Union. This American-Russian primacy proved short-lived. The eventual relaxation of the Cold War, the remarkable comeback of the states of Eastern and Western Europe, and the growing strength and assertiveness of China, all combined to produce an entirely new configuration of world politics. The American-Russian primacy gave way to a new pluralism that represented essentially a return, at least in a political sense, to the global regionalism that had characterized world affairs during the millennia before 1500.

I. WARTIME UNITY

During the war years the Western powers and the Soviet Union were forced to present a common front against the menace of a mortal enemy. Manifestations of their cooperation were the twenty-year mutual-aid pact signed by Great Britain and the Soviet Union in May, 1942, and the decision of the Russians in May, 1943, to abolish the Communist International, which they had established in 1919 to overthrow world capitalism. More important was the agreement reached by Britain and Russia in October, 1944, when the advance of the Red Army up the Danube Valley was forcing the Germans to evacuate the Balkan Peninsula, with Communist-led resistance fighters filling in the vacuum. The prospect of a Communist-dominated Balkans prompted Churchill to meet with Stalin in Moscow, where the two leaders quickly agreed upon spheres of influence in the disputed peninsula. Bulgaria and Rumania were to be in the Russian sphere, and Greece in the British; Yugoslavia was to be a buffer zone under joint British-Russian influence. Thus Churchill was forced, by the exigencies of an unfavorable strategic situation, to accept Soviet predominance in the northern Balkans in order to preserve Britain's traditional primacy in Greece.

At the same time that Churchill was bargaining with Stalin in Moscow, British troops were beginning to land in Greece. They advanced northward on the heels of the retreating Germans, but found the Greek resistance forces preceding them in all the towns and cities. No opposition was offered by these forces, led by disciplined Communists who obediently followed the current Kremlin line. Despite the compliance of the Greek resistance forces, the fact remained that they were the preponderant military power in the country as the Germans withdrew. This was an intolerable situation for Churchill, who resolved to secure the disarming of the resistance forces in order to transfer state power to the legal royal government in Athens. Various disarmament formulas were proposed, but none satisfied both sides. This dispute precipitated an armed clash that developed into the bitter and bloody Battle of Athens. British and Indian troops were rushed in from Italy, and, after a month of fighting, the resistance forces withdrew from the Athens area.

On February 12, a peace agreement (the Varkiza Pact) was signed by which the resistance troops surrendered their arms in return for a promise of elections and a plebiscite on the question of the return of the king. Thus Churchill secured the sphere allotted to him in Moscow: Greece was to be on the side of the West during the postwar years. Equally significant was Stalin's eloquent silence while Churchill was dispersing the leftist resistance fighters. The British-Russian deal on the Balkans was in operation and was working.

The fighting in Athens had barely ceased when, in February, 1945, Roosevelt, Churchill, and Stalin met at Yalta for the last of their wartime conferences. With the Allied armies converging upon Germany from all sides, the problems of a postwar settlement now had to be considered specifically and realistically. As regards the Far East, Stalin agreed to declare war against Japan within sixty days after the end of hostilities in Europe, and in return, Russia was to regain various concessions and territories lost to Japan in 1905. The conference postponed decision on most issues concerning Germany, including reparations and frontiers, but did agree that the country should be divided into four occupation zones.

Most of the negotiating at Yalta concerned the newly liberated countries in Eastern Europe. Stalin was in a strong position in this area, for his armies had done the liberating and were in actual occupation. Given this context, the agreements that were made on Eastern Europe were, on paper, eminently satisfactory from the Western viewpoint. As regards frontiers, Russia was to receive the Polish territory east of a modified Curzon Line, which had been drawn after World War I but subsequently ignored. Poland was to be compensated with territory in East Germany; this was agreed upon in principle, though a final and specific decision was postponed. As regards the Polish and Yugoslav governments, Stalin agreed that the Communist regimes already established under Soviet auspices should be broadened by the admission of representatives from the West-oriented governments-in-exile. The latter were understandably apprehensive about this arrangement, which left the Red Army and the Communist governments in physical and legal control. Their doubts were met, in theory, by a broad statement of policy known as the Yalta Declaration on Liberated Europe. This committed the three powers to assist the liberated peoples of Europe "to form interim governmental authorities broadly representative of all democratic elements in the population and pledged to the earliest possible establishment through free elections of governments responsive to the will of the people. . . ."

Taken at face value, this Declaration represented a substantial concession on the part of Stalin. Despite his domination of Eastern Europe he had consented to free elections that might well bring to office anti-Soviet governments. The substance of this concession, however, was negligible because it was interpreted very differently by the various signatories. The United States interpreted it literally—that is, free elections and no spheres of influence in Eastern Europe. The United States was free to take this position because it was not bound by the agreement reached by Churchill and Stalin in Moscow the previous October. Britain, on the other hand, was ambivalent about the Declaration because the Moscow agreement had enabled her to secure her position in Greece. Yet the Declaration was alluring, because, if literally enforced, it would give Britain a chance to regain positions in Rumania and Bulgaria that she had abandoned. Stalin, by contrast, clung to the Moscow agreement and regarded the Declaration as mere window dressing. He had scrupulously kept quiet while the British crushed the Greek resistance forces, and now, in return, he expected the Western powers to respect his primacy in Eastern Europe. His concern for a Russian security zone as opposed to the American insistence on free elections was a chief cause for the disruption of the Grand Alliance in the months to come.

II. UNITED NATIONS AND PEACE TREATIES

Meanwhile the wartime Allies had been cooperating in the organization of the United Nations. The final charter was signed by the representatives of 50 nations at the conclusion of the conference held in San Francisco from April to June, 1945. By 1974 UN membership had risen to 138, the majority of the newcomers being the newly independent states of Asia and Africa.

The UN, like its predecessor the League of Nations, was set up to accomplish two basic tasks: to preserve peace and security, and to cope with international economic, social, and cultural problems. The latter was entrusted to the Economic and Social Council, which set up numerous specialized agencies, including the International Labor Organization; Food and Agriculture Organization; UN Educational, Scientific, and Cultural Organization; World Health Organization; and International Monetary Fund.

Like the League of Nations, the UN has been quite successful in these various nonpolitical activities. But again like the League, the UN has had a spotty record in its main job of keeping the peace. It has helped to prevent all-out war between the Great Powers by providing a medium for maintaining rapport. It has stopped fighting in areas such as Indonesia, and Kashmir, where vital interests of the major powers were not involved. But it was not able to forestall a series of local, or "brushfire," wars in Korea, Algeria, Vietnam, and the Middle East. Nor was there any consultation of the UN during the highly dangerous Cuban crisis of 1962. The basic difficulty of the UN, as of the League, was that in a world of sovereign states it could provide machinery for settling disputes but could not compel use of the machinery. Consequently, the major powers went their separate ways, organizing their rival security systems and reacting independently to each crisis.

Despite the drift to the Cold War, the foreign ministers of the victorious Allies did succeed in signing peace treaties on February 10, 1947, with Italy, Rumania, Hungary, Bulgaria, and Finland. All the treaties imposed reparations on the defeated countries, limited their armed forces, and redrew their frontiers. Italy lost the Dodecanese Islands to Greece, Saseno Island to Albania, small enclaves to France, and Venezia Giulia and the countryside surrounding Trieste to Yugoslavia. Her African colonies were placed under the temporary trusteeship of Great Britain, their ultimate status to be determined later.

In the Balkans, Bulgaria restored the Greek and Yugoslav territories that she had occupied, but she acquired southern Dobruja, which she had lost to Rumania in 1919. Rumania lost Bessarabia (which had been Russian from 1812 to 1918) and the northern Bucovina (inhabited largely by Ukrainians) to the Soviet Union, but she regained northern Transylvania, which Hungary had seized during the war. Other territorial changes in Eastern Europe not covered by the satellite treaties included the acquisition by Russia of the predominantly Ukrainian Carpathian-Ruthenia from Czechoslovakia, and of the three Baltic states—Latvia, Lithuania, and Estonia. Though Russia claimed the Baltic states on the ground that they had been a part of the Tsarist empire, the Western powers withheld official recognition of their annexation.

Perhaps these treaties will be remembered in the future for the fact that they sanctioned the new Communist regimes in Eastern Europe. Churchill had frequently declared during the war that he would not allow the Soviet zone to extend westward to a line from Stettin in the north to Trieste in the south. Yet this is precisely what the Western powers accepted when they signed the peace treaties at Paris. In doing so they recognized a new balance in Europe—a balance in which Bucharest, Sofia, and Budapest, along with Prague and Warsaw, now looked toward Moscow rather than toward Paris or Berlin.

The satellite treaties were not followed by corresponding pacts with the other enemy countries, and especially with Japan and Germany. The breakdown in peacemaking reflected the growing dissension between East and West. This, in turn, may be explained to a large degree by the immense power vacuums in Europe and Asia following the collapse of the German and Japanese empires. Vacuums are as unnatural and transitory in the political world as in the physical. They obviously were destined to be filled as soon as the fighting ceased. The question was how and by whom.

This vital question involved fundamental readjustments of power relationships. Under the best of circumstances such readjustments are difficult to arrange and fraught with danger, as evidenced by the crises following the Napoleonic Wars and World War I. Now, after World War II, the process of readjustment was made even more complicated and perilous by the addition of ideological issues to the traditional power struggle.

A region of major conflict was Eastern Europe, which Russia viewed as her security zone, and where she used her Red Army to install "friendly" dependent governments. More serious was the East-West clash in Germany, which had been divided into four zones. When the occupying powers faced the concrete problems of administering the country, they discovered basic differences in aims and policies. The Russians wanted substantial reparations and also a social revolution that would transform their zone, and the whole nation if possible, into another dependent People's Democracy. For this reason they favored a centralized German state that would facilitate its eventual communization. The French, like the Russians, were determined to exact heavy reparations, but they preferred a loose federative union, which they regarded as less dangerous to their national security. The British and the Americans were with the French in favoring a federative state, but they opposed both the French and the Russians in economic matters.

The issue came to a head over reparations. It had been agreed at the Potsdam Conference in July, 1945, that Russia was to receive $10 billion indemnity from Germany, to be collected from German foreign assets and through the removal of industrial equipment—from the Russian zone, and from the Western zones insofar as the equipment was not needed by the local economies. The Russians promptly proceeded to dismantle and ship East German factories to their own country, and also to tap current German factory output. The latter practice was a violation of the Potsdam agreement, as was also the refusal by the Russians to allow any inspection of the East German economy. In retaliation, the Americans and the British stopped the delivery of reparations from their zones in May, 1946, and repeatedly raised the permitted level of German industry. The next step occurred in December, 1946, when the British and the Americans combined their zones into an economic "Bizonia."

By early 1947 the four-power administration of Germany had broken up. In an effort to resolve the conflict, a Big Four conference was held in Moscow in March, 1947. The Americans and the British insisted on the economic unification of Germany; the French and the Russians were opposed. After six weeks of futile wrangling, the conference adjourned. Its failure, together with the proclamation of the Truman Doctrine at the same time, mark the beginning of the Cold War.

III. COLD WAR IN EUROPE

The most dramatic manifestation of the oncoming Cold War was President Truman's intervention in the Greek Civil War in March, 1947. Communist-led guerrillas had appeared the preceding fall in the mountains of northern Greece. One reason for the renewed civil strife was the wretched economic condition that drove many impoverished peasants to the rebel ranks. Another was the deteriorating international situation, which led the Soviet bloc to incite and aid the guerrillas against the British-supported Athens government. Finally there was the rightist persecution of political opponents despite the provision for amnesty and normal political procedures in the Varkiza Pact, which terminated the Battle of Athens.

These circumstances engendered considerable popular support for the insurrection, which spread from the northern mountains to the Peloponnesus and the larger islands. The situation became critical when on February 24, 1947, the British government announced that it could not afford the large-scale aid necessary to ensure victory over the rebel bands. Without further aid from London, the Athens regime probably would not have survived the year. President Truman met the emergency by proclaiming the doctrine named after him. Enunciating the principle that "it must be the policy of the United States to support free peoples who are resisting attempted subjugation by armed minorities or by outside pressures," he stated that "the very existence of the Greek state is today threatened," and requested Congress to appropriate $400 million for aid to Greece and Turkey. Thus Britain surrendered her century-old primacy in Greece, and the United

States assumed the responsibility for preventing the extension of Communist influence in the eastern Mediterranean.

The task proved more onerous than anticipated despite lavish American military and economic aid to Athens. Both the 1947 and 1948 campaigns proved inconclusive. In 1949 the balance shifted decisively in favor of the government. The Tito-Stalin split led Marshal Tito to close the Yugoslav border and stop all aid to the guerrillas who had sided with Stalin. At the same time the Athens armies were being retrained by American officers to fight a mobile offensive war instead of garrisoning key towns and communication routes. Thus, in the fall of 1949 the national armies were able to drive the guerrillas from their mountain strongholds and to reach and seal the northern frontiers.

The counterpart to the Truman Doctrine in the economic sphere was the European Recovery Program, commonly known as the Marshall Plan. By the time of its termination on December 31, 1951, a total of $12.5 billion was spent in support of the West European economy. This extraordinary investment, together with the human and material resources of Europe, made possible a rapid recovery that raised production and living standards to above prewar levels. But from the viewpoint of East-West relations, the Marshall Plan marked the final step toward the Cold War. The offer of aid had been directed to all countries, irrespective of ideology. Moscow, however, interpreted the offer as an anti-Communist maneuver and ordered back the Czechs and Poles who had been inclined to respond. Instead, Moscow established in January, 1949, the Council for Mutual Economic Assistance (Molotov Plan), as the Eastern counterpart to the Marshall Plan.

Thus the line was drawn between the Communist and Western worlds. The Cold War now was in full swing, and for the next half decade one crisis followed closely on another in tragic sequence. In February, 1948, the Communists eliminated the last bridgehead of Western influence in the Soviet sphere when they seized full control in Czechoslovakia. That small republic had tried to steer a middle course between East and West, but the attempt ended when the Communists used their control of the police and of their militant "action committees" to take over the government. The venerable President Eduard Beneš, who had led his country also in the prewar period, was succeeded by the Communist leader Gottwald, and thus all of Eastern Europe, except Finland, was now in Communist hands.

Even more dramatic than the Communist takeover in Prague was the protracted Berlin Airlift crisis that began in June, 1948. Having failed to dissuade the British and Americans from setting up a separate West German government, the Russians retaliated by cutting off railway and road access to the three Western sectors of Berlin. The Americans replied with an unprecedented airlift that supplied the food, coal, and other essentials needed by the two million people in the Western sectors. By the spring of 1949 the success of the airlift was apparent, and in May the Russians called off the blockade. In September, the Federal Republic was officially launched in West Germany, and in the next month the Democratic Republic was established in the East. Thus the Cold War had split Germany in two.

These various manifestations of Communist aggressiveness—the coup in Czechoslovakia, the Berlin blockade, and the continuing civil war in Greece—persuaded the Western powers that some defensive alliance system was necessary. Hence, the signing of the North Atlantic Treaty in Washington on April 4, 1949. The treaty included the United States, Canada, Britain, France, Belgium, the Netherlands, Luxembourg, Italy, Portugal, Denmark, Iceland, and Norway. These twelve original powers were joined later by Greece and Turkey (1951) and by West

Germany (1955). The treaty provided that "an armed attack against one or more" of the signatories, in Europe, North Africa, or North America, "shall be considered an attack against them all."

Meanwhile, the Soviet Union had made corresponding political and military arrangements in Eastern Europe. Even before the end of the war Stalin had concluded mutual assistance pacts with Czechoslovakia, Yugoslavia, and Poland, and by 1948 similar pacts were signed with the former Axis satellites—Bulgaria, Rumania, and Hungary. In May, 1955, a more formal and comprehensive military alliance was concluded between Russia and the East European countries. This was known as the Warsaw Pact and constituted the Eastern response to the North Atlantic Treaty. Thus Europe as well as Germany was cut in two by the Cold War—the Western half armed and organized under the aegis of the United States and the Eastern under that of the Soviet Union.

IV. COLD WAR IN THE FAR EAST

In 1950, the focus of the Cold War shifted from Europe to the Far East. By this time a balance had been reached in Europe between East and West. But in the Far East the balance was upset by a momentous development—the triumph of the Communists in China. Just as the Bolshevik Revolution was the outstanding by-product of World War I, so the Chinese Communist Revolution was the outstanding by-product of World War II.

Chiang Kai-shek had become the master of China in 1928, but from the outset his Kuomintang regime was threatened by two mortal enemies, the Communists within and the Japanese without. It was during the war years that Chiang's regime was irretrievably undermined. Chiang traditionally had depended on the support of the conservative landlord class and of the relatively enlightened big businessmen. The latter were largely eliminated when the Japanese overran the east coast, and Chiang was left with the self-centered and short-sighted landlords of the interior. His government became increasingly corrupt and unresponsive to the needs of a peasantry wracked and aroused by years of war. In contrast to the decaying Kuomintang, the Communists carried out land reforms in their territories, thereby winning the support of the peasant masses. They had a disciplined and efficient organization that brought order out of political and economic chaos in the areas under their control. Also their leadership in the anti-Japanese struggle won them popular support as patriots dedicated to ridding the country of foreign invaders and to restoring China's unity, pride, and greatness.

Such was the situation when Japan's surrender in August, 1945, set off a wild scramble by the Nationalists and Communists to take over the Japanese-occupied parts of China. The Communists occupied the countryside around the major cities, being helped by the Russians, who turned over to them the arms the Japanese had surrendered in Manchuria. The Nationalists, aided by the transportation services of the United States Navy and Air Force, won all the main cities, including Nanking, and also rushed troops north to Manchuria. The latter move was a strategic blunder. The Kuomintang forces found themselves in indefensible positions and were forced in the fall of 1948 to surrender to the Chinese Red Army. A chain of comparable military disasters followed in quick succession. The Communist armies swept down from Manchuria through the major cities of North China. By April, 1949, they were crossing the Yangtze and fanning out over South China. The Communist steamroller advanced even more rapidly in the south than in the north. By the end of 1949 it had overrun all of mainland

China. Chiang fled to the island of Taiwan (Formosa), while in Peking the Communist leader, Mao Tse-tung, proclaimed the People's Republic of China on October 1, 1949.

These developments represented a setback for the postwar American policy of the containment of Communism on a global scale. In Japan, however, the postwar occupation was dominated by the United States. Japan, in contrast to Germany, was governed by a single Supreme Command of the Allied Powers, which included Allied representatives. The Supreme Commander, General Douglas MacArthur, and the bulk of the occupation forces were American. MacArthur's instructions were to disarm and demilitarize the country, develop democratic institutions, and create a viable economy. By 1951, when the occupation had attained most of these objectives, a peace treaty was concluded and signed by the United States and most of the Allies, with the notable exception of China and the Soviet Union, who considered the terms overly generous. The treaty restored Japanese sovereignty, but only over the four main islands. There were no military or economic restrictions, except that the United States was permitted to maintain military bases in Japan. The United States also gained trusteeship over the Ryuku and Bonin islands and over Japan's former Pacific mandates. Japan relinquished the Kuril islands and southern Sakhalin (which had been allotted to Russia) as well as Formosa, but the future disposition of these islands was left open. In effect, this treaty made Japan the main bastion of the American position in the Far East. In support of this bastion the United States spent about $2 billion in the first six years after the war. With the demand for a wide variety of goods during the Korean and Vietnamese wars, Japan made such remarkable economic progress that by 1970 it had become the third greatest industrial power in the world, surpassed only by the United States and the Soviet Union.

In the Far East, as in Europe, then, World War II was followed by Cold War. Russia backed Mao Tse-tung, albeit belatedly, while the United States vainly attempted to maintain Chiang Kai-shek as master of China. Conversely, in Japan the United States dominated the occupation and utilized it to further her interests, while the Soviet representatives impotently protested. Once the outcome had apparently been settled in both countries, there was hope, as expressed by Secretary of State Dean Acheson, for "the dust to settle" and for a balance to be reached, as had been done in Europe. The hope was shattered when in 1950 fighting broke out in Korea and the Cold War became hot.

The tragedy of Korea is that its location has made it a natural bridge between China and Japan. Repeatedly it has been fought over by the two countries, and occasionally by Russia also. Since 1895—and formally since 1910—Korea had passed under Japanese rule. Thereafter it was in effect a colony, though unique in that it was under Asian rather than European domination. During World War II, at the 1943 Cairo Conference, the United States, Britain, and China declared that, "in due course," Korea should once more be free and independent. But a generation of Japanese rule had left Korea without the necessary experience for self-government. The victorious Allies decided, therefore, that for a period of not more than five years Korea, though independent, should be under the trusteeship of the United States, Russia, Britain, and China.

With the surrender of Japan, American and Russian troops poured into Korea. For purposes of military convenience the 38th parallel was set as the dividing line in their operations. The coming of the Cold War froze this temporary division in Korea as it did in Germany. The Russians set up in their zone a regime dominated by the Communist New People's Party. In the south, the Americans leaned on English-speaking Koreans, who usually were members of the conservative upper class. In August, 1948, a Republic of Korea was proclaimed in the south, with Dr. Syngman Rhee as president. A month later the North Koreans formed their People's Democratic Republic under Kim Il-sung. A UN commission attempted without success to mediate between the regimes headed by these two men. So strong were the feelings that the commission warned in September, 1949, of the danger of civil war.

On June 24, 1950, civil war did begin, when North Korean troops suddenly crossed the 38th parallel in order to "liberate" South Korea. The next day the UN Security Council adopted an American resolution calling for an immediate ceasefire and the withdrawal of the North Koreans to the 38th parallel. On June 27 the Security Council asked UN members to "furnish such assistance to the Republic of Korea as may be necessary to repel the armed attack and to restore international peace and security in the area." Forty UN member states responded to the Security Council's appeal and provided supplies, transport, hospital units, and, in some cases, combat forces. But the main contribution, aside from that of South Korea, came from the United States, and General MacArthur served as commander in chief.

The course of the Korean War fell into two phases—the first before, and the second after, the Chinese intervention. The first phase began with the headlong rush of the North Korean forces down the length of the peninsula to within fifty miles of the port of Pusan at the southern tip. Then on September 14, 1950, an American force landed at Inchon, far up the coast near the 38th parallel, and in twelve days retook the South Korean capital, Seoul. The North Koreans, their communications severed, fell back as precipitously as they had advanced. By the end of September the UN forces had reached the 38th parallel and on October 8 they crossed the 38th parallel and quickly occupied Pyongyang, the North Korean capital. By November 22 they reached the Yalu River, the boundary line between Korea and the Chinese province of Manchuria.

At this point the second phase of the Korean War began with a massive attack by Chinese "volunteers" supported by Russian-made jets. The Chinese drove southward rapidly in what looked like a repetition of the first phase of the war. Early in January, 1951, they retook Seoul, but the UN forces now recovered and held their ground. In March, Seoul once more changed hands, and by June the battle line ran roughly along the 38th parallel. By mid-1951 it was apparent that a stalemate prevailed at the front. Large-scale fighting petered out, and armistice negotiations started. After two years of stormy and often-interrupted negotiations, an armistice agreement was concluded on July 27, 1953. The terms reflected the military stalemate. The line of partition between North and South Korea remained roughly where it had been before the war. The Western powers had successfully contained Communism in Korea and had vindicated the authority of the United Nations. The Chinese had secured North Korea as a Communist buffer-state between Manchuria and Western influences. And meanwhile, most of the Korean countryside had been laid waste and about 10 per cent of the Korean people had been killed.

V. RELAXATION OF THE COLD WAR

In 1953 the Cold War began to subside. One reason was the death in April, 1953, of Joseph Stalin, who had become increasingly paranoid and inflexible in his later years. The younger men who succeeded him were ready for a relaxation of both the Cold War abroad and the dictatorship at home. At the same time, the new Eisenhower administration was replacing that of Truman in the United States. This also contributed to the international "thaw," for Eisenhower was able in July, 1953, to make a compromise peace in Korea, whereas Truman would have found this extremely difficult because of domestic political considerations. The following month the Soviet government announced that it also possessed the secret of the hydrogen bomb. Paradoxically, this strengthened the movement for a settlement, for it was known that the hydrogen bomb exploded by the United States at Bikini was 750 times more powerful than the Hiroshima atomic bomb, which had killed 78,000 people. All but the most fanatic Cold Warriors sensed that war no longer was a feasible instrument of national policy.

The deterring effect of the H-bomb was manifested during the 1962 Cuba crisis, precipitated when American air reconnaissance revealed that Russian missile bases were under construction in Cuba and that a large part of the United States soon would be within range. It became clear that neither country wanted war when Soviet vessels bound for Cuba altered course and the United States permitted a Soviet tanker to proceed when satisfied that it carried no offensive weapons. Finally, on October 28, Khrushchev announced that he had ordered Soviet missiles withdrawn and all Soviet bases in Cuba dismantled under UN inspection, in return for the ending of the United States blockade and a pledge not to invade Cuba.

Although the Cuban crisis ended peaceably, it was a very near thing—so near that it stimulated several agreements for the limitation of nuclear weapons: controls on tests of nuclear weapons (1963), prohibition of nuclear weapons in space (1967), Latin America made a nonnuclear zone (1967), nonproliferation of nuclear weapons beyond the nations already possessing them (1968), prohibition of emplacement of nuclear weapons on the seabed (1971), and prohibition of the use of biological weapons (1971). These agreements together helped to lessen substantially the international tensions of the Cold War.

VI. EUROPE ITS OWN MASTER

The slackening of the Cold War in turn lessened the rigidity of the opposing blocs and gradually undermined the American-Russian domination of the globe. The Western European states, no longer so apprehensive of the danger of Russian invasion, did not feel so dependent upon Washington and were more ready to formulate and pursue their own policies. To a lesser extent this was true also of the Eastern European states vis-à-vis Russia, which explains in part the Polish and Hungarian outbreaks in 1956. More spectacular and significant was China's breakaway from Russia, ending the hitherto monolithic unity of the Communist world.

The Western European states were able to become increasingly independent of the United States not only because of the waning Cold War but also because of their own growing economic strength, which allowed them more maneuverability in political matters. West European prosperity was based on American aid under the Marshall Plan, on the introduction of American production and managerial techniques, and on the organization of the Common Market. Originally the Common Market comprised six members (Italy, West Germany, the Netherlands, Belgium, Luxembourg, and France), but in 1973 it was expanded to include also Britain, Ireland and Denmark. Thus the Common Market now is a bloc of 195 million people, and an economic power comparable to the United States.

These factors together explain the remarkable growth of Western Europe from an economic dependency to an economic rival of the United States. During the two decades 1950–60 and 1960–70, per capita GNP increased by the following percentages: United States, 1.4 and 2.7; France, 3.6 and 4.7; Italy, 5.2 and 4.8; and West Germany, 6.8 and 3.8. Likewise the shares held of the noncommunist world's total gold reserves fluctuated as follows during the years 1950, 1960 and 1970: United States, 68, 47, 30; France, 2, 4, 10; Italy, .8, 8, 8; and West Germany, 0, 6, 11. Equally symptomatic was the fact that in 1971, for the first time this century, the United States had a deficit in foreign trade. This amounted to 2 billion dollars, but in 1972 the deficit soared to 6.4 billion dollars. This in turn weakened the dollar in the international money markets and led to its devaluation.

The change in economic relationships between Western Europe and the United States led to a corresponding change in political relationships. This was particularly true of France under de Gaulle, who pursued independent policies in every field. In 1963 he vetoed Britain's application for entry into the Common Market, charging that the inclusion of Britain would mean, ultimately, "a colossal Atlantic Community under American dependence and leadership." De Gaulle likewise rebuffed American policy makers by developing his own atomic weapons and aerial striking force. In order to be free to build up this independent military power, de Gaulle rejected the test ban treaty signed in Moscow in 1963 by the United States, Britain, and Russia. Along the same lines, he extended full diplomatic recognition to Communist China on January 27, 1964, despite obvious American disapproval. George Pompidou, who succeeded de Gaulle as President in 1969, was less aggressive but still quite independent.

German politics also reflected the Cold War relaxation and the increasing independence of Western Europe with the coming to office in 1969 of Willy Brandt, leader of the Social Democrat Party. Hitherto, the Christian Union Party had reigned supreme, especially under Konrad Adenauer, a zealous ally of Dulles in waging the Cold War. Brandt reversed this course, particularly after the unexpectedly large majority he received in the November 1972 election. In the following months he implemented his bold new Eastern Policy with repercussions throughout the continent. This involved recognition of the Communist-ruled German Democratic Republic and hence of a Germany divided permanently into two states. It involved also normalizing relations with Moscow and its Eastern European allies, even though this meant acknowledging the irrevocable loss of the eastern territories now part of the Soviet Union and Poland. This normalization made possible the admittance into the United Nations in September 1973 of both the Federal Republic of Germany and the German Democratic Republic.

While Western Europe was becoming independent of the United States, Eastern Europe was gaining a measure of autonomy from the Soviet Union. Here also the change was made possible by the American-Russian military stalemate and by the easing of the Cold War. An additional important factor in Eastern Europe was the change in leadership in the Soviet Union. The death of Stalin in 1953, and the eventual emergence of Nikita Khrushchev as his successor, marked the beginning of a new era not only in Soviet domestic affairs but also in the relations between the Soviet Union and its East European satellites.

On February 25, 1956, Khrushchev exploded a bombshell when, addressing the Twentieth Congress of the Soviet Communist Party, he excoriated the dead Stalin for excessive self-glorification, for assorted acts of treachery and terrorism, and for incompetent leadership during World War II. The tirade was followed by a deStalinization campaign and by an ideological "thaw" allowing artists and writers more freedom in criticizing Soviet society. Foreign Communist leaders, hitherto tightly controlled by the Kremlin, also began to assert themselves, thereby transforming the relations between the Soviet Union and its satellites.

The first anti-Soviet outbreak in Eastern Europe had occurred in 1948 when Tito successfully asserted the independence of his Communist state from Kremlin dictation. Thanks to strong popular support at home and to generous economic aid from the West, Tito was able to resist Soviet pressure and to establish Yugoslavia as a nonaligned state. The next break occurred in Poland where the "national" Communist leader, Wladyslaw Gomulka, was able in 1956 to win a degree of autonomy, though not equal to the nonalignment of Yugoslavia. Poland enjoyed autonomy in domestic affairs but remained definitely a Communist state and a dependable member of the Warsaw Pact.

In contrast to this peaceful compromise reached in Poland, the nationalist-minded Communists of Hungary provoked a violent confrontation in which they were crushed. Unlike the Poles who were content with autonomy within the Soviet orbit, the Hungarians demanded a Western-type democracy, completely free from commitments to Moscow or to the Warsaw Pact. The Russians, viewing this as an intolerable threat to their East European security system, sent their tanks into Budapest in 1956 and installed Janos Kadar as the new and dependable Communist leader. During the following years Kadar was able to evolve a relationship with Russia similar to that of Gomulka, while at home he attracted considerable popular support by easing controls and raising living standards.

This relaxation of Soviet political domination of Eastern Europe had its counterpart in the economic and cultural fields. Under Stalin, satellite states had been ruthlessly exploited by a variety of unequal trade treaties and development arrangements that operated in favor of the Soviet Union. After the 1956 turmoil in Poland, Hungary, and other Eastern European countries, this pattern was quickly changed. Trade treaties and development projects were renegotiated and made more equitable. Each country was allowed gradually to make its own decisions regarding the pace and course of economic development. Industries no longer had to be integrated with those of Russia or the other Communist countries. Instead the trend was toward more independent national development, more leeway to both industry and agriculture, and more trade with the West. Similar relaxation occurred in the field of culture with cultural agreements concluded with Western countries, less frequent jamming of foreign broadcasts, increase in tourism, greater freedom to foreign correspondents, and freer circulation of Western films, books, and periodicals.

In August, 1968, this trend toward liberalization in Eastern Europe was abruptly reversed with the invasion of Czechoslovakia by the Soviet army together with East German, Hungarian, Polish, and Bulgarian units. The invaders ended the "democratic socialist revolution" launched in Prague in January, 1968, by Alexander Dubcek. Perhaps the Russians were motivated by genuine concern that the new Czech regime might drift into the Western camp. Certainly they feared that the new freedom in Czechoslovakia might strengthen popular demand throughout Eastern Europe for similar freedom and thus endanger the existing Communist regimes. In any case, the Soviets justified the invasion with their so-called Brezhnev Doctrine, which reserved the right to invade any socialist neighbor that they considered to be abandoning their camp.

Despite the Czech invasion and the Brezhnev Doctrine, the Soviet position in Eastern Europe is far from being as dominating as during the Stalin era. Public opinion in Czechoslovakia remains overwhelmingly anti-Soviet, as is demonstrated vociferously on all public occasions. Yugoslavia continues on her course of independent neutralism between East and West. Rumania is relatively constrained because of her common border with the Soviet Union. Yet she has paraded before the world her cordial relations with the United States and China, and also, she has refused to allow the Warsaw Treaty powers to conduct army maneuvers on her soil. On the occasion of the signing of a friendship treaty with Russia in July, 1970, Rumania specifically rejected the Brezhnev Doctrine with the statement, "Every people has the right to solve its own problems by itself without interference from the outside."

VII. CHINA CHALLENGES RUSSIA

The year after the victorious Chinese Communists established their People's Republic in 1949, they signed a thirty-year treaty of "friendship, alliance, and mutual assistance" with the Soviet Union. Under its terms, the Russians helped China to build a large modern army and to develop her industries, though it should be noted that the Russians gave loans and not grants. In 1960 this alliance began to show signs of disruption, and in the following year the Russians started withdrawing their technical experts from China. Worst of all, from the Chinese viewpoint, the Soviets refused to share their atomic weapons or the technical information and resources necessary for their manufacture. Thus the quarrel between the two giants grew rapidly to an outright schism, including ideological vituperation and open rivalry all over the globe.

The roots of this fateful rift in the Communist world appear to be partly a conflict of national interests and partly a conflict of ideologies. The national interests primarily involve clashing frontier claims concerning the following: the eastern margins of the Pamir highlands, some islands at the confluence of the Amur and Ussuri rivers, and almost the entire frontier with Mongolia. These territories, formerly a part of the Chinese empire, were annexed by Tsarist Russia during the nineteenth century, and now are claimed by Communist China.

Probably of greater significance in the long run than these frontier disputes is the Russian-Chinese clash in ideology. Chinese communism is quite different from the Russian variety, for Mao's unique contribution has been the "Sinification of Marxism" or the adaptation of Marxism to Chinese needs. This has led to many differences between Moscow and Peking in theory and in practice. Whereas the Russians have clung to traditional Marxist-Leninist dogma that revolution must be led by, and based upon, the proletariat, Mao assigned the lead role to the peasants, and naturally so, given the overwhelmingly peasant character of Chinese society. Thus while the 1917 Bolshevik Revolution involved the sudden seizure of power in Moscow and Leningrad, the Chinese Revolution, by contrast, was a protracted peasant guerilla war during which the countryside was won long before the cities.

This difference in revolutionary strategy led, after the revolution, to a corresponding difference in social organization and objectives. Years of revolutionary warfare in China stimulated a new vision of man and of society—a vision of an egalitarian, nonelitist Communist order in which the individual is motivated by the desire for social service rather than personal gain. Although the Soviet-type Five Year Plans were successful in furthering industrialization and raising productivity, Mao was unwilling to accept the increasing income differentiation and bureaucratic elitism on which these plans were based. This explains the Great Leap Forward of 1958 and the Cultural Revolution of 1966 in China, with their slogans such as "organization without bureaucracy" and "serve the people." The

Russians regarded this as utopian romanticism doomed to failure, which was one reason they stopped their aid to China. But Maoism has not failed, as predicted in Moscow and the West. Economic growth continues at a high rate, and China's egalitarianism and communalism are creating a society that is winning the admiration of visitors such as David Rockefeller, chairman of the board of Chase Manhattan Bank. In August 1973, after a business trip in China, he reported: "The social experiment in China under Chairman Mao's leadership is one of the most important and successful in human history. How extensively China opens up and how the world interprets and reacts to the social innovations and life styles she has developed is certain to have a profound impact on the future of many nations."[4]

This new China is an even greater challenge to Russia than to the West, for it represents an alternative and challenging type of Communism. "Over the last two decades," declared Premier Chou En-lai to the 10th Congress of the Chinese Communist Party on August 24, 1973, "the Soviet revisionist clique, from Khrushchev to Brezhnev, has made a socialist country degenerate into a social imperialist country . . . socialism in words, imperialism in deeds."[5] Thus the Chinese offer their revolution and their society as the way out for other peoples—a model for avoiding the backsliding of Soviet society.

China has challenged Russia not only in matters of doctrine but also for the allegiance of the approximately 90 Communist parties of the world. Moscow claims the support of about three-quarters of these parties, but the Chinese contend that half of the 42.5 million Communist party members of the world are on their side. The Chinese do enjoy the advantage in the underdeveloped Third World of being nonwhite and nonaffluent, in contrast to the Americans and the Russians. They have exploited this advantage effectively, as suggested by Brezhnev's message to the fourth conference of nonaligned nations held in Algiers in August 1973. Brezhnev complained that the Soviet Union and the capitalist powers were being lumped together, in the manner of Chinese propaganda. "There is a particular danger," declared Brezhnev, "in the efforts to divide the nonaligned countries from the socialist states [a category from which the Russians exclude China] and from the Soviet Union and to deprive the developing countries of their natural and surest allies."[6] Brezhnev's concern points up the degree to which China, the pawn of international diplomacy for over a century, today is challenging the two greatest powers of the world.

VIII. END OF BIPOLARISM

By the 1970s—only three decades after World War II—a drastically new configuration of world politics was beginning to emerge. The bipolarization of world power that prevailed in the immediate postwar years had already evaporated. Europe no longer was a pawn—or two pawns, East and West—on the global chessboard, nor was China a satellite nor even a junior partner of the Soviet Union.

Dramatic manifestations of the new global configuration were President Nixon's 1972 visits to Peking and Moscow, and Brezhnev's 1973 visit to Washington. Following these exchanges, Nixon spoke repeatedly of a new global balance of five Great Powers: the United States, the Soviet Union, China, Europe, and Japan. This is a far cry from the immediate post-World War II years when Henry Luce was hailing with confidence the "American century," and when every country that was not actively pro-American was considered to be anti-American.

Equally significant was the Chinese interpretation of the new global interrelationships. Far from welcoming their inclusion in the ranks of the new Big Five, they welcomed the revolutionary movement in the Third World, and they warned against what they termed the "hegemonic" aspirations of the two superpowers, "imperialistic" America and "social imperialistic" Russia. In his August 24, 1973 report to the 10th Congress of the Chinese Communist Party, Premier Chou En-lai declared:

> The present international situation is one characterized by great disorder on the earth. . . . The U.S.-Soviet contention for hegemony is the cause of world intranquility. It cannot be covered up by any false appearances they create, and is already perceived by an increasing number of people and countries. It has met with strong resistance from the Third World. . . . The awakening and growth of the Third World is a major event in contemporary international relations.

If all these world developments are viewed in the light of the foregoing analysis of world history during the past five centuries, they suggest a new phase in the evolution of global relationships. (See map, "World of New Global Relationships.") It will be recalled that prior to Europe's fateful transformation and expansion, several regions had coexisted either autonomously or in complete isolation—the autonomous European, Moslem, and Confucian regions; the largely isolated sub-Saharan Africa, and the completely isolated Americas and Australia. After Columbus and da Gama and Magellan, this compartmentalization gave way to ever increasing interaction and integration directed and exploited by Europe. By the nineteenth century this trend had culminated in the unprecedented hegemony over the entire globe by a few great powers of Europe. The two world wars shattered this European dominance and replaced it with only a decade or two of bipolar predominance by Moscow and Washington—the brevity of this phase reflecting the constantly accelerating tempo of world events.

SUGGESTED READING

D. F. FLEMING, *The Cold War and Its Origins, 1917–1960,* 2 vols. (Doubleday, 1961); J. FREYMOND, *Western Europe Since the War* (Praeger, 1964); J. L. GADDIS, *The United States and the Origins of the Cold War* (Columbia Univ., 1973); H. R. HUNTER, *Security in Europe* (Indiana Univ., 1973); G. F. KENNAN, *Russia and the West* (Little, 1961); G. KOLKO, *The Politics of War: The World and U.S. Foreign Policy 1943–1945* (Random House, 1969) ; W. LAFEBER, *America, Russia and the Cold War* (Wiley, 1968); R. LOWENTHAL, *World Communism: The Disintegration of a Secular Faith* (Oxford Univ., 1964).

chapter forty-one

Decline and Triumph
of the West

The Europeanization of Asia has produced the revolt of Asia against Europe.—René Grousset

In one sense, the course of twentieth century history represented the decline of Europe. London, Paris, and Berlin no longer dominated world news. No longer did they control world empires. Their armies and navies and alliance systems had ceased to dominate the globe. In 1860, for example, Western Europe was responsible for 72 per cent of the world's total industrial output; by 1913 the percentage had dropped to 42; by the eve of World War II, to 30; and by 1960, to 25. It was self-evident that Europe's nineteenth century global hegemony had ended, and ended forever: there is no possibility of Europe's regaining her colonial empires or re-establishing her former military and economic predominance. On the other hand, Europe had not fallen from primacy to subservience, as had appeared likely to happen immediately following World War II. To the contrary, although Europe was suffering relative decline in her military, economic, and political power, her culture was sweeping the world as never before.

Europe was entering a period of triumph as well as decline: her ideas, techniques, and institutions were spreading throughout the globe more rapidly than at any time in the past. Fundamentally, this represented the diffusion of Europe's three great revolutions—the Industrial, the Scientific, and the Political—which earlier had given her the power, the drive, and the knowledge to expand all over the world and to conquer the great colonial empires (see Chapters 24 and 25). But Europe's epochal success had boomeranged: for the colonial empires, by their very existence, facilitated the diffusion of the three revolutions. The subject peoples, profoundly affected by these revolutions, had reacted by selectively adopting some of their features in order better to resist the intruding West.

The Industrial Revolution spread in the nineteenth century from England to Europe and the United States, and in the first half of the twentieth century to Japan and the British Dominions. Following World War II, this diffusion accelerated rapidly. As each new country won political independence, it soon realized that this meant little unless supplemented by economic independence.

575

Thus every Third World leader, whether Nehru in India, Sukarno in Indonesia, Nkrumah in Ghana, or Nasser in Egypt, introduced some type of economic plan in order to stimulate industry and attain the cherished economic independence.

Science also spread rapidly from Europe, and, indeed, has become the one body of knowledge that all peoples have been anxious to acquire. Its objective methodology has made it acceptable to non-Western peoples who, by contrast, may not be interested in European art or religion or philosophy. Science has been eagerly sought after also because it constitutes the basis for advance in technology and general economic development. Thus, Europe has lost its monopoly of science; in the mid-sixties, more scientific work was being done in the United States and the Soviet Union than in any Western European country. Between 1945 and 1973 inclusive, thirty-three Americans won Nobel prizes in physiology and medicine, twenty-seven in physics, and sixteen in chemistry. British scientists were the runners up in each field, with eleven, six, and fourteen Nobel prizes in these areas. The scientific revolution also has begun to make itself felt in non-Western countries. India and China, for example, have won one and two Nobel Prizes respectively, in science. China especially has made outstanding advances in recent years: A-bomb in 1964, H-bomb in 1967 (one year ahead of France), synthesizing of biologically active insulin in 1965 (beating German and American competitors), production of integrated circuits in 1968 (the same year as the Soviets), and orbiting an artificial satellite in 1970 (ahead of all Western Europe).

More significant than Nobel Prizes and spectacular scientific breakthroughs is the gradual diffusion of scientific knowledge and practices among the masses of people in non-Western areas. In Malaya, backwoods medicinemen, or "bomohs," have begun to rely on modern medicine as well as traditional incantations to cure disease. Having received instruction by government agencies concerning anti-malarial drugs, vitamin pills, antiseptic lotions, and the rudiments of hygiene, they are returning to their villages with graduation badges marking their new status as "medical assistants." They are making effective use of their new knowledge and first-aid kits, even though they are still accompanying their treatments with the age-old incantations to give science a gloss of magic.

Likewise in China the entire educational system, formal and vocational, is geared towards inculcating a scientific attitude, towards replacing traditional superstitions with rational explanations arrived at within a framework of causal relationships. A British scientist who visited China in 1965 reported:

In the old days the peasants regarded a diseased crop as a visitation from the gods and did nothing about it. Now, every production team in the commune I was visiting had its own member trained to recognize the most common insect pests and types of plant disease, and to know what remedial steps to take if he found them. Everywhere in China the people are being taught not only that the laws of nature can be understood by man, but that man can often use this knowledge for his own ends. The significance of this realization on a mass scale may yet prove one of the most important accomplishments of the Chinese Communists.[1]

Europe's third revolution, the political, also has been sweeping the entire globe. The most obvious manifestation of this political awakening has been the burgeoning nationalism expressed in the colonial revolutions and the end of empires (see Chapter 39). But nationalism has by no means been the only wind blowing from the West. A variety of other isms have been enveloping the globe, including constitutionalism, communism, socialism, and military authoritarianism. The first of these enjoyed a brief vogue with the wave of democratic enthusiasm immediately after World War II. In country after country, however, the parliamentary regimes succumbed to military dictatorships or to Marxist, one-party rule. This trend, it should be noted, also had ample precedent in Europe. With the exception of Czechoslovakia, every country in Central and Eastern Europe was by 1939 under one form or another of authoritarian government. Nasser, Sukarno, and General Ne Win had their counterparts in Stojadinović, Metaxas, and Marshal Pilsudski. In both cases, corrupt and ineffective parliamentary systems together with the lack of the necessary economic and social foundations led to the imposition of dictatorial rule.

Despite the variety of institutional forms, all the new countries have had one common political characteristic: the gradual awakening and activization of the masses regardless of whether they were participating formally in their governments. This is the essence of the political revolution—the passing of the age-old concept of a divinely ordained division of humanity into rulers and ruled. In more general terms, it means replacing the isolation, ignorance, and acquiescence of traditionalism with the participation, knowledge, and initiative of modernism. This political revolution is reflected each day in newspaper reports, as evidenced by the following headlines from *The New York Times:*

LATVIANS PROTEST RUSSIFICATION *(Feb. 27, 1972)*
TEAR GAS DISPERSES ZULU RIOTERS NEAR DURBAN *(Feb. 3, 1973)*
UGANDA ATTACKS BRITAIN AT COMMONWEALTH TALKS *(Aug. 7, 1973)*
GUEVERA STATUE UNVEILED IN WORKERS AREA IN CHILE *(Nov. 9, 1970)*
BLACK PROTESTS MOUNTING IN SOUTH AFRICA *(May 16, 1973)*
WORLD GYPSIES RESIST "GENOCIDE BY ASSIMILATION" *(June 18, 1971)*
ZAMBIA SEEKS MORE CONTROL OF COPPER *(Sept. 1, 1973)*
CULT OF KENNEDY GROWING IN AFRICA *(April 2, 1968)*

We may conclude that behind Europe's decline has been Europe's triumph. The one led naturally and inevitably to the other. If Europe has lost its place as the dominant force in the world, the basic reason has been the diffusion throughout the world of Europe's three great revolutions. Furthermore, this diffusion has continually been gaining in momentum, because for the first time it has affected the masses of the people. Until the twentieth century only an insignificant leisure class was participating in the process of westernization. Only this handful comprehended the meaning of the West from their knowledge of European languages and literatures, and their travels in European lands. In the postwar years, by contrast, a growing proportion of the masses were being involved actively and consciously.

The explanation is to be found partly in the factories where they have found employment and the highways that have been ending their isolation. But equally important have been the new mass media of tabloids, radio, and movies which have overshadowed the old class media of books and travel. Westernization has gained its tremendous impetus by becoming dependent not on Oxford colleges and Paris salons, but on loudspeakers blaring out on illiterate yet responsive multitudes in village squares. New regimes and leaders have begun purposefully to exploit the mass media to the utmost in order to mobilize popular support for their revolutionary programs. "It is true," stated President Nasser, "that most of our people are still illiterate. But politically that counts far less than it did twenty years ago. . . . Radio has changed everything. . . . Today people in the most remote villages hear of what is happening everywhere and form their opinions. Leaders cannot govern as they once did. We live in a new world."[2]

Nasser's "new world" now has been taking form all over the globe. It is the product of Western ideas and technology and reflects both the triumph and the decline of the West.

SUGGESTED READING

I. ADELMAN and C. T. MORRIS, *Economic Growth and Social Equity in Developing Countries* (Stanford Univ., 1973); G. BARRACLOUGH, *An Introduction to Contemporary History* (Penguin, 1965); G. M. FOSTER, *Traditional Cultures and the Impact of Techno-logical Change* (Harper, 1963); M. JANSEN, ed., *Changing Japanese Attitudes Towards Modernization* (Princeton Univ., 1964); D. LERNER, *The Passing of Traditional Society: Modernizing the Middle East* (Free Press, 1958); M. MEAD, ed., *Cultural Patterns and Technical Change* (New Amer. Library, 1955); L. S. S. O'MALLEY, *Modern India and the West: A Study of the Interaction of their Civilizations* (Oxford Univ., 1941); F. SCHURMANN and O. SCHELL, *The China Reader*, Vol. 3, *Communist China* (Random House, 1967); H. SCHILLER, *Mass Communications and American Empire.*

Notes

CHAPTER 1

[1] F. Boas, "Racial Purity," *Asia,* **XL** (May, 1940), 231.

CHAPTER 3

[1] L. R. Binford and S. R. Binford, *New Perspectives in Archeology* (Aldine, 1968), p. 328.

CHAPTER 4

[1] R. Linton, *The Study of Man* (Appleton-Century-Crofts, 1936), p. 353.

CHAPTER 6

[1] Adapted from J. Hawkes and L. Wooley, *Prehistory and the Beginnings of Civilization,* UNESCO History of Mankind, Vol. 1 (Harper & Row, 1963), p. 467; and V. Gordon Childe, *Man Makes Himself* (New American Library, 1951), p. 149. Mentor Book.
[2] E. R. Service, *The Hunters* (Prentice-Hall, 1966), p. 69.
[3] R. Redfield, *Peasant Society and Culture* (Univ. of Chicago, 1956), p. 79.
[4] O. Handlin, *The Uprooted* (Little, Brown, 1951), p. 7.
[5] *The New York Times,* December 25, 1957. Copyright 1957 by The New York Times Company. Reprinted by permission.
[6] V. Gordon Childe, *What Happened in History* (Penguin, 1942), p. 130.
[7] V. Gordon Childe, *op. cit.,* p. 131.
[8] V. Gordon Childe, *What Happened in History,* p. 69.
[9] W. H. and C. V. Wiser, *Behind Mud Walls 1930–1960* (Univ. of California, 1964), pp. 117–18.

CHAPTER 7

[1] Cited by R. Ghirshman, *Iran* (Penguin, 1954), p. 182.
[2] H. Frankfort, "The Ancient Near East," in *Orientalism and History,* ed. D. Sinor (W. Heffer & Sons, 1954), p. 12.

CHAPTER 8

[1] Plato, *Laws,* III, 692.
[2] Cited by F. M. Cornford, *Greek Religious Thought from Homer to the Age of Alexander* (J. H. Dent, 1923), p. 85.
[3] Cited by C. J. Singer, *A History of Biology* (H. Schuman, 1950), p. 4.
[4] *Politics,* I, 5, 2, 1254a; I, 5, 8, 1256b.
[5] Thucydides, *The Peloponnesian War* (trans. B. Jowett), Book I, Chap. 22.
[6] Polybius, *The Histories* (trans. W. R. Paton), Book V, 104.
[7] Cicero, *First Part of the Speech against Gaius Verres at the First Hearing* (New York, 1928), Chap. V.
[8] A. Piganiol, *L'Empire Chrétien* (Presses Universitaires de France, 1947), p. 422.
[9] R. S. Lopez, *The Birth of Europe* (Evans, 1967), p. 23.
[10] *Life of Marcellus,* from *Plutarch's Lives,* Vol. 3, trans. J. and W. Langhorne (London, 1821), pp. 119 ff.
[11] Lévy, *The Economic Life of the Ancient World,* p. 99.
[12] Lopez, *The Birth of Europe,* p. 20.

CHAPTER 11

1 J. M. Keynes, *Essays in Persuasion* (Harcourt, 1932), pp. 360–61.
2 A. H. M. Jones, "The Decline and Fall of the Roman Empire," *History*, XL, No. 140 (October, 1955), 220.
3 Cited by F. Klemm, *A History of Western Technology* (George Allen and Unwin, 1959), p. 23.
4 W. W. Rostow, *The Process of Economic Growth*, 2nd ed. (W. W. Norton, 1962), pp. 311–12.
5 E. O. Reischauer and J. K. Fairbank, *East Asia, The Great Tradition* (Houghton Mifflin, 1958), p. 136.
6 F. Braudel, *Civilisation materielle et capitalisme, XVᵉ–XVIIIᵉ siècle* (Librairie Armand Colin, 1967), I, 116.
7 R. Lopez, *The Birth of Europe* (M. Evans, 1967), p. 58.

CHAPTER 12

1 H. Yule, ed., *Cathay and the Way Thither*, Hakluyt Society, Series 2, XXXVII (London, 1914), 152, 154.
2 *Novum Organum*, Book I, aphorism 129.
3 Cited by C. R. Beazley, *The Dawn of Modern Geography* (John Murray, 1901), II, 366.
4 Adapted from C. R. Beazley, ed., *The Texts and Versions of John de Plano Carpini and William de Rubruquis* (Hakluyt Society, 1903), ex. ser. vol. 13, pp. 109–111.

CHAPTER 13

1 Cited by A. Mieli, *La science arabe* (Brill, 1939), p. 376.
2 Cited by B. Lewis, *The Arabs in History* (Hutchinson's University Library, 1950), p. 148.
3 Cited by Lewis, *op. cit.*, p. 146.

CHAPTER 14

1 *Matthew Paris's English History*, trans. J. A. Giles (London, 1852), I, 312–13.
2 *Travels of Marco Polo*, trans. R. Latham (Penguin, 1958), p. 225.
3 Ibn Khaldun, *Muqaddimah*, trans. F. Rosenthal (Pantheon, 1958), 250–58.
4 M. Meyerhof in *The Legacy of Islam*, ed. T. Arnold and A. Guillaume (Clarendon, 1931), p. 354.

CHAPTER 15

1 Cited by S. Vryonis, Jr., *Byzantium and Europe* (Harcourt, 1967), pp. 190–92.
2 S. H. Cross, *The Russian Primary Chronicle*, Harvard Studies and Notes in Philology and Literature, XII (1930), 199.
3 Cited by P. Miliukov, *Outlines of Russian Culture* (University of Pennsylvania Press, 1942), I, 16.

CHAPTER 16

1 Cited by L. C. Goodrich, *A Short History of the Chinese People*, rev. ed. (Harper & Row, 1943), p. 200.

CHAPTER 17

1 Cited by R. S. Lopez, *The Birth of Europe* (Lippincott, 1967), p. 146.
2 Cited by L. White, "Dynamc and Virgin Reconsidered," *American Scholar* (1958), p. 192.

3 A. G. Keller, "A Byzantine Admirer of 'Western' Progress: Cardinal Bessarion," *Cambridge Historical Journal,* XI (1955), 343–48.
4 Cited by J. H. Parry, *The Age of Reconnaissance* (World, 1963), p. 36.
5 Cited in manuscript by L. V. Thomas, *Ottoman Awareness of Europe, 1650–1800.*

CHAPTER 18

1 P. Bohannan, *Africa and Africans* (American Museum of Science, 1964), pp. 67–68.
2 Leo Africanus, *A History and Description of Africa,* Vol. III, ed. R. Brown (Hakluyt Society, 1896), p. 825.
3 Ibn Battuta, *Travels in Asia and Africa, 1325–1354,* trans. H. A. R. Gibb (Routledge, 1929), pp. 329–30.
4 Cited by T. Hodgkin, "Kingdoms of the Western Sudan," in *The Dawn of African History,* ed. R. Oliver (Oxford Univ., 1961), p. 43.
5 Cited by B. Davidson, *Africa in History: Themes and Outlines* (Macmillan, 1968), p. 63.
6 T. Hodgkin, "Islam in West Africa," *Africa South,* II (April–June, 1958), 98.
7 Davidson, *op. cit.,* p. 125.
8 Cited by K. O. Dike, *Trade and Politics in the Niger Delta, 1830–1885* (Oxford Univ., 1956), p. 7.
9 Adam Smith, *Wealth of Nations* (Edinburgh, 1838), p. 286.

CHAPTER 19

1 P. Farb, *Man's Rise to Civilization as Shown by the Indians of North America from Primeval Times to the Coming of the Industrial State* (Dutton, 1968), p. 231.
2 *Ibid.,* p. 179.
3 J. I. Lockhart, trans., *The Memoirs of the Conquistador Bernal Diaz del Castillo* (J. Hatchard, 1844), I, 142.
4 R. M. Adams, "Early Civilizations, Subsistence, and Environment," in *City Invincible,* ed. R. M. Adams and C. H. Kraeling (Univ. of Chicago, 1960), p. 270.
5 Cited by C. Turnbull, *Black War: The Extermination of the Tasmanian Aborigines* (Melbourne Univ., 1948), pp. 2–3.

CHAPTER 20

1 Cited by E. W. Bovill, *Caravans of the Old Sahara* (New York: Oxford Univ., 1933), p. 143.
2 W. deG. Birch, ed. and trans., *The Commentaries of the Great Afonso Dalboquerque* (Hakluyt Society, 1888), III, 116–17.
3 E. G. Ravenstein, ed. and trans., *A Journal of the First Voyage of Vasco da Gama, 1497–1499* (Hakluyt Society, 1898), pp. 69–70.
4 Cited by K. M. Panikkar, *Asia and Western Dominance* (G. Allen; New York: Day, 1953), p. 42.
5 E. J. Hamilton, "American Treasure and the Rise of Capitalism (1500–1700)," *Economica,* No. 27 (November, 1929), pp. 347–48.
6 Cited in *The New Cambridge Modern History* (Cambridge Univ., 1957), I, 454.
7 S. J. and B. H. Stein, *The Colonial Heritage of Latin America* (Oxford Univ., 1970), p. 20.

CHAPTER 21

1 "The Complete English Tradesman," cited in *The New Cambridge Modern History* (Cambridge Univ., 1957), VII, 59.
2 J. M. Keynes, *A Treatise on Money* (Harcourt, 1930), II, 159.

CHAPTER 22

1 R. J. Kerner, *The Urge to the Sea* (Univ. of Calif., 1942), p. 86.
2 Cited by G. V. Lantzeff, *Siberia in the Seventeenth Century* (Univ. of Calif., 1940), p. 105.

CHAPTER 23

1 Cited by F. Whyte, *China and Foreign Powers* (Oxford Univ., 1927), p. 38.
2 Cited by A. C. Wood, *A History of the Levant Company* (Oxford Univ., 1935), p. 230.
3 H. Blount, "A Voyage into the Levant," in *A General Collection of the Best and Most Interesting Voyages . . .* , ed., J. Pinkerton (London, 1808–14), X, 222.
4 Cited by A. Reichwein, *China and Europe: Intellectual and Artistic Contacts in the Eighteenth Century* (Knopf, 1925), p. 152.
5 Cited by L. S. S. O'Malley, ed., *Modern India and the West* (Oxford Univ., 1941), p. 546.
6 Cited by Reichwein, *op. cit.,* p. 151.

CHAPTER 24

1 J. B. Conant, *Science and Common Sense* (Yale Univ., 1951), p. 25.
2 Cited by F. L. V. Baumer, ed., *Main Current of Western Thought* (Knopf, 1954), p. 251.
3 Cited by J. D. Bernal, *Science in History* (Watts, 1954), pp. 277–78.
4 T. Sprat, *The History of the Royal Society of London, for the Improving of General Knowledge* (London, 1734), p. 72.
5 *Sidereus nuncius,* trans. E. S. Carlos (1880). Cited by M. Nicolson, *Science and Imagination* (Cornell Univ., 1956), p. 15.
6 A complimentary poem by Johannes Faber. Cited by Nicholson, *op. cit.,* p. 19.
7 Cited by Nicholson, *op. cit.,* p. 30.
8 Voltaire, *Ignorant Philosopher.* Cited by W. C. Dampier, *A History of Science and Its Relations with Philosophy and Religion* (Macmillan, 1944), p. 214.
9 A. L. Lavoisier, *Elements of Chemistry,* trans. Robert Kerr (Edinburgh, 1970). Cited by A. R. Hall, *The Scientific Revolution* (Beacon, 1954), p. 332.
10 H. Spencer, *Illustrations of Universal Progress* (New York, 1865), p. 3.
11 Charles Darwin, *Origin of Species* (New York, 1872), I, 3.
12 Charles Darwin, *The Descent of Man and Selection in Relation to Sex* (Appleton, 1888), pp. 630–31.
13 Cited by H. S. Dinerstein, "The Sovietization of Uzbekistan," in *Russian Thought and Politics,* ed. Hugh McLean, Martin E. Malia, and George Fischer (Harvard Slavic Studies, Vol. IV), p. 503. Reprinted by permission of the publishers. Copyright 1957 by the President and Fellows of Harvard College.
14 H. Butterfield, *The Origins of Modern Science, 1300–1800* (Bell, 1957), p. 179.
15 Cited by S. B. Clough and C. W. Cole, *Economic History of Europe,* 3rd ed. (Heath, 1952), p. 66.
16 Cited by H. Heaton, *Economic History of Europe,* rev. ed. (Harper, 1948), p. 484.
17 C. Merz, *And Then Came Ford* (Doubleday, 1929), pp. 198–99. Copyright 1929 by Doubleday & Company, Inc. Reprinted by permission of the publisher.
18 Cited by L. Huberman, *We, the People,* rev. ed. (Harper, 1947), p. 218.
19 Cited by S. Zavala, "The Frontiers of Hispanic America," in *The Frontier in Perspective,* ed. W. D. Wyman and C. B. Kroeber (Univ. of Wisconsin, 1957), p. 40.
20 Cited by Huberman, *op. cit.,* p. 263.

CHAPTER 25

1 Cited by G. Wint, *The British in Asia* (Institute of Pacific Relations, 1954), p. 18.
2 Sir Edwin Sandys, in a speech in Parliament. Cited by H. J. Laski, *The Rise of Liberalism* (Harper, 1936), p. 117.
3 Zagorin, "The English Revolution, 1640–1660," *Journal of World History,* II (1955), 907.
4 A. S. P. Woodhouse, *Puritanism and Liberty* (Dent, 1938), p. 55.
5 Cited by M. Kraus, *The North Atlantic Civilization* (Van Nostrand, 1957), p. 34.
6 T. Kolokotrones and E. M. Edmonds, *Kolokotrones, Klepht and Warrior* (1892), pp. 127–28.
7 Cited by B. C. Shafer, *Nationalism: Myth and Reality* (Harcourt, 1955), p. 105.
8 Cited by D. W. Morris, *The Christian Origins of Social Revolt* (Allen, 1949), p. 34.

CHAPTER 26

1 Cited by B. Pares, *A History of Russia* (Knopf, 1953), p. 117.
2 Cited by F. Nowak, *Medieval Slavdom and the Rise of Russia* (Holt, 1930), p. 91.

CHAPTER 27

1 Mehmed Pasha, *Ottoman Statescraft: The Book of Counsel for Vezirs and Governors*, ed. and trans. W. L. Wright (Princeton, N.J.: Princeton Univ., 1935), p. 21.
2 Ch. Photios, *Apomnemoneumata peri tes Hellenikes Epanastaseos* [*Memoirs on the Greek Revolution*] (Athens, 1899), I, 1.
3 Cited by H. Temperley, "British Policy Towards Parliamentary Rule and Constitutionalism in Turkey," *Cambridge Historical Journal*, IV (1932), 186.

CHAPTER 28

1 Cited by K. Goshal, *The People of India* (Sheridan, 1944), p. 129.
2 Cited in A. B. Keith, ed., *Speeches and Documents on Indian Policy 1750–1921* (Oxford Univ., 1922), I, 209.
3 Cited by E. Stokes, "The First Century of British Colonial Rule in India," *Past and Present*, February, 1973, p. 153.
4 Cited by W. T. de Barry *et al.*, *Sources of Indian Tradition* (Columbia Univ., 1958), p. 601.

CHAPTER 29

1 S. Teng and J. K. Fairbank, *China's Response to the West: A Documentary Survey, 1839–1923* (Harvard Univ., 1954), p. 28. Reprinted by permission of the publishers. Copyright 1954 by the President and Fellows of Harvard College.
2 Cited by J. R. Levenson, *Confucian China and Its Modern Fate* (Univ. of Calif., 1958) p. 105.
3 Cited by J. K. Fairbank, "China's Response to the West: Problems and Suggestions," *Journal of World History*, III (1956), 403.
4 Cited by R. Tsunoda *et al.*, *Sources of the Japanese Tradition* (Columbia Univ., 1958), p. 644.

CHAPTER 30

1 Cited by T. W. Wallbank, *Contemporary Africa* (Van Nostrand, 1956), p. 25.
2 Cited by W. L. Langer, *European Alliances and Alignments, 1871–1890*, 2nd ed. (Knopf, 1956), p. 286.

CHAPTER 31

1 Elgin to Bruce, September, 1852. W. P. M. Kennedy, ed., *Statutes, Treaties and Documents of the Canadian Constitution, 1713–1929* (Oxford Univ., 1930), p. 514.
2 H. L. Stoddard, *It Costs To Be President* (Harper, 1938), p. 164.
3 H. C. Lodge, *Studies of History* (Boston, 1884), p. 352. Cited by H. L. Mencken, *The American Language: An Inquiry into the Development of English in the United States*, 4th ed. (Knopf, 1946), pp. 20–21.
4 *Report, Royal Commission on National Development in the Arts, Letters and Sciences 1949–1951* (Ottawa: 1951), p. 18.
5 *The New York Times* (November 16, 1959).

CHAPTER 32

1 Surendranath Banerjea, cited in L. S. S. O'Malley, *Modern India and the West* (Oxford Univ., 1941), p. 766.
2 Cited by R. Emerson, *From Empire to Nation* (Harvard Univ., 1960), p. 403.
3 Cited by J. Israel, " 'For God, for China and for Yale'—The Open Door in Action," *American Historical Review*, February, 1970, p. 801.
4 W. T. Stead, *The Last Will and Testament of Cecil John Rhodes* (London: 1902), p. 190.
5 E. G. Browne, *The Persian Revolution of 1905–1909* (Cambridge Univ., 1910), pp. 120, 122, 123.

CHAPTER 33

1 Cited by L. Albertini, *The Origins of the War of 1914*, trans. and ed. I. H. Massey (Oxford Univ., 1953), II, 21.
2 Cited by R. S. Baker, *Woodrow Wilson and World Settlement* (Doubleday, 1922), III, 451.
3 Charles Seymour, ed., *The Intimate Papers of Colonel House* (Houghton, 1928), IV, 389.
4 Cited by K. M. Panikkar, *Asia and Western Dominance* (Day, 1953), p. 262.
5 Cited *ibid.*, p. 364.
6 Cited by R. Emerson and M. Kilson, "The American Dilemma in a Changing World: The Rise of Africa and the Negro American," *Daedalus*, Vol. 94 (Fall, 1965), 1057.

CHAPTER 36

1 Cited by S. and B. Webb, *Soviet Communism: A New Civilization* (Gollancz, 1937), II, 605.
2 Harrison E. Salisbury in *The New York Times*, September 29, 1953. Copyright 1953 by The New York Times Company. Reprinted by permission.
3 London *Times*, February 4, 1932.

CHAPTER 37

1 Anthony Eden, *Facing the Dictators* (Houghton, 1962), p. 636.
2 K. von Schuschnigg, *Austrian Requiem* (Putnam, 1946), p. 36.
3 Churchill, *op. cit.*, p. 376.
4 *The New York Times* (Aug. 27, 1939).

CHAPTER 38

1 M. Muggeridge, ed., *Ciano's Diary 1939–1943* (Heinemann, 1947), p. 297.
2 Cited by A. Dallin, "The Fateful Pact: Prelude to World War II," *The New York Times Magazine* (August 21, 1949), p. 40.

CHAPTER 41

1 C. H. G. Oldham, "Science and Education in China," in *Contemporary China*, ed. R. Adams (Random House, 1966), pp. 306–7.
2 Cited by D. Lerner, *The Passing of Traditional Society: Modernizing the Middle East* (New York: Free Press, 1958), p. 214.

Index

Hyksos, 35, 49

Iberian peninsula, 257
  decline of, 267-70
  expansion of Europe and, 258-60
Ibn Battuta, 133
  on the people of Mali, 206-207
Ibn Khaldun, on science vs. religion, 156-57
Ibn-Saud, Sultan of the Nejd, 470
Ignatiev, Count Nikolai, 368
Imperialism, New, 331-36
Inca Empire, 215-17, 260-61, 265-66
India Act, 391-92
India and the Indians, 6, 52, 96-98, 259-64,
    271, 293, 387-89, 446-47
  Anglo-French rivalry in, 279
  British in, 283-84, 334-35, 339, 389-98, 478-80
  Gupta Age, 98-99
  independence of, 545-46
  Maurya Empire, 95-96
  nationalism of, 395-98, 478-80
  renaissance leaders, 394-95
Indian Mutiny (1857), 391, 446
Indians, American, 6-7, 14, 16, 21, 425-26 (see
    also the Americas)
Indies, Council of the, 266-67
Indochina, 61, 151, 172, 183, 402, 548
Indus civilization, 38-39, 52, 90-91
Industrial Revolution, 225, 298, 303, 308, 316-
    36
  diffusion of, 325-26
  effects of, 326-36
  First stage, 320-22
  Second stage, 322-24
Industry:
  in England, 280
  in France, 280-81
  rise of production, 1860–1913, 328 table
Innocent III, Pope, 168, 194
Intelligence in man and animal, 9
Inventions:
  Chinese, 129-30
  Industrial Revolution and, 320-24
Iran, 477 (see also Middle East)
Iraq, 474 (see also Middle East)
Iron metallurgy, African, 22, 203-204
Isabella of Spain, 195, 258, 260
Islam, 135-45, 154-57, 204-207, 256-58 (see also
    Religion)
Israel, 558-59 (see also Palestine)
Italy and the Italians, 259, 308, 475
  and Ethiopia, 516-17
  and fascism, 490-92
  and Germany, 514
  in World War II (see World War II)
Ivan III, 169-70
Ivan IV (the Terrible), 273, 287, 291, 362

Jacobins, 350
Jainism, 94, 97
James of England, 339-40
James II of England, 340
Janissaries, 378
Japan and the Japanese, 128, 260, 275, 326,
    399, 446
  and China, 180-84, 370, 401-402, 411-12, 481,
    483
  and England, 409-12
  feudalism in, 182-83
  isolation of, 183-84, 407-409
  Manchuria and, 511-14
  and Russia, 366, 370-71, 412-13, 486

Japan and the Japanese (cont.)
  and United States, 409, 511-14
  in World War II (see World War II)
Jassy, Treaty of, 292
Java man, 13
Jews, 66, 141-43, 269, 378, 380-81, 474-75
  and dispute with Arabs, 556-59
  immigration, 475
  in Palestine, 474-75
Jinnah, Mohammed Ali, 480, 546
John of Montecorvino (Friar), 132
Joseph II of Austria, 292, 343
Judaism, 66, 136 (see also Jews; Religion)
Julius Caesar, 81, 83
Justinian the Great, 119, 159, 166

Kadar, Janos, 571
Kellogg-Briand Pact, 496, 513-14
Kenyatta, Jomo, 552
Kerensky, Alexander, 458-60
Keynes, John Maynard:
  on origins of capitalism, 272
  on technological stagnation, 112
Khan Kuchum, 287-88, 291
Khrushchev, Nikita, 501, 570-71
Khufu (Cheops), 35
King William's War, 281
Kissinger, Henry, 559
Korea, 172, 180, 183, 401, 412-13
Korean War, 567-68
Kublai Khan, 128, 132-33, 151-53, 177
Kuchum-Kainarji, Treaty of, 292
Kuomintang Party, 406, 481-83, 566
Kushan Empire, 97, 106

Labor supply, British, 319, 325
Lafayette, Marquis de, 348
Lamarck, Jean de, 313
La Salle, Robert Cavelier, Sieur de, 278
Laski, Harold, 468
Latin America, 430-31, 433-38
  wars of independence in, 427
Lausanne Treaty, 472
Laval, Pierre, 515-16
Lavoisier, Antoine Laurent, 312
Law, Codes of, 33-34, 36, 78, 84, 166
League of Augsburg, War of the, 281
League Covenant, 464-65
League of Nations, 464-66, 474, 495-97, 513-17,
    523, 525, 556
LeClerc, Georges Louis, 311
Legalists, doctrines of the, 103-105
Lend-Lease Act (1941), 534
Lenin, Nikolai, 365-66, 457-60, 467-68, 487,
    499-500
Leo Africanus, 206
Leo I, Pope, 118
Leo III (the Isaurian), 160
Leo III, Pope, 120
Leo X, Pope, 192, 195
Leopold of Belgium, 417-19
Liberalism, 338, 354-55
Liebig, Justus von, 312
Lilburne, John, 340
Linnaeus, 311
Linschoten, Jan Huyghen van, 275
Lin Tse-hsu, 400, 402
Livingstone, Dr. David, 417
Lloyd George, David, 485
Locarno Pacts, 495-97
Locke, John, 343
Lombard League, 191, 194

589

Long Parliament, 339-40
Louis XIV of France, 277, 281-82, 310
Louis XVI of France, 347-50
Louis Phillipe, 355
Luce, Henry W., 445
Lumumba, Patrice, 551-52
Luther, Martin, 195
Lvov, Prince Georgi, 458-59
Lyell, Charles, 313-14

McAdam, John, 322
MacArthur, General Douglas, 567-68
Macauley, Thomas Babington, 393-94
MacDonald, Ramsey, 493, 505
Macedonia, 32
McMahon, Sir Henry, 470
Madeiras, the, 259, 267
Magellan, Ferdinand, 264-65
Maine, Sir Henry, 359
Malacca, 259, 262, 275
Mali empire, 205-207
Manchuria, 172, 369-71, 483, 511-14
Mandates, World War I, 466
Mao Tse-tung, 483, 567, 572-73
Marcellinus, Ammianus, on the Huns, 117
Marconi, Guglielmo, 323
Marco Polo, 127, 133-34, 151, 155-56, 177, 260
Marcus Aurelius, 83, 85
Marie Antoniette, 349-50
Mark Antony, 83
Marshall, General George C., 535
Marshall Plan, 569
Martel, Charles (the Hammer), 119, 139
Marxism and Karl Marx, 314, 356-58, 468, 487
Masaryk, Jan, 490
Mau Mau, 552
Maurya, Chandragupta, 92, 95-96
Maurya Empire, 91, 95-96
Mawali, 139-40
Maxwell, James Clerk, 323
Mayan Empire, 215
Mazzini, Giuseppe, 468
Medicine:
  ancient Greek, 74
  Islamic, 142
Mehemet Ali, 382-83
Menes, 34-35
Mensheviks, 365-66, 459-60
Merovingians, 118
Mesopotamia, 26-34
Metcalf, John, 322
Michelangelo, 192
Middle East, 6, 17-18, 48-50
  colonial revolutions in, 556-59
  post–World War I revolutions in, 469-78
  Western influence on, 374-86
Middle Kingdom, Egypt, 35
Mill, John Stuart, 468
Ming dynasty, 127-28, 177-80
Minh, Ho Chi, 547-48
Minoan civilization (*see* Crete)
Missionaries:
  in India, 96-98
  in Middle East, 379
Mitanni Empire (*see* Hurrians)
Mogul Empire, 279, 283, 387, 389
Mohammed, 131, 136-38 (*see also* Islam)
Mohenjo-Daro, 38-39
Molotov, Vyacheslav M., 525
Monarchies, national, rise of, 193-95
Mongols, 46, 127-29, 132-33, 146-57, 169, 176-77, 361

Monomotapa, 207-208
Monroe Doctrine, 333, 367
Montcalm, Louis, Marquis de, 279-80, 282-83
Montezuma, 265
Montgomery, Sir Bernard, 537, 540
Morse, Samuel F. B., 322
Moslems, 126-45, 207, 256-61, 279, 285-88, 369, 389, 397
Mountbatten, Lord Louis, 546
Muraviëv, Count Nikolai, 368
Muscovy Company, 273, 276
Mussolini, Benito, 491-92, 514-18 (*see also* World War II)

Nanda dynasty, 91-92, 95
Nantes, Edict of, 319
Naoroji, Dadabhai, 396
Napoleon I of France, 350-52, 382-83
Nasser, Gamal Abdel, 557, 559, 577
Nationalism, 338, 351-53
Navigation, schools of, 307
Navigation Acts, 277
Nazi Party, 506-508, 514, 522-23 (*see also* Hitler; World War II)
Necker, Jacques, 348
Negroes, 21, 202-209, 220, 364, 420
  in New World, 331, 425-26
Nehru, Jawaharlal, 479
Neolithic age, 4-5, 15-16, 19-22, 41-44
Nerchinsk, Treaty of, 289, 366-67, 400
Nero, 83, 86
Netherlands and the Dutch, 263, 268-69
  England and, 281
  Golden Century of, 274-77
  Portugal and, 274-76
  and trade, 274-75
  and West European expansion, 271-74
Neuilly Treaty, 464
Newcomen, Thomas, 321
New Economic Policy (NEP), 499-500
New France, 434
New Kingdom, Egypt, 49
Newton, Isaac, 303, 310
New World (*see* Americas)
New Zealand, 431-32
Nicholas I of Russia, 364
Nicholas II of Russia, 368
Nicholas IV, Pope, 132
Nicholas V, Pope, 192, 264
Nile valley, civilization in, 34-36
Nixon, Richard, 548-49, 573
Nkrumah, Kwame, 550
Nomads, 45-53, 256
Nonconformists, in England, 319
Normans, 144, 158, 162-63
North Africa, 475-76 (*see also* Africa)
North Atlantic Treaty, 566
Norway, 120, 190
  in World War II, 529-30
Nubia, 155, 208
Numeral system, 99, 141-42

Oceania, racial distribution in, 425 table
October Manifesto, 372
Odyssey, the, 57
Omar, Caliph, 138-39
Opium War of 1839–1842, 367-68, 400-401
Origins of man, 8-10
Ostrogoths, 118-19
Ottoman Empire, 158-59, 165, 291, 301, 374-84, 469-70
Owen, Robert, 356

Paine, Thomas, 344
Pakistan, 480, 545-46
Paleolithic age, 4, 10-13, 15
Palestine, 66, 144, 152, 159-60, 470-71
  and Arab dispute, 473-75, 556-59
Pan-German League, 450
Papal bulls, 194-95, 264, 272
Papen, Franz von, 508
Paris, Matthew, on Mongol invasion of Europe, 151
Paris, Peace of (1763), 283-84, 343-44, 390
Park, Mungo, 416-17
Pasteur, Louis, 313
Patton, General George, 539-40
Pauthier, Guillaume, on the Chinese, 302
Pax Mongolica, 128-129, 132-33, 155, 197
Pax Romana, 83, 89
Pearl Harbor, 534-35
Peking man, 13
Peloponnesian War, 72, 76
Pepin the Short, 119
Pericles, 71-72
Perry, Admiral Matthew, 409
Pershing, General John, 461
Persia, 32, 50, 57-60, 71-72, 76, 129, 138-39, 384-86, 476-78
Persian Wars, 72
Peru, 267
Peter the Great of Russia, 289, 292, 362-63, 367
Petrarch, 192
Philip II of Spain, 268
Philip of Macedon, 73
Philip V of Macedon, 81
Philotheus, on the Russian Orthodox Church, 170
Phoenicians, 49, 59-60, 80, 129
Pitt, William (the Elder), 282
Pizarro, Francisco, 266
Plant life, 16-19
Plassey, Battle of, 283, 389-90
Plato, 74, 76, 143, 306, 356
  on Greek unity, 72
Pleistocene age, 9-10
Plutarch, on mechanics, 87
Poland, 490
  and Russia, 486
  in World War II, 528-29
Political relations, global, by 1763, 298-300
Political Revolution, 1763–1914, 303-4, 337-58
Polybius:
  on history, 58
Pompidou, Georges, 570
Population:
  Industrial Revolution, effects on, 326-27
  Siberia, 1622–1763, 291 table
Portugal and the Portuguese, 258-60, 264-65, 271, 418
  in Asia, 260-63
  colonial empire of, 425, 552-53
  decline of, 267-70
Prehistoric era, 1-2
Priestly, Joseph, 312
Principi, Gavrilo, 451-52
Printing, 192
  invention of, 130
Privateers, 277
Protestantism and Protestants, 268, 274, 280
  (*see also* Religion)
  in England, 339-41
Prussia, 281-82, 292
Ptolemy, 142
Punic Wars, 80-82

Puritans, 339-40
Pygmies, 7, 14, 21-22, 203-4, 208-9
Pyramids, 35
Pyrrhus of Epirus, 80

Queen Anne's War, 282

Rabban Bar Sauma, 133
Race differentiation, 14
Races, distribution of, 14, 21-22, 294-95
Raleigh, Sir Walter, 288
Ramakrishna, 395
Ranade, M. G., 396
Raphael, 192
Ray, John, 311
Reformation, the, 192, 195-96
Religion, 12, 21, 27-28, 33, 35-36, 40, 42, 53-54,
  58, 62-68, 74-75, 78, 130-32, 136-37, 141,
  161-62, 165, 167-69, 181, 187, 191-94, 387
  (*see also* names of religions)
Renaissance, the, 192-93, 306-7
Restoration, the, 340
Revolutions, post World War I, 469-83
Reza Shah, 477-78
Rhazes (al-Razi), 142
Rhodes, Cecil, 432-33
  on building empires, 332, 445
Ribbentrop, Joachim von, 526
Rif tribesmen, 475-76
River valleys, rise of civilizations in, 6
Rockefeller, David, 573
Roman Empire, 32, 79-89, 115-16
Romel, General Erwin, 536
Roosevelt, Franklin, 505 (*see also* World War II)
Roosevelt, Theodore, 438, 445
Rousseau, Jean-Jacques, 343
Rowlatt Acts, 478
Roy, Ram Mohan, 393, 395
Royal Society, the, 307-8, 310
Rubruquis, William de, 131-32
Rumania, and World War II, 514-15, 532
Russia and the Russians, 167-70, 257, 294 (*see also* Union of Soviet Socialist Republics)
  and Asia, 285-92, 366-71
  and China, 289, 368, 481-83, 572-74
  and Communism (*see* Lenin)
  and England, 361-66
  and France, 351
  geography of, 285-87
  industry in, 364-65, 369, 498-502
  and Japan, 412-13
  and Persia, 476-77
  and Revolution of 1905, 371-73
  and revolutions of 1917, 456-61
  and United States, 367
  in World War I, 453-61, 467-68
  in World War II (*see* World War II)
Russian Orthodox Church, 290, 361
Russian revolution, 371-73, 456-61
Russo-Japanese War, 366, 369-71, 412-13, 446

Saint-Simon, Henri de, 356
Saladin (Salah ad-Din), 144
Saracens, 256
Saragossa, Treaty of, 265
Sarajevo, 451-53
Sargon of Akkad, 29, 32
Schlieffen Plan, 453-54
Schliemann, Heinrich, 36
Schmalkaldic League, 195
Scientific Revolution, 1763–1914, 303-16